Mindwaves

Mindwaves

Thoughts on Intelligence, Identity
and Consciousness

Edited by
Colin Blakemore
and Susan Greenfield

Basil Blackwell

British Library Cataloguing in Publication Data

Mindwaves: thoughts on intelligence,
identity and consciousness.
   1. Psychology, Physiological   2. Mind
and body   3. Brain
   I. Blakemore, Colin II. Greenfield, Susan
   128'.2 QP376

   ISBN 0-631-14622-9

Library of Congress Cataloging in Publication Data

Mindwaves: thoughts on intelligence, identity, and
consciousness.

   Includes index.
   1. Consciousness. 2. Brain. 3. Intellect.
4. Thought and thinking. 5. Artificial intelligence.
I. Blakemore, Colin. II. Greenfield, Susan.
[DNLM: 1. Artificial Intelligence. 2. Brain–physiology.
3. Consciousness. 4. Intelligence. 5. Thinking.
BF 455 M663]
BF 311.M554   1987   128   86-18387
ISBN 0-631-14622-9

Typeset in 10 on 11½ pt Ehrhardt by Gecko Limited, Bicester, Oxon
Printed in Great Britain by Page Bros (Norwich) Ltd

Contents

Part 3   Machines: Could They Have Minds?

Part 4   Ideas: How Brains Could Have Minds, and Why

Part 5   Problems: What is Mind?

Preface

The idea behind this book came from a meeting of three Susans – Greenfield, Hurley and Lazy. The Lazy Susan sat on the table of a Chinese restaurant in Oxford, dividing the scientist (Susan Greenfield) from the philosopher (Susan Hurley). Their conversation turned to one topic on which they thought they should have common knowledge – how the brain makes the mind – but they found that they were separated by more than a dish of Wonton soup. Their backgrounds gave both of them a fascination with the subject, but each a very different way of looking at it.

The conversation ran back and forth, revealing brain research and philosophy to be more or less like two mountaineers clambering up the same peak but from different sides, each virtually unaware of the efforts of the other or the advantages of joining forces. Brain research has, as its ultimate goal, the explanation of how an animal's brain determines its behaviour. The school of psychology called behaviourism taught that this might be done by treating the hardware of the nervous system as a kind of 'black box'. A resourceful electronic engineer, confronted by a box containing an electrical circuit, might be able to give a very full description of what it does (amplification, filtering, oscillation, etc.) just by testing the signals that come *out* of the box when various signals are put in. But the brain of the simplest vertebrate animal is infinitely more complex than the kind of electronic circuitry that can be characterized in this way.

Behaviourism ground to a halt, partly because even the humble laboratory rat proved too resourceful, too thoughtful, too rich in insight to be treated as if it were a mindless machine. Most behaviourists had denied the necessity of postulating mental states, even perceptions; but somehow the need to see behaviour in terms of *intentions* kept intruding. The psychology of behaviour has recently returned to its nineteenth-century roots in the current fashion for 'cognitive' explanations of the actions of animals, as well as people. Brain researchers of all sorts have been forced to take seriously mentalistic explanations of behaviour and most of them see perception, intention, thought and will to be legitimate subjects of interest for the rapidly-growing subject of neuroscience. Indeed the nature of consciousness may come to be seen as the central problem of research on the brain.

Philosophy has had longer to think about thought, but is no closer to a generally agreed solution of the mind–brain problem. The dualism of Descartes put the automatic and the volitional aspects of behaviour into separate categories, the first due to 'reflex' connexions within the brain, the second to spiritual influences on the clockwork of the nervous system. By contrast, the positivism of linguistic philosophy, exemplified by Gilbert Ryle's remarkable book, *The Concept of Mind*, attempted to exorcise the ghost in the machine by treating dualistic or 'first-person' accounts of human behaviour as mere errors of category and language. Positivism and behaviourism were very close in their aspirations, but both have failed to provide the kinds of explanations that would make people change their minds about how their own minds work! In the private world of mental experience, 'first-person' concepts work very well; they are infinitely more cheering than the idea that the mind is nothing more than the actions of a black box and that will is an illusion or self a fantasy. But that brings us back to the fundamental questions. If mind is not brain, what is it? How can personal experience be reconciled with material explanations of behaviour? What does choice mean in a system, however complex, of causal, physical interactions?

The techniques of neuroscience have grown rapidly in sophistication and the explosion of knowledge about the brain leaves scientists themselves gasping at the task of keeping up to date with the flood of facts. It is all too easy, then, for philosophers to construct naive or implausible theories of the relationship of mind to brain, simply through their ignorance of scientific results. The isolation of most neuroscientists from the significance of philosophy is even more alarming. Transported by the elegance of their narrow experimental methods, they are in danger of banality when it comes to the broader issues.

The outcome of the unresolved discussion in the Chinese restaurant was typically academic – what was needed was a *seminar*! Susan Greenfield proposed a modest plan to invite a philosopher to come and preach in the Department of Physiology, but that soon escalated into a programme for a series of evening discussions, under the general title 'Minds and Matters', spanning two Oxford terms. Each session took the form of a pair of complementary or opposed presentations, usually by a scientist and a philosopher, followed by a vigorous debate, often continuing over wine until well after midnight. We hope that these meetings did a great deal to bring together people who otherwise might never have met; certainly the audiences were large and diverse. It is no surprise that the local Oxford community provided many of the speakers, but we also had visitors from as far afield as New York, Hungary, Berkeley and even Cambridge! We are particularly grateful to John Searle from the University of California, who took time to come and speak in Oxford during his visit to record his series of Reith Lectures, which were broadcast on BBC Radio at the end of 1984 and which stimulated so much interest in the philosophy of mind. He summarizes his controversial views in his chapter in this book.

The loyalty of the audiences and the verve of the discussions made it clear that the seminars were both timely and productive. It was Kim Pickin, then Philosophy Editor of Basil Blackwell, who convinced us that the series should be published, to extend the debate to a wider audience. To our surprise, the majority of the speakers agreed to write chapters for this book and we thank them all. The credit must go to them for the originality of this collection. Any editorial failings are ours. We have tried to preserve the spirit and flavour of the seminars with their atmosphere of dialogue and debate. But we have regrouped the contributions into five sections to help the reader to pick and choose. It was our idea to illustrate the book (to the bemusement of some of the authors): our intention was not simply to enliven the book but to use pictures to illuminate ideas.

Many friends and colleagues helped us in our preparation of the seminars and this book. Susan Hurley and Paul Seabright (then both at All Souls College, Oxford) and Nick Rawlins (of the Department of Experimental Psychology and University College, Oxford) were un-flagging in their enthusiasm and support. We thank Andrew Last (then a research student) and Jan Greenslade (Steward of the University Labora-tory of Physiology) for their help with the practical organization of the seminars, Ann Watson for secretarial help, and the staff of Basil Blackwell for their professional support. Finally we are grateful to our colleagues in Oxford who not only tolerated our eccentricity in attempting to wed science and philosophy but came to the talks and brought their minds to bear on the problem of mind.

It would be arrogant to suggest that a collection of essays, even as diverse and extensive as these, could solve the problems of consciousness and the nature of mind. However, we hope that it will at least give you, the reader, something to think about. As James Thurber said, 'It is better to ask some of the questions than to know all the answers'.

Contributors

Editors: Colin Blakemore, Department of Physiology and Susan Greenfield, Department of Pharmacology, University of Oxford

Michael Argyle, Department of Experimental Psychology, University of Oxford
Horace Barlow, Physiological Laboratory, University of Cambridge
Gordon Claridge, Department of Experimental Psychology, University of Oxford
Stephen Clark, Department of Philosophy, University of Liverpool
John Crook, Department of Psychology, University of Bristol
Marian Stamp Dawkins, Department of Zoology, University of Oxford
Sir John Eccles, Switzerland
Hans Eysenck, Institute of Psychiatry, University of London
Brian Farrell, Corpus Christi College, Oxford
Jeffrey Gray, Institute of Psychiatry, University of London
Richard Gregory, Department of Anatomy, University of Bristol
Peter Hacker, St John's College, Oxford
Roy Harris, Worcester College, Oxford
Ted Honderich, Department of Philosophy, University College London
Jennifer Hornsby, Corpus Christi College, Oxford
Nicholas Humphrey, London
Edward Hundert, Cambridge, Massachusetts
Philip Johnson-Laird, Medical Research Council Applied Psychology Unit, Cambridge
John Krebs, Department of Zoology, University of Oxford
Rodolfo Llinás, New York University School of Medicine
János Szentágothai, Semmelweiss University Medical School, Budapest
Colin McGinn, Corpus Christi College, Oxford
Donald MacKay, Department of Communication and Neuroscience, University of Keele
Nicholas Mackintosh, Department of Experimental Psychology, University of Cambridge
Euan Macphail, Department of Psychology, University of York
Derek Parfit, All Souls College, Oxford
Roger Penrose, Department of Mathematics, University of Oxford
Paul Seabright, All Souls College, Oxford
John Searle, Department of Philosophy, University of California, Berkeley
Anthony Storr, Green College, Oxford
Herbert Terrace, Department of Psychology, Columbia University
Larry Weiskrantz, Department of Experimental Psychology, University of Oxford

Part 1
Persons: What Makes an Individual?

The nature of people as persons stands as a major issue in moral philosphy. Judeo-Christian traditions, combined with the libertarian, individualistic cultures of the Western world have raised human beings to the status of works of art – unique, valuable, every one a different creation. The person, or more accurately the self, *is also a fundamentally important concept in the philosophy of mind. Selves are the things that have and use minds; that is, at least, the way things are felt to be. We have the impression that our actions on the world depend on our own self-wills: each human being has, or is, a unique agent that employs mental states as both a window on events in the world outside, and a way of reacting to those events. The words that we use to describe mental events such as 'perceive, 'know', 'believe', 'fear', and 'decide', imply that there is an operator that* does *the perceiving, the knowing, the believing and so on. The operator is self.*

Putting aside any theological issues, what problems does 'personhood' or 'selfness' pose for the science of the brain? In other words, what is happening in (or to) the nervous system of a person when he or she says, 'I want . . .' or 'I think . . .', or for that matter 'I hate . . .' or 'I love . . .'? One approach to the entire problem is simply to dismiss the concept of self as an error of linguistic convention. We go about doing things that we describe as wanting, thinking, etc., but there may be no literal agent of these actions: in these terms 'I' is no more an active thing than is the 'it' of expressions like 'It is three o'clock.' Such attempts to exorcise 'The Ghost in the Machine' cannot conceal the fact that the bodies of people act as if *their actions were campaigns planned by a single, omnipotent commander.*

In a sense, the nervous system is no more than a monstrous jumble of wires, each connecting inputs (sense organs) to outputs (muscles, etc.). But we are far from simple slaves to a multitude of independent, automatic, 'reflex' reactions. We don't jerk along in a fit of uncoordinated responses to anything and everything that happens around us. Somehow the whole potential cacophony of actions usually gets orchestrated into a disciplined melody of movements. What we feel to be happening is that the imagined self of such statements as 'I am going for a walk' is the conductor of our neuromuscular systems, the decision-maker, the chooser. And when we think of other people and what it is about their behaviour that makes each unique, we attribute those differences to the individual nature of the self of each. Our book starts, then, with this central question: What is a person?

The description and analysis of errors and perturbation have played an honourable part in the history of science. Deviations in the orbits of heavenly bodies, and variations and mutation in plants and animals provided crucial data in the early days of astrophysics and genetics respectively. In the same way, individual differences in behaviour and changes in personality associated with disease or injury might cast light on the relationship between self and brain. For instance, is there any evidence from damaged brains that the machinery of self occupies some particular corner of the nervous system? Donald MacKay, engineer, psychologist and philospher, looks critically at the fascinating cases of 'split-brain' people – patients with severe epilepsy who have been treated, as a last resort, by the surgical cutting of the corpus callosum, the enormous bundle of nerve fibres that connects together the two cerebral hemispheres. Anatomically, these people now have the most advanced part of the brain, presumed to be the seat of the self, split in two. Each half-brain receives sensory information from the opposite half of the body and the opposite side of the visual world, and in turn regulates the movements of the opposite hand and half-body. Do such people have two minds, two selves, two wills? Superficially their actions are remarkably normal but the careful observations of Roger Sperry and his colleagues at the California Institute of Technology in the 1960s, showed that each half brain-body could act independently in certain circumstances. MacKay, though, stops short of crediting them with two free wills.

From a philosophical standpoint, Derek Parfit reasons that a split-brain human may have two streams of consciousness, but that the enquiry about whether he or she is one or two persons is misconceived. The crucial question is whether anyone is a person. Parfit himself doubts the whole concept of personhood and his arguments (with some excursions into science fiction) lead him to sympathize with the Buddhist view that our familiar concept of persons is a fallacy.

The other contributions to this first section are concerned with how we assess the nature of the person in another human being and with the borderline between normal and abnormal minds. Gordon Claridge, a psychologist interested in abnormal behaviour, questions the fashionable Laingian explanations of madness in terms of errors in society, because they fail to take account of the growing evidence for physiological disturbances of brain function in schizophrenia. However, he is also unhappy with purely 'organic' accounts of schizophrenia, and he suggests that disturbed mental states reflect exaggerated brain functions that can be detected in the behaviour of apparently quite normal people. Much of Hans Eysenck's work has been concerned with the reliable assessment of personality. He describes the approach here and uses it to identify the biological and social factors that influence the way people behave.

The usual avenue for the recognition and assessment of personhood in others is through social interaction. Though spoken language is clearly the most important means of transfer between people of factual information about the world, non-verbal communication plays a major role in signalling and interpreting emotional states and attitudes. Social psychologist Michael Argyle describes this subtle but rich form of communication, and argues that some signals are basically innate but have become modified by cultural rules.

Sigmund Freud started his career by studying the anatomy and physiology of the nervous system: it is natural to see his subsequent work in psychoanalysis as an extension of the scientific method. Freud's ambition was indeed to create a 'science of the mind', which would bear comparison with physics and *chemistry. Psychiatrist Anthony Storr suggests that psychoanalysis cannot be scientific. Love, fantasy and human understanding – the data of analytical theory – cannot be measured objectively or treated scientifically. Understanding a person is different from understanding a phenomenon in physics or even a disease. Philosopher Brian Farrell looks critically at another claim made on behalf of psychoanalysis, that it has given the humanities a new image of man, and specifically that analytical theory has the power to explain important events in history. Just as Storr questions the value of analytical theory within conventional science, so Farrell doubts its explanatory power in history and the arts. We need a new theoretical approach to the nature of the human person.*

Unfortunately biologists spend most of their time ignoring the subtle individual differences between animals of the same species, in order to discover the physiological mechanisms that they have in common. Brain research, based as it is on animal studies, may give us insight into the origin of mental states and the location of the brain structures responsible for mind. But we are far from an ideal scientific approach to that socially important aspect of the human mind – the question of what makes the character of other people.

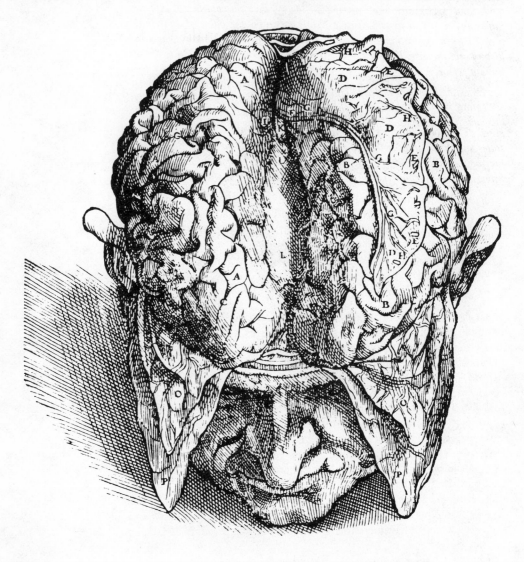

1

Divided Brains – Divided Minds?

Donald MacKay

*Donald MacKay, who graduated from St Andrews University in 1943, was
Emeritus Professor in Keele University's Research Department of Communication and Neuroscience, which he founded in 1960. The Department
combines the approaches of Physiology, Psychology and Computer Science in
the investigation of brain mechanisms, particularly those of vision and
hearing. After three years of radar research during the Second World War,
Donald MacKay taught Physics in the University of London for 14 years
before moving to Keele. He was one of the founding editors of the international
journal* Experimental Brain Research, *and of the* Handbook of Sensory
Physiology *(Springer, 1971). He has frequently broadcast on radio and TV,
and his books include* Information, Mechanism and Meaning *(MIT Press,
1969),* Human Science and Human Dignity *(Hodder, 1979) and*
Brains, Machines and Persons *(Collins, 1980). Donald MacKay died on
6 February 1987.*

What is it about our brains that makes people – you, and me –
psychological unities? In the theory of Descartes it was our possessing a
single central pineal gland, through which traffic was supposed to pass
between the machine he took our bodies to be and the non-material soul
in which lay our personal identity. Nowadays we find this theory
unconvincing; but what to put in its place is far from clear. We now know
that visual and other sensory information from the left side of our bodies
is projected mainly to the right cerebral hemisphere, and from the right
side to the left hemisphere; yet we normally perceive our sensory
environment as a seamless unity. Movements of the left hand or leg are
normally controlled by the right hemisphere and vice versa. But although
we know what it means to be (sometimes) 'in two minds', and to perform
quite complex actions 'absent-mindedly', our dominant impression (unless something goes badly wrong with our nervous system) is that we are
individually and solely in command of the repertoire of action afforded by
our bodies.

The fact that the brain is divided into two roughly symmetrical
hemispheres, and that surgical removal of one hemisphere does not
abolish consciousness, suggests that the task of mediating our conscious
experience is somehow shared between the hemispheres, if indeed they
have anything to do with it. The fact that the hemispheres are linked by

*The corpus callosum (marked L) as illustrated in Andreas Vesalius' De Fabrica (1543). This great
bundle of millions of nerve fibres, which joins together the two cerebral hemispheres, is cut in
'split-brain' patients.*

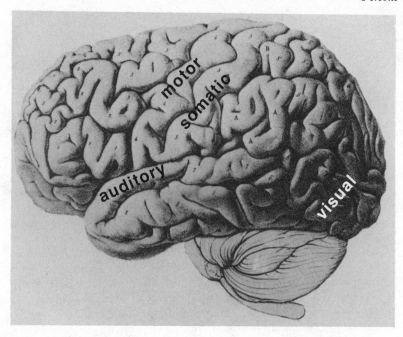

Figure 1.1   The left side of the human brain as drawn by the French anatomist Louis Pierre Gratiolet (1815–65), who named many of the convolutions or folds of the cerebral cortex. Labels have been added to show the main regions concerned with sensation and movement. The motor *strip (where electrical stimulation causes jerky movements of parts of the body) lies in front of a deep diagonal cleft called the central sulcus, which marks the boundary between the frontal lobe (in front) and the parietal lobe (behind). Immediately behind the central sulcus is the* somatic *sensory cortex, which receives sensory signals from the skin and the rest of the body. Another deep cleft, the Sylvian fissure, separates the frontal and parietal lobes from the temporal lobe (below). At the upper lip of the termporal lobe lies the* auditory *cortex, receiving input from the ears. The rear portion of the cerebral hemisphere is the occipital lobe, which is mainly concerned with vision. The primary* visual *cortex lies tucked in at the back, on the inner surface of the occipital lobe.*

the multi-million fold connections of the corpus callosum invites a guess that these may help to maintain the unity of normal conscious experience; but it was only when neurosurgeons ventured to cut these connections in a few epileptic patients, with a view to preventing the spread of seizures from one side to the other, that their importance in man could be experimentally demonstrated.

Divided Brains

As is now common knowledge, the effects under controlled conditions were dramatic.[1,2] When the patient stared at a dot at the centre of a projection screen, so that words (names of objects) flashed briefly to left and right of the dot were transmitted respectively to the right and left occipital lobes (figure 1.2), he could verbally report only the word on the right. This in itself was not surprising, as it was known that in most people the organization of speech requires use of the left hemisphere, which in these patients was presumably cut off from the information in the other. What excited Roger Sperry and his collaborators was the finding that in

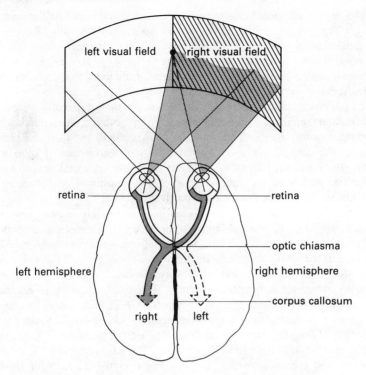

Figure 1.2　This simplified diagram shows the way in which visual information from the two eyes feeds into the brain to provide each hemisphere with a view of the opposite *half of the visual field. It is a strange quirk of the organization of the brain that each side of the cerebral hemispheres is concerned with the opposite side of the body and of the sensory world. In the* left *hemisphere the motor cortex controls the muscles of the* right *side of the body, and the somatic cortex receives information from the right half of the skin surface. The left hemisphere, at least in the majority of people, also contains the machinery for controlling speech.*

Imagine a person with both eyes staring fixedly at a point straight ahead. The image of the right side of the visual field (shown shaded in this diagram) falls on the left half of each retina, as shown, and the nerve fibres leaving these two, corresponding half-retinae pass into the left *hemisphere: this involves the fibres from the right eye crossing over in the structure called the optic chiasma. Similarly the right hemisphere views the left half of the visual field. Although we are normally never aware of it, our visual world is split down the middle in this way. The* corpus callosum, *the huge bundle of nerve fibres which connects the two hemispheres, presumably plays a part in unifying our perception of the visual field and in sending information about things in the left visual field (delivered first to the right, speechless hemisphere) across to the left side so that the owner of the brain can describe those things in words. If a picture of an object is briefly flashed in the left visual field of a split-brain person (whose corpus callosum has been cut) he or she cannot say what the object was but they can reach behind a screen with the left hand and select the correct object from a number of others! Is it right to think of such a person as having two minds, two streams of consciousness, two selves – but one of them voiceless? (redrawn from Springer and Deutsch,* Left Brain, Right Brain, *fig. 2.4 revised edn 1985).*

some cases, although unable to speak the word flashed to the left of the dot, the patient could use his left hand correctly to retrieve the object it named, from a collection accessible behind a curtain. This implies that the right hemisphere, though unable to organize speech, can recognize at least some words and use the information to determine movements of the left hand. Further tests showed that with a so-called 'split brain' it is possible for a human being to pursue disparate and even conflicting goals with the left and right halves of his body, while vocally denying all knowledge of what the left half (regulated by the right hemisphere) is doing. Sperry described such patients as having 'two free wills in one cranial vault',[3] and the popular press spread the word that each beneficiary of the operation was now in reality 'two persons'.

I see no objection in principle to the science-fiction speculation that if a human nervous system could be *completely* bifurcated, and each half left in working order, the resulting structure might embody two distinct persons, as in the case of Siamese twins. In the real-world case of split-brain patients, however, I doubt whether any of the evidence to date requires or justifies such a drastic interpretation of their condition. My grounds for doubt are partly experimental and partly theoretical.

What cash-value would we normally attach to talk of 'two persons'? Each would have, at a minimum, to be a centre of conscious awareness and, at least in principle, a terminal of dialogue – someone who could be met, interrogated, informed, argued with and so forth. Moreover, each must be not just a receiver of sensory information and a generator of bodily movements but an evaluator of both. Evaluation is a crucial ingredient of personal agency. In a primitive form it can of course be carried out in a simple servo-mechanism such as an automatic pilot. Persons, however, are autonomous and conscious evaluators, in the sense that at least to some extent they are able to set and readjust their own norms and criteria according to changing circumstances, in the light of long-range plans. Most significantly for our purpose, talk of 'two persons' implies the possibility in principle of *dialogue between them*, wherein (as Buber would put it) each comes to know the other as 'thou'.[4]

A Fresh Approach

This last consideration suggested a few years ago a fresh experimental line of approach to the question whether split-brain patients were 'two persons' in any effective sense.[5] What would happen, I wondered, if we tried through external communication channels to 'introduce' one half-patient to the other? Could they engage in meaningful dialogue? If so, could it be made to reveal an autonomous capacity for normative self-determination in each 'half'? By courtesy of Roger Sperry and Michael Gazzaniga, my wife, Dr Valerie MacKay, and I were able to spend several months in testing a variety of split-brain patients in Pasadena and New York on these lines.[6,7] Gazzaniga and co-workers had long ago shown,[8,9] both in monkey and man, that two separated hemispheres could apply incompatible criteria of evaluation to the same stimulus, and that the two half-patients could express disparate preferences in the same situation. To cut short a long story, we also found abundant evidence of independence between the systems that coordinated motor action and sensory information in the two 'halves', and signs of independent and even disparate programmes of goal-pursuit and criteria of evaluation. We were able to show that the two 'halves' could cooperate in shared projects such as driving a plotting-pen round a course, with the left hand controlling motion in one direction and the right hand motion in the other. We found in four of the patients we tested that each 'half' could solve simple arithmetic addition or subtraction problems flashed simultaneously to the two sides, signalling results by using the fingers of the two hands (behind a curtain). One patient was even able to add two numbers on the left while simultaneously subtracting two others on the right, and vice versa. But despite all encouragements we found no sign at all of recognition of the other 'half' as a separate person, nor of independence at the normative level where priorities and criteria of evaluation are themselves evaluated – the characteristic human activity with which we associate the term 'will'.

Recent experiments by Gazzaniga and colleagues have suggested that where (as described above) the right hemisphere can cope with printed words, it may also be superior in other cognitive skills (such as the ability to recognize unfamiliar faces and to carry out subtle line-orientation tasks) compared with the majority of right hemispheres studied, which show no linguistic competence. 'A neural system that does not possess language is limited in its cognitive skills.'[10] This offers a further warning against thinking of the 'split' left and right half-systems as simple mirror-images of one another, or expecting them to behave as two persons might.

Cross-cueing

In order to assess experimental evidence in this area, it is vital to allow properly for what is called 'cross-cueing'. This can happen whenever activity under the control of one hemisphere generates signals accessible to the other, in such a way that information can be transferred 'externally' to make up for the loss of the corpus callosum. This may occur quite involuntarily, as when a female patient to whose left half-field Gazzaniga showed a naughty picture found herself blushing and giggling without being able to account for it vocally, and resorted to embarrassed confabulation.[11] It can, however, be developed into a skilled art by much-studied patients. In one of our experiments, we flashed a series of 3-letter words (for only about 150 ms each) to the left field of a split-brain patient, LB, and invited him to try to vocalize them. Given half a minute or more after each word, LB could achieve almost perfect performance. We noticed that he spent much of his time in shaking his head around, and my wife asked him privately what this meant. Although he denied being able to see the letters, he explained he could 'write them with his nose' (the movements of his head being controlled by the knowing, but speechless, right hemisphere). If he had time to do that, he (that is, his articulate left-hemisphere system) could then read them off. Presumably in this case information from sense organs in his neck muscles and semicircular canals, which would give the game away, was projected to both hemispheres. In any case, it must be remembered that a significant visual input projects to the collicular system in the roof of the midbrain (figure 1.3), where it serves among other things to guide eye movements, whose consequences are shared on both sides. Thus innumerable possibilities exist, under normal unrestrained conditions where the eyes are free to move around, for information to 'leak' between the left and

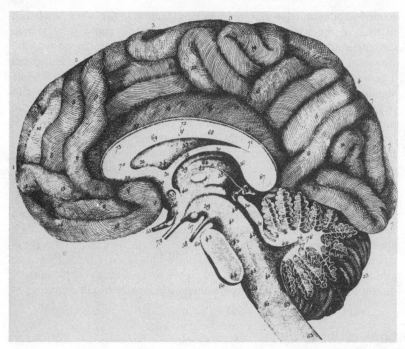

Figure 1.3   The illustration by the French anatomist Felix Vicq d'Azyr (1748–94) shows an inside view of the right half of the human brain, cut completely down the middle. The corpus callosum is the white shape (numbered 67, 68, 69 etc.) and number 50 marks a structure called the superior colliculus *in the part of the brain below the cerebral hemispheres called the midbrain. Some optic fibres from the eyes run to this structure, which is thus a secondary visual centre, evolutionarily more primitive than the visual areas in the cerebral cortex. In humans the superior colliculus plays a part mainly in controlling movements of the eyes and other more or less automatic visual functions.*

right cerebral half-systems. The surprising thing is that such clean dissociations of function can be demonstrated once proper precautions have been taken, especially when we remember that these half-systems have to share not only un-split basal structures in the brain, below the level of the cerebral hemispheres, but also the control of one mouth, one gut, and much else.

To minimize the risk of cross-cueing and guesswork, it is necessary to make the range of stimuli as large as possible, and to ensure that both half-systems are kept busy simultaneously. With this end in view, we carried out one set of experiments in Sperry's laboratory in which a patient was presented with pairs of flashed pictures to left and right of the fixation point, representing outlines of the human body. Each picture had a red dot in a different part of the body, and the patient's task was to name vocally the part so identified, and also to point to it on her own body using her left hand. Since the images accessible to the right hemisphere/left-hand system differed from those she vocally described, the patient usually heard herself saying something contradictory to what her left hand was indicating. This brought out an instructive clue to the degree of 'independence of will' between the two sides. When the mouth got in first, the left hand obediently pointed to the spot it had named; when the left hand was first, and the mouth then named a different spot from the one pointed to, the hand would slide almost furtively to the named spot. From this and other evidence it appears that in cases of cognitive conflict, the speaking half-system is generally the unchallenged 'top dog'.

Goal-conflict

In another series of experiments we trained each half-system to use one finger of the appropriate hand to move a (separate) lever so as to bring two pointers into line with 'target numbers' on a central vertical scale, the targets for the two hands being flashed simultaneously to left and right of the fixation point. After this task had been learnt for a whole sequence of target pairs, we silently clamped the two levers together, and were able to record on strain gauges a strong physical conflict between the two hands as each half-system struggled to achieve its designated target. (Interestingly, if the clamp was fixed from the outset, the patient settled spontaneously into a routine in which she indicated each of the two rival targets in turn, with no sign of physical strain between the two levers.)

At first sight this might be taken as impressive evidence of 'duality of will'; but on reflection we realized that it was exactly the kind of behaviour one might expect of an organist, for example, if some pestiferous scientist were secretly to clamp two of his stops together, so that when he tried to push one in with his left hand and pull the other one out with his right, he met with resistance. Nobody would dream of taking this as evidence that the organist had 'two free wills'! What matters, of course, is how the disparate left and right goals are specified. In the case of the organist, they are set at a single superordinate level, perhaps by an act of 'will' informed by the music he is reading. In the patient they are set by the numbers flashed to left and right of his fixation, and no exercise of free will, either single or double, need come into the picture (apart from the patient's free decision to play the required game).

Dialogue between Half-systems

Our most ambitious tests of the degree of normative independence between left and right half-systems were carried out in 1981 on a cooperative and intelligent patient, JW, then aged 27, who had had his corpus callosum, but not his anterior commissure, sectioned four years earlier.[7] Preliminary tests confirmed that he could not vocally report any visual stimuli flashed to the left of his fixation point, though his left hand could correctly point to or retrieve objects represented by these stimuli. When a single numeral randomly selected from the range of 0 to 9 was flashed for 150 ms a short distance to the left of the fixation point, simultaneously with a distractor (one or more letters of the alphabet) flashed at the corresponding position on the right, JW reported vocally that he saw only the distractor. Both vocal and right-manual responses were normal for stimuli flashed to the right half-field.

Each half-system in turn was then trained to participate in a guessing game of the '20 questions' type in dialogue with one experimenter (E).

(1) E first assumed the role of 'guesser', attempting to name a 'mystery number' written by the second experimenter on a piece of paper in free view of JW. E invited JW to use his left hand to point to the appropriate answers on a card also in free view, bearing the words 'go up', 'go down', 'OK'. The left hand proved immediately capable of providing reliable feedback in this mode.

(2) E then invited JW to 'guess a number between 0 to 9 which I have been shown'. In response to each guess by JW, E pointed mutely to one of the three messages on the card. JW quickly learnt to adapt his vocal guesses so as to home in on the correct answer under this mute feedback from E.

(3) Finally, single digits between 0 and 9 were flashed as before to JW's left half-field, with distractors to the right; and E proposed that JW should fulfil both roles, using his mouth (controlled by the left hemisphere) to make guesses and his left hand (controlled by the right hemisphere) to offer feedback by way of the card so as to guide the guessing process. JW found no apparent difficulty in fulfilling this dual role, although it was notable that all his guesses were addressed to E, who invariably had to prompt him to use his left hand to answer. He proved well able to 'talk himself down' on to the correct target each time, frequently showing satisfaction by a smile when the target was finally named. A useful check that he was not just play-acting (which seemed in any case improbable) was provided by an episode when his mouth guessed '1' and his left hand pointed to 'go down'. JW complained vocally that there were 'no more numbers down there', and had to be reminded of the possibility of '0' (which was the correct answer).

These results showed that a form of low-level dialogue, exchanging information by question and answer, could be sustained between the two half-systems. They did nothing, however, to answer the question whether the two half-participants had the kind of 'independence of will' possessed by two normal human players on opposite sides of a guessing game.

Duality of Will?

An ideal demonstration of such 'duality of will' would be the capacity to bargain: that is, to struggle to induce changes in one another's evaluative criteria or priorities as distinct from merely struggling physically in pursuit of conflicting goals.

Accordingly, E next proposed to JW that 'the left hand (LH) should be paid by the right hand (RH) for each item of information'. RH was provided with an open box containing a limited supply of tokens, and told to pay one token into a similar box on the left for each correct instruction provided by LH. RH was rewarded (with additional tokens) in inverse proportion to the number of guesses required to identify each flashed numeral. Any occasional mistakes made by LH were penalized by repaying three tokens per mistake to RH.

As elaboration of the game in this way proved congenial to JW, we next introduced the possibility of evaluative conflict by proposing to 'ask the left hand whether it would like to be paid more for each answer'. LH was asked to reply by pointing to a card representing one, two and three tokens; and it immediately indicated 'three tokens'. As this soon had the (foreseeable) effect of rendering RH bankrupt and halting the game, E then said, 'Let's ask the left hand whether it would settle for less.' LH immediately pointed to 'two tokens'; but at the same time, and apparently as an integral part of the action, JW's mouth said, 'Sure, make it two tokens.' This was typical of the impression conveyed throughout this second phase of the experiment – that although JW's LH and RH were substantially separate at the cognitive level, their priorities gave no evidence of being under the supervision of two independent systems.

It is of course impossible to draw firm conclusions from such negative findings. What our results bring out, I think, is the inadequacy of all existing evidence, including ours, to justify claims that the two half-systems *do* embody 'two free wills'. Perhaps JW's own spontaneous comment, offered more than once, is illuminating: 'Are you guys trying to make two people out of me?'

At this stage I should perhaps draw some threads together. The evidence we have reviewed makes it clear, I think, that cutting the corpus callosum divides the cerebral organizing system responsible for sensori-motor coordination, selection and pursuit of goals (both concrete and abstract), performance of mental tasks such as addition and subtraction, and evaluation of the outcomes of actions. We might be tempted to ask what more is needed in order to demonstrate that there are in such patients at least two 'streams of conscious experience', if not two 'free wills'. How, it may be said, could anything play on either side of a '20 questions' game, or add numbers, or retrieve symbolically named objects, without being conscious?

Action without Consciousness

My doubts have a twofold origin. First, clinicians have known for many decades of cases where a patient during an epileptic fit could automatically perform complex tasks such as preparing a chocolate drink or even taking clinical notes, while judged by other criteria to be unconscious.[12] This raises the question whether evidence of such capacities can ever be logically sufficient to justify attributions of conscious experience to their possessors. After all, in these days there are many computer programs that can match or surpass ourselves in similar performances without persuading most of us that they have conscious experience!

Secondly, even the crudest skeleton information-flow map of the organization of human behaviour forces upon us a distinction between what we might call the 'executive' and the 'supervisory' levels of brain function.[5,6,13] The executive level is required to organize goal-directed activities, both concrete and abstract, and evaluation of their outcome in terms of current criteria and priorities. The supervisory level is required among other things for the ongoing evaluation and revision of criteria of evaluation themselves – that is, for the adjustment of priorities – and for the updating of the current 'state of conditional readiness' of the lower levels to match the demands made by the sensory input. On this basis, for example, what is *perceived* is internally represented or 'modelled' implicitly by the constraints it imposes on the state of conditional readiness, and is distinguished from the myriad sources of sensory input that are not perceived, by the matching response whereby the supervisory system updates the state of conditional readiness to reckon with it.[14,15] We are *conscious* only of those objects and features of our world that elicit this supervisory matching response, even though many other sensory stimuli may also elicit and steer lower-level executive action without our being conscious of them or their origins. (Think for example of the unconscious sensorimotor coordinations involved in riding a bicycle while looking for a house with a particular number.) Along these lines it would seem more parsimonious to describe a split-brain patient not as 'two people' or 'two free wills', but as one person who is liable in certain circumstances to show a peculiarly elaborate form of absent-mindedness.

How Many Self-supervisory Systems?

You can probably see by now the working hypothesis behind my sceptical argument. It is that what makes people like you or me a psychological unity, as far as our brains are concerned, is our having only one self-supervisory system to determine our overall priorities. How the activity of this system gives rise to our conscious experience is to me totally mysterious;[16] but you can see that if the hypothesis were true, one could expect quite detailed correlations between the physical patterns of self-supervisory traffic and the changing contents of conscious experience.

By speaking of a 'system' here I mean something embodied, not so much in particular anatomical structures, as in particular cooperative patterns of information-flow. A crude analogy might be the sort of oscillation that can arise if a public-address loudspeaker feeds back to its microphone. Here the cooperative oscillating system is formed by the amplifier plus the air-path from loudspeaker to microphone, and cannot be identified solely with certain electronic structures. In a similar sense, the (vastly more complex) cooperative information-flow structure that embodies our conscious experience could be expected in many cases to extend out beyond our skin and back through the environment in which we are consciously active.

While it would also normally entail traffic to, between, and from cortical areas, this evaluative supervisory flow system could be expected particularly to involve those deeper structures, such as the limbic/hypothalamic system (see figure 3.1), which are known to be closely associated with emotional states, and which are not split by cutting the corpus callosum.

To put this in slightly more concrete terms, we can crudely picture the human central nervous system as a structure shaped like a capital Y, but with the corpus callosum normally forming a bridge between the upper ends of the Y, which of course represent the two cerebral hemispheres. Multiple pathways are known to run in both directions along all three arms of the Y. If the only direct correlate of conscious experience were cortical activity, then it would be plausible that cutting the corpus callosum should bring two separate 'streams of consciousness' into being. If, however, as I am arguing, the physical correlate of our conscious experience is likely to be the cooperative to-and-fro traffic between cortical and deeper levels of neural activity (that is, levels below the junction of the two arms), then although removal of the callosal bridge could be expected to bring separate left and right executive systems into being, it would give no reason to doubt the continued unity of the conscious person. It is only if the neural equipment for self-supervisory normative activity were known to be completely duplicated (in *each* hemisphere), at cortical levels normally linked by the corpus callosum, that we could plausibly regard split-brain patients as two people.

Thinking on these lines, then, what we would want to ask about such patients is whether the surgical operation has so completely split the cooperative self-supervisory system (whatever it turns out to be) whose activity mediates the conscious experience of normal people as to set up two independent self-supervisory flow systems. As I hope my story has shown, this is not an easy question to answer experimentally; but I hope it is also clear why I doubt whether existing evidence is adequate to answer it affirmatively.

References

1 Gazzaniga, M. S., Bogen, J. E. and Sperry, R. W. (1962) Some functional effects of sectioning the cerebral commissures in man. *Proceedings of the National Academy of Science*, 48: 1765–9.
2 Gazzaniga, M. S. (1970) *The Bisected Brain*. New York: Appleton-Century-Crofts.
3 Sperry, R. W. (1966) In J. C. Eccles (ed.), *Brain and Conscious Experience*, p. 304. New York: Springer.
4 Buber, M. (1937) *I and Thou*. Edinburgh: T. & T. Clark.
5 MacKay, D. M. (1980) Conscious agency with unsplit and split brains. In B. D. Josephson and V. S. Ramachandran (eds), *Consciousness and the Physical World*, pp. 95–113. Oxford: Pergamon.
6 MacKay, D. M. (1978) The dynamics of perception. In P. A. Buser and A. Rougeul-Buser (eds), *Cerebral Correlates of Conscious Experience*, pp. 53–68. Amsterdam, New York, Oxford: Elsevier.
7 MacKay, D. M. and V. (1982) Explicit dialogue between left and right half systems of split brains. *Nature*, 295: 690–1.
8 Gazzaniga, M. S. and LeDoux, J. E. (1978) *The Integrated Mind.* New York: Plenum Press.
9 Gazzaniga, M. S. (1972) *Am. Scient.* 60: 311–17.
10 Gazzaniga, M. S. and Smylie, C. S. (1984) What does language do for a right hemisphere? *Handbook of Cognitive Neuroscience*, pp. 199–210. New York: Plenum Press.
11 Gazzaniga, M. S., *The Bisected Brain* pp. 105–6.
12 Penfield, W. (in discussion). In J. C. Eccles (ed.), *Brain and Conscious Experience*, p. 253.
13 MacKay, D. M. (in discussion) In ibid., pp. 312–13.
14 MacKay, D. M. (1956) Towards an information-flow model of human

behaviour. *Brit. J. Psychol.* 47: 30–43. Reprinted in W. Buckley (ed.) (1968) *Modern Systems Research for the Behavioral Scientist*, pp. 359–68. Chicago: Aldine.

15 MacKay, D. M. (1970) Perception and brain function. In F. O. Schmitt (editor-in-chief), *The Neurosciences: Second Study Program*. New York: Rockefeller Univ. Press, pp. 303–16.

16 MacKay, D. M. (1982) Ourselves and our brains: duality without dualism. *Psychoneuroendocrinology*, 7: 285–94.

2

Divided Minds and the Nature of Persons

Derek Parfit

Derek Parfit, who was born in 1942, has been a philosopher at All Souls College, Oxford for many years. He has also taught frequently in the United States. The main subjects on which he has worked have been rationality, morality, personal identity, and future generations. These are the subjects of his book Reasons and Persons, *published by Oxford University Press in 1984.*

It was the split-brain cases which drew me into philosophy. Our knowledge of these cases depends on the results of various psychological tests, as described by Donald MacKay.[1] These tests made use of two facts. We control each of our arms, and see what is in each half of our visual fields, with only one of our hemispheres. When someone's hemispheres have been disconnected, psychologists can thus present to this person two different written questions in the two halves of his visual field, and can receive two different answers written by this person's two hands.

Here is a simplified imaginary version of the kind of evidence that such tests provide. One of these people looks fixedly at the centre of a wide screen, whose left half is red and right half is blue. On each half in a darker shade are the words, 'How many colours can you see?' With both hands the person writes, 'Only one'. The words are now changed to read, 'Which is the only colour that you can see?' With one of his hands the person writes 'Red', with the other he writes 'Blue'.

If this is how such a person responds, I would conclude that he is having two visual sensations – that he does, as he claims, see both red and blue. But in seeing each colour he is not aware of seeing the other. He has two streams of consciousness, in each of which he can see only one colour. In one stream he sees red, and at the same time, in his other stream, he sees blue. More generally, he could be having at the same time two series of thoughts and sensations, in having each of which he is unaware of having the other.

This conclusion has been questioned. It has been claimed by some that there are not *two* streams of consciousness, on the ground that the sub-dominant hemisphere is a part of the brain whose functioning involves no

The Daibutsu (Great Buddha) *at Kamakura, Japan, constructed in 1252. Derek Parfit's denial of the concept of a person is remarkably similar to a central tenet of Buddhist philosophy (photograph by Colin Blakemore).*

consciousness. If this were true, these cases would lose most of their interest. I believe that it is not true, chiefly because, if a person's dominant hemisphere is destroyed, this person is able to react in the way in which, in the split-brain cases, the sub-dominant hemisphere reacts, and we do not believe that such a person is just an automaton, without consciousness. The sub-dominant hemisphere is, of course, much less developed in certain ways, typically having the linguistic abilities of a three-year-old. But three-year-olds are conscious. This supports the view that, in split-brain cases, there *are* two streams of consciousness.

Another view is that, in these cases, there are two persons involved, sharing the same body. Like Professor MacKay, I believe that we should reject this view. My reason for believing this is, however, different. Professor MacKay denies that there are two persons involved because he believes that there is only one person involved. I believe that, in a sense, the number of persons involved is none.

The Ego Theory and the Bundle Theory

To explain this sense I must, for a while, turn away from the split-brain cases. There are two theories about what persons are, and what is involved in a person's continued existence over time. On the *Ego Theory*, a person's continued existence cannot be explained except as the continued existence of a particular *Ego*, or *subject of experiences*. An Ego Theorist claims that, if we ask what unifies someone's consciousness at any time – what makes it true, for example, that I can now both see what I am typing and hear the wind outside my window – the answer is that these are both experiences which are being had by me, this person, at this time. Similarly, what explains the unity of a person's whole life is the fact that all of the experiences in this life are had by the same person, or subject of experiences. In its best-known form, the *Cartesian view*, each person is a persisting purely mental thing – a soul, or spiritual substance.

The rival view is the *Bundle Theory*. Like most styles in art – Gothic, baroque, rococo, etc. – this theory owes its name to its critics. But the name is good enough. According to the Bundle Theory, we can't explain either the unity of consciousness at any time, or the unity of a whole life, by referring to a person. Instead we must claim that there are long series of different mental states and events – thoughts, sensations, and the like – each series being what we call one life. Each series is unified by various kinds of causal relation, such as the relations that hold between experiences and later memories of them. Each series is thus like a bundle tied up with string.

In a sense, a Bundle Theorist denies the existence of persons. An outright denial is of course absurd. As Reid protested in the eighteenth century, 'I am not thought, I am not action, I am not feeling; I am something which thinks and acts and feels.' I am not a series of events, but a person. A Bundle Theorist admits this fact, but claims it to be only a fact about our grammar, or our language. There are persons or subjects in this language-dependent way. If, however, persons are believed to be more than this – to be separately existing things, distinct from our brains and bodies, and the various kinds of mental states and events – the

Bundle Theorist denies that there are such things.

The first Bundle Theorist was Buddha, who taught 'anatta', or the *No Self view*. Buddhists concede that selves or persons have 'nominal existence', by which they mean that persons are merely combinations of other elements. Only what exists by itself, as a separate element, has instead what Buddhists call 'actual existence'. Here are some quotations from Buddhist texts:

At the beginning of their conversation the king politely asks the monk his name, and receives the following reply: 'Sir, I am known as "Nagasena"; my fellows in the religious life address me as "Nagasena". Although my parents gave me the name . . . it is just an appellation, a form of speech, a description, a conventional usage. "Nagasena" is only a name, for no person is found here.'

A sentient being does exist, you think, O Mara? You are misled by a false conception. This bundle of elements is void of Self, In it there is no sentient being. Just as a set of wooden parts Receives the name of carriage, So do we give to elements The name of fancied being.

Buddha has spoken thus: 'O Brethren, actions do exist, and also their consequences, but the person that acts does not. There is no one to cast away this set of elements, and no one to assume a new set of them. There exists no Individual, it is only a conventional name given to a set of elements.'[2]

Buddha's claims are strikingly similar to the claims advanced by several Western writers. Since these writers knew nothing of Buddha, the similarity of these claims suggests that they are not merely part of one cultural tradition, in one period. They may be, as I believe they are, true.

What We Believe Ourselves to Be

Given the advances in psychology and neurophysiology, the Bundle Theory may now seem to be obviously true. It may seem uninteresting to deny that there are separately existing Egos, which are distinct from brains and bodies and the various kinds of mental states and events. But this is not the only issue. We may be convinced that the Ego Theory is false, or even senseless. Most of us, however, even if we are not aware of this, also have certain beliefs about what is involved in our continued existence over time. And these beliefs would only be justified if something like the Ego Theory was true. Most of us therefore have false beliefs about what persons are, and about ourselves.

These beliefs are best revealed when we consider certain imaginary cases, often drawn from science fiction. One such case is *teletransportation*. Suppose that you enter a cubicle in which, when you press a button, a scanner records the states of all of the cells in your brain and body, destroying both while doing so. This information is then transmitted at the speed of light to some other planet, where a replicator produces a perfect organic copy of you. Since the brain of your Replica is exactly like yours, it will seem to remember living your life up to the moment when you pressed the button, its character will be just like yours, and it will be in every other way psychologically continuous with you. This psychological continuity will not have its normal cause, the continued existence of your brain, since the causal chain will run through the transmission by radio of your 'blueprint'.

Several writers claim that, if you chose to be teletransported, believing this to be the fastest way of travelling, you would be making a terrible mistake. This would not be a way of travelling, but a way of dying. It may not, they concede, be quite as bad as ordinary death. It might be some consolation to you that, after your death, you will have this Replica, which can finish the book that you are writing, act as parent to your children, and so on. But, they insist, this Replica won't be you. It will merely be someone else, who is exactly like you. This is why this prospect is nearly as bad as ordinary death.

Imagine next a whole range of cases, in each of which, in a single operation, a different proportion of the cells in your brain and body would be replaced with exact duplicates. At the near end of this range, only 1 or 2 per cent would be replaced; in the middle, 40 or 60 per cent; near the far end, 98 or 99 per cent. At the far end of this range is pure teletransportation, the case in which all of your cells would be 'replaced'.

When you imagine that some proportion of your cells will be replaced with exact duplicates, it is natural to have the following beliefs. First, if you ask, 'Will I survive? Will the resulting person be me?', there must be an answer to this question. Either you will survive, or you are about to die. Second, the answer to this question must be either a simple 'Yes' or a simple 'No'. The person who wakes up either will or will not be you. There cannot be a third answer, such as that the person waking up will be half you. You can imagine yourself later being half-conscious. But if the resulting person will be fully conscious, he cannot be half you. To state these beliefs together: to the question, 'Will the resulting person be me?', there must always *be* an answer, which must be all-or-nothing.

There seem good grounds for believing that, in the case of teletransportation, your Replica would not be you. In a slight variant of this case, your Replica might be created while you were still alive, so that you could talk to one another. This seems to show that, if 100 per cent of your cells were replaced, the result would merely be a Replica of you. At the other end of my range of cases, where only 1 per cent would be replaced, the resulting person clearly *would* be you. It therefore seems that, in the cases in between, the resulting person must be either you, or merely a Replica. It seems that one of these must be true, and that it makes a great difference which is true.

How We Are Not What We Believe

If these beliefs were correct, there must be some critical percentage, somewhere in this range of cases, up to which the resulting person would be you, and beyond which he would merely be your Replica. Perhaps, for example, it would be you who would wake up if the proportion of cells replaced were 49 per cent, but if just a few more cells were also replaced, this would make all the difference, causing it to be someone else who would wake up.

That there must be some such critical percentage follows from our natural beliefs. But this conclusion is most implausible. How could a few cells make such a difference? Moreover, if there is such a critical percentage, no one could ever discover where it came. Since in all these cases the resulting person would believe that he was you, there could never be any evidence about where, in this range of cases, he would suddenly cease to be you.

On the Bundle Theory, we should reject these natural beliefs. Since you, the person, are not a separately existing entity, we can know exactly what would happen without answering the question of what will happen to you. Moreover, in the cases in the middle of my range, it is an empty question whether the resulting person would be you, or would merely be someone else who is exactly like you. These are not here two different possibilities, one of which must be true. These are merely two different descriptions of the very same course of events. If 50 per cent of your cells were replaced with exact duplicates, we could call the resulting person you, or we could call him merely your Replica. But since these are not here different possibilities, this is a mere choice of words.

As Buddha claimed, the Bundle Theory is hard to believe. It is hard to accept that it could be an empty question whether one is about to die, or will instead live for many years.

What we are being asked to accept may be made clearer with this analogy. Suppose that a certain club exists for some time, holding regular meetings. The meetings then cease. Some years later, several people form a club with the same name, and the same rules. We can ask, 'Did these people revive the very same club? Or did they merely start up another club which is exactly similar?' Given certain further details, this would be another empty question. We could know just what happened without answering this question. Suppose that someone said: 'But there must be an answer. The club meeting later must either be, or not be, the very same club.' This would show that this person didn't understand the nature of clubs.

In the same way, if we have any worries about my imagined cases, we don't understand the nature of persons. In each of my cases, you would know that the resulting person would be both psychologically and physically exactly like you, and that he would have some particular proportion of the cells in your brain and body – 90 per cent, or 10 per cent, or, in the case of teletransportation, 0 per cent. Knowing this, you know everything. How could it be a real question what would happen to you, unless you are a separately existing Ego, distinct from a brain and body, and the various kinds of mental state and event? If there are no such Egos, there is nothing else to ask a real question about.

Accepting the Bundle Theory is not only hard; it may also affect our emotions. As Buddha claimed, it may undermine our concern about our own futures. This effect can be suggested by redescribing this change of view. Suppose that you are about to be destroyed, but will later have a Replica on Mars. You would naturally believe that this prospect is about as bad as ordinary death, since your Replica won't be you. On the Bundle Theory, the fact that your Replica won't be you just consists in the fact that, though it will be fully psychologically continuous with you, this continuity won't have its normal cause. But when you object to teletransportation you are not objecting merely to the abnormality of this cause. You are objecting that this cause won't get *you* to Mars. You fear that the abnormal cause will fail to produce a further and all-important fact, which is different from the fact that your Replica will be psychologically continuous with you. You do not merely want there to be psychological continuity between you and some future person. You want to *be* this future person. On the Bundle Theory, there is no such special further fact. What you fear will not happen, in this imagined case, *never* happens. You want the person on Mars to be you in a specially intimate way in which no future person will ever be you. This means that, judged from the standpoint of your natural beliefs, even ordinary survival is about as bad as teletransportation. *Ordinary survival is about as bad as being destroyed and having a Replica.*

How the Split-Brain Cases Support the Bundle Theory

The truth of the Bundle Theory seems to me, in the widest sense, as much a scientific as a philosophical conclusion. I can imagine kinds of evidence which would have justified believing in the existence of separately existing Egos, and believing that the continued existence of these Egos is what explains the continuity of each mental life. But there is in fact very little evidence in favour of this Ego Theory, and much for the alternative Bundle Theory.

Some of this evidence is provided by the split-brain cases. On the Ego Theory, to explain what unifies our experiences at any one time, we should simply claim that these are all experiences which are being had by the same person. Bundle Theorists reject this explanation. This disagreement is hard to resolve in ordinary cases. But consider the simplified split-brain case that I described. We show to my imagined patient a placard whose left half is blue and right half is red. In one of this person's two streams of consciousness, he is aware of seeing only blue, while at the same time, in his other stream, he is aware of seeing only red. Each of these two visual experiences is combined with other experiences, like that of being aware of moving one of his hands. What unifies the experiences, at any time, in each of this person's two streams of consciousness? What unifies his awareness of seeing only red with his awareness of moving one hand? The answer cannot be that these experiences are being had by the same person. This answer cannot explain the unity of each of this person's two streams of consciousness, since it ignores the disunity between these streams. This person is now having all of the experiences in both of his two streams. If this fact was what unified these experiences, this would make the two streams one.

These cases do not, I have claimed, involve two people sharing a single body. Since there is only one person involved, who has two streams of consciousness, the Ego Theorist's explanation would have to take the following form. He would have to distinguish between persons and subjects of experiences, and claim that, in split-brain cases, there are *two* of the latter. What unifies the experiences in one of the person's two streams would have to be the fact that these experiences are all being had by the same subject of experiences. What unifies the experiences in this person's other stream would have to be the fact that they are being had by another subject of experiences. When this explanation takes this form, it becomes much less plausible. While we could assume that 'subject of experiences', or 'Ego', simply meant 'person', it was easy to believe that there are subjects of experiences. But if there can be subjects of experiences that are not persons, and if in the life of a split-brain patient there are at any time two different subjects of experiences – two different Egos – why should we believe that there really are such things? This does not amount to a refutation. But it seems to me a strong argument against the Ego Theory.

As a Bundle Theorist, I believe that these two Egos are idle cogs. There is another explanation of the unity of consciousness, both in ordinary cases and in split-brain cases. It is simply a fact that ordinary people are, at any time, aware of having several different experiences. This awareness of several different experiences can be helpfully compared with one's awareness, in short-term memory, of several different experiences. Just as there can be a single memory of just having had several experiences, such as hearing a bell strike three times, there can be a single state of awareness both of hearing the fourth striking of this bell, and of seeing, at the same time, ravens flying past the bell-tower.

Unlike the Ego Theorist's explanation, this explanation can easily be extended to cover split-brain cases. In such cases there is, at any time, not one state of awareness of several different experiences, but two such states. In the case I described, there is one state of awareness of both seeing only red and of moving one hand, and there is another state of awareness of both seeing only blue and moving the other hand. In claiming that there are two such states of awareness, we are not postulating the existence of unfamiliar entities, two separately existing Egos which are not the same as the single person whom the case involves. This explanation appeals to a pair of mental states which would have to be described anyway in a full description of this case.

I have suggested how the split-brain cases provide one argument for one view about the nature of persons. I should mention another such argument, provided by an imagined extension of these cases, first discussed at length by David Wiggins.[3]

In this imagined case a person's brain is divided, and the two halves are transplanted into a pair of different bodies. The two resulting people live quite separate lives. This imagined case shows that personal identity is not what matters. If I was about to divide, I should conclude that neither of the resulting people will be me. I will have ceased to exist. But this way of ceasing to exist is about as good – or as bad – as ordinary survival.

Some of the features of Wiggins's imagined case are likely to remain technically impossible. But the case cannot be dismissed, since its most striking feature, the division of one stream of consciousness into separate streams, has already happened. This is a second way in which the actual split-brain cases have great theoretical importance. They challenge some of our deepest assumptions about ourselves.[4]

Notes

1 See MacKay's contribution, chapter 1 of this volume.

2 For the sources of these and similar quotations, see my *Reasons and Persons* (1984) pp. 502–3, 532. Oxford: Oxford Univ. Press.

3 At the end of his *Identity and Spatio-temporal Continuity* (1967) Oxford: Blackwell.

4 I discuss these assumptions further in part 3 of my *Reasons and Persons*.

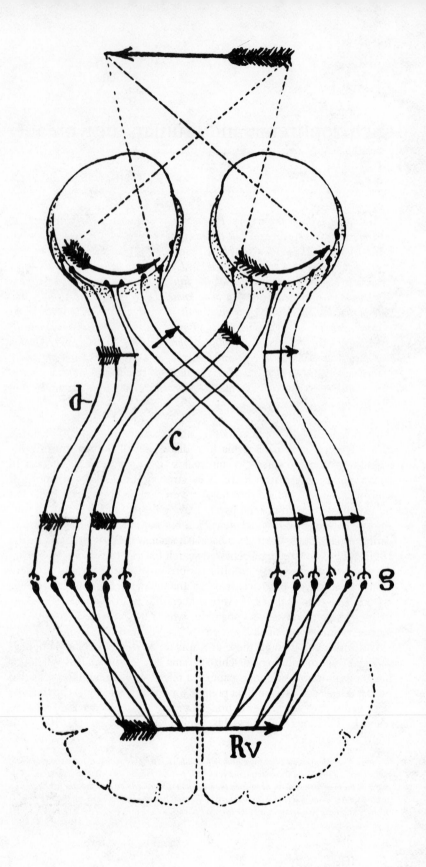

Schizophrenia and Human Individuality

Gordon Claridge

Gordon Claridge trained in Psychology at London University, first at University College and then at the Institute of Psychiatry, where for a while he was research assistant to Hans Eysenck. His subsequent career as both academic researcher and practitioner in Clinical Psychology has resulted in a unique blend of experience, enabling him to bring to bear on the clinical phenomena of mental illness a wide knowledge of psychological theory and experimentation. His current interest is in applying this experience to the understanding of schizophrenia, a disorder on which he takes a radically different view from that currently adopted in British psychiatry. Gordon Claridge is Lecturer in Abnormal Psychology at Oxford University and a Fellow of Magdalen College. He is the author of several books, the most recent of which is Origins of Mental Illness, Temperament, Deviance and Disorder *(Blackwell, 1985).*

Twenty years ago, at the height of the antipsychiatry movement, inclusion of a reference to schizophrenia in a discussion of human individuality would not have seemed so unusual as it does perhaps today. In contemporary psychiatry there is a strongly influential opinion that schizophrenia will indeed turn out to be an organic brain disease that has no useful referent in normal psychology or normal mind/brain relationships. This is not an original viewpoint, but merely represents a return to earlier explanations. Partly as a backlash against the antipsychiatry of the 1960s we are now seeing a renewed search for the 'cause' of schizophrenia and we currently have on offer various possibilities: viruses, enlargement of the brain ventricles or other anatomical defects of the nervous system, and abnormalities of every conceivable neurochemical, especially the transmitter substance dopamine, which has provided us with the longest running story of all.[1]

Unfortunately, none of these attempts to identify a specific pathophysiology or neuropathology in schizophrenia has yet succeeded. We have a few thousand more scientific papers to read – and the organizations that fund research are a few million pounds (or dollars) worse off – but it is not clear that we are any nearer to understanding schizophrenia than we were when R. D. Laing published his book *The Divided Self* in 1960.[2] For

The great Spanish anatomist Santiago Ramón y Cajal (1852–1934) published this diagram in his major treatise Histologie du système nerveux *(1911–12). It shows, in a simplified form, the way in which the projection of nerve fibres from the eyes into the brain delivers a view of the left half of the visual field (the arrow head) to the visual area in the right hemisphere (Rv), and information from the right half-field (the arrow tail) to the left hemisphere.*

example, while it is probably true that dopamine systems in the brain *are* functionally disturbed in schizophrenia, it now seems more than likely that this merely reflects some non-specific increase in the activity of the central nervous system that accompanies any form of mental derangement, even acute anxiety. A virus may certainly contribute to the aetiology in a small proportion of cases, but there is little evidence for this – and even less that it can explain the syndrome as a whole. And the case for enlarged ventricles seems just as weak: a study recently reported in the *British Journal of Psychiatry* suggested that the brain ventricles of some schizophrenics may actually be *smaller* than normal![3]

I believe that there are two reasons why this new 'organic' phase in schizophrenia research has failed in its objectives. One reason is that those working in the field have rarely matched their conceptualizations and explanations of schizophrenia to the complexity of the condition. Anyone who has worked with schizophrenics will know how difficult it is to make sense of (or indeed even obtain stable measurements of) quite simple overt physiological responses in a disorder that is so variable – not only across individuals but also in the same individual from one occasion to the next. The problem becomes even more evident when it is transposed to attempts at understanding what might be going on in the *higher* parts of the nervous system – which presumably mediate most of the significant psychological features of schizophrenia. For in schizophrenia we find complicated disorders of perception, attention, thought and language; weird belief systems driven by inappropriate emotion; and an altered concept of the self in relation to others. It is not inconceivable that all of these effects are due to a single chemical imbalance (or virus) in the brain; but the idea seems inherently unlikely and in any case ignores several important features of schizophrenia which I shall elaborate on here.

The second reason why narrowly focused medical research has failed to explain schizophrenia is that, in its hurry to turn its back on antipsychiatry, it was too ready to reject one of the more important contributions of the radical psychiatry movement. I am referring to the idea, implicit in the writings of the antipsychiatrists, that there is some *continuity* between normal and schizophrenic mental functioning. This view was articulated in two ways. One was in the suggestion that the label 'schizophrenic' is to some extent arbitrary, its use being partly dependent on shifting social criteria of madness. The other was by showing that, if you listen carefully even to acutely disturbed schizophrenic persons, what they say does make some sense when looked at as an expression of their own individuality and their own attempt to interpret the world around them: for example, ideas that are apparently paranoid and delusional may indeed spring from the schizophrenic's hypersensitivity to interpersonal events which, while certainly misinterpreted, may nevertheless have a basis in reality. Where the antipsychiatrists themselves failed, of course, was in refusing to make any reference to the brain; unnecessarily as it turns out, since, as I shall show, a concern with the neuropsychology of schizophrenia does not in the least imply acceptance of the conventional disease models of psychiatric disorder which writers like Laing and Szasz so bitterly opposed.

Perhaps I can now turn to some more substantive evidence for the theme I have just introduced: that there is an essential continuity between the normal and the schizophrenic, such that the study of one can give us valuable insights into the other. Hans Eysenck, in chapter 4, mentions one way in which this idea has gained ground in abnormal psychology when he refers to the dimension of 'psychoticism', identified by him in the course of his statistical analyses of the personality traits that can be found in normal people. He and I have not always agreed on the exact interpretation of the personality traits which he ascribes to this 'psychoticism' dimension.[4,5] However, our differences of opinion are of a technical kind, rather than being a fundamental disagreement about the existence of 'psychotic' personality traits in normal people. In any case, as I know Professor Eysenck would be only too willing to acknowledge, his own work really only puts into a modern form a perspective on schizophrenia that has existed ever since Eugen Bleuler coined the term earlier this century. Thus Bleuler himself used the description 'schizoid' to refer to the fact that some individuals seemed to show cognitive and emotional tendencies that were schizophrenic in quality, though stopping short of manifest insanity. Shortly afterwards Kretschmer brought the idea into personality theory as part of his proposal that 'schizothymia' could be recognized as a general personality characteristic.

Other schools of thought in clinical psychiatry have also pointed in the same direction. To many observers the exact boundaries of schizophrenia have always seemed somewhat blurred, and psychiatrists frequently encounter patients in whom the symptoms of neurosis or personality disorder intermingle with psychotic elements. The early psychoanalysts recognized such individuals as people who were not quite psychotic but who were too disturbed to respond to conventional forms of psychotherapy. There is now growing evidence that these patients probably form part of a spectrum of psychotic states, including schizophrenia, making up a group of so-called 'borderline states'.[6] The Americans have always been more sympathetic to this idea than British psychiatrists and they have recently introduced new categories of 'borderline' into their DSM-III, the latest revision of their classification of psychiatric disorder. One of these borderline categories – 'schizotypal personality disorder' – is defined according to symptoms that are clearly schizophrenic in quality: as shown in table 3.1, they include such characteristics as peculiar emotional reactions to others, odd styles of communication, transient sensory illusions, and so on.

This description of 'schizotypal personality disorder' refers, of course, to continuity within the *clinical* sphere; that is, among individuals who are already recognized as being psychiatrically disturbed. But for several years now my colleagues and I have been investigating the possibility of measuring similar characteristics which we believe can be observed to a lesser degree in *normal* people. Recently, using the DSM criteria shown here as a template for devising questionnaire items, we have constructed a personality scale that can be used quite successfully to select individuals who, while psychiatrically healthy, nevertheless show schizotypal traits.[7] Later I will return to this questionnaire and describe some further uses we have made of it in our research on schizotypy and schizophrenia.

3.1: DSM-III diagnostic criteria for schizotypal personality disorder

---

At least four of the following:
1 Magical thinking, e.g. superstitiousness, clairvoyance, telepathy, 'sixth sense', 'others can feel my feelings' (in children and adolescents, bizarre fantasies or preoccupations);
2 Ideas of reference;
3 Social isolation, e.g. no close friends or confidants, social contacts limited to essential everyday tasks;
4 Recurrent illusions, sensing the presence of a force or person not actually present (e.g. 'I felt as if my dead mother were in the room with me'), depersonalization, or derealization not associated with panic attacks;
5 Odd speech (without loosening of associations or incoherence), e.g. speech that is digressive, vague, over-elaborate, circumstantial, metaphorical;
6 Inadequate rapport in face-to-face interaction due to constricted or inappropriate affect, e.g. aloof, cold;
7 Suspiciousness or paranoid ideation;
8 Undue social anxiety or hypersensitivity to real or imagined criticism.

Before doing so, however, I would like to mention briefly one further argument in favour of the continuity view of schizophrenia. This comes from genetics. There is now considerable evidence that heredity plays some part in schizophrenia – not in any unique sense, merely contributing in much the same way as it does to other forms of human variation. Thus, the most convincing explanation of the genetic data on schizophrenia is that offered by Gottesman and Shields.[8] Their view is based on a genetic model – the polygenic model – that is commonly used to explain the inherited component in continuously variable traits, like intelligence and blood pressure, as well as some forms of systemic disease, such as essential hypertension: the model assumes that many genes, acting together and present in varying number, are responsible for differences in the observed strength of the characteristic in question. Applied to schizophrenia, the theory therefore proposes that what is inherited is a varying degree of *liability* to the disorder, which becomes manifest as frank psychotic illness in those individuals who have a very heavy genetic disposition; and even then only as a result of an interaction between life stress and biological susceptibility. The notion of dimensionality contained in such a model is, of course, entirely consistent with the borderline or spectrum idea of varying *clinical* manifestation of schizophrenic symptoms. It would also account for the existence of a continuum of psychotic or schizotypal traits in the sphere of normal personality, since according to the polygenic theory we would indeed expect the genes for schizophrenia to find some attenuated phenotypic expression among the general population.

Of course, the apparent continuity in schizophrenia referred to so far covers a quite limited set of observations; namely, the dimensionality of rather superficially described personality and cognitive characteristics that can be traced from the normal to the manifestly psychotic. But it does provide a starting-point for asking more searching questions. One such question, of particular relevance here, concerns the extent to which we can find a useful referent for schizotypy (and hence schizophrenia) in the central nervous system. Psychologists pursuing this problem have usuallly done so at the intermediate level of the *conceptual* nervous system, which they hope can act as a model for what is going on in the *real* nervous system. And those like myself, especially persuaded by the continuity theory of psychotic behaviour, have tried to construct conceptual nervous system models that can encompass both schizophrenia as a clincial disorder and the manifestation of its underlying traits in normal personality differences.[9] Empirically, this has involved using a fairly obvious research strategy; namely trying to identify some feature of the response of the central nervous system that can be observed in diagnosed schizophrenic patients and then looking to see whether it can also be found in normal individuals selected according to some external criterion indicating that they are high in schizotypy or, to use Professor Eysenck's term, psychoticism.

Much of the earlier research for which we adopted this strategy concentrated on fairly simple psycho-physiological responses that implicate basic nervous processes like arousal, sensation and perception. There we have shown that quite distinctive patterns of unstable psycho-physiological responding, demonstrable in schizophrenics, can also be observed in some normal subjects, including the first-degree relatives (children or siblings) of schizophrenics – a group which, on genetic grounds, would be expected to contain an especially high number of schizotypal individuals.[5,10,11] Of course, the conclusions we can draw from these observations about mind/brain relationships in schizophrenia are limited, since the conceptual nervous system models put forward to explain such findings have been rather simplistic. In keeping with much of the theorizing by psychologists about schizophrenia, the models have generally referred their explanations to fairly *low-level* brain structures like the limbic system, which is known to be intimately involved in the control of the sensory, attentional and emotional responses studied by psycho-physiologists (see figure 3.1). Thus it is reasonable to suppose that deviant functioning in such areas of the brain as the limbic system probably do mediate some of the more basic anomalies of perception and arousal found in schizophrenia.

Our more recent research has moved along somewhat different lines, however, and has involved extrapolating from recent findings which suggest that the organization of the two cerebral hemispheres is different in schizophrenia.[12] It is well established that the two halves of the brain subserve different psychological functions, the left hemisphere for example being specialized for language. However, there is now a good deal of evidence that, when examined on tests that demand the processing of linguistic material, schizophrenics show unusual patterns of hemisphere asymmetry: the results suggest either a deficiency in, or even a reversal of, the left hemisphere's normal superiority in carrying out this kind of task. We were therefore interested to see whether we could show similar forms of cerebral organization in some otherwise normal people, chosen because they were high in schizotypal traits. There were two reasons why this approach appealed to us, compared with our earlier concentration on simpler psycho-physiological processes. First of all, it took us closer to the *higher* nervous system and therefore to that part of the brain that clearly mediates the really important psychological features of schizophrenia.

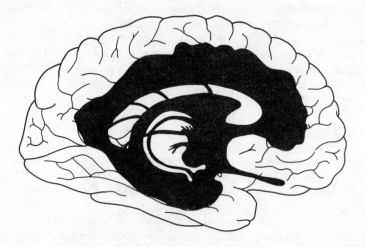

Figure 3.1   The left hemisphere of the human brain is seen from the inside after the brain has been divided along the midline. The principal regions included in the limbic system *are shown in black (redrawn from Ottoson, 1983,* Physiology of the Nervous System, *Macmillan Press, London, Oxford University Press, New York, fig. 19.1, 287).*

Secondly, it seemed to offer a richer set of possibilities for exploring the neuropsychological connection between schizophrenic disorder and schizotypal personality.

The most consistent finding with schizophrenic patients has come from studies using the divided visual field technique, described in chapter 1 by Donald MacKay, to compare the speed and accuracy with which verbal stimuli are processed when presented first to the left or to the right hemisphere. It has been observed that, when tested on this kind of task, schizophrenics tend to show either a left-hemisphere inferiority or, as mentioned above, some degree of reversed asymmetry for verbal processing; that is, a slightly superior response to stimuli presented to the *left* visual field and therefore first to the *right*, normally language-inferior, hemisphere. However, an experiment carried out some years ago by my colleague Paul Broks showed that this unusual hemisphere asymmetry is not confined to schizophrenics: it can also be demonstrated in normal schizotypal subjects, selected on the basis of the questionnaire mentioned earlier.[13] The experiment employed a conventional divided visual field technique and involved presenting nonsense syllables separately to each half-field, the measure of the subject's response being the accuracy with which each stimulus was recognized. The index of asymmetry was calculated as a 'laterality coefficient' representing the relative difference between the number of stimuli correctly recognized in the two fields of view. This measure was found to correspond closely to subjects' schizotypy scores, in such a way that the higher the schizotypal rating the weaker was the apparent left-hemisphere superiority for verbal processing. In other words, schizotypal normal individuals did indeed appear to perform somewhat like schizophrenics.

Since carrying out that experiment we have replicated it successfully and also undertaken further studies using other kinds of stimulus material.[14,15] So far all of the evidence seems to point in the same direction. It shows *either* that schizotypal normals are like schizophrenics – where the same experiment has been done with patient groups – *or* that their patterns of brain asymmetry are opposite to what one would expect, based on previous research on hemispheric function in normal subjects. Given the way in which we derived the schizotypy scale, this seems to suggest that what has been regarded as a sign of schizophrenic 'disease' is merely a form of brain organization that schizophrenics have in common with some normal people. If we add to this the other, psycho-physiological, evidence mentioned earlier, then it seems that we have a good case for arguing that in brain function, as in behaviour, there is some continuity between the schizophrenic and the normal.

Where does this take us in our search for an understanding of schizophrenia and human individuality? Even the studies of hemisphere function in psychotic *patients* have generated a large number of different theoretical models and, as usual in schizophrenia research, we have an explosion of fact and little in the way of comprehension. One interpretation of the data on language processing is that schizophrenics have some deficit in the left hemisphere, perhaps of a structural kind. But this seems unlikely, for two reasons. First of all, it would be difficult to explain the results just mentioned on normal subjects, unless it were assumed that some psychologically healthy people have the same deficit. And, secondly, it can be shown that the hemisphere asymmetries found on divided visual field tests are not necessarily *fixed*. Instead, they may fluctuate in extent and direction and may, indeed, be partly dependent on the psychological state of the individual, such as the degree of arousal prevailing at the time. Thus, in a recent unpublished study in our laboratory we found that on repeated testing on a divided visual field task, identical to that just described, the schizophrenic can eventually begin to perform 'normally'; that is, show the more usual left-hemisphere superiority for verbal processing. All of this suggests, not a structural defect, but that there is a much more dynamic set of mechanisms at work determining the apparent anomalies of hemisphere organization in schizophrenia.

Another explanation is that in schizophrenia there is some unusual form of inter-hemispheric *communication*. There are actually two versions of this hypothesis. One draws an analogy with the so-called 'split-brain' patient (referred to in chapter 1 by Donald MacKay) and argues that in schizophrenia the two hemispheres may be functionally separated.[16] The other version of the hypothesis suggests the opposite: that in schizophrenia there is *too much* communication, too much 'cross-talk', as it were, between the hemispheres.[17] Personally, I find this second version of the 'communication hypothesis' more appealing. Although at present rather vaguely stated, it does seem to offer more possibilities for trying to understand the phenomenology and aetiology of schizophrenia. And it might also give us a better clue to how psychosis, as a pathological state, could arise out of properties of the brain which in themselves are part of its normal functioning but which in extreme degree have the capacity to mediate the deviant psychological experiences found in schizophrenia. Vague though it is, I would like to examine the hypothesis in a little more detail, while issuing a caveat that what follows is extremely speculative.

Suppose it were the case that individuals differed in the facility with which information flowed between the two hemispheres, perhaps as a genetically determined characteristic. This would have a number of important consequences. During development it might lead to differences in the extent to which important functions like language become lateralized and therefore in the degree to which the symbolic internalization of external reality is predominantly taken over by one side of the brain. In some cases it might even lead to a dual representation of language, a dual conceptual system, and even a dual concept of the self. Here, incidentally, I am *not* proposing anything akin to 'dual personality' – in the clinical sense – or two personalities literally residing in opposite halves of the brain. Rather what I am suggesting is that the development of the *unity* of the self may be fragmented, leading to the sort of quality which Laing talks about as 'ontological insecurity', which causes many schizophrenics – and incidentally many borderline patients – to ask questions like 'Who am I?'

Schizophrenic *illness* might therefore be a state in which the cross-talk between the two systems becomes so intense that the brain as a whole becomes confused and can no longer make sense of the external world. The state itself might fluctuate, of course, and depend on a number of triggering factors, such as increased emotional arousal, which could serve to exacerbate the inter-hemispheric 'cross-talk'. This fluctuating characteristic might explain what is indeed the case in schizophrenia, that the patient's appreciation of reality, his stream of thought and use of language are often all extremely patchy, varying – often from moment to moment – between the sensible and the bizarre.

I should say that I have talked to at least two schizophrenics whose self-reports would fit the explanation just given. The first described having two personalities, which *he* actually did locate on opposite sides of his head. One of these personalities he described as his 'true' personality, which dealt with the real world but which was constantly in conflict with a second, alien, personality having its own set of ideas, motives and beliefs. The man suffered from almost continuous hallucinations in the form of voices from his second personality urging him to do things which his 'realistic' personality tried to resist. The other schizophrenic, although less articulate, told a similar story and, interestingly, located *his* voices in his left ear!

The idea, flowing from these introspections, that auditory hallucinations may represent a second language system talking to the person, is one that has been seriously discussed by Green and his colleagues, a group of psychologists who have made an important contribution to research on inter-hemispheric communication in schizophrenia.[18] They base their conclusion partly on the results of that work and partly on evidence that when schizophrenics hallucinate it is possible to record covert speech in the form of whispering and also to detect physiological activity in the region of the vocal musculature.[19] It may therefore indeed be the case that when schizophrenics hallucinate they are actually talking to themselves and that the content of the hallucinations reflects a secondary ideational system gaining access to consciousness.

One further merit of the 'cross-talk' hypothesis to which I have referred is that it might allow for the sort of graded variation that would be necessary if we are to support a continuity view of schizophrenia. Degrees of dual representation of the world might indeed lead to degrees of duality of the self, in the sense in which I defined it earlier. In the normal schizotype this might be perfectly healthy but it might become progressively maladaptive as we move along the continuum towards schizophrenia. If we take, for example, the borderline states, one of the primary features of these conditions is *ambivalence*; that is, the existence side by side of quite contradictory feelings and attitudes. The schizoid personality has also been described in the same way. For example, Manfred Bleuler recently referred to the 'ambitendencies' in the schizophrenic personality; what he called '. . . the inner shambles and disunity'; the person saying 'I want what I don't want' or 'Being alone is horrible; I want to be alone'.[20] It is conceivable that such conflict of impulse has, as its counterpart in the neurological domain, a 'divided brain', each part competing for attention in consciousness to the extent that mental chaos prevails.

Of course, whatever explanation we give of the hemisphere data – or, indeed, of any other data – about schizophrenia, there is still a huge gap between schizotypy and clinical psychosis. There is even a big gap between clinical psychosis and the so-called borderline states. If we are to sustain a continuity view then we have to be able to give a credible explanation of how the dispositional qualities that I have referred to here as 'schizotypy' get translated into schizophrenia and why, once that occurs, it persists, often into chronic illness. As a starting-point for trying to explain this transition I would again like to draw upon a self-report: this time of a person of my acquaintance who had a schizophrenic breakdown as a young man and who can talk with some authority about the question since he also happens to have once trained as a physiologist.

His view is that there are really two stages or two components in schizophrenic breakdown. The first, he suggests, has a transient, dynamic quality and involves disturbance of fairly basic psycho-physiological processes, like perception and emotional arousal: the person experiences a sense of heightened awareness, altered selective attention and other disturbances of consciousness which many early schizophrenics have described as a 'flooding' of the mind with thoughts and sensations. Such changes might be initiated fairly low down in the nervous system and correspond to the kind of phenomena that 'limbic system theories' of schizophrenia, to which I referred earlier, have tried to explain. However, there is then a next stage when these relatively low-level events are elaborated by the higher nervous system: for example, the person may develop delusional beliefs based on his earlier misperceptions, often in an attempt to explain them rationally to himself. Unlike the first stage, such changes have a more permanent quality because they become 'hard wired' into the nervous system as memories, attitudes and styles of thought, ready to be energized again should some relevant event, or increase in arousal, cause them to be reawakened.

This view of schizophrenia accounts, I believe, for a number of important features of the condition. It explains, for example, why, once set in motion, the progression into illness is difficult to reverse. Although it may be possible to damp down the underlying, dynamic element – say with drugs – the more permanent representation of psychotic thoughts in the higher nervous system remains, forming part of the individual's personality and cognitive structure. The theory also helps to explain the variable, and often patchy, time-course of schizophrenia, as well as its varying degree of severity in different individuals. Thus, there is presumably a continuous feedback between the two components just referred to, their mutual interaction producing a vicious circle of cause and effect that pushes some especially prone individuals further and further away from reality. In others, however, the process may be less insidious or even stop short of manifest psychosis, being seen rather as those disorders of the personality that have been labelled 'borderline'.

Of course, the account just given of schizophrenia does not specifically refer to theories of hemisphere function in the brain; nor does it explain the existence of schizotypal traits in personality and how these may be consistent with normal, or even superior, psychological adjustment. On the first point, it is possible to argue, I believe, that a person's liability to schizophrenia crucially depends on the extent to which a firm sense of external reality has become internalized in childhood; and this process, I have suggested, may reflect, in the physiological domain, the properties of communication between the two cerebral hemispheres. This would mean that individuals whose internal representation of reality is already ambiguous might be especially liable to misconstrue sense data from the external world, especially at particular periods in life, such as adolescence, when the sense of self is in any case uncertain and when dynamic neural processes controlling affectivity are undergoing dramatic change.

As for schizotypy as a normal personality characteristic, it is not unusual for mental disorder to have elements of adaptiveness – anxiety is a simple example – and elsewhere I have argued that this may be true of schizophrenia: not because schizophrenia itself is adaptive but because the biological and psychological traits underlying it might, if occurring in moderate degree, form part of the rich array of qualities that contribute to Man's individuality.[21] Among such qualities I would include, as many other observers have, some that enter into the creative process, the schizotypal mind (and brain) perhaps being peculiarly adapted to handle the ideational juxtapositions required in original thought.

The suggestion here – that normal schizotypy and schizophrenic disorders are not incompatible concepts – raises a more general issue about conventional notions of disease in psychiatry and further underlines an earlier point: that much current research on schizophrenia may be wrongly focused in its quest for the 'cause' of the condition. Most investigators – and this includes psychologists as well as more medically orientated workers – have proceeded according to the principle that it is necessary to seek evidence of *defect* in schizophrenics, ways in which they are impaired relative to other people. Yet I would suggest that, easy though this may be to demonstrate, it can lead to a false impression about the nature of schizophrenia. For there are now several studies showing that in some situations schizophrenics can achieve levels of performance that are actually *superior* to those of normal people. This is true on some types of cognitive task, one such example being found in a recent study of perceptual processing in schizophrenic patients.[22] There the subjects were required to count the number of elements (lines) in a series of briefly presented visual displays. The lines were either horizontal or vertical, the two types of element in a particular display either being randomly mixed or arranged adjacently in groups of a similar type. The purpose of the study was to examine a suggestion from an earlier experiment that during perceptual processing schizophrenics rely solely on a piecemeal or 'local' analytic strategy, rather than, as is more usual, going through an initial phase of 'global' analysis in which the overall gestalt of a stimulus configuration is first apprehended before being examined in detail. In the experiment being referred to here this hypothesis was confirmed, schizophrenics being largely unaffected by whether or not the line elements in the displays used were arranged into adjacent groups of similar type. More interesting, however, as shown in figure 3.2, the schizophrenics performed significantly *better* on the task than the control subjects, especially under conditions where the horizontal and vertical elements in the displays were randomly mixed – and therefore where it was actually to the subject's detriment to seek a pattern in the arrangement of the lines before trying to count them. In other words, it seems that the schizophrenic's excessive attention to detail might actually be an advantage in certain circumstances.

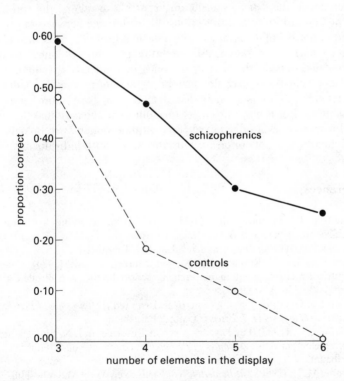

Figure 3.2   Performance curves of schizophrenic and control subjects on the perceptual task described in the text. The graphs show the proportion of correct responses (vertical axis) as a function of the number of elements displayed (horizontal axis), under conditions where the elements were arranged in random fashion and no prior perceptual organization was possible. Note that although, as expected, both groups scored progressively fewer correct responses as the size of the display increased, schizophrenic patients performed uniformly better throughout (from data by Schwartz Place and Gilmore, Journal of Abnormal Psychology, *1980, 3, 409–18).*

In a somewhat different vein, but also illustrating the occasional 'superiority' of schizophrenic perception, another recent study tested out subjects' ability to discriminate between genuine and sham expressions of emotion in other people.[23] It turned out that schizophrenics were better than normals at telling when the emotion was genuine. This particular finding is interesting because it illustrates especially well an apparent paradox in the continuity model of schizophrenia for which I have argued here; namely the fact that the schizophrenic's serious failure of social and psychological functioning seems irreconcilable with it having arisen out of processes that we would normally judge to have the qualities of excellence. That in the instance just quoted the latter are associated with disorder rather than health is perhaps merely an indication that it is not entirely adaptive to be too attuned to other people's feelings!

In general, what the two studies just described seem to suggest is that the underlying quality of schizophrenia is not a defect at all, but an exquisite sensitivity of the nervous system, which, due to a combination of events, gets translated into an *appearance* of deficit as the individual progresses into a state that we recognize, quite rightly, as illness. But we are only justified in labelling it as such on the grounds that the person has passed some threshold at which normal functioning has become painfully unpleasant to the self or socially unacceptable to others: the threshold may be both arbitrary and precarious, the difference between sanity and madness not being as great as we would like to think. This ineluctable connection between the healthy and the psychotic – long accepted, incidentally, outside the narrow confines of academic psychology and organic psychiatry – may not just be of significance as a model for understanding serious mental disorder. It may have more profound implications. For it may indeed yet turn out to be the case that the study of schizophrenia will offer us, whether as philosophers, psychologists or physiologists, some of our clearest insights into human individuality.

References

1 Meltzer, H. Y. and Stahl, S. M. (1976) The dopamine hypothesis of schizophrenia: a review, *Schiz. Bull.* 2: 19–76.

2 Laing, R. D. (1960) *The Divided Self.* London: Tavistock.

3 Reveley, A. M., Reveley, M. A. and Murray, R. M. (1984) Cerebral ventricular enlargement in non-genetic schizophrenia: a controlled study. *Brit. J. Psychiat.* 144: 89–93.

4 Claridge, G. (1981) Psychoticism. In R. Lynn (ed.), *Dimensions of Personality. Papers in Honour of H. J. Eysenck.* Oxford: Pergamon.

5 Claridge, G. (1983) The Eysenck psychoticism scale. In J. N. Butcher and C. D. Spielberger (eds), *Advances in Personality Assessment*, vol. 2. Hillsdale, NJ: Erlbaum.

6 Stone, M. H. (1980) *The Borderline Syndromes.* New York: McGraw-Hill.

7 Claridge, G. and Broks, P. (1984) Schizotypy and hemisphere function. I. Theoretical considerations and the measurement of schizotypy. *Person. individ. Diff.* 5: 633–48.

8 Gottesman, I. I. and Shields, J. (1982) *Schizophrenia: The Epigenetic Puzzle.* Cambridge: Cambridge Univ. Press.

9 Claridge, G. (1967) *Personality and Arousal.* Oxford: Pergamon.

10 Claridge, G. and Clark, K. (1982) Covariation between two-flash threshold and skin conductance level in first-breakdown schizophrenics: relationships in drug-free patients and effects of treatment. *Psychiat. Res.* 6: 371–80.

11 Claridge, G., Robinson, D. L. and Birchall, P. (1985) Psychophysiological evidence of 'psychoticism' in schizophrenics' relatives. *Person. individ. Diff.* 6: 1–10.

12 Gruzelier, J. (1983) A critical assessment and integration of lateral asymmetries in schizophrenia. In M. Myslobodsky (ed.), *Hemisyndromes. Psychobiology, Neurology, Psychiatry.* New York: Academic Press.

13 Broks, P. (1984) Schizotypy and hemisphere function. II. Performance asymmetry on a verbal divided visual-field task. *Person. individ. Diff.* 5: 649–56.

14 Broks, P., Claridge, G., Matheson, J. and Hargreaves, J. (1984) Schizotypy and hemisphere function. IV. Story comprehension under binaural and monaural listening conditions. *Person. individ. Diff.* 5: 665–70.

15 Rawlings, D. and Claridge, G. (1984) Schizotypy and hemisphere function. III. Performance asymmetries on tasks of letter recognition and local-global processing. *Person. individ. Diff.* 5: 657–63.

16 Galin, D. (1974) Implications for psychiatry of left and right cerebral specialisation. *Arch. gen. Psychiat.* 31: 572–83.

17 Wechsler, B. E. (1980) Cerebral laterality and psychiatry: a review of the literature. *Amer. J. Psychiat.* 137: 279–91.

18 Green, P., Hallett, S. and Hunter, M. (1983) Abnormal interhemispheric integration and hemispheric specialisation in schizophrenics and high-risk children. In P. Flor-Henry and J. Gruzelier (eds), *Laterality and Psychopathology.* Amsterdam: Elsevier/North-Holland.

19 McGuigan, F. J. (1966) Covert oral behaviour and auditory hallucinations. *Psychophysiol.* 3: 73–80.

20 Bleuler, M. (1984) What is schizophrenia? *Schiz. Bull.* 10: 8–9.

21 Claridge, G. (1985) *Origins of Mental Illness. Temperament, Deviance and Disorder.* Oxford: Blackwell.

22 Schwartz Place, E. J. and Gilmore, G. C. (1980) Perceptual organization in schizophrenia. *J. abn. Psychol.* 89: 401–18.

23 LaRusso, L. (1978) Sensitivity of paranoid patients to non-verbal cues. *J. abn. Psychol.* 87: 463–71.

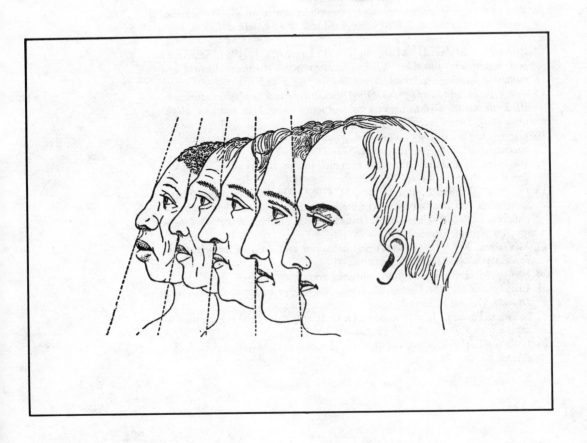

4

Individuality

Hans Eysenck

Hans Eysenck was born in Berlin in 1916, but left Germany in 1934 as a political protest against the Hitler regime. He studied in Dijon and Exeter before obtaining his BA and PhD degrees in Psychology at the University of London. He founded the Department of Psychology at the newly created Institute of Psychiatry in 1955, and was Professor in the University until his retirement in 1983. His main research interests have been in personality and individual differences, intelligence, behavioural genetics, behaviour therapy, and social attitudes. He has written or edited some 40 books, and has published over 800 articles. He founded two psychological journals, Behaviour Research and Therapy, *and* Personality and Individual Differences.

One of the most obvious things about human beings (as well as other animal organisms, and even plants) is their *individuality*, that is the fact that they differ in very many ways. Williams has amassed a great deal of evidence on biochemical individuality,[1] but individual differences are perhaps even more noticeable in such fields as intelligence,[2] personality,[3] and physique.[4] Differences along these various lines have been studied by psychologists for many years, usually following one of two quite different approaches. The 'idiographic approach' has been to treat each individual as *unique*, to deny the meaningfulness of analyses along the lines of abilities, traits, etc., and quite generally to treat psychology as a *Geisteswissenschaft* (a branch of the humanities). The nomothetic approach has been that of analysing behaviour in terms of traits, abilities, and other latent variables which cannot be observed directly but are inferred from regularities of behaviour. This approach has been identified with the dictates of *Naturwissenschaft* (natural science). The idiographic approach has failed to produce any kind of agreed and meaningful results, and we shall here be concerned only with the nomothetic approach.[5]

Personality description in terms of traits involves *uniformities of behaviour*, and these can be measured directly, or related by observers, or be measured by means of self-report questionnaires. Such an analysis must in the first instance be *descriptive*, and it has revealed three major dimensions of personality which have received many different names, but which emerge from studies carried out by large numbers of investigators,

---

After the publication of Darwin's Origin of Species *there were many attempts to find differences in the anatomy of various human races and animal species that might be an indication of their presumed levels of evolution. For some time the 'facial angle' (the angle of a line joining the brow and the upper lip) was thought to be a reliable measure of the state of advancement of a person. From* Natural History of the Human Races *(1869) by John J. Jeffries.*

using different measuring instruments and different methods of analysis.[6] In the terminology that I introduced, these major dimensions are labelled P (Pyschoticism, as opposed to ego-control), E (Extraversion, as opposed to introversion), and N (Neuroticism, as opposed to emotional stability). The nature of these dimensions can be seen from the traits that have been found to intercorrelate with each other and define the dimensions (figure 4.1). Thus extraverts are characterized by being sociable, lively, active, assertive, sensation-seeking, carefree, dominant, surgent and venturesome, for instance, while introverts are the opposite in each case, with ambiverts somewhere in between.

Many psychologists are content to leave the matter here, and to regard the principles of classification involved as primarily a matter of the *psyche*, that is, of mental orientation. Others, including myself, have rather followed the precept of T. H. Huxley: 'No psychosis without a neurosis', that is, no psychic event without an underlying physical event. The principles governing this approach, and a survey of research supporting it, are set out elsewhere.[7,8] This approach, often called 'reductionist' (because it attempts to link biological and social phenomena, thus 'reducing' the latter to the former), is in fact much more complex than the term would suggest.

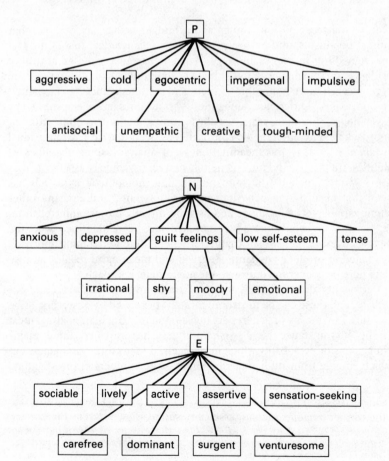

Figure 4.1 The personality dimensions of Psychoticism *(P),* Neuroticism *(N) and* Extraversion *(E) are each characterized by a number of personality traits.*[5]

We begin with the obvious statement that man is a *biosocial* organism, that is, that his actions and his behaviour generally are determined in part by biological constraints (hunger, thirst, sex) and in part by social constraints (rules, laws, mores). Biological factors clearly influence behaviour in social situations, but equally behaviour influences underlying biological factors. Androgens (male hormones) in part determine a man's desire for intercourse, but frequency of intercourse also determines in return to some extent the amount of testerone. Similarly, testerone determines dominance in social situations, but failure in social situations may cause a reduction in testerone.[9] Clearly the term *reductionism* oversimplifies the situation. We are not simply proposing that all human conduct, including cognition and consciousness, can be reduced to physical factors completely; this would be a philosophical position held by naive realists but incapable at the moment of scientific proof or disproof. What is being maintained, rather, is that biological systems interact with what for the moment we may perhaps call 'mental' systems and behaviour, and that this interaction is not all in one direction. The evidence for such a proposition needs of course to be specific, and a great deal of such material is already available and may serve to explain individual differences in personality and intelligence.

Let us consider just one of the three major dimensions of personality, namely extraversion–introversion. There is no particular logical reason why sociability should be correlated with physical activity, assertiveness with carefreeness, or liveliness with assertiveness. It would logically be perfectly possible for a person to be sociable and non-assertive, physically active but not carefree, etc. We must therefore search for a *causal* element to explain the observed relationship, and I have suggested that differential levels of cortical arousal, mediated by the reticular formation (the part of brain thought to be responsible for regulating the level of arousal and attention) may be partially responsible for individual differences in extraversion–introversion.[7,8] The fact of differences in cortical arousal, usually measured by means of the electroencephalogram (EEG, or 'brain waves'), is of course not in dispute; high levels of arousal are characterized by fast, low-amplitude alpha waves at a frequency of about 10–12 cycles per second, and low levels of arousal by slower high-amplitude alpha rythmns. What the theory suggests is that high arousal is characteristic of introverts, and is partly responsible for their behaviour, while low levels of arousal are typical of extraverts, and in turn mediate their behaviour.

Consider, as an example, figure 4.2, which in diagrammatic form relates levels of sensory stimulation to hedonic tone (pleasantness versus unpleasantness). As the middle curve illustrates, most people have a high positive hedonic tone (pleasure) to intermediate levels of stimulation, with a negative hedonic tone (dislike) for very high or very low levels, characteristic respectively of pain and sensory deprivation. The optimal level of sensory stimulation (O.L. in figure 4.2) is displaced to the *left* for introverts, to the *right* for extraverts, because the high level of arousal of the former *amplifies* incoming sensory stimulation, whereas the low level of cortical arousal of the latter *reduces* the effects of incoming sensory stimulation. At the given level of sensory stimulation, e.g. A or B in figure

4.2, where for the average person the hedonic tone is indifferent, introverts and extraverts will respectively be affected positively or negatively, in opposite directions.

Two predictions may be deduced from this hypothesis. First, extraverts will be more tolerant of pain, introverts more tolerant of sensory deprivation; this has been demonstrated to be true in many investigations.[7] Second, introverts will seek for lower levels of stimulation, extraverts for higher levels, in order to achieve maximum positive hedonic tone. This prediction too has been verified in several experimental studies.[8]

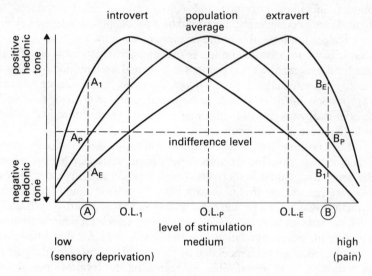

Figure 4.2 Hedonic tone *is related to the intensity of sensory stimulation, reaching a peak at some particular level of stimulation, dependent on the degree of extraversion.*[5]

This is a fairly direct set of predictions from the model; even more direct, of course, are psychophysiological studies carried out on extraverts and introverts, respectively, to test directly the hypothesis of greater cortical arousal of introverts. This literature has been reviewed by Stelmack, with largely positive results.[9] More indirect is another mode of reasoning, which argues that many laboratory phenomena in experimental psychology are affected by levels of arousal, and can hence be used to test the hypothesis.[3] Pavlovian conditioning is a good example; high levels of arousal mediate quick and strong conditioning, whereas low levels of arousal are unfavourable to the formation of conditioned reflexes. Figure 4.3 shows the results of a study testing the hypothesis that introverts, having higher cortical arousal, would show quicker eye-blink conditioning (i.e. conditioning of the eye-blink reflex to a tone) than would extraverts; it is quite clear that the results bear out the hypothesis.[10] Indeed, the study also supported a hypothesis, based on Pavlov's principle of transmarginal inhibition, namely that with very strong intensities of the unconditioned stimulus there would be a *reversal* in performance, with extraverts now showing higher rates of conditioning than introverts; as figure 4.4 shows, this was actually found when the strength of the unconditioned stimulus was greatly increased.[10]

Personality and behaviour can of course be influenced by drugs, in predictable ways.[11,12] Stimulant drugs like dexamphetamine sulphate should have an *introverting* (arousing) effect, and hence facilitate conditioning, while depressant drugs like amobarbital sodium should have the opposite effect. Figure 4.5 shows the outcome of such an experiment, including also a placebo treatment; it will be seen that the predicted effects do occur.[13]

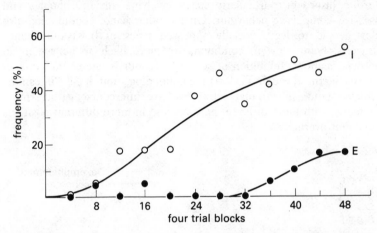

Figure 4.3   These graphs plot the frequency of occurrence of the conditioned eye blink response (the involuntary blinking of the eyes in response to a brief warning sound – the unconditioned stimulus – presented just before a puff of air to the eyes – the unconditioned stimulus) was measured during successive presentations. In this experiment[10] the unconditioned stimulus was a very gentle air puff and introverts (I) developed the conditioned reflex much more rapidly than extraverts (E).

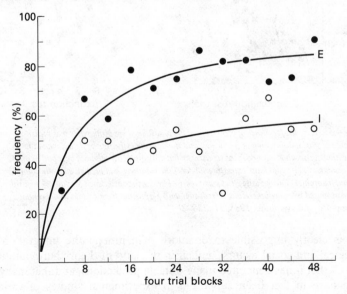

Figure 4.4   When the unconditioned stimulus was a strong puff of air, extraverts (E) developed a conditioned eye blink reflex more quickly than introverts (I).[10]

The theory linking personality and conditioning is particularly important, because conditioning has been found to mediate many social effects, such as those of crime[14] and neurosis.[15] Another important area in which conditioning seems to mediate behaviour is sex.[16] An account of theories linking these various areas is given in my paper entitled 'The Social Application of Pavlovian Theories'.[17] Briefly, what I suggest is that Pavlovian conditioning mediates the acquisition of neurotic responses and symptoms, particularly in introverts with a high degree of neuroticism; hence the frequently observed relationship between introversion and neurotic disorders, particularly states involving anxiety, phobias and obsessive–compulsive behaviour. On the other hand, conditioning also helps people to learn socially approved types of behaviour; hence extraverts, being slow to condition, are more likely to behave in an antisocial manner. Inhibition of sexual behaviour is one of the conduct patterns learnt through Pavlovian conditioning, and hence it can be predicted (and shown) that extraverts have intercourse earlier, more frequently, with more different partners and in more different positions than do introverts.

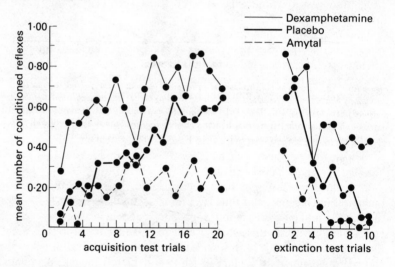

Figure 4.5   Here the frequency of occurrence of the conditioned eye blink reflex was measured during the period of initial acquisition or 'training', and then during extinction or decay, when the unconditioned stimulus was presented repetitively but without being followed by a puff of air. Acquisition was more rapid and extinction slower if the volunteer had been given a stimulant drug (Dexamphetamine). The opposite effect was produced by a depressant drug (Amytal). A neutral placebo produced intermediate results[13] (redrawn with permission from Franks and Trouton J. Comp. Physiol., Psychol., *1958, 51: 220–2).*

It is clearly impossible to do more than hint at the integration of biological and social factors implicit in the kind of theory here outlined; the fact that it has generated many testable predictions, and that many of these have in fact been supported in experimental studies of various kinds, suggests that some such integration is in fact taking place, and that causal theories of social behaviour must be based on the fundamental premise of man as a biosocial organism. Such facts as those mentioned here do of course have a bearing on the mind–matter controversy, but I shall delay a discussion of this until I have examined some facts in the field of intelligence measurement.

Any reasonable account of intelligence must begin with the recognition of the tripartite nature of this concept. A similar division could be made with respect to the concept of personality, but it has been more frequently used in relation to intelligence, where the three types of intelligence, A, B and C, have been distinguished. Intelligence A (*biological intelligence*) is the underlying biological structure of the central nervous system and the cortex, which allows learning, remembering, problem-solving and other cognitive processes that are basic to human intelligence to take place. Intelligence B (*social intelligence*) constitutes the social application of intelligence A, complicated by educational, socio-economic and cultural influences and determinants, by personality variables, and by the myriad other influences that occur in everyday life. Intelligence C (*psychometric intelligence*) is the intelligence measured by IQ tests of various kinds.[2] It will be clear that discussion can proceed on an intelligent basis only if participants make it clear which type of intelligence they are discussing. Much unnecessary conflict has arisen because such clarification was not attempted.

Most work on human intelligence has been concerned with social intelligence, often to the almost complete neglect of biological intelligence.[18] This has led to the growth of a technology of intelligence measurements that lacked a scientific basis; IQ tests are very useful for many practical purposes, but they have no firm basis in science, and the type of measurement they represent is based entirely on a comparative basis – Tom is brighter than Harry; there is a complete failure to develop a system of measurement which is based on physical magnitudes. The weaknesses of this approach have been outlined many times, and they have led to a great deal of criticism.

In recent years attempts have been made to find direct measures of biological intelligence, and thus lay a more scientific basis for theories of the concept and measures of individual differences in intelligence. Barrett and I have reviewed this work elsewhere,[19] and I have presented the theoretical implications of this work for an understanding of intelligence and cognition generally.[20] Here I wish to note merely the major findings. Very high correlations have been observed between IQ tests, on the one hand, and certain measures of the *averaged evoked potential*, on the other. An evoked potential is a set of brain waves related to a particular event, such as the pattern of waves precipitated by a sudden visual or auditory stimulus. Usually what is measured is the latency (delay between stimulus and evoked potential) and amplitude of these waves: by and large, *fast latencies* and *high amplitudes* have been found to be correlated, although not very highly, with IQ. Both are to some extent dependent on *variability* of measurement. Because these evoked brain waves are very tiny and are obscured by the background electrical 'noise' of the brain, many separate evocations have to be averaged in a computer in order to obtain a meaningful recording. But when there is considerable variability from one recording to the next, the peaks and troughs in the traces do not coincide well and this reduces the amplitude of waves in the averaged record. In the original work, amplitude and latency were related to IQ along the traditional lines pioneered by Binet; in other words, as children grow older, the amplitude of the averaged evoked potential increases, the latencies decrease, and variability decreases.

More recent work has formulated a variety of theories giving rise to somewhat different measures of the evoked potential, and these have revolutionized the field by giving very much higher correlations with IQ.[21] One such hypothesis is that of error-free transmission of information through the cortex; errors in such transmission would increase the variability of the averaged evoked potential, decrease its complexity, and also produce lower IQ values in psychometric tests of intelligence. There is a good deal of indirect evidence for this hypothesis, and appropriate measures of the evoked potential correlated extremely highly with the Wechsler IQ test on a group of 219 15-year-old schoolchildren with an average distribution of intelligence.[22]

Another paradigm suggests that high neural adaptability, characterized by evoked potentials with much smaller than average amplitude when the stimulus producing the potential is *expected* by the observer, but much larger than average amplitude to unexpected stimuli, would be correlated with good performance in IQ tests. This correlation, too, has been demonstrated to be quite high, as has the correlation predicted in another, related theory, suggesting that *habituation* to a series of identical stimuli, as shown by gradual diminution of the amplitude of the evoked potential, would be more rapid in high-IQ than in low-IQ subjects.[23]

These various studies of human variability, concentrating on personality and intelligence, do not solve the problem of the mind–body relation in its philosophical perspective. Most scientists in the field have adopted for heuristic reasons either the dual aspect or the epiphenomenal point of view, rather than any form of monism. The data certainly would be most readily interpretable in terms of some form of dual-aspect theory as formulated by Spinoza, but apart from showing some indissoluble relationship between body and mind, the data certainly do not settle the argument, which must remain indeterminate as presented. What does emerge as indisputable is the biosocial nature of human behaviour, and its dependence on both biological and social factors. That this is so has become particularly clear in the resolution of the old debate about nature and nurture, which should of course never have been interpreted as postulating the complete predominance of either. What was needed right from the beginning, and what has now become available in modern behavioural genetics, was an algorithm that allocates portions of the total variance in bodily form or behaviour amongst the population to various genetic and environmental components, and thus discloses the genetic architecture of behaviour. Clearly this goes well beyond the simplistic device of calculating heritabilities; what is needed is a detailed allocation of portions of the variance to the additive genetic variance, to dominance, epistasis and assortative mating; a division of the environmental variance into between-family and within-family environmental variance; and above all an attempt to estimate the various interactions possible between heredity and environment. The work of the Birmingham School of

Biometrical Genetical Analysis has solved most of the problems inherent in this approach, and we now have a great deal of knowledge about the genetic factors, the environmental factors, and their interaction, for both personality and intelligence.[2,8]

While there are some similarities in the genetic analysis of personality and intelligence, there are also many differences. The similarity that is most noticeable is the great contribution of additive genetic factors, in the fields of both personality and intelligence. Beyond that, however, differences predominate. Thus non-additive factors like dominance and assortative mating are prominent in the field of intelligence, but almost entirely absent in the field of personality. On the environmental side, too, there are differences. Thus between-family environmental variance contributes a great deal to the phenotypic variance in the field of intelligence, but nothing in the field of personality; within-family environmental variance is important for personality, where it contributes practically the whole of the environmental variance, but it is relatively unimportant in the field of intelligence.

Along these lines, then, psychologists are approaching the problems of mind and matter. There is no attempt to solve the problem in its philosophical sense, but a determination to arrive at a better understanding of the way in which behaviour is determined by social and biological factors, to get insight into the way these factors cooperate and interact, and to formulate laws and theories that would enable us to predict the behaviour and actions of different individuals according to the way they are constituted. While only a beginning has been made along these lines, much progress has already been achieved, and the problem certainly seems a soluble one.

References

1 Williams, R. J. (1956) *Biochemical Individuality*. London: Chapman & Hall.
2 Eysenck, H. J. (1979) *The Structure and Measurement of Intelligence*. New York: Springer.
3 Eysenck, H. J. (ed.) (1976a) *The Measurement of Personality*. Lancaster: MTP.
4 Sheldon, W. H., Stevens, S. S. and Tucker, W. B. (1940) *The Varieties of Human Physique*. New York: Harper.
5 Eysenck, H. J. and Eysenck, M. W. (1985) *Personality and Individual Differences*. New York: Plenum.
6 Royce, J. R. and Powell, A. (1983) *Theory of Personality and Individual Differences: Factors, Systems and Processes*. Englewood Cliffs, NJ: Prentice-Hall.
7 Eysenck, H. J. (1967) *The Biological Basis of Personality*. Springfield, Ill.: C. C. Thomas.
8 Eysenck, H. J. (ed.) (1981) *A Model for Personality*. New York: Springer.
9 Eysenck, H. J. and Wilson, G. (1979) *The Psychology of Sex*. London: Dent.
10 Eysenck, H. J. and Levey, A. B. (1972) Conditioning, introversion–extraversion and the strength of the nervous system. In V. D. Nebylitsyn and J. A. Gray (eds), *Biological Bases of Individual Behaviour*, pp. 206–20. New York: Academic Press.
11 Eysenck, H. J. (ed.) (1963) *Experiments with Drugs*. Oxford: Pergamon.
12 Eysenck, H. J. (1983) Psychopharmacology and personality. In W. Janke (ed.), *Response Variability to Psychotropic Drugs*. Oxford: Pergamon.
13 Franks, C. M. and Troughton, D. (1958) Effects of amobarbital sodium and

dexamphetamine sulphate on the conditioning of the eyelid response. *J. Comp. & Physiol. Psych.* 51: 270–2.

14 Eysenck, H. J. (1977) *Crime and Personality*, 3rd edn. London: Routledge & Kegan Paul.

15 Eysenck, H. J. (1977) *You and Neurosis*. London: Temple Smith.

16 Eysenck, H. J. (1976b) *Sex and Personality*. London: Open Books.

17 Eysenck, H. J. (1983) The social application of Pavlovian theories. *Pavlovian Journal of Biological Science*, 18: 117–25.

18 Sternberg, R. J. (1982) *Handbook of Human Intelligence*. Cambridge: Cambridge Univ. Press.

19 Eysenck, H. J. and Barrett, P. (1985) Psychophysiology and the measurement of intelligence. In C. R. Reynolds and V. Wilson (eds), *Methodological and Statistical Advances in the Study of Individual Differences*. New York: Plenum.

20 Eysenck, H. J. (1984) The theory of intelligence and the psychophysiology of cognition. In R. J. Sternberg (ed.), *Advances in the Psychology of Human Intelligence*, vol. 3. Hillsdale, NJ: Erlbaum.

21 Eysenck, H. J. (ed.) (1982) *A Model for Intelligence*. New York: Springer.

22 Hendrickson, E. (1982) The biological basis of intelligence. Part 11: Measurement. In H. J. Eysenck (ed.), *A Model for Intelligence*.

23 Shafer, E. W. P. (1982) Neural adaptability: a biological determinant of behavioural intelligence. *Int. J. Neurosci.* 17: 183–91.

5

Innate and Cultural Aspects of Human Non-verbal Communication

Michael Argyle

Michael Argyle is Reader in Social Psychology at Oxford University, and a Fellow of Wolfson College.

After being educated at Nottingham High School and Cambridge, and serving in the RAF, he has been teaching Social Psychology at Oxford since 1952, and has built up an active research group. His research has been into the detailed analysis of human social interaction–non-verbal communication, social skills, long-term relationships, cultural differences, and failures of social performance in mental patients. He has been active in promoting social psychology in Britain, and in the growth of social skills training.

He is the author of a number of books, for example Bodily Communication *(1975), and many journal articles. He has been visiting professor at universities in the USA, Canada, Australia and elsewhere, and travels frequently to lecture and carry out cross-cultural research.*

The study of non-verbal communication (NVC) has its origins in cooperation between social psychologists and zoologists, with some help from anthropologists and psychiatrists. The first international conference on the subject was held in Oxford, in 1969, organized by Professor Ralph Exline and myself. Since then the two sides have divided, zoologists to study the evolutionary origins of NVC in animals, as explained by John Krebs in his chapter in this book, while social psychologists have been concerned with human non-verbal communication. This has some unlearnt components, for example certain facial expressions, but in addition there are effects of learning from the culture, as in the case of most gestures. In addition human beings communicate by means of language, but this is coordinated with and supported by an intricate set of non-verbal signals. Non-verbal communication in humans has four main functions – communicating emotions and attitudes to other people, supporting speech, self-presentation, and rituals. I will deal with these in turn, and look at the biological and cultural components.

Communicating Emotions and Interpersonal Attitudes

One of the main functions of non-verbal communication in animals and

The power of non-verbal communication. Arthur Scargill, then leader of the Yorkshire miners, speaking on a picket line at an industrial dispute in 1977 (© S & G Press Agency Ltd).

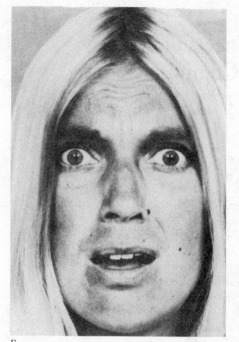

Fear

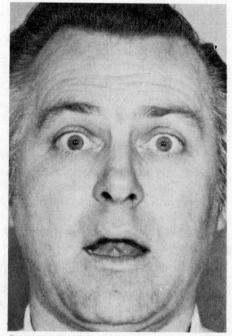

Surprise

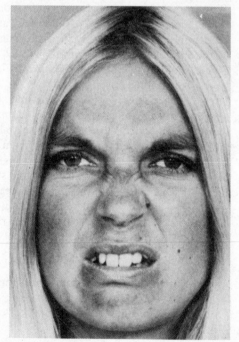

Figure 5.1   Facial expressions for emotions[2] (reprinted with permission from Ekman and Friesen Unmasking the Face, *1975, Prentice-Hall).*

Disgust

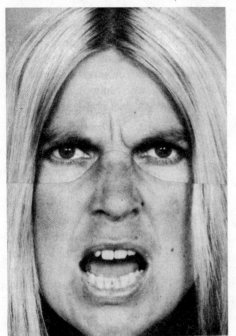

Anger

Happiness

Sadness

men is to communicate emotions and attitudes. Ekman and Friesen[1,2] have located six basic facial expressions for emotion – happiness, sadness, fear, surprise, anger and disgust/contempt (figure 5.1). Izard[3] has found two more – interest and shame. The main interpersonal attitudes are friendly, hostile, superior, inferior and loving.

These emotions and attitudes are *encoded* mainly into facial expressions and tone of voice, but also into gaze, proximity, bodily contact and bodily posture. The signals are then *decoded*, more or less successfully, by receivers – the people observing or hearing the sender. Encoding and decoding are different processes and I shall consider them separately below (figure 5.2). Tests for ability to do them are also quite different.

Figure 5.2   Encoding and decoding[5] (redrawn with permission from Argyle, 1975, Bodily Communication, Methuen).

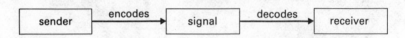

It is a matter of degree how far any particular non-verbal signal is really a case of intentional *communication*. For example, pupil dilation, which is a sign of sexual attraction, cannot be controlled, and is therefore a sign or an element of behaviour, rather than communication. Gestures are mainly deliberate, and are mostly learnt from the culture: they are clearer cases of communication. It is now recognized that posed and spontaneous non-verbal signals are rather different, and have a different neurological basis. Most normal human non-verbal communication is a mixture of the two, since spontaneous signals are overlaid with the effects of learning and attempts to control or modify them.[4]

The great importance of human non-verbal communication is shown by the finding that some of the main deficiencies in the social behaviour of socially inadequate mental patients lie in this sphere – they smile less, look less and gesture less than normal people. The capacity to send the appropriate non-verbal signals is an important part of social skill, sometimes by masking true feelings by the expression of different ones. Non-verbal communication is particularly important for making friends. A series of experiments has shown that non-verbal signals like facial expression and tone of voice have a much greater impact in communicating a friendly attitude than equivalent verbal messages.[5] Non-verbal communication is of course much less important for communicating detailed information, as in lectures, as opposed to indicating the attitude of a speaker to his listeners.

A hint of the balance between inheritance and learning can be obtained from problems of communication between cultures. Although the main non-verbal signals have much the same meaning in different cultures, this is not true of gestures, while the levels of touching, gaze and proximity may be rather different, and some facial expressions may be inhibited or exaggerated. Training courses for dealing with different national or ethnic groups often include training in non-verbal communication, as does training in social skills for socially inadequate mental patients, and for many professions – police, doctors, teachers and others. A typical training laboratory is shown in figure 5.3.

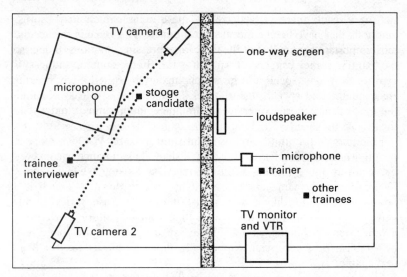

Figure 5.3   Social skills training laboratory[6] (redrawn with permission from Argyle, 1983, The Psychology of Interpersonal Behaviour, Penguin).

Encoding

Research on encoding is done by putting subjects into some emotional or attitudinal condition, and then recording their non-verbal communication. Creation of genuine emotions can be achieved by showing films which are funny, disgusting, etc.[4] Posed emotions can be studied, for example by asking subjects to communicate emotions while counting from one to ten, or to send verbally ambiguous messages with a particular meaning – for example, 'I'm feeling cold, aren't you?' to mean 'please come and warm me with your bodily warmth'.[7]

It is clear that the face is the most informative area for the expression of emotions and attitudes. There is evidence that some facial expressions are innate: infants who have been born both blind and deaf have been found to smile, laugh and cry. The combination of smiling and looking is a most powerful social signal, and is given by 3-week-old infants, perhaps to ensure that their caretaker looks after them. The eight emotions listed earlier are found in all cultures studied, including some very remote ones; their members can enact emotions in a way recognizable to us, and can pick the 'right' photographs to go with stories.[1] Facial expression is regulated by about 20 muscles, innervated by the facial nerve, which is controlled directly from the motor cortex. Spontaneous facial expressions are also affected by impulses from the reticular formation and other brain centres.[8] The main way in which facial expressions differ in different cultures concerns the occasions on which they are displayed. Ekman found that Japanese people in the company of others did not show the expected facial signs of disgust when shown disgusting films; but they did show disgust if they thought they were alone. We have found Japanese subjects 'inscrutable', even to each other; they could decode British and Italian senders better than they could other Japanese![9] This is all due to 'display rules'; in Japan it is considered rude to show sadness, anger or other negative emotions.

While the face is very well controlled, the voice and the body are less so. As a result there is 'leakage' to these areas, which may express emotions that have been concealed in the face. The voice is the second most important channel, after the face, for expressing emotions. It does so by 'paralinguistic' aspects of speech style. For example, sadness is expressed by slow speed and low pitch, anxiety by raised pitch, breathy voice quality and speech disturbances.[10] Since this is a leaky channel, these signals are more expressive of genuine emotions and attitudes than those from the face.

Emotions and attitudes are also expressed by gaze. We look more at people whom we like, less at those we dislike.[11] Dominance is conveyed by relatively more looking while talking, less looking while listening. Depression and shame are expressed by looking down.[12] Touch is a powerful signal for liking and sexual interest; its use varies greatly between cultures, and the British are a 'non-contact' culture. Proximity is another signal for liking, as is a sideways spatial position; dominance can be established by occupying symbolically important places, like the head of the table.

Gaze, face, proximity and other non-verbal cues combine together to give one overall message of, for example, liking or intimacy. Any one of these signals can substitute for another, so that, for example, if two people are moved further apart they look at each other more.[13]

'Body language' has received much popular attention, but in fact posture is a relatively unimportant non-verbal cue. The main message it conveys is degree of tension or arousal rather than any specific state, though certain postures have been found to communicate boredom (leaning back, legs stretched, head on hand), and disagreement (arms crossed) (figure 5.4).[14]

There are considerable individual differences in the ability to encode non-verbal communication. This ability can be measured by finding the percentage of signals, spontaneous or posed, that can be correctly decoded by a group of judges. As far as spontaneous sending is concerned, extraverts and women have been found to be good, depressives and other mental patients poor. For posed sending, socially skilled people and those in jobs involving dealing with people are good.[4,15] Training in sending non-verbal signals is straightforward. For facial expressions a collection of photos of faces for modelling, and a mirror, are needed for the first stage, followed by use of a video-tape-recorder. Training the voice can be done by copying tape-recordings, followed by making recordings of, for example, reading a newspaper to portray different emotions.[16]

Decoding

It can be assumed that in the course of evolution the capacities to send and receive developed together. The ability to decode facial expression appears at an early age. Rhesus monkeys who have been reared in isolation react differently from normal to photographs of monkey facial expressions.[17] Human infants start to discriminate different facial expressions at 5–6 months, perhaps as a result of maturation rather than learning.

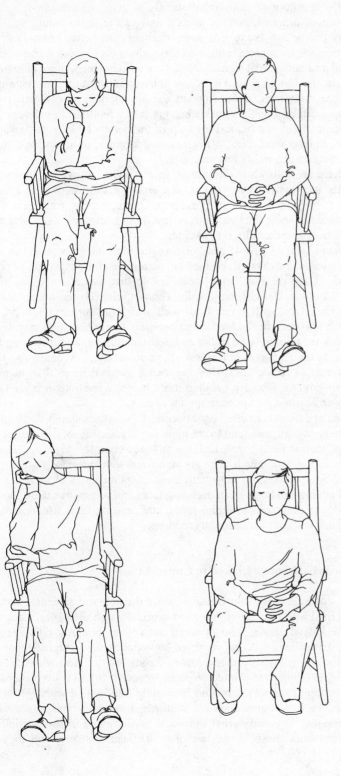

Figure 5.4 Some human postures[14] (reprinted with permission from Bull, 1983, Bodily Movement and Interpersonal Communication, *Wiley).*

The decoding of non-verbal signals is quite sophisticated; it takes account of other signals, of speech and of the surrounding situation. Many people are aware that some channels are better controlled than others, and pay more attention to leaky channels like voice and body. If verbal and non-verbal signals conflict, as we have seen, more attention is paid to the non-verbal. The same non-verbal message can have quite different meanings, depending on the situation. A direct glance at a stranger can be a threat signal (when given by a football fan to a supporter of the other side), a request for help (if the person looking has collapsed on an underground train), a heterosexual advance, or an attempt to gain the attention of a waiter or a chairman.[12]

There are individual differences in the ability to decode non-verbal signals accurately. Tests consist of a series of short audio- and video-tapes to be judged. Some tests use posed performances, while others use spontaneous ones; the two kinds of test do not correlate well,[4] and must be measuring rather different abilities.

Socially skilled people are good at decoding posed signals, possibly spontaneous ones as well. Women are better decoders, especially of posed signals. They are also 'polite' decoders, in that they attend more to the face than to leakier channels, while men put relatively more emphasis on vocal cues. Girls shift to this facial/vocal weighting during childhood, and women who decode like men are unpopular. The explanation may be that females are trained to be polite and accommodating, and this extends to receiving the messages others want them to receive.[15] Women also react differently to tactile cues: they like being touched more than men do. Female patients who are handled more before operations recover faster afterwards, while the opposite applies to men.[18]

Mental patients are often poor decoders. Neurotics simply don't attend to others enough, and tend to see more social rejection, of themselves and others, than is really there. Delinquents are very insensitive, for example not realizing how much they are annoying someone else until a fight starts. Some psychotics engage in gross misperceptions of what is going on. Training can be given in decoding faces and voices, by asking trainees to judge photographs or audio-tapes, and drawing their attention to the facial or vocal cues for different emotions.

Non-verbal Signals Linked to Conversation

This section is about 'conversation', since the non-verbal signals here are concerned with language in use, and especially with dialogues. Language can be looked at as a kind of social behaviour, though a rather special kind. Utterances can be regarded as 'speech acts', signals that are intended to influence other people in some way.[19] And when actually spoken, as opposed to printed on paper, speech acts and conversations are accompanied, supported by and intricately coordinated with non-verbal signals, such as tones of voice, gestures, head nods and minor facial expressions. The non-verbal signals to be discussed in this section are different from those of the last: they are faster-moving, and they are closely linked to speech. It is not possible to say very much about the innate/cultural division here. The capacity for speech appears to be innate, but it is also learnt, mainly from close interaction between infant and mother; the non-verbal accompaniments develop at the same time. This non-verbal system is quite similar in different cultures, though the meanings of gestures are very different.

Non-verbal Accompaniments of Speech

There is a major difference between written and spoken language – the latter has a lot more NVC. And 'we speak with our mouths but we converse with our whole bodies'.[20] A speaker elaborates, disambiguates or comments on his verbal utterances mainly by non-verbal vocalizations and gestures. The relevant vocalizations here are 'prosodic' signals – (a) pitch, which indicates syntax and ending of utterances; (b) stress, showing which words are to be emphasized, in what might otherwise be ambiguous utterances, for example, 'they are *hunting* dogs' as opposed to 'they are hunting *dogs*'; and (c) timing, especially short pauses, which indicate grammatical pauses, and can also give emphasis.

While people talk they also use their hands. 'Illustrative gestures' are used to indicate shapes, sizes, directions and to point, for example to describe a spiral staircase. We found that senders could communicate shapes better if they were allowed to use their hands, especially for shapes for which there are no words; and the effect was greater for Italian subjects.[21]

Emblems

Emblems are mostly hand, or hand-to-face gestures, with arbitrary meanings, but which stand for one word or a group of words. Where illustrative gestures are similar in form to their referents, emblems usually are not. There is a lot of cultural variation in the meaning of emblems. The 'hand-purse' (palm upward, fingers inclined together) can mean 'good' (Greece), a question (Italy), 'slowly' (Tunisia) and 'lots' (Spain) (figure 5.5).

An important set of head gestures are those for 'yes' and 'no'. 'No' is signalled by shaking the head in most of Europe, but by tossing it back in Greece and southern Italy. The geographical divide is a small range of hills marking the limit of Greek occupation of Italy in the classical period.[22]

Some emblems have a meaning through an association with the gesture; for Arabs it is very rude to show the sole of the foot, since this means 'you are like the dirt on the sole of my foot'. The Greek open-hand gesture is even ruder, meaning 'I would like to rub excrement in your face'.

Emblems are used in place of speech for several reasons – at a distance (greeting), in broadcasting, war, underwater swimming, etc. It is not known why the Italians make so much use of emblems while they are speaking.

Figure 5.5   Some gestures
with variable meaning[22]
(reprinted with permission from
Morris et al., 1979, Gestures,
Jonathan Cape).

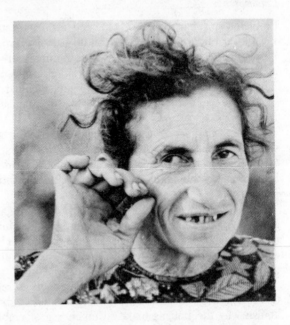

Back-channel Signals

While one person is speaking, others are listening, and the latter give off a rapid flow of back-channel, or feedback, signals at the same time. These are mostly spontaneous, though there is some degree of deliberate control of what is sent, especially by sophisticated interactors. The main channels are: non-verbal vocalizations ('I see', 'really', etc), head-nods, glances and changes of facial expression, especially of mouth and eyebrows. Several kinds of information are sent: (a) 'listening behaviour' indicating that the listener is still attending, or pretending to – consisting of head-nods, grunts and glances; over the telephone there is much more vocalized listening behaviour, to compensate for loss of visible cues; (b) feedback, giving a commentary, showing how far the listener agrees (smiles), disagrees (frowns), is surprised (eyebrows raised), puzzled (eyebrows lowered), etc. by what has just been said; (c) listeners cooperate by reflecting the meaning of what has been said, for example, by looking sad if it was sad, smiling if it was funny.[23]

The Coordination of Gaze with Speech

A speaker cannot observe head-nods or other non-vocal feedback without looking at the listener. Speakers in fact look at the ends of utterances, and at major grammatical pauses within utterances. For listeners, however, these glances are signals. The 'terminal gaze' at the ends of long utterances is one of the non-verbal full-stop signals. For the speaker, his gaze is used to open a channel, while for the listener who is gazed at it is a signal.[24] The listener's glances similarly are taken as signals by the speaker that the other is attending. This is a quite different aspect of gaze from that discussed earlier; gaze linked with speech plays a central part in the rapid flow of verbal and non-verbal events in conversation, is crucial in obtained feedback and can be important as a synchronizing cue.

People look nearly twice as much while listening as while talking. The reason is that speakers do not want to be distracted by extra information, especially at the beginning of utterances, while listeners want to receive the non-verbal accompaniments of the utterance and perhaps do some lip-reading too. Powerful people look about as much while talking as while listening, they look relatively less while listening – because what the other says is unimportant, relatively more while speaking – to make sure that the other is listening.[12]

Managing Synchronizing

How do people manage to coordinate their utterances in conversations so efficiently, with few interruptions or pauses? In fact the interval between utterances is typically less than the normal reaction time. We have seen that the terminal gaze is one signal here, but it has been found that it works only if the general level of gaze is rather low, as in hesitant speech.[25] Several other synchronizing signals have been discovered, some verbal, some non-verbal, which seem to be of differing importance under different conditions, and perhaps for different people. The main ones are:

(1) 'Tonal contour', i.e. a fall of pitch, except in most questions, which have a rising pitch. Mrs Thatcher has been found to be interrupted in TV interviews as a result of giving a falling pitch contour in mid-utterance.[25]
(2) Keeping a hand in mid-gesture by a speaker is a powerful suppressor of interruptions.
(3) Sentence structure indicates when the end is coming, especially, though not only, in the case of questions.

It has been found that in male–female conversation nearly all the interruptions are by the male. Is this because women send less clear signals, because men don't receive them, or because they don't care?

The 'Gestural Dance'

There has been some disagreement over the extent to which interactors coordinate their respective bodily movements. As we have seen, there is some degree of coordination on the time-scale of the whole utterance and of complete clauses: listeners look nearly twice as much as speakers, who look mainly at the ends and at grammatical breaks in utterances. Speakers gesture more than listeners. It has also been claimed that there is much finer coordination on a smaller time-scale. While this has not been confirmed for people in groups,[26] there is evidence that the hand-to-face movements of two people engrossed in a conversation are often synchronized in this way (G. W. Beattie, lecture at Oxford).

Self-presentation

Another way in which NVC operates is in sending information about the self. Animals do this too, for example through the impressive appearance of deer antlers. It sometimes takes the form of deliberate display – peacocks showing their feathers. Human self-presentation is done rather differently, mainly by clothes and decoration. While animals do it either to threaten other animals or to attract mates, humans do it more to project their self-image. This is done to obtain immediate rewards, such as getting a job or being approved of, or to make aspects of the self-image public; if these are accepted by others it helps to incorporate parts of the ideal self in the self-image.[27]

Self-presentation could be done with words, but there are two reasons why NVC does it better. First, the words may be untrue, while NV messages are trusted more. Secondly, there is a taboo on overt self-presentation in many cultures, so that if words *are* used they have to be very indirect to be acceptable.

Self-presentation is used to send several kinds of information. Social status or occupational role are shown by clothes and uniforms, for example in hospitals and law courts. Mary Sissons carried out an experiment in which the same person asked a lot of people the way at Paddington station, in two totally differents sets of clothes; his perceived social status varied with the clothes that he was wearing (figure 5.6).[28] Group membership is displayed by T-shirts, badges, ties, etc. It was found that more students at an American college wore the college T-shirt after the college football team had won a game. Personality characteristics are also shown. It was found that girls in the north of England agreed what kind of girl would wear certain items of clothing, whether they were snobbish, fun-loving, rebellious, shy, promiscuous, etc.[29]

Clothes are one of the main channels. They are different from other non-verbal signals in that their meaning keeps changing, as fashion changes. Ties and other badges have meanings which are mainly arbitrary, and are often only recognized by members of the group concerned. 'Oxford University' T-shirts, on the other hand, are not normally worn by members of that place. Bizarre hair styles, whether long, short, dyed or spiked, are linked particularly to membership of deviant groups. Cosmetics – colouring of face, hair, etc. – are used mainly to enhance physical attractiveness, and it does so very successfully. Accents signal social class, real or pretended. Rooms, houses, cars and wives can all be used as part of self-presentation.[5]

Figure 5.6   Social class at Paddington station in London[28] (reprinted with permission from 'Money, wealth and class', D100, © 1971 The Open University Press).

Decoding is done in terms of the decoder's own cognitive categories. Social class is one of the main ones. Physical attractiveness is another, and this influences other judgements – the 'physical attractiveness stereotype'. Attractive people are believed to be more kind, sensitive, interesting, sociable, strong, poised, modest, outgoing, and sexually warmer.[30] There are many other stereotypes, most of them with little factual basis – for example, that people with spectacles are more intelligent.

Rituals

By rituals are meant standardized patterns of social behaviour which are mainly symbolic rather than instrumental, and concerned with religious or occult ideas. Marriage services and religious healing are examples: they produce changes of social relationships or states of mind rather than physical effects. By ceremonies are meant standardized symbolic patterns of social behaviour not concerned with religion. Greetings and gradua- tions are examples.

Animals also have ritualized behaviour. However, human and animal rituals are clearly produced by different mechanisms: animal ritual is the result of biological evolution, human ritual is the result of cultural development; the first is passed on genetically, the second is passed on by tradition and learning – though there may be universal structures underlying human rituals. Human rituals develop much faster than animal rituals. There is also greater individual variation between humans, and innovators and leaders play an important role in changing the tradition. Humans are influenced by ideas, and acts and objects acquire symbolic meanings.

Human rituals are of three main kinds: changing or confirming changes of role or relationship, healing, and religious. They do 'ritual work', for example, when two people have been married, they and everyone else sees the couple as man and wife. Healing rituals in primitive society may actually heal people, of psychosomatic complaints at least. When a visitor has gone through the rituals of parting, and has to return to collect some forgotten object, he does not need to go through the rituals again – the ritual work has been done.[31]

How is this ritual work accomplished? Partly by non-verbal communication. All human rituals make extensive use of it. Take greetings, for example. Field studies by Goffman,[31] and by Kendon and Ferber[32] suggest that greetings have the following components:

(1) *Distant salutation* (non-verbal only). Two people sight each other, a distant salutation like a wave or smile may be made, one or both approach.

(2) *Approach and preparation* (non-verbal only). Gaze is averted, they groom themselves, and an arm may be brought across the front of the body; in the final approach there is mutual gaze, smiling, the head is set in a special position, and the palm of the hand is presented.

(3) *Close phase* (verbal and non-verbal). Stereotyped utterances are exchanged ('Hello', 'How nice to see you'), usually with bodily contact – handshake, embrace or kiss.

(4) *Attachment phase* (mainly verbal). There is less stereotyped conversation, establishing the identity and status of the other if necessary, enquiring after his recent activities, enquiring purpose of visit, looking after his immediate needs, for example providing him with seat or drink.

In *rites de passage*, where individuals undergo a change of status or of relationships, they may put on symbolic objects (gown, wedding-ring), and be blessed by a touch from the priest or other official. The power of the priest is amplified by non-verbal signals, like touch, gaze, impressive costume, and place at the front and centre of the action.

In healing rituals for barren women in Zambia an elaborate set of NV symbols is used, including dolls in gourds and the blood of a cock. This includes a number of symbols; for example, the calabashes represent wombs, the death of the cock represents the end of the patient's being troubled by a spirit, red clay is used representing menstrual blood, and in another part of the ritual castor oil is used – which is also used to anoint couples before marriage and to massage new-born infants. Each of these objects has powerful emotional associations or metaphorical meanings.[33]

Christian religious rituals include familiar symbols – bread and wine, the cross. Other religions use sacrifices, symbols for birth and death, sun and moon, and so on. It is common to use music, incense, darkness, candles, silence and special postures, to evoke religious feelings.

Non-verbal communication in ritual has meaning in two main ways: (a) similarity, metaphor or analogy, for example, wine for blood, water for purification, putting on a ring; (b) arbitrary associations, for example, flags and crests representing colleges or countries. In rituals which are concerned with social relationships, these symbols indicate social groups, or relations between people. There is no objective means of deciding on the meaning of these rituals. It seems most probable that a ritual can have a number of different meanings at the same time – the same act or object can have a large number of metaphorical links. Turner suggests that symbols can 'condense' several meanings simultaneously, both analogical bodily meanings and arbitrary reference to social groups.[33] In this way group values become charged with emotion, while basic emotions become ennobled through being linked with social values.

Why is non-verbal communication used in ritual? Because it evokes powerful emotional feelings, and is thus able to do the ritual work of changing relationships, healing, and the rest. Rituals can be described in words and initiated in words, but as Raymond Firth said, gestures 'have a significance, a propriety, a restorative effect, a kind of creative force which words alone cannot give'.[34] Words add to the meanings of non-verbal signals, and in religious ritual this consists typically of a combination of verbal and non-verbal, where the two kinds of meaning are combined. This adds the precision of words to the emotive power of bodily signals.

Why Do Humans Use NVC?

We have the power of language, which can carry far more information, so why bother with non-verbal communication? The non-verbal channel is biologically older, and was presumably already doing a very effective job before language appeared on the scene. That job was primarily communicating emotions and interpersonal attitudes. Language can do this too, but it has certain disadvantages. Non-verbal signals for love and hate, for example, immediately put the recipient into an emotional state of biological readiness, while the corresponding words simply set off a lot of complex thought processes. Non-verbal signals are received near, and often below, the threshold of conscious awareness, and interpersonal relations are negotiated smoothly and without embarrassment; furthermore these signals do not commit the sender to a particular degree of intimacy as words would do.

Non-verbal signals linked to language introduce a second channel, which is very useful for communicating feedback, and handling synchronizing, without interrupting the conversation. Illustrative gestures are resorted to when words are lacking, emblems when there is need for silence, or when words are not expressive enough.

Self-presentation is mainly done non-verbally because words are easily spoken and may be untrue. Non-verbal signals are trusted more, though they may be misleading too. Expensive jewellery is evidence that the wearer is rich, an Etonian tie makes it likely that the wearer attended that school. A person dressed as a punk *is* a punk, since that is mainly what a punk is.

Rituals use non-verbal communication because in some way this enhances the ritual work. It is achieved through the powerful body imagery – of opening up people to one another by the bodily contact of a greeting, in the symbolism of blood, birth, etc., of healing, and in the strong emotions evoked by religious music and symbols.

References

1 Ekman, P. (1982) *Emotion in the Human Face*, 2nd edn. Cambridge: Cambridge Univ. Press.

2 Ekman, P. and Friesen, W. V. (1975) *Unmasking the Face*. Englewood Cliffs, NJ: Prentice-Hall.

3 Izard, C. E. (1977) *Human Emotions*. New York: Plenum.

4 Buck, R. (1984) *The Communication of Emotion*. New York: Guilford.

5 Argyle, M. (1975) *Bodily Communication*. London: Methuen.

6 Argyle, M. (1983) *The Psychology of Interpersonal Behaviour*, 4th edn. Harmondsworth: Penguin.

7 Noller, P. (1984) *Nonverbal Communication and Marital Interaction*. Oxford: Pergamon.

8 Rinn, W. E. (1984) The neuropsychology of facial expression: a review of the neurological and psychological mechanisms for producing facial expression. *Psychological Bulletin*, 95: 52–77.

9 Shimoda, K., Ricci Bitti, P. and Argyle, M. (1978) The intercultural recognition of emotional expressions by three national groups – English, Italian and Japanese. *European Journal of Social Psychology*, 8: 169–79.

10 Scherer, K. R. (1979) Nonlinguistic indicators of emotion and psychopathology. In C. E. Izard (ed.), *Emotions in Personality and Psychopathology*. New York: Plenum.

11 Exline, R. and Winters, L. (1965) Affective relations and mutual glances in dyads. In S. Tomkins and C. Izard (eds), *Affect, Cognition and Personality*. London: Tavistock.

12 Argyle, M. and Cook, M. (1976) *Gaze and Mutual Gaze*. Cambridge: Cambridge Univ. Press.

13 Argyle, M. and Dean, J. (1965) Eye-contact, distance and affiliation. *Sociometry*, 28: 289–304.

14 Bull, P. (1983) *Body Movement and Interpersonal Communication*. Chichester: Wiley.

15 Rosenthal, R. (ed.) (1979) *Skill in Nonverbal Communication: Individual Differences*. Cambridge, Mass.: Oelgeschlager, Gunn & Hain.

16 Trower, P., Bryant, B. and Argyle, M. (1978) *Social Skills and Mental Health*. London: Methuen.

17 Sackett, G. P. (1966) Monkeys reared in isolation with pictures as visual input: evidence for an innate releasing mechanism. *Science*, 154: 1468, 1471–3.

18 Whitcher, S. J. and Fisher, J. D. (1979) Multidimensional reaction to therapeutic touch in a hospital setting. *Journal of Personality and Social Psychology*, 37: 87–96.

19 Austin, J. (1962) *How to Do Things with Words*. Oxford: Oxford Univ. Press.

20 Abercrombie, K. (1968) Paralanguage. *British Journal of Diseases of Communication*, 3: 55–9.

21 Graham, J. A. and Argyle, M. (1975) A cross-cultural study of the communication of extra-verbal meaning by gestures. *Int. J. Psychol.* 10: 57–67.

22 Morris, D., Collett, P., Marsh, P. and O'Shaughnessy, M. (1979) *Gestures: Their Origins and Distribution.* London: Cape.

23 Kendon, A. (1977) *Studies in the Behavior of Social Interaction.* Bloomington, Ind.: Indiana Univ. Press.

24 Kendon, A. (1967) Some functions of gaze direction in social interaction. *Acta Psychologica*, 26: 22–63.

25 Beattie, G. (1983) *Talk: An Analysis of Speech and Non-verbal Behaviour.* Milton Keynes: Open Univ. Press.

26 McDowall, J. J. (1978) Interactional synchrony: a reappraisal. *Journal of Personality and Social Psychology*, 36: 963–75.

27 Arkin, R. M. (1980) Self-presentation. In D. M. Wegner and R. R. Vallacher (eds), *The Self in Social Psychology*. New York: Oxford Univ. Press.

28 Sissons, M. (1971) The psychology of social class. *Money, Wealth and Class.* Milton Keynes: Open Univ. Press.

29 Gibbins, K. (1969) Communication aspects of women's clothes and their relation to fashionability. *Brit. J. Social and Clinical Psychology*, 8: 301–12.

30 Dion, K., Berscheid, E. and Walster, E. (1972) What is beautiful is good. *J. Personality and Social Psychol.*, 24: 285–90.

31 Goffman, E. (1971) *Relations in Public.* London: Allen Lane.

32 Kendon, A. and Ferber, A. (1973) A description of some human greetings. In R. P. Michael and J. H. Crook (eds), *Comparative Ethology and Behaviour of Primates*. London: Academic Press.

33 Turner, V. W. (1966) *The Forest of Symbols.* Ithaca, NY, and London: Cornell Univ. Press.

34 Firth, R. (1970) Postures and gestures of respect. In J. Pouillon and P. Marande (eds), *Echanges et Communications*. The Hague: Mouton.

6

Why Psychoanalysis Is Not a Science

Anthony Storr

Anthony Storr is an Emeritus Fellow of Green College, Oxford, a Fellow of the Royal College of Physicians, and a Fellow of the Royal College of Psychiatrists. His books include The Integrity of the Personality, Human Aggression, The Dynamics of Creation, The Art of Psychotherapy, *and* Jung. *His principal recreation is classical music.*

My purpose is to affirm that, although Sigmund Freud continued to hope that psychoanalysis was, or might become, a science, that hope was doomed to disappointment. Although some of the hypotheses of psychoanalysis can be treated scientifically, that is, subjected to objective assessment and proved or disproved in the same fashion as scientific hypotheses in other fields, this is only true of a minority. For most of the hypotheses of psychoanalysis are based upon observations made in the course of psychoanalytic treatment, and psychoanalytic treatment cannot be regarded as a scientific procedure. Observations made during the course of psychoanalysis are inevitably contaminated with the subjective experience and prejudice of the observer, however detached he tries to be, and cannot therefore be regarded in the same light as observations made during the course of a chemical or physical experiment. It is certainly possible to study human beings as if they were objects merely responding to the stimuli impinging upon them. This is the aim of experimental psychology. But it is not possible to conduct psychoanalysis or any form of psychotherapy in this fashion, for reasons which I shall proceed to outline.

To my mind, Freud's wish to be thought a scientist, and his reluctance to admit that he abandoned that role at an early stage in his career, have had an unfortunate effect. If no one had ever claimed that psychoanalysis was a science, dispute about its status would not have been so intemperate. John Bowlby, who is perhaps the most influential living psychoanalyst, once said that he thought that Freud's attitude had held up the development of psychotherapy by fifty years. Yet Bowlby would be the first to acknowledge the originality of Freud's genius. In order to understand this paradox, it is necessary to glance at some aspects of the development of Freud's thought.

Freud's Early Career

Freud was not only a medical man, but had also been trained in the

Sigmund Freud as a young man (1891). His initial attraction to science may have led to the erroneous view that psychoanalysis is essentially scientific (Mary Evans Picture Library/Sigmund Freud Copyrights).

laboratories of Ernst Brücke, a scientist who, according to his collaborator Emil du Bois-Reymond, had 'pledged a solemn oath to put into power this truth: no other forces than the common physico-chemical ones are active within the organism.'[1] This hard-headed, uncompromisingly deterministic point of view, which has proved so rewarding in the exact sciences of chemistry and physics, was, at that date, a departure from the vitalistic form of biology taught to Brücke and his fellows when they were students. For fifteen years, Freud conducted research, first into the nervous systems of fish, and then into the human central nervous system. Even when he had begun to formulate psychoanalytical ideas, he looked back with regret to his neuro-anatomical days, published a monograph on aphasia (speech disorders due to brain damage) in 1891, and another, major work on childhood cerebral palsy in 1897. Because Brücke's two assistants were relatively young, Freud had little prospect of advancement within that laboratory. On this account, Brücke advised him to practise medicine. Freud's decision to do so was reinforced by his having fallen in love with Martha Bernays, whom he could not marry without increasing his earnings. Freud reluctantly took his medical degree in 1881, and was then appointed a demonstrator in Brücke's Physiological Institute. With so much 'hard' science behind him, it was natural enough that Freud's approach to the study of neurotic symptoms should derive from his medical and scientific training. That is, he approached neurotic symptoms as if they were of the same order as the physical symptoms of organic disease, and at first treated them with the physical methods of treatment then available: hydrotherapy, electrotherapy and massage. In the summer of 1885, Freud applied for, and won, a travelling fellowship, which enabled him to spend the winter of 1885–6 studying in Paris with the famous neurologist Charcot. Charcot had, for some years, been investigating hypnotism, with the object of finding a way of distinguishing between organic and hysterical paralyses. Charcot demonstrated to Freud that *ideas*, although intangible, could nevertheless be causal in neurosis. For when a patient developed an hysterical paralysis, the form which the paralysis took was not determined by the facts of anatomy but by the patient's faulty *idea* of anatomy. Instead of developing a paralysis which could be explained by a lesion of a particular peripheral nerve, he exhibited a paralysis of a limb which corresponded to his *idea* of where his leg began and ended. Moreover, Charcot demonstrated that hysterical paralyses could be artificially reproduced by means of hypnosis. If ideas could cause hysterical symptoms, then ideas might also bring about cures. By means of hypnosis, ideas of health could be forcibly implanted, and Freud found that hypnosis could indeed relieve a number of hysterical symptoms. Freud therefore began to employ hypnosis as his main method of treatment for neurotic disorders, and continued to do so until 1896.

The Beginnings of Psychoanalysis

Hypnosis came to have two aspects. The first was the installation of ideas of health into the mind of the patient – positive suggestions designed to counteract the negative ideas which were causing the symptoms. The second and more important aspect derived from Freud's friend and

Figure 6.1   The French neurologist and pioneer of psychiatry, Jean Martin Charcot (1825–93), demonstrating the hysterical collapse of a young woman at the Salpêtrière Hospital in Paris. Sigmund Freud was one of Charcot's students (photographie Giraudon).

collaborator Josef Breuer. When treating his famous case Anna O (Bertha Pappenheim) with hypnosis, Breuer discovered that if she could be persuaded to recall the very first moment of the appearance of each hysterical symptom, the symptom disappeared. Breuer named this method of treatment 'catharsis'. Hypnosis, therefore, came to be used as a way of getting the patient to recall forgotten origins. Instead of being used as a positive, direct attack upon neurotic symptoms, it became a method of investigation.

Freud and Breuer came to hope that all neurotic symptoms could be abolished in this laborious though essentially simple way. In their first paper in *Studies on Hysteria*, they wrote:

For we found, to our great surprise at first, that each individual hysterical symptom immediately and permanently disappeared when we had succeeded in bringing clearly to light the memory of the event by which it was provoked and in arousing the accompanying affect, and when the patient had described that event in the greatest possible detail and had put the affect into words.[2]

Later, the same technique was applied to obsessional symptoms. In volume III of the Standard Edition, we read of a girl

who had become almost completely isolated on account of an obsessional fear of incontinence of urine. She could no longer leave her room or receive visitors without having urinated a number of times. When she was at home or entirely alone the fear did not trouble her. *Reinstatement*: it was an obsession based on temptation or mistrust. She did not mistrust her bladder, but her resistance to erotic impulses. The origin of the obsession shows this clearly. Once, at the theatre, on seeing a man who attracted her, she had felt an erotic desire, accompanied (as spontaneous pollutions in women always are) by a desire to urinate. She was obliged to leave the theatre, and from that moment on she was a prey to the fear of having the same sensation, but the desire to urinate had replaced the erotic one. She was completely cured.[3]

We can see from this account that, although neurotic symptoms differed from those of physical disease in originating from unpleasant memories or unwelcome or unadmitted emotions, it was nevertheless possible to regard them in much the same light. Just as pneumococci might be regarded as the 'cause' of pneumonia, and abolished by suitable medication, so neuroses were 'caused' by repressed emotions or traumas, and could be abolished by recall of the painful emotions and their discharge; a process which was named 'abreaction'. Moreover, whilst hypnosis remained the technical method for enabling the patient to recover the repressed memories and the unpleasant emotions which had accompanied them, it was possible to teach it in the same way that the technique of removing an appendix could be taught. The psychotherapist could therefore assume the traditional medical role of a skilled professional; a benign authority, giving the patient the benefit of his superior knowledge; benevolent, considerate, but essentially detached.

So long as this view of neurosis could be maintained, it also followed that the patient could be treated as an isolated individual, without reference to his present circumstances or current interpersonal relationships. For, if the cause of neurosis lay in the past, the task of the therapist was merely to facilitate remembrance of things past. Psychoanalysts have often been criticized for only attempting to understand their patients when the latter have been put into an isolated, artificial situation which is remote from ordinary life, and which precludes access to those who know them best, their relatives and friends. But, if it is assumed that neurosis is caused by repressed emotions originating in the past, more particularly in the earliest years of the patient's childhood, it is not unreasonable to disregard current relationships and to create a situation in which recall of the past is facilitated. If a patient's illness is due to an inflamed appendix, the surgeon's task is to locate the appendix and remove it. Descriptions by the relatives of the patient's reaction to pain and illness are unlikely to be relevant.

The Psychoanalyst and the Behaviour Therapist

The case-history of the girl with the obsessional fear of incontinence is not given in any detail. There are many questions about her to which any psychiatrist practising today would like to have the answers. But, as Freud presents the case, we are told that she was completely cured; and this was probably good enough for her as it must be good enough for us. Freud's attitude toward his patient, at this period of history, is similar to that advocated by behaviour therapists today. (Behaviour therapy is a technique of treating neurotic symptoms used by experimental psychologists. It is derived from learning theory and the principles of conditioning through reward and punishment expounded by B. F. Skinner. Claims that its good effects are entirely due to the application of scientific principles rather than to interpersonal interaction are less strident than they were.) Although behaviour therapists think of neurotic symptoms as learnt, maladaptive habits rather than as being caused by repressed emotions, their attitude toward the patient is not unlike that of a physician toward a patient suffering from a physical illness; and this was also Freud's attitude when he began treating such patients. The physician has as his aim the understanding of the underlying cause of whatever symptoms the patient presents, and the abolition of those symptoms by appropriate techniques of treatment. This is entirely proper. There is no need for the physician to get to know his patient as a person, and still less for him to examine his own personality and motives. The physician's ideal is to discover ways of treating disease by methods which can be learnt and applied by any other doctor; methods to which the personality of the doctor is irrelevant. In similar fashion, Eysenck has been heard to say that behaviour therapists should be like dentists: considerate and kind, no doubt; but essentially skilled technicians who apply techniques of treatment which can be learned by any intelligent person, and which can be evaluated by the ordinary methods of science.

This objective, scientific approach is perfectly all right as far as it goes, both in physical disorders and in certain defined types of neurotic disorder. If I consult a physician for asthma, what I want is that he shall be an expert in respiratory disease, and that he shall be able to prescribe what drugs are necessary. If he happens to be skilled in interpersonal relationships and comes to understand me as a person, this is an unsought bonus for which I may be grateful, but which is a secondary gain rather than a prime objective. Behaviour therapists score their greatest successes with specific phobias, especially with those which take origin from defined traumatic incidents, and I am the last person to question their achievements. Indeed, I have considerable sympathy with their point of view. It would be admirable if all forms of neurosis could be treated by objective, scientific techniques which anyone could learn. This was certainly Freud's hope in the early days, and one which he never completely abandoned. However, subjective factors began to interfere with this aspiration, even before the close of the nineteenth century. In a paper entitled 'The Aetiology of Hysteria', published in 1896, Freud states that, having treated some eighteen cases, 'Whatever case and whatever symptom we take as our point of departure, *in the end we infallibly come to the field of sexual experience.* So here for the first time we seem to have discovered an aetiological precondition for hysterical symptoms.'[4] Freud goes on to point out that, in cases in which the onset of hysterical symptoms seemed to have been triggered by something trivial, psychoanalytic investigation revealed that 'at the bottom of every case of hysteria there are *one or more occurrences of premature sexual experience,* occurrences which belong to the earliest years of childhood but which can be reproduced through the work of psycho-analysis in spite of the intervening decades.'[5] Roger Brown has pointed out that this was Freud's last attempt to give figures concerning aetiology, and that, even in this

instance, there were no controls. Brown suggests that there were two
reasons for Freud's change of attitude. First, he discovered that some of
his patients were telling him fantasies, not facts, about their pasts.
Second, Freud had embarked upon his own self-analysis. Freud knew
that, in his own case, the case of the nineteenth patient, the Oedipus
complex had bulked large in childhood. But he also knew that he had not
experienced actual sexual seduction. Accordingly, Freud transferred his
attention from so-called traumatic incidents, of which sexual seduction
had seemed the most important variety, to an examination of the patient's
inner world of fantasy. Psychoanalysis changed from what might be called
a scientific attempt to disclose a causal series of events culminating in the
outbreak of a neurosis, to an exploration of the patient's imaginative world
which could not be categorized as scientific.

The Neuroses are Different Today

These were not the only reasons for supposing that Freud's ideal of
establishing psychoanalysis as a true science of the mind was doomed to
failure. Freud's original hypothesis concerning precocious sexual arousal
was based on dramatic cases of hysteria which are hardly ever seen today.
Why this is so is uncertain; but it has been suggested, rather convincingly,
that it may be connected with the fact that women, however incomplete
their freedom, are at least more emancipated than they were in the days of
Freud. In the nineteenth century, life had very little to offer an intelligent
woman who did not get married, or who was unhappily married.
Condemned to social, as well as sexual frustration, and either despised for
not achieving the status of marriage, or locked into a situation from which
there was no escape, such women expressed their dissatisfaction in
dramatic fashion, developing symptoms which, if they did not get them
what they wanted, at least ensured that they were paid attention.

We have seen that the kind of hysterical symptoms produced by Anna
O and her sisters could, in many instances, be traced to a defined origin
and abolished in much the same fashion as can symptoms of physical
disorders. But the majority of neurotic symptoms are not like this. If a
patient complains of headache, it is legitimate to think of this symptom as
an alien intruder. The same is true of a limited range of neurotic
symptoms, of which specific phobias are the best examples. But most
neurotic symptoms are much more intimately connected with the
patient's personality as a whole and cannot really be understood unless
the patient's personality as a whole is taken into consideration. Consider,
for example, the common symptom of agoraphobia. In some instances,
agoraphobia may take origin from a frightening experience, a so-called
'traumatic incident'. One may expect that a girl who has been sexually
assaulted in the street would be reluctant to venture out alone for a while.
But, in most cases, it will be found that agoraphobia originates from what
Bowlby calls a disturbance in 'attachment behaviour'. That is, inquiry into
the patient's early emotional development will reveal that, as a child,
attachment figures were unreliable or absent, with the consequence that,
instead of developing increasing confidence, the child came to regard the
world as a frightening and unpredictable place into which it was not safe
to venture alone without a supporting arm.

Or consider depression. People who are particularly prone to depression tend to feel both helpless and hopeless in the face of any form of adversity. If one is to understand the reasons why anyone habitually reacts in this way to disappointment, loss or challenge, it is necessary to investigate the emotional climate in which the patient was reared. Although a specific attack of depression may be relieved by physical methods of treatment, the tendency to become severely depressed cannot be understood without taking the whole personality into account; nor can the person be expected to learn to deal better with this tendency because his symptom has been attacked directly with anti-depressant drugs or ECT (electro-convulsive therapy).

As time went on, patients seeking psychoanalysis presented symptoms which were even less defined than agoraphobia or recurrent depression. Today, many patients asking for psychotherapy are not suffering from any definable neurosis but from generalized unhappiness, from tensions at work, or from difficulties in interpersonal relationships. They bring to the psychoanalyst what Thomas Szasz has accurately called 'problems in living', and therefore demand to be understood as persons rather than treated for particular symptoms. Since its establishment in the 1890s, psychoanalysis has moved farther and farther away from the medical model.

Freud's Change of Technique in Treatment

Another important reason for psychoanalysis becoming more concerned with persons as a whole than with neurotic symptoms sprang from Freud's change in technique. I said earlier that Freud continued to use hypnosis until 1896. I should rather have said that he finally abandoned its use in 1896; for, from 1892 onward, he was gradually modifying his technique. Freud's substitution of free association for hypnosis was, I believe, his most momentous therapeutic innovation. The employment of free association compels the therapist to assume a much more passive, less authoritarian role than that conventionally expected of the doctor, and makes the patient take the initiative. Hypnosis is a treatment which is entirely dependent upon the doctor's authority and the patient's compliance. The hypnotized patient recovers because the hypnotist tells him that he will; or recalls the remote past because the hypnotist urges him to do so. The adoption of free association means that the patient is no longer automatically placed in a submissive or childish relation to the therapist. Instead of looking to the therapist for direct advice or specific instructions, the patient learns to use the analysis as a way of understanding himself better and, through this, learning to solve his own problems.

This is the most important consequence of the adoption of free association, but it is not the only one. If a person is encouraged to say everything which comes into his mind without censorship, he will surely talk not only about his symptoms, but about his hopes and fears, his aspirations and disappointments, his successes and failures and everything else which preoccupies him and constitutes him as a unique person. Once again we observe that the emphasis has shifted away from the treatment of neurosis to the consideration of the person as a whole.

Another reinforcement of this shift was Freud's discovery of transfer-

ence. As he proceeded with his psychoanalytic work, he found that he
became emotionally important to his patients in a way which he did not
welcome, but which he reluctantly came to realize was a vital part of
psychoanalytic treatment. Freud at first thought of transference as an
erotic attachment to the analyst, as indeed it can be. However deplorable
this might be, it was, so Freud considered, a useful way of overcoming
resistance. Later, Freud came to think of transference as an artificially
induced neurosis in which the patient repeated all the attitudes which he
had held in early childhood toward his parents. By means of interpretation, Freud strove to convert this repetition into recollection, thus
reducing the intensity of present emotions by affirming that they really
belonged only to the past. Freud wrote: 'The patient, that is to say, directs
toward the physician a degree of affectionate feeling (mingled, often
enough, with hostility) which is based on no real relationship between
them and which – as is shown by every detail of its emergence – can only
be traced back to old wishful fantasies of the patient's which have become
unconscious.'[6] In other words, Freud was striving to discount any
possibility that his patients might be experiencing genuine emotional
feelings toward him in the here-and-now. In fact it is perfectly natural
that patients should genuinely value the analyst in a special way, however
much their picture of him or her may be distorted by past experience.
Many patients in analysis have never experienced the kind of long-term
concern that an analyst gives them. There is no other situation in life in
which one can count on a devoted listener for so many hours. In June
1910, Freud wrote to Pfister: 'As for the transference, it is altogether a
curse.'[7] One can understand why Freud felt this. Instead of his patients
accepting him merely as a trained, skilled operator who could, by means
of his technique, expose the origins, and abolish the symptoms, of their
several neuroses, they made him into a saviour, or a father-figure, or an
idealized lover. What they wanted was not his science, but his love.

Freud's recognition of the phenomena of transference, however
interpreted or explained, once again deflected interest from neurotic
symptoms as such, and steered it in the direction of interpersonal
relationships. Moreover, it soon became obvious that the analyst was not
and could not be the kind of detached observer who was no more affected
by his patient than if the latter was a chemical solution. Jung was the first
of the early analysts to insist that the analyst himself must be analysed.
Analysts, ideally, were supposed to be freed from their own emotional
blocks and prejudices in order to be able to treat their patients satisfactorily. However, Jung insisted, they must always remain open to change
themselves. The analyst must allow himself to be affected by his patient to
be able to help him. He must monitor his own emotional responses by
means of introspection, since his own subjective reaction to what the
patient was saying was a vital means toward understanding him.

This is a far cry from what is demanded of a scientist. In conducting a
chemical experiment, the scientist takes pains to ensure that his own
emotions do not affect the objectivity of his observations. Perhaps his
hopes and fears are deeply aroused by a particular experiment. Perhaps a
Nobel prize depends upon whether a solution turns red or blue. But the
scientist's hopes and fears must not be allowed to influence the detachment with which he notes his results; nor does his own knowledge of

himself affect his understanding of the interacting chemicals. In psychoanalysis, the analyst must, to some extent, regard his patient objectively. But, if he is to understand him, he must take into account his own feelings and his own reaction to the patient's feelings. If he treats the patient in the way in which a scientist treats a chemical solution, he cuts himself off from the sources of information which we all habitually use in understanding each other.

I hope I have made clear how it came about that psychoanalysis became less and less concerned with neurotic symptoms, and more and more concentrated upon persons and interpersonal relationships. Neurotic symptoms have become an entry ticket for embarking upon psychoanalysis, and are largely disregarded once the analysis is under way. Not long ago, I was talking to a senior member of the Tavistock Clinic in London, which is entirely staffed by psychoanalysts. He told me that they were thinking of appointing a behaviour therapist to the staff. I was at first surprised that a therapist trained to use an entirely different approach to treatment should be introduced into a Freudian stronghold. Such a person would, I thought, be an entirely alien figure. Then the light dawned. 'You want the behaviour therapist to get rid of the symptoms,' I said. 'Then you can get on with what really matters – the analysis.'

Understanding Persons Rather Than Symptoms

If one is to understand persons, one is compelled to try to understand their interpersonal relationships. For what we call a person is defined by comparison with, and interaction with, other persons. As John MacMurray put it: 'Persons ... are constituted by their mutual relation to one another. "I" exists only as one element in the complex "You and I".'[8] The growth of what is known as the 'object-relations' school of psychoanalysis bears witness to the change from regarding the patient as a closed system whose difficulties were explained in terms of repression and instinctual fixation to looking upon him as someone whose interpersonal relations have gone awry at an early stage in his development. This change in emphasis has reached its zenith in the work of John Bowlby, whose massive, three-volume work *Attachment and Loss* was completed in 1980. Bowlby's conception of neurosis is couched entirely in terms of disturbed relationships with 'significant others' rather than in terms of 'instinctual fixation'.

Treating symptoms and treating persons are two different exercises. It is possible to sustain an objective, scientific approach to neurotic symptoms, but it is not possible to do so in understanding persons. Because Freud tried to maintain the notion that psychoanalysis was a science and that he was a scientist, this difference has not been made as clear as it should have been, and this has given rise to unnecessary misunderstanding. Eysenck was perfectly right in asserting that psychoanalysis is 'unscientific', but his attack would never have been made if Freud and his followers had not tried to claim that psychoanalysis was a science. Their efforts to do so sprang partly from Freud's original training, and partly from a general over-valuation of the exact sciences which we are only now beginning to correct. Other forms of human endeavour, like history and literature, are equally valuable in an entirely different way. One can hardly imagine that Eysenck would attack poetry for being unscientific, since no one supposes that poetry has anything to do with science.

Why is it that the objective, scientific approach to human beings is insufficient? The behaviourists, of whom B. F. Skinner is the most famous modern example, argue that this is not the case. The original behaviourists tried to adopt a purely determinist, objective approach to human beings, and therefore discarded anything derived from introspection, confining themselves to examining only overt behaviour. This approach demands that human beings be studied as if their behaviour was entirely determined by external forces; as if they were billiard balls possessing no inner life, neither will nor intention. Skinner's view of man is precisely that. His notion of Utopia is one in which the environment is so controlled that appropriate 'contingencies of reinforcement' will automatically produce socially desirable behaviour and general happiness. Skinner writes: 'What is being abolished is autonomous man – the inner man . . . the man defended by the literature of freedom and dignity. A scientific analysis of behaviour dispossesses autonomous man and turns the control he has been said to exercise over to the environment. What is needed is more control, not less. The problem is to design a world which will be liked not by people as they now are but by those who live in it. It is science or nothing.'[9]

Is it? I do hope not. Someone, presumably Skinner, has to decide what kind of world is wanted, and has to design the contingencies of reinforcement which will bring this world into being. I have met Skinner, and reviewed the first volume of his autobiography. I would not want to live in a world designed by Skinner. It is because the behaviourists have taken this strictly deterministic attitude toward human beings that what they have to tell us about ourselves is of so remarkably little interest.

What the Philosophers Say

As I have indicated, it is just possible to sustain a more or less deterministic attitude toward neurotic symptoms, but the philosophers have always realized that such an attitude cannot be sustained when there is any question of interpersonal relationships. For example, P. F. Strawson points out that the psychoanalyst may temporarily adopt, or partially adopt, an objective, impersonal attitude toward those parts of his patient's behaviour which are at first incomprehensible or which the patient cannot control. But once those parts have been understood, and brought into relation with the rest of the patient's behaviour, such an attitude is no longer appropriate. Strawson takes as his example the kind of analyst which Freud originally attempted to be. In his essay 'Freedom and Resentment' Strawson writes:

His objectivity of attitude, his suspension of ordinary moral reactive attitudes, is profoundly modified by the fact that the aim of the enterprise is to make such suspension unnecessary or at least less necessary. Here we may and do naturally speak of restoring the agent's freedom. But here the restoring of freedom means bringing it about that the agent's behaviour shall be intelligible in terms of conscious purposes rather than in terms only of unconscious purposes. This is the object of the enterprise; and it is in so far as this object is attained that the suspension, or half suspension of ordinary moral attitudes is deemed no longer necessary.[10]

In other words, once the psychoanalyst has traced the origin of the symptoms, and brought their meaning and the affects connected with them into consciousness, he is bound to treat the cured patient as a person possessing will and intention; as a being who has the power of choice; not as a being whose behaviour is determined either by factors of which he is unconscious, or by factors external to him, by 'contingencies of reinforcement', as Skinner would call such factors.

In his introduction to *Psycho-Analysis Observed*, Charles Rycroft charts his own progress from considering psychoanalysis as a causal theory to regarding it as a semantic one: that is, from seeing the task of psychoanalysis as uncovering causes to seeing it as a means of making sense of, and understanding, the personalities and communications of patients. If a patient's symptoms are entirely the consequence of unconscious wishes or repressed traumatic incidents, then making the patient conscious of these determinants should, and sometimes does, result in the disappearance of those symptoms, as in the early cases which Freud describes. But, as Rycroft points out,

symptoms are not solely an individual matter, they have a social nexus and function and change in one person may be contingent on change in others. Secondly, in patients other than straightforward psychoneurotics, analysis involves consideration of the whole personality including his conscious values. And thirdly, conscious as well as unconscious motives play a part in the maintenance of neuroses.[11]

Modern psychoanalysts, therefore, are not merely concerned with making what is unconscious conscious, but with understanding persons. If we are to understand persons we must assume that which Skinner and his followers try to eliminate, an inner life which is revealed only through introspection, a life concerned with conscious intention, will, motive, belief and values.

There really is a sense in which understanding a person is different from understanding a disease, an animal, a tree, or even a neurotic symptom. Isaiah Berlin makes the point clearly in his book *Vico and Herder*:

Understanding other men's motives or acts, however imperfect or corrigible, is a state of mind or activity in principle different from learning about, or knowledge of, the external world.

Just as we can say with assurance that we ourselves are not only bodies in space, acted upon by measurable natural forces, but that we think, choose, follow rules, make decisions, in other words possess an inner life of which we are aware and which we can describe, so we take it for granted – and, if questioned say that we are certain – that others possess a similar inner life, without which the notion of communication, or language, or of human society, as opposed to an aggregate of human bodies, becomes unintelligible.[12]

This kind of understanding, as Isaiah Berlin implies, is a refinement and deepening of the kind of understanding we employ every day in our social lives. To adopt an impersonal, scientific attitude toward human beings tells us only about their behaviour: it is to treat them as not possessing an inner life, more particularly, as not possessing will or intention. D. C. Dennett, in his essay 'Mechanism and Responsibility', refers to 'intentional explanations' which 'cite thoughts, desires, beliefs, intentions, rather than chemical reactions, explosions, electric impulses, in explaining the occurrence of human motions.'[13] The impersonal stance, referred to by Dennett as 'mechanistic', can only inform us about another person's behaviour. Although, by adopting this attitude, we may be able to discern *causes* for this behaviour, our explanation cannot be in terms of intention, nor can we determine what this behaviour means to the individual concerned.

In our ordinary day-to-day encounters with individuals, we are bound to adopt the intentional stance. I cannot but assume that I myself have feelings, thoughts, desires, beliefs and intentions; and I must, in the ordinary way, assume that others are similarly constituted. The mechanistic stance is the exception; the intentional stance must be the rule. Anatol Rapoport, in *Fights, Games and Debates*, has pointed out that, when playing a game, we are bound to make what he calls 'the assumption of similarity' about our opponent. Playing a game is impossible unless one can assume that one's opponent intends to win if he can, and that, in trying to achieve this, he will be influenced by the same kind of considerations and have in mind the same kinds of strategy as one does oneself.[14]

Using Intuition and Empathy

Adopting the objective, mechanistic stance toward human beings actually deprives the observer of an important source of understanding. In our exchanges with others, we are bound to rely upon our own subjective experience if we wish to grasp what others are thinking and feeling. We observe behaviour, the signals which others give us. But we interpret those signals, at least in part, in terms of what we ourselves feel or have felt in the past. This is why it is often difficult to understand patients who come from different cultures. It is easy to misinterpret the signals with which we are presented. In contrast, persons who are close to one another, like husband and wife, often develop sensitive antennae, which tell each what the other is feeling without any verbal exchange. Each knows what the other is feeling, not just because the other provides evidence of happiness, sorrow, fatigue, or zest, but because the emotional state of the other has an immediate influence. We care about how those close to us are feeling, in some degree, perhaps, because we possess a measure of altruism, but more especially because their happiness or unhappiness has a direct effect upon our own. Psychoanalysts need to be affected by their patients if they are to understand them, which is one reason why psychoanalysis is an emotionally demanding profession.

Although psychoanalysis which goes beyond a concern with isolated neurotic symptoms is not, and can never be, scientific in the sense in which the so-called 'hard' sciences are scientific, this does not mean that it should be dismissed as hopelessly subjective. Psychoanalysis is a professional discipline: a skill which ought to be practised only by people who have been properly trained. Although the potential psychoanalyst must use his own emotional reactions in understanding his patient, he also has to learn to control those emotional reactions and not permit them to interfere with the patient's discourse. Psychoanalysis is very far removed from ordinary social interaction. Although the skills used by the psychoanalyst are refinements of those we all employ in understanding others, the analyst must learn to be self-effacing. He must not respond to his patient in the same way that he would in social intercourse, but must suppress all responses of his own that do not further the patient's understanding of himself. Psychoanalysis is bound to be one-way traffic, in that the enterprise is designed to benefit the patient without providing any gratification for the analyst other than that of exercising, and being paid for, a professional skill. But the practice of psychoanalysis demands of the analyst all the intuitive, empathic understanding which he can muster. Because such understanding must be derived from his own human experience, the analyst can never employ the detached, cold objectivity which is a mandatory requirement of the exact scientist.

References

1 Quoted in: Sulloway, Frank J. (1979) *Freud, Biologist of the Mind*, p. 14. New York, Basic Books.
2 Breuer, Josef and Freud, Sigmund (1955) *Studies on Hysteria*. In: Freud, Sigmund, Standard Edition, vol. II, p. 6. London: Hogarth.
3 Freud Sigmund (1962) Standard Edition, vol. III, p. 77. London: Hogarth.
4 Freud, Sigmund (1962) Standard Edition, vol. III, p. 199. London: Hogarth.
5 Freud, Sigmund (1962) Standard Edition, vol. III, p. 203. London: Hogarth.
6 Freud, Sigmund (1957) Standard Edition, vol. XI, p. 51. London: Hogarth.
7 Quoted in: Jones, Ernest (1955) *Sigmund Freud*, vol. II. p. 497. London: Hogarth.
8 MacMurray, John (1961) *Persons in Relation*, vol. II, p. 24. London: Faber & Faber.
9 Skinner, B. F. (1971) *Beyond Freedom and Dignity*, pp. 160, 164, 177, 200, 205. New York: Knopf.
10 Strawson, P. F. (1974) *Freedom and Resentment and Other Essays*, pp. 19–20. London: Methuen
11 Rycroft, C. (1966) *Psycho-Analysis Observed*, p. 11. London: Constable.
12 Berlin, Isaiah (1976) *Vico and Herder*, pp. 23, 28. London: Hogarth.
13 Dennett, D. C. (1973) Mechanism and Responsibility. In T. Honderich (ed.), *Essays on Freedom of Action*, p. 161. London: Routledge & Kegan Paul.
14 Rapoport, Anatol (1960) *Fights, Games and Debates*, p. 306. Ann Arbor: Univ. Michigan Press.

The Daily Mirror

THE MORNING JOURNAL WITH THE SECOND LARGEST NET SALE.

No. 2,782.   Registered at the G.P.O. as a Newspaper   MONDAY, SEPTEMBER 23, 1912   One Halfpenny

SUFFRAGETTES MOBBED AND BEATEN IN WALES: HAIR TORN FROM THE HEADS OF MR. LLOYD GEORGE'S INTERRUPTERS.

There were scenes of the wildest disorder at Llanystymdwy on Saturday, when some suffragettes were violently treated by an angry and excited crowd. Llanystymdwy is near Criccieth, where Mr. Lloyd George received his boyhood training, and the occasion was the visit of the Chancellor to open the village institute which he has presented to the parish. The suffragettes had been warned that it would injure their cause if they adopted their usual tactics towards Cabinet Ministers, but they paid no heed to the warning, and suffered in consequence. Those who interrupted the Chancellor were attacked with great fury, their hair being torn out and their heads beaten. One was actually stripped to the waist. The large photograph shows a policeman vainly endeavouring to protect a woman from the infuriated mob. The small one shows a man grabbing and pulling the hair of the same girl.—(Daily Mirror and C.N.)

7

Psychoanalytic Explanation, with Special Reference to Historical Material

Brian Farrell

Brian A. Farrell was born in Cape Town, and came to consciousness in the backveld of South Africa. He survived to graduate at the University of Cape Town, from which he migrated on a Rhodes Scholarship. He spent some time wandering round the Universities of Cambridge, London and Chicago. He taught Philosophy at the University of the Witwatersrand for ten years. When Psychology was at last given a place in an Honours School at Oxford after the war, he was appointed to the Wilde Readership in Mental Philosophy, to help to establish the respectability of the new subject and Honours School. He was later elected a Fellow of Corpus Christi College. He has now retired from all obligatory duties, and is reputed to have two passions – exercise and grandchildren.

I want to take a look at a topic of some general interest about psychoanalysis in Britain and elsewhere. Consider what I shall call, vaguely and with no snobbish implication, any group of educated people, such as can be met in a university. One is liable to find that the people in this group have two different and apparently conflicting views about psychoanalysis. The one view is, in general, sceptical, critical and unfavourably disposed. The other view is sympathetic, interested and favourably disposed. It seems to me that the critical, sceptical view is held, largely, by those whose education has been primarily on the scientific side. The sympathetic view is held, largely, by those whose education has been primarily in the Arts.

I trust you are all familiar with this difference of view about psychoanalysis between the Science-man and the Arts-man. When, for example, one goes into the Department of Experimental Psychology in Oxford, the atmosphere is one of 'remorseless empiricism' (to use the apt expression of one well-known Oxford psychologist); and hence it is one of scepticism about a subject such as psychoanalysis. When one mingles with students of classics or contemporary literature, the atmosphere is liable to be rather different.

What can we say about this difference and apparent conflict of views? What are the chief reasons that go to sustain this conflict? Is it irreconcilable or not?

Two suffragette hecklers assaulted at a political meeting in 1912. Psychoanalysis could mislead us into oversimplifying the whole matter of the opposition to women's suffrage (© photo by Syndication International).

The 'Science-man's' Case

I take it that we are all pretty familiar these days with the Science-man's case against psychoanalysis. I need do no more than just remind you of the gist of his criticism.

Psychoanalysis contains no theory that is scientific in character. This is so whether we look at it as a whole, or at any part of it, such as psychic structure or psychopathology. When we look at the general statements it gives us (for example, about human development – as in the Oedipal story), it is clear that the chief evidence for them comes from the quasi-clinical material of the psychoanalytic session. And this evidence is beset by well-known doubts, which impugn its weight. If we focus on a very well-known part of psychoanalysis, namely, the theory of dreams, we find that scientific inquiry has quite undermined the credibility of this theory. When we look at the potent role that Freud attributes to early childhood experiences, we are landed in doubts again. As Gelder, Gath and Mayou have said recently: 'There is now fairly general agreement that the important period in development is not limited to early childhood, and that relationships outside the family are influential as well as those with parents.'[1] If we look at the allegedly important role of unconscious states, wishes, and so on, in our lives, we are looking at what is popularly regarded, perhaps, as Freud's greatest discovery. But when we move outside the field of the psychopathology of the neuroses, the evidence for this vague and large claim is poor indeed.

Well, from this it is clear, and generally agreed, that the criticisms of psychoanalysis from the Science-man amount to a formidable onslaught. They explain why he takes such a dim view of the subject. On the other hand, it is also widely accepted in the West that these criticisms are not lethal: they do not constitute a knock-down case. The reason for this becomes clear when one remembers and considers the central core of evidence in support of psychoanalysis. This comes from the material of patients in psychotherapy of the analytic type, and from analysands and patients in analysis. This material gives us some grounds to believe that we *do* function as individuals in certain ways to which psychoanalysis has drawn our attention. Thus, we do seem to react to stress and difficulty in ways that are referred to as 'the mechanisms of defence'; and there do seem to be patterns of early experience – often complex and subtle – that go along with later, adolescent and adult patterns of conduct. It is legitimate, therefore, for us to ask about the weight that the quasi-clinical material lends to psychoanalytic theory. And we can legitimately ask about the credibility of the story in its parts or as a whole.[2]

The 'Arts-man's' Case

Now let us turn to the Arts-man with his sympathetic and favourable view of psychoanalysis. What grounds has he for his sympathy and his favourable attitude? Here we enter territory that is, I think, somewhat unexplored, and which is, in certain areas, the subject of considerable controversy in the United States at the present time.

If we press the Arts-man for the grounds for his view, he might answer us on the following lines:

Figure 7.1 Jacob Freud, with his son, Sigmund age 8. Sigmund was to transform our view of human nature by focusing attention on early experience (Mary Evans Picture Library/Sigmund Freud Copyrights Ltd).

In the course of the last seventy years or so, psychoanalysis has given us an entirely new picture of man. The work of Freud, in particular, has transformed our view of human nature, rather as Marx has changed our view of history and society. Psychoanalysis has done this in virtue of the fact that its concepts and discoveries have enabled us to throw light on a great deal in human life and culture that we could not understand before, for it has been applied to many diverse fields, as we all know: to mention a few, the understanding of art, the nature of religion, the psychology of dress, the psychopathology of politics, the origins of racial prejudice. Indeed almost every aspect of culture has been subjected to psychoanalytic elucidation. Furthermore, Freudian ideas have been applied in biographical work, and have been largely responsible for the development of an ostensibly new discipline in the Humanities, namely Psychohistory.

So, the Arts-man could claim, 'Psychoanalysis has helped us to understand the meaning and significance of much in human life that was puzzling before, has helped to explain it, and thereby helped to transform our view of man.'

It seems, therefore, that the Arts-man's sympathy for psychoanalysis is grounded on its (seemingly) great explanatory power outside clinical contexts. But is this grounding a good one? Might is not be the case that the (seemingly) great explanatory power of psychoanalysis is deceptive, to some lesser or greater degree, and that the new psychoanalytic vision of man is deceptive also?

Let us look at an example or two of such psychoanalytic explanations. Though the range of these examples is enormous, and though they differ, no doubt, considerably *inter se*, a few examples may be good enough to exhibit quickly something of the nature of the whole problem.

Consider a relatively simple example – one with which it is easy to get to grips. Consider *part* of the explanation that Lytton Strachey gives of the fact that Elizabeth I never married.[3] You will appreciate that this is a fact about Elizabeth that historians have to account for – given the circumstances of the period (in which a woman ruler was unthinkable, and in which the whole Protestant cause seemed to depend on her having children); and given also the strong heterosexual interests of Elizabeth herself. Why, then, did she not marry? If I may now update Lytton Strachey, his answer, in part and in brief, would be as follows.

When she was 2 years 8 months old, Elizabeth's father (Henry VIII) cut off her mother's head. Consequently, her father became at one and the same time a male figure whom she respected and loved, but also a male figure of a threatening and terrifying character. Hence she came through her Oedipal period with a very serious unresolved conflict in respect of the father-figure. Hence she reached adulthood with a great fear and revulsion in respect of any male who got close to her, and thereby threatened her. A husband would do just this, and hence would be viewed as a danger. Consequently, she could flirt with men and love them (in the way she did Leicester), but she could never marry one. This psychological conflict is sufficient to account for her not marrying.

Now it can be argued that Strachey's explanation gives us a coherent narrative that gets rid of the puzzle about Elizabeth by making sense out of the facts. But is it a *true* story? What reason have we to believe that she had this unresolved Oedipal conflict, and that, if she had, it played any important part in her remaining single?

To begin with, I gather we do not know whether, in the Court at the time, she knew her mother and her father well and closely enough for the typical pattern of Oedipal relations to develop, with which psychoanalysis is standardly concerned.[4] On the other hand, we should have to take Strachey's explanation seriously, perhaps, if there were no other plausible explanation available.

But there is! As every schoolboy historian knows, when Elizabeth I came to the throne, her overriding task was to preserve the unity and independence of the kingdom. We have good reason to believe that she was a very ambitious woman – determined to succeed and to be a great ruler. Marriage to an Englishman or to a foreigner was only too liable to recharge internal antagonisms and/or to make the country dependent on a foreign power. With the ghastly mistakes before of her sister Mary and of Mary Queen of Scots, it was only too clear to Elizabeth – with her formidable intellect – that marriage was *not* in the best interests of the country. In addition, too, there were the reports that came to her later about her mother's end, her experience at eight of Katherine Howard's death, and her closeness as an adolescent to the scaffold in the Tower, along with the execution of her adolescent lover, Seymour. All this must have contributed to render her, in Black's words, 'a woman . . . schooled to self-repression, and prudence and mistrust'.[5] Accordingly, she must have realized that private passions are not for princes or princesses. As Neale has said, 'in the long run, it was *the weal of the Kingdom* and the limits of practical politics that directed her judgement'.[6]

Figure 7.2   Henry VIII, *by Hans Holbein, painted about 1536, the year of the execution of Anne Boleyn. Their daughter Elizabeth was two years eight months old. As well as being a respected and loved father figure, Henry was now a threatening and terrrifying male (reprinted with permission of the Weidenfeld Archive).*

Figure 7.3 Queen Elizabeth I *as princess, about 13 or 14 years old (artist unknown). Why did she never marry? The apparent explanatory power of psychoanalysis is illusory (reproduced by gracious permission of Her Majesty the Queen).*

This alternative explanation, or something like it, is widely accepted. When faced by it, Strachey's Oedipal account looks simple-minded to a degree. We can speculate, of course, about how her (alleged) Oedipal conflict fed into and strengthened her own concern to control her private passions. But this is mere speculation. The Oedipal story is not needed, and seems to add little, if anything, to our understanding of Elizabeth's failure to marry. Therefore, we have to conclude that the explanatory power of psychoanalysis in this example is illusory.

On the other hand, it is clear what sort of *additional* evidence we need to support the Oedipal explanation, and what sort we need to disconfirm it. To support it, we need, for example, hitherto unknown letters from Elizabeth in which she reveals attitudes to men and marriage that are characteristic of Oedipal fears and difficulties. To disconfirm the explanation, we need, for example, evidence that Ben Jonson was right in saying (according to Strachey) that 'she had a membrana on her, which made her uncapable of man'. For, if this were so, it suggests that, whatever role her feelings about men played later in her adulthood life, she knew full well that in marrying she would give up her independence and freedom to rule without securing the Protestant succession. Since, in particular, we can state what sort of evidence is required to confirm or disconfirm Strachey's explanation, we can say that his application of psychoanalysis is a reasonable one. The illumination it offers may be negligible or non-existent, but at least it is an explanation that is open to rational inquiry – to rational confirmation and disconfirmation.

Let us look next at a very different example of psychoanalytic explanation – one which highlights the central difficulties facing the Arts-man in his attempt to use psychoanalysis for explanatory purposes.

The example is to be found in a recent book, *The Psychoanalysis of Culture*, by a sociologist, C. R. Badcock.[7] I cannot begin to present the argument of this book adequately in a few paragraphs, and I do very much hope that I will not be unfair to the author in anything I say about his work. Badcock takes up what he regards as Freud's suggestion in *Civilisation and its Discontents*, and applies psychoanalysis to the examination and explanation of culture. In doing this, he takes the view that culture goes through the same stages of development as the individual. He starts with primitive man, accepts Freud's case in *Totem and Taboo*, and concentrates on the social phenomena of religion in the West. He summarizes his account in a table (table 7.1). This table contains five columns, and I shall concentrate on the columns headed Religion and Individual Development. Note that the stages in the development of religion parallel the stages in the development of the individual. Note also that each stage, reading downwards, goes along with (to use Freud's notions) a psychological advance towards maturity in the form of a renunciation of instinct. At the same time, each stage reveals a return of the repressed from the stage but one before it.

I shall now just pick out briefly a few features of this table to illustrate what Badcock has in mind. Take the change from Animism to Totemism. This happens through the killing of the father by the sons in the primal horde. This generates, through guilt and deferred obedience, the reinstatement of the father in the totem, and the introduction of the incest taboo – thereby producing the Oedipus complex for the whole race of man.

Look at Pastoralism in the column headed Economy. Pastoralism involves the domestication of animals, and these must not be killed. They come to stand for the father – they are sacred – and so we have the rise of a monotheism and a God doing duty for a punitive super-ego. Badcock pays particular attention to Judaism as a special form of monotheism. Now the 'good news' of the Christian gospel were the tidings of great joy that man was now, at least in fantasy, free from Oedipal guilt, because a

7.1: The social phenomena of religion in the West

Economy	Original Oedipal orientation	Religion	Individual development	Corresponding psychopathology
Foraging		Animism	Primal narcissism	
		↓		
Hunting	+♂	Totemism	Oedipal period	Anxiety hysteria (animal phobia)
		↓		
Cultivation	−♀	Polytheism		
		↓	} Latency	
Pastoralism	+♀	Monotheism		Obsessional neurosis
		↓		
(Mixed farming)		Catholicism		Paranoia
		↓	} Adolescence	(Obsessional complications)
Capitalism	−♂	Protestantism		Obsessional neurosis (paranoid complications)
		↓		
		Psychoanalysis	Maturity	

Advance in renunciation of instinct → Return of the repressed

Source: C. R. Badcock, *The Psychoanalysis of Culture*

Son of God had borne the guilt and had paid the penalty in his stead. Christianity involved a renunciation of self, in the altruism of the New Testament, and this was an advance in the power to control our instincts. But Christianity also went along with a return of the repressed in its polytheism. There were now three Gods; and later we had the Virgin Mary and a whole host of heavenly figures.

The development of Protestantism was an advance in the renunciation of instinct, in that it involved a repression of submissive, passive homosexual tendencies, as well as the masochism of the Cross. At the same time there was a return of the repressed in the form of the severe super-ego of monotheism.

The next and final stage in the advance of instinct consists in the advance of the reality principle – 'a victory of the rational consciousness of the Ego'. This is the stage of cultural maturity, where we are no longer dependent on the fantasies involved in religious beliefs. This stage is represented by psychoanalysis. Since Catholicism contained something to gratify every aspect of man's mind, there will be a complete return, in this last stage, of all that was repressed before, and an abreaction of all the emotions connected with this repressed material. Psychoanalysis will be as comprehensive – as catholic (with a small 'c') – in its scope as Catholicism.

Badcock ends with a picture of the future of psychoanalysis in our education and culture, and concludes the book with these words:

. . . it is I think clear that if the arguments advanced in this book are in any way to be relied upon they strongly suggest that psychoanalysis is destined to play a role in world-history of the first importance. Certainly, it is my belief that if psychoanalysis ceased to be merely a department of modern medicine and became instead a system of education and the basis of culture the universal neurosis which we call 'civilization' would have been largely resolved and the psychoanalysis of man would have been brought to a provisional, but successful conclusion.[8]

Well, what are we to say to all this? Without going into details (which I am not competent to do anyway), I think the historian of religion is likely to protest that Badcock's account is a highly selective one. He has picked out certain aspects of a *very* large and enormously complex story – aspects which enable him to apply or fit his psychoanalytic categories. Hence his account of religious history is a very distorted one. If this objection is correct, then Badcock's narrative fails, because it has not covered all the data by a very long way. Moreover, is it a coherent account? He speaks of whole cultures and religious epochs as being under the influence of 'instinct'. But the word 'instinct' in ordinary discourse and in psychoanalytic theory applies to the individual organism. How then can we talk coherently of the instinct of a culture or epoch? To make sense out of this, we would have to tinker with, or water down, the meaning of the word 'instinct' in some serious way, and then it would be uncertain whether this new, watery concept of instinct could do the work Badcock wants the word to do. Similar considerations apply, of course, to the expression 'return of the repressed', which plays a key role in Badcock's account. It is evident, therefore, that he is faced by some very large conceptual difficulties.

But whatever we may think of this work, it has at least one virtue. It raises in an acute form the central problem that faces the Arts-man when we use the concepts of psychoanalysis. When is it legitimate to use them to explain features of our lives, and when is it not? The hostile critic is liable to protest that, if Badcock's sort of account is acceptable, then *anything* is acceptable! Anything goes!

Let me add in passing that Freud himself did utter a caution and a warning in one place, at least, about this sort of explanation. In *Civilisation and its Discontents* he said:

I would not say that such an attempt to apply psycho-analysis to civilised society would be fanciful or doomed to fruitlessness. But it behoves us to be very careful, not to forget that after all we are dealing only with analogies, and that it is dangerous, not only with men but also with concepts, to drag them out of the region where they originated and have matured.[9]

Likewise, whereas Badcock sees psychoanalysis as bringing to an end 'the universal neurosis' of civilization, Freud concludes with a warning:

My courage fails me, therefore, at the thought of rising up as a prophet before my fellow-men, and I bow to their reproach that I have no consolation to offer them; for at bottom this is what they all demand – the frenzied revolutionary as passionately as the most pious believer.[10]

Three Criteria for the Legitimacy of Psychoanalytic Explanations

How, then, are we to distinguish an application of psychoanalysis by the Arts-man that is legitimate from one that is not? I shall make a few tentative suggestions, in the form of some vague criteria.

Let me consider only the application to an individual person or an item, such as a work of art. Here the criteria for the application of psychoanalysis to an individual inside the clinical situation seem to resemble the criteria for its application outside of the situation; and the latter is what the Arts-man is interested in.

(1) The application of psychoanalysis is legitimate if, and only if, by applying its notions, we can construct a coherent narrative about the individual, which covers the data about the individual that require to be ordered and explained.

This criterion is vague to a degree. For one thing, what fixes the data to be covered? It is difficult enough to agree on them in the clinical situation; it is much more difficult to do so outside it. With historical figures, for example, the data would seem, to some extent, to be relative to the views, interests, etc. of the particular historian. What is a datum for one is not necessarily a datum, or just the same datum, for another.

Moreover, when one applies psychoanalytic notions, there is a tendency to reconstruct the situation surrounding the individual – by filling in the gaps in the data in the light of analytic theory and expectations. But of course this makes for circularity, and so diminishes the weight of the psychoanalytic explanation that is offered.

In addition, this criterion is not sufficient to legitimize the application of analytic theory, because – as we have seen – other plausible, non-psychoanalytical narratives may be available. Hence we need something more.

(2) The application of psychoanalysis is legitimate, if we cannot handle the data without it.

This criterion has to be treated with caution. The distinction between 'can and cannot handle' may not be clear-cut in any given instance; and even if we have an alternative explanation available, it may nevertheless still be worth while applying psychoanalysis merely to discover what new features, if any, they highlight, and what new inferences they suggest.

But, even if the psychoanalytic narrative satisfies criteria (1) and (2), it may remain a speculative exercise. These two criteria are not sufficient to make us take it seriously. For this, again, we need something more.

(3) We must be able to specify the sort of material that will confirm or disconfirm the narrative. We can call this the confirmation criterion.

It has an obvious corollary. The closer we are to the actual discovery or uncovering of such confirming or disconfirming material, the more seriously must we take the explanation; and the less justified we are in treating it as just a speculative exercise.

What now about the psychoanalytical explanation of group and social phenomena generally? For example, what about white prejudice against non-whites in South Africa; the origin of clothes; the rise of Hitlerism; the conditions that maintain capitalism? Can we explain these and other group phenomena in a way that heeds Freud's warning about the dangers of arguing by analogy?

I confess I do not know the answer to this question. It is evident at once that it is difficult to apply the criteria suggested above to group phenomena. How, for example, are we to determine – in a way that does not help to prejudge the case for or against psychoanalysis – the data that make up white racial prejudice in South Africa? Much more serious, can we state the sort of material that will confirm or disconfirm, say, MacCrone's analytic explanation of this prejudice, as it existed in the 1920s and 1930s?[11] Can we do this for MacCrone's modest and clear-cut story, any more than we can for Badcock's sweeping and vague one? Clearly these questions face us with serious logical and methodological issues.

Now consider quite a different sort of example. Suppose I use psychoanalysis to try to explain the present, and very striking, role that Diana, Princess of Wales plays in British culture. Suppose I say: 'She is a person on to whom we project our unconscious wish, with its related fantasies, to identify with an ideal mother – to identify with a young Madonna and child – especially now that the picture of the traditional Virgin and Child has lost its hold in our very secular culture.'

We have to remember that our society is, of course, a very heterogeneous one, containing people of different sorts from varied backgrounds. If this Freudian story of mine, or something like it, about the Princess is to be of any value, we must know what people in our society it is referring to. And the story must also satisfy the confirmation criterion (3). But my story is weak on both counts. It is unclear what people it is referring to, and what evidence of a psychosociological sort is required to support or upset it. Until we are clearer about these matters, it remains uncertain whether my analytic story about the Princess of Wales is really worth offering, let alone taking seriously. Similarly, for the many other stories of this sort – Flugel on the origin of clothes, Fromm on the rise of Hitlerism, Brown on capitalism as an anal culture, and Badcock on the development of religion.[12] Hence it is doubtful whether we can claim *simpliciter* that psychoanalytic accounts of large-scale social phenomena have much explanatory power.

Figure 7.4 The Virgin and Child, *by Giovanni Bellini. The ideal mother, whose hold is lost in our very secular culture.*

The Problem of Psychohistory

At this stage let me return to the historian. We may find her or him puzzled about, or even laughing at, our hunt for the criteria to distinguish the legitimate from the illegitimate uses of psychoanalysis. 'My job', he or she may say, 'is to write what my fellow-historians will regard as "good" history. If, when I use Freudian notions, I can write good history as well, that is sufficient for me. The trouble with Lytton Strachey is that, when he applied analytic theory, he wrote bad history. And most of what is called psychohistory today is very bad indeed.'[13]

Let us not embarrass the historian at this point by asking her or him to clarify the distinction between good and bad history. Instead, let us try to get some further illumination about the whole matter by glancing at a recent example of what is regarded (I understand) as 'good' history, and which claims to use psychoanalytic notions. The example is given us by Professor Peter Gay, of Yale University, in his book *The Bourgeois Experience. Victoria to Freud* – the first volume in a large enterprise.[14]

In this book, Gay sets out to 'examine' bourgeois sexuality from about 1820 up to 1914. For this purpose, he says his 'most rewarding

Figure 7.5   Diana, Princess of Wales, and Prince William. Can psychoanalysis be used to explain her striking role as that of a modern-day Madonna? (© Keystone Press Agency).

documents are . . . private diaries, family correspondence, medical texts, household manuals, religious tracts, and works of art'. He takes these to be indicative of what is going on in bourgeois culture in general. He then purports to apply psychoanalytic notions in order to move from the manifest content of these items to their latent content – in order 'to tease out underlying unconscious fantasies', and the like. In short, he claims to use 'a set of methods and of propositions' from Freud so as 'to wrest from the past its recondite meanings and to read its full orchestrated score'. What he then gives us is a very interesting account, one that obviously throws fresh light on the period, and to which these few remarks of mine do not do justice. For one thing, it shows that the Victorians were far from being as stuffy and inhibited about sexual matters as is generally supposed.

However, this whole enterprise is pervaded by doubts and difficulties. It is difficult enough to be reasonably sure about the truth of a psychoanalytic interpretation when dealing with an item from an individual analysand in the psychoanalytical situation, with its full context and backing of the clinical material. It is much more difficult to be reasonably sure about the truth of an analytic interpretation of the usual sorts of records left by a deceased person to the historian.

Gay purports to apply Freudian 'propositions' to 'wrest from the past its recondite meanings'. If he is to succeed, then it is very advisable indeed, if not necessary, that the psychoanalytic propositions he uses should be true, or should approximate to the truth. If not, they will be liable to mislead him, and his readers, in some greater or lesser degree. Now Gay is far from being clear and precise about what propositions he does use. But a study of his text suggests that the propositions he employs are ones to which the Science-man does indeed take serious exception. Thus, for example, Gay describes the opposition from men to women's suffrage, and suggests that it was due, in part, to an Oedipal fear – viz. the fear of 'castration by woman' (*sic*). But the Science-man would claim that the Oedipal story is still unproven, and that there is some reason to believe the castration part of it is false. Because of this, Gay's use of Freudian theory, in this instance, is liable to mislead us into oversimplifying the whole matter of the opposition to women's suffrage. Gay faces the objection that, by reading the bourgeois experience with the aid of the particular psychoanalytic propositions he uses, he may be giving us a serious *misreading* of this experience.

In trying to apply Freud and analysis, Gay makes use of psychoanalytic concepts of Defence, such as reaction formation and identification with the aggressor. It is well known that these concepts are very difficult to handle. For they are not used to pick out classes of conduct that can be precisely specified. They are used to pick out typical patterns, or clusters, of conduct.

Now the analytic situation does generally provide the analyst with the material that encourages him to recognize an instance of conduct as part of a typical pattern, and that gives him reasonable grounds for claiming that it is an instance of reaction formation, or repression, or identification with the aggressor, or whatever it may be. The historian is not, typically, in this fortunate situation. It is doubtful whether his material generally

Figure 7.6   The 'castrating woman' triumphant! Samson and Delilah, *by Max Liebermann, 1902. This Oedipal fear might be offered to explain men's opposition to women's rights (photograph by Ursula Edelmann, reproduced by permission of the Städelsches Kunstinstitut Frankfurt).*

offers him the sort of contextual pattern, or cluster, he requires to give him reasonable grounds for applying a concept of Defence to some item. In these circumstances, it may be tempting for a historian to disregard the constraints that the contextual pattern imposes on the use of the concepts of Defence. Such disregard is liable to lead to their misuse and debasement.

It is tempting, perhaps, to reply that this whole problem could be overcome if historians were themselves analysed – a course that Gay seems to recommend. But this will not help. For, whether the historian be a trained analyst or not, the problem he faces in applying the concepts of Defence to the historical material is not primarily that of skilfully identifying the relevant patterns. It is that of obtaining sufficient historical material to give him the pattern he requires to justify him in applying a concept of Defence at all. It is difficult to see how his analytic training will help him to find such material. Hence, it is difficult to see how his training in itself will help him to handle these concepts adequately. Moreover, historians may be inclined to protest that an analytic training is a dangerous enterprise for a historian to undertake. For though the training may extend his or her sensitivities in one way, it is also liable to restrict them severely in another, since he or she is liable to acquire psychoanalytic blinkers, along with the unshakeable, but unproven, conviction that, by looking through these blinkers, he or she can now come to grips with the realities of human nature.

In general, therefore, I suspect a historian may be inclined to say of Gay's work that, in so far as he uses psychoanalytic notions, his history is suspect or even bad. But in so far as he relies on his very sensitive historical nose, and the sophisticated common sense of our time, he writes good history, and produces something well worth while. In the light of this, I would advise any historian who is tempted to make use of analysis to be quite clear about what he is proposing to do, and to be aware of the sorts of troubles he is liable to run into. Indeed, it is not easy to see how he can avoid the sorts of troubles that afflict Gay's interesting work, if he tries to travel down this difficult road.

This enquiry into the logic of psychoanalytic interpretation gives rise quite plainly to an obvious suggestion. It suggests that, if we are to apply psychoanalysis *outside* the clinical situation, we must be less ambitious than Gay. The safest and wisest thing for us to do is to apply it only in biographical work – where the material satisfies certain conditions. The material or data about the person concerned should be fairly plentiful and relatively fixed – just as it is in the clinical situation at any one time. The person should present anomalies, which our apparatus of ordinary notions cannot explain and remove – thereby making it appropriate to resort to psychoanalysis. In these circumstances, the account we offer will, no doubt, also resemble one that is provided in clinical contexts, in that it will enable us to tell what further material will go to confirm or disconfirm the analytic narrative contained in our biography.[15]

Conclusions

I hope that I have managed by now to give you some appreciation of the Arts-man's view of psychoanalysis. It is clear that, when he sets out to explain some item, or items, in a non-clinical domain, he engages in a somewhat hazardous exercise; and I hope I have shown what some of these hazards are like.

It is evident that they are sufficient to undermine seriously the 'new picture of man' that the Arts-man believes Freud has given us. They undermine the picture by showing that it is poorly grounded. For it is based largely on interpretation of non-clinical material in human communities, and these interpretations are generally hazardous and liable to be poorly supported. Moreover, these interpretations make use of generalizations and notions that are themselves poorly grounded, and even mistaken. Hence the 'new picture of man' is not only poorly grounded but also liable to be misleading. We should be well advised, therefore, not to allow this picture to seduce us, but to retain our sceptical detachment from it.

On the other hand, I think it is also evident that, when the Arts-man uses psychoanalysis with care, he can nevertheless often help to explain what is puzzling, and help us to see things in new and interesting ways. He can do so even though the weight to be attached to his explanations is not as great, in general, as he may like to suppose. When analysis is used with care, its explanatory power is not illusory either. Hence, given his purposes, the Arts-man is justified in general in being favourably disposed to psychoanalysis.

By now it should be evident, too, that the conflict of views between the Arts-man and the Science-man reflects a difference of purpose. The Arts-man is interested in applying analysis for ordering and explanatory purposes. The Science-man – outside strictly therapeutic contexts – is not concerned to apply psychoanalysis at all. He is concerned to discover what contribution psychoanalysis can make to the scientific understanding of the bio-psychological system that constitutes the human individual. He finds that this contribution is small. Naturally, therefore, he stresses the limitations of analysis, and has an unfavourable view of it. In all this, the Science-man is doing the unpopular thing of helping us to face reality – the reality of our still enormous ignorance about ourselves. His influence is sobering and beneficial.

I hope that what I have said is sufficient to show that the difference of view between the Arts-man and the Science-man is neither irreconcilable nor unfortunate. For the Arts-man, psychoanalysis has a legitimate but limited role; for the Science-man, it remains a psychology whose status is doubtful. As long as its status remains doubtful, psychoanalysis will help us to maintain our excitement and interest in the nature of human functioning in all its variety. I hope we can agree that this excitement and interest is a good thing.

Postscript

Professor Gay has explained and defended the place of psychohistory in historical enquiry in his book *Freud for Historians* (Oxford Univ. Press, 1985). I think the interested historian will learn a lot from this work; but I doubt whether it does much to remove the difficulties facing psychohistory, which I raise in this chapter.

Notes and References

Among those who have helped me with this chapter, I am especially indebted to Brian Harrison and Peter Gay. But the views expressed in it are mine alone.

1 Gelder, M., Gath, D. and Mayou, R. (1983) *The Oxford Textbook of Psychiatry*. Oxford: Oxford Univ. Press.
2 Farrell, B. A. (1981) *The Standing of Psychoanalysis*. Oxford: Oxford Univ. Press.; Fisher, S. and Greenberg, R. P. (1977) *The Scientific Credibility of Freud's Theories and Therapy*. New York: Harvester Press, Basic Books; Kline, P. (1981) *Fact and Fantasy in Freudian Theory*. London: Methuen.
3 Strachey, Lytton (1928) *Elizabeth and Essex*. London: Chatto & Windus.
4 Cf. Larissa, J. Taylor-Smither (1984) Elizabeth I: a psychological profile. *Sixteenth Century Journal*, 15, no. 1. In this article – by a psychoanalytically oriented historian – the writer assumes 'a basic contiguity between the patriarchal nature of family life in the 16th century and that of fin-de-siècle Vienna'; but (as far as I can tell) offers little new material to support this assumption. I am indebted to Mrs Loach, of Somerville College, for this reference and her help.
5 Black, J. B. (1955) *The Reign of Elizabeth 1558–1603*. Oxford: Clarendon Press.

6 Neale, J. E. (1934). *Queen Elizabeth I.* London: Cape.
7 Badcock, C. R. (1980) *The Psychoanalysis of Culture.* Oxford: Blackwell.
8 Ibid.
9 Freud, S. (1929/30). *Civilisation and its Discontents.* Standard Edition, vol. XXI, ch. 8. London: Hogarth.
10 Ibid.
11 MacCrone, I. D. (1937) *Race Attitudes in Southern Africa.* London: Oxford Univ. Press.
12 Flugel, J. C. (1930) *The Psychology of Clothes.* London: Hogarth; Fromm, E. (1942) *The Fear of Freedom.* London: Kegan Paul; Brown, N. O. (1959) *Life against Death.* London: Kegan Paul; Badcock, C. R. (1980) *Psychoanalysis of Culture.*
13 On psychohistory and discussion about the value of psychoanalysis for historians, see, for example: *The Journal of Psychohistory, passim*; Stannard, D. E. (1980) *Shrinking History: On Freud and the Failure of Psychohistory.* London: Oxford Univ. Press; Lowenberg, P. (1980) Psychohistory. Ch. 17 in Kammen, M. (ed.), *The Past Before Us.* Ithaca, NY: Cornell Univ. Press; Friedlander, S. (1978) *History and Psychoanalysis.* New York and London: Holmes and Meier.
14 Gay, P. (1984) *The Bourgeois Experience. Victoria to Freud*, vol. 1. New York: Oxford Univ. Press.
15 For the classic example, see: Freud, S. (1957) Leonardo and a memory of his childhood. Standard Edition, vol. XI. London: Hogarth. For an examination of it, see: Farrell, B. A. (1963) Introduction to Freud, S. *Leonardo*, pp. 11–88. Harmondsworth: Pelican Books. Reprinted in Morris Philipson (ed.) (1966) *Leonardo da Vinci: Aspects of the Renaissance Genius*, pp. 224–75. New York: Braziller.

Part 2

Animals: How Do They Think, and Do They Have Minds?

'Cats and monkeys, monkeys and cats – all human life is there.' So wrote Henry James. What may have been intended as a tongue-in-cheek criticism of the naïve interpretation of animal behaviour actually sums up rather well the fundamental tenet of biology since Darwin – continuity. Human beings share about 98 per cent of their DNA, the material of the genes, with gorillas and the other great apes, and more than half with the tiny fruit fly. The genes contain the instructions that build the body so it is not surprising that the chemical structure, metabolic systems and physiological principles of operation of a human being have much in common with those of much humbler beasts.

Darwin taught us that successful structures and functions (or more accurately the genes responsible for them) have been discovered, preserved and refined through natural selection. Biological evolution, from single-celled organisms to higher mammals, seems to have tinkered on like a manic automobile maker, finding a million new ways of fitting together the basic bits and pieces and dressing them up to produce ever more intricate and rich machinery. Well, if people are this year's model of last year's obsolete animal, how much do human beings have that is genuinely new? Perhaps our most preciously human attributes are just the tail fins and spoilers that make this year's version look different from last. Under the shell, things are much the same.

Animals have indeed taught us a great deal about how our cells and bodies work. But what about the brain, and thence the mind? Does the principle of biological continuity apply there too? We are far from understanding completely how the nervous system is constructed during development, but the genes obviously play an enormous part in building the brain. So, if we look at the brains of animals we see all sorts of similarities to the human brain, not just in the lumps and lobes but in the basic physics and chemistry of nerve cells and the connections between them.

Then why shouldn't the principle of continuity apply to minds too? Animals obviously do a good job of getting around the world. They act as if they comprehend their environment, have needs and know about how to satisfy them. Judged by their behaviour, animals (or at least higher mammals) appear to have intentions *too. This part of our book asks whether animals think in the way that we do, and whether their behaviour reveals the presence of minds.*

To propose that animals have minds is to say that their actions are best understood in terms of theories that ascribe to them certain mental predicates, such as knowledge and belief. Nick Mackintosh, a behavioural psychologist, shows that, in these terms, even Pavlovian conditioned reflexes can be interpreted to mean that animals as modest as the laboratory rat have minds of a sort. Psychological experiments on chimpanzees suggest that they

*understand general rules and relationships rather well and that they may
have minds much like ours.*

*During the past 20 years or so some highly publicized research on
chimpanzees has even challenged the notion that language is a uniquely
human faculty. Allen and Beatrice Gardner at the University of Reno in
Nevada trained a young chimp called 'Washoe' to use the hand gestures of
American Sign Language for the deaf to communicate with her human foster
family. Then many other psychologists went on to show that chimps and
gorillas could apparently use a variety of symbolic forms of representation to
express their thoughts and needs. Nick Mackintosh believes that, given the
evident intelligence of apes and their ability to understand generalizations, it
would be rash to assert that they lack the intellectual capacity to master many
features of human language. However, Herbert Terrace, a behavioural
psychologist who conducted a lengthy project on a chimpanzee learning sign
language, denies that such experiments demonstrate a true capacity for
language in apes. He argues that they cannot use symbols as* names *for
represented objects and ideas, or construct original and grammatical sentences.
However, even though he denies genuine language in animals, he also
challenges the simplistic view of hard-line behaviourists, who have claimed
that animals need no mental experiences, no internalized 'cognitive' representation of their environment. He describes recent research on rats and pigeons
that shows that they do have some form of internal (non-linguistic)
representation of events in space and time, which makes their imagined
mental world much richer than the classical behaviourists would have
thought.*

Animals, then, may perceive *the world in much the same way that we do,
even if unable to convert their perceptions into the generalized symbolic
representation and expressive form of true language. But what of their
emotional worlds, and their feelings? Benedict Spinoza believed that animals
have feelings, but so different in nature from our own that we need take no
account of them. Moral philosopher Stephen Clark argues that we should not
be misled by using the same words to describe animal and human behaviour
and emotions. Clark demonstrates that ethical evaluation of what animals
feel can be conducted rationally, within an ethic of respect for the other lives
and natures that share the world with us.*

*Marian Dawkins, a zoologist, also tackles the important issue of animal
suffering. She shows that it is possible to approach this question calmly on the
basis of evidence rather than anthropomorphic dogma. Our ethical response to
an animal (such as a battery hen or a laboratory subject) ought to be
dependent on objective evidence that it can and does suffer. With simple
experimental techniques it is possible to ask animals to express their own
feelings and preferences – with some surprising results. Dawkins argues that,
among animals, minds that think and minds that suffer are one and the same.
If this is true it raises important general questions about the character of mind
and suggests that the capacity for conscious emotion (as opposed to blind, reflex
changes of mood) may depend on reflective thought. If we start out by giving
moral consideration to organisms that we suspect can suffer, we shall probably
end up valuing most, in a moral sense, those animals that think and reason
too.*

Ethologist John Krebs returns to the question of animal communication –

not the heady issue of whether apes have true grammar, but the rich but stereotyped displays or signals that animals use to communicate with each other about territory, sex and so on. Krebs rejects the view that such strong ritualized signals developed simply to provide clear, unambiguous messages and proposes instead that they evolved as a result of an escalation of social roles. Animals play the parts of 'actor' or 'reactor'; 'actors' use signals to manipulate the behaviour of 'reactors', while 'reactors' become sales-resistant. The outcome, as in human advertising, is exaggerated displays.

The last two chapters in this section, by psychologist Euan Macphail and philosopher Jennifer Hornsby, are concerned with the nature of animal intelligence and thought. Comparative psychologists have tried to demonstrate qualitative differences in intellect between animal groups in the hope that such differences could yield insights into the processes and evolution of intelligence. Macphail thinks that this quest for distinct variation has failed and that intelligence has not changed in nature up the animal scale (at least not until human beings). He considers the mental lives of goldfish and rats, and finds that these two very different species can both form expectancies and both make decisions. Hornsby, on the other hand, suggests that our naïve opinions about animal intelligence cannot be dislodged as easily as Macphail supposes, and that simple experimental situations (such as the conditioning procedures used by psychologists) do not reveal the full complexities of intellectual judgement. Means, ends and insight are relevant but much harder to evaluate.

What emerges from this section is a view of animals far from both the empty machines envisaged by behaviourism and the furry little humans of fairy tales. Animals are masters of their own behaviour, which is as rich as it needs to be for the lives that they live. Just as animals share with man a large fraction of his genes, so they display, through their behaviour, powers of understanding that make it difficult to believe that they have no mental lives at all. The principle of continuity makes it inconceivable that the human mind has no precedent in the biology of animals.

8

Animal Minds

Nicholas Mackintosh

Nicholas Mackintosh is Professor of Experimental Psychology at the Univer-sity of Cambridge. He was educated at the University of Oxford, where he also taught, and has held teaching positions at the University of Sussex, Dalhousie University and, more briefly, the Universities of Pennsylvania, California at Berkeley and Hawaii, and at Bryn Mawr College. His major research interests have been in animal learning, beginning with work on discrimina-tion learning in collaboration with Stuart Sutherland, and later more generally on conditioning, on which he has written two books. He has, intermittently, done research on animals marginally more exotic than the standard laboratory rat or pigeon, such as octopuses and crows. This is sparked by an interest in the classical problem with which animal psychology began, namely the question of mental or intellectual continuity between man and other animals. This has also led to occasional work on intelligence testing in people.

Introduction

I take as my starting-point the following assumption: the ascription of mental predicates to another person is a matter of interpreting their behaviour in certain ways. We observe the behaviour of another, what he does in certain circumstances and would do if these circumstances were to change, what he has done in the past and might be expected to do in the future; we observe his actions, gestures, facial expressions and, in the case of most people, what he says. And at the end of the day we believe that we can interpret these actions and this behaviour in terms of certain mental predicates, that he has certain beliefs, wishes, intentions, motives and so on. The ascription of these terms constitutes, in a loose sense, a theory to account for his behaviour.

Animal psychologists are in the business of observing the behaviour of animals, of predicting what that behaviour will be under novel experimen-tal circumstances and of developing theories to account for that be-haviour. For the past 100 years or more the most successful and influential theory was one that denied the need to apply common mental predicates to non-human animals. Their behaviour, it was argued, could be quite sufficiently understood without appeal to concepts such as

Ivan Petrovic Pavlov (1849–1936), the Russian psychologist who pioneered experiments on conditioning in animals. His work was to provide the basis for a whole school of thought concerning learning and behaviour (Mary Evans Picture Library).

knowledge, belief or intention. That theory was classical reflex theory, which asserted that all behaviour can be analysed as a set of responses to stimuli, the output triggered by an antecedent input. The theory is both powerful and appealing, for with suitable complications and additions it appears to provide an explanation of a very wide range of animal behaviour, and it does so in a hard-nosed, seemingly objective manner, appealing to known facts about the operation of the nervous system and eschewing idle speculation and anthropomorphic intrusions. Thus the concept of drive or motivation is introduced to explain why the same stimulus may elicit different responses on different occasions, as when the sight of food fails to elicit a normal salivary response when a dog has recently been fed to satiation, or the appearance of a territorial intruder elicits aggression only at certain times of the year. And the basic facts of learning are readily handled by supposing that new stimulus–response connections can be established, either by simple contiguity whenever a stimulus is sufficiently often followed by some new response, as in Pavlov's account of conditioning, or by a combination of contiguity and the strengthening action of a subsequent reinforcing event as in Thorn-dike's Law of Effect.

Conditioning and learning are seen by stimulus–response theory, not as the acquisition of new knowledge about the world, but simply as the acquisition of new behaviour. Pavlov's dog salivating to the sound of the bell does not know that the bell signals the imminent delivery of food; the rat pressing a lever in a Skinner box does not know why he is pressing the lever or what will happen when he does. Both have simply been conditioned to perform a new response. Although there was always a small number of opponents to this dominant tradition in the theory of conditioning and learning, until recently they remained a small minority. But fashions in experimental psychology change, and the study of animal learning and behaviour has in the past 20 years followed much of the rest of psychology through a 'cognitive revolution'. There is always a temptation to be mildly sceptical of the claims of fashionable revolutionaries, but beneath the froth there is a fairly solid body of evidence which suggests that the stimulus–response analysis misses out on important features of conditioning. Conditioning does, after all, involve the acquisition of new knowledge about the world. The behaviour of animals in conditioning experiments makes it natural and reasonable to ascribe mental predicates such as knowledge and belief.

Conditioning as the Acquisition of Knowledge About the World

I shall give two examples, one from Pavlovian or classical conditioning, the other from operant or instrumental conditioning. In the Pavlovian conditioning experiment, the CS (see box below) is sugar-flavoured water, which a thirsty rat will normally drink with great avidity (see table 8.1). But in this experiment, it is followed by the injection of a drug, lithium chloride, which makes the rat ill. As a consequence of the pairing of these two events, the rat rejects sugar-flavoured water.

8.1

Experimental procedures			Outcome
1 Sugar		Lithium	Aversion to sugar
2 Sugar .... Salt .... Lithium			Aversion to salt No aversion to sugar
3 Sugar .... Tone .... Lithium			Aversion to sugar

---

Classical and Instrumental Conditioning (see also chapter 13)

In conditioning experiments, the experimenter delivers some biologically significant event or 'reinforcer', for example food or water, to a
hungry or thirsty animal, or a mildly painful or distressing event such
as a brief electric shock or an injection of a drug which induces
nausea. The distinction between classical and instrumental conditioning lies in the rules which determine when the reinforcer is delivered.
In classical conditioning, its occurrence is signalled by another
stimulus (the conditional stimulus or CS), but it is delivered regardless
of the animal's behaviour. Nevertheless, successful conditioning is
evident from an appropriate change in the animal's behaviour towards the CS: Pavlov's dogs came to salivate to the bell (the CS)
which signalled the delivery of the food reinforcer. In instrumental
conditioning, the occurrence of the reinforcer is dependent on the
animal's performance of a particular response designated by the
experimenter. In the Skinner box, the hungry rat must press a small
lever in order to obtain a pellet of food. Successful conditioning is
evident from an appropriate change in this designated response.

In common with other conditioning preparations, the aversion conditioned to a novel-flavoured substance depends on this flavour being the
best available predictor for the rat of its subsequent illness. For example,
while a rat will condition an aversion to sugar-flavoured water even
though a relatively long time gap separates its consumption from the rat's
subsequent illness, if the rat consumes some other novel substance during
this interval, say salt-flavoured water, he will condition an aversion to the
salt flavour rather than to the sugar flavour. It is as though the rat
attributes his illness to the most recently consumed novel substance. A
special feature of this particular conditioning preparation, however, is that
rats are very much more likely to associate their illness with the flavour of
something they have recently consumed rather than an arbitrary, external
stimulus. For example, if a tone or buzzer is sounded while a rat is
drinking plain, unflavoured tap water, this fact will not be associated with
subsequently induced illness, and the rat, when recovered from his
illness, will consume water quite readily whether or not the tone is
sounded. As one might expect, therefore, such an experience will not
interfere with the conditioning of an aversion to a previously consumed

novel flavour. If the rat drinks sugar-flavoured water, and then plain water while a tone is sounded, he will still condition an aversion to the sugar flavour.

The stage is now set for the critical condition I wish to emphasize. Peter Holland has shown that if rats are given the opportunity to associate the presentation of the tone with the consumption of salt-flavoured water, then the occurrence of the tone, as in the bottom row of table 8.1, will now prevent conditioning of an aversion to the sugar flavour.[1] Instead, when subsequently tested, the rat will display an aversion to the salt flavour – which itself has never been paired with illness. It is as though the prior pairing of tone and salt solution ensures that when the tone is presented again on the conditioning trial, it evokes a central *representation* or *image* of that salt flavour, which is then available for association with illness, to the detriment of conditioning to the earlier consumed sugar solution. It is, if you like, a demonstration of conditioning to a 'hallucinated stimulus'. For my present purposes, its point is that it surely requires us to say something new about what happened when tone and salt solution were initially paired. It cannot be enough to say that this pairing caused the tone to elicit a new response or pattern of behaviour, but rather a new image or central representation of what had occurred in its presence. It would not be unreasonable to say that the rat now believes that tone and salt solution go together.

The experiment on instrumental conditioning I wish to describe (table 8.2) also involves the conditioning of an aversion to a novel-flavoured substance, but for a different purpose. Consider a rat in a standard Skinner box that provides him with the opportunity to perform two different responses which will be rewarded in two different ways (that is, with two different 'reinforcers'). If he presses the lever, he will be rewarded with food pellets; if he pulls on a chain hanging from the ceiling he will be rewarded with sugar solution. By appropriate arrangement of these contingencies, the experimenter can ensure that the rat will perform both of these responses, now earning a pellet of food, now a small quantity of sugar water, at a steady rate throughout each experimental session. According to the terminology of Thorndike, the experimenter has established two *stimulus–response habits*: the sight of the lever now evokes approach and press, the sight of the chain evokes approach and pull; both habits have been stamped in by the automatic action of the consequent reinforcement.

8.2

	Stages of experiment		Test and outcome
	1	2	
	Lever-press → food Chain-pull → sugar	Sugar → Lithium	Choice of lever and chain, rat chooses lever

In the next phase of the experiment, an aversion is conditioned to one of these reinforcers. The lever and the chain are removed from the box, the rat is fed, let us say, sugar solution and subsequently injected with lithium. After a few days of this treatment, a strong aversion is conditioned and the rat refuses to drink the proffered sugar water. In the final phase of the experiment, the lever and chain are put back, and the rat is allowed to perform the two previously trained responses. But this is a brief test session and neither response produces its previously rewarding consequence. The question is simply which response will the rat choose to perform. Common sense suggests that the rat might refrain from pulling the chain, because chain pulling produced sugar solution and this is no longer valued by the rat. Common sense is right: this is exactly what the rat does.[2,3] But Thorndike's account predicts no such effect: if all that the rats have learnt is to perform two responses when placed in the Skinner box, they are in effect credited with no knowledge about the consequences of these actions, and the only way in which they would stop chain pulling while continuing to press the lever is if they were given the opportunity to perform the two responses with the original reinforcers still being presented. Lever pressing would be maintained because still followed by a reinforcing consequence; chain pulling would extinguish because now followed by an aversive consequence.

The results of these instrumental experiments thus imply that a rat has learnt to perform a particular response for a particular reinforcer, or can reasonably be described as *knowing* what are the consequences of that action. Holland's experiment on Pavlovian conditioning similarly implies that if two stimuli have been paired, presentation of one evokes a representation of the other. The process of conditioning is one whereby animals learn about the relations in time between events in their environment, and can predict one event from the occurrence of the other. Conditioning cannot be reduced to the acquisition of new responses; it involves the acquisition of knowledge about the world.

Experiments on conditioning are widely regarded, even by experimental psychologists, as both boring and simple. The description of Pavlov's dog drooling helplessly at the sound of the bell, or of laboratory rats trundling their way through a maze by a process of blind trial and error has done nothing to improve their image. It is quite true that conditioning experiments provide as simple an instance of associative learning as one could hope to find, although the laws of association that they reveal are notably more complex and interesting than those of contiguity and constant conjunction advanced by classical associationist philosophy.[4] But if even in supposedly simple conditioning experiments we find behavioural evidence of the acquisition of knowledge about the world, what might we not expect to find in our animals if we studied them in more interesting and complex situations? One answer, which will certainly seem disappointing to many, is conditioning in disguise. Once we have acknowledged that conditioning itself is a more complex and interesting process than we have thought, it will be that much harder to substantiate the claim that the behaviour of an animal in an apparently more complex experiment cannot be understood in terms of conditioning theory. The case of language learning by apes provides an instructive example.

Language Learning as Conditioning

Herbert Terrace, in chapter 9 in this book, had more to say on this topic, and says it with greater authority than I can. I wish only to comment on one or two aspects. It is common to hear it argued that apes cannot have learnt anything approximating to human language because their behaviour is simply the product of conditioning. If what they do can be understood in terms of conditioning theory, then it cannot be language that they have learnt, since we know perfectly well that real language cannot be explained in associationist terms. The trainer describes the chimpanzee as having learnt sentences, as producing sequences of manual signs, or symbols on a computer terminal, corresponding, for example, to the sentence 'Please give me drink'. But this is an over-rich interpretation: a more neutral and accurate description would be to say that the chimpanzee has discriminated between sequences of arbitrary stimuli or responses that produce reward and sequences that do not, and this is a far cry from understanding the meaning of sentences.

The distinction is a real one, but conditioning theory is not confined to this second interpretation. That is a characterization of the chimpanzee's behaviour in terms of stimulus–response theory and it is as easy to prove it false here as it was in the cases I have considered earlier. The chimpanzee Sarah has been taught by David Premack to use plastic tokens, apparently to refer to various objects, both animate and inanimate in her environment (herself, her trainers, apples, bananas, chocolate, balls, buckets, etc.) as well as some of their attributes (red, yellow, round, square, etc.).[5] She is not to be described as having learnt to perform certain arbitrary responses in the presence of various objects because rewarded for doing so. She surely *knows* the meaning of these tokens. Asked questions about an apple, Sarah responds correctly by noting that its colour is red, its shape round, and so on. The critical observation is that she can respond in exactly the same way to the token for an apple (which happens to be a blue triangle), again answering that its colour is red, its shape round, etc. There can be little doubt that the plastic token *calls to mind* the object to which it refers or, if you will, with which it has been associated. Sarah can list the attributes of that absent object, because use of the token is not an arbitrary response stamped in by reward whenever she sees an apple; she knows that the token in some sense stands for the apple.

Similarly, the chimpanzees Sherman and Austin, who have been taught by Sue Savage-Rumbaugh to operate symbols on a keyboard to ask for objects,[6] can take turns as sender and receiver, one requesting an absent object, the other going to fetch that object when so requested. They can surely be said to know what these symbols refer to even in the absence of the objects to which they refer. But rats in an instrumental conditioning experiment can with equal propriety be said to know that performing one response will produce one consequence and performing a different response will produce a different consequence, and in the absence of either consequence will choose which response to perform, depending on the value that they now set upon those consequences.

The original argument was that the apes cannot be said to have learnt a language because their behaviour can be understood in terms of a relatively crude and impoverished theory of conditioning, and we know that real language cannot be so understood. The argument fails because their behaviour cannot be explained in these simple terms – but then neither can that of the rat in a conditioning experiment. Does it follow that rats and pigeons could be taught language as readily as chimpanzees, because language really can be understood as a product of simple processes of conditioning?

What Else Does Language Require?

I am not so foolish as to press this argument. Without pretending to be exhaustive, it is worth suggesting two critical aspects of language that lie outside the scope of such a theory, and thus beyond the powers of an animal whose learning is restricted to such processes. One of them, at least, I judge to lie within the chimpanzee's ability.

A critical question asked of apes supposedly learning language is whether they can understand and generate sentences, that is, strings of words whose meaning is determined by their syntactic structure, for example by word order. David Premack has shown that chimpanzees can discriminate between different sequences of signs,[5] but then, as Herbert Terrace points out, there is little doubt that pigeons can do much the same. They can be trained to peck at four coloured lights in a particular sequence (for example, green, white, red, blue) because that sequence, and no other, is followed by food reward. Has Sarah achieved anything more than Terrace's pigeons? Has she learnt that the same words in different orders convey different meanings, in accordance with certain syntactic rules, or has she simply learnt that certain sequences of signs predict reward and others do not? But what, anyway, is the distinction between these two interpretations?

Consider the following piece of anecdotal evidence. The chimpanzee Lucy, trained in sign language by Roger Fouts, will sign 'Roger tickle Lucy'. When Fouts one day, instead of granting her request, signed back 'No. Lucy tickle Roger', she at first seemed not to understand, but eventually went over and tickled him. A single, anecdoctal example of a chimpanzee apparently understanding the new meaning of a novel sequence of signs establishes rather little. But it illustrates, I think, what we should require of the chimpanzee if we were to grant her understanding of syntax. She must *generalize* the rule that changing the order of a string of signs has a predictable effect on the meaning of that string. She must understand that the meaning of any string of signs, A–B–C, is related to the meaning of its transform, C–B–A, in something like the same way that the meaning of another string, D–E–F, is related to F–E–D (and so on for any related string of signs in her vocabulary). This, of course, is a far cry from learning that one particular sequence of four coloured lights predicts reward and all other sequences do not. And there is good reason to question whether a pigeon could learn the general rule. But there are no such reasons for questioning the chimpanzee's ability, for it requires little more than Sarah has already demonstrated.

Sarah is adept at solving what are conventionally called 'matching-to-sample' discriminations. Shown one object, say an apple, as sample, she

*Figure 8.1   Ally and Bruno
are young male chimpanzees
who live at the Institute of
Primate Studies in Norman,
Oklahoma. They are being
taught American Sign
Language for the deaf by Roger
Fouts and his colleagues. Here
they give the gesture for 'listen'
when their teacher points to his
watch (photograph from the
Institute of Primate Studies,
University of Oklahoma).*

will select, when offered a choice between two further objects, another apple and a banana, the one that is the same as, or matches, the sample. And she can match on the basis, not just of physical similarity, but also of an attribute or even a relationship. Shown half an apple as sample, she will select a half-filled jug of water rather than a whole apple as instantiating the matching role. And she has also shown that she understands that the relationship between two diagrams (a large red triangle and a large blue triangle) is the same as that between two others (a small red circle and a small blue circle). This matching of relationships extends to the relationships between objects in the world: Sarah will select a key as the object that stands in the same relationship to a padlock as a can opener does to a tin can.[7,8] Sarah, in other words, is capable of solving analogies, of seeing that A is to A' as B is to B'. But it was precisely this ability to see that the relationship between A–B–C and C–B–A is the same as that between D–E–F and F–E–D that we required as evidence of grasping some rudiments of syntax.

The perception of relationships and of the similarity of the relationships between disparate groups of objects or signs is not a process greatly illuminated by traditional theories of conditioning. And there is reason to question whether it is one uniformly available to all species. Pigeons, for example, have so far provided only the most meagre evidence of being able to solve the generalized matching-to-sample discrimination even on the basis of physical similarity.[9,10] There is thus good reason to believe that the learning of language does require processes extending beyond those of simple conditioning, and that these processes are more likely to be found in some animals than others.

But there is even better reason to believe that no animal has yet *used* tokens or gestures in the way that the youngest child uses language. Children use words as an extension of other ways of communicating shared interests and intentions, as a means of drawing an adult's attention to something that has attracted their attention, or of commenting on the world and their thoughts about it. By and large, as Terrace has noted, signing or token-using apes are doing nothing of the sort; they are performing responses in order to obtain rewards. Language is a medium (one of several) of social interaction between people. Apes do not appear to interact with people in the same way. This resounding platitude does need stressing, for not only does it remind us that there are important aspects of language that no animal is likely to display, it also implies that there must be an important sense in which an animal's mind differs from ours. But that difference is not necessarily one of cognitive process: the fact that children and apes *use* language for quite different purposes does not necessarily imply that the processes by which they *learn* a language (at least to begin with) are so very different.

Conclusion

I should conclude by stressing one other rather obvious point. My argument has been that the behaviour of animals, even of laboratory animals such as rats and pigeons in boring experiments on conditioning, is such that we should have rather little hesitation in ascribing to them knowledge of, and beliefs about, the world. But this does not imply that I have provided a scientifically adequate theory of the rat's behaviour when I say that he knows about the consequences of his actions. This is not necessarily an appropriate language for scientific analysis. I have not been trying to provide a formal theory of the rat's behaviour, but rather to note that any such theory should not be one which specifically denies the propriety of ascribing such mental predicates to animals.

Notes and References

1 Holland, P. C. (1983) Representation-mediated overshadowing and potentiation of conditioned aversion. *J. exp. Psychol.: Animal Behavior Processes*, 9: 1–13.
2 Adams, C. A. and Dickinson, A. (1981) Actions and habits: variations in associative representation during instrumental learning. In N. E. Spear and R. R. Miller (eds), *Information Processing in Animals: Memory Mechanisms*, pp. 143–65. Hillsdale, NJ: Erlbaum.
3 Colwill, R. M. and Rescorla, R. A. (1985) Post-conditioning devaluation of a reinforcer affects instrumental responding. *J. exp. Psychol.: Animal Behavior Processes*, 11: 120–32.
4 There have been many laws of association, but contiguity and conjunction are among the most popular. The first states that ideas or events will be associated only if they occur close together. This contiguity may be both temporal – the events must occur (nearly) at the same time – and spatial – they must occur in the same place. Both temporal and spatial contiguity have been shown to exert a powerful influence on conditioning. The law of constant conjunction asserts simply that association between two events depends on their repeatedly

occurring together, and not apart; there is little doubt that this too is an important ingredient of successful conditioning. What is more interesting is that contiguity and conjunction do not provide a sufficient account of conditioning. In Holland's experiment cited earlier, for example, the temporal relation between the rat's drinking sugar-flavoured water and receiving the injection which made him ill was constant in all conditions of the experiment. But whether or not the rat associated sugar flavour and illness depended on what else happened in the interval between the two. For a fuller account of the laws of association as they apply to conditioning, see Mackintosh, N. J. (1983) *Conditioning and Associative Learning.* Oxford: Oxford Univ. Press.

5 Premack, D. (1976) *Intelligence in Ape and Man.* Hillsdale, NJ: Erlbaum.

6 Savage-Rumbaugh, E. S., Rumbaugh, D. M. and Boysen, S. (1978) Symbolic communication between two chimpanzees (*Pan/trogladytes*). *Science,* 201: 641–4.

7 Gillan, D. J., Premack, D. and Woodruff, G. (1981) Reasoning in the chimpanzee: I. Analogical reasoning. *J. exp. Psychol.: Animal Behavior Processes,* 7: 1–17.

8 Woodruff, G. and Premack, D. (1981) Primitive mathematical concepts in the chimpanzee: proportionality and numerosity. *Nature* (London), 293: 568–70.

9 D'Amato, M. R., Salmon, D. P. and Colombo, M. (1985) Extent and limits of the matching concept in monkeys (*Cebus apella*). *J. exp. Psychol.: Animal Behavior Processes,* 11: 35–51.

10 Mackintosh, N. J., Wilson, B. and Boakes, R. A. (1985) Differences in mechanisms of intelligence among vertebrates. *Philosophical Transactions of the Royal Society of London.*

9

Thoughts Without Words

Herbert Terrace

Herbert Terrace is a Professor of Psychology at Columbia University in New York. He gained his bachelor's and master's degrees from Cornell University and his doctorate from Harvard, where he studied with the noted behaviourist B. F. Skinner. From 1973 to 1975 he served as President of the Society for the Experimental Analysis of Behavior. He is co-editor of Psychology and Human Behavior *(with T. G. Bever), of* Animal Cognition *(with H. L. Roitblat and T. G. Bever), and of* The Biology of Learning *(with P. Marker). He has published articles on his research in discrimination learning and its by-products, autoshaping, the linguistic competence of apes and cognitive processes in animals. This article is a shortened version of one entitled 'Animal Cognition: Thinking without Language' which appeared in the* Philosophical Transactions of the Royal Society of London, *1985, B 308: 113–28.*

Unlike human beings, animals cannot speak about their thoughts. The only indication that animals think is indirect evidence, gleaned from their behaviour. Scientists and laymen approach such evidence with deep-seated and contradictory attitudes. One point of view, usually attributed to Descartes, regards animals as unthinking mechanical beasts. Behaviour is elicited automatically by stimuli that originate in the animal's internal or external environments. However complex or elaborate the animal's behaviour, it can always be reduced to some configuration of *reflexes* in which thought plays no role. Descartes also argued that an animal, no matter how intelligent, lacked the capacity to learn language, the vehicle of human thought.

Darwin's theory of evolution, on the other hand, acknowledges the possibility that animals can think. In comparing man and animals, Darwin argued that it is just as logical to say that the human mind evolved from animal minds as to say that human anatomical and physiological structures evolved from their animal counterparts.

Until recently, there has been little concrete basis for choosing between the contradictory positions of Descartes and Darwin. During the past two decades, however, students of animal behaviour have provided two important answers to the venerable question 'can an animal think?'. For the first time, ample evidence is available of the existence of animal thought.[1,2] Yet there is considerable agreement that apes, considered by

The chimpanzee, Nim, with his teacher-companion Herbert Terrace (photograph © Susan Kuklin, 1979).

many psychologists to be man's most intelligent relatives, are unable to master the basic features of human language.[3,4,5] This state of affairs raises a fascinating question that can be asked of animals in general: 'What is the non-linguistic medium of animal thought?'. This question poses obvious problems of definition regarding thought and language. For the moment, I shall focus on language and try to justify my claim that it is absent in animals. Once we understood what is absent, we shall, at the very least, see the importance of developing non-linguistic models of animal cognition.

Ape Language Projects

Though linguists, philosophers, psycholinguists and psychologists have yet to agree on a rigorous definition of language that encompasses its many complexities, there is general agreement that the most distinctive feature of human languages is the provision they make for creating new meanings by combining arbitrary words into sentences according to arbitrary grammatical rules. In contrast to the fixed character of various forms of animal communication, the meaning of a word is arbitrary. A sentence characteristically expresses a semantic proposition through words and phrases, each bearing a well-defined but nevertheless arbitrary relation to one another (for example, in some languages, actions can precede objects; in others, actions follow objects).

Our ability to create and comprehend novel sentences has prompted many linguists to argue that human grammatical competence is innate and species-specific.[6] It was in this neo-Cartesian *Zeitgeist* that the various recent ape-language projects were started.[7,8] Accordingly, it was not surprising that a general goal of those projects was the demonstration of grammatical competence in apes. As we shall later see, that goal took too much for granted regarding an ape's non-grammatical linguistic competence and stimulated the various ape-language projects to set goals for themselves that were unrealistically ambitious. It is only recently that researchers in this area have redirected their efforts toward more productive lines of inquiry.[9]

The initial results of the various ape-language projects produced exciting evidence of an ape's ability to create sentences.[10] For example, in an early diary report, the Gardners noted that their chimpanzee Washoe, who had been taught in American Sign Language for the deaf (ASL), used her signs 'in strings of two or more ... in 29 different two-sign combinations and four different combinations of three signs'. That report prompted Roger Brown, the Harvard psychologist and expert on language in children, to comment: 'It was rather as if a seismometer left on the moon had started to tap out "S–O–S".'[11] Indeed, Brown compared Washoe's sequences of signs to the early sentences of a child, in particular with respect to their structural meanings (for example, agent-action, agent-object, action-object, and so on).

Other projects reported similar combinations of two or more symbols. The chimpanzee Sarah, studied by David Premack, produced strings of plastic chips representing words, such as MARY GIVE SARAH APPLE.[12] Duane Rumbaugh *et al.* taught a juvenile female chimpanzee named Lana to use an artificial language of 'lexigrams', each of which consisted of an arbitrary geometric configuration superimposed on one of six coloured backgrounds.[13] After learning to use individual lexigrams, Lana was taught to produce sequences such as PLEASE MACHINE GIVE M & M (M & Ms are a variety of candy!). Subsequently Francine Patterson reported that Koko, a young female gorilla she taught to use American Sign Language, also produced many combinations of two or more signs.[14]

The Imitative and Non-spontaneous Nature of an Ape's Signing

By 1980, it became apparent that the evidence purporting to show that apes can create sentences could be explained without any reference to grammatical competence. I and my colleagues analysed approximately 20,000 combinations of two or more signs made by a young chimpanzee Neam Chimpsky (Nim for short) who, like Washoe, had been reared by his human surrogate parents in an environment in which ASL was the major medium of communication.[5,15] Superficially, many of Nim's combinations appeared to be generated by simple finite-state grammatical rules – for example, MORE + X; transitive verb + me or Nim, etc.. However, a frame-by-frame analysis of videotapes of Nim's signing with his human companions revealed that he responded mainly to the urgings of his teacher to sign and that much of what he signed was a full or partial imitation of his teacher's prior gestural utterance. Thus, unlike a child at Roger Brown's stage 1 of language acquisition,[16,17] Nim's signing was mostly non-spontaneous and imitative.

The conclusions of Project Nim were criticized by other investigators attempting to teach apes to use sign language, on various methodological grounds.[18,19] However, none of those investigators has revealed enough of their own procedures to allow one to evaluate the significance of their criticisms of Project Nim,[20,21] and my conclusions have yet to be countered with positive evidence of spontaneity in the production of sequences of gestures.

Rote Sequences versus Sentences

Different considerations led to a rejection of the view that Sarah's and Lana's sequence were sentences. After analysing a corpus of approximately 14,000 of Lana's combinations that were collected by a computer, Thompson and Church concluded that those combinations could be accounted for almost completely by two non-grammatical processes.[22] One is *conditional discrimination*, learning to make a discriminative response to one value of a compound stimulus, for example, pushing the lexigram GIVE in the sequence PLEASE MACHINE GIVE X (X= apple, chocolate, banana, etc.) when a food appears in a vending machine as opposed to the lexigram SHOW, when a screen is lowered so as to produce the sequence PLEASE MACHINE SHOW SLIDE (or MOVIE). The other non-grammatical process is *paired-associate learning*, learning to use an arbitrary symbol as a means towards the end of obtaining some reward in the presence of a particular stimulus. Which of six stock sentences occurred could be predicted by the circumstances in which Lana would try to obtain some incentive. For example, if the object was in view in the machine, the stock sequence would be of the form PLEASE MACHINE GIVE X or PLEASE MACHINE GIVE PIECE OF X. If there was no object in view, the appropriate sequence would be PLEASE PUT INTO MACHINE X. If an experimenter was present, the stock sequence would be of the form PLEASE Y GIVE X. In addition, Lana learned paired associates, each consisting of a particular lexigram and a particular incentive, for example, apple, music, banana, chocolate, and so on. These lexigrams were inserted in the appropriate position (usually the last of the stock sentence).

Further evidence that Lana's and Sarah's sequences were not sentences came from studies (described in more detail below) demonstrating that even pigeons can be trained to respond in an arbitrary sequence to four simultaneously presented coloured lights, red, green, yellow and blue, whose positions are changed from trial to trial.[23,24] Mention of a pigeon's sequence-learning ability is not to imply that a pigeon could approach a chimpanzee's ability to learn various conditional discriminations that specify which arbitrary sequence is to be emitted in which context. Nor is it meant to imply that a pigeon could master even a single sequence as rapidly as could a chimpanzee. Indeed, there is strong evidence to the contrary.[25] There is also no reason to assume that pigeons and chimpanzees use similar strategies in learning to produce a sequence.

These qualifications should not, however, detract from the fact that, in each case, what is learned is a *rote sequence*. It would be just as erroneous to interpret a rote sequence of pecks to the colours red, green, yellow and blue, in that order, as a sentence meaning PLEASE MACHINE GIVE GRAIN as it would be to interpret the sequence that a person produces while operating a bank cash machine as a sentence meaning PLEASE MACHINE GIVE CASH. In sum, a *rote* sequence, however that sequence might be trained, is not necessarily a sentence.

What Do the Words of an Ape's Vocabulary Mean?

In a searching review of their own work and that of other projects, Sue Savage-Rumbaugh and her colleagues not only questioned the validity of evidence purporting to show that apes can produce and comprehend sentences but also doubted whether, at the level of individual elements of their vocabularies, the apes studied in any project (their own chimp, Lana, included) used those elements as actual *words*. By questioning the lexical status of an ape's use of signs of ASL, of plastic chips, or of lexigrams, they identified a basic problem of interpretation that is common to all of the projects that sought to demonstrate that apes could master simple features of human languages. Indeed, a strong case can be made for the hypothesis that the deceptively simple ability to use a symbol as a name required a cognitive advance in the evolution of human intelligence that was at least as significant as the advance(s) that led to grammatical competence.

The Development of a Child's Vocabulary: the Behaviourist View

Thanks, in large part, to a precoccupation with the emergence of grammatical competence in children, developmental psycholinguistics have paid relatively little attention to the process of acquiring a lexicon or vocabulary *per se*. It is, of course, true that ample information is available regarding the kinds of words children learn and at what rate they do so.[26,27,28] However, most psychologists, at least implicitly, assume that some version of a 'behaviourist' account of the growth of vocabulary would suffice to explain how children learn their initial vocabulary.

At first glance this might seem to be a reasonable state of affairs since there is general agreement that, unlike sentences, words are learnt individually. Accordingly, why not invoke principles of associative learning to account for vocabulary acquisition? On this view, a child associates the speech of a parent with primary reinforcers (rewards) such as physical contact, food, or the removal of distressful stimulation. As a consequence, the parent's vocalizations become reinforcing.

At the same time, the child's vocalizations are presumed to be reinforced directly, by the parent providing one of these primary reinforcers, by the parent's attention or by the parent's vocalization. Initially, virtually any instance of an infant's babbling is reinforced. As the infant becomes older, the parent 'shapes' the child's vocabulary to approximate adult sounds. In addition, those infant's vocalizations that resemble parent's speech are self-reinforcing. Gradually, the frequency of the infant's vocalizations that resemble sounds uttered by a parent increases while the frequency of those sounds which differ from the sounds uttered by the parent decreases.[29]

Naming versus Learning

At best, the behaviourist view of vocabulary acquisition is an explanation of paired-associate learning (using an arbitrary symbol in the presence of a stimulus to obtain a reward). What is missing from the behaviourist view is the speaker's *intention* in using a word. Saying something and meaning what you say are obviously two different kinds of response. In most human discourse, a speaker who utters a name expects the listener to interpret the speaker's utterance as a reference to a jointly perceived object. It should therefore come as no surprise that the function of much of a child's initial vocabulary of names is to inform another person, usually a parent, that the child has noticed something.[30] In many instances, the child refers to the object in question spontaneously, with obvious delight, and shows no interest in obtaining the object. The child appears not only to enjoy sharing information with her or his parent but also to derive intrinsic pleasure from the sheer act of naming. As I shall argue later, these aspects of uttering a name have not been observed in apes, and there is reason to doubt whether the most intensive training programme imaginable could produce an ape who would approach a child's natural ability to refer to objects as an end in itself. The sounds that a human infant emits, when learning to talk, are not even truly imitative of the parent's speech and they often function as names rather than requests, which casts further doubt on the behaviourist view of word acquisition.[28,31]

How Children Learn to Use Language

An obvious truism about language learning is that it draws on certain kinds of non-linguistic knowledge. For example, before learning to speak, an infant acquires a repertoire of instrumental behaviour that allows her or him to manipulate or approach various objects. An infant also learns how to engage in various kinds of social interaction with her parents – for example, being able to look where the parent is looking or pointing. Eventually, the child learns to point at things that she would like her parent to notice. In short, the infant first masters a social and conceptual world on to which various kinds of linguistic expression are later mapped.

The rapidly expanding literature on the pre-linguistic development of the child makes it clear that the process of naming emerges from the highly structured interactions between an infant and her parents. Especially relevant are interactions in which the parent is able to direct the infant's attention to particular objects. For example, when an infant is roughly four months old, a parent can direct attention to an object simply by looking at it. Subsequently, the parent can accomplish the same end by pointing to an object. Often the parent will comment about the object while pointing to it or moving it towards the infant. Stress on the spoken name of the object to which the parent seeks to direct the infant's attention makes the infant come to discover that a stressed vocalization is a signal that there is 'something to look at'. Likewise, highly ritualized games whereby an object is made to disappear and later reappear (typically, with distinctive vocal accompaniments) also facilitates a parent's control over an infant's attention. As the infant gets older, her contribution to these interactions increases. At first she may only point to an object in response to the parent's pointing or vocalizing. Subsequently, the child may utter non-standard vocalizations while looking or pointing at the object presented by the parent. Eventually, the child learns to repeat the object's name as provided by the parent, while the child and the parent jointly attend to that object.[32]

During the course of a long series of object-oriented interactions with her parents, an infant not only learns to direct her attention to objects that are presented by her parent but she also learns that her response to such objects, whether pointing, babbling or saying the actual name of the object, is recognized by the parent as a sign that she has noticed the object. In short, the infant learns that her response to an object has much in common with her parent's response to the same object. In that sense, the child learns the conventions of reference, first non-verbally and subsequently at a verbal level.

Can Referring be Taught?

In a provocative discussion of how children learn to name objects, John

MacNamara concludes that referring to an object (the act of communicating that one's attention is directed to a particular object) is not learnt.[30] Instead he regards referring as a 'primitive of cognitive psychology'. What is learnt is reference: the conventions of using symbols and words that do the work of referring.

Verification of MacNamara's view of learning names awaits much further research, but it is certainly interesting to consider the extent to which learning theory can account for a child's ability, first to understand that her parent is referring to a particular object and subsequently to master pre-verbal techniques for directing her parent's attention to a particular object. As commonplace as such skills may seem, it is not obvious how one can teach them. To argue that referential behaviour is 'shaped' begs the question of what rudimentary forms of referential behaviour can be used as a point of departure for the shaping process. To acknowledge that such a rudimentary form exists is to agree with MacNamara that the act of referring is a given. At best, principles of learning might be invoked to characterize how a parent adds to the variety and complexity of situations in which referring occurs.

The Function of Symbols for Chimpanzees and Children

The hypothesis that the act of referring is a given and that it is also a necessary precursor of naming provides an important basis for comparing the use of symbols by children and chimpanzees. Like children, chimpanzees appear to show evidence of object-recognition soon after birth. It is also quite easy to direct their attention to a particular object by looking at it, by pointing to it or by moving it into the chimpanzee's line of sight. However, informal observations suggest that their main reaction is acquisitive.[15] When confronted with an object, familiar or otherwise, an infant ape will make soft reflexive hooting noises and either reach for the object or try to approach it. Typically, the object is explored orally and manually. Beyond such explorations there is no evidence that suggests that an infant ape is interested in communicating, to another ape or to its human surrogate parent, the fact that it has noticed an object, *as an end in itself*. To be sure, chimpanzees will communicate with one another about food locations,[33] or about objects of prey.[34] It is, however, important to recognize that such communication is in the service of some concrete end and is not intended simply to inform a companion that something has been noticed.

The absence of natural referential skills that are independent of concrete ends makes all the more remarkable the kinds of symbol use that an ape can master, such as the use of generic terms that apply to symbols for particular foods and tools.[35] They have also shown some rudimentary intentional communication in highly structured play situations.[9]

Naming as a Precursor of Syntax

At some point in the evolution of human intelligence infants were able to relax their acquisitive reactions to an object of interest and simply indicate to a parent that they noticed it. Whatever the origin of that kind of reaction, it clearly exerted a significant influence on the evolution of

Figure 9.1   Nim signs 'me hug cat' to his teacher, Susan Quinby (photograph by Herbert Terrace).

language. Foremost, it provided a psychological basis for activities between an infant and her parent for engaging in activities based on their joint perception of an object. As we have seen, such activities are important precursors of reference to objects and events with names.

If a child had not developed the ability to use a name to register what she saw and if the sole function of her speech was to demand things, it is hard to see why she would combine words according to a grammatical rule. Since a single word should suffice as a demand or as a warning of some danger, the child would have had no need to learn to speak syntactically. Obviously, the same argument applies to apes and indicates why it was premature to have expected that an ape might master even the most primitive grammatical rules.

In theory one could, of course, argue that a highly structured system of demands might require syntactic rules – for example, a request for the red plum from the far tree, as opposed to the green apple under the near bush, and so on. Such a state of affairs is implausible for a variety of reasons. To the extent that such specific desires occur in the natural world, they could be dealt with by eye-gaze, pointing, facial expressions, some combination thereof, or by a process of elimination of alternative incentives. Thus, it is not clear what natural function a hypothetical demand system of such complexity might serve. Further, any attempt to teach such skills in a laboratory environment would seem to tax the ability of any known primate other than man.

A different state of affairs exists in those situations in which there is a desire simply to transmit information about a relationship between one object or action and another, or about some attribute of an object, or about past or future events. In these instances, a single word would not suffice. Hence the functional value of syntax.

Representations as Evidence of Animal Thinking

For reasons far more elementary than those advanced by the contemporary neo-Cartesian school of linguistics, we have seen that Descartes was correct in denying that animals lack the capacity to learn a human language. However, Descartes's contention that animals cannot think was based as much on their inability to master a language as it was on his view that their behaviour consisted of nothing more than a mechanical system of reflexes. That view in particular became the creed of twentieth-century behaviourists.[36,37,38,39] Their models, however, obviously assumed a more realistic view of the nervous system than was available to Descartes. Like Descartes, modern behaviourists saw no need to appeal to cognitive structures that intervened between a stimulus and a response so long as their models of conditioned behaviour could predict reliably the occurrence of a particular response.

An important tension in the modern study of behaviour is one that resulted from a tug of war between behaviourists and cognitively orientated psychologists as to the validity of instances of animal behaviour that were purported to be exceptions to reflex models of behaviour. The significance of such exceptions was recognized more than 70 years ago by Walter Hunter, an early behaviourist, who observed that 'if comparative psychology is to postulate a representative fact . . . it is necessary that the stimulus represented be absent at the moment of response. If it is not absent, the reaction may be stated in sensory-motor terms.'[40] By stipulating that 'the stimulus represented be absent at the moment of response', Hunter required that the only cue available was one that the animal itself generated as some *representation* of the absent stimulus. That representation would function just as a genuine external stimulus might in evoking appropriate behaviour. It is important to ask why Hunter saw no need to argue for internal representation (in the brain) of an *external* stimulus when it *does* reliably precede a response and is present as the animal responds. Like Skinner and other behaviourists, Hunter answered with the logic of parsimony: our ability to *predict* or to explain behaviour is not enhanced by appealing to a representation of a stimulus if that stimulus is available when the organism responds.

Of course, an animal must store a *memory* of a stimulus in order to be able to react similarly to it on two different occasions. It is, however, necessary to distinguish between an animal's ability to generate, or at least to maintain, a representation of some previously experienced stimulus

Figure 9.2 B. F. Skinner on his seventieth birthday.

that is present when the response in question occurs, and its ability to respond when that stimulus is *absent*.

Hunter himself found little evidence that animals can represent features of their environment, but recent experiments on animal memory provide compelling support for the idea that animals do form representations.

Learnt Sequences of Responses: the Traditional View

Of particular interest are experiments involving integrated sequences or responses. Though natural behaviour typically occurs in integrated sequences of actions, learning theorists have concerned themselves mainly with individual repetitive responses such as bar-presses and key-pecks. Integrated sequences of response are regarded as *chains* of discrete responses.[37,38,39,41,42] On this view, an animal that learns a sequence of responses has simply learnt to respond appropriately to a series of successively presented stimuli (each dependent on the animal's own preceding actions), and nothing more. For example, a rat that learns to run through a maze need not have any knowledge of the plan of the maze.

Animal Behaviour that Traditional Chaining Theory Cannot Explain

The Radial Maze

David Olton's experiments on a rat's behaviour in a radial maze provide an important departure from traditional maze studies.[43,44,45] Consider a maze in which eight runways radiated from a common starting-point – like the spokes around the hub of a wheel. Each runway was identical and was baited with equal amounts of food that could not be seen from the entrance to the runway. After a few days in the maze, Olton's rats, on the average, re-entered less than one alley per trial before all the food was consumed. They must have remembered which alleys they had already entered, even though they used different sequences of exploration each time. How does the rat remember which arms it has already visited? Subsequent clever experiments showed that the rat's choice could not be attributed to any particular external cue such as the smell of each alley. They were not simply conditioned responses to some feature of the environment. The rats must have formed some kind of internal representation of the maze.

Serial Learning

A rat's ability to create and use a map of food locations is clear evidence that, while foraging, it is not simply making a series of mindless responses, each triggered by some environmental cue. But however remarkable this ability may seem, it sheds no light on an animal's ability to learn *particular* sequences. Young children, for example, find it easy to learn all kinds of arbitrary sequences by rote, such as nursery rhymes or telephone numbers.

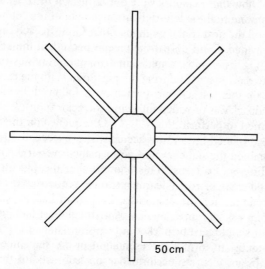

Figure 9.3   A diagram of the radial maze, viewed from above. Eight corridors, each baited with a pellet of food at the end, radiate from a central box, into which a rat is placed. The rat is rewarded for choosing to enter each arm only once (redrawn from Olton and Samuelson, Journal of Experimental Psychology: Animal Behavior Processes, *2, 97–116,* © *1976 by the American Psychological Association, adapted by permission of the authors).*

My colleagues and I have used pigeons to study those kind of sequences, which also resemble the rote sequence that chimpanzees were trained to perform to obtain reward (for example, MARY GIVE SARAH FOOD). The procedure we used differed significantly from conventional chaining paradigms, which do *not* require the animal to memorize the sequence that defines a particular chain. For example, in learning to run through a normal maze, a rat has only to learn what to do at various choice points. Since each choice point can be distinguished, the rat's task can be characterized as learning to solve a set of discrimination problems in which the discriminative stimuli are encountered successively.

In contrast to the traditional successive-chaining paradigm, in which discriminative stimuli and the opportunity to make a particular response are encountered one at a time, we used a simultaneous-chaining para-digm, which presents, at the same time, all of the stimuli and all of the things needed for each response. Conventional successive-chaining paradigms ensure that each correct response produces *feedback* (that is, information for the animal about the correctness of its response), which typically results in the automatic replacement of the current discrimina-tive stimulus by the next one. By contrast, an essential feature of the simultaneous-chaining paradigm is that it provides no differential step-by-step feedback following each response.

In the first studies to employ a simultaneous-chaining paradigm,[23,24] we trained pigeons to learn a 'list' of coloured lights. Each trial consisted of the presentation of an array of four colours (A, B, C, D), each randomly positioned on different response keys. To obtain food, the pigeon had to respond to each array by pecking in the sequence A–B–C–

D regardless of how those colours were positioned on the response keys. For example, on one trial the left–right arrangement of the colours might be B, C, A, D; on the next trial it might be D, B, C, A. In each case access to food was provided if and only if the pigeon pecked all the keys in the order A–B–C–D. If the subject made an error the array was turned off and a new array was presented during the next trial. With the exception of the response to the last colour (which was followed by food), no differential feedback was provided following correct responses.

Pigeons learned to perform the A–B–C–D sequence on the arrays on which they were trained at levels of accuracy that exceeded 70 per cent, and they maintained the same level of performance even if the keys were arranged in different patterns. This showed that the pigeon had not simply mastered a set of rotely learnt response sequences to the arrays used during training, for the only basis the pigeon had for choosing a particular colour was its representation of what colour it had just pecked and what colour should next be pecked.

A pigeon's ability to form a representation of the sequence was also demonstrated by its accurate performance on 'sub-sets' of the original sequence, for example, B and D, A and D, C and D, and so on. On arrays presenting B and D, in which the required sequence was B–D, the pigeon had neither the advantage of the normal starting colour nor, having pecked B, the advantage of an adjacent element. Just the same, accuracy of performance was as great on arrays requiring the sequence B–D as it was on arrays requiring the sequence A–B.

Difference between Human and Animal Representations

Though our knowledge of animal representations is embarrassingly meagre, we can be fairly confident that animal representations differ from those generated by human beings in two important respects. Most studies of human memory use verbal stimuli. Even when non-verbal stimuli are used, memory may be facilitated by verbal mnemonics and control processes. In the absence of such mnemonics and control processes, it seems foolhardy to assume that animals rehearse stimuli verbally or that there is much overlap between animal and human encoding processes. It also seems clear that cognitive processes in animals may be more limited by biological constraints than those of their human counterparts.

In the radial maze, for example, an important basis of the rat's ability to avoid previously visited alleys is an unlearnt 'win–shift' strategy that it follows when searching for food. While a win–shift strategy is not sufficient to explain the highly efficient performance of Olton's rats, it appears to be a necessary condition. This becomes evident when comparing the performance of pigeons in a similar radial maze. Pigeons appear to be 'win–stay' animals and hence are considerably less efficient than rats in avoiding previously visited alleys.[47] Given the pigeon's ability to home, it seems more plausible to attribute its poor performance in the radial maze to its 'win–stay' tendency than to a poorer ability to represent spatial locations.

Putting aside the contribution of a win–shift strategy, it is unclear that the rat's ability to perform a radial maze efficiently has very much in common with such superficially similar human abilities as remembering elements of arbitrary lists – for example, which of a group of people have yet to be called on the telephone, which errands have yet to be performed, and so on. At present, we have no basis for assuming that a rat's ability to keep track of alleys that it has visited could generalize to tasks that require other responses (for example, bar pressing) or to the many kinds of arbitrary non-spatial tasks that language makes possible in the case of humans.

Virtually all of the examples of representation in animals described earlier warrant similar caution when it comes to extrapolating to human cognitive processes. For example, others who study pigeons have noted that the processes that they use to form concepts may differ considerably from those used by human subjects.[48,49,50] In the case of a pigeon's ability to represent a group of elements in performing a serial learning task, it is unlikely that its representation of these elements has much in common with human representations of serially ordered elements. Both involve representation and both involve sequences. There is, however, good reason to assume that, unlike the pigeon, human subjects encode each element of the sequence verbally.

These, and other problems suggested by recent demonstrations of animal cognition, leave us with a baffling but fundamental question. Now that there are strong grounds to dispute Descartes's contention that animals lack the ability to think, we have to ask just how animals *do* think. In particular, how do they think without language? Learning the answer to that question will provide an important biological benchmark against which to assess the evolution of human thought.

References

1 Hulse, S. H., Fowler, H. and Honig, W. K. (eds) (1978) *Cognitive Processes in Animal Behavior*. Hillsdale, NJ: Erlbaum.
2 Roitblat, H. L., Bever, G. T. and Terrace, H. S. (1984) *Animal Cognition*. Hillsdale, NJ: Erlbaum.
3 Premack, D. (1979) Species of intelligence: debate between Premack and Chomsky. *The Sciences*, 19: 6–23.
4 Savage-Rumbaugh, E. S., Rumbaugh, D. M. and Boysen, S. (1980) Do apes use language? *American Scientist*, 68: 49–61.
5 Terrace, H. S., Petitto, L. A., Sanders, R. J. and Bever, T. G. (1979) Can an ape create a sentence? *Science*, 200: 891–902.
6 Chomsky, N. (1966) *Cartesian Linguistics: A Chapter in the History of Rationalist Thought*. New York: Harper & Row.
7 Gardner, R. A. and Gardner, B. T. (1969) Teaching sign language to a chimpanzee. *Science*, 165: 664–72.
8 Premack, D. (1971) On the assessment of language competence in the chimpanzee. In A.M. Schrier and F. Stollnitz (eds), *Behavior of Nonhuman Primates*, vol. 4, pp. 186–288. New York: Academic Press.
9 Savage-Rumbaugh, E. S., Pate, J. L., Lawson, J., Smith, T. and Rosenbaum, S. (1983) Can a chimpanzee make a statement? *J. exp. Psych. Gen.* 112: 457–87.
10 Ristau, C. A. and Robbins, D. (1982) Language in the great apes: a critical review. *Adv. Study Behav.* R12: 141–255.
11 Brown, R. (1970) The first sentences of child and chimpanzee. In R. Brown

(ed.), *Selected Psycholinguistic Papers*, pp. 808–22. New York: Macmillan.

12 Premack, D. (1976) *Intelligence in Ape and Man*. Hillsdale, NJ: Erlbaum.

13 Rumbaugh, D. M., Gill, T. V. and von Glasersfeld, E. C. (1973) Reading and sentence completion by a chimpanzee (*Pan*). *Science*, 182: 731–33.

14 Patterson, F. G. (1978) The gestures of a gorilla: language acquisition in another pongid. *Brain Lang.* 5: 72–97.

15 Terrace, H. S. (1979) *Nim*. New York: Knopf.

16 Brown, R. (1973) *A First Language*. Cambridge, Mass.: Harvard Univ. Press.

17 Bloom, L. M., Rocissano, L. and Hood, L. (1976) Adult–child discourse: developmental interaction between information processing and linguistic knowledge. *Cont. Psychol.* 8, 521–22.

18 Gardner, B. T. (1981) Project Nim: who taught whom? *Cont. Psychol.* 26: 425–6.

19 Patterson, F. G. (1981) Ape language. *Science*, 211: 86–7.

20 Terrace, H. S., Petitto, L. A., Sanders, R. J. and Bever, T. G. (1981) Reply to Patterson. *Science*, 211: 87–8.

21 Terrace, H. S. (1982) Evidence for sign language in apes: what the ape signed or how well was the ape loved? *Cont. Psychol.* 27: 67–8.

22 Thompson, C. R. and Church, R. M. (1980) An explanation of the language of a chimpanzee. *Science*, 208: 313–14.

23 Straub, R. O., Seidenberg, M. S., Terrace, H. S. and Bever, T. G. (1979) Serial learning in the pigeon. *J. exp. Analys. Behav.* 32: 137–48.

24 Terrace, H. S. (1984) Simultaneous chaining: the problem it poses for traditional chaining theory. In R. J. Herrnstein and A. Wagner (eds), *Quantitative Analyses of Behavior*. Cambridge, Mass.: Ballinger.

25 Pate, J. L. and Rumbaugh, D. M. (1983) The language-like behavior of Lana: is it merely discrimination and paired-associate learning? *Anim. Learn. Behav.* 11: 134–8.

26 Brown, R. (1956) The original word game. In J. Bruner, J. Goodnow and G. Austin (eds), *A Study of Thinking*, Appendix. New York: Wiley.

27 Clarke, E. (1983) Non-linguistic strategies and the acquisition of word meanings. *Cognition*, 12: 161–82.

28 Nelson, K. (1973) Structure and strategy in learning to talk. *Mon. Soc. Res. Child Dev.* Ser. 1, No. 149: 38.

29 Winitz, H. (1969) *Articulatory Acquisition and Behavior*. New York: Appleton-Century-Crofts.

30 MacNamara, J. (1982) *Names for Things*. Cambridge, Mass.: Bradford, MIT Press.

31 Bloom, L. and Lahey, M. (1978) *Language Development and Language Disorders*. New York: Wiley.

32 Bruner, J. S. (1983) *Child's Talk*. New York: Norton.

33 Menzel, E. W. (1979) Communication of object-locations in a group of young chimpanzees. In D. A. Hamburg and E. R. McGowan (eds), *The Great Apes*, pp. 359–71. Menlo Park, Calif: Cummings.

34 Telecki, G. (1973) *The Predatory Behavior of Wild Chimpanzees*. Lewisburg, Pa.: Buckness Univ. Press.

35 Savage-Rumbaugh, E. S., Rumbaugh, D. M., Smith, S. T. and Lawson, J. (1980) Reference – the linguistic essential. *Science*, 210: 922–5.

36 Pavlov, I. P. (1917) *Conditioned Reflexes*. London: Oxford Univ. Press.

37 Guthrie, E. R. (1952) *The Psychology of Learning*. New York: Harper & Row.

38 Hull, C. L. (1943) *Principles of Behavior*. New York: Appleton-Century-Crofts.

39 Skinner, B. F. (1938) *The Behavior of Organisms*. New York: Appleton-Century-Crofts.

40 Hunter W. S. (1913) The delayed reaction in anaimals. *Behavior Monographs*, 2, no. 6.
41 Spence, K. W. (1956) *Behavior Theory and Conditioning*. New Haven: Yale Univ. Press.
42 Logan, F. A. (1960) *Incentive*. New Haven: Yale Univ. Press.
43 Olton, D. S. and Samuelson, R. J. (1976) Remembrance of places past: spatial memory in rats. *J. exp. Psychol.: Animal Behavior Processes*, 2: 97–116.
44 Olton, D. S. (1979) Mazes, maps and memory. *Amer. Psychol.* 34: 588–96.
45 Olton, D. S. (1978) Characteristics of spatial memory. In S. H. Hulse, H. Fowler and W. K. Honig (eds), *Cognitive Processes in Animal Behavior*. Hillsdale, NJ: Erlbaum.
46 Terrace, H. S., Straub, R. O., Bever, T. G. and Seidenberg, M. S. (1977) Representation of a sequence by a pigeon. *Bull. Psychol. Soc.* 10: 269.
47 Bond, A. B., Cook, R. G. and Lamb, M. R. (1981) Spatial memory and the performance of rats and pigeons in the radial-arm maze. *Anim. Learn. Behav.* 9: 575–80.
48 Herrnstein, R. J. and Villiers, P. A. de (1980) Fish as a natural category for people and pigeons. In G. H. Bower (ed.), *The Psychology of Learning and Motivation*, vol. 14. New York: Academic Press.
49 Lea, S. E. G. and Harrison, S. N. (1978) Discrimination of polymorphous stimulus sets by pigeons. *Quart. J. Exp. Psychol.* 30: 521–37.
50 Morgan, M. J., Fitch, M. D., Holman, J. G. and Lea, S. E. G. (1976) Pigeons learn the concept of an 'A'. *Perception*, 5: 57–66.

10

The Description and Evaluation of Animal Emotion

Stephen Clark

Stephen R. L. Clark is Professor of Philosophy at Liverpool University, and author of Aristotle's Man, the Moral Status of Animals, The Nature of the Beast *and* From Athens to Jerusalem *(all published by Oxford University Press) and* The Mysteries of Religion *(forthcoming from Basil Blackwell). He has been a scholar of Balliol, a Fellow of All Souls College, Oxford, and a Lecturer at Glasgow University. His main projects are to demonstrate the relevance of metaphysical, epistemological and ethical speculation to the hard necessities of practical and scientific life, and to advocate a radical alteration in our attitude to other animals, and the world of nature. He has a wife, three children and three cats.*

What follows is my imagined conversation with two authors, a philosopher and a psychologist. The philosopher, Benedict Spinoza, is one I respect; the psychologist, Howard Liddell, sometime professor of psychobiology at Cornell, writes like a humane and intelligent man. I emphasize this point, that I have no grudge against either, because I am going to criticize their moral views. It is my experience that people who hold to some version of the 'boo–hurray' theory of ethics – which is to say, a good many scientists – always take moral criticism to be a form of personal insult: I do not, and it is not.

'Animals are not Human'

First the philosopher:

The emotions of animals that are called irrational differ from the emotions of men as much as their nature differs from human nature. Horse and man are indeed carried away by lust to procreate, but the former by equine lust, the latter by human lust. So too the lusts and appetites of insects, fishes and birds are bound to be of different kinds.[1]

Spinoza's reason for thinking this is not the banal fact that equine lust typically has horses for its objects, and human lust has people, nor yet that rather different behaviour is required of lustful fish, insects and humans –

The display of a cat, terrified by a dog (from Charles Darwin's The Expression of the Emotions in Man and Animals, *1872).*

Figure 10.1   The Dutch philosopher Benedict de Spinoza (1632–1677) (Mary Evans Picture Library).

though these points are important – but rather that both lusts are bound up with each creature's basic endeavour to maintain and improve its own life. To lust as a horse is to want to be, as a horse, nor do such creatures have any option in the matter, nor capacity to consider their own lusts, and correct or cultivate them. The joy of one kind is different from the joy of another, because kinds are essentially distinct. This is not the place to comment on Spinoza's species-essentialism, a doctrine he took over from the medieval tradition, but not from Aristotle, whom modern taxonomists usually blame for it.[2]

Virtue is human power, which is defined solely by man's essence; that is, it is defined solely by the conatus whereby man endeavours to persist in his own being. Therefore the more every man endeavours and is able to preserve his own being, the more he is endowed with virtue.[3]

The principle of seeking our own advantage teaches us to be in close relationship with men, not with beasts or things whose nature is different from human nature, and that we have the same right over them as they over us. Indeed, since every individual's right is defined by his virtue or power, man's right over beasts is far greater than their rights over men. I do not deny that beasts feel; I am denying that we are on that account debarred from paying heed to our own advantage and from making use of them as we please and dealing with them as best suits us, seeing that they do not agree with us in nature and their emotions are different in nature from human emotions.[4]

Hating humans is never good, but Spinoza expressly allows that we may even hate all others, that is, desire their destruction.[5]

Spinoza's argument, as always, is a subtle one, and I am not sure that I have entirely understood it. It is an additional irony that his general outlook and philosophy seem to support recent environmentalist and 'deep ecology' movements. It is Spinoza's eventual conclusion, after all, that our highest good lies in contemplation of the whole, and understanding of our place in it. 'Things are not more or less perfect to the extent that they please or offend human senses, serve or oppose human interests.'[6] At the same time, as you have seen, he rules out any obligation to consider the needs or interests of non-human creatures. Indeed, 'the requirement to refrain from slaughtering beasts (or doing them any other hurt or harm) is founded on groundless superstition and womanish compassion rather than on sound reason.'[7] The very fall of Adam, on Spinoza's account, came

when he came to believe that the beasts were like himself (and) straightway began to imitate their emotions and to lose his freedom, which the Patriarchs later regained under the guidance of the spirit of Christ, that is, the idea of God, on which alone it depends that a man should be free and should desire for mankind the good that he desire for himself.[8]

There seem to be two arguments advanced for excluding non-humans from rational consideration, the Hobbesian and the moralistic. The Hobbesian first: if any of us are to achieve our individual advantage we need a civil association of the like-minded, an assurance that others will not aim to overmaster us, and a constant challenge and example to our intellectual powers. We do not need to consider, and ought not to consider, any of the feelings or emotions or life-projects of other creatures, since they can be no general threat to us (of a kind that can be obviated by a compact of mutual forbearance and assistance), and cannot share in the general good of mankind (namely, the increase of knowledge and sound learning). We are still in a Hobbesian state of nature with all other creatures.

Second, the moralistic: Spinoza explicitly dissociates himself from the Cartesian view that animals do not have feelings but that if they did we should be bound to take account of them. He acknowledges – indeed he insists – 'that in the animal world we find much that far surpasses human sagacity and that sleepwalkers do many things in their sleep that they would not dare when awake – clear evidence that the body, solely from the laws of its own nature, can do many things at which its mind is amazed'.[9] But he did not conclude that it was 'unnecessary' to postulate a mental aspect to what went on physically: extension and thought, and the laws of extension and thought, were two aspects of the one infinite universe. Physical and mental explanation were not mutually exclusive. If we are at once mental and physical beings, there is no good reason to deny that animals too are subjects of experience, in their degree: what physical difference is there to go along with so vast a mental gap?

It is worth digressing for a moment to emphasize this point. A surprising number of people still seem to think that offering an explanation in terms of intentions or feelings or the like is somehow incompatible with an explanation in terms of physiological condition, as if intentions occupied space to the exclusion of nerve fibres. That something is happening at the neurophysiological level as I write this essay is obvious. We might even have a usable theory which would reveal that what went on was all that physically could go on. This would not show that I had no intentions or feelings in the matter. There are many levels of true description, from the chemical to the political, and which of these – if any – offers a truer explanation is not something that can be settled by experiment. Intentions and feelings may be non-spatial (that is, spiritual) items associated with physical states (a dualistic doctrine that some commentators now pretend appeals only to the senile, though no final argument has been produced against it). They may be characteristic properties of states which are neither simply physical nor simply mental, or even the very same states of matter that the neurophysiologist describes, though experienced from another point of view. Whatever the nature of such intentions and feelings may be, there is at least no reason to think that what has a physical explanation or description cannot also have a mental one. It follows that you cannot prove that an animal is not conscious merely by saying that its motions are in accordance with biochemical laws. Nor can you suppose that animals are like us physically, but that there is no need to think them (broadly) like us mentally, without admitting merely magical conjunctions into the universe: it just happens that consciousness has lighted on us, but not on creatures obedient to the same physical laws. The onus, as Spinoza saw, has to be on those who wish to deny all feeling to the non-rational in the face of outward similarity.

But though animals, on Spinoza's account, can feel, and though we might speak of many emotions that they shared with us, those emotions were of another kind than ours, and could not rationally matter to us. This is what I have called the moralistic argument. He may have been influenced by a point that he adduces elsewhere, which is also used as the basis of a quite atrocious argument by David Hume:

> Every one looks with admiration upon traits in animals which he would execrate and regard with aversion if displayed by men, such as the wars of bees and the jealousy of doves. For while these are forbidden to men, we regard the animals as all the more perfect because they are thus endowed.[10]

*Figure 10.2   A Celebes black ape (*Cynopithecus niger*) in a calm mood (above) and expressing its pleasure while being caressed (below). Although monkeys and apes bare their teeth in anger, Darwin thought that the human smile may have originated from the less exaggerated grimace that indicates pleasure.*

The animals behave in ways that can be described by using human moral terms, 'war', 'slavery', 'harem', 'incest', but they do not display any vice in so doing. What they do is not the same as what we might wickedly do, nor are animal 'acts of virtue', loyal and affectionate behaviour to 'spouse' or 'child', acts in the same sense as ours. Where Hume argued that since animals did the same things as we did, but without condemnation, moral evaluation must be in the eye solely of the beholder, Spinoza (more plausibly) would deny that they really did the same things at all, as not having the same things in mind, nor capable of the same reasonings. Sociobiologists who think it obvious that a sultan's harem is the same sort of thing as a walrus's, or that the human ban on 'incest' is of a piece with the disinclination of female chimpanzees to mate with too-familiar males, should take Spinoza's warning seriously. It is not a merely verbal point, but a correct observation that, for example, humans commit incest by mating with stepchildren or deceased wives' sisters or clan-members, and that female aversion to too-familiar males has precisely nothing to do with maintaining the ban.

A further digression: there is a point, for Spinoza, when we shall have to agree that everything is as perfect as it could be, just as it is, and that our attitude to animals, appreciating them as what they are, without condemning them for what they cannot help and which is no imperfection in them, should also be our attitude to human 'malefactors'. These latter will still suffer for their 'crimes', but the rational man acknowledges

> that a horse is excusable for being a horse, and not a man; nevertheless he needs must be a horse, and not a man. He who goes mad from the bite of a dog is to be excused; still, it is right that he should die of suffocation. Finally, he who cannot control his desires and keep them in check through fear of the law, although he is to be excused for his weakness, nevertheless cannot enjoy tranquility of mind, and the knowledge and love of God, but of necessity be lost.[11]

The man who lives not by reason but in obedience to passion lives as if he were an animal, or nearly so. Though animals cannot be blamed for so doing, humans have a higher capacity, for re-ordering their lives by a calculation of their global advantage, and sharing in political and theoretical debate. To think immediate sense-experience, to which level animals are confined, important is to lose sight of a higher perfection. Animals can neither be condemned nor morally admired, and their concerns ought not to concern us. 'Sexuality', Kant remarked for similar reasons, 'exposes us to danger of equality with the beasts.'[12]

Figure 10.3   David Hume (1711–1776) (Mary Evans Picture Library).

Animals are Rather Like Humans

Let us turn from Spinoza, plausibly called the first 'modern' philosopher, so many of whose ideas have conditioned the thought and practice of people who think themselves severely 'practical', to Howard Liddell, the experimental psychologist:

There is no doubt from our observation of hundreds of sheep and goats that the mildest electrical stimulation of the skin of the limbs is interpreted as gravely threatening. Such a minimal startle stimulus to the forelimb of the untrained animal leads to vehement aggression or attempts to escape through leaping or struggling if this is physically possible.[13]

Pavlov's classical conditioning procedure leads, if long enough continued, to emotional bankruptcy and chronically disabling behaviors in the experimental animal. We have succeeded in precipitating such chronic emotional disorders (or experimental neuroses) in sheep, goats, pigs and dogs.[14]

On one occasion, Liddell reports, the goat-keeper was startled and upset by the sudden 'anxious apprehension' displayed by a particular goat who had hitherto been fond of him. The goat, he knew, 'was not mistreated by punishment or rough handling' in the laboratory: what he did not know was that the goat was being systematically stressed by repeated electrical shocks, and 'had begun to carry its troubles back to the barn'.[15] Liddell did not beat his animals, and seems concerned to make it clear that the shocks were, in themselves, mild ones. Presumably he thought it wrong to inflict particularly severe pains on animals, at least when lesser pains would serve, though the only reason I can see for thinking it wrong to do so is that the animals would have been made miserable – as they were by what Liddell did do to them. By his own account, the sheer monotony of the experiment imposed 'almost intolerable discomfort' on the experimenters, a fact he mentions to help explain why the animals came out of it so badly disturbed.[16] His techniques could be guaranteed to produce experimental neurosis. In one set of experiments individual lambs were taken from their mothers (leaving the other twin of each pair as a control), and subjected to the usual stresses. Predictably, the deprived lambs coped less well with those stresses than the controls, became lethargic, unsociable, incompetent, and died young.

Liddell makes the usual, ritual acknowledgement that there is no scientific demonstration that, say, a dog shares any of our feelings or thoughts,[17] though he adds that a psychiatrist has similar problems with the behaviour of acute psychotics. Neither animal psychologist nor psychiatrist can expect rational, verbal answers to their questions. But his insistence on making sure that the stimuli are, in themselves, mild ones, and his claim that the neuroses are similar in outward manifestation and inner cause (he instances 'self-imposed restraint'), suggests that he has no real doubts that animals can feel. He also insists that it is 'obvious that words such as loneliness, companionship and gregariousness when used to characterize animal behavior are evaluative rather than descriptive. They are used to avoid circumlocution.'[18] The use of 'evaluative' here leaves me very uncertain of his meaning, and I can offer only the following four possibilities. There may well be others.

First, he may mean that such terms reach beyond what can be immediately sensed and described, that they name theoretical entities which may serve to explain the immediate empirical data. Notoriously, what counts as empirical or theoretical is highly context-relative. That this book is a material object is, in ordinary conversation, a datum, hardly worth mentioning unless there is a chance that it is a hologram; in other contexts, it is a theoretical interpretation of immediate sense-data. Even the most hard-nosed of animal psychologists had better sometimes be prepared to notice that an animal is very angry, very miserable, or very affectionate, even if these assertions can be understood as going beyond the immediately accessible data. We do that all the time. That an animal genuinely confronts us as a subject of experience, that we are present to it in something like the way that it is present to us, is something that does not logically follow from any lower level of description, any more than the thesis that this book genuinely confronts us as a physical object strictly follows from any report of sense-data. We may nonetheless rely upon it. My own suspicion, incidentally, is that 'loneliness' and the rest will turn out to name internal complexes that might also be studied, under different and more esoteric names, by psychologists: 'loneliness' is that complex induced in sociable animals (including us) by prolonged dis-sociation from companions.

Secondly, he may mean to say that what identifies the animal's emotional condition as 'lonely', 'gregarious' and the rest is that it bears the same relation to the rest of the animal's life and its society as loneliness does to ours. What is at issue is analogy, not homology, similarity of function not similarity of internal structure and ancestry. So Konrad Lorenz wrote:

> Psychologists have protested that it is misleading to use terms such as falling in love, marrying or being jealous when speaking of animals . . . [But] since we know that the behaviour of geese and men cannot possibly be homologous – the last common ancestors of birds and mammals were extremely primitive reptiles with minute brains and certainly incapable of any complicated social behaviour – and since we know that the improbability of coincidental similarity can only be expressed in astronomical numbers, we know for certain that it was more or less identical survival value which caused jealousy behaviour to evolve in birds as well as in man . . . These terms refer to functionally determined concepts, just as do the terms 'legs', 'wings', 'eyes', and the names used for other bodily structures that have evolved independently in different phyla.[19]

This functional interpretation of 'emotion-words' and the like has a long and respectable history, and does eliminate the pseudo-problem that, if such words had only introspectible feelings as their referents, no one would ever know if we were using the words in the same sense as each other, or as our own past selves. Pure functionalism, of course, with its implication that there are no such introspectible realities at all, has its own problems. But the general thesis, that such terms apply not solely in virtue of undiscoverable similarities between occult mental processes but in virtue of functional analogies between public, and social, activities, is a good one.

Thirdly, Liddell may intend to say that understanding an animal, or even a person, involves an exercise of imaginative sympathy over and above mere reportage, or theory about causes and functions. To speak of loneliness is to evaluate the situation in which the animal finds itself, from that animal's imagined viewpoint. This is undoubtedly a dangerous exercise, and a good Spinozist should have no difficulty pointing out that it is very difficult to divest ourselves of our human nature so as to 'see things' as the animal does. What right have we to assume that the animal even perceives things, as such, at all or has anything remotely resembling our long-term plans? The proof, perhaps, lies in seeing how well experienced and imaginative people do manage to cope with animals. It is no surprise that we are quite good at it, since our species has for millenia gained many of its advantages through being able to predict the behaviour of prey and domestic animal.

Finally, Liddell may mean – and it is useful to me to assume that he did – that imputing loneliness is to make a value-judgement, to say that this is a condition to be pitied, as being one that we should hate to be in ourselves. In referring to the animal's condition only in suitably sterile ways we would be standing back from sympathetic involvement, possible agreement with the animal's view. In doing so, we are not – as psychologists sometimes seem to think – refraining from making a judgement, and concentrating on the 'facts': we are actually endorsing a particular evaluation, that the animal's condition is not a thing that rational people would worry about. We can neutralize that endorsement, but if we don't, it stands, and no one listening to us will be in much doubt of our moral view.

Ethical Evaluation is not Irrational

The act of evaluating is not essentially irrational, and people can often be shown that the particular evaluations they had made were in one way or another misplaced: they were inconsistent, ill informed, partial, or arbitrary. A good deal of harm has been done in this area by mistaken use of the notion of the 'naturalistic fallacy', which has been taken to mean that there can never be good reason for any evaluation, which must therefore be merely 'personal' and 'arbitrary'. This was, emphatically, not G. E. Moore's meaning.[20] It is one thing to agree that there are no logically self-evident principles from which we can demonstrate, by strict deduction, particular moral truths. It is quite another to deduce from this truism the particular moral judgement that one ought never to rely upon sound reasoning in the pursuit of ethical decision. We have long ago given up the fantasy of founding all science upon logically self-evident principles. Why should we be so scared of non-demonstrative but reasonably persuasive argument in ethics and politics?

Do we ever have information to be sure (within the limits set by general epistemological scepticism) that an animal's emotional condition is one to be pitied? 'Pity', said Spinoza, 'is pain accompanied by the idea of ill that has happened to another whom we think of as like ourselves.'[21] It follows from his general system that 'the man who lives by the dictates of reason endeavours, as far as he can, not to be touched by pity',[22] though pity is a necessity in those not moved by reason, by the calculation of their own advantage as members of civil and intellectual society. Spinoza may have intended to imply that there were three levels of benevolent action: those moved by reason act to promote the advantage of humankind; those moved by proper pity, founded on a correct assessment that the sufferer is like themselves, that they might be in as bad a state, act, emotionally, to help a fellow-human; those moved by 'womanish compassion' weep at an animal's distress, making themselves of one kind with the animal and projecting their sentimental fantasy on to the animal.

The question whether it is right to pity an emotionally disturbed animal, and correspondingly wrong to create that disturbance, rests on the prior question, is such a one really like us? Presumably a sexually repressed, lethargic, obsessively ritualizing animal is only badly off in so far as there is some other state it might be in which is a less impeded, more assisted manifestation of its nature. There is an observable difference between a lamb that frisks away from and back toward its mother, acting out the pattern of its growing life, and a lamb that lies still, cowers in dark corners, cannot cope with additional stress, and so on,[23] even though both behaviours are responses to the environment, and both are, in a sense, 'in a lamb's nature', there to be evoked. In refusing to give any weight to our sympathy with the neurotic lamb, our delight in the happy lamb, Spinoza implicitly relied on the following theses: (a) that the rational man should delight in what must be, should see the neurotic lamb as a perfect expression of nature's workings at that point (as was Belsen); (b) that any impulses we have to such sympathy is not to be delighted in, but rather repressed. But these theses are in conflict. If we ought to appreciate things just as they are, we ought to acknowledge our own natural sympathies, evoked by the same sort of cues that evoke pity for human distress. If, on the other hand, it is possible for us to be depraved, relative to that species-nature which allows us higher joys and perfections, it is also possible for animals to miss out on the fulfilment of their species-natures, what is possible for them as what they are. If we ought to be moved by the thought of our defect, why not by the thought of theirs? If they were genuinely of a wholly alien kind, we could indeed have no clue to how they might be well or badly off. We do have such clues, and they are not aliens. Nor is it, in the long run, at all likely that we would be better human beings if we excised our impulses of pity, our appreciation of the things they appreciate.

Let us suppose that Spinoza was right to take his stand on egoistic principle, though there is no final argument to prove that egoism is more rational than any other project. The good, for each of us, is what we must have for our true advantage. It is to my advantage to live in peace with my neighbours and join with them in political and intellectual endeavour. But why is it not also to my advantage to awaken in myself (or not to repress) a feeling for the manifold, partial lives that go to make up the whole sweep of the living universe? 'Concern for the well-being and health of animals cannot be dismissed as sentimentality: indeed, it may often make sound practical and economic sense'[24] – though it is a fallacy to imply that it would be irrational to take the health and well-being of animals as one's end if this did (or to the extent that it does) conflict with other goals. Economics is not the science of what we should desire, but the art of putting a price on what we desire. Other advantages aside, is it really so obvious that human beings who treat all other creatures as their enemies or slaves live happy lives? If we can so readily and effectively read the feelings of our domestic and farmyard kin – a skill which has obvious evolutionary advantages – is it not best to agree that they do, after all, feel very much as we would feel if we lived under their disabilities? What the sheep goes through as she waits, in harness and monotony, for yet another shock, is not beyond conjecture, and the refusal to pity this condition is not obviously correct.

It is not my intention to leave you with the thought that we ought always to act out of pity. Spinoza was right so far: those who act out of immediate emotions, of pity, or anger or affection, may fail to see the wider context in which acting so is not going to do any good. The virtuous person does indeed act out of his or her considered judgement of what should be done, for the advantage of all, and in obedience to such rules as prevent us straying too far. But pity and affection, shared jokes and shared miseries are part of the apparatus that brings us information about the world we live in, and the sort of things that surround us. Simply to redescribe what we would otherwise and honestly see as misery so that it no longer matters to us is not the mark of reason, but of self-deceiving emotion, a magical endeavour to make things as we would have them without the trouble and difficulty of really doing so. Spinoza's challenge can be turned around: it is the person who refuses to see his or her own kinship with the beasts, and who denies that such miseries matter, who is denying reason. The world was not made exclusively for us, and our true good lies in enjoying and caring for the good in all things.

References

1 Spinoza, B. (1982) *Ethics and Selected Letters*, tr. S. Shirley, ed. S. Feldman, 3p57s (i.e. part 3, proposition 57, scholion). Indianapolis: Hackett.
2 Balme, D. E. (1980) Aristotle's biology was not essentialist. *Archiv für Geschichte der Philosophie*, 62: 1ff.
3 Spinoza, *Ethics and Selected Letters*, 4p20d.
4 Ibid., 4p37sl.
5 Ibid., 4p45s.
6 Ibid., 1p36s.
7 Ibid., 4p37s.
8 Ibid., 4p68s.
9 Ibid., 3p2s.
10 Ibid., Letter 19, 237. See Hume, D. (1888) *Treatise of Human Nature*, ed. L. A. Selby-Bigge, 3.1.1. Oxford: Clarendon Press. Cf. Clark, S. R. L. (1985) Hume, animals and the objectivity of morals. *Philosophical Quarterly*, 35: 117–33.
11 Spinoza, *Ethics and Selected Letters*, Letter 78, p. 254.
12 Kant, I. (1930) *Lectures on Ethics*, tr. L. Infeld, p. 164. London: Methuen. Cf. Clark, S. R. L. (1983) Humans, animals and 'animal behavior'. In H. B. Miller and W. H. Williams (eds), *Ethics and Animals*, pp. 169–82. New Jersey: Humana Press.
13 Liddell, H. (1956) *Emotional Hazards in Animals and Men*, p. 6. Springfield, Ill.: C. C. Thomas.
14 Ibid., p. 15.
15 Ibid., p. 53.
16 Ibid., p. 42.
17 Ibid., p. 19.
18 Ibid., p. 38.
19 Lorenz, K. (1983) *The Foundations of Ethology*, p. 90. Berlin: Springer.
20 See Clark, S. R. L. (1984) Morals, Moore and MacIntyre. *Inquiry*, 26, pp. 425–45.

21 Spinoza, *Ethics and Selected Letters*, 3AD18.
22 Ibid., 4p50d.
23 Liddell, *Emotional Hazards*, pp. 22f.
24 Dawkins, M. (1981) Welfare of animals. In D. McFarland (ed.), *Oxford Companion to Animal Behaviour*, pp. 598–600. Oxford: Oxford Univ. Press.

11

Minding and Mattering

Marian Stamp Dawkins

Marian Stamp Dawkins is Fellow in Biological Sciences at Somerville College and teaches animal behaviour in the Animal Behaviour Research Group of the Department of Zoology in Oxford. She does research into the behaviour of hens, with an emphasis on behavioural measures of welfare. She has recently written a book, Unravelling Animal Behaviour, *about the more problematical aspects of the behaviour of animals, and has written another,* Animal Suffering, *on the even more problematical subject of the assessment of when animals are suffering. Marian Dawkins is a member of the Farm Animal Welfare Council and of the Ethical Committee of the Association for the Study of Animal Behaviour. She is firmly convinced that biology in general and the study of behaviour in particular have an important part to play in ensuring that non-human animals get a fair deal from human ones.*

Moral Attitudes to Animals

In few areas of our lives are our ethical values so tangled and confused as in our attitudes to animals of species other than our own. We may like to think that we have straightforward principles guiding all our behaviour and that our moral attitudes are consistent and logical. But where animals are concerned, our moral decisions are often so confused and conflicting that they resemble a bowl of spaghetti, with ends and intertwining strands, the precise relationships of which are not at all clear.

We have only to think of various different sorts of animals to show up our inconsistencies. There are demonstrations against killing baby harp seals, but there are no comparable campaigns to stop the killing of rats. Many people are quite happy to eat pigs or sheep but horrified by the idea of eating dogs or horses. Animals that are noble-looking like stags or cuddly like rabbits tend to be better regarded than animals that look mean or ugly. Animals that look like us or that are rare tend to get more ethical consideration than those that look alien or are just very common. There is even some ethical mileage to be gained from simply being large. An animal that is large *and* rare *and* cuddly, like the Giant Panda, becomes the symbol of all the animals we are concerned about. Try justifying or accounting for all these beliefs and the analogy with spaghetti becomes apparent.

Amongst all this confusion, however, two strands can be discerned,

How much do things matter to a battery hen? (© Poultry World*).*

Figure 11.1   If culling seals is an outrage, why don't we feel the same way about rats? (photograph courtesy of Greenpeace)

two ethical bases for our treatment of animals. Both these ethical strands involve attributing various aspects of mind to other organisms and both are closely bound up with our ethical responses to other human beings.

The first of these moral strands is that we value other animals which are clever or which show evidence of the ability to reason. We are more likely to take ethical notice of an intelligent animal than one which is stupid. In fact, many people comfort themselves and justify treating animals in a certain way by saying 'Well, they are not very clever, are they?', implying that if an animal is not clever, it is not worth bothering about ethically.

This view has also played an important part in the history of thought about the treatment of animals. Many philosophers have emphasized the moral value that should be given to the ability to reason and the ability to think. One of the most influential philosophers in this respect was René Descartes, who clearly expressed the view that because non-human animals cannot speak, they cannot reason or think either: 'speech is the only certain sign of thought hidden in a body. All men use it, however stupid and insane they may be, and though they may lack tongue and organs of voice; but no animals do.'[1]

He also believed that the absence of a reasoning soul meant that animals did not count for very much ethically either:

Please note that I am speaking of thought, and not of life or sensation. I do not deny life to animals, since I regard it as consisting simply in the heat of the heart;

and I do not deny sensation, in so far as it depends on a bodily organ. Thus my opinion is not so much cruel to animals as indulgent to men . . . since it absolves them from the suspicion of crime when they kill or eat animals.

Even though Descartes wrote this over 300 years ago, his ethical dismissal of animals by virtue of their lack of ability to speak and therefore to think continues to be very important.

But evidence of intelligence is not, of course, the only attribute of mind that people feel should be given ethical value. The second very important strand which can be discerned is to value other organisms that show evidence of the ability to suffer and to feel pain. We tend to say that something is morally wrong if, given that there are no mitigating circumstances, we have evidence that preventable pain or suffering is being caused. This view has a long history. One of the most influential of its exponents was Jeremy Bentham, who directly attacked the idea that we should base our ethical decisions on whether animals could reason and argued, as in the following often-quoted passage, that they should be based instead on the capacity to suffer: 'a full-grown horse or dog is beyond comparison a more rational, as well as a more conversible animal than an infant of a day or a week, or even a month old. But suppose they were otherwise, what would it avail? The question is not, Can they *reason?* nor, Can they *talk*, but Can they *suffer?*'[2]

So out of the tangled mess of people's attitudes to animals, we can discern these two very important ideas. One is that we should value, in a moral sense, other beings that have the capacity to reason and to think; the other is that we should value other beings not because they are intelligent but if they have the capacity to suffer. Both of them, in varying proportions, are to be found in people's everyday and perhaps not very explicit attitudes to animals. Both of them are to be found in the more academic philosophical writings about animals. And both of them involve attributing properties of mind to other beings whether human or non-human and making distinctions about how different ones should be treated on the basis of whether we believe them to possess these attributes or not. The possession of a mind that thinks or a mind that feels does, for almost everyone, affect the ethical decisions that are arrived at about the possessor of that mind. From the ethical spaghetti of our moral consciences, these two attributes stand out as worthy of moral consideration.

Suffering and Morality

Now, for a moment, I want to put the reasoning criterion, the Cartesian one, to one side. I want to examine the Bentham criterion that it is the capacity to suffer that matters ethically, not the ability to reason. I want to pursue this argument and see where it gets us. And what I shall argue is that, despite what we may initially think, giving ethical value to the ability to suffer will in the end lead us to value animals that are clever. Even if we start out by rejecting Descartes's reasoning criterion, it is the reasoning animals that are the ones most likely to possess the capacity to suffer.

My justification for this view will come essentially from a consideration of how we might be able to recognize when any animal is suffering at all.

But before I do this, I would like to make two general points, to anticipate possible objections. The first is that in reply to the objection that we can never actually know what another animal experiences emotionally, the answer is that of course we cannot, any more than we can know what other people experience. The point I want to make is not that there are not difficulties in attributing emotional feelings to other people, but rather that these difficulties are only slightly less than those of deciding whether other animals have emotions and feelings. We all of us assume that we can have a fairly good idea about what other people are feeling, despite the fact that those feelings are essentially private. What I shall focus on is the *difference* in the kind of evidence we might have about feelings in other sorts of animal. In other words, I want to avoid the general philosophical problems of 'other minds'. I want to focus instead on whether there really are more problems with some kinds of other minds than with other kinds of other minds.

The second general point I want to make is about the general *un*importance of language in our attribution of emotions to other people. English is full of phrases that pour contempt on words as true indicators of real emotion. 'Mere words' or 'mouthing' are examples of how little credence we give to them. We are far more impressed by what people do than by what they say. 'Actions speak louder than words', 'He put his money where his mouth is', 'Voting with their feet' are all phrases that show that we think that what people do is a better indication of what they are feeling than what they say. This point is perhaps best made by reference to the classic joke letter written by someone to his girlfriend: 'I would cross the widest seas just to hear your voice. I would climb the highest mountain just to look into your eyes. I'll be over on Thursday if it's not raining.'

Words are cheap. What matters is what people do. And the things that impress us about what people do – voting with their feet, or giving up a great deal in order to gain something – are precisely the things that animals can do too. Animals that cannot speak can vote with their feet, express preferences and forgo one thing in order to gain something else, as I shall show later on. Even those philosophers who have put a great deal of emphasis on language as being necessary to thought and reasoning have not said that words are necessary to having feelings. And so we should not be put off trying to study feelings in species which do not have words because words do not seem to be that important anyway.

There are, however, problems in attributing feelings to other organisms, human or non-human, and considerable dificulties in defining exactly what we mean when we say they may be 'suffering'. In the case of human beings, we talk about people 'suffering' from hunger, 'suffering' from a bereavement, 'suffering' from heat, 'suffering' from cold, 'suffering' from overwork, and so on. Clearly, when talking about human beings, we use the word to cover a very wide range of different states – different causes, different emotions, different behaviour. So it is worth asking what they all have in common that enables us to give them this one label of 'suffering' before we try to come up with a definition that might be applied to non-human animals.

About the only thing that they all have in common is that they are all extremely unpleasant. They are all states in which people would rather not be and which they would probably try to get out of if that were possible. It is important to emphasize the *extremely* unpleasant nature of these states because a mild itch which lasted for only a short time might be vaguely unpleasant but could hardly be described as giving rise to 'suffering'. But if someone had an itch that dominated their lives and prevented them from sleeping or doing any work, then we would say that they 'suffered' from the itch. So in asking whether we are justified in attributing the mental state of suffering to animals, we are really asking whether we have any evidence that they experience very unpleasant emotional states strong enough and worrying enough to them to warrant the term 'suffering'.

Evidence for 'Suffering'

There are three sources of evidence we can use to help us decide whether an animal is suffering: its general state of health, its physiology and its behaviour. I shall describe these only very briefly here as I have dealt with them fully elsewhere,[3,4] and I would like to emphasize that they provide only indirect evidence. We obviously cannot expect to have direct evidence of subjective feelings in other organisms, but we can, with care, accumulate indirect evidence in the same sort of way we do for other people.

The first and most obvious sign of suffering in both people and other kinds of animal is appearance and general state of health. If an animal is diseased, injured or emaciated, then this is in itself good evidence that it is suffering. The problem with using physical health (or lack of it) to decide whether an animal is suffering or not is that, of course, it is not the disease or injury itself that constitutes the suffering. It is the accompanying mental state. An animal or person may be injured in the sense of being physically damaged and yet show no apparent signs of pain. Soldiers can be wounded in battle and yet, at the time, report little or no pain. Anaesthetics obviously mitigate pain. Conversely, people complaining of severe and constant pain can sometimes baffle their doctors because they have no sign of tissue damage or abnormality at all. Damage to the body does not always go with the highly unpleasant experience we call 'suffering from pain'.

It would, however, be a mistake to use our ignorance about the precise mechanisms of pain perception to push aside the effect that disease and injury can have on animals. Signs of intense pain in both human and non-human animals are easy to recognize. The Littlewood Committee, a British Government committee which was set up to look at experiments on animals, listed the signs of pain in animals as: squealing, struggling, convulsions, and so on.[5]

If animals show gross disturbances of health or injuries together with any or all of these symptoms, then that is a very powerful first piece of evidence that they are suffering. To give a specific example, the transport of animals such as pigs and cattle from the farm where they have been reared to a slaughterhouse can sometimes result in weight loss and injury so severe that some of the animals die. In such circumstances, the case that the animals suffered during the journey is very difficult to refute. In fact, the main problem with using physical ill-health as a criterion of suffering is not that the animals may be perfectly all right despite being diseased or injured. The main problem with it is that it may be insufficient – animals may look perfectly healthy but still be undergoing intensely unpleasant mental experiences, perhaps because they have been confined for a long time in a small cage or been repeatedly subjected to the sight of a predator. It is this possibility – that not all mental suffering may show itself in gross and obvious disturbances of physical health – that has meant that people have looked for other ways of trying to decide when an animal is suffering.

A second source of evidence we have is from physiology. Even before gross and obvious disturbances of health set in, it may be possible to detect physiological changes such as changes in hormone levels, in the ammonia content of muscles, in heart rate or brain activity. In other words, it may be possible to see a whole set of changes going on beneath the skin, if we have the right physiological techniques to detect them. Now, although this appears to be a very promising source of evidence, there are several problems with using physiology in this way. One is that making the physiological measurements may itself be traumatic for the animal, if only because some kind of measuring instrument has to be attached to the animal. But by far the most serious theoretical objection is that we are still left with a large gap between the physiological measurements we can make and the mental state of 'suffering' that we are trying to infer. We can measure hormones and heart rate until we are blue in the face, but we still will not have got to the nub of the problem, which is whether we are dealing with a mind that experiences what we call suffering.

For this reason, people have turned increasingly to a third sort of evidence, which may be able to answer more convincingly the question we really want answered: Is the animal indeed experiencing intensely unpleasant emotional states? This evidence is its behaviour.

Behaviour has a long history in this context. Charles Darwin entitled his book on animal behaviour *The Expression of the Emotions in Man and Animals*. Many people since have felt that what animals *do* is the key to what they are feeling. There are many different ways in which behaviour has been used in this way, many different kinds of behaviour, that is, which have been thought to give evidence of animal mind. There is not space here to go into all of them and I want therefore to concentrate on just one, because I feel that it is this one which comes closest to giving us firm evidence for such states in animals without speech. In case I give a misleading impression, I would like to emphasize that I am not putting it forward as the only thing we need study about animals. In view of the fallibility of any of the evidence about other minds, we have to look to many different sorts of evidence all taken together, such as the physical health and physiological evidence I have just mentioned.

I have already indicated the fact that, as far as other human beings are concerned, we are particularly impressed by certain things that they do – voting with their feet, forgoing a desirable commodity for a later reward, and so on – showing us in some tangible way how strongly motivated they are to do something. Some of the things that impress us about people can also be done by animals that lack speech. One of the clearest examples of this is given in a study by A. P. Silverman on mice, rats and hamsters, which was a purely serendipitous discovery.[7] The experiment was not done to discover anything about animal minds; it was in fact carried out to look at the toxicity of tobacco smoke. Rats, mice and hamsters were kept in small containers and streams of cigarette smoke were blown at them. The animals then took matters into their own hands: almost all of them learnt to stop the stream of smoke by plugging up the tubes with their own faeces! Over and over again they would push faeces up the tubes and one hamster actually asphyxiated itself because the tubes were, as well as the source of drafty smoke, the only source of oxygen. The animals were clearly expressing what they thought of what was being done to them and words would simply have been superfluous.

While this was an accidental discovery, it is also possible to set up experiments in which one deliberately tries to find out what animals think of what is being done to them. Pigs, for example, can easily learn to operate switches that alter the light levels or heating in their pens.[8] In this way they can tell us what sort of heating and lighting regime they prefer. But this is not really all we are after. As I said earlier, 'suffering' is not just a mildly unpleasant state. We call it suffering only if we have evidence that it is very unpleasant – if, for example, we have evidence that the animal will cross an electric grid, go without food, do almost anything to get to or away from something. So what we need is a method by which animals can not only express a preference, but tell us how strong or weak that preference is.

Asking the Animals

I would like to illustrate this idea of asking an animal how much something matters to it by using a particular example. This is in fact a rather curious example because it involves a negative result. The animals effectively said that something was not particularly important to them, even though well-meaning humans had thought it was.

The example comes from part of a study to investigate the difficult problem of whether hens 'suffer' in battery cages. There are many things about battery cages that have caused people to claim that egg-laying hens suffer in these cages. The birds have very little space to move around in, they are crowded together, they stand on sloping wire floors and they have nowhere to scratch, dustbathe or perch. I chose to look at one particular feature – the lack of anywhere to scratch or dustbathe. Hens kept outside or in large litter pens spend a lot of their time scratching around and I therefore suspected that the lack of litter in battery cages might cause the hens to suffer. Sure enough, when I gave them a choice between a cage with a wire floor and one with litter in which they could scratch, they chose the litter-floored cage.[9,10] In fact they would enter a tiny cage (so small that they could hardly turn round) if this was the only way they could gain access to litter. Even birds which had been reared all their lives in cages and had never before had experience of litter chose the cage with litter on the floor.[11] Although this was suggestive, it was not enough. I had

Figure 11.2 Battery farming. Horrifying to many people, but what do the hens think? (© Poultry World).

to show that not only did the hens have a preference for litter but also that they had a preference which was strong enough to say that they might suffer if kept without it.

Hens were then offered a slightly different choice. This time they had to choose between a wire-floored cage which had food and water and a litter-floored cage without food and water. Their behaviour was monitored over a period of eight hours and the time they spent in the two cages was measured. The result was that they spent a lot of time in the litter cage, with much less time being spent in the wire cage, even though this was the only place they could feed and drink. Then a complication was introduced. The birds had to 'work' to move between the cages. They either had to jump from a corridor or push through a curtain of black plastic. So changing from one cage to another now had a cost. Preliminary results were surprising. The hens still spent the same amount of time in the wire cage with food as previously when there was no difficulty in entering it. But they spent hardly any time in the litter cage. They simply didn't seem prepared to work or pay any cost to get into the litter cage. They were willing to pay a cost to enter the wire cage with food, however. This suggests that they will choose litter when they can obtain it with no cost, but do not think it is worth paying a cost for. This preliminary result is now being followed up, but, together with the unwillingness that hens show to perform an operant response for litter,[12] it casts severe doubt on the idea that litter is really all that important to battery-caged hens and that they suffer without it. Quite contrary to what I had expected, the birds seemed to be saying that litter did not really matter to them. They would choose litter if it was easy to get at but would not really bother if they had to make any effort. This is to be contrasted with their response to food, where they showed very clearly that even if I made them work, they would gain access to it.

But, positive result or negative result, what I want to bring out of this example is the method – the importance of getting the animal to vote with its feet and evaluate how much something is worth to it. I want to suggest that a working definition of 'suffering' is now possible. Animals can be said to suffer if they are kept in conditons that they will work hard to get out of if given the opportunity, or if they are kept in conditions without something that they will work hard to obtain if given the opportunity. 'Working hard' can be defined in some way such as expending energy, going without food, etc. This puts flesh on the earlier definition of suffering as a very unpleasant emotional state, because it says that we can conclude that the animal is suffering only if the animal is both in an unpleasant emotional state and actually does something to get itself out of that state.

Clever Animals are the Ones that Suffer

Following on from this, the animals for which I believe we should have the greatest ethical responsibility are those animals which can show that things matter to them. This neatly marries together the Cartesian view that we should value animals that are clever and Bentham's view that we should value animals that have the capacity to suffer. Suffering by the emotional mind is revealed by animals that have enough of a rational mind to be able to do something about the conditions that make them suffer.

I suggest that because we can best determine whether animals suffer through their ability to evaluate their environments and work out how to get the things they need or get away from the things that are the cause of their suffering, even the Bentham view eventually ends up favouring clever animals at the expense of ones that are less able to show what matters to them.

This may sound as though I am being heartless – discriminating against animals which may suffer but not have the wit or the ability to do anything about it. The reason I do not think I am being heartless is that I suggest that such animals are unlikely to exist.

Consider for a moment the evolutionary significance of the capacity to suffer and feel pain – to undergo, as I have defined it, intensely unpleasant emotional experiences. This capacity did not just arrive in organisms at random. It is not a cross they have to bear with no attendant advantages. One of the trademarks of ethologists is that they stress the effect that natural selection has had on all aspects of animal life. Without being able to say precisely what the survival value of suffering is, it seems that it probably had something to do with the mechanisms of escape, avoidance or anticipation of future dangers. Animals with the capacity to suffer are, I suggest, better able to remove themselves from present danger or learn how not to get into danger in the future. If this is correct, it is also likely that organisms without the capacity to do anything to remove themselves from a source of danger would not evolve the capacity to suffer. There would be no evolutionary point in a tree which was having its branches cut off having the capacity to suffer in silence. The tree cannot throw people off, run away or strike out at its attackers. It is the *doers* that suffer, the active evaluators, those that can work out what steps need to be taken that have, as part of their armoury, the capacity to undergo intensely unpleasant emotional states. This is because un-pleasant emotional states are the signals of body damage and danger. The more an animal is able to do, that is, the more complicated its methods of weighing up the environment, the more developed its warning and alarm systems are likely to be.

The important thing for those of us who work with animals is that we have to put the right questions to them and to give them the opportunity to tell us whether the things that we do to them matter and, which is more important, how much they matter.

I would like to suggest that the best evidence we can hope to obtain about whether we are dealing with a mind that can suffer is whether or not it has the capacity to show that at least something matters to it. And this, as I have argued, is best revealed by the extent to which it is able to evaluate the world and work out how to bring about a change in its world. We will find, even if we give ethical value to organisms that suffer, that we will at the same time be valuing organisms that are clever too.

References

1 Descartes, R. (1970) *Philosophical Letters*, ed. A. Kenny, p. 245. Oxford: Oxford Univ. Press.
2 Bentham, J. (1789) Introduction to *Principles of Morals and Legislation*. London.
3 Dawkins, M. S. (1980) *Animal Suffering: the Science of Animal Welfare*. London: Chapman & Hall.
4 Dawkins, M. S. (1985) The scientific basis for assessing suffering in animals. In P. Singer (ed.), *In Defence of Animals*, pp. 27–40. Oxford: Blackwell.
5 Littlewood, S. (Chairman) (1965) *Report of the Departmental Committee on Experiments on Animals*. Cmnd. 2641. London: HMSO.
6 Darwin, C. (1965) *The Expression of the Emotions in Man and Animals*. Chicago: Univ. Chicago Press.
7 Silverman, A. P. (1978) *Anim. Behav.* 26: 1279.
8 Baldwin, B. A. and Ingram, D. L. (1967) *Physiol. and Behav.* 2: 15.
9 Hughes, B. O. (1976) *Appl. Anim. Ethol.* 2: 155.
10 Dawkins, M. S. (1981) *Br. Poult. Sci.* 22: 255.
11 Dawkins, M. S. (1983) *Br. Poult. Sci.* 24: 177.
12 Dawkins, M. S. and Beardsley, T. (1986) *Appl. Anim. Beh. Sci.* 15:351.

The Evolution of Animal Signals

John Krebs

John Krebs is University Lecturer in Zoology and E. P. Abraham Fellow of Pembroke College, Oxford University. He graduated from Oxford in 1966 and, having stayed on for a DPhil, taught at the University of British Columbia and at the University of North Wales before returning to Oxford in 1975. His research is on various aspects of animal behaviour and ecology, including bird song, learning and memory, and foraging behaviour. In 1984 he was elected a Fellow of the Royal Society.

In this chapter I shall discuss the evolutionary origin and development of animal signals. The starting-point will be the interpretation of signal evolution developed by ethologists such as Konrad Lorenz and Niko Tinbergen in the 1930s, 1940s and 1950s.[1,2] The task that these workers undertook was to try to account for the origin and evolution of the displays and signals used by animals. By displays and signals (I shall use those two terms interchangeably) I mean the movements, postures, body patterns, sounds, scents, electrical impulses, and so on, that are used by animals in communicating with one another. I am not going to define communication at this stage, because I think it will become clear very shortly what is meant by this term with respect to animals.

Signals are Derived from Other Behaviours

Ethologists studying signal evolution worked mainly with birds, mammals and fish, and primarily focused their attention on the communicatory behaviour involved in courtship and in aggressive interactions. An immediately striking feature of many aggressive and courtship signals is that they are bizarre. For example, if you watch a pair of fighting cocks engaged in battle, one may suddenly break off from the physical contest of pecking and chasing to preen or peck at the ground, actions that are as incongruous and out of context as would be a boxer combing his hair or eating a snack in the middle of a championship fight. Nor is this an atypical example: dogs mark their territories by urinating, birds by singing. Birds of some species court their partners by wiping their beaks, others by pointing to the heavens, and others by bobbing up and down as if constipated. Why, the ethologists asked, have such bizarre behaviour

Ethologist Konrad Lorenz with his devoted greylag geese. The birds have been 'imprinted' to follow Lorenz, rather than their natural mother, because of contact with him early in life (photograph by Dimitri Kasterine, courtesy of BBC Hulton Picture Library).

patterns come to be used as signals? Is it just a matter of chance? Could *any* bit of behaviour have equally well been chosen by evolution to become a signal? The answer for ethologists such as Lorenz and Tinbergen was an emphatic 'no': signals are not picked at random from the behavioural repertoire, they are *derived* from particular kinds of precursor. This was the first main point of the ethological interpretation of signal evolution: certain kinds of behaviour patterns are more likely than others to be sequestered during evolution as the raw material for signal evolution. By simply observing closely the detailed form and structure of signal movements it was inferred that the precursors of signals were often activities that directly reflected the animal's internal state at the moment it performed the ancestral display. Often these activities were ones characteristic of what might loosely be called 'motivational stress' or, to use the term favoured by ethologists, 'motivational conflict'. By this is meant that the activities were responses that an animal might show when it is at a moment of indecision or is under some challenge from the immediate environment (the environment in this case usually being another individual). For example, there are the well-documented autonomic responses (that is to say, responses controlled by the 'involuntary' or autonomic nervous system which controls the function of internal organs such as the heart, stomach and bladder) to stress such as increased rate of breathing, sweating and urinating. Similarly, at moments of ambivalence an animal might 'dither', might show incomplete 'intention' movements, or might rapidly alternate between alternative courses of action. These are the kinds of activities that formed the raw material for displays. One can immediately see how this view provides a satisfying account of the bizarre signals that initially seemed so puzzling: the ancestral dog, when confronted with a frightening rival, urinated uncontrollably, and this has taken on the meaning of a signal used in aggressive encounters. The ancestral bird in the same situation breathed rapidly, producing squeaks or croaks through rapid exhalation which have later become the elaborate songs now used by many species in proclaiming ownership of a territory.

Signals are Ritualized

Identifying such assumed precursors was the first half of the ethological analysis of signal evolution. The second half was to try to explain why signals evolved away from their ancestral form once they had originated. From various kinds of evidence, for example by comparison of closely related species, it was concluded that the ancestral signal movements have, during the course of evolution, become *ritualized*. This is a technical term in the ethological literature referring to a syndrome of changes. Ritualized signals are exaggerated, repetitive, stereotyped and of high amplitude when compared with their ancestral precursors. Take bird song as an example: the ancestral grunt or whistle associated with rapid breathing has evolved into a highly stereotyped, complex, repeated musical sound. The same kind of change can be traced for most displays: a simple ancestral preening movement may be enhanced by bright colours on the body, an ancestral dither may have evolved into a dance akin to that of a whirling dervish.

What are the evolutionary selection pressures that cause signals to become ritualized? The answer, according to the view of ethologists, was this. Ritualization has two effects: one is that it ensures that the recipient of the display actually detects it and the other is that it reduces the chance that the recipient will misinterpret the display. In short, ritualization *increases the clarity and reduces the ambiguity* of signals and hence is of selective advantage during evolution.

Behaviour or response	Example of display	
1. Intention movement	Sky pointing in the gannet	
2. Ambivalent behaviour	Oblique threat posture of black headed gull	
3. Protective response	Primate facial expressions	
4. Autonomic response (e.g. sweating, urinating, rapid breathing)	Vocalisations (from rapid breathing). Scent marking	
5. Displacement activities	Preening in duck courtship	
6. Redirected attack	Ground pecking in herring gulls	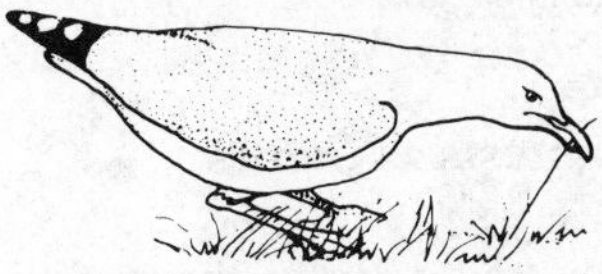

Figure 12.1 Examples of the kinds of behaviour patterns and other responses from which displays in birds, fish and primates are thought to have evolved (from data in Hinde, 1970, Animal Behavior *2nd edn McGraw-Hill, redrawn in Krebs and Davies,* Introduction to Behavioural Ecology, *Blackwell Scientific, 1984).*

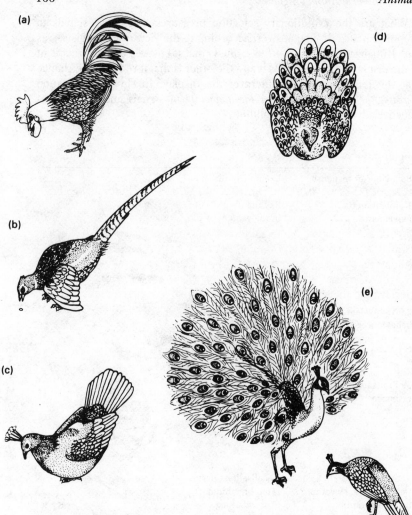

Figure 12.2   *The ground-pecking behaviour of phasianid birds illustrates the origin and ritualization of a display. (a) The least ritualized form is shown in the male domestic fowl. It scratches the ground with its feet and pecks at small stones (perhaps originally a displacement activity). This attracts the female. (b)The male ring-necked pheasant attracts females by means of a similar display. (c) The impeyan pheasant and (d) the peacock pheasant both emphasize the pecking display with rhythmic bobbing of the tail/or head. (e) The peacock shows little of the ancestral movement. The male spreads his enormous tail and points his beak towards the ground (observations of Cullen, 1972, redrawn in Krebs and Davies,* Introduction to Behavioural Ecology, *Blackwell Scientific, 1984).*

Contests as Games

Now this view of the evolutionary cause of ritualization remained the established interpretation from the time it was spelled out in the early 1950s until the mid-1970s. But then a new, closer look at the processes involved in the evolution of behaviour led to a rather different point of view. One novel approach came from the work of John Maynard Smith, who was concerned not with communication as such but with analysing contests or fights between animals.[3] He had the clever idea of thinking about contests as games in which each combatant attempts to maximize its pay-off. One advantage of this metaphor is that it focuses attention on a crucial feature of the evolutionary process: when, as is often the case, the interests of two individuals do not coincide, the logic of natural selection suggests that self-interest would prevail at the expense of cooperation. In a contest, for example, each individual might be expected to follow a course of action that would maximize its own chances of winning (or gaining the most benefit) at the expense of the other. Now, as you know, one of the elementary principles of a game in which you are trying to outwit your rival over a series of 'rounds' is that you should not give away your intentions: you are unlikely to win at poker if you tell your rival what cards you have. Instead, it is better to play 'poker-faced'. Applying this line of reasoning to the evolution of ritualized signals, Maynard Smith saw an alternative interpretation for the stereotypy of ritualized signals. Rather than seeing stereotypy as a way of decreasing ambiguity of a signal, Maynard Smith saw it as a way of *increasing* signal ambiguity. By performing the signal in a highly stereotyped way the animal conceals its exact state (for example, the balance between whether to flee or attack): it plays poker-faced.

Manipulation and Arms Races

Another, more general re-evaluation of the evolution of ritualized signals, developed by Richard Dawkins and myself,[4] took a similar tack to Maynard Smith in that we viewed communication from the point of view of benefits to the individual. We saw communication as the means by which one individual, the *actor*, exploits the muscle power of another, the *reactor*. In other words we viewed communication as a form of *manipulation*. The point is dramatically illustrated by thinking about a baby cuckoo in its host's nest. A cuckoo nestling looks nothing like its foster parents' nestlings, and yet it is cared for by the fosters as though it were a genuine offspring. Nor is this without cost to the parents; in fact they are more or less committing genetic suicide: most small birds survive for only one breeding season, so one season lost in rearing a cuckoo is a lifetime's genetic representation thrown away. Why, then, do foster parents continue to feed cuckoos? Surely the selection pressure to discriminate against cuckoos is so enormous that all parents would rapidly become 'rejectors'. Dawkins and I suggested that one way to interpret this apparent paradox is to say that the cuckoo manipulates its foster parents against their own interest. By this we meant that, during evolution, cuckoos have discovered the kind of stimulus that triggers off parental effort in the foster parents. In spite of strong selection against being parasitized, there have to be *some* stimuli that release parental behaviour and cuckoos seem to have found these and used them to their own advantage.

The cuckoo problem was, of course, well known before we discussed it, but we differed from previous writers in suggesting that cuckoo manipulation, far from being an anomaly requiring special attention, is in fact typical of many kinds of communication. Communication, we argued, often involves two roles, which might be called 'manipulator' and 'victim'. Cuckoo-like behaviour may, for example, be typical of interactions between parents and their offspring. As Bob Trivers pointed out some years ago,[5] a parent, being equally related in genetic terms to all its brood of offspring, should value them all equally (at least in the case where they are all the same age) and allocate its care accordingly. Each individual offspring, on the other hand, values its own survival more than that of its siblings (in genetic terms it is more closely related to itself than to its siblings). This is the evolutionary stage on which conflicts of interest between parent and offspring are acted out. The loud, incessant begging of a hungry nestling may be more than simply a sign saying 'I need food'; it may be a manipulative signal that has evolved as a result of selection on the young to garner more food than the parent is selected to give.

Figure 12.3   A cuckoo removing the host's egg before laying her own. (redrawn from the Field Guide to Birds of Britain, *published by Reader's Digest Ltd, London).*

An immediate problem with this point of view is that it suggests that while communication is good for the manipulator role it is bad for those who happen to be playing the reactor role. I use the term role here because, of course, the same individual may switch from one role to another in an instant. Why, in other words, are victims susceptible to manipulation? Could not counter-strategies to being manipulated have evolved over the generations? Further, why are victims manipulable in the first place? Dawkins and I saw the answer to the second question, that of the origin of susceptibility, in the following terms. If you think of how signals might have started, how they first evolved, the likely path is that they evolved because reactors gained a benefit through using giveaway cues to predict the future behaviour of actors. To go back to the game metaphor for a contest, if you were in the position of being able to predict your opponent's next move, you would be at a great advantage. If, for example, you knew that bared teeth were followed on the whole by a bite, you could take appropriate evasive action at the first glimpse of teeth.

Because there *are* statistically identifiable laws of transition from one behaviour to another, this is a feasible scenario. Recall also that, according to the ethological view, the movements that were to become signals were often ones that occurred at moments of indecision; in other words, they were just the kinds of behaviour that would be useful to focus on if one were out to predict future courses of action of an individual. The advantage of anticipating the future reactions of other individuals is a possible selective pressure for the evolution of consciousness: as Nicholas Humphrey has suggested, the capacity for conscious thought allows an individual to 'rehearse' in its mind the possible reactions that would be elicited from others by a particular action.[6]

Given that signal evolution started with reactors anticipating actor behaviour by reading tell-tale cues, how might evolution have proceeded? What kind of change might have occurred in the behaviour of actors to counter the advantage gained by reactors from their ability to anticipate? One possibility, the one that Maynard Smith emphasized, is for actors to play poker-faced: selection might have favoured ways of concealing the tell-tale cues. Another outcome is the one that Dawkins and I proposed: if animal A predicts the behaviour of B and reacts appropriately, the path is open for B to manipulate the reactions of A. This evolutionary sequence could be visualized as follows: one dog detects the incipient attack of another by the glimpse of bared teeth and retreats; this paves the way for dogs to cause rivals to retreat simply by tooth-baring. (I am thinking here of a change over many generations and not implying learning or modification within the lifetime of an individual.) This is not the end of the evolutionary sequence: if actors can get rivals to retreat by tooth-baring and take advantage of it, there will be selection for sales resistance on the part of reactors, for reluctance to retreat from bared teeth. By analogy with human advertising, the counterploy to sales resistance is to increase the sales pitch, to make the signal louder, more repetitive, more conspicuous, in fact to modify it in any way that will overcome the raised threshold of the reactors. You will have noticed that I have now reached the point of explaining how signals become ritualized: they are the outcome of the manipulation–sales resistance arms race I have just described!

To sum up briefly, according to the classical ethological view, ritualization occurred as a product of selection for unambiguous messages, while according to the alternative view, they arise in the way that human advertising signals arise, as a product of the co-evolution of sales resistance and persuasion.

The evolutionary arms race I have just described is, however, not the only possible route for the evolution of signals. A rather different outcome might be expected when the actor and reactor actually share a common interest in signalling and receiving the signal. I have assumed so far that individuals involved in communication do not share an interest in the same outcome. This seems reasonable for signalling associated with competition for food, mates, and so on, as well as for many kinds of communication which at first sight appear cooperative and on closer analysis are not, such as that between parent and offspring. However, suppose for a moment that the communicating individuals to a large

In the wilds, an animal's roar lets everyone know he's there. What man needed was a civilized way to roar. Now he has it: Musk by English Leather.® Earthy. Primitive. Fiercely masculine. Let it provoke your instincts.

And there's a complete line of grooming gear. So you can roar with Musk soap, roar with deodorant, and rrroar with After Shave or Cologne.

Figure 12.4 Manipulation through advertising. The message has to be vivid and exaggerated to overcome our raised sales resistance.

extent share an interest in the same outcome (by this I mean that the same outcome increases the evolutionary fitness of all parties involved). Members of an ant colony, for example, share an interest in rapid and efficient communication about the approach of an enemy, since the future genetic representation of any individual depends crucially on the survival of the colony as a whole. Similarly, established territory-holding neighbours in a population of blackbirds might mutually benefit by 'agreeing' on the location of boundaries and maintaining them by signalling rather than by a daily battle. (It is in fact a common observation that established neighbours in many species hardly take any notice of one another.)

The evolution of this kind of cooperative signal might be expected to proceed along different lines from that of the non-cooperative signals discussed so far. The starting-point is the same: the ancestral reactors gained an advantage by anticipating the behaviour of ancestral actors through responding to giveaway cues. But now imagine what might happen if actors actually benefit from reactor anticipation. Instead of selection for concealment of the tell-tale cues, or selection for exaggeration to overcome sales resistance, there would be selection to make the cues more readily detectable. At the same time, selection on reactors would favour the opposite of sales resistance: heightened sensitivity to the cues. In other words, the co-evolutionary interaction here is between decreased response thresholds on the one hand and increased signal clarity on the other. Now add one more consideration. To make any kind of signal, a noise, a scent, a movement or whatever, has a *cost*. The cost may be the energy involved in generating the signal, or it may be the unwelcome attention of enemies that the signal attracts. (There are well-documented instances of predators that rely primarily or exclusively on detecting the mating and aggressive signals of their prey to find them.) In the sales resistance–manipulation arms race the advantage of overcoming sales resistance is great enough for the actor to incur an appreciable cost of signalling, but in cooperative communication there is no need to incur such a cost because the threshold of response of reactors is selected to diminish and not to increase. In fact, as reactor threshold decreases, selection on actors will be to reduce the cost of signalling by decreasing signal amplitude.

In short, the counterpart to sales resistance and manipulation is an evolutionary trend in which increased sensitivity of reactors goes hand in hand with a decrease in signal amplitude and conspicuousness. There is a clear prediction (not to my knowledge tested as yet) that signals identifiable a priori as cooperative should be less obvious than those categorized as non-cooperative.

One can draw an analogy with human communication by contrasting the persuasion and 'hype' of the proverbial used-car salesman with the subtle gestures, undetected by the rest of the group, used by a couple to agree when it is the moment to leave a dinner party. While this analogy underlines the distinction between cooperative and non-cooperative communication, it is important to remember that my discussion refers to the evolutionary history of signals and not to the moment-to-moment dynamics of communication. While there must be some mapping of the short term on to the long term, it is very likely that the dynamics of communication are much more complex than indicated by my broad evolutionary sketch.

The Animal Mind

Before closing, let me turn briefly to the question of communication and the animal 'mind'. Might the study of communication, as Donald Griffin has suggested, provide a 'window on the animal mind'?[7] Without committing myself as to whether it could, or even to whether the question is worthwhile asking, I will make three brief comments. These comments do not refer to the question of attempts to teach chimpanzees and other primates to use man-made languages such as American Sign Language (see Herbert Terrace's chapter in this book), as my brief is to talk about *natural* communication in animals.

The first point is that many signals have, as I discussed earlier, probably evolved from behaviour patterns or other responses (sweating, blushing) that were a more or less direct read-out of the animal's internal state. It could be said, therefore, that at this basic and probably rather uninteresting level, signals convey to the human observer something about the animal's 'mind'. The second point, perhaps a little more interesting, is that the communication system of some species has been used as a tool to study how animals perceive their environment. An example is Keith Waddington's work on honey bees.[8] As is well known, honeybee workers, in one of the most remarkable feats of communication in the animal kingdom, communicate to their sisters in the hive about the distance, direction and quality of food sources. As Karl von Frisch discovered, these aspects of the food source are encoded in the orientation and speed of the dance performed by a returning forager on the hive surface.[9] What Waddington has done is to take the basic relationship between, say, dance speed and food source quality, and then use the bee's dance as a read-out of how it perceives experimental manipulations of the food source: it is possible in this way to ask whether the bee responds simply to the energy value of the food, to a combination of the energy value and the expenditure required to get it, to the energy and the time required to get it, and so on.

The third point is one that was made recently by the philosopher Daniel Dennett.[10] He has suggested that one can analyse animal communication in terms of intentionality, an analysis which he feels might reveal something about how sophisticated animals are in their use of language and therefore perhaps about how their minds work. He illustrates the idea with the following example. A species of vervet monkey in Africa has two kinds of alarm call, one for snakes and one for eagles,

Figure 12.5   The waggle dance of the honey bee, discovered by Karl von Frisch. The bee runs again and again in a figure-of-eight pattern, waggling her abdomen during the straight central section of the dance. The direction of this waggle-run relative to gravitational vertical inside the hive (20° in this case) tells the other bees the direction (relative to the sun) of a good source of food. The length of the waggle-run indicates the distance of the food (photograph © Margaret LaFarge 1980, fig. 34 of Bonner, 1980, The Evolution of Culture in Animals, *reprinted with permission of Princeton University Press).*

both of which are potential dangers. When a monkey gives the snake call, others in the troop look around on the ground and may climb up into the trees, while in response to the eagle call, troop members look upwards and head for the bushes. So other monkeys respond appropriately to the two calls. Dennet's question is how the caller perceives the response of other monkeys. The simplest causal account of calling is what he refers to as the killjoy, bottom-of-the-barrel account: the monkey has a knee-jerk reflex and gives a call whenever it sees a predator, having no regard for the response of others. This is zero-order intentionality. However, it is observed that monkeys do not always give the call when they see a predator; they only do so if there is also at least one other monkey within earshot. This, for Dennett, suggests a slightly higher level of intentionality than the killjoy level. (One could actually question this, since the stimulus needed to release the 'knee-jerk' type of behaviour could be a *combination* of predator *plus* other monkeys in the neighbourhood.) But things can be taken a stage further. One incident was seen in which two troops of monkeys were having a fight; suddenly a member of the losing troop gave an alarm and members of both sides ran to safety. Actually there was no predator around, but the interruption to the fight gave the losers some respite. If, as the anecdote implies, the monkey giving the call could actually appreciate enough of the consequences of calling to use the call deceptively in this way, it would seem that monkeys are well above the knee-jerk reflex level of signalling. However, it must be said that the anecdote remains just that, and no one has yet tried to apply Dennett's analysis in more detail. Whether this kind of approach will reveal much about the animal mind is still a very open question.

References

I thank Richard Dawkins for many stimulating discussions about communication and Colin Blakemore for helpful comments on the manuscript. My research on communication has been supported by the SERC.

1 Lorenz, K. (1958) The evolution of behavior. *Scientific American*, 199: 67–78.
2 Tinbergen, N. (1952) Derived activities: their causation, biological significance, origin and emancipation during evolution. *Quart. Rev. Biol.* 27: 1–32.
3 Maynard Smith, J. (1976) Evolution and the theory of games. *American Scientist*, 64: 41–5.
4 Krebs, J. R. and Dawkins, R. (1984) Animal signals: mind reading and manipulation. In J. R. Krebs and N. B. Davies (eds), *Behavioural Ecology: An Evolutionary Approach*, pp. 380–402. Oxford: Blackwell Scientific.
5 Trivers, R. L. (1974) Parent–offspring conflict. *Amer. Zool.* 14: 249–65.
6 Humphrey, N. K. (1976) The social function of intellect. In P. P. G. Bateson and R. A. Hinde (eds), *Growing Points in Ethology*, pp. 303–17. Cambridge: Cambridge Univ. Press.
7 Griffin, D. R. (1981) *The Question of Animal Awareness*, 2nd edn. New York: Rockefeller Univ. Press.
8 Waddington, K. D. (1982) Honey bee foraging profitability and round dance correlates. *J. Comp. Physiol.* 148: 297–301.

9 Frisch, K. von (1967) *The Dance Language and Orientation of Bees*. Cambridge, Mass.: Belknap Press.
10 Dennett, D. C. (1983) Intentional systems in cognitive ethology: the 'Panglossian Paradigm' defended. *Brain Behav. Sci.* 6: 343–90.

13

Intelligence: A Comparative Perspective

Euan Macphail

Euan Macphail was born in 1938 in Edinburgh and educated there until 1955. He spent three years as an apprentice to chartered accountants in the City of London before going up to university in 1958. He read Psychology and Philosophy at Balliol College, Oxford, graduating in 1961, and stayed at Balliol as a research student investigating pleasure centres in the pigeon brain, obtaining a DPhil. in 1965. He visited Neal E. Miller's laboratory at Yale as a Nato post-doctoral fellow 1965–6 and, after a further year's post-doctoral research at Oxford, became a lecturer in the University of Sussex in 1967. He moved to York as a senior lecturer in 1976.

My contribution to this book falls into two parts: first, a general account of how I find myself holding what appears to be a distinctly idiosyncratic view of intelligence; and second, a more specific account of a potential contrast between the intellects of non-human animals, involving experiments on fish, rats and pigeons. The first, general, part is best introduced with a brief discussion of the comparative approach to intelligence.

Comparative Studies of Intelligence

One of the major goals of the psychologists investigating intelligence is to be able to answer the question: 'When we solve problem X, what processes are taking place in our minds (or brains)?' It is clear that it will be very difficult to find detailed answers to such a question, and that in turn provides one of the reasons for the use of non-human subjects. It may be that their problem-solving proceeds in a somewhat simpler manner than that of humans; learning theorists have hoped, by analysing the performance of non-humans, to detect what might be regarded as the building-bricks that form the foundations of human intelligence.

The prospect of investigating non-human performance raises in turn the possibility that, just as humans are more intelligent than non-humans, so some non-humans may be more intelligent than others, and not only more intelligent but, perhaps, intelligent in quite different ways. It is the aim of comparative psychologists to discover differences in performance in learning tasks amongst animal groups, and to exploit those contrasts in generating theories about how problem-solving proceeds. Two ways in which contrasts between species might be of theoretical value are as

Ivan P. Pavlov (1849–1936) demonstrates a conditioned dog to students at the Russian Army Medical Academy about 1904 (© Novosti Press Agency).

follows. First, it might be that one group, species A, say, was capable of solving a set of problems which could not be solved by species B. By analysis of the common demands of the set of tasks that differentiated the species, it might be possible to infer the nature of some information-processing device involved in solving one type of problem, a device that was present in species A but not in species B. In this way an important insight into the structure of the intelligence of species A would be gained. A second (related) way in which between-group contrasts might be of theoretical service emerges from consideration of some theoretical analysis, in one species, of a set of phenomena which supposes that the phenomena reflect the operation of a single device. Such an analysis would predict, in general, that in other species either all or none of these phenomena would be obtained. The discovery of a species in which some, but not all, of the phenomena in question were obtained would clearly call the account into question, whereas the discovery of a species in which none of the phenomena was seen would give good support to the analysis.

The discussion of potential advantages of comparative work has so far considered the possibility that some species might possess a device that is absent in other species, that there might be, in other words, qualitative differences amongst animal groups. An alternative possibility, of course, is that there might be quantitative differences amongst groups. In this case, one might expect to obtain the same phenomena, and the same

Figure 13.1   How can the intelligence of an animal be judged? Behavioural psychologists have designed a variety of techniques for training animals, so that their powers of discrimination can be measured. Here a pigeon is watching a circular panel that can be illuminated with lights of various colours. The pigeon must learn to peck the panel when it sees a certain stimulus; when correct the panel peck causes food to be delivered into the tray below (redrawn from Hall, 1983, Behavior, Academic Press, fig. 2.12, 43).

success in problem-solving, in two species, but differences between the species on such measures as the rate at which solutions were arrived at, or the accuracy that could finally be attained. Quantitative differences might be theoretically interesting in validating some proposed index of intelligence such as, for example, brain size.

It was to establish what between-group contrasts had been demonstrated, and with what theoretical implications, that I embarked on a survey of comparative studies of intelligence in vertebrates. Before discussing the results of that survey, one further preliminary issue must be raised. It is hardly necessary to point out that the discovery of a difference of performance between two species on some learning task is not sufficient to show a difference in intellect between the species. Obvious alternative interpretations might appeal to differences in variables associated with motivation, perception or motor control. Indeed, the burden of proof lies with the experimenter to show that a given difference is not due to any such 'contextual variable' and this is because, whereas we know that species do differ in motivation, perception and skill, we do not know that they differ in intellect. It is therefore parsimonious to assume, until evidence accumulates to the contrary, that performance differences are due to contextual variables rather than differences in intellect.

My survey had a somewhat unexpected conclusion.[1] I could find no convincing demonstration of any performance difference between verte-

---

Contextual Variables

Suppose that we decide to use ability to learn a maze for food reward as a measure of intelligence, and compare learning of a maze by, say, rats and dogs. Suppose, further, that the rats make fewer errors than the dogs. But now suppose we find that the number of errors made by the rats varies according to the level of hunger of the rats, and that the number of errors made is in fact higher at some levels of deprivation than the number made by the dogs in the original experiment. Since we can hardly hope to 'equate' the levels of hunger in rats and dogs – nobody would suppose that, for example, two hours of food deprivation would produce identical states of hunger in two different species – it is clearly possible that the original performance difference was due to differences in the hunger-inducing effects of deprivation. And, of course, it is not difficult to imagine numerous other factors which might influence performance, but are independent of intellectual capacity. Such factors are known as contextual variables, and it is hardly surprising that in fact performance in laboratory tests of intelligence *does* vary with alterations in such variables. My survey found that it was possible to show that alterations in contextual variables did produce overlap between the performance levels of different species for the great majority of tests used by comparative psychologists. In other words, I have not simply claimed that an established performance difference *might* be due to some (unspecified) contextual variable; I have been able to show that there are indeed conditions in which different species do achieve comparable levels of performance in most of the 'intelligence tests' used.

brate groups (excluding man) in a learning task, where that performance difference could clearly be ascribed to a difference in intellect, rather than to a difference in effects of some contextual variable. Although there are many tasks that have been successfully mastered by, say, chimpanzees and not by goldfish, it appears either that goldfish have not been tested (in which case we simply do not know how they would perform) or that there are good 'contextual' reasons for the failure of goldfish.

My response to the negative outcome of the survey has been to propose that we should adopt the 'null hypothesis',[2] namely that there are in fact no differences – qualitative or quantitative – among the intellects of non-human vertebrates. Before discussing some of the implications of that hypothesis, I should perhaps devote some space to humans, whose intellect is manifestly superior to that of non-humans. What is the source of this superiority?

Humans, unlike non-humans, use language and there can be little doubt that language enters into the solution of most, if not all, the intellectual problems tackled by humans. Even in those cases in which no overt use of language can be detected, it can be argued that previous use has contributed to the development of the skills or processes that are engaged. If we cannot eliminate the influence of language we should, perhaps, ask the question: why do humans alone acquire language? Two clear possibilities exist: humans may acquire language either because they are (quantitatively) more intelligent or because they possess a species-specific language-acquisition device and so differ qualitatively from other vertebrates. I have argued that if humans were simply quantitatively superior then it should be possible to teach language to non-humans, at least at a basic level.[1] My interpretation of the language-learning studies carried out in non-humans is that they have not yet provided convincing demonstrations of true language acquisition.[3] To be sure, chimpanzees can be taught to emit signs when shown particular stimuli – but this is most economically seen as demonstrating instrumental learning, which occurs in all vertebrates. What remains in doubt is whether non-humans can acquire the rules of grammar, and until that is demonstrated I shall be inclined to argue, first, that the various participants in language-learning programmes (primarily apes) have not demonstrated any capacity not already known to be present in other, 'lower', vertebrates; and, second, that the capacities demonstrated are inadequate for true language acquisition. I conclude then that the major difference, perhaps the only difference, between the human and non-human intellect is qualitative and consists in the possession by humans of a language-acquisition device.

I shall close the general part of this paper with a brief consideration of issues related to our understanding of the brain that are raised by the null hypothesis. It is well known that both the anatomical organization and the size of the brain vary extensively amongst vertebrates and it has been widely supposed that much of that variation is due to changes associated with the gradual evolution of intelligence.

The early comparative neuroanatomists assumed that the 'higher' centres given over to various senses were relatively independent and that, in particular, the forebrain of fishes was dominated by olfaction. The

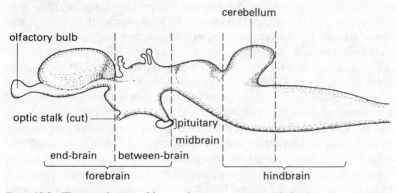

Figure 13.2   The major divisions of the central nervous system in an idealized vertebrate (modified from Romer and Parsons, 1977, The Vertebrate Body, 5th edn, W. B. Saunders fig. 401C, 520, reprinted by permission of CBS College Publishing).

Some Elementary Neuroanatomy

The basic organization of the central nervous system (CNS) is similar in all vertebrates, including humans. Early in its embryonic develop-ment, the CNS is a hollow tube. As development proceeds, a number of characteristic swellings appear at the anterior end of this tube, and these swellings constitute the brain. The posterior end of the tube goes on to form the other part of the CNS, the spinal cord. The brain is conventionally divided into three major regions which are, moving in the anterior–posterior direction, the forebrain, the midbrain and the hindbrain. The forebrain is in turn divided into two regions, the endbrain and the between-brain. The endbrain in mammals is dominated by the neocortex, a relatively thin six-layered surface structure, which envelops the entire forebrain in adults. The principal structure of the between-brain is the thalamus, and the dorsal, or uppermost, part of the thalamus is the region from which information from sensory systems (with the exception of smell) is relayed to specific neocortical sites; olfactory information is transmitted directly from the olfactory bulb to the endbrain.

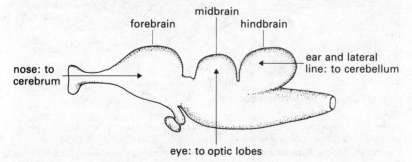

Figure 13.3   A summary of the traditional view of the relationship of the three major sensory systems in fish to the three major subdivisions of the brain (redrawn from Romer and Parsons, 1977, fig. 402, 520).

major centres for vision and hearing were located in the mid- and hindbrain, and the dorsal thalamus, which in mammals forms a major 'relay station' for the transmission of non-olfactory sensory input to the neocortical regions of the forebrain, was small and little developed in fish. This organization would result in difficulty in integration of information from different senses and in the control of behaviour by local, relatively specific, reflexes, with little opportunity, therefore, for the development of a centralized general faculty of intelligence. But neuroanatomical and electrophysiological work over recent decades has shown quite clearly, first, that the fish forebrain is not dominated by olfaction – the pattern of olfactory innervation of fish forebrain in fact shows close parallels to that seen in mammals – and, second, that information from other senses is indeed relayed via the dorsal thalamus to anterior forebrain regions in fish. It is still true that little is known about these non-olfactory projections in fish; but in reptiles and birds, which have been more extensively investigated, there is now very good evidence for marked similarities with mammalian sensory organization. There is, then, good reason to suppose that there exists, in non-mammals as in mammals,

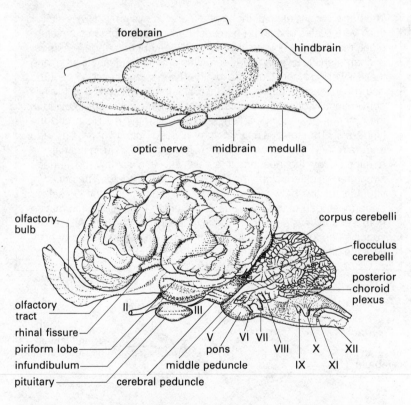

Figure 13.4   Views of the left side of the brain of a rat (above) and a horse (below). Note the absence of folding of the surface of the cerebral cortex in the rat (redrawn from Kalat, 1984, Biological Psychology, 2nd edn, Wadsworth fig. 4.3, 84, and from Romer and Parsons, 1977, fig. 406 B, 523).

adequate opportunity for integration within the forebrain of information from a range of sensory modalities.

A second and rather striking feature of brain organization is the neocortical folding, the rich pattern of gyri and sulci, so obvious in the external appearance of the human brain and much reduced or even absent in animals widely supposed less intelligent, such as cats or rats. It might be supposed that this folding reflects the complexity of neocortical organization associated with a well-developed intelligence. It seems, however, that it is in fact an indirect consequence of increasing brain size. For the thickness of the neocortex varies relatively little with increasing brain size – being about 1 mm in the mouse and 4 mm in the elephant – but the volume of the neocortex varies directly with total brain volume within a given order of mammals. There are differences between orders in relative amount of neocortex, but they are relatively small when compared to differences in neocortical volume related to differences in whole brain volume. Now, given that neocortex shows little variation in thickness, it must, in order to maintain a constant proportion of brain volume as brain size increases, increase its total surface area. This is exactly what happens, with the inevitable consequence that folding occurs. The human brain shows neocortical folding and the rat brain does not, not because humans possess more complex intelligent devices, but because the human brain is bigger than the rat brain. Other mammals with large brains, like horses, with, perhaps, a poor reputation for intellect, also show extensive folding.

The introduction of brain size leads to consideration of the question whether the (supposedly) more intelligent animals, and humans in particular, possess larger brains than less intelligent animals. In fact, the two major determinants of brain size appear to be body weight and class of vertebrate.[4] Mammals and birds of the same body weight have, on average, brains of the same size. Similarly, cold-blooded vertebrates, whether reptile or fish, have brains of comparable size for any given body weight. In general, the brains of warm-blooded vertebrates are approximately ten times larger than those of cold-blooded vertebrates. An interesting exception to this rule is the group of fish known as elasmobranchs (the sharks, skates and rays), whose distribution of brain sizes overlaps the distribution of both the cold-blooded and warm-blooded vertebrates of the same body weight; some sharks, in other words, have brains as large as those of certain mammals of the same weight, other sharks have brains as small as those of some bony fish of the same weight. Within the two major groups – cold- and warm-blooded vertebrates – brain size increases in an orderly way with body size, although increases in brain size do not keep pace with increases in body size, so that small vertebrates tend to possess higher ratios of brain to body weight than large vertebrates. Man does not possess the largest of vertebrate brains – the brains of elephants and whales are larger – although it is true that man possesses a larger brain than any other animal of comparable body weight. There is a case, then, for arguing that man's brain is – relative to body weight – exceptionally large within vertebrates.

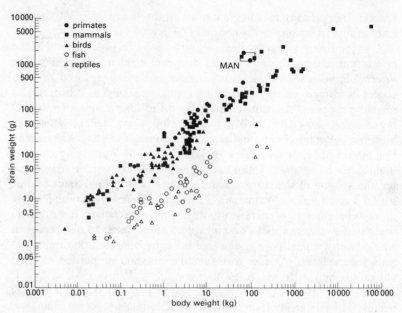

Figure 13.5   The weight of the brain, plotted in grams against the weight of the whole body (in kilograms) for 198 vertebrate species. The rectangle, marked MAN, summarizes results from a sample of human beings: the four points of the rectangle are for two heaviest and the two lightest individuals. Fish and reptiles (shown as white symbols) have smaller brains than birds and mammals of similar body weight, and primates tend to have the heaviest brains of all. Few experts in this field suppose that absolute brain size determines intelligence (the human brain is, after all, smaller than that of the elephant). However, it is widely believed that relative brain size – a measure of brain size that takes into account differences in body weight – might be related to intelligence (redrawn from Jerison, 1969. Brain evolution and dinosaur brains, Am. Nat. 103, and reprinted by permission of the University of Chicago).

Apart from man's position at the top of a ranking of relative brain size, however, the data do not support the view that brain size increased as intelligence evolved, and, more particularly, that brain size increased in the line that led to man. Birds, for example, are no more closely related to man than are living reptiles, yet birds' brains are as large as those of mammals, man's closest relatives. And if (relative) brain size is a major determinant of intelligence, then there should be a marked discontinuity between the intellects of cold-blooded vertebrates and those of warm-blooded vertebrates. But the essence of the case that I am making here is precisely that no such intellectual difference has been demonstrated. It is to that central issue – the failure to detect differences – that this paper will now turn, with a discussion of one specific proposal of a qualitative difference between fish and mammal.

Do Fish Form Expectancies?

The origins of the proposal to be discussed here lay in observations of differences in performance of rats and goldfish following shifts in some pre-established level of reward. One example was found in the reactions of the two species to shifts from high to low reward. Leo Crespi showed that rats trained to run in an alley for a large reward (256 food pellets) showed a rapid reduction in running speeds when they found in the goal box not the large but a small reward (16 pellets).[5] Not only were running speeds reduced, but they in fact fell below those of control rats which had been rewarded with the small reward throughout training. This finding, known variously as the Crespi depression effect or the successive negative contrast effect, posed serious problems for the stimulus–response (S–R) learning theories which were predominant at that time. Such theories held that associative bonds were formed between responses and antecedent stimuli when those responses were followed by reward (a reduction of some drive, such as hunger). The role of rewards was to strengthen or reinforce S–R bonds but not to enter into the association itself: what the animal learned, that is, was simply an association such that a given set of stimuli would elicit a particular response. Such a view found it difficult to explain why running speeds should decline at all upon reduction of reward, much less show a contrast effect. The new reward level, small though it was, should continue to strengthen the previously formed bond, and no plausible mechanism for reduction in strength of the bond was available.

Lowes and Bitterman carried out an experiment using goldfish trained to strike a target (with their noses) for food reward.[6] One group received large reward (40 *Tubifex* worms), and a second group small reward (4 worms), both groups experiencing one trial a day for 22 days. From Day 23 on, both groups received the small reward; a third, control, group

---

Classical and Instrumental Conditioning Procedures

The behavioural techniques used to demonstrate associative learning are conventionally referred to as either classical or instrumental conditioning procedures.

A classical conditioning procedure is one in which the experimenter arranges a contingency between two stimuli, one of which is usually rewarding or punishing. So, for example, a bell may be regularly followed by the presentation of food to a hungry animal, and successful conditioning is demonstrated when the bell obtains salivation in the absence of the food. Notice that in classical conditioning the occurrence of the conditioned response (salivation, in this example) is irrelevant to the delivery of the food.

In an instrumental conditioning procedure, the experimenter arranges a contingency between a *response* and a rewarding or punishing stimulus. So, for example, a hungry rat may obtain food when it depresses a lever, and conditioning is demonstrated when the rate of lever pressing increases above the baseline or spontaneous rate of pressing. In this case, the learned response is *instrumental* in obtaining the reward, and no rewards occur unless the response has occurred.

For the first half of this century, American psychologists concentrated their analyses on experiments using instrumental procedures, while workers in Russia and Eastern Europe concentrated on classical conditioning.

received the large reward throughout. Lowes and Bitterman found that the reduction in reward size had no effect whatever on the response speed of the fish trained with large reward and this despite the fact that, as a result of the pre-shift reward size, they were responding considerably faster than the fish that had received small reward throughout. The fish, in other words, unlike the rats, performed exactly as would be expected according to the 'traditional' S–R theorists.

Why the difference between rats and fish in this task? Any answer to such a question depends, of course, on the theoretical analysis of the phenomenon in question. Bitterman has argued that the difference arises because, although the S–R reinforcement account is sufficient to explain the behaviour of the goldfish, it must be supplemented for rats with the proposition that rats form 'expectancies'.[7] It is the disappointment of expectancies, on this view, which leads to such a sudden and severe disruption of behaviour when reward is reduced.

What, then, are expectancies? It is now generally agreed that in this context expectancies are associations between stimuli, so that the presentation of one stimulus elicits an internal representation of a second stimulus, even in the absence of that stimulus. Formation of such stimulus–stimulus (S–S) bonds is known as classical or Pavlovian conditioning. Bitterman's proposal was, then, that fish are pure S–R animals, incapable of forming S–S bonds.

S–R Behaviourism

Western S–R theories began with Edward L. Thorndike (1874–1949), whose Law of Effect stated that responses that were accompanied or closely followed by satisfaction were connected with the situation in which they occurred. John B. Watson (1878–1958) was influential as a popularizer of S–R behaviourism, although he differed from Thorndike in holding that reward played no role in strengthening S–R bonds: according to Watson, S–R bonds grew in strength simply as a function of repeated contiguous occurrences of the stimulus and the response. Clark L. Hull (1884–1952) made the biggest theoretical impact with his theory, which was a modification of Thorndike's, intended to allow rigorous specification of which events could act as reinforcers of S–R bonds. According to Hull, bodily needs – defined as deviations from the optimum state for the survival of an individual and its offspring – generated drive, and any reduction in drive acted as a reinforcing event.

Two beliefs held in common by the S–R behaviourists are worth noting. The first is that *all* learning consists in the formation of S–R bonds; in other words, all learning is response learning. This belief implies that, whatever the procedural differences between classical and instrumental techniques, all learning is in fact instrumental. The second belief, despite differences on the role of reward in learning, is that rewards were not learnt *about*. In other words, they rejected the common-sense notion that animals behaved in certain ways *in order to* obtain rewards. Modern theorists now accept the common-sense view, and see the critical association in instrumental learning as that between the response and the reward (an R–S association).

Figure 13.6 John B. Watson (1878–1958) (from Bolles, 1979, Learning Theory, *2nd edn, Holt, Rinehart and Winston, 3, 43 and 90, reprinted by permission of CBS College Publishing).*

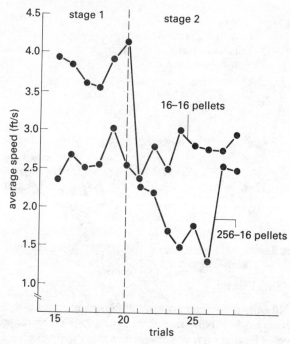

Figure 13.7   This graph shows the speed with which rats ran along a runway during successive trials, to receive food in a goalbox at the far end. During stage 1, one group of rats received 256 food pellets in the goalbox and they ran faster than the other group, which received only 16 pellets. However, during stage 2, when both groups received only 16 pellets, the previously heavily-fed group lost their enthusiasm and their running speeds fell precipitously. Thus the two groups, now being rewarded in exactly the same way, ran at different speeds depending on their past experience (redrawn from Hall, 1983, after Crespi, 1942, fig. 7.9, 237).

Before going on to explore what has become the central issue, namely, whether goldfish can form S–S bonds, I should like to interject some propaganda for animal learning theory. It may sometimes seem as though arguments about the nature of the associations formed by animals performing relatively simple tasks – learning to salivate in response to a bell signalling food, for example – are arid disputes, of interest only to those fascinated by the remarkable theoretical contortions possible on the part of those theorists on either side of any of the many disputes in this area. But the reality, frequently obscured by the language used, is that these arguments have a very real and profound significance for our understanding of the nature of the mental life of animals. If goldfish are pure S–R animals then they possess in effect nothing that we could regard as knowledge. They do not perform actions with any goals in mind, do not envisage consequences of any actions and, indeed, do not make any decisions: their responses are simply elicited by environmental stimuli and their learning amounts only to changing the probabilities with which stimuli will elicit their responses. Fish would, in that case, be blind automata responding in the total absence of any knowledge or understanding of why they were responding. Rats, on the other hand, being capable of classical conditioning, would possess something at least akin to

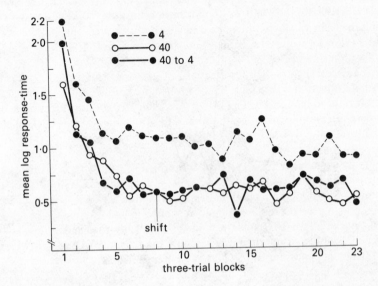

Figure 13.8   Three groups of goldfish were taught to strike a target for a reward of worms. Those rewarded with 40 worms responded more quickly (shorter response-time) than those given 4 worms. However, even when some of the 40-worm goldfish were switched to only 4 worms, at the point marked 'shift', they continued to respond as quickly as before (redrawn from Bitterman, 1975, 'The comparative analysis of learning', Science, 188, fig. 2, 700).

what we might call knowledge: rats would, on seeing a goal box, envisage the reward previously experienced there and approach to the goal box could be seen, at least in part, as a response to that expectancy.

Goldfish do, as a matter of fact, show perfectly good and rapid learning when tested in standard classical conditioning paradigms. The problem is that alternative explanations, other than the obvious explanation that S–S bonds have been formed, are available, explanations that appeal to covert instrumental contingencies. If, for example, a goldfish is exposed to pairings of a light followed by electric shock, the goldfish will rapidly show evidence of learning in that it will move in response to the light. This might be the consequence, of course, of the animal's detecting the association between light and shock, but the analysis is complicated by the fact that movement of the fish may change the intensity of the shock. Shocks are normally delivered to fish through grids placed on either side of a tank, and Woodard and Bitterman have shown that the amount of current transmitted through the fish body varies with the orientation of the fish in the tank.[8] It may be, then, that the conditioned response obtained is one that minimizes the shock and that it emerges because that response in effect is selectively reinforced by a reduction in shock strength. It may be said here in passing that the S–R theory does have great difficulty in accounting for reinforcement by reduction or omission of aversive events since, if events are not expected by the organism, it is hard to see how their non-occurrence can even be detected. The way in which that problem might be overcome by S–R theory forms a set of theoretical contortions with which, fortunately, we need not concern ourselves here; it will be enough to concede simply that the response seen in the light–shock study might be interpreted as an S–R bond reinforced by a reduction in shock magnitude.

Similar problems arise when rewarding events are paired (in a classical paradigm) with neutral stimuli: it could be argued that dogs salivate in response to bells, not because they anticipate (or expect) the food signalled by the bell (an S–S bond) but because the salivation response improves the quality of the reward obtained (by, perhaps, making it easier to swallow), so that the (S–R) bond between the neutral stimulus and salivation is reinforced by the increase in reward magnitude.

How are such S–R interpretations of learning to be ruled out? It is widely agreed that the single most powerful technique available is what is known as 'omission training', and this technique is best illustrated by example. If hungry pigeons are exposed to a procedure in which a keylight is lit for, say, 8 seconds, and is then followed by food reward, the birds rapidly come to peck the lit key. This phenomenon, known as autoshaping, may be interpreted as an instance of S–S learning: the birds learn to expect the food on seeing the light – that is, the light excites a representation of the food. This representation in turn elicits some of the components of the unconditioned response to food, namely, approach and pecking. An alternative account is that, although in fact the food occurs whether or not the birds respond, the response of pecking (which is here supposed initially to occur spontaneously) has been 'adventitiously' reinforced, so that an S–R bond is formed (such adventitious pairings, perhaps, leading to what appears to be 'superstitious' behaviour).

The omission training technique tests the S–R interpretation by introducing the contingency that if the target response (pecking the key in this case) occurs during presentation of the signalling stimulus (lighting of the key), no food is delivered on that trial. Now if a given response is never followed by reward, no S–R bond can be reinforced, according to S–R theory. If pigeons are exposed to such a schedule in the autoshaping paradigm, conditioned key-pecking *is* acquired and persists, despite the fact that every such response prevents the delivery of food. Responding occurs at a lower rate than if the omission contingency is not in force, but this is largely due to the fact that now the overall correlation between the stimulus (lighting of the key) and the food is weakened, there being many trials in which the stimulus occurs but is not (owing to the occurrence of a pecking response) followed by the reward. The persistence of responding by pigeons in such omission training schedules is powerful support for the view that responding is a consequence of the detection by the pigeon of the contingency between the keylight stimulus and food reward – of S–S learning.

The phenomenon of autoshaping is obtained in fish also and Brandon and Bitterman asked whether the introduction of omission training would abolish autoshaped responses in goldfish.[9] They found that, although the rate of response was reduced in omission training, it was nevertheless not abolished: just as in pigeons, autoshaped responding persists in goldfish even if each response prevents food delivery. The most compelling interpretation of this fact is that goldfish, like pigeons, are capable of 'genuine' classical conditioning, that they do form S–S bonds. In fact, Brandon and Bitterman resisted that conclusion and suggested alternative accounts for which they found some rather weak experimental support.

There is no need, fortunately, to go into detail concerning the alternative accounts proposed by Brandon and Bitterman, since Bitterman has himself now conceded that fish are capable of S–S bonds, using a design which provides, he claims, 'what is perhaps the clearest example of S–S association in vertebrates'.[10] The design in question seeks evidence for 'within compound' associations and Bitterman describes one such experiment using goldfish.[11] In Stage 1 of this experiment fish were trained to respond to two stimuli, responses to each of which were rewarded with food. Each stimulus was a compound of a white line which was either horizontal or vertical, on a coloured (red or green) background. So fish might be trained with the horizontal line on the red background, and the vertical line on the green background; other fish would be trained with alternative compounds – but all fish saw each colour consistently associated with one of the line orientations.

In Stage 2 fish were trained to discriminate between two of the stimuli from only one of the dimensions experienced in Stage 1, responses to one stimulus now being rewarded, responses to the other stimulus having no effect. So in Stage 2 fish were trained to discriminate between either horizontal and vertical lines on a black background or between red and green stimuli with no lines present. In Stage 3 the fish learnt a second discrimination, using stimuli from the dimension not used in Stage 2. So a fish trained to discriminate between red and green in Stage 2 would learn, in Stage 3, a discrimination between horizontal and vertical. The positive stimulus in Stage 3 could either be the stimulus which had been paired, in Stage 1, with the positive stimulus for Stage 2, or the stimulus which had been paired, in Stage 1, with the Stage 2 negative stimulus. Now if an association had been formed in Stage 1 between the elements of the compound (a within-compound association), then it should be easier to learn, in Stage 3, a discrimination in which the Stage 3 positive stimulus was the stimulus associated, in Stage 1, with the Stage 2 positive stimulus, than it would be to learn the reverse discrimination. This is precisely the result that Bitterman reports. Given that all stimuli were carefully counterbalanced across groups, differential rates of learning in Stage 3 can be explained only on the assumption that within-compound associations were found in Stage 1.

Goldfish then, like rats, are indeed capable of forming classical associations; they are not pure S–R animals. One question that arises now is why did the Crespi effect fail to appear in goldish? It is not appropriate here to commit much space to a detailed discussion of the Crespi effect, but some indication of the way in which such a discussion might proceed may be given by noting three further facts. First, rats do not invariably show a Crespi effect when shifted from a preferred to a less preferred reward, and there is reason to suppose that one factor in the non-appearance of the effect is the use of rewards (such as different concentrations of sucrose) that appear to produce poorly discriminable memory traces, or after-effects. Second, there is good evidence that the rewards commonly used with goldfish do indeed produce poorly discriminable after-effects. Third, there are now in the literature reports of two successful demonstrations of a Crespi effect in goldfish. In other words, rats sometimes behave like goldfish, goldfish sometimes behave like rats, and there is reason to suppose that a contextual variable, the properties of the reward used, is critical in obtaining the species difference. There are also, it may be added, good theoretical grounds for supposing that the remembered after-effects of reward may in fact be the major, if not the only, causal factor in the Crespi effect.

Can Fish Make Decisions?

I have argued that whereas a pure S–R animal would be a blind automaton, an animal capable of forming S–S associations would possess at least some form of knowledge. But it can be seen that the animal's cognitive capacities, given only the ability to form S–R and S–S bonds, would still be severely restricted. Such an animal's response, whether a consequence of an S–R or of an S–S bond, would simply be elicited by the stimuli perceived: the animal would not *decide* to respond in a particular way; it would, rather, emit responses 'unintentionally', just as a human might salivate at the thought of some tempting food. In recent years learning theorists have reassessed the nature of instrumental learning – response learning – and it is now widely accepted that in rats, at any rate, instrumental learning should be seen as involving the formation of associations between responses and their consequences (food, for example) – as, in other words, involving response–stimulus (R–S) learning. The principal evidence in support of such an account (and in opposition to an S–R account) derives from experiments in which reinforcers are devalued after some response has been learnt (for example by Adams and Dickinson[12]). Suppose, for example, that a hungry rat is trained, in the conventional way, to perform a particular response by rewarding (with food) occurrences of that response. Then, in some other context, the food concerned is devalued by, say, following its consumption by injection of some mild poison, so that that particular food is avoided in subsequent tests. Now return the animal, hungry, to the original task and it is found that response output (in tests in which no food is in fact delivered) is low when compared to control groups (which have experienced the same mild poisoning, but in association with some other food). It can be seen that such a result cannot be accommodated within S–R theory: since the reinforcer does not enter into the association, devaluation of a reinforcer could not affect the strength of a previously formed S–R bond. The correct interpretation of the animal's behaviour would seem to be the common-sense one, that the rat performs the response because it expects a particular reinforcer as a consequence of responding. If the reinforcer is less desirable, then the tendency to respond will decline.

Now if the R–S account of instrumental learning is valid and that account allows that animals may indeed make informed decisions about responding (decisions which would take into account the anticipated consequences of responses), then it becomes of considerable importance that we be certain that fish are indeed capable of instrumental learning. This is more difficult than it might seem, since many instances of what appears to be response learning can be reinterpreted in terms of classical, or S–S, learning. For example, a fish trained to swim from one end of an alley to the other for a food reward may have learnt only the association between the stimuli at the far end of the alley and food: as a result of such an association those stimuli might elicit approach (since this is one of the unconditional responses to food). In other words, the stimuli at the far end would elicit a representation of the food reward, which would in turn elicit approach. To overcome the possibility of such interpretations it is necessary to train responses that cannot be seen as either approach or withdrawal from stimuli associated with reward or punishment. It happens that one of the best examples of such a response is provided by the teleost fish, *Gnathonemus* (an elephant fish, of the mormyrid family). *Gnathonemus* possesses electric organs which discharge spontaneously, and Mandriota, Thompson and Bennett have shown that these fish may be trained to increase the resting rate of organ discharge in the presence of a warning stimulus when increases in rate lead to the avoidance of a punishing reinforcer (electric shock).[13] Control fish, given a series of warning stimuli and shocks which were yoked to those of the 'master' fish in the avoidance condition – but for whom there was no contingency between discharge rate and shock avoidance – showed reliably lower rates of electric organ discharge. Since both groups experienced the same series of stimulus–shock and stimulus–no shock trials, the difference between the groups must be attributed to the detection by the avoidance group fish of the consequence of their response – shock omission. It is important to notice that the singular advantage of the response used in this study is that, since it did not involve movement towards or away from any stimulus, it is reasonable to suppose that 'yoked' fish did indeed receive precisely the same sequence of stimuli (and reinforcers) as their master fish.

Fish, then, are capable of 'genuine' instrumental learning. They can, like rats, detect the consequences of their responses so that it does make sense to suppose that they make decisions about responding and do not simply have responses elicited from them by stimuli. While it was plausible enough to argue some ten years ago that goldfish had impoverished mental lives, the research that has followed up that suggestion has in fact led to a quite different conclusion, one which emphasizes the similarity between their cognitive capacities and those of the species with which they have been contrasted most often, the rat.

Conclusion

I began by making out the case for taking seriously the proposal that there may be no substantive differences in intellectual capacity among non-human vertebrates and by indicating some of the implications of such a null hypothesis. That case was based primarily on the absence of any specific demonstrations of differences in performance that could most plausibly be attributed to differences in intellect. The second part of the paper took one example of a proposed difference in intellect (the absence of expectancies in fish) and argued that the research directed towards that proposal has in the end shown that there is no such difference. The example was selected not only to illustrate the way in which comparative research has proceeded, but to show also the relevance of the proper analysis of apparently simple conditioning tasks to questions of very general and profound significance. Analysis of these tasks leads one to conclude not only that fish and rats possess comparable intellects, but that their common cognitive capacities are such that we may sensibly speak of their being decision-making creatures which form, on the basis of their past experience, expectancies concerning future events, and base their decisions on those expectancies.

References

I am grateful to Peter Bailey and Peter Thompson for their constructive comments on an earlier draft of this chapter, and to the UK Medical Research Council for its support.

In order to avoid cluttering up the text with references, I have made a number of generalizations without citing detailed support. For evidence relevant to claims made in the areas of comparative and physiological psychology, see Macphail,[1] and for claims concerning the nature of classical and instrumental conditioning, see Dickinson[14] or Mackintosh.[15]

1 Macphail, E. M. (1982) *Brain and Intelligence in Vertebrates.* Oxford: Clarendon Press.
2 Macphail, E. M. (1985) Vertebrate intelligence: the null hypothesis. *Philosophical Transactions of the Royal Society of London,* B308: 37–51.
3 Terrace, H. S., this volume.
4 Jerison, H. J. (1973) *Evolution of the Brain and Intelligence.* New York: Academic Press.
5 Crespi, L. P. (1942) Quantitative variation of incentive and performance in the white rat. *Amer. J. Psychol.* 55: 467–517.
6 Lowes, G. and Bitterman, M. E. (1967) Reward and learning in the goldfish. *Science,* 157: 455–7.
7 Bitterman, M. E. (1975) The comparative analysis of learning. *Science,* 188: 699–709.
8 Woodard, W. T. and Bitterman, M. E. (1971) Punishment in the goldfish as a function of electrode orientation. *Behavior Research Methods and Instrumentation,* 3: 193–4.
9 Brandon, S. E. and Bitterman, M. E. (1979) Analysis of autoshaping in goldfish. *Anim. Learn. Behav.* 7: 57–62.
10 Bitterman, M. E. (1984) Learning in man and other animals. In V. Sarris and A. Parducci (eds), *Perspectives in Psychological Experimentation: Towards the Year 2000,* pp. 59–70. Hillsdale, NJ: Erlbaum.
11 Bitterman, M. E. (1984) Migration and learning in fishes. In J. D. McCleave, G. P. Arnold, J. J. Dodson and W. H. Neill (eds), *Mechanisms of Migration in Fishes,* pp. 397–420. New York: Plenum.
12 Adams, C. D. and Dickinson, A. (1981) Instrumental responding following reinforcer devaluation. *Quart. J. Exp. Psychol.* 33B: 109–21.
13 Mandriota, F. J., Thompson, R. L. and Bennett, M. V. L. (1968) Avoidance conditioning of the rate of electric organ discharge in mormyrid fish. *Anim. Behav.* 16: 448–55.
14 Dickinson, A. (1980) *Contemporary Animal Learning Theory.* Cambridge: Cambridge Univ. Press.
15 Mackintosh, N. J. (1983) *Conditioning and Associative Learning.* Oxford: Clarendon Press.

Intelligence – A Reply to Euan Macphail

Jennifer Hornsby

Jennifer Hornsby read Philosophy and Psychology for her first degree and is now a tutorial Fellow in Philosophy at Corpus Christi College, Oxford. She is author of Actions *(Routledge & Kegan Paul, 1980), and her recent published work has been in philosophy of mind and philosophy of language.*

In order that I should remain with the fascinating questions in comparative psychology that Euan Macphail has brought up in the preceding chapter and his book *Brain and Intelligence in Vertebrates*,[1] I shall not attempt a self-contained essay on intelligence: I shall interpret my role as that of commentator.

The Issue

Let me begin by presenting a graphic, if extremely sketchy, view of the central question. Macphail thinks that if we rank the various groups of vertebrates for intelligence, then we get the picture represented by the straight horizontal line in figure 14.1 ('all non-human vertebrates are equally intelligent'). But people in general, I take it, are disposed naively to think that some such picture as that represented by the dotted line would be more accurate. Our question is whether we ought to allow Macphail to persuade us to abandon our naive picture. (In figure 14.1, human beings are left out, because Macphail thinks that they, unlike chimpanzees, *are* more intelligent than fish; humans, then, are not part of the subject matter of the present question.)

It is worth taking note of the style of Macphail's argument for his own picture. Macphail tells us that his 'null hypothesis' ('the hypothesis we should accept in the absence of evidence to the contrary') is that all vertebrates possess identical mechanisms of intelligence. Macphail's claim is that there is in fact no evidence against this null hypothesis; he says that no one has demonstrated that there is a mechanism of intelligence possessed by one vertebrate group and not another. So when he tells us that we ought to abandon our naive picture, this is because he thinks that no experiment has proved his own picture wrong. (In my

Adult chimpanzees show off their intelligence by poking grass stems into a termite nest to catch the tasty insects while a youngster looks on. This drawing by Margaret LaFarge is based on photographs by Jane Goodall, in My Friends the Wild Chimpanzees *(1967) National Geographic Society, Washington, DC, 49, 51, reproduced in Bonner (1980)* The Evolution of Culture in Animals *and reprinted by permission of Princeton University Press.*

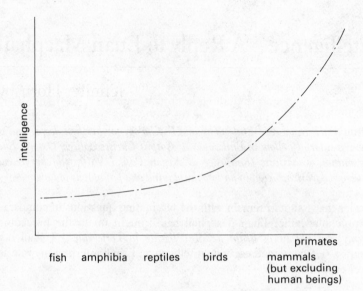

intelligence

fish   amphibia   reptiles   birds   primates
mammals
(but excluding
human beings)

Figure 14.1   Two interpretations of the distribution of intelligence amongst animals of different classes.

Conclusions I shall come to question the dialectical appropriateness of introducing the idea of a null hypothesis where Macphail introduces it.)

Notice that Macphail does not take the null hypothesis to be that *all* animals – vertebrates and invertebrates alike – have identical mechanisms of intelligence. Presumably this is because we can take it for granted that amoeba (say) are less intelligent than chimpanzees: it is only common sense. But if common sense is allowed to impinge in this way upon what the null hypothesis is, then we may wonder why our naive views about vertebrates are not allowed to impinge. At least we should want to ask whether the naive picture has any reasonable grounding in common sense. There is a danger that Macphail, in taking it as 'the null hypothesis' that our naive picture is wrong, may be ignoring all the grounds we have for our picture – whether they are good grounds or bad grounds. So I shall ask whether some of the thoughts we have about animals and about intelligence that give rise to the naive picture rely on a conception of intelligence, or aspects of intelligence, which Macphail's empirical studies do not confront. I shall argue that the conception of intelligence which Macphail employs is a limited one.

I can gesture towards my particular arguments (in the section 'Three Considerations') by mentioning now three particular reasons why Macphail's conception of intelligence seems to me unduly narrow. First, he does not allow for the idea that two mechanisms for intelligence could be of the same sort so far as learning theory is concerned, yet none the less differ significantly in their degree of complexity. Second, he does not allow for the idea of animals who differ from one another in adaptability at the level of the means that they can take towards their ends. Third, he does not allow for any diversity in animals' ends or goals.

Reasons and 'Low-grade Reasons'

I can work towards these points by trying to connect the importance that Macphail sees in the distinction between classical and instrumental conditioning with a phenomenon we find at the human end of things.

The phenomenon I have in mind is that of giving reasons for actions. Each of us, during most of her or his waking life is intentionally doing something. And whenever something is being intentionally done by a person, there is an answer to the question *'Why* is she doing that?'. This answer mentions her thinking (or believing) something or other, and her wanting something or other. 'Why is she crossing the road?' 'She wants some cigarettes, and she thinks that there's a shop on the other side of the road where she can buy some.' 'Why did she say that the train leaves in quarter of an hour?' 'She believes he hasn't noticed the time, and she wants him to hurry.' When human behaviour can be explained in this sort of way, we have instances of rational behaviour. Rational behaviour is surely one form of intelligent behaviour.

How does this relate to animal learning? It seems that where an animal's behaviour is subject to instrumental conditioning, there we want to say that some form of explanation of it in something like the style of reason–explanation is possible. Of course, where the language of conditioning is appropriate, we are unable to give reason–explanations as we know them from the human case; but we still have the idea of an animal's doing something *because* of states that the animal has come to be in. In the case of a fish, I assume it is obvious that we would not want to speak of states of believing and wanting; but we may think nevertheless that fish sometimes behave as they do as a result of an 'informational state' (compare *belief*), and a 'motivational state' (compare *wanting*). The very term 'instrumental' seems to suggest this sort of model. The animal who has been instrumentally conditioned has learnt a means to some end: it is as if it possesses information which in the human case we conceptualize on the pattern of 'If I do such and such, then I shall achieve so and so'; and the animal's having learnt the means corresponds to its being in the informational state that it is in. Its having a biologically definable goal, along with its recent history's leaving some homeostatic mechanism in a certain condition (or whatever), corresponds to its being in a motivational state. My suggestion is that if we take susceptibility to instrumental conditioning to manifest intelligence in an animal (as Macphail does), then that is connected with the fact that we can redescribe what is going on in an instrumentally conditioned animal in the terms of what I shall call low-grade reasons.

This suggestion may appear to assimilate the behaviour of fish too much to human action. So it is worth remarking that the idea of a low-grade reason is one which we could avail ourselves of without recourse to any comparison between non-humans and humans. If animals are to survive and reproduce, they must exist in conditions that are conducive to survival and reproduction – conditions in which they obtain food, avoid predators, meet up with mates, etc. What better way could there be to ensure that such conditions prevail than by having animals in states in which it is more likely that food is obtained, predators avoided, mates met up with? This could be achieved if animals were endowed with a capacity to possess states acquired through interaction with the environment, where these states interacting with motivational states produce responses which make it more likely that goals will be served. When we think of the matter in this sort of way, we can resist any suggestion that we need to attribute to animals such mental states as we take to be distinctively human. Possession of intelligence by an animal and possession of low-grade reasons by an animal can be connected, without our having to assume (for instance) that animals that have been instrumentally conditioned have expectations. The animal makes the response it does in the test situation because it is in a certain informational state and a certain motivational state which make that response appropriate from a biological point of view.[2]

I have introduced the notion of a low-grade reason in order to put into a new perspective the issue I set out at the beginning. What is it in our conception of intelligence that provides for the naive picture? What permits us to think that as one moves along the evolutionary scale of the vertebrates one sees increases in intelligence? Well, if we could find anything as it were intermediate between the minimal low-grade reasons of the merely instrumentally conditionable animal and the full-blown reasons of human beings, then we might gain an idea of how there could be degrees of intelligence midway between that of a fish and of a chimpanzee. (There is no suggestion here that the difference between low-grade reasons and full-blown reasons should be conceived as a matter of degree: only that the contrast between low-grade and full-blown reasons is suggestive if we seek phenomena which furnish differences that can be conceived as a matter of degree.)

Three Considerations

Complexity of Mechanisms

If we think of low-grade reasons as forming systems in animals, then we can expect greater and lesser degrees of complexity in these systems. We might expect that a perceptually highly discriminating animal with a great range of biologically endowed needs and many sorts of movement open to it would have a more complex system of informational and motivational states than a perceptually impoverished animal with few goals and few ways of responding. It seems quite natural to say that the more complexity involved in some of the processes which serve to yield motor responses as a product of interactions with the environment, the more intelligent the animal.

This can perhaps be put in the terms of artificial intelligence. We could think of a program in an animal, or in a computer simulation of an animal, that gets to work on informational and motivational states and yields values for motor responses. In the case of any animal we can ask: 'How complex is the program?' We then seem to have an idea of differing degrees of intelligence. (*Complexity* as applied to computer programs is not a precise or well-defined idea. But firstly, this need not matter if we are only looking for something which is intuitively a matter of degree and which bears on intelligence; and secondly, this is a virtue, if *intelligence* itself is imprecise or ill defined.)

Macphail says that he does not want to apply the word 'intelligent' to processes solely on the grounds that they involve complex information processing.[3] So it is worth pointing out that I do not want to do that either. It is not that the more computationally complex the simulation of just any process in an animal has to be, or that the more computationally complex the simulation of an animal's psychological-states-in-general has to be, the more intelligent the animal is. The idea is rather, firstly, that one portion of a full simulation of what goes on in an animal brain may have to model transitions from perceptions to responses via the having of low-grade reasons; and secondly, that greater complexity in this particular, reason-based portion may contribute to a higher degree of intelligence. Complex perceptual systems, or motivational systems or motor systems in an animal do not in themselves make it more intelligent; but in so far as the potentials of these systems affect the possible inputs and outputs to the relevant sub-program, they are not mere 'contextual variables', which it would be best to try to discount in thinking about an animal's intelligence.[4]

Consider an animal who can grasp an object displaced from it in three-dimensional space even where there is an opaque surface between the animal's eye and the object. We naturally think that this evinces a degree of intelligence that goes beyond what is found in a goldfish. At any rate our naive conception of intelligence allows us to think this. To argue

Figure 14.2 Wolfgang Köhler (1887–1967) studied the cognitive capacity of chimpanzees by giving them problems to solve. Here the chimpanzee Grande *builds a four-storey structure to reach food hanging overhead. Does this kind of complex behaviour prove that apes have insight? (from Köhler's* The Mentality of Apes, *Routledge & Kegan Paul, London, 1925).*

against our naive conception, it is surely not enough to say that for all we know if a goldfish had some analogue of hands, then it could do this too. For given that fish in fact have no parts with which to manipulate objects, we know that fish differ from chimpanzees at least in that they need not contain any program of the complexity of one that actually enables the grasping of hidden objects: they need not, and perhaps they do not. There is an advantage here in talking in computational terms: we can introduce a level of abstraction, the program level, at which we make comparisons, so that we do not have to assume that two sorts of animals have the same perceptual or motor apparatus in order to make comparisons. At the level of abstraction that is appropriate we can raise the question whether a fish's computational resources are of a complexity sufficient to subserve the grasping of objects in space. If the answer were 'No', then *pro tanto* there would be grounds for crediting a fish with less intelligence than a chimpanzee. On Macphail's view, there could be no such grounds.

Means

Animals like us who have language do not merely have reasons for doing things; we can reflect on our reasons. And one of the things that this facilitates is our taking roundabout routes to our ends. For example, if we have some goal, we can do something which is not directly a means to that goal, but which, say, teaches us facts that are likely to make us notice some direct means to our goal. This gives us the idea of an instrumental belief which does not have the simple form 'If I do that, I'll get what I want', but has a more complicated form, say, 'If I do that, I may come to know something, and when I know that I'll be able to do something which will get me what I want.'

As a low-grade analogue of this, we might have the idea of a state of an animal directed towards a sub-goal – not to a biological goal itself, but to being in a condition in which biological goals can be better served. There is no obvious reason why an animal should need a language to be in such a state. But it seems plausible that if an animal had the capacity to possess such states, then *pro tanto* it would be more intelligent than an animal which had no such capacity. It would in a relevant respect be more like us, who are very intelligent.

Observations of rats in mazes are sometimes made in order to see whether they can properly be described as testing hypotheses for solutions to the maze. Such observations could be relevant here. (If the rat does not proceed by random trial and error, then we might want to say that it has a sub-goal of solving the maze, and behaves as it does because it has a reason (low-grade, of course) to find out the solution.) Again, such work as Wolfgang Köhler's on chimpanzees, which was directed at seeing whether animals have insight, seems to be to the point (even if it was misdescribed).[5] At any rate one can imagine evidence for differences between groups of animals in the possibilities of adaptation of their means. Learning theory experiments on the conditioning paradigm will not, I think, give us all the relevant results here.

If learning theory experiments do seem inadequate, perhaps the explanation can be seen by returning again to a comparison with the full-blown reasons of the human being. When we interpret a person's actions, there are three things that may be in question: what the person means to do, what she or he wants, and what she believes. If we find someone's behaviour difficult to understand, then that may be because we did not appreciate which among the things she did she actually meant to do (or whether she meant to do something that she did not in fact do), or because we did not realize what she thought about the situation, or

Figure 14.3   Köhler's chimpanzee Chica *tries a different strategy.*

because we did not know what she wanted. When a psychologist endeavours to condition an animal instrumentally, it is not like this. The psychologist tries to establish a contingency within an animal between a response and a goal; and she can test for the presence of such contingencies only if she predetermines the response and the goal (pellets of food for a rat, oxygenation of water for a fish, or whatever). It is because the goal is bound to be fixed that these experiments are not obviously useful if we want to investigate an animal's capacity for possessing and achieving what I have called sub-goals.

Ends

If an animal's ends or goals have to be independently identifiable and verifiable in the learning theory situation, then the variety of an animal's ends (if there is such variety) is never going to be revealed in learning theory experiments.

What I have to say under the head of *ends* is speculative. But one of the things that makes us, the possessors of full-blown reasons, so very intelligent is that our ends take on a life of their own. The pure mathematician who constructs theories does not construct them because doing so serves some determinate biological goal, or even because she (or he) has some sub-goal *en route* to serving a determinate biological end. Again, when we play tennis and try to win, it is hard to attach any strictly biological or life-preserving or replicating significance to what we do. Our intelligence has a non-instrumental aspect which has come into its own, and all sorts of things happen that cannot be seen as adaptive to independently specifiable ends. In the case of some animals evolutionarily below human beings, it does not seem absurd to think that there is a similar sort of flexibility and biological-underdetermination of ends. If we find ourselves impressed with that idea – as we may be if we watch non-human animals *playing*, for instance – then we cannot disregard it in asking questions about these animals' intelligence.

This sort of consideration may have a place if we are interested in speculating about language, and about how it got on to the scene. Macphail's idea is that there is a language mechanism, and that when that is super-added to one form of intelligence, we get another form, with an attendant qualitative and quantitative leap.[6] I agree with Macphail in thinking that language as we have it makes a quite astounding difference, and that chimpanzees cannot be taught anything like it (see Herbert Terrace's chapter in this book). But perhaps one of the things that makes our naive picture of intelligence initially more attractive than Macphail's is that it does not require us to suppose that language *per se* accounts for the whole of the difference in intelligence between goldfish and ourselves. It does not seem implausible that before a language mechanism could be slotted into an animal, so to speak, the animal would need quite a lot more by way of intellect than a goldfish has. One idea here would be that before an animal could be ready for language, it would need some flexibility of goals.

Conclusions

I have tried to account for the naive picture of animal intelligence by thinking of ways in which animals might differ from one another, and which might properly have some reflection in our view of how (relatively) intelligent those animals are. I have not made any claims about how intelligent or stupid any actual sort of animal actually is, so that I have not tried to show that the naive picture is right. Even if my suggestions are correct, then, they do nothing to overthrow Macphail's picture. But if my suggestions are correct, they would reveal two respects in which his argument could be questioned.

First, we may think that to discover the correct picture of animals' relative intelligence, we should need sometimes to make a different kind of observation from that which Macphail thinks could be used to settle the matter.

Second, we see that it will make a great deal of difference if we refuse to set up the issue in Macphail's way, in terms of a null hypothesis.

Macphail's way of setting up the issue ensures that our naive picture of vertebrate intelligence, not his own picture, is what requires vindication. But why should that be? The term 'null hypothesis' gets its sense in statistical theory: an experimenter who is going to perform a certain sort of significance test on her (or his) data must have it as her strategy to reject the null hypothesis, and accept the alternative hypothesis; if her results prove to be such it is very improbable that they should have been obtained if the null hypothesis were true. But when we evaluate theses about vertebrates' relative intelligence, our position is not that of one about to perform a particular experiment. Our question is 'what is it rational to believe in the light of the evidence (where some of this is experimental, some not)?' Of course, if we want, we can raise the question 'If we had been disposed to believe Macphail's picture, would recent work in comparative psychology force us to abandon our belief?' This in effect is Macphail's question, and he answers it 'No'. But it is different from the question that we must interest ourselves in if our aim is to adjust our beliefs to the evidence. And if the answer to Macphail's question is indeed 'No', then that may be only because we cannot always expect to win the argument if we are confronted with a devil's advocate who forbids us to make a case of our own, and rules that we must first refute his case as it stands.

If Euan Macphail is in the business of persuasion, and wants to dislodge our naive opinions, then I expect he will have less success if he insists that we should start with the assumption that those opinions must derive all their support from experimental evidence than if he presents findings which we should never have been able to predict on the basis of those opinions and encourages us to recognize how impressionistic our grounds are for holding them.

Notes and References

1 Macphail, Euan (1982) *Brain and Intelligence in Vertebrates*. Oxford: Oxford Univ. Press.
2 It may be that some of the psychologists who want to assimilate instrumental conditioning to a simple S–R model want to do so because they think that they will otherwise be lumbered with applying notions like expectancy. I suggest that if we can see instrumental conditioning on the model of low-grade reasons, then we shall neither think of it as purely S–R *nor* suppose that such things as expectations have to be attributed to the animals who show instrumental learning.
3 Macphail, *Brain and Intelligence*, p.4.
4 Notice that where environmental conditions vary, the informational states which make it more likely that biological goals will be served will be states that are responsive to the environment, and in a certain way reflect it. This explains why when we take the notion of a low-grade reason to have application where there is intelligence, the phenomena of *learning* (rather than perception or motor aptitude) can still be given the central place that comparative psychologists attribute to it.
5 Köhler, W. (1925) *The Mentality of Apes*. London: Routledge & Kegan Paul.
6 See Macphail, *Brain and Intelligence*, chapter 8, for a useful review of the work on linguistic capacities in non-human mammals, and chapter 9 for the connections Macphail sees between the hypotheses (a) that a linguistic capacity distinguishes humans from all other vertebrates, and (b) that there are no differences of intelligence between non-human vertebrates.

Part 3
Machines:
Could They Have Minds?

We saw in the previous part that observations on animals sometimes give insight into the nature of the human mind. Now we extend that approach to machines, which crystallize the most important questions about the nature of mind.

However certain we are that people have minds, the only mind that anyone can have direct knowledge of is his or her own. Descartes's famous 'cogito ergo sum' was the apotheosis of his philosophy of doubt. His awareness of the outside world was unreliable and the only thing that he could be certain of was his own existence as a thinking agent. But even other people are part of that untrustworthy outside world. We see and hear them (through our admittedly fallible senses) but can never be sure that they have minds like our own. Only through their actions, their expressions of intention and belief, in short their behaviour, can we guess at their mental lives. To the extent that others act as you would in a given situation, you are inclined to say 'that person must have memories and motivations like mine and make decisions as I do; perhaps he or she also enjoys mental states like mine'.

This classical philosophical problem of 'other minds' thinly disguises a fundamental worry about the nature of mind. Would it be possible to imagine other human beings having the functions of memory, motivation and decision-making, allowing them to get around in the world, but without being conscious or having mental states? And if you could be fooled by such an 'imitation of intention' into thinking that other mindless people are truly conscious, is it self-deceit to believe yourself to have a truly independent agent of intention within you?

If we could demonstrate that thought, consciousness and mental states of all sorts could be produced in a computer, it would surely dispel once and for all the vitalistic notion that mental states are immaterial, spiritual in nature, and uniquely an attribute of human persons. Indeed, computers might be the ideal experimental apparatus with which to work out precisely how mental states are related to the structure and processes in the brain. In principle, it might be possible to model nerve pathways of the brain in the hardware of a computer and to mimic the sequence of operations performed by nerve circuits with the software of the computer program.

Since its inception in the 1950s the new and exciting science of artificial intelligence (AI) has certainly made great strides towards its goal of achieving intelligent performance in computers comparable to that of human beings. There are already programs that can do complex mathematics, that can diagnose blood diseases as well as any doctor, that can play chess at tournament level and that can win the world championship in backgammon.

Indeed in speed, number-power, potential memory capacity and complexity of logical operations, computers already far exceed the capacities of most, if not all, human beings. It's true that when it comes to things like seeing, understanding speech and controlling fine movement, machines are still far from human performance, but most experts in AI believe that it's only a matter of time before those skills too will be done as well by a robot as by a person.

But would a machine that outwardly performs in all respects like a person be conscious and have mental states? And even if it did, how would we be able to tell (any more than we can tell that other humans have minds)?

John Searle recently gave the annual Reith Lectures on BBC Radio (published as Minds, Brains and Science *by BBC Publications) in which he brought this philosophical issue to a wide audience. Here he summarizes his worries about the more extravagant claims of AI. Although he espouses a variant of* identity theory, *arguing that the conscious mind is simply a product and a property of the brain, he derides those who assert that consciousness is incidentally and automatically present in intelligent machines simply* by virtue of the running of a program. *Simulation is not replication.*

Intentions are primary in human life; they are the inspiration and origin of much of what we do. But human intentional states reveal an understanding of the world that man-made machines, Searle argues, cannot have. He draws a distinction between the syntax *of formal symbolic representation in the grammar of a human language or in a computer program and the* semantic *nature of the underlying meaning of human belief and intention. Only minds, he claims,* know *what they are doing.*

One disturbing aspect of Searle's argument is the question of what kind of machines are capable of having minds. After all, the brain indubitably is a physical instrument, and Searle agrees that it has mind as a direct consequences of its physical operations. Then is it only organic machines that can have mind? If so, what is special about machines made out of organic as opposed to inorganic molecules? Also, Searle believes passionately that mental states are of fundamental importance in determining human action; yet he seems to admit that a computer could, in principle, mimic human behaviour completely without the benefit of consciousness.

Richard Gregory, a psychologist who was involved in AI at an early stage, opposes John Searle and particularly argues against the conceptual inertia of the syntax/semantics distinction. He paints a thought-picture of the intelligent machines of the future, not only sharing our world but perceiving it, interpreting it, and getting to understand it as we do.

Philip Johnson-Laird, a psychologist of the new 'cognitive' school, considers specifically what kind of computational architecture could be conscious. He suggests that the brain acts as a parallel hierarchy of finite-state devices that compute asynchronously, with an operating system at the highest level in the hierarchy that has access to a partial model of its own capabilities and that has the recursive machinery to embed models within models. These conditions, he reasons, are necessary for consciousness, but not necessarily sufficient. Consciousness is the property of a class of parallel algorithms (mathematical procedures that can be carried out by a computer), but not of the functions *that they compute, which could always be computed by a serial algorithm. There may be no decisive diagnostic test to reveal whether or not a machine or an organism is conscious.*

Roger Penrose, the mathematical physicist, even questions whether the processes that go on in the brain are necessarily algorithmic and hence capable of replication in a computer. True, brains are part of the natural world and must act according to the laws of physics, but there are well-defined mathematical procedures that are not *algorithmic. Perhaps at the delicate border-line between quantum behaviour and 'classical' behaviour, physical laws themselves are not always algorithmic. The special physics of the quantum–classical borderline may be relevant to certain aspects of conscious behaviour.*

Finally, philosopher Colin McGinn considers the qualitative differences between brains and machines as we currently know them. Knowing how to build a computing machine is not knowing how to build a conscious machine. However, he argues that if consciousness has a physical substrate, it should be possible to build a conscious machine. But even if we are willing to accept that a machine (not just the particular kind of machine that humans brains are) could be conscious, we are still left with two enormous questions: what is consciousness? And what benefit would consciousness bestow on such a machine?

15

Minds and Brains Without Programs

John Searle

John Searle was born in Denver in 1932. He has been Professor of Philosophy at the University of California, Berkeley since 1959. Before that he taught at Oxford where he studied as an undergraduate and graduate student. He is best known for his contribution to linguistic philosophy, in particular his work on the theory of speech acts. He is married with two sons and lives in the foothills of Berkeley with a collection of antique rugs, several cars, much fine wine from the vineyard he helps to run, and a small dog called Russell.

The Gap

The aim of this chapter is to present an interim report on some arguments I have been having with philosophers and people in various other disciplines.[1] I want to begin by placing the issues in a somewhat larger context.

There is a remarkable lacuna in twentieth-century intellectual life. ('Lacuna' is perhaps a euphemism for 'scandal'.) We are quite confident that we can give explanations of human behaviour in ordinary, common-sense terms. So we say such things as, 'That man voted for Ronald Reagan because he thought Reagan would cure inflation.' Such remarks are part of common-sense or grandmother psychology. To give it a fancy name, we could call it 'intentionalistic psychology'. We also suppose that underlying this level of explanation there must be a neurophysiological level of explanation. But we really don't know how to give neurophysiological explanations of ordinary human behaviour. We don't know how to make such claims as, 'The man voted for Reagan because of a condition in his thalamus.' This leaves us in an intellectually embarrassing situation. We are reasonably confident in using grandmother psychology at the higher level and we think there must be a hard science underlying it at the lower level, but we haven't the faintest idea how the lower level works in explaining specific cases of normal human behaviour. We use grandmother psychology all of the time, but we are embarrassed to call it a science. Nobody, for example, has the nerve to go to the National Science Foundation and ask for a grant to do grandmother psychology. Yet we don't know enough about the lower level to make it work. So it seems we have a gap.

$$\frac{\text{intentionalistic psychology}}{\text{neurophysiology}} \leftarrow \text{gap}$$

A Chinese Room (British Library Department of Oriental Manuscripts 15530.c.11).

Some of the great intellectual efforts of the twentieth century have been attempts to get the gap filled – to find something that would be a science of human behaviour, but wasn't common-sense psychology and wasn't neurophysiology either. And if you live long enough, it is interesting to look back and see all the dead carcasses of theories that were supposed to fill the alleged gap. In my lifetime the most spectacular failure was behaviourism. But I also lived through several other failed efforts. There was games theory and there was information theory. I don't suppose anyone reading this is old enough to remember cybernetics, but at one time great claims were made for the future of cybernetics. There was something called 'structuralism', and that was followed by something called 'post-structuralism'. And now there is sociobiology, yet another candidate to fill the gap.

However, the leading candidate right now is called 'cognitive science', and the central research programme in cognitive science is often thought to be artificial intelligence. There are different schools of cognitive science and artificial intelligence, but the most ambitious gap-filling theory is the one that says that work in cognitive psychology and artificial intelligence has now established that the mind is to the brain as the computer program is to the computer hardware. This is a very common equation in the literature: mind/brain = program/hardware. To distinguish this view from more cautious versions of artificial intelligence, I have labelled it 'strong artificial intelligence' ('strong AI' for short). According to strong AI, the appropriately programmed computer with the right inputs and outputs literally has a mind in exactly the same sense that you and I do.

Now this view has something interesting consequences. It has the consequence, for example, that there is nothing essentially biological about the human mind. It so happens that the programs which are constitutive of minds are run in the wetware that we have in our biological machine, our biological computer in the head. But those very same programs could be run on any hardware computer whatever that was capable of sustaining the program. And that has the further consequence that anything whatever, any system whatever, could have thoughts and feelings – and indeed it not only *could have*, but *must have*, thoughts and feelings – in exactly the same sense that we do, provided only that it is running the right program. That is, if you have the right program with the right inputs and the right outputs, then any system running that program, regardless of its chemical structure (whether it is made out of old beer cans or silicon chips or any other substance) *must have* thoughts and feelings in exactly the same way you and I do. And this is because that is all there is to having a mind: having the right program. Now, whenever I attack this view, many people say, 'But surely nobody can believe that.' I'm going to tell you the names of some of the people who believe this, so you won't think I am just attacking a straw man.

Herbert Simon of Carnegie-Mellon University has written on a number of occasions that we already have machines that can literally think, that can think in the same sense that you and I do. Philosophers have been worried for centuries about whether or not you could build a machine that could think, and now we learn that they do it every day at

Carnegie-Mellon. Simon's colleague Alan Newell, in a lecture I heard him give in San Diego at the founding meeting of the Cognitive Science Society, said we have discovered (it is not just some hypothesis we are considering, but we have 'discovered') that intelligence is purely a matter of physical symbol manipulation. So any machine that is capable of manipulating the right symbols in the right way literally has intelligent processes in exactly the same sense that you and I do. Marvin Minsky says that the next generation of computers will be so intelligent that we will be lucky if they keep us around the house as household pets. And Freeman Dyson is quoted in the *New York Times* as having said that since we now know that mental processes, such as consciousness, are purely formal processes, there is an evolutionary advantage to having these formal processes (consciousness, and so on) go on in silicon chips and wires, because that kind of stuff is better able to survive in a universe that is cooling off than organisms like us made out of our messy biological machinery. So the next stage in evolution, on this view, will be made out of wires and silicon. My all-time favourite in this literature (and I recommend the literature to you because it is marvellous) is from John McCarthy, the inventor of the term 'artificial intelligence'. McCarthy has written: 'Machines as simple as thermostats can be said to have beliefs . . .' And indeed, he adds, 'having beliefs seems to be a characteristic of most machines capable of problem solving performance'.[2] So I asked him, 'John, what beliefs does your thermostat have?' I admire his courage. He said, 'My thermostat has three beliefs. My thermostat believes it's too hot in here, it's too cold in here, and it's just right in here.'

Now, I like this thesis for a very simple reason. This equation, mind/brain = program/hardware, is unusual in philosophy because it is a reasonably clear thesis. You can state it with reasonable precision. And unlike most philosophical theses, it is subject to a very simple and, I think, decisive refutation. This is a refutation that I have published elsewhere, but I am going to repeat it briefly because it is not universally accepted in the artificial intelligence community that I have in fact refuted this view. Then I want to go into a deeper issue, and that is this: one of the reasons people believe in strong AI is that they can't see any other way to solve the mind–body problem. I am convinced that one of the sources of the belief that all there is to having a mind is having a computer program is that people can't see any other way of solving the mind–body problem without resorting to dualism. The challenge is often presented to me: 'Well, if you don't accept the artificial intelligence analysis of the mind, then what is your solution to the mind–body problem? Aren't you forced into dualism or mysticism or vitalism or some equally weird view?' So really I have two tasks. I want to refute strong artificial intelligence, and I want to solve the mind–body problem.

The Chinese Room Revisited

The argument against strong AI, I fear, is rather simple. This argument occurred to me when I read Schank and Abelson's book about their story-understanding programs.[3] Some of you will be familiar with this, but I will go over the steps of how their programs work. These very ingenious programs have been designed at Yale University. The programs do what they call 'understanding stories'. The computer is given a very simple story as input. A typical story would be something like the following:

'A man went into a restaurant and ordered a hamburger. When they brought him the hamburger it was burned to a crisp. The man stormed out of the restaurant without paying for the hamburger.'

Then, you ask the computer, 'Did the man eat the hamburger?' And lo and behold, the computer says as output, 'No, the man did not eat the hamburger.' Or you give the computer another story:

'A man went into a restaurant and ordered a hamburger. When he was served the hamburger he was delighted with it, and when he left the restaurant he paid the bill and left a large tip for the waitress.'

If you then ask the computer, 'Did the man eat the hamburger?', the computer says, 'Yes, the man ate the hamburger.' Now notice, in neither story did it say explicitly whether or not the man ate the hamburger. How does it work? It works because the program has in its data base what is called a 'restaurant script'. The restaurant script is a representation of how things normally go on in restaurants. When the computer gets a story, it matches the story against the restaurant script, and then when it gets the question about the story, it matches the question against both the story and the restaurant script. Since it 'knows' how things are supposed to go on in restaurants, it can produce the right answer. The claim that is often made about the programs is that since the machine satisfies the

Figure 15.1   Alan Turing (1912–54) as a young man. He was a pioneer in computer theory whose ideas anticipated the development of artificial intelligence. He conceived of a test (the Turing test) to discover whether a computer has achieved human-level intelligence (photograph Andrew Hodges).

Turing test, the machine must literally understand the story.[4] It must literally understand the story in exactly the same sense that you and I would understand such stories if we were asked such questions and gave good answers.

The Turing Test

The Turing test was designed by Alan Turing to test whether a computer or other system had the same cognitive abilities as humans. As it is usually understood, the test is whether or not an expert would be able to distinguish the machine's performance from that of a human. If not, the machine has the same cognitive abilities as the human. See Roger Penrose's account on p. 261.

It seems to me that there is a very simple refutation of this claim. The refutation is just to imagine that you are the machine. I like to imagine it the following way.

Suppose I am locked in a room. In this room there are two big bushel baskets full of Chinese symbols, together with a rule book in English for matching Chinese symbols from one basket against Chinese symbols from the other basket. The rules say things such as, 'Reach into basket 1 and take out a squiggle-squiggle sign, and go put that over next to the squoggle-squoggle sign that you take from basket 2.' Just to look ahead a moment, this is called a 'computational rule defined over purely formal elements'. Now let us suppose that the people outside the room send in more Chinese symbols together with more rules for shuffling and matching the symbols. But this time they also give me rules for passing back Chinese symbols to them. So, there I am in my Chinese room, shuffling these symbols around; symbols are coming in, and I am passing symbols out according to the rule book. Now, unknown to me, the people who are organizing all of this on the outside of the room call the first basket 'a restaurant script', the second basket 'a story about the restaurant'; the third batch of symbols they call 'questions about the story', and the symbols I give back to them they call 'answers to the questions'. The rule book they call 'the program', themselves they call 'the programmers', and me they call 'the computer'. Now after a while, suppose I get so good at answering these questions in Chinese that my answers are indistinguishable from those of a native Chinese speaker. All the same, there is an important point that needs to be emphasized. I don't understand a word of Chinese, and there is no way that I could come to understand Chinese from instantiating a computer program in the way that I described it. And this is the point of the story: *if I don't understand Chinese in that situation, then neither does any other digital computer solely in virtue of being an appropriately programmed computer, because no digital computer solely in virtue of its being a digital computer has anything that I don't have.* All that a digital computer has, by definition, is the instantiation of a formal computer program. But since I am instantiating the program, since we are supposing we have the right program with the right inputs and outputs, and I don't understand any Chinese, then there is no way any other digital computer *solely in virtue of instantiating the program* could understand Chinese.

Now that is the heart of the argument. But the point of the argument, I think, has been lost in a lot of the subsequent literature developed around this, so I want to emphasize the point of it. The point of the argument is not that somehow or other we have an 'intuition' that I don't understand Chinese, that I find myself *inclined to say* that I don't understand Chinese but, who knows, perhaps I really do. That is not the point. The point of the story is to remind us of a conceptual truth that we knew all along; namely, that there is a distinction between manipulating the syntactical elements of languages and actually understanding the language at a semantic level. What is lost in the AI *simulation of* cognitive behaviour is the distinction between syntax and semantics.

Now the point of the story can be stated more generally. A computer program, by definition, has to be defined purely syntactically. It is defined in terms of certain formal operations performed by the machine.[5] That is what makes the digital computer such a powerful instrument. One and the same hardware system can instantiate an indefinite number of different computer programs, and one and the same program can be run on different hardwares, because the program has to be defined purely formally. But for that reason the formal simulation of language understanding will never by itself be the same as duplication. Why? Because in the case of actually understanding a language, we have something more than a formal or syntactical level. We have a semantics. We do not just shuffle uninterpreted formal symbols, we actually know what they mean.

You can see this by enriching the argument slightly. There I am in the Chinese room shuffling these Chinese symbols. Now suppose that sometimes the programmers give me stories in English and ask me questions, also in English, about these stories. What is the difference between the two cases? Both in the English case and in the Chinese case, I satisfy the Turing test. That is to say, I give answers which are indistinguishable from the answers that would be given by a native speaker. In the case of Chinese, I do that because the programmers are good at designing the program, and in the case of English, I do that because I am a native English speaker. What is the difference, then, if my performance is equivalent in the two cases? It seems to me that the answer to that question is obvious. The difference is that I know English. I know what the words mean. In the case of English, I don't just have a syntax, I have a semantics. I attach a semantic content, or meaning, to each of these words; and therefore I am doing something more than a digital computer can do just in virtue of instantiating a program. I have an interpretation of the words, and not just the formal symbols. Notice that if we try to give the computer an interpretation of the formal symbols, all we can do is give more formal symbols. All we can do is put in more uninterpreted formal symbols. By definition, the program is syntactical, and the syntax by itself is never sufficient for the semantics.[6]

Well, that is my rejection of this equation, mind/brain = program/ hardware. Instantiating the right program is never sufficient for having a mind. There is something more to having a mind than just instantiating a computer program. And the reason is obvious. Minds have mental contents. They have semantic contents as well as just a syntactical level of description.

There is a persistent misunderstanding of my argument which I wish to block immediately. Some people suppose that I am claiming that is is in principle impossible for silicon chips to duplicate the causal powers of the brain. That is not my argument; indeed, it has no connection whatever with my argument. It is a factual question, not to be settled on purely philosophical or a priori grounds, whether or not the causal powers of neurons can be duplicated in some other material, such as silicon chips, vacuum tubes, transistors, beer cans, or some quite unknown chemical substances. The point of my argument is that you cannot duplicate the causal powers of the brain solely in virtue of instantiating a computer program, because the computer program has to be defined purely formally. It is important to emphasize that artificial intelligence, whether strong or otherwise, has nothing whatever to do with the chemical properties of silicon or any other substance. Once the AI partisan concedes that these are even relevant, he has abandoned the thesis of AI. AI is about the 'cognitive' powers of programs. It has nothing whatever to do with the specific chemical properties of hardware realizations of programs.

However, that leaves us with the second question. If we reject the equation and we reject AI as a gap-filler, then what is our analysis of the relationship between the level of intentionality and the level of neurophysiology? Well, the short answer is that the reason the gap-fillers always fail is that there isn't any gap to fill. There isn't any gap between the level of intentionalistic explanations and the level of neurophysiological explanations. But in order to substantiate that, I need, as I promised earlier, to solve the mind–body problem.

Four Puzzles

Before confronting the 'mind–brain problem' head-on I want to step back a minute and ask why this problem has seemed so intractable. Why in philosophy, psychology and neurophysiology, do we still have a mind–body problem? Since Descartes, at least, the general form of the mind–body problem has been the problem of accommodating our common-sense and pre-scientific beliefs about the mind to our general scientific conception of reality. Our scientific conception of the world as a physical system or as a set of interacting physical systems has grown in power and comprehensiveness, and it has seemed increasingly difficult to find any place for mind in this conception. Some of the pre-scientific views that appear to be challenged by the growth of a scientific world-view derive from religion or morality – doctrines such as the immortality of the soul, the freedom of the will, the nature of moral responsibility – and about these issues I will have nothing to say in this discussion. I will be concerned with the narrower, and I believe more pressing, question, how can we square what we know, or seem to know, about the world in general with what we know, or seem to know, about the operation of our own

minds? Quite apart from the speculations of religion and the presupposi-
tions of morality, we know a number of things about our minds, and my
aim is to give a coherent account of the relationships between what we
know about our own minds and what we know about the way the world
works in general. Why then has this narrower, non-religious, non-moral
problem seemed so intractable? Why, to repeat, is there still a mind–brain
or mind-body problem?

The features of our common-sense conception of the mind that seem
hard to assimilate to our general scientific conception of the world are at
least the following four:

Consciousness

I, at the moment of writing this, and you, at the moment of understanding
it, are both conscious. It is just a plain fact about the world that it contains
conscious mental states, but it is hard to see how (mere) physical systems
could have consciousness. How could such a thing occur? How, for
example, could this hunk of grey and white matter inside my skull be
conscious?

Intentionality

Many of my mental states, such as, for example, my beliefs and desires
and my visual perceptions and my intentions, are directed at, or about, or
of objects and states in the world apart from themselves. This feature,
called 'intentionality', is characteristic of human minds. But again, how
could such a thing occur? How could processes in my brain, which after
all consists, in the end, of 'atoms in the void', be *about* anything? How can
atoms in the void *represent* anything? One is inclined to say: things and
processes in the world just are; whether we are thinking of biological
processes such as digestion and sequences of neuron firings or ordinary
physical *things* such as stones and trees, it seems quite impossible that any
of these should be *about* anything. How can *aboutness* be an intrinsic
feature of the world?

Subjectivity

Mental states are characteristically subjective. But it is hard to understand
how the objective physical world, equally open to all competent observers,
should contain anything essentially subjective such as, for example,
conscious mental states. Naively construed, the subjectivity of mental
states is marked by such facts as that I have my states and not yours; mine
are accessible to me in a way they are not accessible to you; I perceive the
world from my point of view, not from your point of view, etc. How can
subjectivity be a real part of the world?

Intentional Causation

Even if there were such things as mental states, it is hard to see how they
could make any real difference in the world. Could anything, so to speak,
as 'gaseous' and 'ethereal' as a conscious mental state have any impact on

a physical object such as a human body? How could mental phenomena ever push objects around or have any other physical significance? Wouldn't mental states, even if they existed, be just epiphenomenal?

Let us call these problems, respectively, the problems of consciousness, intentionality, subjectivity and intentional causation. Though not all mental states have all of these four features, they are none the less real and typical features of mental phenomena. We know, for example, that people are often in a state of consciousness, that, for example, they often have thoughts and feelings which refer to objects and states of affairs outside themselves, that they apprehend the world from a subjective point of view, and that their thoughts and feelings make a difference to their behaviour. I believe any account of the mind–brain problem must, at a minimum, be able to account for all of these facts.

On the view of mental states adopted in this essay, mental states and processes are real biological phenomena in the world; as real as digestion, photosynthesis, lactation or the secretion of bile. The aim of this chapter is not to show in detail how such biological phenomena are related to the neurophysiological processes of the brain – no one knows in detail how they are related – rather its aim is the more modest one of showing how it is even possible that mental states could be biological phenomena in the brain. I believe it is a typical but unstated tacit assumption behind many of the implausible contemporary doctrines concerning the mind – doctrines such as behaviourism or strong artificial intelligence – that it is simply impossible to accommodate a naive common-sense account of the mind with an overall scientific world-view. And I believe that it is the sense of desperation caused by the feeling that no coherent account can be given which accommodates common-sense mentalism with hard science that leads people to say the implausible, and sometimes silly, things they say about the nature of the mind. The view that I am about to expound of the relation of mind and brain is consistent with what is known about brain functioning and also consistent with a general biological approach to biological phenomena. My approach does not, like strong AI, try to treat the mind as something formal or abstract; nor does it, like certain forms of functionalism, try to treat the mind as simply a neutral set of causal powers with no intrinsically mental characteristics. Frankly, I think that the approach I am about to present is pretty much an obvious and common-sense view, and until I got involved in these recent polemics, I had assumed that it was widely accepted, so widely accepted as to hardly be worth a separate statement. Nonetheless, my previous formulations of it have been characterized by my critics as 'mysticism' (Ringle)[7], 'sophistry' (Dennett)[8], 'religious' (Hofstadter)[9], etc. Perhaps, therefore, it is worth spelling out the position in some detail so that anyone can see that these charges are quite unfounded. I need hardly emphasize that I am not the first person to hold this sort of view, and similar biological approaches to the mind–body problem can be found at least as far back as the nineteenth century.

The Brain and its Mind

How does the brain work? In detail, no one knows. I have an amateur's ignorance of the subject, but even the best experts are up to the present time baffled by what one would think are the most fundamental questions. What exactly is the neurophysiology of consciousness? Why do we need sleep? How exactly are memories stored in the brain? Why does alcohol make us drunk? Why does aspirin relieve pain? As recently as 1978, a famous neurophysiologist, David Hubel, wrote: 'There are [areas of the brain] the size of one's fist, of which it can almost be said that we are in the same state of knowledge as we were with regard to the heart before we realized that it pumped blood.'[10] Furthermore, in our ignorance, we grope for metaphor and analogy, usually based on the latest technology. Thus, nowadays, the most fashionable view is that the brain is a digital computer, but in my childhood I was assured that it was a kind of telephone switchboard; Charles Sherrington compared the brain to a telegraph system and to a jacquard loom; Sigmund Freud compared it to hydraulic pumps and electromagnetic systems; Leibniz compared it to a mill and I am told that certain Ancient Greeks thought the brain functioned like a catapult. The very latest view among neurophysiologists is that the brain functions like a Darwinian natural selection system.

However, though there is much to learn, we are not totally ignorant, and in a discussion such as this we need to remind ourselves of a few elementary things about the brain. Like all organs, the brain consists of cells. However, unlike other organs, the brain and the rest of the nervous system consist in large part of very special kinds of cells, neurons. By current estimates there are probably between 50 and 100 billion neurons in the human brain. Neurons come in a bewildering variety of types, but the typical garden-variety neuron consists of a cell body, or soma, with two types of long fibres sticking out of it, a single axon, and a number of dendrites. Neurons come in contact with each other at certain small bumps called synapses. The axons and dendrites don't actually fuse together at synapses but the axon characteristically has on it a little protuberance, the bouton, that abuts on to the dendrite, the tiny gap between them being the synaptic cleft. There are also synapses on the soma. Some neurons in the cerebellum have as many as 200,000 synapses on one cell. One of the basic functions of the neuron is the transmission of electrical impulses, that is, brief, 'all-or-nothing' changes in electrical potential. Each electrical impulse passes from the soma along the axon. However, in most neurons the electrical impulse does not pass directly from one neuron to the next; rather the electrical impulse, upon reaching the bouton, causes the release of small amounts of fluid from little compartments in the bouton, the synaptic vesicles, into the synaptic cleft. The release of these fluids, the neurotransmitters, at the synapses, can have either an excitatory or an inhibitory effect on the next neuron in line. If excitatory, it will tend to cause the next neuron to fire or increase its rate of firing. If inhibitory, it will tend to prevent the neuron from firing or decrease its rate of firing. From a functional point of view, the important thing is not that the neuron fires, because many neurons fire all the time anyway. What is important are the variations in the *rate* of neuron firings; specifically, variations in the rate of axon firing from the sum of excitations and inhibitions in dendrites.

It is important to emphasize this point because several authors have erroneously supposed that the all-or-nothing character of the firing of

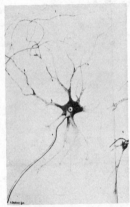

Figure 15.2   A typical garden variety neuron. Otto Deiters drew this picture, remarkably accurate for the time, in 1865. He carefully dissected individual nerve cells from the spinal cord of an animal (probably an ox). The drawing shows the cell body (with its nucleus inside), the long axon (a) and the numerous branching dendrites. Deiters thought that he saw other fine axons (b) sprouting from the dendrites, but these were probably the terminations of the fibres of other neurons ending in synapses on the dendrites.

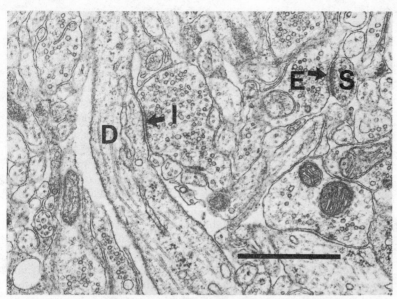

Figure 15.3 Connections between neurons in the cerebral cortex of a rat. This electron micrograph (prepared by Alan Larkman) shows an enormously magnified view of the tangle of axons and dendrites in the cortex. The horizontal bar at the bottom right represents one thousanth of a millimetre. The shape labelled D is one of the dendrites (see fig. 15.2) of a cell in the cortex. It is contacted by the terminal of an axon, marked I, which contains many tiny oval vesicles containing a chemical transmitter substance, which is released into the narrow gap between terminal and dendrite, in the region shown by the arrow, when each nerve impulse arrives at the terminal. The membranes of the terminal and the dendrite are equally thickened in the area of contact, which is thought to be characteristic of an inhibitory *synapse, whose transmitter substance decreases the activity in the next nerve cell. Nearby is a clear view of another synaptic contact between an axon terminal (marked E) and a round knob-shaped process – probably one of the 'spines' which cover the dendrites of many cortical cells. In this case the membrane of the axon is much less thickened than that of the spine in the region of contact (arrow), which indicates that this is an excitatory synapse.*

nerve impulses constitutes evidence that the principles of brain functioning are those of a digital computer.[11] Nothing could be further from the truth. As far as we know, the functional aspect of the neuron is the non-digital variation in the rate of firing.

On the traditional account of the brain, the account that takes the neuron as the fundamental unit of brain functioning, the remarkable thing about the relationship between the brain and the mind is simply this. All of the enormous variety of inputs that the brain receives – the photons that strike the retina, the sound waves that stimulate the sensory cells of the inner ear, the pressure on the skin that activates nerve endings for pressure, heat, cold and pain, etc. – all of these inputs are converted into one common medium: variable rates of neuron firings. Furthermore, and equally remarkable, these variable rates of neuron firing relative to different neuronal circuits and different local conditions in the brain produce all of the variety and heterogeneity of the mental life of the human or animal agent. The smell of a rose, the experience of the blue of the sky, the taste of onions, the thought of a mathematical formula – all of these are produced by variable rates of neuron firing, in different circuits relative to different local conditions in the brain. Now what exactly are these different neuronal circuits and what are the different local environments that account for the differences in our mental life? In detail, no one knows, but we do have good evidence that certain regions of the brain are specialized for certain kinds of experiences. The visual cortex plays a special role in visual experiences, the auditory cortex in auditory experiences, etc. Vision is one of the best understood (or least inadequately understood) functions of the brain and in the case of vision there appear to be quite specialized neurons in the visual cortex capable of responding to specific different features of visual stimuli. Suppose that auditory stimuli were fed to the visual cortex and visual stimuli were fed to the auditory cortex. What would happen? As far as I know, no one has ever done the experiment, but it seems reasonable to suppose that the auditory stimulus would be 'seen', that is, that it would produce visual experiences, and the visual stimulus would be 'heard', that is, it would produce auditory experiences, in both cases because of specific, though largely unknown, features of the visual and auditory cortex respectively. Though this hypothesis is speculative, it has some independent support if you reflect on the fact that a punch in the eye produces a visual flash ('seeing stars') even though it is not an optical stimulus.

In my layman's view the amount of knowledge we now have about the nature and functioning of neurons is quite impressive: however, there is now a lot of evidence that, in order to understand the role of the brain in mental life, we need to understand the functioning of the brain at higher levels than that of individual neurons, and in particular among the various higher levels we need to understand the functioning of systems of neurons organized into neural networks or neural circuits. For many functions of the brain the unit of functioning is not the single cell but the network of cells and, at this level, brain functioning is a matter of interaction between a large set of neural networks. The best anatomical evidence for the existence of more or less independently functioning networks, at least in the cortex, is the existence of neural modules in the form of vertically oriented columns, cylinders or slabs of cells in the cortex.[12] As Gerald Edelman says, 'The greatest achievement in thinking about the cortex, the greatest revolution, is that the cortex is not just a continuous horizontally disposed sheet, but is vertically organized as stacks of slabs or columns.'[13] These modules may vary in the number of neurons they contain, from as few as 50 neurons to as many as 50,000 or even more. On the modular view the real significance of the neuron is in the contribution it makes to the functioning of the module.

I have no idea if the combination of the neuronal account and the modular account or perhaps some other account is the correct account of brain functioning. But one conclusion emerges clearly from even the most cursory investigation of the functioning of the brain: *mental phenomena, whether conscious or unconscious, whether visual or auditory, pains, tickles, itches, thoughts, and all the rest of our mental life, are caused by processes going on in the brain.* Mental phenomena are as much a result of electrochemical processes in the brain as digestion is a result of chemical processes going on in the stomach and the rest of the digestive tract. I think this is an obvious fact about how the world works and yet its full implications are not generally realized by students of artificial intelligence, cognitive science or philosophy. It is also important to emphasize that the relevant causal processes are entirely internal to the brain. Though *in fact* mental events mediate between external stimuli and motor responses, there is no *essential* connection. A man could, for example, have a terrible pain without having either a pain stimulus of the peripheral nerves or any pain behaviour. This simple fact is sufficient to discredit the entire behaviourist tradition in philosophy.

To substantiate this at least a little bit, let us tell a part of the causal story for one type of conscious mental phenomenon: pain. Pain signals are transmitted from sensory nerve endings to the spinal cord by two types of fibres: A delta fibres which are specialized for prickling sensations and C fibres which are specialized for burning and aching sensations. In the spinal cord they pass through the tract of Lissauer and terminate on the neurons of the cord. As the signals go up the spine and enter the brain

Figure 15.4   René Descartes (1596–1650) conceived of the body, including the brain, as a machine, capable of automatic (reflex) reactions to events in the world. This illustration, from the 1662 edition of the Treatise of Man, *shows the way in which the heat of a fire (A) causes disturbance of sensory nerve fibres in the hand (B), and transmission of a message up to the brain, 'just as, pulling on one end of a cord, one simultaneously rings a bell which hangs at the opposite end'. Descartes thought that this tugging would in turn open pores in the walls of the fluid-filled cavities (the ventricles) of the brain, causing 'animal spirit' to flow out through what Descartes believed were hollow tubes in the centres of other nerves connected to the muscles of the body. This liquid was then thought to inflate the muscles and cause various reflex reactions such as withdrawing the injured hand or moving the other arm across to protect it. This description, even if adequate to explain the* behaviour *associated with pain, says nothing about the sensation itself. That was supposed to be caused by simultaneous disturbance of the pineal gland (the oval shape at the back of the head), which acted as the interface between the material body and the spiritual soul.*

they separate into two pathways, the prickling pain pathway and the burning pain pathway. Both pathways pass through a structure called the thalamus but, beyond that level, prickling pain is more clearly localized in the somatic sensory cortex, specifically, somatic area 1, whereas the burning pain pathway transmits signals not only upwards into the cortex but also laterally into the hypothalamus and other basal regions of the brain. In consequence of these differences it is much easier to localize a prickling sensation, whereas burning and aching pains can be more distressing, perhaps because they activate more of the nervous system. The actual sensation of pain appears to be caused both by the stimulation of the basal regions, especially the thalamus and the stimulation of the somatic sensory cortex.

Now for philosophical purposes, it is essential to hammer this point home: sensations of pain are caused by a series of events that begin at free nerve endings and end in the thalamus and other regions of the brain. Indeed, as far as the actual sensations are concerned, the events inside the central nervous system are quite sufficient to cause pains, as we know from both phantom limb pains,[14] and from the pains caused by artificially stimulating relevant portions of the brain. And what is true of pain is true of mental phenomena generally. To put it crudely, and counting the rest of the central nervous system as part of the brain for the purposes of this discussion, everything that matters for our mental life, all our thoughts and feelings are caused by processes inside the brain. As far as the causation of mental states is concerned, the crucial step is the one that goes on inside the head, and not the external stimulus. And the argument for this is simply that if the events outside the brain occurred but caused nothing in the brain, there would be no mental events, whereas if the events in the brain occurred the mental events would occur even if there were not outside stimulus.

I believe these points are obvious, but they are inconsistent with two very common views about the mind. One view treats external causation as the essential form of causation for mental contents. But on the present account the external causal chains are only important to the extent that they actually impact on the central nervous system. Another widely held view is that there cannot be a causal relation between mind and brain states, because mental states just are brain states and the form of the identity relation in question precludes the possibility of any psycho-physical causal relations. For example, many materialist philosophers used to claim that pains just *are* C fibre stimulations, whereas on the present view, C fibre stimulations are not *identical* with pains but are *part of the causes* of (certain kinds of) pain.

But then let us ask the next obvious question: if pains and other mental phenomena are caused by neurophysiological processes, what are the phenomena themselves? Well, in the case of pains, they are obviously very unpleasant sorts of sensations; but that answer leaves us unsatisfied because it doesn't, so to speak, tell us how to locate pains and other mental phenomena relative to the rest of the world we live in. How do pains fit into our overall ontology? Once again, I think the answer to this question is obvious, though it will take some spelling out. To our first claim, namely that pains and other mental phenomena are caused by brain processes, we need to add a second claim: *pains and other mental phenomena are features of the brain.*

One of the primary aims of this discussion is to show how *both* of these propositions can be true together. There are different levels of philosophical puzzlement that such a pair of theses can generate. At one level we can be puzzled as to how mental and physical phenomena can stand in causal relations when one is a feature of the other. Wouldn't it lead to the dreaded doctrine of *causa sui?* That is, wouldn't it imply that the mind caused itself? At bottom most of our puzzlement comes from a misunderstanding of the nature of causation. It is tempting to think that whenever A causes B there must be two discrete events, one identified as the cause, the other identified as the effect; that all causation functions on the model of a bolt of lightning causing a clap of thunder; and if we have this crude model of causation we will be tempted to think that the causal relations between the brain and the mind force us to accept some kind of dualism; that events in one realm, the 'physical', cause events in another realm, the 'mental'. But this seems to me a mistake. And the way to remove the mistake is to get a more sophisticated concept of causation. To do this, let us turn our attention away from mind–brain relations for a while to observe some other sorts of causal relationships in nature.

Macro- and Micro-properties

A common distinction in physics is between micro- and macro-properties of systems. Consider, for example, the desk in front of me, or the creek that flows outside my office window. Each system is composed of micro-particles and the micro-particles have features at the level of molecules and atoms as well as subatomic particles. But each system also has certain properties such as solidity in the case of the table, or liquidity in the case of the creek, which are macro-properties or surface properties, of the physical systems. Some, but not all, macro-properties can be causally explained by the behaviour of elements at the micro-level. For example, the solidity of the table in front of me is (causally) explained by the lattice structure of the molecules of which the table is composed. Similarly, the liquidity of the water is (causally) explained by the behaviour of the H_2O molecule movements. Not all macro-properties have a causal explanation in terms of micro-behaviour. For example, the velocity of the creek is not explained by the movement of the molecules but rather by the angle of the slope, the pull of gravity and the friction provided by the creek bed. But in the case of those macro-features that are causally explained by the behaviour of elements at the micro-level, it seems to me that we have a perfectly ordinary model for explaining the puzzling relationships between the mind and the brain. In the case of liquidity and solidity, we have no difficulty at all in saying that the surface phenomena are *caused by* the behaviour of elements at the micro-level and at the same time that the surface phenomena *just are* (physical) features of the systems in question. My preferred way of stating this point is to say that the surface feature F is *caused by* the behaviour of micro-elements M, and at the same time is *realized in* the system of micro-elements. The relations between F and M are causal but at the same time F is simply a higher-level feature of the very system which consists in elements M.

In objection to this one might say F just is, just is identical with, features of M. So, for example, we might define solidity as the lattice structure of the molecular arrangement. This point seems to me correct but not really an objection to the analysis that I am proposing. It is a characteristic of the progress of science that an expression that is originally defined in terms of surface features of a phenomenon, features accessible to the senses, is subsequently defined in terms of the micro-structure that causes the surface features. Thus, to take the example of solidity, the table in front of me is solid in the ordinary sense that it is rigid, it resists pressure, it supports books, it is not easily penetrable by most other objects such as other tables, etc. Such is the common-sense notion of solidity. Now in a scientific vein one can define solidity as whatever micro-structure causes these gross observable features. One can then say either that solidity just is the lattice structure of the system of molecules and that solidity so defined causes, for example, resistance to touch and pressure; or one can say that solidity consists of such things as rigidity and resistance to touch and pressure and is caused by the behaviour of elements at the micro-level. This shift from causation to definitional identity is very common in the history of science. Consider the following pairs: lightning is caused by an electrical discharge – lightning just is an electrical discharge; the colour red is caused by photon emissions with a wavelength of 600 nanometres – red just is a photon emission of 600 nanometres; heat is caused by molecule movements – heat just is the mean kinetic energy of molecule movements.

If we apply these lessons to the study of the mind it seems to me that there is no difficulty in accounting for the metaphysical relations of the mind to the brain in terms of a causal theory of the brain's functioning to produce mental states. Just as the liquidity of water is caused by the behaviour at the micro-level, and yet at the same time is a feature realized in the system of micro-elements, so in exactly that sense of 'caused by' and 'realized in' are mental phenomena caused by processes going on in the brain at the neuronal or modular level but they are realized in the very system that consists of the neurons organized into modules. And, just as we need the micro–macro distinction for any physical system, for the same reasons we need the macro–micro distinction for the brain. Though we can say of a system of particles that it is solid or liquid, we cannot say of any given particle that this particle is solid, or this particle is liquid. In exactly the same way, as far as we know anything at all about it, though we can say of a particular brain that this brain is conscious or this brain is experiencing thirst or pain, we cannot say of any particular neuron that this neuron is in pain, this neuron is experiencing thirst. To repeat this point, though there are enormous empirical mysteries about how the brain works in detail, there are no logical or philosophical or metaphysical obstacles to accounting for the relation between the mind and the brain in terms that are completely familiar to us from the rest of nature. Nothing is more common in nature than for surface features of a phenomenon to be caused by and realized in a micro-structure, and those are exactly the relations that are exhibited by the relation of mind to brain. The intrinsically *mental* features of the universe are just higher-level *physical* features of brains.

The Possibility of Mental Phenomena

Let us now return to the four problems that seem to face any putative solution to the mind–brain problem.

How is Consciousness Possible?

The best way to show how something is possible is to show how it is actual, and we have already given a sketch of how pains are actually caused by neurophysiological processes going on in the thalamus and the sensory cortex. Why is it then that many people feel dissatisfied with this sort of answer? I think that by pursuing an analogy with an earlier problem in the history of science we can dispel this sense of puzzlement. For a long time many biologists and philosophers thought it impossible, in principle, to account for the phenomena of life on purely biological grounds. They thought that in addition to the biological processes some other element must be necessary, some *élan vital* must be postulated in order to lend life to what was otherwise dead and inert matter. It is hard today to realize how intense the dispute between vitalism and mechanism was even a generation ago, but today these issues are no longer taken seriously. Why not? Is it simply because we synthesized urea (the first organic compound to be synthesized), and this proved that organic compounds could be produced artificially? I think not. I think rather it is because we have come to see the biological character of the processes that are characteristic of living organisms. Once we understand how the features that are characteristic of living beings have a biological explanation, it no longer seems mysterious to us that inert matter should be alive. I think that exactly analogous considerations should apply to our discussions of consciousness. It should seem no more mysterious in principle that this hunk of inert matter, this grey and white oatmeal-textured substance of the brain, should be conscious than it seems to us problematic that this hunk of matter, this collection of nucleic acids, proteins and other molecules stuck on to a calcium frame, should be alive. The way, in short, to dispel the mystery is to understand the processes. We do not yet fully understand the processes, but we understand the *character* of the processes, we understand that there are certain specific electrochemical processes going on in the relations among neurons or neuron-modules and perhaps other features of the brain, and that these processes are causally responsible for the phenomenon of consciousness.

How Can Atoms in the Void Have Intentionality?

As with our first question, the best way to show how something is possible is to show how it is actual. Consider thirst. As far as we know anything about it, at least certain kinds of thirst are caused in the hypothalamus by sequences of neuron firings. These firings are in turn caused by the action of the peptide hormone angiotensin II in the hypothalamus, and angiotensin II, in turn, is synthesized by renin, which is secreted by the kidneys. Thirst, at least of these kinds, is caused by a series of events in the central nervous system, principally the hypothalamus, and is realized in the hypothalamus. Notice that thirst is an intentional state. To be thirsty is to have, among other things, the desire to drink. Thirst has propositional content, direction of fit, conditions of satisfaction, and all the rest of the features that are common to intentional states.

As with the 'mysteries' of life and consciousness, the way to master the mystery of intentionality is to describe in as much detail as we can how the phenomena are caused by biological processes while at the same time they are realized in biological systems. Visual and auditory experiences, tactile sensations, hunger, thirst, sexual desire and olfactory experiences are all caused by brain processes and realized in the structure of the brain, and all are intentional phenomena. I am not saying we should lose our sense of the mysteries of nature; on the contrary, the examples I have cited are all in a sense astounding. But I am saying that they are neither more nor less mysterious than other astounding features of the world such as the existence of gravitational attraction, the process of photosynthesis or the size of the Milky Way.

Subjectivity

The puzzle about subjectivity can be stated quite simply. Since the seventeenth century our conception of reality has involved the notion of total objectivity. Reality, on this view, is that which is accessible to any competent observer. Indeed, in some versions, reality is that which is objectively measurable. Now the question is: how do we accommodate the subjectivity of mental states within this picture; how do we square the fact that each of us has real subjective mental states with an objectivist conception of the real world? The solution to this puzzle can be stated equally simply. It is a mistake to suppose that the definition of reality should exclude subjectivity. If science is the name of the set of objective and systematic truths we can state about the world, then the existence of subjectivity is just an objective scientific fact like any other. If a scientific account of the world attempts to describe how things are, then one of the features of the account will be the subjectivity of mental states, since it is just a plain fact about biological evolution that it has produced certain sorts of biological systems, namely human and certain animal brains, that have subjective features. My present state of consciousness is a feature of my brain and in consequence is accessible to me in a way that it is not accessible to you, and your present state of consciousness is a feature of your brain and is accessible to you in a way that it is not accessible to me. Thus the existence of subjectivity is an objective physical fact of biology. It is a persistent mistake to try to define 'science' in terms of certain features of existing scientific theories. But once this provincialism is perceived to be the unscientific prejudice it is, then any domain of facts is a subject of scientific investigation. If, for example, God existed, then that fact would be a fact of science like any other. I do not know whether God exists, but I have no doubt at all that subjective mental states exist, because I am now in one and so are you. If the fact of subjectivity runs counter to a certain definition of 'science', then it is the definition and not the fact which we will have to abandon.

Intentional Causation

The problem of intentional causation for our present purpose is the problem of how to give an account of the mental that avoids epiphenomenalism. How, for example, could anything as gaseous and ethereal as a thought give rise to an action? The answer is that thoughts are not gaseous and ethereal. Their logical and intentional properties are solidly grounded in their causal properties in the brain. Because mental states are physical states of the brain, they can cause behaviour by ordinary causal processes. They have both a higher and a lower level of description, and each level is causally real.

Once again, we can use an analogy from physics to illustrate these relationships. Consider hammering a nail with a hammer. Both hammer and nail must have a certain kind of solidity. Hammers made of cotton or butter will be quite useless, and hammers made of water or steam are not hammers at all. Solidity is a real causal property of the hammer and not something epiphenomenal. But the solidity itself is caused by the behaviour of particles at the micro-level and is realized in the system of micro-elements. The existence of two causally real levels of description in the brain, one a macro-level of mental neurophysiological processes and the other a micro-level of neuronal physiological processes, is exactly analogous to the existence of two causally real levels of description of the hammer. Consciousness, for example, is a real causal property of the brain and not something epiphenomenal. My conscious attempt to perform an action such as raising my arm causes the movement of the arm. At the higher level of description, the intention to raise my arm has the movement of my arm as its condition of satisfaction and it causes the movement of the arm. At the lower level of description, a series of neuron firings which originate in the cortex causes the release of the transmitter substance acetylcholine at the 'end plates' where the axon terminals of motor neurons connect to the muscle fibres; this in turn causes a series of chemical changes that result in the contraction of the muscle. As with the case of hammering a nail, the same sequence of events has two levels of description, both of which are causally real and where the higher-level causal features are both caused by and realized in the structure of the lower-level elements.

Traditional Categories

I have so far resisted using the traditional vocabulary of dualism, monism, physicalism, etc. in attempting to characterize the view argued for in this chapter. However, it may be useful to see how these views relate to the traditional categories. In a discussion of these matters at the Philosophy of Mind conference at New York University, Hilary Putnam from Harvard characterized the view put forward here as (1) property dualism; (2) emergentism; (3) supervenience. I think it will deepen our understanding of the issues if we consider each of these assessments in turn.

Property Dualism

If 'property dualism' is simply the view that the world contains some physical features which are mental – my present state of consciousness, for example – and some physical features which are non-mental – the weight of my brain, for example – then my view can correctly be described as property dualism. Nonetheless, I believe that there is something deeply misleading about this characterization. 'Property dualism' seems to imply that there are two and only two types of properties in the world, physical and mental, and that is emphatically not the view that I hold. On my view, mental properties just are higher-level physical features of certain physical systems in the same sense that solidity and liquidity are higher-level physical features of certain physical systems. Thus mental properties are physical properties in the sense that liquidity and solidity are physical properties. This view, it seems to me, is correctly described not so much as property dualism, but as *property polyism*. That is, there are lots of different kinds of higher-level properties of systems, and mental properties are among them. To put this point another way, on my view the words 'mental' and 'physical' are not properly opposed to each other, because mental properties, naively construed, are just one class of physical properties, and physical properties are correctly opposed not to mental properties but to such other features as logical properties and ethical properties, for example.

Emergentism

Similar considerations apply to the question whether or not we should think of mental properties as in some way emergent. It all depends on what you mean by 'emergent'. If we are to think of any higher-level feature of a system such as solidity, liquidity, etc. as emergent, then in that sense I believe states of consciousness, intentionality, subjectivity, etc. are indeed emergent properties of certain biological systems. In fact, if we define emergent properties of a system of elements as properties which can be explained by the behaviour of the individual elements but which are not properties of elements construed individually, then it is a trivial consequence of my view that mental properties are emergent properties of neurophysiological systems. However, traditionally, emergentism is often regarded as implying something mysterious; it is taken as implying that there is some mysterious non-physical process that produces a peculiar kind of property. Emergentism, in short, tends to go with the more mysterious aspects of dualism, and in that sense I am denying that my view can correctly be characterized as emergentism. If emergentism is taken to imply that there is something mysterious, something lying outside the scope of physical or biological sciences as they are normally construed, in the existence of emergent properties, then it seems to me clear that mental properties are not emergent in that sense.

Supervenience

The doctrine of the supervenience of the mental on the physical is the doctrine that there can be no mental differences without corresponding physical differences: if a system is in two different mental states at two different times, then it must have different physical properties at those two times. This view is a consequence of the thesis that mental phenomena are caused by and realized in the brain, for if the effects are different the causes must be different. Indeed, it seems to me a merit of the view advanced here that the supervenience of the mental is simply a special case of the general principle of the supervenience of macro-properties on micro-properties. There is nothing special or arbitrary or mysterious about the supervenience of the mental on the physical; it is simply one more instance of the supervenience of higher-order physical properties on lower-order physical properties. If a bowl of water is ice at one time and liquid later, then there must be a difference in the behaviour of the micro-particles to account for this difference. Similarly, if I want a drink of water at one time and later do not want a drink of water, there must be a difference in my brain to account for this difference in my mental states.

Consequences for the Philosophy of Mind

Some mental concepts, such as, for example, *having a pain* or *believing* that so and so, denote entities that exist entirely in the mind. Others such as *seeing* or *knowing* also refer to mental phenomena but they require that additional conditions be met in order that the concept be applicable. So, for example, to say that X knows that P implies more than that X believes that P; it implies, among other things that P is true, and the truth of P cannot, in general, be solely a matter of what goes on in the mind of X. To say that X sees that P implies that X has a visual experience of a certain sort, but it also implies that it is the case that P. Let us call such concepts whose truth conditions depend only on what goes on in the mind 'pure mental concepts' and let us call such mental concepts as those whose truth conditions require extra-mental phenomena 'hybrid mental concepts'. Now since hybrid mental concepts all contain by definition a mental component, to the extent that we are discussing the nature of the mind, we can carve off that mental component and examine it separately. For every hybrid mental concept there is a corresponding pure mental concept which captures the purely mental component of the hybrid concept. As far as the mind proper is concerned, we can confine our discussion entirely to pure mental concepts and the pure mental states which are the denotations of pure mental concepts. Whenever a mental phenomenon is present in the mind of an agent – for example, he is feeling a pain, thinking about philosophy or wishing he had a cold beer – causally sufficient conditions for that phenomenon are entirely in the brain. And indeed the thesis that mental phenomena are caused by and realized in the brain has the consequence that, for any mental phenomenon whatever, causally sufficient conditions are in the brain. Let us call this principle *the principle of neurophysiological sufficiency*. Now if this principle is true, then many current theories in the philosophy of mind will turn out to be false, because they are inconsistent with this principle. For example, several philosophers following Wittgenstein and Heidegger have tried to explain the intentionality of mental phenomena in terms of social relationships. But how are we to take this explanation? If we take it as claiming that social relationships are necessary for, or constitutive of, mental life, then we know that it must be false, because social relationships are relevant to the causal production of intentionality only in so far as they impact on the brains of human agents; and the actual mental states, beliefs, desires, hopes, fears and the rest of it have causally sufficient conditions that are entirely internal to the nervous system. This is not to deny that social relations are crucial for the production of many forms of intentionality such as, for example, language. Children can learn

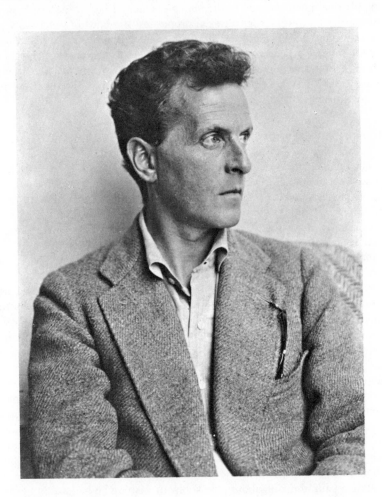

Figure 15.5 Ludwig Wittgenstein (1889–1951).

a language and use it only if they are exposed to other people who also use language. But the thesis that there are forms of intentionality that require a social base needs to be interpreted so that it is consistent with the claim that intentionality is a purely internal product of internal physiological processes. These views are not necessarily inconsistent; they can be interpreted as just ways of describing different aspects of the same phenomenon. The mistake is to suppose that the social relations can somehow or other replace or substitute for what goes on in the brain.

An even more prominent implicit denial of the principle of neurophysiological sufficiency is the entire tradition that has been built around Wittgenstein's claim that 'an inner process stands in need of an outward criterion'.[15] So, for example, Norman Malcolm has tried to give a non-internal account of dreaming,[16] Elizabeth Anscombe has tried to explain intentions in terms of outward behaviour,[17] and Anthony Kenny has tried to explain many emotions in terms of their social setting and behavioural consequences.[18] But it is hard to interpret any of these analyses in ways that are consistent with the principle of neurophysiological sufficiency. Whatever other features dreams have, they are caused by neurophysiological processes. And the same goes for intentions and emotions such as fear and anger. Now perhaps we might interpret the views of Kenny, Malcolm and Anscombe as simply describing constraints on our having a *vocabulary* for discussing mental phenomena. And perhaps we might interpret Wittgenstein's claim as the claim that a *vocabulary* for inner processes stands in need of outward criteria. But if we take these claims as claims about the *nature* of the mental phenomena themselves – that one can't have a dream or have an intention or be angry except when certain external conditions are satisfied, conditions external to the brain, that is – then we know these theses must be false because of the principle of neurophysiological sufficiency. What goes on in the head must be causally sufficient for any mental state whatever.

And, of course, this Wittgensteinian tradition is itself part of a larger tradition of seeking behaviouralistic or quasi-behaviouralistic analyses of mental concepts. And once again, we know from the principle of neurophysiological sufficiency that these efforts are doomed to failure. We cannot define mental phenomena in terms of their behavioural manifestations, because we know that it is always possible to have the phenomena independently of having any behavioural manifestations.

Some Conclusions

The main polemical aims of this chapter regarding the relations of minds and programs can be swiftly summarized. In order that there be total clarity, I will state a set of 'axioms' and derive the relevant conclusions.

Axiom 1. Brains cause minds

This is simply a very crude statement of the empirical fact that the relevant causal processes in the brain are sufficient to produce any mental phenomenon. It is important to re-emphasize that, where pure mental phenomena are concerned, there is no essential connection between these internal causal processes that are sufficient for mental phenomena and the causal input–output relations of the whole system. In principle, we could have all of our mental life without any of the appropriate stimuli or any of the normal external behaviour.

Axiom 2. Syntax is not sufficient for semantics

This is a conceptual or logical truth that articulates the distinction between the level of formal symbols and the level of meaning.

Axiom 3. Minds have contents; specifically, they have intentional or semantic contents

Axiom 4. Programs are defined purely formally, or syntactically

Now from these obvious points we can derive some controversial conclusions.

Conclusion 1. Instantiating a program by itself is never sufficient for having a mind (by Axioms 2, 3 and 4)

This conclusion by itself is sufficient to refute Strong Artificial Intelligence.

Conclusion 2. The way the brain functions to cause minds cannot be solely by instantiating a program (Axiom 1 and Conclusion 1)

Conclusion 3. Any artefact that had a mind would have to have causal powers (at least) equivalent to those of the brain (by Axiom 1, trivially)

Conclusion 4. For any artefact that had a mind, the program by itself would not be sufficient for having a mind. The artefact would have to have causal powers equivalent to the brain (by Conclusions 1 and 3)

Anyone who wishes to challenge the central theses owes us a precise specification of which 'axioms' and which derivations are being challenged.

Notes and References

1   This chapter is based on a lecture delivered in Oxford at a time when I was in Britain for the purpose of taping the 1984 Reith Lectures for the BBC, and it was not originally intended for separate publication. There is considerable overlap of the material in the Reith Lectures and the material in this lecture. The lectures have since been published as *Minds, Brains and Science* (BBC Publications, 1984; Harvard Univ. Press, 1984). I apologize to the listeners and readers of the Reith Lectures for the repetition. I am publishing this article separately, in part because Colin Blakemore and Susan Greenfield have convinced me that it might make a useful contribution to the volume, in spite of the repetition of material published elsewhere, and in part because it gives me the opportunity to expand and explain further several of the points that were made in the Reith Lectures.

2   McCarthy, John (1979) Ascribing mental qualities to machines. Stanford Artificial Intelligence Laboratory Memo AIM-326, p. 2. *Computer Science Department Report*, no. STAN-CS-79-725, March 1979.

3   Schank, R. C. and Abelson, R. P. (1977) *Scripts, Plans, Goals and Understanding*. Hillsdale, NJ: Erlbaum.

4   I do not mean to imply that either Schank or Abelson makes this claim.

5   'Language understanding' programs characteristically have a 'syntax', a 'semantics', and in some cases even a 'pragmatics'. This is, of course, quite irrelevant to the present point, since all three levels are computational, i.e. 'syntactical' in the sense in which I am now using the word.

6   Some truly desperate people in AI have proposed that it is not *I* who

understand but the *whole room*; i.e. the system containing me, the program, the bushel baskets, the window to the outside, etc. But this reply is subject to exactly the same objection. Just as I do not have any way of getting from syntax to semantics, neither does the whole system. The whole system has no way of knowing what any of these formal symbols actually *mean*.

7 Ringle, Martin (1980) Mysticism as a philosophy of artificial intelligence. Commentary on Searle's 'Minds, brains, and programs'. *The Behavioral and Brain Sciences,* 3: 444.

8 Dennett, Daniel (1980) The milk of human intentionality. Commentary on Searle's 'Minds, brains, and programs'. *The Behavioral and Brain Sciences,* 3: 428.

9 Hofstadter, Douglas R. (1980) Reductionism and religion. Commentary on Searle's 'Minds, brains, and programs'. *The Behavioral and Brain Sciences,* 3: 433.

10 Hubel, D. (1978) Vision and the brain. *Bulletin of the American Academy of Arts and Sciences,* April 1978, 31, no. 7: 18.

11 Oppenheim, Paul and Putnam, Hilary (1958) Unity of science as a working hypothesis. In Feigl, Scriven and Maxwell (eds), *Minnesota Studies in the Philosophy of Science,* vol. 2, Concepts, Theories, and the Mind–Body Problem, p. 19. Minneapolis: Univ. of Minnesota Press.

12 See Szentagothai's chapter in the book.

13 Edelman, Gerald (1982) Through a computer darkly: group selection and higher brain function. *Bulletin of the American Academy of Arts and Sciences,* October 1982, 36, no. 1: 28.

14 Phantom limb pains are pains suffered by amputees which feel as if they were coming from the, now non-existent, limb.

15 Wittgenstein, Ludwig (1973) *Philosophical Investigations,* tr. G. E. M. Anscombe. New York: Macmillan.

16 Malcolm, Norman (1959) *Dreaming.* London: Routledge & Kegan Paul.

17 Anscombe, G. E. M. (1963) *Intention.* Ithaca, NY: Cornell Univ. Press.

18 Kenny, Anthony (1963) *Action, Emotion and Will.* London: Routledge & Kegan Paul.

In Defence of Artificial Intelligence – A Reply to John Searle

Richard Gregory

Following service in the RAF in the Second World War, Richard Gregory read Moral Sciences at Cambridge (Philosophy, and Experimental Psychology under Sir Frederic Bartlett). After two years' research with the Medical Research Council at Portsmouth, he received a University Lectureship at Cambridge and a Fellowship at Corpus Christi College.

Gregory started and ran the Special Senses Laboratory in the Department of Experimental Psychology at Cambridge. He worked on a variety of projects on visual and perceptual problems, and invented several optical instruments.

Gregory has been a Visiting Professor at three American universities: MIT, UCLA and NYU. In 1967 he become Professor of Bionics at Edinburgh. Feeling the lack of government funding for artificial intelligence, he moved in 1970 to Bristol, as Professor of Neuropsychology, to set up the Brain and Perception Laboratory, working mainly on vision and hearing, with clinical implications. He has served on Ministry of Defence committees on aviation and radar.

Gregory is founder and scientific Director of the Bristol EXPLORATORY, a science and technology centre which opened to the public in February 1987. His interests centre on phenomena: *how to show them effectively, investigate them, and explain them in terms of adequate philosophy. The study of perception appeals to him because there are clear, beautiful phenomena to observe and measure, and mind-stretching questions of how observers – we and, most likely, future intelligent machines – are related by information and knowledge to the universe.*

The enterprise of Artificial Intelligence (AI) aims to understand what we might call Brain Intelligence (BI) in terms of concepts and techniques of engineering. The fundamental assumption is that the living brain is a kind of machine, though many of its processes may remain to be invented, and so be understandable in engineering terms. This, at the very start, leads to a doubt of how deep such explanations can be: for to what depth do accounts in terms of engineering explain familiar inventions such as radio or lasers? Even the humble bicycle has its mysteries. Nevertheless, when

Freddy, the ambitious robot developed in the early 1970s by the artificial intelligence group at Edinburgh University. Freddy had a video camera as its 'eye' and computer-controlled pincers for its hand. One of Freddy's advanced features was the way in which it could build up an internal 'representation' of the world. Here Freddy begins the task of assembling the parts of a toy car (photograph Department of Machine Intelligence, University of Edinburgh).

we can bring principles of science to bear on practical problems, to produce working solutions, we do at once have a powerful test that these principles are relevant and likely to be on the right lines – if not entirely adequate for a full explanation. This is not to say that by *copying* we gain understanding (useful as a Xerox machine is, it entirely lacks wisdom); but when we can *design* a working machine we can reasonably accept that we have acted on, and so demonstrated for our satisfaction, some valid understanding.

Nearly 20 years ago we designed and built (though my own part was small) an ambitious robot, called Freddy, in the Department of Machine Intelligence and Perception in the University of Edinburgh. The Department was set up by Donald Michie, Christopher Longuet-Higgins and myself, and it was financed by the British Science Research Council and the Nuffield Foundation. We worked closely with the first AI laboratories in America, especially with Marvin Minsky at MIT and John McCarthy at Stanford. Using the newly available electronic digital computer, we tackled the ancient questions of minds in matter empirically by trying to design and build working intelligent machines. If we, or our successors, succeeded, then clearly no philosophical objection to the possibility of AI could be valid. It is, however, a curious fact that with each advance accepted criteria for 'intelligence' tend to move back, so machines that would have been unbelievably intelligent a few years ago may now be regarded as inadequate for demonstrating mind in matter. This is so of chess-playing computers, which a few years ago would have been unbelievable miracles, but now are available for the price of a book or two. Are they intelligent? Do they understand what they do? Just what problems do engineers and computer programmers have to solve to demonstrate intelligence in a man-made machine?

Figure 16.1   Richard Gregory in Edinburgh at the time of the AI Laboratory.

Though the robot Freddy was built in Edinburgh, the enterprise was cut short – in part by a philosophical argument, couched in mathematical terms, put forward by the highly distinguished mathematician Sir James Lighthill. The argument was that since any practical computing machine must have a finite number of operating states (such as the positions of its switches), it will inevitably run out of capacity – as problems generate trees of possibilities which grow exponentially – to generate a 'combinatorial explosion' which must saturate the machine and bring it to a halt. The obvious counter to this argument is that, if brains have only a finite number of states, they also must suffer from the combinatorial explosion – and so they cannot be intelligent either! Sir James Lighthill's argument does, however, have weight: it is necessary to suppose that brain intelligence (BI) depends on strategies for preventing overwhelming growth of the tree of possibilities. But if this is so for brain intelligence – why not also for artificial machine intelligence? Indeed, the problem of how to limit the combinatorial explosion is central to AI, and it can be extremely difficult. It is far from solved; but it does not rule out intelligence for machines any more than it can for brains. Following experience of the effects of this argument on the subsequent funding of the AI enterprise, both in this country and in America, I am now wary of any such general objections. Certainly they should not be allowed to block this, one of the most exciting developments of current science, by default.

In general, I do not think philosophy – and especially linguistic philosophy, using arguments based on verbal usage – has the power to make empirical statements. Whether a man-made machine can be intelligent is an empirical question, which is essentially outside philosophical jurisdiction. Specifically, if we succeed in making such a machine, then clearly it is possible. And if, up to some time *t* (such as now, or in ten or a hundred years time) we have failed, it may nevertheless remain possible, though perhaps with diminishing probability, for the future. So we can have perpetual optimism! We should, however, note that there *can* be very general overriding objections showing that something is unattainable; the clearest case is the impossibility of perpetual motion given the 2nd law of thermodynamics.[1] But if Brain Intelligence is accepted as physically based, AI cannot be like this, for the brain is an 'existence theorem', proving by the fact of its own existence the possibility of physically based intelligence and ability to read meaning in symbols. We know intelligence is possible – so no such valid objection as the thermodynamic impossibility of perpetual motion can apply to AI. This reveals the point that any claim that AI is impossible, such as that made by H. L. Dreyfus,[2] would have to show that the brains of intelligent organisms have properties that cannot be reproduced in a man-made machine. I am assuming that AI is possible simply because BI exists. If John Searle is claiming, in the preceding chapter, that in spite of even his own BI intelligence AI is impossible, we should rebut his notion that intelligence is only possible in biological living matter – or give up the AI enterprise.

Here I shall try to defend 'strong AI' – that it is possible to design and build computer-based machines that are intelligent and can read meanings in symbols. This is to say that intelligence is not necessarily embodied in living organisms, or in protoplasm, but may occur in a computer system based on silicon, or indeed any other material. This of course puts the emphasis on processes rather than substance; but there must be physical mechanisms to carry out the processes. The 'strong' claim is that any physical system that is capable of carrying out the necessary processes can be meaningfully intelligent – even if it is 'made of old beer cans', as John Searle puts it.

Have the various philosophical objections already been rebutted by practical successes? For example, was the robot Freddy sufficiently intelligent? With its single television camera eye, it could recognize a variety of fairly simple-shaped objects over a wide range of orientations. It could in this way select wooden parts for building a model car, or a model boat – including such skills as putting axles on wheels and inserting the axles into the body of the car. This it did starting with the parts in a random heap, which it would sort, selecting what it needed at each stage of assembling the models. From a simple touch sense in its hand it could, to a limited extent, explore by touch, mainly to re-calibrate its visual world. It depended, however, very much on prior instructions for its knowledge base; thus it was taught specific skills (such as inserting the axles into the car body, and removing its hand which got in the way of pushing the wheels home, which needed a special manoeuvre to extricate it). But perhaps this is not so different from teaching *children* skills and how to play games and make things. They too depend greatly on knowledge fed to them, much being conveyed by symbols. Freddy had some of the skills of a child aged three or four; but not, of course, by any means *all* the child's skills. Did it have sufficient to be child-like intelligent? Will Freddy's robot children do well enough to convince the AI sceptics? Much depends on what they demand of 'intelligence' and what they claim is uniquely BI, never to be attained by AI.

John Searle makes the broad (negative) claim that computer-machines can have syntax, but can never ever have semantics. In other words, that they can follow *rules*, such as those of arithmetic or grammar, but not understand what to us are *meanings* of symbols, such as words. Considering a pocket calculator, used for calculating the area or volume of a room, he surely rightly suggests that although the machine can handle numbers, to come up with the right answer, it does not know what 'area', or 'volume', or 'room' mean. So although it can follow rules of arithmetic the calculator lacks semantics. On this we would surely all agree. But would we all agree that *no* calculator, or chess computer, could have semantics – that the moves it responds to, and makes, could *never* have meaning for it? The issue is whether this limitation must apply to all present and future programmable computers, including robots with sensory systems, and with the ability to learn from their experience.

Here we may turn to human perception and understanding. Before the shared dream and realization of the Freddy robot, my notions on these kinds of questions were greatly affected by studying the rare case of SB, a man, effectively blind from infancy through opacity of the corneas of his eyes, who received corneal transplants when he was an adult aged fifty-two. I studied the development of his subsequent perception with my colleague Jean Wallace.[3] In brief, we found that after surgery he could immediately recognize objects that he already knew by touch – but that he was effectively blind to previously unfamiliar objects. Most striking, he could immediately name capital letters – which he had learnt by touch, when a boy in the blind school. He could not, however, recognize lower-case letters (of any size) and these he had *not* been taught at the blind school. He could also tell the time visually, which he was skilled at doing by touch with a special watch. For objects, or parts of objects, that he had been unable to experience before the operations on his eyes, he was effectively blind. We concluded that visual perception requires stored knowledge for the neural signals from the eyes to have meaning in terms of external objects; and that normally this is learnt in infancy and childhood – especially by exploratory touch – so that the eye's signals can have significance, by being correlated to objects and events of the external world.

The effective blindness to non-correlated objects, or features, was remarkably similar to Ludwig Wittgenstein's 'aspect blindness'. In our own experience (or lack of it!) this is the curious non-seeing of features, or of whole objects, in what are called 'ambiguous figures' – such as the Necker cube, which spontaneously switches its orientation in depth, or Jastrow's duck-rabbit, which is seen sometimes as a duck, at other times as a rabbit. While it is accepted as a rabbit, the duck features are scarcely seen: they disappear into 'aspect blindness'. This is even more dramatic

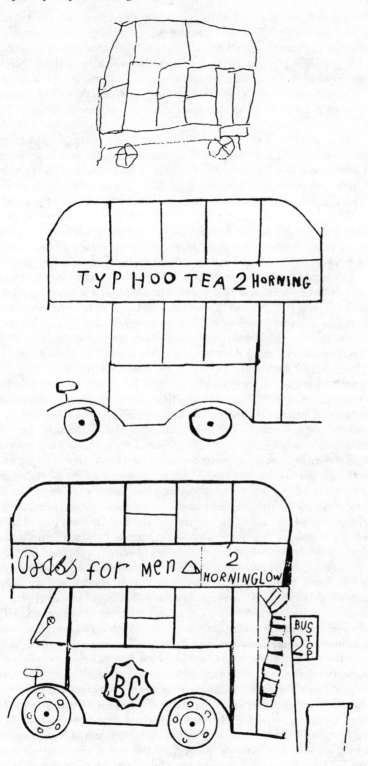

Figure 16.2 R. L. Gregory and J. G. Wallace studied the 'recovery' of vision in a man, S. B., who had his sight restored by a corneal graft after a long period of blindness. The first drawing is S. B.'s attempt at a sketch of a double-decker bus, made 48 days after the operation. All the features shown were probably previously known to him by touch. *The front, which he would not have explored by touch, is missing (from Gregory and Wallace, 1966,* Eye and Brain: The Psychology of Seeing, *reprinted by permission of Weidenfeld and Nicolson.*

The second drawing was made six months later. Now S. B. adds writing, and the 'touch-image' of spokes on the wheels has been corrected, but he still cannot draw the engine cover.

A year later (last drawing) there is yet more detail but the very front of the engine is still absent.

in Rubin's face-vases, which disappear in turn, sinking into the 'ground' of the invisibility of 'aspect blindness', to emerge from nothing as materializing ghosts, seen 'figures'. Thus Wittgenstein asks of an imaginary aspect blind person presented with the reversing skeleton Necker cube figure: 'Ought he to be unable to see the schematic cube as a cube? For him it would not jump from one aspect to another. The "aspect-blind" will have an altogether different relationship to pictures from ours.'[4]

Interestingly we found that SB – the man who optically gained sight when adult – did not experience reversals of these, to us, ambiguous figures such as the Necker cube. For him they were meaningless patterns of lines, and in general pictures were hardly seen as representing objects. From this I have argued, in some detail,[5] that phenomena of perceptual ambiguity are highly useful for empirical investigations of meaning. Wittgenstein compares such visual 'aspect blindness' with experiencing – or not experiencing – meanings of words. In any case, we may include sensory signals, as well as words and numbers, as symbols to be read.

Let's return to the computer. If a computer is fed with, or discovers for itself, facts or parameters of a world, why should it not interpret its data much as we do? Should it not also suffer similar ambiguities, as alternative interpretations of its data are entertained in turn? This might suggest that it is reading meaning from its sensory inputs much as we do. This happens with many AI programs.

John Searle sometimes expresses his attack on AI by limiting it to 'formal programs'. If by *'formal* programs' he means programs lacking parameters or empirical data relating them to the world, or to a particular problem or whatever, then clearly any possibility of reading signals or symbols is ruled out – both for machines and organisms. But this limitation to 'formal programs' is surely too restricted to be interesting outside pure logic or formal mathematics. For AI this point is trivial, as AI programs, like us, obviously must have knowledge of the world to deal with the world. So this could hardly be John Searle's message. But this does seem to be the implication of the Chinese room. For consider bringing up a *baby* in the Chinese room: how could it learn the meanings of the Chinese, or any other symbols, in such a restricted environment? There is a great deal of evidence that years of active exploration in infancy are essential for human beings to learn to read meanings in the neural signals from their senses. (The only known exceptions are where knowledge is inherited, as for instinctive behaviour, but this is also the result of experience and so is not *essentially* different in this context.) The Chinese room environment, extended to perception as a whole, would prevent correlations between symbols and events being developed, as the room has no view of the outside world, or any opportunity for exploring by touch, or other adequate senses, to build up a store of knowledge about the world and relate this to Chinese or any other symbols. The man in the Chinese room would be like a dictionary in which each word is defined by other words, but none has significance through experience. (It would be like Bertrand Russell attempting to have Knowledge by Description, but lacking the necessary Knowledge by Acquaintance to give it significance.) The Chinese room parable does not show that computer-based robots

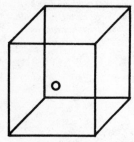

Figure 16.3   The Necker cube. This is a pattern with two alternative three-dimensional interpretations. Does the face marked with the small circle lie at the front or the back of the cube? The visual system cannot settle for one answer, though it never accepts both at the same time. This kind of hypothesis-making goes on throughout normal perception but usually there is sufficient information in the retinal image to lead to a unique solution (from Eye and Brain: The Psychology of Seeing, *reprinted by permission of Weidenfeld and Nicolson).*

cannot be intelligent as we are – because *we* wouldn't be intelligent from this school either.

One might say that *pure* mathematics has only syntax without semantics, and that *applied* mathematics takes on semantics as it represents conceptual models (of *bridges*, dynamics of the solar system or whatever) with parameters which may give it appropriateness to the world. Inappropriate conceptual models, and errors of parameters, will generate the discrepancies of illusions – which can be highly revealing for reading mind in the matters of other organisms and of AI machines. Perhaps paradoxically, illusions are first-rate evidence of ability to read meaning from sensory signals, or other symbols; for occasional *misreading* implies ability to read. Kinds of misreading (kinds of errors or illusions) provide evidence of how data and organized knowledge are applied for reading meanings. When an AI vision machine suffers illusions similar to ours, we have suggestive evidence that the procedures and knowledge followed and used for its seeing are much like our own. So the AI of the machine meets the BI of man, in shared procedures and knowledge for seeing and recognizing objects, perhaps in time to share rich perceptual and conceptual models of the world.

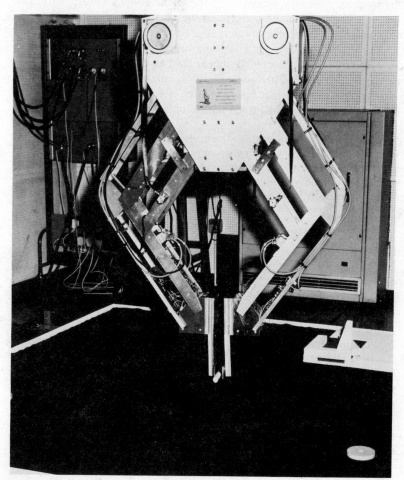

Figure 16.4   Freddy the robot puts the final touches to the toy car he is building. We may come to regard the ever more sophisticated successors to Freddy as conscious and mindful, as well as simply intelligent (photograph Department of Machine Intelligence, University of Edinburgh).

But these considerations may not reach the nub of Searle's position. Like all philosophers – and this can be useful – John Searle is a guardian of semantic inertia. But he uses this (a danger of semantic or conceptual inertia!) to limit the science of AI to pre-AI thinking. Thus he writes:

Marvin Minsky of MIT says that the next generation of computers will be so intelligent that we will 'be lucky if they're willing to keep us around the house as household pets'. But my all-time favourite in the literature of exaggerated claims on behalf of the digital computer is from John McCarthy, the inventor of the term 'artificial intelligence'. McCarthy says 'even a machine as simple as a thermostat can be said to have beliefs'. I admire McCarthy's courage. I once asked him 'What beliefs does your thermostat have?' And he said 'My thermostat has three beliefs – it believes it's too hot in here, it's too cold in here, and its just right in here.'[6]

John Searle comments: 'now as a philosopher, I like these claims for a simple reason. Unlike most philosophical theses, they are reasonably clear, and they can be simply and decisively refuted.' But is it possible to *refute* McCarthy's notion that a thermostat can have beliefs? Clearly this turns on what we allow as a 'belief' – or rather on whether we are willing to extend its usual range of application from man, to animals, to thermostats. Semantic inertia is useful for protecting words; but it can generate the unfortunate conceptual inertia to which philosophers are singularly prone, presumably as they are too seldom *bethumped* (as King John would put it) by facts or conceptual developments of science. Personally I do not object to saying, at least as a try-on, that thermostats have beliefs. It might dispel some of the obscurantist mystery of 'belief'.

John Searle claims that his refutation of strong AI – defined as 'the mind is to the brain as the program is to computer hardware' –

has nothing whatever to do with any particular stage of technology. The nature of the refutation is completely independent of any state of technology. It has to do with the very definition of a digital computer, with what a digital computer is . . . A computer program is only syntactical, and minds are more than syntactical. Minds are semantic, in the sense that they have more than a formal structure, they have a content.

But is it impossible for a machine to have 'intrinsic meaning', or 'content'? Considering, as an example, an automatic pilot, John Searle argues that this only *simulates* flying the plane, as it lacks the power to read symbols or information 'intrinsically'. But is this so? Surely it accepts signals of many kinds, and it makes decisions on data – so surely it *actually* flies the plane. If one asks whether it has the rich content of a human pilot's mind, one can indeed be sure it hasn't, for it is not worried about missing an appointment and it will not be feeling tired or interested in the air hostess. But in accepting and acting on navigational and other data it *is* a pilot. So in so far as being a pilot requires a mind, it must have a mind. It may be a very limited mind, and this is so also for the chess computer, though we regard chess as an intellectual skill; but it is actually performing, and not merely simulating mind-tasks. So a chess computer and an autopilot have (if limited) 'intrinsic' meaning, as they can act, of their own accord, on symbols.

Let's take this a step further, considering a word processor. It clearly does *not* understand our symbols. We know this because *it does not know how to spell*. If I type – 'I am write and John Searle is knot' – it is clear that my word processor has not spotted that 'write' and 'knot' are incorrectly spelled, *in this meaning-context*. Machines for taking dictation are now on the edge of technology. Will we have to rationalize our spelling, or will they, like a human typist, come to appreciate context-meanings to make their spelling appropriate to sense? What will they do in ambiguous sentences? Will they make *deliberate* puns? When they do, I shall accept, against any philosophical argument, that AI has arrived.

Is the 'semantic inertia' of philosophy, which objects, for example, to saying that thermostats have beliefs, any more than a failure to follow the development of new concepts? Why should we be convinced, on verbal-usage grounds, that computer-based robots cannot have minds – unless we believe that such wisdom is built into normal language? This would be to say that such wisdom is built, a priori, into *us*. But the infinite surprises of science show very clearly that we have no such a priori widsom, so language must continuously change to keep pace with new discoveries and changing concepts, or it becomes misleading. Language is inertial and not, like observation, experiment and invention, look-ahead.

A philosopher might, however, just as scientists do every day, object to certain statements on grounds of violating accepted *concepts*. Thus Searle's objection to a thermostat having beliefs might not only be that the word 'belief' is not normally applied to thermostats, or other engineering devices; but, far more significant, that there are *conceptual* objections to thermostats or man-made devices in general having such human-like characteristics. This he would have to justify on theoretical, conceptual grounds. (Whether this would be philosophy rather than science is a moot – and hence a mute – point.) It could in any case be argued that although semantic and conceptual inertia are useful for maintaining communication, and ensuring directed thinking, occasionally widening the use of words such as 'belief' is a good way to test our conceptual insights and assumptions and develop them in creative new ways.

Considering meaning in mind, John Searle essentially distinguishes between *intrinsic* and *derived* contents – suggesting that only brain-minds have intrinsic contents. Thus *we* have to read the significance in the *calculator's* numbers. But I have suggested that this is not so for the chess computer, nor the autopilot. They act for themselves, without human intervention or interpretation. Working autonomously, the first can beat most of us in an intellectual game and the other can take us safely across oceans, or into space and back. So how is it appropriate to say that they lack 'content' – or to state that they cannot read symbols? If this stricture is intended only to apply to 'formal programs' – which are denied data – then the discussion has no bearing on intelligence or meaning, whether BI or AI. So the 'formal program' cannot be sensibly (though he sometimes seems to say it is) the nub of Searle's position.

Finally, although John Searle denies that any present or future digital computer will be intelligent, he allows that intelligence, with intrinsic meaning and so on, is a possibility for 'Martians'. But how can we know that a Martian will not be made of silicon, and then more or less identical to a present or future IBM computer? Searle's contention is that the

Martian might be fully intelligent, though a computer cannot be intelligent, because the Martian will have a *biological origin*. This, he holds, can fit it for intrinsic mental content. But isn't this a form of vitalism? Isn't it a return to special properties of substance, or of special origin, which biology has been struggling for so many years to avoid? Our origins are certainly important for what we are now; but surely it is only what we are *now* that matters for our present intelligence, understanding and mental content. Presumably we might have attained our present intelligence from different origins, even from having been made in a thermostatically controlled factory and programmed by John McCarthy – provided we were not brought up in a Chinese room preventing us from exploring the world.

References

1 See Feynman, R. P. (1964) *Lectures on Physics*. Reading, Mass.: Addison-Wesley.
2 Dreyfus, H. L. (1963) *What Computers Can't Do: The Limits of Artificial Intelligence*. New York: Harper & Row (revised 1979).
3 Gregory, R. L. and Wallace, Jean (1963) *Recovery from Infant Blindness: A Case Study*. Experimental Psychology Society Monograph II. Cambridge: Heffer. (Reprinted in: Gregory, R. L. (1972) *Concepts and Mechanisms of Perception*. London: Duckworth.)
4 Wittgenstein, L. (1953) *Philosophical Investigations*. Oxford: Blackwell.
5 Gregory, R. L. (1981) *Mind in Science*, esp. pp. 378–95. London: Weidenfeld & Nicolson.
6 Searle, J. (1984) *Mind, Brains and Science*. London: BBC Publications.

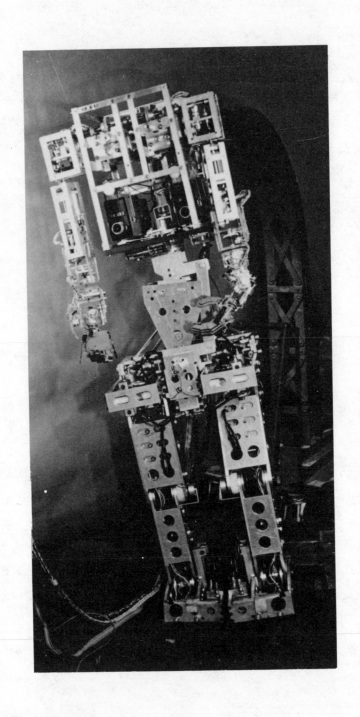

17

How Could Consciousness Arise from the Computations of the Brain?

Philip Johnson-Laird

Phil Johnson-Laird was born in Rothwell (near Leeds) in 1936. He is married to a librarian, and has two children. He left school at the age of 15 and worked as a quantity surveyor for five years. Subsequently, he had a variety of jobs – some as an alternative to National Service – before going in 1961 to read Psychology at University College London. He wrote his doctoral thesis there under the supervision of Peter Wason; they later worked on a joint project that led to the publication of their book, The Psychology of Reasoning *(1972). In 1971, he was a Visiting Fellow at the Princeton Institute of Advanced Study, where he began a collaboration with George A. Miller on the theory of meaning; they were co-authors of* Language and Perception *(1976). After seven years on the faculty of University College London, he moved to Sussex in 1973, where he was subsequently appointed Professor of Experimental Psychology. He has continued to carry out research on language and inference, with a particular emphasis on using experimental results to guide the development of computer models of mental processes (see his* Mental Models, *1983). He is currently Assistant Director of the Medical Research Council Applied Psychology Unit, Cambridge.*

Introduction

Consciousness lies at the centre of the mind–body problem, because without it there would be no such problem – or, at least if there were, we would be unaware of it. Despite its centrality, however, consciousness is profoundly puzzling, and one immediate problem about it is to determine what needs to be explained. You might suppose that the answer is obvious: what is needed is a theory that explains what consciousness is, and how it depends on the operations of the brain. Unfortunately, there do not seem to be any obvious criteria by which to judge the success of such a theory. A theory of perception, in contrast, can be judged by testing whether its account of, say, stereoscopic vision or visual illusions measures up to the facts. But what specific phenomena should a theory of consciousness cast light on? It is perhaps this lack of criteria that lends respectability to those who, whether they be ancient behaviourists or modern materialists, argue that consciousness is an unfounded myth, and

'Wabot' – the Waseda University biped robot. There is nothing highly problematical about automatic behaviour, but there is a puzzle as to how an organism can possess self-awareness.

that it can be dispelled by the property study of nerve, muscle and behaviour. In my view this attitude of ruthless anti-mentalism is a mistake. What is needed instead is both a set of tractable problems for a theory of consciousness to explain and a new approach to constructing theories – an approach based on computational considerations. In this chapter, I will outline four major problems of consciousness and then present a computationally based theory designed to resolve them.

Four Problems of Consciousness

The first problem is what I shall refer to as the problem of 'awareness'. It is to account for the distinction between what one can and cannot be aware of. There are some things that readily enter consciousness, whereas others evidently cannot enter it. You can be aware of the contents of perception – that, for example, you are reading words on this page, but you cannot be aware of the process of perception – of the intricate chains of events that converts the retinal image into an informative representation of the world. There may be good evolutionary reasons for why that should be so: if you see a tiger, it is best to take rapid avoiding action, without reflecting on the process of perception. If the process were introspectible, it would inevitably be slower since it could not depend on events happening in parallel, and you might stop to check whether the tiger was illusory. It pays to act first and to leave the psychologists to answer the questions afterwards. Of course, whether or not there are unconscious mental events is a matter of controversy, and some theorists have identified mental phenomena solely with consciousness. Everything else, they claim, is a matter of neurophysiology. Maybe. But one is bound to ask about the status of the neurophysiological events underlying consciousness, and particularly about the mysterious power by which a purely neurophysiological state representing, say, a telephone number stored in memory can be transformed into consciousness when the telephone number is called to mind. Since both states represent the same content, it seems preferable to talk of unconscious mental states and processes. If readers find this usage objectionable, then they may substitute some other terminology. It remains necessary nevertheless to give an account of the distinction between what one can and cannot be aware of.

The second problem, which I shall refer to as the problem of 'control', is to draw a similar distinction between what one can and cannot consciously control. There are those behaviours that are voluntary, that we choose to do on the basis of a conscious intentional decision, and there are those behaviours that – much as we should sometimes like to control them – are involuntary. It is, for instance, difficult to feel a particular emotion simply because one has decided to do so. And, to raise a topic that is almost taboo in psychology, individuals appear to differ in their will-power: some people have considerable control over their behaviour, whereas others, like Oscar Wilde, can resist everything except temptation. The majority of us perhaps vary from one domain to another. What needs to be explained is how an organism can have only partial 'control' over its behaviour.

The third problem is *self*-awareness. On the one hand, you can be aware of what is going on in the world, and, on the other hand, you can be aware of yourself acting in the world or aware that you are aware of it. (Can you be aware that you are aware that you are aware? Perhaps.) There is a clear introspective contrast between being so involved in a situation – so dominated by what one is doing or perceiving – that one is hardly aware of one's self, and of the state of self-awareness. Paul Valéry may have been right when he argued that a whole philosophy could be based on this contrast, a philosophy that is captured in his rejoinder to René Descartes: sometimes I am, sometimes I think. There is nothing problematical about mechanical behaviour: it underlies Descartes's distinction

Figure 17.1 René Descartes (1596–1650), the first recognizably modern philosopher, who posed a sharp distinction between mind and body (Mary Evans Picture Library).

between mind and body. He argued that the body is an automaton, but the mind has free will and therefore lies outside the realm of scientific explanation.

The fourth and final problem that a theory of consciousness should address is the nature of intentionality. To act intentionally is presumably to decide to do something for some reason and in consequence do it. The problem here is to explain what is missing from certain sorts of well-understood goal-seeking behaviour. For example, there are programming languages, such as PLANNER and PROLOG, which make it easy to devise programs whose behaviour is driven by goals: a specific goal leads to the creation of sub-goals, whose achievement may call for the satisfaction of still further sub-goals, and so on. Some computer scientists have argued that such programs have intentions and beliefs; for example, John McCarthy, who devised LISP, the first computer language of artificial intelligence, even claims that thermostats have rudimentary beliefs. Ingenious as such devices are, this attribution seems mistaken. What one wants from a theory of consciousness is an account of what is missing from goal-driven programs that distinguishes them from truly intentional entities.

17.1: An example of a procedure for controlling a robot in a PLANNER-like programming language. The details have been simplified.

PROGRAM	Its interpretation
(CONSEQUENT (X Y)(ON ?X ?Y)	To put one object, X, on top of another, Y
(GOAL (CLEARTOP ?Y))	Ensure that nothing is on top of Y
(GOAL (GRASP ?X))	Grasp X
(GOAL (MOVE-TO ?Y))	Move it to the top of Y
(GOAL (LET-GO-OF ?X))	Let go of X

The Theory of Computability

My strategy in trying to advance a hypothesis about these four problems will be to rely on the theory of computability, which preceded by a decade the invention of programmable digital computers. It is clear that all explanations have to take something for granted, and that many psychological explanations take too much for granted. Alonzo Church and Alan Turing, along with many other logicians, were interested in the question of how to minimize what has to be taken for granted in order to be able to carry out any computation. Church proposed the following conjecture: any procedure that can be described explicitly can be computed with recursive functions (see table 17.2); Turing offered a similar conjecture framed in terms of a class of automata that have come to be known as 'Turing machines' (see Roger Penrose's chapter in this book). It turned out that the two conjectures were equivalent because anything that can be computed with recursive functions can be computed with a Turing machine, and vice versa. The details of the computational machinery need not detain us: Turing machines are, however, the abstract ancestors of the modern digital computer. Hence, the Church–Turing thesis implies that any explicitly described procedure can be implemented in a computer program. This thesis cannot be proved, because it takes the intuitive idea of an explicit description of a procedure and offers a theoretical analysis of it. However, the thesis could be falsified, though in fact it has endured for nearly fifty years, and all the different analyses of the same intuitive notion have turned out to be provably equivalent to one another.

17.2: A summary of the theory of recursive functions

I The theory assumes that there is some method (its details are taken for granted) of computing three simple things:
   (1) The zero function, which yields the value 0 given an input of any natural number (0, 1, 2, 3, . . .)
   (2) The successor function, which yields the number that follows any natural number, e.g. the successor of 0 is 1, the successor of 1 is 2.
   (3) The set of identity functions, each of which, given a string of input arguments, returns the identical value of one of them as specified by its position in the string; e.g., one identity function takes two arguments and returns the value of the first of them, another takes two arguments and returns the value of the second of them, and so on.

II More complex functions are built up by combining these basic functions in three different ways:
   (1) The *composition* of functions: the outputs of one or more functions become the inputs of another function; e.g., the function +2, which adds 2 to any number, is equivalent to (successor (successor X)), i.e. the successor of the successor of X.
   (2) *Primitive recursion*: a new function is defined by giving its value for some constant, typically 0, and then showing how to compute its value for the successor of n from its value for n. The factorial function $n!$ (where, for example, $3! = 3 \times 2 \times 1$) can be recursively defined thus:
      Factorial (0) = 1
      Factorial ($n + 1$) = ($n + 1$) $\times$ Factorial (n)
   (3) *Minimization*: the value of a new function is equal to the smallest value of an argument for which another given function yields the value 0. For example, the function that yields the largest integer not exceeding half the size of X can be defined as: the minimization of Y in $X - 2Y - 1$; e.g., the smallest integer not exceeding half of 5 is 2 since the minimization of Y in $5 - 2Y - 1$ is 2. The computation of a minimized function calls for the use of what programmers call a 'while'-loop: *while* the result is not 0, the value of Y is incremented and the value of the function computed again.

III It is a remarkable fact that any computer program whatsoever can be built up from the set of basic functions in I and the three building-blocks of composition, primitive recursion and minimization.

Mental Processes as Computations

Why should a thesis about computation matter to psychology? The answer lies in an assumption that goes back to Kenneth Craik, and that underpins the bulk of cognitive psychology. Craik proposed in his book *The Nature of Explanation*[1] that the essential characteristics of the human mind are that it translates aspects of the external world into internal representations, processes these representations so as to yield others, and, if need be, translates derived representations back into behaviour. He argued that the essence of the mind is that it has this particular functional organization. Granted this assumption, which is also to be found in the

more recent philosophical doctrine of functionalism, it follows that mental processes are essentially computations that construct, manipulate and interpret representations of the world.

The Church–Turing thesis and the doctrine of functionalism allow us to divide the space of logical possibilities concerning consciousness into a series of dichotomies (see figure 17.3). The first dichotomy is whether or not consciousness is scientifically explicable. If you assume that it is scientifically explicable, then the next dichotomy is whether or not the Church–Turing thesis is correct. Some theorists appear to believe that it is false, since they argue that there cannot be a theory of consciousness that is computable – presumably they consider that any scientific account of consciousness will have to rely on non-computable procedures. Whether or not they are right about consciousness is perhaps of less interest than their implicit claim that the general form of the Church–Turing thesis is false. Granted that the thesis is correct, then the final dichotomy rests on Craik's functionalism. If you believe it to be false but accept the Church–Turing thesis, then presumably you hold that consciousness could be modelled in a computer program in the same way that, say, the weather can be modelled: it would be wrong to suppose that a program could exhibit consciousness, just as it would be wrong to expect a computer model of the weather to exhibit actual meterological phenomena, for example, for fog to start pouring from the machine. If you accept functionalism, however, then you should believe that consciousness is a computational process. You should accept that if the appropriate sort of computer were to be programmed in the right way, then it would be conscious.

Figure 17.2 Cambridge psychologist Kenneth Craik (1914–45). He argued that any system might be regarded as 'mental' regardless of the materials from which it was built, if it could carry out the following sequence of operations: (1) translate aspects of the external world into internal representations; (2) process these representations so as to yield others; (3) if need be, translate derived representation back into behaviour (photograph by Ramsey and Muspratt, Cambridge).

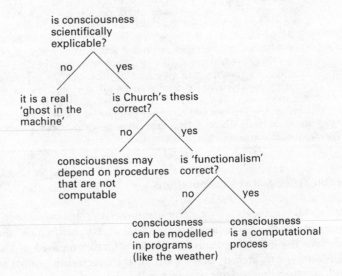

Figure 17.3 A series of theoretical dichotomies.

There are no decisive a priori considerations either in favour or against this proposition: all the philosophical arguments ultimately depend upon the respective philosopher's intuitions. The sensible strategy is accordingly to accept the strongest possible hypothesis on a tentative basis and to see where it leads. In particular, if consciousness is a computational process, then we must ask about the particular computational architecture that is necessary to support it. There are a number of principles at stake here and I will develop each of them in turn before attempting to summarize them.

The Computational Architecture of the Brain

There is abundant psychological and neurophysiological evidence implying that the mind depends on computations carried out *in parallel* by the brain. To consider just one psychological example, speech depends on the formulation of some idea worth expressing, the selection of the appropriate words and syntax, and the utterance of the resulting morphemes in a correct phonological manner. Each of these aspects of speech – from the choice of words to the control of the muscles in the vocal apparatus – is highly sensitive to context, and each calls for an exquisite timing and interrelation with the other processes. There is indeed an overwhelming case that lexical, grammatical and phonetic processes occur not one after the other in a sequence of operations that occur only one at a time, but rather in parallel like a series of processes on a conveyor belt that gradually fashion an utterance out of an idea.

The most general form of a parallel computational architecture consists of a set of simple processing devices (automata with only a finite number of distinct states) wired up to each other so as to allow data to be transmitted amongst them. Since the brain is a finite organ, then the computational systems that it embodies must be finite, too. One of the consequences of this organization is that one processor cannot observe the detailed workings of another. They merely pass messages to one another. Likewise, of course, one processor cannot interfere with the internal computations of another. Hence, the system will not behave in a radically unpredictable manner: its behaviour may reflect an interaction among different variables but these interactions will be relatively weak. The system is also likely to be asynchronous, that is, there is no need for a central clock that controls the behaviour of all the processors; instead, each processor springs to life just as soon as it receives the data needed to carry out its computations, and, in the interim, it lies dormant.

One danger with parallel processing, familiar to computer scientists now that they have started to build parallel computers, is that the computational system may get into various sorts of pathological configuration. For instance, suppose the situation arises in which one processor, A, is waiting for data or for a signal from another, B, which in turn is waiting to hear from the first one (see figure 17.4). In this case, the two processors are locked together in a 'deadly embrace', neither able to respond until the other does. Nature ensures that such pathologies do not occur in primitive nervous systems, since any gross pathologies at the level of neuronal wiring will be weeded out by natural selection. But the mind is a system that can learn; it can devise new procedures, and if, as seems likely, it assigns them to parallel processors, there is no way in which natural selection could prevent the pathological allocation of a procedure to a set of processors. An obvious solution is to promote one processor to monitor others and to override them if they become pathologically configured. Consciousness may owe its origin to the emergence of such a monitoring device from the web of parallel processors. The monitoring principle is likely, however, to pervade the entire system, and accordingly to give rise to a hierarchical organization of parallel processors.

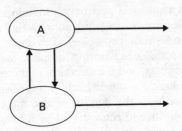

Figure 17.4   A 'deadly embrace' between two processors computing in parallel.

Computation and the Four Problems of Consciousness

Awareness and Parallel Computation

The parallel architecture that I have so far described is compatible with a number of psychological phenomena, and it helps us to resolve the problem of awareness. If awareness depends on the computations of one processor, or even on one sub-set of processors, then the internal operations of the remaining processors will be outside awareness. Moreover, given a hierarchical architecture as postulated, is it natural to suppose that the outputs of many processors have no direct contact with the system mediating awareness at the top of the hierarchy? One part of the mind is indeed unaware of others; and instances of dissociation between the parts can be observed in cases of self-deception, and particularly in their neurotic counterparts, the hysterias. The classical description of hysterical paralyses – those that arise not from damage to the nervous system, but from a form of unconscious defence – is to be found in Freud. But sceptics might also consult Lord Adrian's account of how he cured hysterical paralyses brought on by 'shell-shock' in the First World War[2]. (See also the chapter by Sir John Eccles, p. 293.) Adrian appreciated that his patients were not malingering and that the best chance of curing them was to outwit their unconscious minds. He accordingly devised a treatment that consisted of brushing the paralysed limb with a wire brush through which there passed a mild electrical current. He told the soldiers that the treatment always worked, and exuded a general air of confidence and authority. His success rate was indeed over 90 per cent.

Another more recently discovered form of dissociation is the phenomenon of 'blind sight'. Damage to a certain part of the brain may yield a large blind spot in the visual field. Yet, if patients are forced to guess the location of a spot of light shining within the area of this blind spot, they are able to do so remarkably well: all that appears to be missing is their awareness of what they are seeing (see Weiskrantz, this volume). A further form of dissociation sometimes occurs after an epileptic attack: patients can carry out skilled behaviour (for example, driving a car) but only like an automaton, and with no capacity to make intentional decisions. Finally, the so-called 'cocktail party' phenomenon provides a more mundane illustration of how mental computations occur outside awareness. At a party, you can be paying attention to somebody talking to you, but your attention will be diverted if someone in a neighbouring conversation mentions your name. Despite its prosaic nature the pheno-menon is difficult to explain unless your mind contains a parallel device that is sensitive to your name and that lies dormant until the right phonological pattern brings it to life. Its activation leads to an involuntary switch of attention to the source of the stimulus.

Conflicts cannot arise in serial computation, but they can occur between parallel processors; for example, if the ring-like nervous system of a starfish is cut into two separate arcs, the two halves of the creature are likely to move in opposite directions. If conflicts are resolved by proce-dures built into the general architecture of the system, the two character-istic modes of resolving them will account for the problem of control and phenomena of the will. On the one hand, in a hierarchy of parallel processors, those lower down can initiate behaviour without the controll-ing influence of the operating system, which is not in direct communica-tion with them, as when a response occurs despite our attempts to control it. Likewise, a goal formulated by a high-level processor may fail because of the autonomy, not to say recalcitrance, of automata at a lower level. On the other hand, a conflict may be resolved in favour of the high-level processor, with the result that an effort of will succeeds.

The next step in the argument concerns the nature of the processor at the top of the parallel hierarchy. In real computers, the highest level of control consists of an operating system – a set of programs that allow a human operator to interact with the machine, for example, to load a program and to execute it. The human operating system, however, is largely autonomous: it makes the decisions. This propensity depends on the mind's operating system – consciousness – having access to a model of its own high-level capabilities. The system has a partial model of itself.

The concept of a mental model goes back to Craik,[1] and to his idea that an internal representation consists of a model of the external world. There is evidence that the comprehension of discourse depends on the construction of a model of the state of affairs it describes, and that deductive inferences are made by formulating informative conclusions based on such models and then establishing that there are no other models of the premises that refute those conclusions.[3] In order to understand discourse about other people's beliefs and particularly what they believe about someone else's state of mind – for example, 'He believes that she thinks that . . . he is guilty' – it is necessary to build a model of someone else's model, and then in turn to embed that model within another, and so on. The central notion in the present theory is accordingly that the operating systems of mental computational devices first have a model of their own capabilities; and, second, can embed that model within itself.

17.3: A simple inference based on constructing a mental model of the premises

Step 1   Imagine a state of affairs that is described by the premises, e.g., 'Some of the professors are scientists. All the scientists are experimenters'. The first premise can be represented by a model containing an arbitrary number of individuals:

```
professor  =  scientist
professor  =  scientist
(professor)   (scientist)
```

The content of the second premise can be added to the model:

```
professor  =  scientist  =  experimenter
professor  =  scientist  =  experimenter
(professor)   (scientist  =  experimenter)
                            (experimenter)
```

Step 2   Find a relation in all the models of the premises so far constructed that is not stated explictly in the premises, and formulate a conclusion expressing it:

'Some of the professors are experimenters'

Step 3   Search for an alternative model of the premises that falsifies the putative conclusion. If there is no such model, the conclusion is valid; if such a model can be found, then return to step 2.

The example has a small finite model, and it is easy to discover that there is no alternative model of the premises that severs the link from professors to experimenters. Hence, the conclusion is valid.

The idea of a program, or automaton, that can print out a complete description of itself is familiar to computer scientists, but it is clear that human beings do not have introspective access to anything like a complete description of their mind's internal workings (though Minsky seems to propose such a theory)[4]. However, much as we can build models based on our understanding of phenomena, we can also build models – incomplete and sometimes even erroneous – that represent our own capabilities. Self-awareness, the sense of being aware of one's self, depends on our ability to perceive ourselves as perceiving or acting on the world. It arises in the present framework when the operating system has access to a model of itself perceiving or acting on the world. The force of the word 'model' here is that what is embedded within the operating system is an incomplete representation of the mind sufficient only to create the unique subjective experience of self-awareness. One of the developments in computer science since these ideas were first proposed is the design of so-called 'reflective' languages that appear to have this property: an embeddable model of a procedure can be used by the procedure itself.[5]

This account of self-awareness illuminates the last of the four problems: the nature of intention. An intention is presumably a conscious, or self-aware, decision to act so as to try to achieve a particular goal. Hence, if a computational system is to have intentions, it must be able to represent a hypothetical state of affairs, that is, a goal, and possess a system for planning a sequence of behaviours that will achieve the goal. These requirements are satisfied by programming languages that enable a programmer to devise goal-directed programs. The requirement of a self-aware decision is more subtle: the computational device needs an operating system that, first, has a model of the system, including its ability to set up goals, devise plans to achieve them, and execute those plans; second, that can decide that it itself, the operating system, should act so as to bring about that state of affairs; and, third, that is aware that the system itself is able to make such decisions. What the system needs is therefore a goal-directed planning ability, such as one finds in certain programs, together with an operating system of the kind that I have described.

Conclusion

In summary, the computational architecture of the brain that I am positing consists of a parallel hierarchy of finite-state devices that compute asynchronously. At the highest level in the hierarchy, there is an operating system that has access to a partial model of its own capabilities, and that has the recursive machinery to embed models within models. These conditions certainly appear to be necessary for consciousness. It remains an open question whether they are sufficient. They imply, however, that consciousness is the property of a class of parallel algorithms, but not of the functions they compute, which could always be computed by a serial algorithm. This conclusion has an interesting corollary: there may be no decisive diagnostic test to reveal whether or not an organism is conscious. Granted that behaviour depends on mental processes, the same computations could be computed by a serial device that lacks a conscious mental life.

References

1 Craik, K. (1943) *The Nature of Explanation*. Cambridge: Cambridge Univ. Press.
2 Adrian, E. D. and Yealland, L. R. (1917) The treatment of some common war neuroses. *Lancet* (June), 3–24.
3 Johnson-Laird, P. N. (1983) *Mental Models*. Cambridge: Cambridge Univ. Press; Cambridge, Mass.: Harvard Univ. Press.
4 Minsky, M. L. (1968) Matter, mind, and models. In M. L. Minsky (ed.), *Semantic Information Processing*, Cambridge, Mass.: MIT Press.
5 Smith, B. C. (1984) Reflection and semantics in LISP. Conference Record of the Eleventh Annual Association for Computing Machinery Symposium on Principles of Programming Languages, pp. 23–35. Salt Lake City, Utah.

18

Minds, Machines and Mathematics

Roger Penrose

Roger Penrose was born at Colchester, Essex, in 1931, the second of four children of the geneticist Lionel S. Penrose and Margaret (née Leathes). He was supposed to become a doctor (as an antidote to all the chess-playing in the family – and his secret ambition had been to be a brain surgeon), but he liked puzzles and geometry and so became a mathematician instead. After stints at Cambridge, London (mainly Birkbeck College) and elsewhere, he became, in 1973, Rouse Ball Professor of Mathematics at Oxford (and, later, part-time Lovett Professor at Rice University, Houston, Texas). He has worked on black holes, pentagonal crystals, twistors and other aspects of mathematical physics. He has collected the odd prize, medal or FRS, but fortunately no honorary degrees. He has three sons but is divorced. Though he is considered an expert on space and time, he claims to be unable to organize either.

Now that the fruits of electronic computer technology are beginning to impinge on various aspects of our daily lives, it is becoming particularly topical to address the question of whether such computers can be said actually to think. To what extent are our own thought processes like the functioning of a computer? Are computers likely soon to acquire genuine intelligence? May they soon exceed our own abilities in this respect? Does it matter what a 'thinking device' is actually made of, or is its computational algorithm all that counts? Indeed, to what extent is it appropriate to analyse our own thought processes in terms of such computational algorithms? My purpose here is to make some remarks relevant to these matters.

Algorithms and Turing Machines

First, I should explain what is meant by a *computational algorithm* (or recursive process). Basically, this is an operation that can be performed by a computer – though one has to be a little bit careful because, strictly for the purpose of the definition, we mean a computer with an unlimited

---

In a remarkable series of experiments, D. A. Baylor, T. D. Lamb and K.-W. Yau demonstrated the electrical responses of individual rod photoreceptors from the eye of the toad in response to the absorption of single photons of light – the smallest indivisible units of light energy. This photograph shows a small fragment of toad retina with one of the rods sucked up into a glass tube containing fluid connected to a sensitive amplifier detecting any electric current flowing through the rod. A bright bar of light is shone on the glass tube, so that light falls on the rod and sets off an electrical response (photograph supplied by the authors, reprinted by permission of the Journal of Physiology).

memory store which is allowed to continue for an unlimited time without wearing out. All this can be made precise in terms of the abstract mathematical object known as a *Turing machine* (which is the concept on which modern electronic computers are actually based).[1] In a Turing machine, any algorithmic process is broken down into elementary steps, where at each step the operation to be carried out is perfectly clear-cut and immediate, and so also is the procedure for moving on to the next elementary step. There is, moreover, a concept referred to as a *universal* Turing machine – which is some particular Turing machine with the capacity to imitate any other Turing machine. All one needs to do is to feed the universal machine first with a positive integer, say N, and it will then behave, in effect, as though it were the Nth Turing machine. Modern general-purpose computers are, in essence, universal Turing machines.

Algorithm

An entirely mechanical mathematical procedure, which is completely well defined in operation and which can be applied automatically without any additional decisions, judgements or random choices having to be made. The word comes from the name of a ninth-century Arab mathematician *al-Khowârizmi*. He was the author of a Persian textbook on algebra.

In our present century, the British mathematician, logician and code-breaker Alan Turing (1912–54) formalized the notion of algorithm in terms of the concepts which has become known as a (universal) Turing machine. This logical concept lies at the heart of all modern general-purpose computers.

The word 'algorithm' refers to a procedure for solving mathematical problems in a specified class, where there is a clear-cut rule to follow at each stage – that is to say, it is a procedure which can be carried out by a Turing machine. As an example, there is the well-known procedure referred to as *Euclid's algorithm*, which finds the highest common factor of two positive integers. Divide the smaller integer into the larger one; take the remainder; divide that into the previous smaller one; take the remainder again, and so on until the division goes exactly. The final (non-zero) remainder is the required highest common factor. It is very simple to write a flow diagram for this procedure (see box). We are familiar with many far more complicated (and extremely impressive) procedures that can now be carried out by computers. But these procedures are still composed of the same standard elementary clear-cut steps at each stage. (It can happen that sometimes such calculations simply go around in loops and do not terminate. Or perhaps they may just expand without limit. In such cases the calculations will not be as useful as an algorithm. For a proper algorithm we should be assured of an answer in a finite time in each case.)

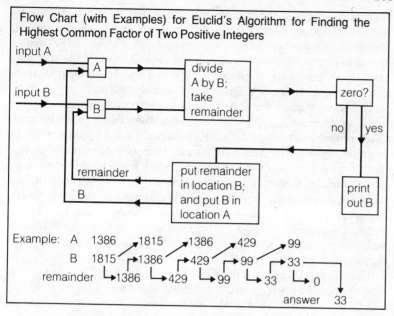

Flow Chart (with Examples) for Euclid's Algorithm for Finding the Highest Common Factor of Two Positive Integers

input A

input B

A

B

divide A by B; take remainder

zero?

no   yes

remainder

B

put remainder in location B; and put B in location A

print out B

Example: A   1386   1815   1386   429   99
          B   1815   1386   429   99   33
     remainder   1386   429   99   33   0

answer   33

The Turing Test

I shall need to consider what is known as the Turing test.[2,3] This is intended to be an objective way of deciding whether a computer could validly be said to have been programmed to 'think'. The idea is that the computer and a human subject are both to be hidden from the view of a perceptive experimenter. The experimenter can communicate with either of the two subjects, human or electronic, but is not told which is which.

Figure 18.1   The Turing test: the experimenter, depicted at the right, has to decide which of two hidden subjects is a computer and which is a human being.

The questions that the experimenter puts and the answers that the subjects provide are each conveyed in an impersonal way – say, typed in and displayed on a screen. The experimenter, by such suitable questioning, is to decide which is the human subject and which is the electronic one. If the experimenter cannot reliably tell which is which, then the computer (or computer's programmer) has passed the test.

Of course, part of the skill involved in getting the computer to pass would be to make it *suppress* the kind of answers that a computer could easily provide, but which an ordinary human subject could not. If, for example, the experimenter were to ask some complicated arithmetical question, the computer would have to 'pretend' not to be able to answer it easily. And, of course, the computer would have deliberately to 'lie' sometimes – such as in replying to the direct question 'Are you a human being?' But all that would be the easy part. The hard part would be in getting the computer to give convincing answers to questions that could be answered easily in a 'common-sense' way by an ordinary average human subject.

The 'strong AI (artificial intelligence) point of view'[3,4] asserts not only that it is merely a matter of (a comparatively short) time before a computer will be able to pass the Turing test, but also that once it has done so, terms such as

thought
understanding
awareness
happiness
pain
compassion
pride

could then be applied as validly to the computer as to the human subject. Such a viewpoint provides a very 'operational' approach to such questions. But strong-AI supporters would argue that the operational approach is necessary for cutting away the nebulous and shoddy thinking that pervades discussions in this kind of area – and it provides, instead, a rigorous and scientifically testable framework.

We recall that any universal Turing machine can, if supplied with an appropriate program, imitate any other Turing machine. Moreover, present-day general-purpose electronic computers are, in effect, already instances of universal Turing machines. Thus all that is now needed, from the point of view of *hardware*, for a modern computing machine, is a large enough store and a sufficient rapidity of operation that it can carry out its instructions adequately fast. Thus, so the strong-AI argument goes, it is merely the nature of the computer's program – that is, its software – which determines whether 'thinking', 'understanding', or any other of the terms in our list, has become appropriate to a modern computer's functioning.

Searle's Chinese Room

Not everyone accepts this view, however. In particular, John Searle in his chapter in this book and elsewhere,[5] has argued strongly that 'under-standing' cannot simply be a matter of the carrying out of an appropriate 'program' or 'algorithm'. He cites his example of the 'Chinese room'. This is a thought experiment based on some computer program (such as that of Roger Schank) which can correctly answer simple but not quite direct questions about certain elementary stories which Searle takes in Chinese. Searle envisages the program being enacted by the manipulation of Chinese symbols to obtain the desired answers. We may ask whether a computer following such a program can actually be said to 'understand' the story. The strong-AI answer would appear to be 'Yes'. But Searle says 'No'. For the electronics of the computer are replaced in Searle's thought experiment by a human worker – or perhaps by a room full of human workers, none of whom understands Chinese – each putting counters with Chinese symbols on them in various bins – and taking them out again –according to a set of instructions given to the workers in a book of rules printed, say, in English. The workers clearly do not understand the story since none of them understands Chinese. Still less does the room itself understand the story!

In my opinion, Searle has quite a strong case. But it is not a totally overwhelming one. The computer programs that do exist at present, and which are designed to provide answers to simple questions about such a restricted class of stories, are possibly just simple enough that one might reasonably envisage a person, or perhaps a room full of people carrying out the appropriate instructions. But when an actual Chinese person comprehends a Chinese story, the algorithm that is being carried out in that Chinese person's head – if, indeed, the followers of 'strong AI' are correct in believing that it *is* some algorithm – must be incomparably more complicated. The complication might be so great that imitation by a room full of human workers is simply out of the question. (It is not unknown in physics that totally new effects can arise, with 'big' systems, that are not discernible at all at a smaller scale.) Nevertheless, I feel that Searle is probably correct in maintaining that 'understanding' is not just a question of the carrying out of some appropriate algorithm – and still less is it merely a matter of the *output* of an algorithm. (Different algorithms can sometimes produce identical outputs.) It would seem, if this is the case, that 'understanding' is *not* just a question of *software* (that is, of programs or algorithms), but that the *hardware* should also be important. By 'hardware' is meant the actual physical construction of the object – either computer or brain.

I am not sure that Searle would put it quite like that – I am rather freely interpreting what I take to be his position (or the implication of his position) – but according to a viewpoint such as his, one would seemingly be driven to believing that a computer designed to follow the logical operation of every detail of the workings of a human brain would itself *not* achieve 'understanding' even though that *person* whose brain is under consideration may claim to be attaining understanding in some matter. The difference between this brain and this computer would not lie in the algorithms they are performing – since these are taken to be identical – but (presumably) only in their actual physical construction, that is, in their 'hardware'. (This contrasts markedly with the 'strong-AI' views expressed by, for example, Douglas Hofstadter.[4])

Non-algorithmic Functioning

My own viewpoint is not really the same as this. While I do indeed believe that the nature of the hardware is likely to be vitally important, I do not think that this can be separated from the question of software. I shall try to argue that if the 'hardware' is chosen appropriately, then its functioning is not something that is describable in terms of a computational algorithm at all. How this could come about I shall try to indicate shortly. For the moment, let us assume that non-algorithmic functioning *is* possible, and that a conscious human (or non-human) brain may well be non-algorithmic in its behaviour.

One of the implications of this viewpoint is that I do not really expect that an ordinary algorithmic computer could properly pass the Turing test at all. I should, however, at least qualify that statement. It could well be that a sufficiently clever program will some day be able to fool a perceptive experimenter for some of the time. It depends to some extent on how long the experimenter is allowed to continue the questioning in one single test and on how probing and sustained that questioning is allowed to be. Also, one could imagine a situation in which a computer is involved in a long succession of failures of the Turing test, but then the various answers provided by the human subject are 'studied', 'analysed' and 'remembered' by the computer and subsequently trotted out, perhaps with some random element, as the computer's 'own' answers at some later date. It is perhaps unfair to expect the experimenter to continue to ask original types of questions indefinitely and it is easy to imagine that after a long succession of separate tests the experimenter could get fooled. Somehow I regard this as 'cheating' and not 'properly' passing the test – though I admit the distinction is a bit vague. At least I doubt that many would regard *such* passing of the test as providing good evidence that the computer was actually 'thinking' or 'understanding' in the normal human way.

My own view is that if 'machines' are ever built that can *properly* (and consistently) pass the Turing test, then such 'machines' would have to incorporate the same non-algorithmic elements as are present (I am claiming) in conscious human thinking. More precisely what I mean by 'non-algorithmic elements' I shall have to explain later. For the moment let me just say that I do *not* mean simply *random* elements. I mean instead that some essentially non-algorithmic behaviour inherent in physical laws is being called upon.

The Active Role of Consciousness

In claiming that conscious thinking can invoke such non-algorithmic behaviour I am, in effect, tacitly claiming that consciousness is *functional*; that is, rather than being merely an 'accidental' feature of our particular (say, biological) construction – or, perhaps, as the strong-AI point of view might have it, being a necessary concomitant of sufficiently complex or high-level modes of computation ('thinking'?) – consciousness (I claim) has an *active* role to play in behaviour. Such a viewpoint seems to be rather unpopular with scientifically minded people (the *passive* role of consciousness being readily admitted), perhaps because it seems to imply that this active role of consciousness goes 'outside science' – that is, that the laws of physics must be suspended in order to allow this conscious 'self' to affect the body's behaviour. However, I am making no such suggestion, as we shall see. The philosophical distinction between consciousness playing an active role, or merely a passive one, is perhaps a delicate one. I shall not concern myself with that question here. My use of the word 'active' in this context has mainly a motivational significance. I think it is a useful way of thinking about consciousness, particularly in connection with the question of how consciousness can have arisen as a result of natural selection.

I should make the (obvious) point that a good deal of the (very complicated) activity that goes on in our heads is not in fact conscious. A good deal of our behaviour is the immediate result of unconscious rather than conscious 'thinking'. When I say that consciousness is playing an active role I mean that the kind of behaviour which seems necessarily to be accompanied by conscious thought is different in character from that which does not. One of the things that makes this difficult to analyse, however, is that activities which at *one time* may have required consciousness may, later on, be carried out entirely unconsciously. Driving a car is one obvious example, or riding a bicycle, or (presumably) walking. Such activities are commonly carried out when one *is* conscious though not actually conscious of the activities themselves. Yet there is still a marked difference in the manner in which they are carried out, according to whether or not one's consciousness is actually brought to bear on those activities. This is clear from the manifestations of those circumstances when it is not so brought to bear, such as in day-dreaming. Moreover, consciousness may be absent altogether, such as in sleep-walking or (more pathologically) cases of epileptic 'fugue', in which a sequence of actions is automatically carried out. Here, the absence of conscious direction can be particularly manifest in the resulting behaviour.

Figure 18.2 In states such as sleepwalking, the effects of lack of conscious direction can be particularly manifest.

There is, moreover, a clear and perhaps rather trivial way in which the activities of conscious things can differ from those of unconscious things. For conscious things have this habit of sometimes going around worrying about questions of 'self', etc. – not all the time, no doubt, but at least at critical moments when the matter is brought up with them. This is, in a sense, often the way in which one is persuaded that some other object *is* actually conscious! Of course, it would be a simple matter to program a computer merely to go around muttering 'worry, worry, worry . . . self, self, self' . . . but it is hard to see why natural selection should trouble to produce creatures which do such things it if were not, in some sense, an important ingredient of consciousness itself – a consciousness that is no doubt naturally selected, for quite other reasons.

What is Consciousness Needed for?

Though it is hard to be precise about the distinction between that kind of activity which seems to require consciousness and that which does not, I should like to list some suggestive terms that we do, in the ordinary way, use for one such kind of activity or the other:

consciousness not needed	*consciousness needed*
'automatic'	'common sense'
'following rules mindlessly'	'judgement of truth'
'programmed'	'understanding'
'algorithmic'	'artistic appraisal'

I suppose, to a neurophysiologist, one might try to suggest that the activities in the left-hand column might be carried out by the cerebellum (see Rodolfo Llinás' chapter), whereas those on the right require some activity of the cerebrum. I doubt that it is quite as simple as that, but there is likely *some* truth in it. (Perhaps one could describe what an 'algorithm' is to a neurophysiologist by saying that it is an activity that could be carried out by a cerebellum!)

The distinction is not, however, even as clear-cut as I have presented it. It seems to me to be manifest that there are many unconscious factors which enter into our conscious judgements. Matters of experience, prejudice, intuition, and even our normal use of logic, seem to be involved in our judgements in ways that we are commonly not aware of. Perhaps it is the case, as many would suggest, that even the conscious parts of these judgements are still algorithmic, but just incomparably more complicated – or 'higher-level' – than are the unconscious ones.

Personally, I would strongly doubt that consciousness can be just a reflection of the complexity of an algorithm. I am also doubtful that the term 'higher-level' is, in itself, greatly helpful as a means of distinguishing the putative 'conscious' algorithms from the unconscious ones. For the 'level' that one assigns to a logical operation is largely a matter of one's interpretation of it – or of the 'meaning' that one attributes to it (that is, semantics) – rather than something that the computation itself intrinsically possesses.

With regard to the question of complexity, there is a property of

Figure 18.3   The conscious self seems, in some respects, to be like the chairman of some large corporation who is presented only with highly processed and simplified data.

conscious thinking that I have always found puzzling, namely that things *seem* to need to be very *simple* in order that our conscious judgements can take effect. Somehow, the complicated operations are all done for us unconsciously and only the final ruling between some simplified alternatives seems to be carried out by the conscious mind. It is rather like a chairman of a large corporation, who insists on being presented with highly processed and simplified data, and then makes all the 'important' decisions. I do not suppose that it is really quite like that. There is somehow a lot of information in those seemingly vague and 'over-simplified' sense impressions ('*gestalts*') that one's consciousness is continually being presented with (or perhaps actually 'is'). Yet there *is* something about having to keep thoughts simple in our conscious thinking. I am continually struck by such commonplace statements as: 'how can I be expected to think of more than one thing at a time?' Somehow it is intrinsically difficult – and even regarded as obviously so – to keep more than one thing consciously in mind at a time. This is a very puzzling feature of conscious thought, if consciousness is to be merely a matter of complication, since there is no difficulty at all about keeping a huge number of vastly complicated *unconscious* processes going on at once, as is continually the case in one's ordinary activity. But *consciously*, one seems to be able to keep only one thing in mind at a time. It would appear that to deal with several things at once the conscious mind needs to flip backwards and forwards between them rather than deal with them concurrently. There is a curious 'oneness' or perhaps 'globality' of conscious thought which appears to be among its characteristic features. I shall have a comment to make later of possible relevance to this.

Computer Models of the Brain

To see what all this might have to do with the suggested computer models of the brain, I shall need to examine briefly the physiological basis of such

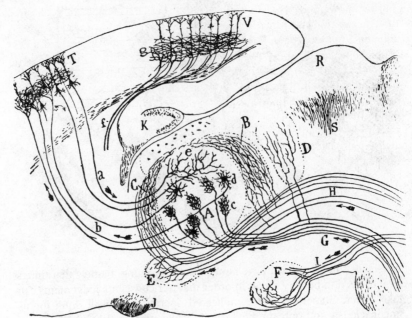

Figure 18.4   Huge numbers of nerve fibres connecting a great many neurons. This diagram (1911) by the Spanish anatomist Santiago Ramon y Cajal shows one side of the brain, cut through from back to front. It illustrates a tiny proportion of the different types of nerve cells, with fibres carrying in sensory information and carrying out motor signals.

models. The picture that is normally presented involves huge numbers of nerve fibres connecting a great many neurons; here the nerve fibres are modelled as wires carrying electric currents and the neurons as the logical switching units that occur, in computers, at the junctions of such wires – and which provide the logical (and hence also arithmetical, etc.) operation of the computer. The present view seems to be that single neurons do not correspond just to the most basic logical units ('and', 'or', 'not', etc.) but to some more complicated combinations. This would not affect the general picture. However, there does seem to be an additional ingredient in that the firing of neurons appears to involve a *random* element. What comes out is not just a function of what goes in, but all one can say is that there is a *probability* so-and-so of such-and-such an outcome, for any given input signal. Thus one seems to have, in effect, a Turing machine with a *randomizer* instead of a Turing machine proper.

However, there are mathematical results which say that the randomizer does not really give us anything new in the sense of being able to compute things that one could not compute without the randomizer. In any case, what is in practice normally done in modern computers, when some random ingredient is needed in a calculation, is to supply what are called 'pseudo-random' numbers – the results of some calculation which are, to all intents and purposes, indistinguishable from 'truly' random numbers. Alternatively, one could incorporate some physical random input such as the decay times of atoms in some radioactive source. It seems hard to believe that this would make any difference in practice.

All this seems to suggest that the modelling of the brain by a Turing machine is a reasonable procedure. Indeed, I think that it *is* a very worthwhile thing to try to do. There are, however, certain objections that one can make to taking this analogy too literally. In the first place, a Turing machine needs an infinite store, whereas the capacity of the brain, though very large, is clearly finite. On the other hand, one could also allow an unlimited supply of pieces of paper for writing notes on. Of course one could query whether in practice this *is* strictly unlimited (which it is not). But the real limitation is likely to be the *time* it takes to do a computation, not the number of pieces of paper that are allowed to be used. A computation that takes $10^{10^{10}}$ years to perform using some well-defined algorithm is not going to be much use in practice – and algorithms can, indeed, often be absurdly slow. The general theoretical discussion of computability by algorithms is very much concerned with what can be done in principle and not really with how long (in the sense of how many steps) it takes to carry out a computation.

Complexity

This leads us into another area of mathematics known as *complexity theory*, which *is* concerned with this very type of question. Given a well-defined class of mathematical problems for which there does exist an algorithm for solving them, and for which the 'size' of the problem is characterized by some positive n, we may ask how long the algorithm takes as a function of n. For example, the time might be roughly proportional to $\log n$, or n, or n^3, or 2^n, or $n!$, or n^{n^n}. In the last few of these cases the algorithm would rapidly become useless for moderately large values of n. In complexity theory, one of the aims would be to find algorithms in which this function of n does not grow too rapidly, where some algorithm may be already known which is perhaps inefficient in this respect – or else to find absolute limitations to possible improvements of this kind. Clearly these questions have some importance in the matter of what can be computed *in practice* by either a human or electronic computer. But even complexity theory is not exactly concerned with the practicality of algorithms, since it deals only with their efficiency in the limit of very large values of n.

The excessive slowness or memory requirements of certain algorithms would seem to be to the disadvantage of the human who chooses to use them, more than they are to the electronic computer, since inefficient 'brute force' operations are carried out much more efficiently and amenably by the latter. It is a more human quality to try to see one's way around having to do such things – for example, by finding shortcuts, or even by building computers to carry out such burdensome tasks!

Gödel's Theorem

Is there evidence, then, for ways in which the human procedure of conscious thinking might actually be *more* effective than the purely algorithmic computer picture of things? Is there even any clear evidence that conscious thinking is actually any *different* at all from something entirely algorithmic? My personal view is that there *is* such evidence, though none of it is uncontroversial. It would take too long to expound on these matters to any adequate degree, but I should like to make a few comments about Gödel's theorem, which I believe to have some genuine relevance to this.

Gödel's argument is concerned with the question of the provability of mathematical statements by means of some pre-assigned system of precise formal procedures.[6] For definiteness, let us take these mathematical statements to be propositions about arithmetic – statements of the form: for all integers $a, \ldots, c$, there exist integers $d, \ldots, f$, such that for all ... etc., then some arithmetical relation between $a, \ldots, c, d, \ldots, f, \ldots$ holds. The statements of 'Fermat's last theorem' or the 'Goldbach conjecture' have this general form. The pre-assigned proof procedures are supposed to have the property that their correct application or otherwise can be checked by some algorithmic procedure, that is, by a Turing machine. Assuming that these procedures are actually all valid (that is, that they lead only to *true* arithmetical propositions), Gödel's argument contrives to produce another arithmetical proposition that is *not* obtainable by the procedures, yet is manifestly *also true*!

What Gödel's argument *seems* to show is that the way in which we decide that mathematical statements are true is not algorithmic. It most definitely does show that there is no algorithmic procedure (a Turing machine) which can generate *all* the true propositions of arithmetic and no false ones. It is often argued, on the other hand, that there is no evidence that human mathematicians can do any better. Yet it is a remarkable fact that the very argument by which Gödel establishes his result provides a specific arithmetical proposition that any mathematician following the Gödel argument *sees* to be true. By following the argument, a *new* method of proof is seen to be valid, which goes beyond whatever collection of methods had been accepted previously.

But why, then, can one not simply get a computer also to follow this Gödel argument and itself 'see' the truth of any new Gödel proposition? The catch lies in 'seeing' that the Gödel argument, in any specific realization, has actually been correctly applied. The trouble is that the computer does not have a way of judging truth; it is only following rules. It does not 'see' the validity of the Gödel argument. It does not 'see' *anything* unless it is conscious! It seems to me that in order to appreciate the validity of the Gödel procedure – or, indeed, to *see* the validity of *any* mathematical procedure – one must be conscious. One can follow rules without being conscious, but how does one *know* that those rules are legitimate rules to follow without being, at least at some stage, conscious of their meaning?

This matter has a bearing on the 'simplicity' inherent in conscious thinking that I referred to earlier. I am not sure that 'simplicity' is really the correct term, but I am unable to think of an appropriate alternative. The 'simple' thoughts that I am referring to are often hard to formulate in a precise way. They are things that one would often be hard-put to program on a computer. 'Common sense' is a good example. The central idea underlying the Gödel argument is another. There are many things in mathematics and science that could come under this heading. It is a question of conceptual simplicity, perhaps, though specific realizations of the 'simple' ideas may well lead to extreme complication in detail (as they do with the Gödel argument).

Physical Laws

The main argument *against* human mathematicians being able to achieve what a computer cannot rests, as far as I can see, on the idea that it should be possible *in principle* to follow whatever physical processes are going on in a person's head by some precise computation, even if one does not know the details of which computation that might be. The argument goes beyond any specific model of nerves and neurons and refers directly to the physical laws that are operative on a human scale. One has the picture that the material of a brain is composed, after all, of a vast number of particles which move around and bounce off one another, all according to very precise laws. Some of the particles are charged and are deflected in precise ways by a pervading electromagnetic field; and this field itself propagates according to the marvellously precise Maxwell equations. Is this not a highly mechanistic picture in which the future state can be computed – albeit only in principle – from the state at any earlier time? The time-evolution of any system, whether it be a precisely constructed machine or a biological system, would appear to be adequately governed, at the relevant level, by the deterministic laws of classical physics. Are we not being presented here simply with a vast computing machine?

It seems to be the prevailing view that classical physics should be adequate for describing behaviour on the scale relevant to a human brain. Nevertheless, it could be the case that *quantum mechanics* is actually needed. In my own view, it is highly likely that quantum phenomena *are* actually involved in the workings of the brain. It seems to be the case that single quantum events can be responsible for the triggering of nerve impulses. (In the visual system, a sensation of light can be triggered by something like five photons being absorbed by the rod photoreceptors of the retina; but even just a single photon can produce a detectable electrical response in a rod and could suffice to produce a visual sensation were it not for an inbuilt mechanism for suppressing or ignoring signals of that sensitivity – otherwise one would be flooded with irrelevant 'noise'.) How might this 'computer picture' be affected if a quantum description needs to be adopted?

Standard quantum mechanics,[7] in the way that one has actually to apply the theory, employs two distinct modes in which a system can evolve. The first is Schrödinger evolution (or, using a different but equivalent form of description, Heisenberg evolution – the more general comprehensive term would be 'unitary' evolution). According to Schrödinger evolution, the state of a system evolves according to a perfectly well-defined deterministic law. Everything is governed by a differential equation, the situation being very similar to that for the classical Maxwell equations, and again the 'computer picture' would seem appropriate. However, to get agreement with observation, one must bring in the second mode of evolution, which is referred to as 'state-vector reduction' (or wave-function collapse). The theory is not at all clear about when this second mode must be brought in. Phrases like 'when an observation is made on the system' are invoked in order to give us some indication of when this should be. But it is not very clear what kind of systems have 'observer status' and can so set off the 'state-vector

---

A Brief History of the Development of Quantum Theory

Max Planck 1900	black-body spectrum requires that light be emitted and absorbed in units of energy $E = h\nu$ where ν = frequency, h = (Planck's) constant
Albert Einstein 1905	postulates that electromagnetic fields consist of photons and predicts photo-electric effect
Niels Bohr 1913	('old' quantum mechanics) explains atomic spectra on basis of assumption that angular momentum of orbital electrons is quantized in units of $h/2\pi$
Prince Louis de Broglie 1923	postulates wave nature of particles
Wolfgang Pauli 1925	exclusion principle for electrons
Werner Heisenberg 1925, 1927	matrix mechanics, uncertainty principle
Erwin Schrödinger 1926	Schrödinger wave equation
Max Born 1926	probability interpretation of wave function
Paul Dirac 1927, 1928	general transformation theory, equation for electron, beginnings of quantum field theory

---

reduction' mode of evolution. It is this second mode that involves all the probabilities and the indeterminism that many people find so troublesome. The lack of determinism also makes it clear that state-vector reduction is not really consistent with Schrödinger evolution. One might like to imagine that when the observer is also treated as being part of a quantum system, evolving according to Schrödinger evolution, then the second mode could be dispensed with. But this appears not to be so, because Schrödinger evolution is deterministic whereas state-vector reduction is not.

I do not propose to enter into the endless discussions that these questions lead into. But if, for the moment, we simply accept that there are these two modes of evolution, then where does this lead us for our 'computer picture' of the brain? It seems that the interjection of this second mode at various times introduces an essentially random element, so we are apparently presented not with a Turing machine model, but with a Turing machine with a randomizer.

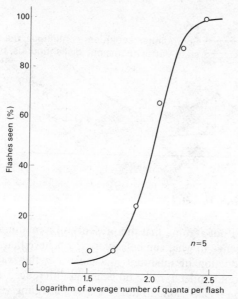

Figure 18.5   *In 1942, the physicist Selig Hecht and his colleagues, S. Shlaer and M. H. Pirenne, reported the result of a remarkable experiment. They wanted to discover the smallest amount of light that can be seen by the human eye when fully dark-adapted. The observer (in this case Maurice Pirenne) looked at the dim flash and this graph plots the percentage of flashes that he saw according to the number of quanta or photons of light entering the cornea of his eye (2.0 on the horizontal scale indicates 100 quanta). A large fraction of the quanta are absorbed before they reach the rods and cones in the retina. The curve drawn through the points is derived theoretically on the assumption that only five quanta are needed for the flash to be seen. Since the flash covered a large number of rods in the retina, the chance of any one rod catching more than one of the five quanta was extremely low. So, the conclusion was that rods in the human eye must be capable of producing a signal on the capture of a single quantum of light (redrawn from the* Journal of General Physiology, *1942, 25, 891–40).*

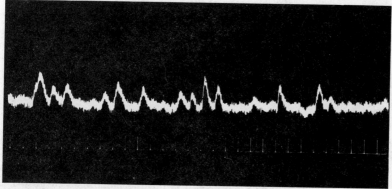

Figure 18.6   *For these recordings of the electrical responses of a single rod from the eye of a toad, the light intensity was reduced to the level at which the rod absorbed only one photon,* on average, *for each flash. Because of the probabilistic nature of light emission the actual number of photons hitting the rod would inevitably vary; sometimes none, often one, sometimes two, rarely three, and so on. The blips on the lower trace, occurring every 30 seconds, indicate the moment of each flash, while the upper trace is the amplified recording of electric current flowing through the rod. Sometimes there is no current, often a small response, sometimes one roughly twice as large, occasionally one about three times the size. Presumably these signals reflect the number of* individual *photons caught by the rod. Here is a direct demonstration of the ability of photoreceptors to respond to single photons of light (based on results published in the* Journal of Physiology, *1979, 288, 613–34).*

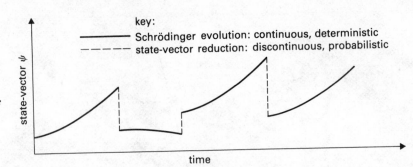

Figure 18.7 A strange picture of the evolution of the physical world – as described by conventional quantum mechanics.

Non-algorithmic Physics?

However, was I not arguing that the presence of a randomizer makes no essential difference to what can be achieved? I believe that this is so, and that the introduction of quantum mechanics, in the way that I have presented it would, indeed, make no essential difference. But in my view (and I am by no means alone in this) there is something very incomplete about quantum theory as it stands. It is a question of where the borderline falls between a quantum description and classical descriptions of things – a question of when a system should be described quantum-mechanically and when classically (the latter behaviour cannot properly be deduced from the former) – and of what to do with that borderline. I am of the opinion that a *new theory* is really needed in order to cope with such matters (and I believe that one can begin to make suggestions as to where to look for such a theory).[8] It seems to me to be quite on the cards that such a theory might involve operations with a non-algorithmic evolution!

Moreover, I think that this quantum–classical borderline could well be highly relevant in the workings of the brain. Whereas the firing of nerve signals can apparently be triggered by quantum events, it is the usual view that the signals themselves are 'large enough' to be treated as classical phenomena. However, the triggering of the next nerve signal could again involve single quantum events, and so on. I am not trying to say anything very specific here. But it seems to me to be highly likely that the quantum and quantum–classical aspects of physics ought not to be ignored in these discussions.

Quantum physics involves many highly intriguing and mysterious kinds of behaviour. Not the least of these are the quantum correlations (see box below) which can occur over widely separated distances.[9] It seems to me to be a definite possibility that such things could be playing a role in conscious thought-modes. Perhaps it is not too fanciful to suggest that quantum correlations could be playing an operative role over large regions of the brain. Might there be any relation between a 'state of awareness' and a highly coherent quantum state in the brain? Is the 'oneness' or 'globality' that seems to be a feature of consciousness connected with this? It is somewhat tempting to believe so. (Such a view might provide a way of resolving the 'teletransportation paradox', according to which a person is teletransported by photon signals to a distant

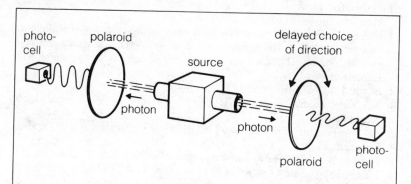

photo-cell   polaroid   delayed choice of direction

source

photon

photon

polaroid   photo-cell

Quantum correlations: in the experiment of Aspect and his colleagues the polarizations of photons from a common source are measured some twelve metres apart. The photons behave as one still-connected entity up until they are detected, their polarizations being correlated with each other in a way which is inconsistent with their being separate objects (diagram highly schematic).

planet, but the instructions to destroy the 'original copy' of the person are disobeyed![10] Would such a hypothetical operation produce two absolutely identical versions, in different places, of a single *person*? What would happen to his consciousness? If a mental state is like a quantum state, then the paradox could be resolved. For *in principle* quantum states cannot be copied – or, rather, they can be copied *only* at the expense of destroying the original state.)

Finally, I should remark that even in classical physics, the relation between determinism and computability (algorithmic behaviour) is not at all as clear-cut as might be felt from the above discussion. Some mathematical results by Pour-El and Richards indicate that a non-computable evolution can sometimes arise even with very simple classical-type deterministic systems.[11] The precise status of these results in the present context is not clear to me. But they do at least highlight the important point that perfectly well-defined precise physical laws can sometimes result in non-algorithmic behaviour. Deterministic behaviour does *not* at all imply algorithmic (that is, computable) behaviour. (There are, indeed, many things in mathematics that are well defined but not algorithmic.) It is my guess that some non-algorithmic physical process may well be being harnessed in the workings of the conscious mind.

Notes and References

1 Turing, A. M. (1937) On computable numbers, with an application to the *Entscheidungsproblem*. *Proc. Lond. Math. Soc.* 2, 42.
2 Turing, A. M. (1950) Computing machinery and intelligence. *Mind*, 59; reprinted in A. R. Anderson (ed.), (1978) *Minds and Machines*. New York: McGraw-Hill.

3 Hofstadter, D. R. Jr. (1979) *Gödel, Escher, Bach: An Eternal Golden Braid* Hassocks, Sussex: Harvester.

4 For a collection of articles exhibiting a range of views on this question, see Hofstadter, D. R, Jr and Dennett, C. M. (eds) (1981), *The Mind's I.* For an extreme 'strong-AI' view, see Hofstadter's article: A conversation with Einstein's brain.

5 Searle, J., in ibid, also chapter 15, this volume.

6 See Nagel, E. and Newman, J. R. (1959) *Gödel's Proof.* London: Routledge & Kegan Paul.

7 See, for example, Polkinghorne, J. C. (1984) *The Quantum World.* London: Longman.

8 Penrose, R. (1985) Gravity and state-vector reduction. In R. Penrose and C.J. Isham (eds), *Quantum Concepts in Space and Time,* Oxford: Oxford Univ. Press. Press.

9 Aspect, A. and Grangier, in ibid.

10 See the introduction to ref. 4. and Derek Parfit's chapter in this book.

11 Pour-El, M. B. and Richards, I. *Adv. in Math.* 39 (1981): 215–39; 48 (1983): 44–74.

19

Could a Machine be Conscious?

Colin McGinn

Colin McGinn took a First in Psychology from Manchester University in 1971, and went on to complete an MA in Psychology there in 1972. He then switched to Philosophy, obtaining a BPhil at Oxford in 1974. While at Oxford he was awarded the John Locke prize. He taught at University College London from 1974 to 1985, visiting several American universities during this period. He is now Wilde Reader in Mental Philosophy at Oxford. His books are The Character of Mind *(1982),* The Subjective View *(1983),* Wittgenstein on Meaning *(1984). Apart from philosophy, his main interest is literature.*

I want to make some sobering remarks about an intoxicating question – the question that forms my title. It seems to me that, on reflection, this question does not have the interest it is popularly thought to have. Its power to excite stems largely from unclarity about what is being asked. In particular, we need to be clear what we mean by 'machine'.

I have formulated the question in terms of the notion of *consciousness*, but this too needs to be clarified. I could equally have asked whether a machine could have a mind. These formulations have a generality which disguises the diversity of the phenomena. For the question must be whether a machine could think or feel or perceive or will or create or imagine – or do whatever else we customarily dub 'mental'. And it is not obvious that each of these attributes will be equally accessible to a machine; they raise different issues and make different requirements. It is not even clear that consciousness belongs essentially to all of them – we are familiar with the idea of unconscious beliefs and desires, for example. In order to keep my question within manageable proportions I shall focus on a specific attribute of mind, namely subjectivity; and by this I shall mean what Thomas Nagel has meant in saying that for an entity to have subjectivity is for there to be something it is *like* to be that entity.[1] I do not pretend that this notion is particularly explanatory or even very clear (that is part of the problem we face in this area), but I think it will serve to identify the kind of question I mean to be asking. Could a machine enjoy a distinctive 'phenomenology'? Could things *seem* a certain way to a machine – as the world seems a certain way to us and to bats? Could a machine be a subject of experience?

We can interpret the word 'machine' in a narrow sense and a wide

A Dalek – one of the evil robots from the BBC Television series Doctor Who. *Could a machine be evil without being conscious? Could the world seem a certain way to a Dalek, as it seems a certain way to a human being or a bat? (© BBC, 1983).*

Figure 19.1   Stonehenge: a 'machine' in the widest sense – the intentional product of some kind of intelligence (Mary Evans Picture Library).

sense. In the narrow sense we mean the kinds of device that have actually been constructed by human beings: motor cars, typewriters, aeroplanes, nuclear weapons, pocket calculators, office computers. Could any *such* device be conscious? Well, *is* any such device conscious? Surely not, as even the most ardent enthusiast of the word processor would agree. And if not, then *extensions* of such devices, built by the same principles, will not be conscious either. Some people believe that consciousness is a *computational* property, but they do not believe that present-day computers and extensions thereof are conscious; the technology needed for implementing the computational properties in which consciousness consists lies (they would say) in the distant future. I shall return to this question; for now I am saying merely that consciousness is not to be found in the *current* extension of the word 'machine'. Nobody today knows how to design a machine that is conscious.

In the wide sense of 'machine' we mean anything, actual or possible, that is an *artefact*, that is, the intentional product of some kind of intelligence. Artefacts thus contrast with naturally occurring objects. The question then is whether an artefact could be conscious. This question can be considered in two parts: (a) could a *human* artefact be conscious, and (b) could an artefact of *any* conceivable intelligence be conscious? On the first question I would say that the matter is entirely an empirical one: it concerns whether human beings ever in fact achieve enough in the way of scientific and technological knowledge. It is like asking whether we shall ever travel to another galaxy. The second question is the one that raises the issue of principle, for it asks whether the *concept* of an artefact is such as to exclude the possession of consciousness. And here I think a quite definite answer is possible: certainly an artefact could be conscious. All that is required is an intelligence of sufficient ingenuity and know-how. Suppose there were an intelligence clever enough to create beings physically just like us (or bats). Then I think this intelligence would have created conscious beings. Or consider the doctrine of creationism: false as it undoubtedly is, it is surely not self-contradictory. If we are the artefacts of God, this is not a reason to suppose ourselves unconscious. After all, there is a sense in which we *are* artefacts: for we are the products of natural selection operating upon inorganic materials to generate brains capable of subserving consciousness. It is, if anything, *harder* to see how consciousness could result naturally than to see how it could have been wrought by intelligence, as proponents of the argument from design have always maintained. At any rate, all intelligence needs to do to create conscious beings is to recapitulate what natural selection did mindlessly. There is thus no problem of principle about an artefact being conscious.

Why is the distinction between artefact and natural object irrelevant to the question whether an entity is conscious? Because of the following principle: the intrinsic nature of an object is logically independent of the manner of its genesis. Conjoin this with the claim that whether an entity is conscious is solely a matter of its intrinsic nature and you get the result that an artefact could be conscious. In other words, if we know that an entity a has the same intrinsic physical nature as a conscious being b, then we know that a is conscious in the same way as b, quite independently of whether a and b came into existence in the same way. This principle is an application of what has come to be called the *supervenience* of the mental on the physical: if x and y have the same physical constitution, and x has mental property P, then y must also have P.[2] How x and y came to have that physical constitution is irrelevant to whether they both have P. Hence whether something is an artefact is irrelevant to the question whether it is conscious.

It is important to note that my reason for holding that an artefact could be conscious is *not* that I take myself to have any theory or explanation of what it is about the brain that makes it the basis of consciousness. It is not that I can see what feature makes the brain conscious and can therefore see how to build a machine which incorporates this feature. On the contrary, as I shall explain later, I do not believe that we do possess such knowledge of the brain. All I am saying is that supervenience assures us that the brain has *some* property which confers consciousness upon it; I do not say that I know *which*. Granted this degree of materialism (quite a modest amount, actually), there is no obstacle to artefactual conscious-ness. If you duplicate the brain you duplicate whatever it is about it that confers consciousness, and there is no reason to think the duplication must occur *naturally* if the duplicate brain is to have this unknown feature.

Any residual misgivings about this claim must, I think, devolve upon the assumed degree of materialism. How *can* consciousness depend on the brain in this way? This is a good question, in the sense that it is a hard question to answer. But it is not a question about machines and consciousness; rather, it is an expression of that old set of anxieties known as the mind–body problem. And it would be a mistake to convert these (legitimate) anxieties into a denial that artefacts could be conscious. The question about machine consciousness does indeed sharpen and vivify the mind–body problem, but the problem was there anyway and independently. It is just as hard to see how an entity constructed naturally from mere matter can be conscious as it is to see how an intentionally created material object can be. But we know that the former is possible, because we have seen it done. *How*, we don't know.

There is a different question that might be being asked by the sentence 'Could a machine be conscious?' It might be the question whether only *living* things can be conscious. Must a conscious being be animate, organic, alive? This is not the same as our last question, since we were allowing then that an artefact could be alive, that is, be a biological entity. The present question is whether, however an entity came into existence, it could be conscious only if living. Certainly this is one way in which the word 'machine' is used, conjuring up as it does images of cogs and pulleys, microchips and computer screens. Wittgenstein makes some suggestive remarks about this question in his *Philosophical Investigations:*

. . . only of a living human being and what resembles (behaves like) a living human being can one say: it has sensations; it sees; is blind; hears; is deaf; is conscious or unconscious. (¶281)

We do indeed say of an inanimate thing that it is in pain: when playing with dolls for example. But this use of the concept of pain is a secondary one. Imagine a case in which people ascribed pain *only* to inanimate things; pitied *only* dolls! (¶282)

Look at a stone and imagine it having sensations. One says to oneself: How could one so much as get the idea of ascribing a sensation to a thing? One might as well ascribe it to a number! – And now look at a wriggling fly and at once these difficulties vanish and pain seems able to get a foothold here, where before everything was, so to speak, too smooth for it. (¶284)[3]

Clearly Wittgenstein is here making a conceptual link between being conscious and being alive. Let us examine this idea.

What, to begin with, is meant by 'living'? This question belongs to the philosophy of biology, and it is not altogether easy, but I think the following is along the right lines: an entity counts as a living thing just if it is made up of a system of interacting parts which control the growth and repair of the entity by means of some process of part duplication (cell reproduction), these parts deriving their substance from exogenous materials (food). No doubt this definition could be improved and refined, but for our purposes it will do as it stands. For the question is whether any *such* conditions could be necessary for the possession of consciousness (these conditions are obviously not *sufficient* for consciousness because plants and micro-organisms, which surely are not conscious, do satisfy such conditions). Now is there a *conceptual* connection between life, as so defined, and consciousness?

Here I think we feel pulled in two directions. On the one hand, it is hard to see how there *could* be a conceptual connection between something's being conscious and its being alive in the defined sense. For what have growth and repair and cellular structure got to do with the possession of subjectivity? Why should things seeming a certain way to a creature conceptually require that the body of the creature be structured in the way defined? On the other hand, Wittgenstein does appear to have hold of a sound intuition: how can what is dead and inert be a subject of conscious states? Surely the reason we ascribe consciousness as we do – to human beings and other animals but not to stones and pocket calculators – has something essential to do with being alive or not. I think we can resolve this tension by adopting an intermediate view, the view indeed which a careful reading of Wittgenstein's words suggests. This intermediate view says that a conscious being must either be alive or must resemble what is alive, where the resemblance is between the *behaviour* of the things in question. In other words, only of what behaves *like* a living thing can we say that it is conscious. This claim connects consciousness with life, but not with what constitutes life; rather, with what manifests or expresses it. A non-living thing might therefore in principle qualify for the ascription of consciousness, so long as it behaved like a living conscious thing, for example ourselves. Only such an entity could *invite* the ascription of consciousness. It is presumably because of a tacit acceptance of this idea that we are so prone to count the robots of science-fiction films as conscious beings: they do not live, but they act as if they do.

But if we accept this idea, *why* do we? Why does the ascription of consciousness depend upon sufficiently lifelike behaviour? The reason, I think – and here again I follow Wittgenstein – is that our concept of a conscious state is the concept of a state with a certain sort of behavioural *expression*. We cannot really make sense of a conscious stone because the stone does not behave in ways we can recognize as expressive of its supposed consciousness. Think here of facial expressions: these are so integral to our notion of an emotion that we just do not know what to make of the suggestion that an IBM 100 might be angry or depressed or undergoing an adolescent crisis. The problem is not that the IBM is inanimate, not made of flesh and blood; the problem is that it is not embodied in such a way that it can express itself (and putting it inside a lifelike body will not provide for the right sort of expressive link-up). But I think that if we *could* make a non-living thing that behaved exactly like a fly, then we would have as much reason to attribute conscious states to it as we do to a living fly: whether its body could repair itself by cellular replacement is neither here nor there.

I conclude, then, that being biologically alive is not a necessary condition of consciousness, but that it is necessary that a conscious being should behave like a living thing (of a certain sophistication).

What Makes the Brain Conscious?

Earlier I confessed ignorance about what properties of the brain make it the 'seat of consciousness'. I now want to criticize some attempts to be more positive on this question, in particular the thesis that consciousness is a computational property of the brain.

Let me first flog a dead horse – dead horses can still teach sound lessons. The most naive view of what makes the brain conscious is that it contains some special *substance* that makes it so. Thus it might be supposed that chemical analysis of the brain will turn up some especially subtle and ethereal substance, ectoplasmic in nature, which explains consciousness. This idea is both empirically false and conceptually misconceived. It is empirically false because the brain does not contain any such radically special kind of substance – generally speaking it has the same kind of chemical composition as other organs of the body. And it is conceptually misconceived because even if there were such a unique substance in the brain, this would not be the *kind* of thing to explain consciousness: for how could *any* chemical substance *be* consciousness? So plainly it cannot be the chemical properties of the brain – which chemical substances compose it – that explain consciousness. The materials of the brain are of the same kind as those found in non-conscious nature, so how could they explain why consciousness is found in the brain but not elsewhere (for example, the kidneys)? It follows that, no matter how well we come to understand the chemistry of the brain, this will not enable us to understand consciousness.

Reflections such as these have led philosophers (and others) to seek a different kind of brain property which might explain conscious pheno-mena. Thus there developed the doctrine known as *functionalism*. Instead of identifying consciousness with the material composition of the brain, we should identify it with certain higher-order properties of the brain, namely the (supposedly) more abstract *causal* properties possessed by physico-chemical states of the brain. The first-order physico-chemical properties are admittedly of the wrong kind to constitute consciousness, but their causal roles will do better: they will, among other things, have the desired specificity. Pain, for example, is a higher-order property of physical states which consists in having a certain pattern of causes and effects, as it might be mediating bodily injury and avoidance behaviour. To build a machine that feels pain it will then suffice to install mechanisms that mediate input and output in this way. Functionalism has been subjected to a good deal of critical discussion, and I do not have space here to recapitulate the usual criticisms. I will just make one central point: it does not seem plausible to claim that possession of functional properties is *sufficient* for the possession of consciousness. For isn't it entirely conceivable that something should have the functional properties of chemical structures in the brain and yet not be conscious? Nor is it surprising that this should seem possible, since the functionalist's causes and effects are themselves just physico-chemical events. True, states of the brain have different causal roles from states of the kidneys, but the causal roles of *both* are defined in terms of physical causes and effects; so how can the former 'give rise' to consciousness while the latter do not? The kidneys have a characteristic pattern of inputs and outputs, and hence higher-order functional properties; so why aren't the kidneys a second centre of consciousness? The problem again is that the suggested properties are not specific enough to the brain, and anyway turn out upon examination to be the wrong *kind* of properties to determine conscious-ness.

Computationalism

What *other* sort of property might the brain have which makes it uniquely the organ of consciousness? This property will have to be specific to the brain, and it will have to be of the right 'kind'. The idea that has been gaining adherents is that the brain has (in addition to material and functional properties) computational properties; and it is these that 'underlie' the presence and operations of consciousness.[5] In particular, it is held that *thinking* is a computational process. This thesis has a direct bearing on the question of machine consciousness, because if we can design computing machines and consciousness is computation, then we know, at least in general outline, how to *design* a conscious machine: we simply (!) build in the computational structure of the brain. In order to evaluate this thesis we need to get more exact about what a computational property is.

To say that the brain carries out computations is, presumably, to say that certain physical processes may be described as (literally) performing mathematically describable operations: the brain does sums. Thus the optical system calculates (say) the distance of an object from information about the magnitudes of certain variables to which the retina is sensitive, for example, size in the retinal image. So we can say of a physical process or structure in the brain: 'It just calculated that the distance of x was d on the basis of the light having intensity i.' Such ascriptions attribute propositional content, signified by the clause following 'calculated that', to physical processes and structures in the brain. It is natural to suppose that such propositional contents are represented in a system of internal symbols, so that the brain's computations (like the kind we do externally on paper) involve the manipulation of these symbols. It further appears that the brain is performing a great many such computations at any given time, and that their results are typically integrated into higher-level computations; there is, in the jargon, much 'parallel processing'. A computer likewise, it is said, performs computations (that's why it's called a *computer*), and so the brain is rightly described as a computer. The claim then is that mental attributes, in particular consciousness, can be identified with such computational processes: to have a mind is to instantiate a computer program. Is this view plausible?

Let me first warn against a potential *non sequitur*. From the fact that the brain is a computer and the fact that the brain has mental attributes it does not follow that those attributes are computational in nature. For it may be that the brain's computational properties, like its material composition, do not constitute mentality – they simply coexist with it. Nor do we get an identification from the fact (if it is one) that computations are part of the causal background of conscious mental phenomena. We need more than this for a genuine identification (such as is exemplified by the identification of water with H_2O or heat with molecular motion). But now *could* consciousness be identifiable with cerebral computations? I think not, but before I say why let me dissociate myself from two other critical responses that are sometimes made to the computational theory of mind.

I do not, first, wish to question the literal and non-derivative truth of ascriptions of computations to subconscious physical processes in the brain. I think that the brain really does carry out subconscious computations, quite independently of our so describing it – it is not merely *as if* it does. Content is thus not the prerogative of the properly mental (as *information* is not in the mathematical theory of 'communication'). And so far as I can see, these computations need a medium, that is a system of internal symbols, for example symbols standing for light intensities at the retina.

Secondly, I do not object to the computational theory for the same reason John Searle does in his 'Chinese room' argument.[6] His argument is that a computer program is a set of rules for performing *syntactic* operations on symbols, and therefore instantiating a computer program can never add up to the possession of *semantic* properties; hence intentionality cannot be explained in terms of computations. With one part of this argument I completely agree: you can't get semantics out of syntax alone; so *if* a computer program deals only in syntax it cannot confer semantic features such as our conscious intentional states have. However, it does not follow that the symbols manipulated by a computer program cannot have semantic properties – all that is shown is that they cannot have these in virtue of the rules of the program. The clear-headed computational theorist will agree with Searle about the non-semantic character of program rules but point out that the symbols manipulated can have other sorts of property too, and these might be what give the symbols semantic features. Thus a symbol in the visual system might get to stand for light intensity at the distal source in virtue of the extrinsic causal links between that symbol and circumambient objects. Internal manipulations don't determine reference, but causal relations to the environment might. And there is no reason why such an account of semantic properties should be unavailable in respect of computing machines. On this way of looking at the matter, computing machines might have intentionality – that is, world-directedness – but not simply because of the program they instantiate. To put it differently, when the visual system computes that p (where p stands for a proposition) this is a matter not just of syntactic features of its internal code but also of how the symbols of the code are related to the subject matter of p. Since I believe that the brain does compute, I think that it must have semantic properties, and so there must be something about it that *confers* these properties. Accordingly, my objection to the computational theory of mind cannot be that it cannot provide for semantic intentionality.

My objection is in a way simpler than this. The problem I see is how such computational processes as those in the retina and central visual system could ever explain the existence of conscious subjectivity. Since such computations go on without subjectivity – they are subconscious – how could their presence be sufficient to explain subjectivity? How can consciousness be got from something that does not essentially involve consciousness? A pocket calculator computes but isn't conscious, so how could consciousness be a matter of computations? If computations can go on without consciousness, they cannot be *sufficient* for consciousness. Such computations may indeed be possessed of semantic features, but this falls short of there being something it is like for that which performs these computations.

To this objection it will be replied that not just *any* kind of computation is sufficient for consciousness – consciousness requires a special *sort* of computational complexity or structure. Thus it has been claimed that integrated parallel processing is what makes for consciousness, or again the existence of a self-scanning unit which monitors what is going on in the brain's various computational departments.[7] But it seems to me that these sophistications do not evade the fundamental problem, namely that such properties could be instantiated in the absence of consciousness. And the reason for this is simply that they are of the wrong *kind* to explain the phenomenon of subjectivity. You can't get the 'qualitative content' of conscious experience – seeing red, feeling a pain, etc. – out of computations in the nervous system. No matter how many pocket calculators you put together, and however you link them up, you won't get a conscious experience out of them – how could you? The difficulty here is one of principle: we have no understanding of how consciousness could emerge from an aggregation of non-conscious elements such as computational devices; so the properties of these devices cannot *explain* how consciousness comes about or what it is. It may indeed be true that, as a matter of fact, organisms get to be conscious just when their brains reach a certain level of computational complexity, as it is true that consciousness seems to require a certain degree of physiological complexity; but this observation does nothing to *explain* how consciousness depends upon computational complexity, as a like observation about physiological complexity does not. A proper theory of consciousness in terms of properties of the brain should make it *intelligible* that the brain is the basis of consciousness, but the computational properties of the brain do not furnish such a theory: it remains a mystery how cerebral computations could give rise to consciousness, as much a mystery as how mere matter could form itself into the organ of consciousness.[8]

It follows from what has just been said that knowing how to build a computing machine is not knowing how to build a conscious machine. So we do not know the design of a conscious machine. We do not know this because we do not know what makes the brain conscious. If we knew what properties of the brain made *it* conscious, then we would know the design of a machine that would be conscious – where the machine in question might precisely duplicate the physical nature of the brain. The two questions go together. Still, the brain is a physical entity and it is conscious, so it must have *some* design feature, presumably 'physical' in nature (whatever that might mean), that *makes* it conscious. My point has been that we do not at present know what that feature is, and so we do not at present know how to build a machine which matches this achievement of the brain's. But this is not to say that a machine could not be conscious. It needs merely to be the same kind of machine as the brain is, whatever that kind is.

References

1 See his 'What is it like to be a bat?', in *Mortal Questions* (1979) Cambridge:

Cambridge Univ. Press.

2 See Davidson, Donald (1980) Mental events. *Essays on Actions and Events*, p. 214. Oxford: Clarendon Press.

3 Wittgenstein, L. (1953) *Philosophical Investigations*. Oxford: Blackwell.

4 For a survey and criticism, see Block, Ned, Troubles with functionalism. In Ned Block (ed.), *Readings in Philosophy of Psychology*, vol. 1. Cambridge, Mass.: Harvard Univ. Press.

5 See Johnson-Laird, P. N. (1983) *Mental Models*, esp. chapter 16. Cambridge: Cambridge Univ. Press and his chapter in this book.

6 See Searle, J. (1984) *Minds, Brains and Science*. London: BBC Publications; also his second Reith Lecture, 'Beer cans and meat machines', reprinted in *The Listener*, 14 November 1984.

7 This would appear to be Johnson-Laird's position, *Mental Models*.

8 The argument of this paragraph owes much to Thomas Nagel's 'Panpsychism', in *Mortal Questions*.

Part 4
Ideas: How Brains Could Have Minds, and Why

Like kidneys, spleens and hearts, minds must surely be useful to people or animals that have them. The mind is hardly likely to be a redundant, inherited vestige of some previously valuable feature of a distant ancestor – a kind of mental appendix! Following evolutionary dogma it must then be the useful product of a selective process, conferring a biological advantage on those that have it. In part 4 we tackle the philosophy and the biology of mind and consciousness.

No area of human enquiry has rivalled the philosophy of mind in its ability to generate '-isms'; but the batallions of schools of thought about thought reduce to two great armies – the materialists and the dualists. Materialist theories see mind as part of the physical world; dualists see it as fundamentally different in nature.

At the time of its conception by René Descartes in the seventeenth century, dualism was a liberating force because it freed every natural phenomenon except mind (or soul) from the constraints of religious dogma. The blossoming of science and medicine in the following 100 years was partly due to this liberation of the material world. Moreover it also heralded modern biology because it encouraged the idea that the body and organs of man are essentially similar to those of animals. What man has that elevates him above the beasts is a soul that can grab the wheel of the brain, step on the throttle or stamp on the brakes for the sake of controlling his animal instincts. Animals are mere machines, slaves to their reflex reactions to sensory signals (a concept that Descartes also introduced). Man alone has a spiritual agent within him that takes over when it comes to things like choice, moral judgement and free will.

Most brain researchers of today would find the explicit dualism of Descartes little more than an historical joke, especially his idea that the pineal body, a tiny structure in the middle of the brain, is the syphon of the soul, pushing the magical fluids inside the brain in one direction or the other in order to steer the brutish brain. More popular now is some version of identity theory, suggesting that mind and brain are expressions of a single system, the conductor and driver of a one-man bus.

Sir John Eccles, distinguished neuroscientist who won the Nobel Prize for his study of the transmission of signals between nerve cells, is spirited in his defence of dualism. He finds identity theory unacceptable and advocates dualist-interactionism (an approach described in detail by Eccles and Sir Karl Popper in their book The Self and Its Brain. *He envisages the world of subjective experience as distinct from the material world, but interacting with it in special areas of the cerebral cortex. In these terms, simply thinking should produce neural activity in the cortex, and Eccles describes experiments that could be assumed to support this prediction. New techniques for measuring localized nervous activity in the living human brain show that merely imagining sequences of movement without carrying them out, or concentrating attention on some part of the body in expectation of a touch, causes activity in particular regions of the cortex.*

Eccles believes that interactionism of this sort need not contradict the laws of physics: he takes ideas from the quantum physicist Henry Margenau and suggests that thought could act like the 'probability fields' of quantum mechanics on the contacts between nerve cells, where signals are transmitted between them.

Larry Wieskrantz, neuropsychologist, also seeks evidence about the nature of consciousness from studies of living brains, but brains that have been damaged by strokes or other forms of injury. He tells the extraordinary story of patients who can make sensory discriminations or learn things, but who, because of their brain damage, are unaware of their abilities – unconscious of their perception or memories. They act as if a 'monitor' in the brain had been disconnected – the monitor of consciousness. The evolutionary advantage of this monitoring function is that it permits reflection, consideration, the comparison of events separated in space or time: in short, it allows thought.

János Szentágothai, a Hungarian neuroanatomist, reckons that the 50 billion or so nerve cells in the human brain and the $10^{13} - 10^{14}$ connections between them provide substrate enough for the creation of self, without any need to postulate non-material forces. A neural system capable of exhibiting mind would, he argues, have to be distributed widely through various parts of the brain and would have to consist of a hierarchy of self-organizing networks of nerve cells. He describes his own research on the ability of even tiny grafts of 15–50 randomly scattered nerve cells to organize themselves into functional circuits. The individual modules *of thousands of nerve cells, of which the cerebral cortex is made up, may constitute the self-organizing units needed for the construction of mind. Thus Szentágothai takes a solidly materialist line but is well aware of the problem that remains: how can mindfulness, if created from* the operations *of the brain, act back by 'downward causation' on the system that has made it, in order to impose the actions of will on the brain?*

Rodolfo Llinás, a biophysicist, develops the idea that the coordinates of the outside world become 'embedded' in the brain to form internal semantic representation with predictive power. Indeed he proposes a specific theory for how networks of neurons can become organized in this way, based on current knowledge of the physiological properties of nerve cells and on a branch of mathematics known as tensor theory.

Horace Barlow, neurophysiologist, and Nicholas Humphrey, psychologist, both tackle the questions of the biological advantage of consciousness and how it might have emerged under selective pressure during evolution. They both come to the conclusion that the essential role of conscious reflection is in the management and control of our social behaviour, and that interactions and communication between brains are necessary for consciousness. It occurs in single minds because each individual constructs models of the principle characteristics of other individuals, which it then interacts with internally. Consciousness is shared with others not in a mystical or paranormal way but simply as a consequence of the reciprocal control of the modelled minds on an individual's introspection. Models of other minds are necessary for even the most private introspections.

Where Barlow and Humphrey diverge is on the issue of the reliability of conscious reflection. For Humphrey the 'inner eye' of consciousness provides the basis of insight into one's own behaviour and the ability to interpret in mentalistic terms and hence to predict the behaviour of other members of the species. Barlow, however, points out that some aspects of social interaction involve deliberate attempts to conceal true feelings, and that even our own introspective experiences of, say, pain and love, tell us little about the biological function of the behaviour associated with them.

Finally, John Crook, whose interests bridge the gap between psychology and anthropology, considers the emergence of conscious awareness through biological evolution, arguing that consciousness is the subjective aspect of cognitive systems of representation and is probably present in a number of advanced species. He reviews the phenomenological, physiological and ethological evidence for the appearance and refinement of awareness and self-awareness.

In the first three parts of this book we have considered how we might recognize the presence of mind in people, animals and machines; daunting though this problem is, it is only the siren that warns us of philosophical minefields and biological barbed wire ahead. We still face the issues of what mind is and what use it could be. The first question is both a thought-problem (rightly the subject of philosophical conjecture) and an empirical question (about the mechanisms that make mind). The second question is essentially teleological.

20

Brain and Mind, Two or One?

Sir John Eccles

Sir John Eccles has spent a long lifetime studying the brain in order to discover how it could possibly be the material substratum of our rich mental life: experiencing, thinking, acting, imagining, enjoying, feeling, and more specifically of our absolutely unique personhood. Eccles became vividly aware of the challenge in 1920 when he was only 17 and a student of medicine in Melbourne University. After much study it became evident that the scientific knowledge of the brain was hopelessly inadequate as a basis for any rational psychology and philosophy of the mind–brain problem. So, after graduating in medicine in 1925, Eccles departed for Oxford to work under Sherrington, then the world master in neuroscience. Now 60 years later and after a Nobel Prize for his work on basic neuroscience, Eccles is still enthralled by his life-long task of attempting to throw light on this fundamental problem of the nature of our spiritual self and how it interacts with the brain in a manner more intimate and intricate than we can imagine. In the last year Eccles has been greatly excited by suggestions of the quantum physicist Henry Margenau as described in this chapter. He senses a gleam of light where there had hitherto been impenetrable darkness.

Introduction

In the title of this discussion 'two' would refer to dualistic interactionism with the mind and brain as two distinct entities, whereas 'one' would refer to the many materialistic theories of the mind: radical materialism or the three materialistic theories that recognize the existence of mind or mental events, but give it no independent status (figure 20.1). According to the above three materialistic theories of the mind, mental states are an attribute of matter or the physical world, either of all matter as in panpsychism, or of matter in the special state in which it exists in the highly organized nervous systems of animals and man. One variety of this, epiphenomenalism, need not be further considered, having been replaced in recent decades by the identity theory that was first fully developed by Herbert Feigl.[1] Furthermore I reject the denial of all mental events, radical materialism, as an absurdity. Sir Karl Popper states that 'all four assert that the physical world (World 1) is self-contained or *closed* . . . This

Sir John Eccles (right) in 1957 with Lord Adrian (1889–1977), then Professor of Physiology at Cambridge, who was a pioneer in the study of the physiology of the brain (photographed by Owen and Moroney for the Ciba Foundation Symposium on The Neurological Basis of Behaviour, *1957).*

World 1 = All of material or physical world including brains
World 2 = All subjective or mental experiences
World 1_P is all the material world that is without mental states
World 1_M is that minute fraction of the material world with associated
      mental states

Radical Materialism:	World 1 = World 1_P; World 1_M = 0; World 2 = 0.
Panpsychism:	All is World 1–2; World 1 or 2 do not exist alone.
Epiphenomenalism:	World 1 = World 1_P + World 1_M
	World $1_M \rightarrow$ World 2
Identity theory:	World 1 = World 1_P + World 1_M
	World 1_M = World 2 (the identity)
Dualist-interactionism:	World 1 = World 1_P + World 1_M
	World $1_M \rightleftarrows$ World 2; this interaction occurs
	in the liaison brain, LB = World 1_M.
	Thus World 1 = World 1_P + World 1_{LB}, and
	World $1_{LB} \rightleftarrows$ World 2

Figure 20.1 A diagrammatic representation of brain–mind theories.

physical principle of the closedness of the physical World 1 ... is of decisive importance ... as the characteristic principle of physicalism or materialism.'[2] Popper then goes on to give a critical account of all materialistic theories of the mind.

It has been difficult to discover statements by philosophers that relate to the precise neural events that are assumed to be identical with mental events. The clearest expression was given by Feigl:

The identity thesis which I wish to clarify and to defend asserts that the states of direct experience which conscious human beings 'live through', and those which we confidently ascribe to some of the higher animals, are identical with certain (presumably configurational) aspects of the neural processes in those organisms ... processes in the central nervous system, perhaps especially in the cerebral cortex ... The neurophysiological concepts refer to complicated highly ramified patterns of neuron discharges.[3]

Mario Bunge in his version of the identity theory, which he calls emergentist materialism, states: 'The set of mental events is a subset of the events in the plastic neural systems of the animal.'[4] In his careful study of central state materialism David Armstrong chooses not to define in detail the parts of the brain in identity with neural events, speaking only of the physico-chemical system of the brain, and does not attempt any cerebral localization.[5]

Empirical Testing

In an Alpbach discussion workshop in August 1984 organized by a distinguished identity theorist, Professor Gerhard Vollmer of Giessen, the question was raised whether there could be experimental testing of predictions from the dualist-interactionist hypothesis (figure 20.2) on the one hand and the identity hypothesis on the other. A simple diagram (figure 20.3A) was constructed embodying the essential features of the identity hypothesis. In accord with Feigl, there was agreement that mental–neural identity occurs only for neurons or neuron systems at a high level of the brain, especially in the cerebral cortex. These neurons

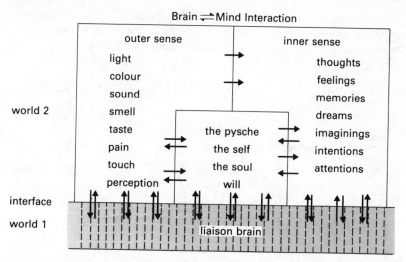

Figure 20.2   Information-flow diagram for mind–brain interaction in the human brain. The three components of World 2 (outer sense; inner sense; and the psyche, self or soul) are shown on the diagram with their communications indicated by arrows. Also shown are the lines of communication across the interface between World 1 and World 2, that is from the liaison brain to and from these World 2 components. The liaison brain has the columnar arrangement indicated by the vertical broken lines. It must be imagined that the area of the liaison brain is enormous, with open or active modules numbering over a million, not just the two score here depicted.

can be called *mental–neural event (MNE) neurons*, whereas other neurons in the brain, and in particular neurons on the input and output pathways, would be simple *neural event (NE) neurons*, as in figure 20.3B. It would be predicted from the identity hypothesis that MNE neurons would be distinctive because in special circumstances their firing would be in unison (identity) with mental events. But of course this firing would be in response to inputs from other neurons, MNE or NE, and is in no way determined or modified by the mental events. This is the *closedness of the physical world* referred to by Popper.

In this chapter I shall be describing remarkable experimental work that strongly suggests that certain neurons or neuron systems in the cerebral cortex seem to be MNE neurons, being distinctively related to intentional or attentional mental states.[6,7] In the diagram (figure 20.3A) the identity theorists would have to postulate that the firing of the MNE neurons would be entirely explicable as responses to NE inputs or to other MNE neurons of the higher brain.

What then is the position of the dualist-interactionist? It would be the crucial difference that the MNE neurons would have, in addition to the MNE and NE inputs, an input from mental events (ME) *per se* (see figure 20.3B). The firing of MNE neurons would exhibit a response that is different from what it would be in the absence of the mental events of intention or attention. There is evidence that this indeed does occur both for intentions activating neurons of a part of the frontal lobe of the cerebral hemispheres called the *supplementary motor area* (SMA),[8,6] and for attentions activating neurons, probably of the mid-prefrontal area (another region in the frontal lobe), that project to the appropriate attention neurons of the somatosensory area, the strip of cortex that receives sensory information from the skin and deep tissues.[7]

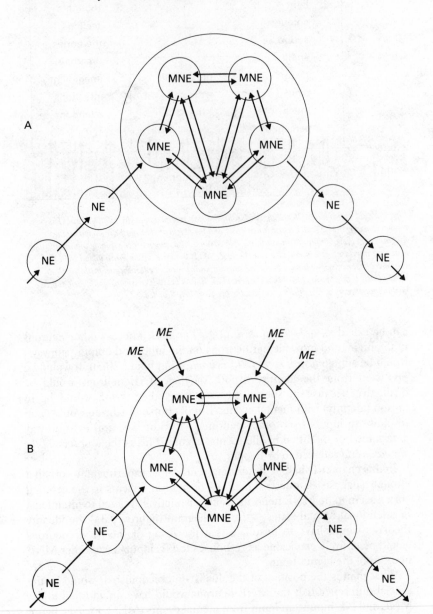

Figure 20.3   Diagrams of brain–mind theories. A. The identity theory. B. Dualist – interactionism. Assemblages of neurons are shown by circles. NE represents conventional neurons, which respond only to neural events. MNE are neurons that are associated with both mental and neural events and are grouped in a larger circle representing the higher nervous system. In B, ME arrows represent mental influences acting on the neural population that is associated with both mental and neural events. All other arrows in A and B represent the ordinary lines of neural communication, which are shown in reciprocal action.

Radio-Xenon Technique

A solution of radio-xenon is injected into the internal carotid artery and so the brain blood vessels on that side become radioactive for about 45 seconds, as is detected by a helmet of 254 Geiger counters over the scalp. From these data there can be constructed a map of the brain surface showing the regions of increased blood supply to the cerebral cortex, which gives a reliable mapping of the cerebral activity.

Figure 20.4 shows the position of the supplementary motor area (SMA) of the left cerebral hemisphere, in the medial part of the frontal cortex just anterior to the motor area of the hind limb. By a radio-xenon technique Roland and his colleagues recorded the regional cerebral blood flow over one side of the cerebral hemispheres of human observers.[6] In figure 20.5B there is seen to be a highly significant increase of about 20 per cent in the local blood flow of the SMA region when the subject was

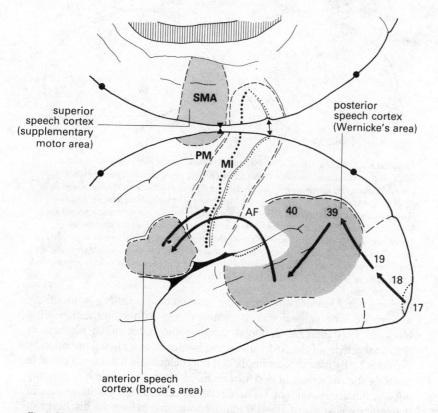

Figure 20.4   The left hemisphere seen from the lateral side with the frontal lobe to the left. The medial side (inner surface) of the hemisphere is shown as if reflected upwards. The primary motor cortex, MI, lies in the precentral cortex just anterior to the central sulcus (see fig. 1.1) and extends deeply into it. Anterior to MI is shown the premotor cortex, PM, with the supplementary motor area, SMA, largely on the medial side of the hemisphere (modified from Penfield and Roberts).[9]

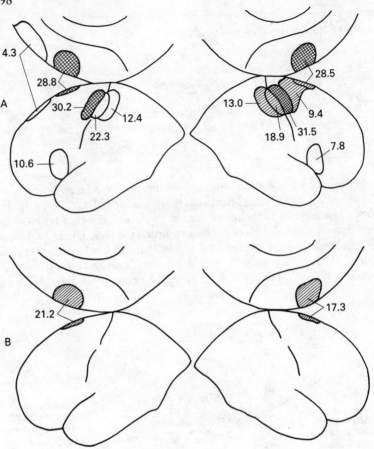

Figure 20.5   A: These diagrams of the left and right hemispheres of the brain (arranged as in fig. 20.4) show changes in local blood flow, reflecting changes in the activity of the populations of nerve cells, during the motor-sequence test described in the text, performed with the hand opposite to the brain hemisphere. The outlined brain areas are regions of increased blood flow, the density of shading indicating the magnitude of the change. The figures show the average percentage increases in blood flow, corrected for the overall increase in flow, for measurements from five different left hemispheres and ten right.[6] B: Similar diagrams showing the change in local blood flow (for three left hemispheres and five right) during internal programming of the same motor-sequence task, i.e. simply imagining carrying out the movements without actually doing them. Now the increase in blood flow is restricted to the region called the supplementary motor cortex.[6]

carrying out a learnt complex motor task mentally, entirely without any movement. The subject was at complete rest with vision and hearing blocked. This increase in blood supply is an index of an increase in neuronal activity of the SMA under the influence of a mental intention by the subject. By means of an implanted microelectrode it has been possible to study the responses of SMA neurons of a monkey while it is carrying out a voluntary movement.[8] There is an increase in the discharge rate of many neurons at about 50–100 milliseconds (ms) before the discharge of neurons in the nearby motor cortex that eventually would cause the willed movement.[10,11] Ethical considerations preclude the carrying out of such an experiment on a human subject; however, the recording of electric and magnetic fields over the human scalp during repetitive voluntary movements also points to the SMA as the site of action of the mental intention.[12]

Figure 20.6 shows a remarkable finding of Per Roland; when the human subject was attending to a finger on which a just detectable touch stimulus was about to be applied, there was an increase in blood flow over the part of the somatosensory cortex that receives signals from the fingers, as well as in the mid-prefrontal area. These increases must result from the mental attention because no touch was applied during the recording. Thus figure 20.6 gives a clear demonstration that the mental act of attention can activate appropriate regions of the cerebral cortex.

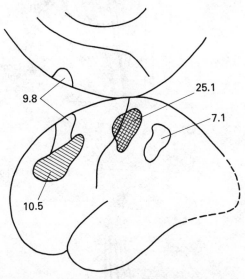

Figure 20.6   These brain diagrams made by Per Roland, 1981 (arranged like those of fig. 20.5) show the average percentage increase in local cerebral blood flow while the human volunteer simply attended to somatic sensations from the body, without any actual peripheral stimulation. Results from eight subjects have been averaged.

The identity theorist is committed to the doctrine that mental events *per se* cannot generate neural events figure 20.3A), which is the doctrine of *the closedness of World 1*. The experience of an intention to move would, in these terms, have to be attributable simply to the activity of an assemblage of NME neurons in the SMA. One may ask what causes these neurons to fire impulses and so bring about a voluntary movement. To this question the identity theorist has no answer except to say that there must be other as yet unidentified neuronal centres containing NME neurons that fire before the SMA, which is merely an evasion of the problem. Another possible answer is that the SMA activity is due to chance; but can one accept chance as the invariable cause of our voluntary movements?

By contrast the experimental findings are in accord with prediction from dualist-interactionism. Each mental event of intention (ME in figure 20.3B) initiates the firing of a set of neurons of the SMA that through the various known pathways cause the 'correct' motor cortical neurons to discharge impulses down the pyramidal tract (figure 20.7) to cause the desired voluntary movement.[10,11] Similarly, the dualist-interactionist is able to account for the action of the mental event of attention on the neurons of the prefrontal lobe. It is assumed, but not proven, that this is the site of the interaction and that the neurons of the touch area of the cerebral cortex were secondarily activated.[7]

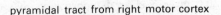

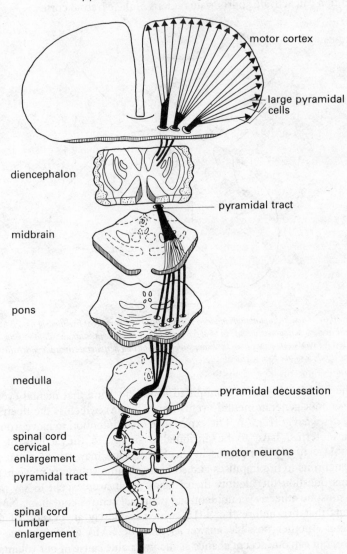

Figure 20.7   Diagram of the course of the major movement pathway, the pyramidal tract, from the right motor cortex. The fibres in this tract come from large cells in the cortex. In the medulla, at the base of the brain, most of the fibres cross over and pass down in the dorsolateral column of the spinal cord on the opposite side.

Conservation Laws of Physics

As originally defined, such physical entities as mass, energy, momentum were believed to be 'conserved' in a closed physical system. Now mass and energy are convertible on the Einstein equation, $E = mc^2$.

However, the monistic critics argue that insuperable difficulties are encountered by the hypothesis that immaterial mental events can act in any way on material structures such as neurons. Such a presumed action is alleged to be incompatible with the conservation laws of physics, in particular of the 1st law of thermodynamics. This objection would certainly be sustained by nineteenth-century physicists. Unfortunately it is rare for a quantum physicist to risk an intrusion into the brain–mind problem. But in a recent book the distinguished quantum physicist Henry Margenau makes a fundamental contribution.[13] It is a remarkable transformation from nineteenth-century physics to be told 'that some fields, such as the probability field of quantum mechanics, carry neither energy nor matter'. He goes on to state:

In very complicated physical systems such as the brain, the neurons and sense organs, whose constituents are small enough to be governed by probabilistic quantum laws, the physical organ is always poised for a multitude of possible changes, each with a definite probability; if one change takes place that requires energy, or more or less energy than another, the intricate organism furnishes it automatically. Hence, if there is a mind–body interaction, the mind would not be called upon to furnish energy.

In summary Margenau states:

The mind may be regarded as a field in the accepted physical sense of the term. But it is a nonmaterial field. It cannot be compared with the simpler nonmaterial fields that require the presence of matter (e.g. gravity). . . Nor does it necessarily have a definite position in space. And so far as present evidence goes it is not an energy field in any physical sense, nor is it required to contain energy in order to account for all known phenomena in which mind interacts with brain.

Vigil Coma

After severe damage to the midbrain such as can be produced in a traffic accident, the victim does not recover from the immediate unconsciousness, but remains unconscious for an indefinite period with a flat electroencephalogram, though the cerebral cortex may have little or no damage. Its inactivity is explained by the failure of activation by the midbrain reticular system which projects via the thalamus and so up to the cortex.

These considerations should eventually answer the objections of the materialists or physicalists who are imbued with nineteenth-century physics. However, dualist-interactionism has still to face up to the problem of how a non-material entity, the mind, can act with discriminative effectiveness on neurons, albeit only some specialized neurons in higher levels of the brain. We know that, when there is no background activity in the cortical neurons, there is no interaction with the mind, as is most strikingly shown in vigil coma. So we can assume that the mental events achieve interaction with the neural events of spatio-temporal patterns of activity of the awake cerebral cortex.[11] Even in one cortical module with its 4,000 or so neurons, there must be an ongoing intense dynamic activity of unimaginable complexity. Although we know the outlines of the neuronal structure of a module,[14,15] there has as yet been only a very limited study of the physiology. All that we can surmise is that mental events acting as a field in the manner postulated by Margenau could effect changes in the spatio-temporal activity of a module without violating conservation laws. There could be, for example, a balance of patterned increases and decreases of neuronal activity in adjacent microsites of a module.

Cortical Module

The large area (2000 cm^2) of the cerebral cortex, with 10,000 million neurons, is subdivided into functional columns or modules across its thickness of about 0.3cm. A module can be regarded as a functional unit because it tends to function in that way in communication with other modules of the same or opposite cerebral hemisphere (see figure 22.3).

A further objection has been made by Mario Bunge that 'every information flux rides on some physical process',[4] that is, information from non-material mental events could not be transmitted to the brain. But, as stated above, this objection cannot apply to the probability field of quantum mechanics, and according to Margenau the mind may be regarded as some such field.

Synapse and Vesicles

Each neuron of the cerebral cortex receives close functional contacts from as many as 10,000 synapses on the surface of its dendrites and soma. Each of these synaptic contacts is in the form of a fine nerve fibre ending or in minute bouton (about 0.002 mm across) on its surface, usually on a small spine projecting from its surface. These boutons are filled with about 20,000 synaptic vesicles containing a high concentration of a specific transmitter substance. One vesicle can be completely ejected (quantally) into the narrow synaptic cleft and so can effectively act on the neuron, either exciting it or inhibiting it (see figure 15.3).

The suggestion that the mind operates as a probability field brings into consideration earlier conjectures of Eddington,[16] based upon the uncertainty principle of Heisenberg, that were developed further by Eccles,[17] in the light of the discoveries that the synaptic unit of action was a vesicle of transmitter of about 400Å in diameter with a mass of about 3×10^{-17}g. If the uncertainty principle is applicable to an object of this size, then it was calculated that the uncertainty in the position of such a vesicle would be of the order of 30Å in 1 millisecond. The intricate process of quantal emission of transmitter from a synaptic vesicle involves action across the presynaptic membrane, which is about 50 Å across, and the times of action are in the order of a millisecond.

There has been a precise study of the emission of a synaptic vesicle from a bouton when a single impulse in a muscle afferent fibre causes it to eject its contents on to a motoneuron of that muscle (figure 20.7). Julian Jack, Steve Redman and associates have made an analysis of this event and have discovered that a nerve impulse has merely a probability rather than a certainty of causing the emission of one quantum or vesicle.[18] Calculated probabilities range from 0.05 to 0.5 for the 4 synapses made by one afferent fibre on a neuron.

Evidently this level of refinement of synaptic physiology opens up the possibility of being able to account for the mind–brain interaction in terms of the action of non-material fields, such as the probability field of quantum mechanics.[13] All that would be required for an effective action of a mental event on a neuron would be an alteration of the probabilities of quantum release, which could be accomplished by a non-material agent such as a mental intention. Hence it can be concluded that modern physics presents no insuperable objection to dualist-interactionism, though it must be appreciated that we are only at the beginning of our attempts to understand the *interaction* of mental events with neural events. Meanwhile dualist-interactionism is to be preferred to all materialistic monisms because it accounts for such experimental findings as intention and attention, which are indubitably mental events causing changes in the activity of neurons. Thus the final conclusion is that brain and mind are two, not one.

References

1 Feigl, H. (1967) *The 'Mental' and the 'Physical'*. Minneapolis: Univ. Minnesota Press.

2 Popper, K. R. and Eccles, J. C. (1977) *The Self and Its Brain*. Berlin, Heidelberg, London, New York: Springer Internat.

3 Ibid., p. 79.

4 Bunge, M. (1980) *The Mind–Body Problem*. Oxford: Pergamon.

5 Armstrong, D. M. (1968) *A Materialist Theory of the Mind*. London: Routledge & Kegan Paul.

6 Roland, P. E., Larsen, B., Lassen, N. A. and Skinhøj, E. (1980) Supplementary motor area and other cortical areas in organization of voluntary movements, in man. *J. Neurophysiol.* 43: 118–36.

7 Roland, P. E. (1981) Somatotopical tuning of postcentral gyrus during focal

attention in man. A regional cerebral blood flow study. *J. Neurophysiol.* 46: 744–54.

8 Brinkman, C. and Porter, R. (1979) Supplementary motor area in the monkey: activity of neurons during performance of a learned motor task. *J. Neurophysiol.* 42: 681–709.

9 Penfield, W. and Roberts, L. (1959) *Speech and Brain Mechanisms.* Princeton: Princeton Univ. Press.

10 Eccles, J. C. (1982) The initiation of voluntary movements by the supplementary motor area. *Arch. Psychiatr. Nervenkr.* 231: 423–41.

11 Eccles, J. C. (1982) How the self acts on the brain. *Psychoneuroendocrinology*, 7: 271–83.

12 Deecke, L. and Kornhuber, H. H. (1978) An electrical sign of participation of the mesial 'supplementary' motor cortex in human voluntary finger movement. *Brain Res.* 159: 473–6.

13 Margenau, H. (1984) *The Miracle of Existence.* Woodbrige, Conn.: Ox Bow Press.

14 Szentágothai, J. (1978) The neuron network of the cerebral cortex. A functional interpretation. *Proc. R. Soc. Lond.* B201: 219–48.

15 Szentágothai, J. (1983) The modular architectonic principle of neural centers. *Rev. Physiol. Biochem. Pharmacol.* 98: 11–61.

16 Eddington, A. S. (1935) *New Pathways in Science.* Cambridge: Cambridge Univ. Press.

17 Eccles, J. C. (1970) *Facing Reality.* New York, Heidelberg, Berlin: Springer.

18 Jack, J. J. B., Redman, S. J. and Wong, K. (1981) The components of synaptic potentials evoked in cat spinal motoneurones by impulses in single group Ia afferents. *J. Physiol.* 321: 65–96.

21

Neuropsychology and the Nature of Consciousness

Larry Weiskrantz

Larry Weiskrantz took his first degree in Swarthmore, USA, in 1949. After a period of postgraduate research in Oxford he returned to Harvard where he completed a PhD. He subsequently occupied various senior posts at Oxford and Cambridge and for the last 20 years has held the Chair of Psychology in Oxford. In 1980 he was elected to the Royal Society.

Anyone who presumes to address the question of the nature of consciousness soon finds that it is a topic about which it is very difficult to say anything new, so often and for so long has it been searchingly pursued, but it is also almost impossible to say anything entirely old, because everyone has his own particular angle on it. Various people have tried to exorcize the word, but it is very much part of our vocabulary and it remains as a persistent challenge to neuroscientists to try to think of just what aspects of neural organization are related, and how, to changes in whatever the ordinary person means by levels or qualities of consciousness.

Crudely speaking, and leaving aside for now the complex questions of neural organization, historical approaches to consciousness have taken three routes. Firstly, it is said we all in some sense know what we mean by our own consciousness, we have our own awareness or self-awareness and through a complicated process of inference we assume that other creatures who appear to behave more or less the way we do must also have consciousness. So it is one kind of inferential approach based on a complex kind of social interaction. 'I think, therefore I am. As others also seem to exist, therefore they think.' But there is a second kind of view of old and distinguished vintage that asserts that consciousness of other creatures is a property more or less directly present in ordinary perception, as part of our phenomenal observation, or at least readily derived it. Darwin, for example, said that 'we have seen the senses and intuitions of various emotions and faculties such as love, memory, attention, curiosity, imitation, reason, etc. of which man boasts may be found in an incipient, or even sometimes in a well-developed condition, in the lower animals.'[1] And Jennings, who in a classical work at the turn of the century wrote with enormous knowledge about the way (mainly) invertebrate creatures work, was quite convinced from his direct observation: 'If *Amoeba* were a large

Animal training sometimes results in behaviour that can all too easily be anthropomophically interpreted in terms of conscious intention. Photograph of a rabbit playing a piano by Mike Salisbury.

Figure 21.1   An irreverent view of Charles Darwin from the magazine Vanity Fair *at the time of great public interest in his theory of evolution (1871).*

animal, its behaviour would at once call forth the attribution to it of states of pleasure and pain, of hunger, desire, and the like, on precisely the same basis as we attribute these things to the dog.'[2] Along similar lines, he later warns us that if *Amoeba* 'were as large as a whale, it is quite conceivable that occasions might arise when the attribution to it of the elemental states of consciousness might save the unsophisticated human being from destruction that would result from lack of such attribution'.[3]

Jennings's views also provide a transition to the third route, namely, one that considers the evolutionary and adaptive value of consciousness. Thus he says, 'we usually attribute consciousness ... because this is useful; it enables us practically to appreciate, foresee, and control [an

Figure 21.2 The zoologist and physiologist George Romanes (1848–94), photographed in 1891. His claim that consciousness depended simply on a capacity to learn would not satisfy most neuroscientists or engineers today (Mary Evans Picture Library).

animal's] actions much more readily than we could otherwise do'.[3]

The question remains, *what* is it we are attributing, what do we mean when we assign this kind of property to another human or to any other creature? And what is it about this property that makes it useful? And this is where the difficulty arises, because the criteria are as broad as those for adaptive behaviour itself, and it is very difficult to find any in modern discussions that were not also put forward at least 100 years ago, although it is possible to find some from that period that would no longer satisfy us today. Romanes, for example, said that it was based on the capacity to learn,[4] which would not satisfy most neuroscientists or engineers today as a *sufficient* criterion, because quite simple mechanical toys can be constructed with such a property. Lloyd Morgan said it was capacity for choice,[5] which would also raise similar doubts in a computer age, although Morgan's usage probably was deeper than that involved in the design of computer software. More recently, possession of ethical values has been advanced as a criterion, which might then admit the dolphin and some other creatures; but there are, of course, difficulties about defining

Figure 21.3 William James (1842–1910), American philosopher and psychologist, who concluded that even a headless frog must be conscious (Mary Evans Picture Library/ Society for Psychical Research).

or evaluating ethical values, even in man. William James had a rather complex view.[6] He first of all said that the cerebral cortex was the organ of consciousness, but then when he was pressed for a criterion he said that it was based on 'the pursuance of future ends and the choice of means for their attainment'. And this led him to conclude quite logically, on the basis of evidence from Pfluger and Lewes and the other contemporary physiologists of the end of the nineteenth century, that the headless frog must be conscious, because it shows adaptive behaviour: it was reported that if it was stimulated on one limb and that limb was prevented from removing the source of irritation, another limb spontaneously substituted itself to carry out the purposeful activity. So he concluded that the spinal cord of a frog has conscious intelligence. When I put this to a physiological colleague he said, 'Well it may well be true but it is very difficult to address the question to the frog's head, now detached.' But it does raise precisely the question of just why a frog with a head should be considered to be more conscious than one without on the basis of precisely defined criteria.

A view that has become increasingly popular in recent years links evolution with an emergent property, which assumes that as nervous systems evolve they become more and more complicated, and that at some stage, not exactly clear when, somehow this mysterious property of self-awareness or consciousness becomes an attribute of the nervous system. But exactly how one recognizes it when it happens remains the problem.

At the other extreme (and this species of philosophical argument still exists, sometimes but not always linked with reductionist views) is the position that consciousness is just an epiphenomenon – what T. H. Huxley called the steam-whistle on the locomotive: it has no effect on the engine of the locomotive but is just there as an ancillary and powerless gadget.[7] Lloyd Morgan challenged Huxley very directly and asked, if it is useless, why did it ever evolve? And any evolutionist has to answer that argument.

Well why did it evolve? One view often discussed these days is that advanced earlier by Michael Chance and Alison Jolly,[8] and more recently by Nicholas Humphrey,[9] that somehow the pressures from social complexity made it useful, perhaps necessary, for consciousness to evolve. The fact that we are complicated social creatures produces this extraordinarily strong need for each of us to attribute consciousness to other creatures so that we can try to predict their behaviour by role-playing and other forms of thought. And being able to do so generates important advantages for survival. I would like to take just the opposite point of view, namely that creatures are indeed socially complicated throughout the whole vertebrate kingdom, but that most other creatures except man have very good ways of dealing with it. Man, in fact, is the only creature that perversely gets into social difficulty of any really serious kind, and one reason for this is because he is conscious and can think about all the social complications that he might confront, or deviously try to exploit for gain or for protection. And so I think the social complications are a consequence of the powers of consciousness rather than the other way around. It is the fact that we have the capacity to think and be aware and consider what other people might be thinking about us that produces, I think, the uniquely human condition of paranoia. I do not know that paranoia, as a really damaging social–psychiatric condition, exists in any creature other than man, and human beings can have it only because their consciousness is so highly developed.

I would like to stress a view about one essential property of attributed consciousness, and the one from which powerful evolutionary advantages derive, namely the view that Lloyd Morgan himself put. Lloyd Morgan is often cited as being a rather austere critic of people who are a little bit loose with their terminology, and is well known for his canon of parsimony, but in fact I think he had a broad range of quite creative insights, and he is very rarely quoted in full. The position I would like to adopt was put by him (quoting Mivart) this way: 'If a being has the power of thinking "thing" or "something", it has the power of transcending space and time. Here is the point where intelligence ends and reason begins.'[10] For my purposes, 'conscious awareness' can be substituted for 'reason' in this sentence.

The Evidence from Damaged Brains

What I would like to do now is turn to some observations of neurological patients which, while they relate to just one restricted aspect of the problem of consciousness, raise the issue of the existence and the importance of knowledge of what it is one is doing, that is, knowledge of one's own capacities and one's own acts. Such observations, because they are concerned with the effects of damage to known neural structures, also provoke us to think about those neural structures and the type of organization in which they are embedded. I will deal with these observations of patients briefly, and then return to Lloyd Morgan's theme.

There are patients with brain damage, and they are clinically very striking, who have the capacity to learn quite adaptive skills and to carry out discriminative acts. If we were carrying out the very same acts, we would certainly be able to report and to communicate about those acts not only to others but to ourselves, that is, to think about them. These patients, in contrast, seem to have the capacity to learn and to perform in various ways but they are detached from awareness of doing so. We all know that a great deal of what we do in everyday life has just that character. In fact it would be a terrible waste of cerebral tissue and processing capacity to spend one's time thinking about all the skills that one has acquired. It would be a waste for us to recite, every time we spoke, the fact that we have indeed learnt every single word we were uttering; we no longer have a conscious memory of that; we have a skill. If we had to think, 'well now, that is interesting; I can remember learning the English language and I can remember when I acquired a new word', and so forth, we would never get through a conversation. Or we would never be able to drive a car or indeed efficiently carry out any complicated skill. And there are a huge number of bodily responses of which we have no awareness at all. After all, the pupils of our eyes are responding enormously vigorously throughout our entire day, and I do not know anyone who has ever reported an awareness of what his pupil is doing. In fact it doesn't behave like a mere photocell, changing only in relation to the level of light entering the eye: it also responds to the sight of pretty things, to beauty, to touch, and to all sorts of emotional disturbance. It has even been used as an index in marketing research, because it has been reported that, when a picture is taken secretly of someone's pupil when he is looking at goods in the supermarket, the diameter of the pupil correlates with the attractiveness of the product, and thus one can predict the sales values, say, of certain types of packaging. There is nothing inherently strange in the fact that we do lots of complicated things without awareness. What is strange is finding that there are patients who do things that we *are* normally aware of but of which they are not. There are two main types that I would like to review briefly.

The 'Amnesic Syndrome'

The first are patients who suffer from the 'amnesic syndrome'. It can be caused by a large number of different agents, such as herpes simplex encephalitis – which is a very devastating form of it – by chronic alcoholism, by various kinds of poison. Surgeons can induce it if they ablate both medial temporal lobes of the brain, or just one lobe if the other one happens to be defective. We know the brain structures that must be damaged if the amnesic state is going to occur. You can also see this syndrome in an extreme form in very elderly or pre-senile patients, such as those with Alzheimer's Disease (although they have other problems as well), but it can occur in a pure form in young people and to a very extreme degree. The most striking clinical feature is that these patients, despite retaining normal intelligence and perceptual and cognitive skills, report not remembering anything at all from minute to minute; it really is a crippling disorder. You can be talking to such patients, then leave the room and come back in a minute: the patient does not recognize you at all and admits of no memory of having seen you. So devastating is this clinical condition that for a long time it was thought that these patients were incapable of learning anything at all. But gradually it has become clear that in fact they are capable of learning a large variety of new things, and of doing so quite efficiently. For example, they can be subjected to classical Pavlovian conditioning of a sort that each of us would surely report remembering, which they seem to acquire at normal rates. They show verbal learning, they show perceptual learning, they show motor skill learning, and they retain these over long periods of time, sometimes for weeks or months.[11] But the only person who does not acknowledge that anything has been learnt or display any recognition of this fact is the patient himself. So there is a very clear dissociation between the capacity to learn and to retain, on the one hand, and the patient's knowledge of that fact, on the other.

'Blindsight'

The other type of patients I wish to describe suffer from lesions in the first way-station in the cerebral cortex at which visual inputs are normally received, the striate cortex or first visual cortical area ('V-1'). There is a very orderly projection of the visual field mapped on to this region of cortex. For a long time it was thought that such patients were rendered blind, absolutely blind, in that part of the visual field corresponding to the damaged portion of the projected map in the striate cortex. But in some patients, at least, it has proved possible to demonstrate that they have a very good capacity to discriminate, to detect visual events in this 'blind' area, to locate them in space, to make judgements about the orientation of lines or gratings, to detect the onset and termination of movement, and even to do simple pattern discriminations. And yet there is no acknowledgement of any such capacity at all: subjects say when questioned that they are just guessing and playing the experimenter's game when he insists on their saying 'yes' or 'no' when a light is flashed briefly in their 'blind' field, or insists on their saying whether a grating is horizontally oriented or non-horizontally oriented, or insists on their reaching to the spot where the 'invisible' flash occurs on a screen, none of which they can actually *see*. Indeed with the first patient that my associates and I tested,[12] we did not (and still do not) give the patient knowledge of results during the test; when he was told his results afterwards he just expressed open astonishment. He thought he was just guessing. We called the phenomenon 'blindsight'. There are various gradations of this capacity which I cannot review in detail here but which have been recorded elsewhere.[13] For example, under some conditions the patient will say that he does not 'see', but has a 'feeling' that something is there, and sometimes he may even achieve a strange kind of visual exprience. A similar kind of phenomenon has been reported with damage in another sensory system – the somatosensory system – which has been called 'blindtouch'. That is, the patient can locate touch stimuli on his skin, although he has no awareness of actually being touched.

Criticisms

Recently it has been claimed that this evidence is based on artefact, and because the matter has been raised rather heatedly I want to write just a word or two about this attack.[14] One argument is that we do not know where the patient's lesion is precisely, or whether the cortex has been only incompletely damaged. This is true: none of these patients (fortunately) has died yet, and so post-mortems have not been done; but I shall later mention some evidence that suggests that one can make pretty good guesses about this point. The other argument is rather more serious: it is that the investigators who reported 'blindsight', and there are now a goodly number of such reports, have not controlled for diffusion or scatter of light in the eye or stray light in the environment that reaches an intact part of the visual field, and it might be that the object is responding to such subtle cues. I think the evidence against that argument is really very strong. There are several lines of evidence, but perhaps the best is based on a natural built-in control provided by a structure in each eye called the *optic disc*. This is *truly* and absolutely blind because it is where the optic nerve fibres penetrate the retina and hence where there are no

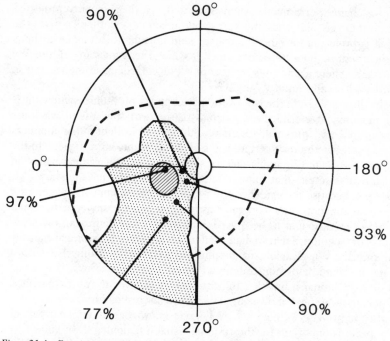

Figure 21.4   Experiments on 'blind-sight'. Here we see a plot of the visual field of the left eye of a patient who had suffered damage to a large part of the primary visual cortex (the striate cortex) *in his right hemisphere. The patient stared fixedly at the centre of a hemisphere (shown here as the large circle) while a small light was presented at different points on the hemisphere to determine the limits of the visual field of the left eye, shown as a dashed line. The brain damage has caused a* scotoma *or area of blindness, shown by the dotted region. Visual stimuli presented within this region were not consciously 'seen' (although the hatched region indicates an area within the scotoma where presentation of a stimulus produced a 'feeling' that something had happened). Then a small spot of light was briefly flashed, 30 times each, at the positions within the area of blindness marked by spots. Under controlled conditions, where guessing would produce only 50 per cent correct judgement, the patient had to say whether the light had been presented or not, even though he never consciously saw it. The figures show that he was correct between 77 per cent and 93 per cent of the time – well above chance performance. On the other hand, the score was only 43 per cent (indistinguishable from pure guesswork), if the light was deliberately presented so that its image fell in the middle of the optic disc (where the optic nerve fibres pass out through a hole in the back of the eye and which is therefore literally blind). The conclusion is that the visual ability of this patient within the 'blind' area, though very limited and unconscious, was genuine and could not be accounted for by scattering of light on to the seeing part of the retina, since that should have happened to an equal extent for the light falling on the optic disc.*

receptors and no vision. This natural 'blindspot' is small, only 5° by 7° in angular size, which gives one a well-defined blind area within which to estimate how much effective light scatter there can be with a particular stimulus.

If you have a spot of light that absolutely disappears when its image falls on the optic disc, you can really be sure that there is no discriminable scatter beyond about 2°. Now it usually happens that the optic disc, the natural blindspot, in one eye falls within the 'blindsight' field of a patient with damage in the visual cortex. A small spot of light therefore can be directed randomly either to the true 'blindspot' or to the apparently blind region immediately surrounding it. When studied in this way, the patient shows chance performance when asked to detect the spot when projected on to the true 'blindspot' but very good detection performance when the light is projected into the 'blindsight' field outside it. But as far as he is concerned, he does not know which is which: he is guessing all the way through. There are various other compelling control experiments, and so I do not have any doubt about this point.[15]

In the context of criticism of the observations on human patients it is illuminating to consider the original reason why 'blindsight' was ever discovered and pursued. Originally, there was evidence that monkeys could still discriminate certain types of visual events after damage to the striate cortex, and by and large they show just about the same capacity, in quantitative terms, that human patients with 'blindsight' can show.[13] It was just because the evidence from experiments on animals suggested a residual function after cortical damage that human subjects, who had always been thought to be quite blind, were reassessed using the same kinds of techniques that we had used to demonstrate the residual capacity in animals. What came as a genuine surprise was not only that such a capacity could be demonstrated in a 'blind' field caused by striate cortex lesions in humans, but that the patients themselves were disconnected from any awareness of the stimuli they were discriminating.

In the primate we have relatively good knowledge about what part of the brain is important for the residual visual function, and we know that the residual capacity can be detected even in the complete absence of striate cortex. And, as it happens, some of the patients in whom positive evidence of 'blindsight' has been reported are also highly unlikely to have any striate cortex whatever left in one hemisphere, because they had their entire cerebral cortex surgically removed from that hemisphere (to alleviate otherwise uncontrollable epilepsy or other disruptive pathology).[16] There is, incidentally, no inherent mystery about how the residual 'blindsight' might be mediated in the nervous system in the absence of striate cortex: the eye sends six or seven different outputs to various regions of the brain, especially to areas called the tectum and pre-tectum in the midbrain, that bypass the striate cortex. Presumably these areas, which would survive damage to the cerebral cortex, are responsible for the visual function in such patients.

Well, what are the implications of these two classes of patients, those with 'amnesic syndrome' and those with 'blindsight'? Both demonstrate really quite striking capacities in the absence of the patient's own conscious knowledge. The person can process information if it leads to a straightforward and unambiguous route from stimulus to response, in the absence of 'thought'. What I think has become disconnected is a monitoring system, one that is not part of the serial information-processing chain itself, but which can monitor what is going on. I think that is the kind of neural organization one is looking for in order to explain awareness. The presence of such a system might be assessed in the following way: imagine that we had to discriminate between, say, a horizontal and a vertical grating, and had to press one of two keys to indicate which orientation had been presented; we would have no difficulty also in indicating on a *third* key whether we were 'seeing' the difference or merely 'guessing'. This is where we would differ from the 'blindsight' patient who might be able to make the judgement of orientation quite accurately but deny seeing the pattern at all. Similarly, the amnesic patient could make a response based on stimulus information to which he had previously been exposed, but his third key would indicate 'guessing' and not 'remembering'.

Where Does 'Monitoring' Occur?

Where is the brain structure involved in monitoring? I do not know. But I think that is the kind of organization that one has to look for, and I think that the point in the nervous system at which it is likely to emerge is not in the striate cortex, because that is too early in the chain, but at the first place at which information from the whole of the visual field comes together. (The striate cortex in each hemisphere has input from only one *half* of the visual field.) We know where that coming together is in the monkey, and therefore we have some guesses where it occurs in man. In the monkey it is part of the cortex that lies in the inferior regions of the temporal lobe – several synapses beyond the striate cortex of each hemisphere – that first combines information from both half-fields, and therefore can deal with the whole visual world as an entity. It is within this region, in fact, that we have reason to think that the neural representations of external objects takes place.[17]

It is all very well to speculate on the basis of such observations of these patients, with whom we can converse about their experiences, or lack of them, in relation to their impressive residual capacities. I have said that a monkey with comparable brain lesions also demonstrates comparable residual capacities; indeed, it was because of the work on animals that much of the human clinical work was pursued. But how could we know whether the sort of 'monitoring system' that I have suggested constitutes consciousness is connected or not in a non-verbal animal? We have no way of conversing with the monkey, or at least no one has solved that problem yet. But I think there may be an interesting lead which has come from an ingenious idea put forward by some Canadians, Beninger and colleagues.[18] They have, in effect, allowed laboratory rats to do what they like and then asked them if they knew what they were doing. Actually they did not let them do quite anything they wished, but four possible things that rats do quite frequently and naturally without training: (1) face-washing; (2) rearing up; (3) walking; or (4) remaining immobile. So the animals had a choice of one of four things to do when they wished, and they could do any one of the four in any order that they wished. But in order to get food reward, after they performed any one of these acts they had to press one of four different levers, so as to indicate what it was they had done. And the rats *could* do that. Now I do not know whether a sea slug or crab could do that – I very much doubt it – or a frog, or a pigeon. I would be very surprised if a monkey could *not* do it. And I know if we gave that kind of test to an amnesic patient he would fail if there was even a short delay between the first act and the key-press. So I think there may be a methodology which could be developed to ask animals to indicate what it is they know about their own behaviour; or, for that matter, about

Figure 21.5 Does a rat know what it's doing? According to the experiments of R. Beninger and his colleagues this rat does know that it is washing its face (© Arthur Christiansen, Frank Lane Picture Agency).

another animal's behaviour; and beyond that, in principle at least, about their own behaviour in relation to another animal's behaviour.

Even here, there is a difficulty that is, in itself, quite revealing. One highly adaptive feature of everyday life is the strong tendency to transform as much of our behaviour as possible into automatic routines. Achieving this, after all, will leave a cognitive system of limited capacity free to deal with those problems that still require thought. Quite complicated conversations can become automatic and, in a sense, unconscious, as in sleep-walking or in verbal exchanges about the weather. Many highly skilled persons, such as aircraft controllers, carry out highly complex but routine verbal exchanges without thinking and probably would have difficulty in reporting them after a delay if there were not some ancillary form of recording. And so the same thing might happen with any highly practised sequence, even in a rat. Tony Dickinson and others have invented one approach to trying to decide whether a sequence has reached this automatic state for a rat.[19] The strategy is to see whether the animal can adapt to a disturbance in a remote part of the chain or whether, alternatively, it continues to reel off its responses in an automatic way. For example, the value of the reward can be sharply increased or decreased to see if the animal nevertheless still persists in performing by 'force of habit', even though the end goal is no longer the same. In practice no doubt one will need a whole set of criteria, but conceptually I think there are ways of supporting and investigating the distinction between a capacity or a skill and a monitoring of that skill.

The Adaptive Value of 'Monitoring'

Let me finish by asking what might be the evolutionary significance of the 'monitoring' function that creates conscious experience. I think its adaptive significance is just the one that Lloyd Morgan put forward, that it enables the animal to think about his own behaviour and others' behaviour, to communicate if it has words, as we do, so as to link objects and events in time and space that would otherwise be separated; in other words, to think and to reflect. The 'blindsight' patient, lacking the awareness of the discriminative skills that the 'blind' field actually possesses, has no image of his current visual experience to link to any other visual events. He cannot compare or match by 'picturing'. Nor can the amnesic patient relate his current behaviour – even though it is affected by learning – to other 'memories'. This is one reason why amnesic patients are so severely incapacitated, despite evidence of such impressive residual capacities, and why they need chronic custodial care. ('Blindsight' patients are very rarely ever 'blind' in more than a half-field of vision, and so they can readily adjust by using their intact half-field.) The 'monitoring system', to paraphrase Lloyd Morgan, is where intelligent processing ends and consciousness begins. But also implicit in this formulation is that action must be capable of redirection as a result of 'monitoring'; the monitor is not just another of Huxley's epiphenomenal steam-whistles. 'Monitoring' reflects a form of neural organization with a hierarchical capacity for control. Also implicit is the fact that sheer complexity of the nervous system, *per se*, is not a sufficient condition for such an organization to be generated as an emergent property, although it may be that only the more complex nervous systems can be so organized as to allow 'monitoring' and hierarchical control. Indeed, the very specific and circumscribed character of the neuropathological condition that dissociates a capacity from an acknowledged awareness, in itself, speaks against sheer complexity of the nervous system being a sufficient condition for emergence. This is especially so given that other discrete sites of pathology give rise to quite different and dissociable disorders of cognition that are, as it happens, just as revealing about other aspects of the structure of the mind.

There is just one final point that ought to be touched on, so that I can fire the first shot before standing in the firing line of others. We all know the problem with the little homunculus in the brain: it is the problem of the infinite regress. Who looks in on *him*, and so forth and so forth? I embrace the infinite regress; I have no worry at all about having another monitor looking at a set of other monitors, in thinking about thinking, and having an elaboration of hierarchical levels of organization, and hence of varying levels of abstraction in thought. It is not a little man doing the looking, but a part of the nervous system itself that monitors other neural networks, rather than being firmly enmeshed as a link in a closed serial chain of processing. It is a matter of organization rather than of peeping Toms.

References

1 Darwin, C. (1871) *The Descent of Man*. London: John Murray (pp. 125–6 of 1894 edn).

2 Jennings, H. S. (1904) *Behaviour of the Lower Organisms*. Bloomington: Indiana Univ. Press.

3 Ibid.

4 Romanes, G. J. (1882) *Animal Intelligence*. London: Kegan Paul, Trench.

5 Morgan, C. Lloyd (1890) *Animal Life and Intelligence*. London: Edward Arnold.

6 James, W. (1890) *The Principles of Psychology*. London: Macmillan (p. 8 of 1901 edn).

7 Quoted by Morgan, C. Lloyd (1900) *Animal Behaviour*, p. 308. London: Edward Arnold.

8 Chance, M. R. A. and Jolly, A. (1970) *Social Groups of Monkeys, Apes, and Men*. London: Cape.

9 Humphrey, N. (1983) *Consciousness Regained*. Oxford: Oxford Univ. Press.

10 Morgan, C. Lloyd, *Animal Life and Intelligence*, p. 375.

11 Warrington, E. K. and Weiskrantz, L. (1982) Amnesia: a disconnection syndrome? *Neuropsychologia*, 20: 233–48.

12 Weiskrantz, L., Warrington, E. K., Sanders, M. D. and Marshall, J. (1974) Visual capacity in the hemianopic field following a restricted occipital ablation. *Brain*, 97: 709–28.

13 Weiskrantz, L. (1980) Varieties of residual experience. *Q. J. exp. Psychol.* 32: 365–86.

14 Campion, J., Latto, R. and Smith, Y. M. (1983) Is blindsight an effect of scattered light, spared cortex, and near-threshold vision? *Brain Behav. Sci.* 6: 423–86.

15 Weiskrantz, L. (1983) Evidence and scotomata. *Brain Behav. Sci.* 6: 464–7.

16 Perenin, M. T. and Jeannerod, M. (1978) Visual function within the hemianopic field following early cerebral hemidecortication in man. I. Spatial localization. *Neuropsychologia*, 16: 1–13.

17 Weiskrantz, L. and Saunders, R. C. (1984) Impairments of visual object transforms in monkeys. *Brain*, 107: 1033–72.

18 Beninger, R. J., Kendall, S. B. and Vanderwolf, C. H. (1974) The ability of rats to discriminate their own behaviours. *Canad. J. Psychol.* 28: 79–91.19.

19 Dickinson, A. (1985) Actions and habits: the development of behaviour autonomy. In L. Weiskrantz (ed.), *Animal Intelligence*, pp. 67–78. Oxford: Oxford Univ. Press.

22

The 'Brain–Mind' Relation: A Pseudoproblem?

János Szentágothai

János Szentágothai was born in Budapest in 1912, where he also attended his primary and secondary schools. He trained at Budapest University Medical School, gaining his MD in 1936. In the early part of his studies he was apprenticed to the Anatomy Department under the eminent Hungarian neuroanatomist Michael von Lenhossék, and became obsessed with tracing neural connections with the aid of axonal and synaptic degeneration (considered as a 'crazy enterprise' at that time). The first edition of J. F. Fulton's Physiology of the Central Nervous System *(1938) convinced him that neuroanatomy made sense only if confronted and combined at every step with neurophysiology. He became Professor of Anatomy at Pécs University in 1946 and Chairman of the Anatomy Department in 1947. In 1963 he took over the chairmanship of the first Anatomy Department at the Semmelweis University Medical School, Budapest. By that time tracing of neuronal connections had become an established routine approach in neuroanatomy, so that his interest switched to the functional architecture of neuron networks. He has been a member of the Hungarian Academy of Sciences since 1948, and was elected as its president during the period 1977–85. He holds numerous foreign or honorary memberships of the traditional academies both of East and West, including Foreign Membership of the Royal Society.*

> **There are no 'unintelligent' animals; only careless observations and poorly designed experiments.**

Taking Stock (Neurobiological Phenomenology)

Presumably all the readers of this book know what a *brain* is, but probably none of us, including the authors, could claim that she or he completely understands or can even correctly define the term *mind*. And yet everybody having even rudimentary knowledge of animal behaviour cannot but be overwhelmed by the versatile, purposive, self-programmed, and highly adaptive behaviour of virtually all animals. As long as they are

Székely and Czéh showed that if a small piece of the embryonic spinal cord of an amphibian was grafted, together with an embryonic limb bud, on to the back of another animal, the small group of transplanted nerve cells became interconnected and sent out fibres to the muscles of the extra limb. The tiny network of nerve cells then spontaneously generated impulses that caused more or less co-ordinated movements of the limb.

acting within their particular ecological spheres, all animals learn very quickly (usually after less than 10 trials), recall almost instantaneously, and show an 'intelligence' bordering on real insight of the situation, its potential dangers, and possibilities of reward. When confronted with tasks outside their own ecological sphere, animals are poor performers, are reluctant to behave as expected, and more often than not reproduce only mechanically what has been taught to them at the cost of inordinately large efforts. Spontaneity and playfulness – performance 'for its own sake' – can be seen in natural situations over a wide spectrum of animal species, and where this is not obvious to us, it may well be the result of our poor observation and anthropomorphic biases.

It seems dubious, to say the least, that the remarkable 'wholeness' and 'purposefulness' of animal behaviour could occur without a unified 'level of representation' – in other words, without an internal model of the world, including some kind of model of the animal itself. Short of this, the animal would be little more than a collection of reflexes (even if interconnected and interacting with each other), and of genetically inbuilt drives and behavioural programs – little more than a sophisticated biological robot.

There is probably no need to try to convince anybody that such a view would be untenable. But how can one imagine a 'level of representation' corresponding to such concepts as *wholeness* and *self*? The only possible route into this world of discourse is through our own consciousness. We have no key to the understanding of any other consciousness, even in our own species, including our closest relations, apart from the means of communication specific to our species. Although each of us is probably right in assuming that she or he is unique, we also act and behave under the intuitive insight (strengthened by an immense body of more objective, although circumstantial evidence) that all other human beings have the same type of subjective experience (even if language, social environment, and cultural tradition make very considerable differences in detail). The nervous systems of all animals are built of the same matter and on the same structural, functional, genetic and metabolic principles. So there is little reason to deny the same representational level of wholeness and of self to any other animal – possibly down to the simplest forms. In nervous systems less complicated than our own the repertoire and sophistication of possible internal models and states would presumably be simpler, although still sufficient to correspond to the demands of the special ecological niche of the animal.

It is the level of representation of wholeness, self and purpose of the animal that I here propose as the equivalent of the ambiguous term (or concept) 'mind'. This is tantamount to the assumption that mind must be present, however rudimentary in content, in all living beings endowed with a nervous system. We should be aware, of course, that in adopting this concept of mind we have to break away radically from our conventional anthropomorphic notions of our own human consciousness. Modern ethology has demonstrated a vast gulf between primates and sub-primates in the degree of understanding of the nature of 'self' and an even wider gulf between the still rudimentary self-consciousness of a non-human primate (amounting to insight into the difference between self and non-self) and the true human self-awareness. But, however large these differences, there is no reason to deny a certain level and degree of reflection of 'wholeness' in lower animals.

Emergence

I have used the terms 'representation' and 'reflection' virtually synonymously, but 'representation' specifically conveys the idea of something *emerging* from many things happening in a distributed form on levels below. Over the past two decades the terms 'emergent' and 'emergence' have been introduced (or, more correctly, reintroduced, since the concept has an earlier history) by Roger Sperry,[1] and incorporated into the framework of an explicitly formulated theory by Mario Bunge.[2] In spite of its great importance, the concept of emergence does not solve the problem of this level of reflection of the unity of 'self' (here divested of its anthropomorphic connotations), nor does it point to its location in particular neural centres. It does not clearly indicate whether what emerges has to be classified as an entirely different 'world' or category from that of matter (as Sir Karl Popper and Sir John Eccles advocate[3]), or whether it can be ultimately reduced to the material world, as Bunge believes.[2] In other words, the concept of emergence does not resolve the conflict between neo-Cartesian dualism and materialist monism.

As a humble neurobiologist, I do not want to enter the philosophical side of the debate, but perhaps a scientific approach can throw some light on the issue. I do not think that there is any material (or non-material) substrate of my own inner self except the roughly 50,000,000,000 nerve cells in the human nervous system, with the 10^{13}–10^{14} synaptic connections between them. We have to stay with these facts, at least for the time being, although we cannot rule out some major new discoveries in the future about the structure and the function of neural systems that would radically change our understanding. Nor do I think that there is any fundamental difference between the biological and functional characteristics of nervous systems throughout the animal kingdom. The miracle of a higher-order organization entered the world with the nervous systems of the flatworms, where the long phylogenetic process of the evolution of central nervous systems began.

The development of complex nervous systems in the course of evolution, with an ever-increasing diversity of possible behaviours, is nothing short of miraculous: consider the immense range of behavioural types from the highly independent patterns of life in some species to the varieties of cooperativeness in the social behaviour of other closely related species. On the surface, such behaviours may appear strictly determined by genetic inheritance; and yet even such rigidly pre-programmed behaviours show a very considerable range of extremely sophisticated plasticity (such as the ability to learn, memorize and to transmit experience to fellow-members), which is essential for the survival of both the individual and the entire group.

Approaches to the Brain–Mind Problem

It is fascinating to trace the circuitous and labyrinthine route that the knowledge of the higher functions of the neural system has taken recently, beginning with the impasse of behaviourism, through the great enthusiasm with which cybernetics was received in the late forties and early fifties (as well as the later disenchantment), to the present state of 'chaos'. 'Chaos' is not meant here to be derogatory, but to characterize various individual attempts at solving the age-old problem of the relationship between brain and mind, many of which are admirable achievements in my opinion; by 'chaos' I mean here simply the great variety of proposed solutions, which are difficult to enumerate and even more difficult to classify. Those who are interested in this problem should be most grateful to Mario Bunge for his clear outline of the various views and theories (see table 22.1).[2]

It is obviously impossible for me to discuss here adequately the many different philosophies offered even in the last 25 years. I have, though, to make one exception – Sir Karl Popper's and Sir John Eccles's remarkable book *The Self and Its Brain*.[3] This is not because I am in complete (or near-complete) agreement with the explanation that they offer of the brain–mind relationship, but because I basically approve of the logical strategy taken by these two distinguished authors, and of the great importance that they attribute to this subject for the survival of mankind. I have already implicitly stated one significant point of disagreement with Popper and Eccles: in my view man is the end-result of a long and marvellous evolution from rather primitive neural systems towards the unique miracle of the brain of *Homo sapiens sapiens*. I do not think that consciousness or even self-awareness starts with man. Its rudiments have to be there with the very existence of the 'neural'.

If understood and used metaphorically, the *three-world concept* envisaged originally by Popper and elaborated by Eccles is a fascinating view of great beauty, which may be of heuristic value. But taking it literally, and following the thought through to its ultimate consequence of an explicit dualist (interactionalist) view of the human mind is a different matter (and what about the rudimentary 'minds' of all animals?). We should have to leave the domain of legitimate science and enter that of religion and faith.

Some may ask whether seeing man as part of the animal kingdom would not detract from (or even destroy) our admiration for the human brain as a unique feature of the universe. Religious fundamentalists would obviously answer this question in the affirmative. But let me, for the sake of argument, put the issue bluntly as follows: in which view would our admiration for the Creation (or even the Creator) be greater: if (1) we retain the explanation from 3,000 years ago that man was made 6,000 years before our time from a piece of clay? or if (2) we assume, as science suggests, that the human brain is the result of 3.5 billion years of evolution? For scientific reasoning, the latter statement is no longer a theory, but a plain, proven fact, although we shall probably disagree for further millennia about the mechanisms through which this evolution came about – whether by a succession of extremely unlikely changes, or whether by means of some kind of initial 'pre-programming'.

22.1: Ten types of explanation of behaviour and mentation (by M. Bunge)

	Philosophy of mind	Explanation of behaviour	Explanation of mentation
M1	idealism, panpsychism, phenomenalism	Manifestation of the workings of a spirit (individual or world-wide). No precise laws	Autonomous and spontaneous activity of the mind coverable by law containing only mentalist predicates
M2	Neutral monism, double aspect view	Behaviour and mentation manifestations of the workings of a being neither material nor mental, explainable with a single set of laws with two projections or translations (behavioural and mentalist)	
M3	Eliminative materialism, behaviourism	Outcome of stimuli, hence describable by S–R laws (no intervention of CNS)	Mentation non-existent, hence not to be explained
M4	Reductive materialism	Motor outcome of physical CNS events, hence explainable in physical terms	Physical activity of the CNS
M5	Emergent materialism	Motor outcome of biological CNS events, explainable with the help of biological laws, some of which contain new predicates	Biological activity of plastic sub-systems of CNS, explainable with the help of biological laws containing new predicates
D1	Mutual independence of body and mind	Biological events explainable in purely physiological terms plus possibly theological ones	Mental events explainable in purely mentalist terms plus possibly theological ones
D2	Psychophysical parallelism. pre-established harmony		
D3	Epiphenomenalism	Motor outome of CNS events	Non-motor effect of CNS activity
D4	Animism	Motor outcome of mental events (e.g. intending and wishing)	Unexplainable except possibly in supernatural terms
D5	Interactionism	Under dual control of body and mind. Only partially explainable	Autonomous though influenced by bodily events. Unexplainable by science

Before attacking the objective directly, I shall consider, very briefly, the principal trends that neural organization has followed during evolution (although I shall not venture into any discussion of unicellular organisms).[4,5] Such an approach gives valuable insight into the way in which the nervous system has become organized.

In the simplest multicellular forms (Coelenterates) the nervous system appears as a fairly homogeneous, widespread network. Apparently diffuse

Self-organization in Tissue Recombination Experiments

In the experiments that I did with György Székely,[8] a fragment of tissue from the embryonic neural tube (primitive spinal cord) of a newt was transplanted into the dorsal fin of another larva of the same species (*Triturus vulgaris* or *Pleurodeles waltli*) with an embryonic limb bud implanted nearby. When the limb bud developed into an extra limb, attached to the host animal's fin, the muscles of the limb became innervated by the prospective motor nerve cells of the grafted piece of neural tube nearby. (Only neurons containing the appropriate transmitter substance, acetyl choline, can successfully innervate skeletal muscle.) The limb soon began to move and to show the 'epileptiform' activity (random twitches or bursts of successive contractions) first described by Paul Weiss.[7] In our own experiments the fragments of central nervous tissue were taken from larvae at a relatively late stage of development and subsequent histological examination of the preparations showed only a few (15–50) randomly scattered neurons in the graft, without any organized structure. Fewer than 20 surviving neurons, from which only two or three were motor neurons, fully sufficed to create this characteristic spontaneous activity. Occasionally, sensory nerve fibres from the skin of the fin of the host animal became entangled with, and connected to, the graft of nervous tissue. In those cases, 'reflex' movements of the extra limb could be produced by stimulating the host animal's fin. However, in most cases, no such reflexes were ever seen during weeks of careful daily observation: the activity of nerve cells in the graft, leading to the twitching movements, must have been truly 'spontaneous'. The movement patterns of the implanted limbs were entirely random both with respect to timing and to which joint of the transplanted limb was moved. Each transplanted spinal cord/limb preparation, though, developed some characteristic overall pattern of movement. Local

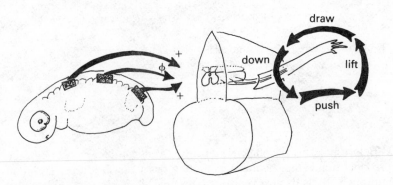

Figure 22.1   In their experiments on transplanted fragments of amphibian nerve cord and limb bud, Székely and Czéh[10] found that sequences of limb movements characteristic of walking occurred only if the nerve graft had been taken from an embryonic segment that would normally become connected with a forelimb or hindlimb (the two transplantations marked with plus signs in the diagram above). Sensory input was not necessary for this activity.

application of a solution of strychnine (a drug that interferes with inhibition in the nervous system) to the skin covering the neural transplant resulted in much more vigorous twitching of the limb, with protracted 'convulsive states'. We inferred, then, that this strychnine effect was due to the presence in the graft of local inhibitory nerve cells, influencing the tiny nerve network.

Already at the time we were doing this work (1962) we realized that these grafts were devoid of sensory input and nevertheless were able to become active. 'Spontaneous' activity of certain nerves and muscles (for instance heart muscle) had been known for a long time, so we did not attach particular significance to this phenomenon.

Somewhat later, Székely and Czéh refined their techniques and explored systematically which parts of the transplanted neural tube were essential for generating real 'walking-type' patterns of limb movement.[10] It turned out that the grafts of developing neural tube had to retain their organized structure (the central canal had to be preserved); and secondly, the tissue had to be taken from those parts of the developing spinal cord of the donor that would normally innervate either fore- or hindlimbs (transplants of mid-thoracic segments, which do not normally connect to either limbs, were unable to produce any coordinated movement of limbs). Thirdly, sensory input was not necessary for walking-type movement. The two symmetrical halves of a neural tube implant could connect with a pair of implanted limbs and move them both, but only in synchronous manner.

As shown later by Brändle and Székely,[11] the typical alternation of the limb pairs seen in normal walking depends on the presence in the graft of a few additional segments of the neural tube located above the limb segments. Hence, the limb-bearing segments of the tube contain the 'step generator', and alternation of steps in a pair of analogous limbs requires an additional 'step-alternation generator'.

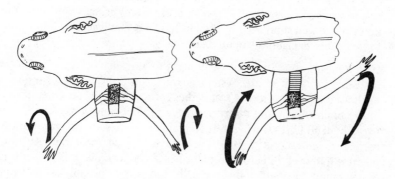

Figure 22.2   Brändle and Székely [11] transplanted whole sections of the embryonic trunk, with limb buds attached, into the flank of a host animal of the same species. The limbs of the graft produced only oar-like movements (diagram, left), unless an additional piece of the embryonic spinal cord was included, in which case the limbs moved in natural alternation (right).

neuron networks are retained in all higher forms – for example in the neural plexus of the gut.

The first major trend in 'neural evolution' was *centralization* (appearing in the flatworms), which led quickly to the development of centralized neural organs (as opposed to the peripheral nervous system, which contains receptors, sensory nerves, and motor nerves controlling muscles and glands). The second general trend was *cephalic dominance*, that is, the gradual predominance gained by parts of the nervous system at the head end, with the *transposition* of the most important (higher) functions into those regions of the brain. This trend, which is evident in all the major phyla of the animal kingdom, was made possible – in the vertebrates – by the development of a cranium as a protective case for larger central organs at the front end of the animal. Even this was only an interim stage of brain evolution and was soon superseded, in the mammals, by *corticalization* (the formation and spectacular development of the cerebral cortex).

Possible Requirements of Systems that Might Underlie Mind

Today, all neurobiologists, psychologists, behavioural and cognitive scientists, and philosophers engaged in the study of mental phenomena would surely accept (even if only tacitly) that *the nervous system is not (primarily) a reflex machine*. But if not a 'reflex machine', what is it?

Let me be positive and try to define the requirements of a *neural system* that is more than purely a 'reflex robot':

Requirement 1: Such a system has to be distributed through various parts of the brain, mainly because the other alternative (precise localization) does not fit the facts. Vernon Mountcastle and Gerald Edelman, in their book *The Mindful Brain*,[6] summarized the known facts about the mammalian brain and concluded that whatever is considered as mind must be localized in or tied to a distributed system.

Requirement 2: Such a system has to be built of *hierarchically arranged sub-systems of self-organizing neuron networks*. Many aspects of this requirement are so well supported by established facts that it seems almost trivial to try further to elaborate upon them.

Requirement 3: Such a system ought to have massive capacity for *re-entrance*,[6,21,22] that is, the system ought to have the ability to influence itself via connections to and from other cortical or even sub-cortical areas of the brain. According to my own rough calculations, probably over 80 per cent of all fibres leaving the cerebral cortex are serving direct cortico-cortical re-entrance.[19,20] The total percentage of re-entrant pathways might run to over 90 per cent of all cortical connections. It is probably no exaggeration to assume that virtually every cortical cell has potential access, directly or indirectly, to any other point in the cortex.

Neural systems are more like networks (or cell-assemblies) than simple chain-like sequences of cells. What may look like straightforward sequential chains of nerve cells along pathways in the nervous system are in fact interrupted at each relay nucleus by a rather complex network built by combining divergence and convergence of incoming messages, as well as circuits of local nerve cells (interneurons) arranged in either feedback or feedforward loops.

Self-organization might be a more controversial subject, but its possible significance in neural organization was suggested long ago by the theoreticians in the golden age of cybernetics. In addition, experimental work on nerve tissue recombination and culture (see box p. 328), in which I was involved some time ago, strongly suggested that growing neurons have the capacity for self-organization.[7,8,9]

I have tried to elaborate on the significance of these earlier experiments,[12,13,14] and I am now working with my colleague Péter Érdi to put the concept of self-organization into a larger theoretical framework. To explain the earlier experimental observations (see box) we need to account for the origin of neural activity that could be (self-) organized into dynamic patterns. In the experiments in which transplanted spinal cord and muscle developed rhythmic movement without any sensory input, one had to assume the existence of spontaneous activity in the neurons of the isolated network. Spontaneous (random-like) activity of excitable tissues, although known for a long time, had not been seriously considered earlier as an important aspect of neural functions in vertebrates. So it came as a surprise to realize that the development of networks in neural systems might rely heavily on the spontaneous activity of the constituent nerve cells, and that this 'neural noise' might be put to some important use in promoting self-organization. Very recently Jean Pierre Changeux and his colleagues have included spontaneous activity in neural tissues in an explicit and mathematically formalized theory of so-called 'pre-representations' emerging from spontaneous activity plus some 'resonance' with activity-generated stimulation provided by the environment.[15] The 'tensor theory' of Pellionisz and Llinás (see Rodolfo Llinás' chapter in this book) also suggests that internal representations are set up by interaction between spontaneous activity and sensory input,[16] though those authors question the term 'self-organization', which I have to admit is used purely intuitively in neurobiology.

The term *sub-system* in itself seems to require the presence in neural systems of corresponding anatomical structures. That neural systems are indeed structurally organized, at the level of the gross anatomy of the brain, is so obvious that it needs no description. However, each major part of the brain is known to be further divided into functional sub-regions: for instance, the cerebral cortex contains a number of sensory and motor areas, most of which consist of an 'isomorphic' representation or 'map' of the body or one particular sensory surface (such as the visual field for the visual areas of the cortex). In a more recent development of our knowledge we have come to realize that these large, seemingly isomorphous or 'mapped' centres are built up of a mosaic of smaller, repetitive structural and functional units of nervous tissue, called *modules*. [12,17–20]

Principles of Operation

After this stock-taking of neurobiological phenomena and of the requirements of organization for a neural system capable of 'representation', I

The 'Modular Architectonic Principle' of the Cerebral Cortex

The modular building-block of the mammalian cortex is shown here, stripped down to its bare essentials. The upper part of the figure 22.3 (A) shows the most general principle of nerve fibre connectivity between different 'columns' of nerve cells in the cortex. One class of column contains cells that send fibres to, and receive fibres from, other (distant) parts of the cortex. Such cortico-cortical columns of cells are about 0.2–0.3 mm in width and they extend vertically through the entire depth of the cortex (that is, 2.5–3 mm in the human cortex). Pyramid-shaped cells (about 60 per cent of the entire nerve cell population in the cortex) are the main source of fibres leaving any part of the cortex and these same fibres form the main contingent of axons entering the cortex from below. While these pyramidal cells from the upper (outer) cortical layers send their axons mainly to other cortical regions within the same hemisphere, fibres that run across to the other hemisphere may arise from any cortical layer, and are often only side-branches of fibres that have other destinations. The axons of pyramidal cells in the deeper layers are generally sent to the brain centres below the cerebral cortex. It is generally thought that the fibres of all pyramidal cells have excitatory actions on the cells they connect to.

The lower part (B) of figure 22.3 shows a single cortico-cortical column enlarged, in the shape of a cylinder. The excitatory nerve cells (pyramidal cells – Py) and excitatory nerve fibres and their connections are drawn in outline. A single cortico-cortical fibre (cort-cort) is drawn entering the middle of the column (actually there might be a couple of hundred such fibres for each column). The inhibitory nerve cells with local connections are shown in black. Various types of such inhibitory interneurons have been identified recently. For instance, the larger 'basket cells' (Ba) are lined up in two rows, directly above and below the middle layer of the cortex. They act chiefly on pyramidal cells, reducing activity in the cells in the middle layers of the cortex.

---

can now attempt to outline some of the operative principles that such a system might be based on.

The most basic principle of neural systems is, in my opinion, 'self-organization' in neuronal networks. It is by no means restricted to the highest centres of the brain, but is a general operational principle, present from the most primitive neuron networks in simple animals up to the human cerebral cortex. The first question that arises is, 'what kind of information is being self-organized?' Nervous systems, considered as information-processing and even information-creating devices,[23] have well-defined inputs along sensory channels. But this kind of sensory inflow is only the most conventional mode of input. What about other inputs from genetically in-built 'information' and from traces of past experience: that is, memory? In spite of remarkable efforts and a wealth of interesting observations our scientific knowledge of these aspects is virtually nil. Is memory coded in some way or other in specific molecules?

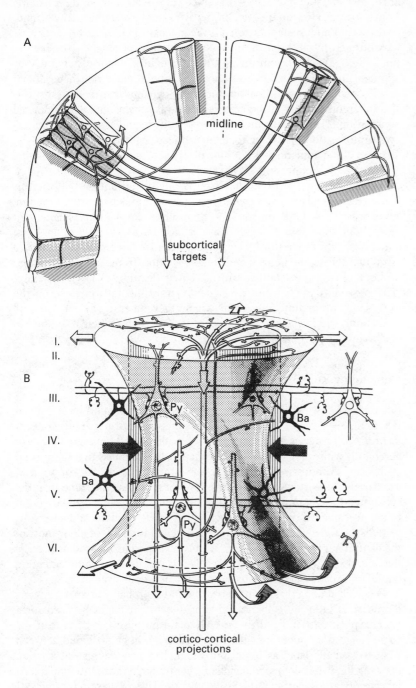

Figure 22.3   The modular *principle of the cerebral cortex. A shows the pattern of interconnection between regions of cortex and between cortex and subcortical structures. B shows in more detail one of the cylindrical modules of which the cortex is composed. The Roman numerals on the left indicate the layers of the cortex. The tendency of excitatory connections to spread further sideways in the shallowest and deepest parts of the cortex and of inhibitory connections (black arrows) to spread more in the middle layers converts the* functional *module into the shape of an hour glass.*

If so, how are such molecules preserved for 70–80 years in the case of a human being? How do they act on the synapses between nerve cells, and, to use a computer metaphor, what is the mechanism of the read-out?

Motivated by my own tissue-recombination experiments (see box on pp. 328–9), I would favour the idea that the neuronal 'noise' generated by spontaneous activity in billions of neurons is the original raw material that is self-organized by neuronal networks into dynamic activity patterns. It is this inherent, self-organized activity of neural systems into which normal sensory input is fed and which is open to genetic and acquired (memory-type) information, whatever their mechanism. More important still – in the case of the human – it is additionally open to all information belonging to 'World 3' of Popper and Eccles.

This interpretation would have the additional advantage that there is some – admittedly still somewhat mystic – relation between 'information' and 'order'.[24] 'Mind' functions – themselves considered as emergent from brain functions – might have a *downward causal effect* on brain functions.[13] In other words, consciousness and thought might interfere with the activity of neuron networks resulting from self-organization, without getting into conflict with accepted (legitimate) laws of nature. The possibility of 'downward causation' from mental functions on the very same brain functions from which they emerge (by 'bottom up' causation), within the accepted laws of nature, is an attractive solution to the brain–mind problem.

Concluding Remarks

Speaking of downward causation from the emergent 'mind level' toward the 'brain level' might create the impression that I introduce this concept in order to bridge a gap existing between the two. However, I have to agree fully with John Searle (see his chapter in this book) that there is no such gap. Although distributed over large parts of the brain (not exclusively the cortex), the reflective level of mind has the same material substrate as the brain, the only difference being that while ordinary brain functions can occur in separate, even rather small, portions of the nervous system, the reflective level (or mind) is a global function of all or most of the central nervous system. There is thus no gap to be bridged as regards the neural substrate of mind: the problem is only how anything emerging on the reflective level can act back upon the neuronal level.

To speak about a real brain theory of mind is probably premature. This discourse is little more than a building-block that might be used for a later, explicitly formulated theory. My main purpose has been to make some suggestions about how the relationship might be imagined between what we usually label as brain and mind. If a two-way causal relation between the two is not in irreconcilable contradiction with the fundamental laws of nature (particularly the 1st and 2nd laws of thermodynamics), I cannot see any reason why acceptance of this notion would *per se* force anybody to make a choice between monism or dualism. Non-scientific questions about the ultimate reasons and purpose of existence (and the universe) do not necessarily come into conflict with whatever one believes to be acceptable for the relationship between brain and mind. These ultimate questions do belong and will continue to belong to the realm of a personal credo. I do not think that at present we can go much further in view of our lack of knowledge about how the nervous system codes and reads out genetically in-built information and information about past experience (memory and learning), and information coded in the complex symbol system of Popper's and Eccles's 'World 3' (language, metalanguage, music, myths, religion, scientific knowledge, etc.). It might suffice to know from accepting the fact of 'downward causation' that we have the choice and are responsible. This is the basic contrast with all other beings of the animal kingdom, for which this World 3 does not exist. Animals are equal to their nature and live in happy ignorance of good and evil. The parable of 'Paradise Lost' is indeed the ultimate and terrifying truth – the beauty and greatness of being human.

References

1 Sperry, R. W. (1969) A modified concept of consciousness. *Psychological Review*, 76: 532–6.

2 Bunge, M. (1977) Emergence and the mind. *Neuroscience*, 2: 501–9.

3 Popper, K. R. and Eccles, J. C. (1977) *The Self and Its Brain*. Berlin, Heidelberg, London, New York: Springer Internat.

4 Párduc, B. (1954a,b, 1955, 1956, 1957, 1958) Reizphysiologische Unter suchungen an Ziliaten I–VII. (a) *Acta Microbiol. Hung.* 1: 176–221; (b) *Acta Biologica Hung.* 5: 169–212; *Ann. Nat. Mus. Natur. Hung.* 6: 189–95; *Acta Biol. Hung.* 6: 289–316; *Acta Biol. Hung.* 7: 73–99; *Acta Biol. Hung.* 8: 218–51.

5 Khosland, D. E. (1974) The chemotractic response as a potential model for neural systems. *The Neurosciences: Third Study Program*, pp. 841–52. Cambridge, Mass.: MIT Press.

6 Edelman, G. M. and Mountcastle, V. B. (1978) *The Mindful Brain*. Cambridge, Mass.: MIT Press.

7 Weiss, P. (1950) The deplantation of fragments of nervous system in amphibians. *J. exp. Zoology*, 113: 397–461.

8 Székely, Gy. and Szentágothai, J. (1962) Experiments with 'model nervous systems'. *Acta Biol. Acad. Sci. Hung.* 12: 253–69.

9 Crain, S. M. (1973) Tissue culture models of developing brain functions. *Development Studies of Behavior and the Nervous System*, vol. 2, Aspects of Neurogenesis, pp. 69–114. New York: Academic Press.

10 Székely, G. and Czéh, G. (1971) Activity of spinal cord fragments and limbs deplanted in the dorsal fin of urodele larvae. *Acta Physiol. Hung.* 40: 303–12.

11 Brändle, K. and Székely, G. (1973) The control of alternating coordination of limb pairs in the newt (Triturus vulgaris). *Brain, Behav. Evol.* 8: 366–85.

12 Szentágothai, J. and Arbib, M. A. (1974) Conceptual models of neural organization. *Neurosci. Progr. Bulletin*, 12: 313–510.

13 Szentágothai, J. (1984) Downward causation? *Ann. Rev. Neurosci.* 7: 1–11.

14 Szentágothai, J. (1985) Theorien zur Organisation und Funktion des Gehirns. *Naturwissenschaften*, 72: 303–9.

15 Changeux, J. P. (communicator): Heidmann, A., Heidmann, T. and Changeux, J. P. (1984) Stabilisation sélective des représentations neuronales per résonance entre 'préreprésentations' spontanées du réseau cérébral et 'percepts' évoqués par interaction avec le monde extérieur. *C. R. Acad. Sc. Paris, t. 299, Série III*, No. 20.

16 Pellionisz, A. and Llinás, R. (1985) Tensor network theory of the metaorgani zation of functional geometrics in the CNS. *Neuroscience*, 16: 245–73.

17 Eccles, J. C. (1981) The modular operation of the cerebral neocortex considered as the material basis of mental events. *Neuroscience*, 6: 1839–56.

18 Szentágothai, J. (1975) 'The module concept' in cerebral cortex architecture. *Brain Res.* 95: 475–96.

19 Szentágothai, J. (1978) The Ferrier Lecture, 1977: The neuron network of the cerebral cortex. A functional interpretation. *Proc. Roy. Soc. Lond.* B201: 219–48.

20 Szentágothai, J. (1983) The modular architectonic principle of neural centers. *Rev. Physiol. Biochem. Pharmacol.* 98: 11–61.

21 Goldman, P. S. and Nauta, W. J. H. (1977) Columnar distribution of cortico-cortical fibers in the frontal association, limbic, and motor cortex of the developing Rhesus monkey. *Brain Research*, 122: 393–413.

22 Goldman–Rakic, P. S. and Schwartz, M. L. (1982) Interdigitation of contralateral and ipsilateral columnar projections to frontal association cortex in primates. *Science*, 216: 755–7.

23 MacKay, D. M. (1982) Ourselves and our brains: duality without dualism. *Psychoneuroendocrinology*, 7: 285–94.

24 Érdi, P. (1983) Hierarchical thermodynamic approach to the brain. *Int. J. Neurosciences*, 20: 193–216.

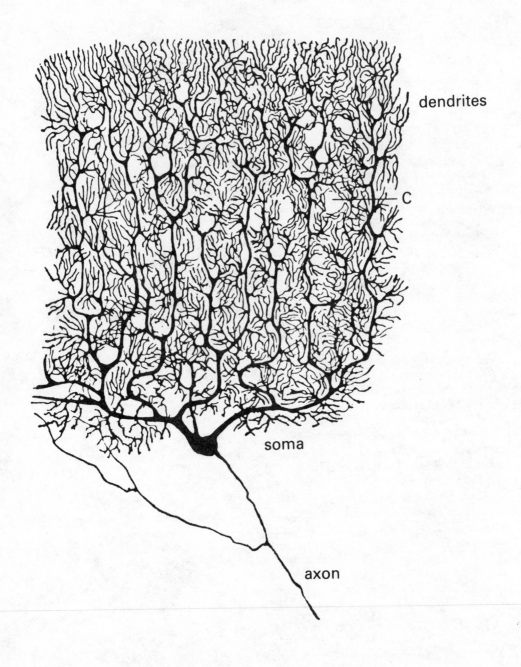

dendrites

C

soma

axon

23

'Mindness' as a Functional State of the Brain

Rodolfo Llinás

Rodolfo Llinás is Professor and Chairman of the Department of Physiology and Biophysics and the Thomas and Susanne Murphy Professor of Neuroscience at New York University School of Medicine. His interests range from biophysical properties of nerve membranes and synaptic transmission through the analysis of mammalian neuronal networks to include cerebellum, inferior olive, thalamus and tectum, as well as different levels of mathematical modelling. Much of his work has been in the biophysics of mammalian central neurons as studied in both in vivo and in vitro preparations. In addition, he has made contributions in both the ontogeny and phylogeny of brain development. His overall interest has been the development of experimentally based theories for brain function and their relation to the body–mind problem.

Introduction

As a neuroscientist, the single most important issue one can address concerns the manner in which brains and minds relate to one another. It is thus quite surprising that this issue attracts so little interest in our field. There are at least two reasons for this apparent lack of interest: (a) neuroscientists consider such issues to be irrelevant to their immediate field of study; or (b) it is considered that the questions have not been sufficiently clarified to allow an unambiguous experimental or even a theoretical approach to their elucidation.

I for one, as a monist, consider 'mindness'[1] to be but one of several global physiological computational states that the brain can generate.[2] An example of another global physiological state, in which 'mindness' is not apparent, is that known as 'being asleep' and yet another is known as dreaming, in which 'cognition' does not relate to the co-existing external reality. Among the above, the 'mindness state' allows complex goal-directed interactions between a living organism and its environment. The more complex the interaction the more involved the 'mindness' state – and yet, it seems to me, never so complex as to transcend the boundaries of the purely material.

The Function of the Nervous System is Geared to Prediction

As a first step in approaching the nature of 'mindness', one may ask, 'what

Ramon y Cajal's drawing of a spectacular neuron – a Purkinje cell from the cerebellum.

is the brain good for?'. The set of possible answers is immense if one considers all the properties that the nervous system displays in each of us. However, on second thoughts, a common denominator may be found which encompasses most aspects of brain function. I personally feel that *prediction* may be such a common denominator. This predictive property seems to be the ultimate and most general of all global functions of the brain. Indeed, it is the ability to anticipate on the basis of incoming sensory stimuli the ultimate outcome of a given change in the external surroundings and to respond to such change with goal-directed actions that ensures survival. In considering the evolution of the brain, the basic property implemented consists of the ability to transform given sensory responses into organized motor events. Even in brainless cellular colonies like the Portuguese man-of-war jellyfish, such a scheme is already

Figure 23.1 Santiago Ramón y Cajal (1852–1934), the founder of modern neuroanatomy. In 1911 he produced a theory of the spinal cord, suggesting that the central nervous system develops by organizing itself around initial motor activity (photograph of Cajal from the University Laboratory of Physiology, Oxford).

present. Indeed, while distinct groups of cells will sense given forms of energy, other (genetically unrelated) groups of cells generate movement (retraction of the tentacles; see figure 23.2) or secretion of a stinging substance used by the colony as a defence mechanism.[3] In the case of the Portuguese man-of-war we have a conglomerate of cellular colonies that organize themselves such that 'sensory' and 'motor' responses will be related to one another, even in the absence of an organized nervous system.

Following this principle of organization, in the primitive nervous systems the simple sensorimotor response is implemented by the interposition between sensory and motor cells of additional connecting nerve cells (interneurons), which serve to reroute and distribute sensory input to different sets of muscle-like cells. The functional advantage provided by an interneuron is that of 'steering with multiple reins'; that is, sensory stimuli impinging on a few sensory cells may activate a small set of such interneurons and evoke a complex motor response involving a large number of contractile elements. Through this multiple forward connectivity the animal becomes capable of executing well-defined gross movements. This initial network already defines the basic properties of sensorimotor transformations.

Figure 23.2   The Portuguese man-of-war is a superorganism recognized by its air float above and its tentacles trailing below. It is a colony of interdependent individual organisms, some specialized for buoyancy, others for feeding, protection or reproduction. There is communication among the individuals and thus the colony as a whole is capable of considerable co-ordination. This is seen every few minutes as the sides of the bright blue float are pulled under water to wet the tissue and material surrounding the gas chamber.

It is delightful to consider that development of a nervous system is in fact very much a property of actively moving organisms (non-sessile organisms), that is, those that do not remain fixed to a particular place, as is the case for plants. This principle is beautifully exemplified by the tunicate (a 'sea squirt') with free-swimming larvae. Herein lies one of the truly extraordinary lessons of biology. In ancestral tunicates as well as in some present forms, the sessile adult form (which is rooted by its pedicle to a stable object in the sea) carries out two main functions: it feeds by filtering seawater (a deeply bureaucratic type of function); and it reproduces by budding (see figure 23.4).[6] Upon reproduction, larvae are free-swimming and possess a brain-like ganglion which can be informed about the environment by peripheral sensory input from a statocyst (organ for balance),[7] a primitive eye, and a notocord (primitive spinal cord). These central nervous structures have the connections necessary to deal with the continuously changing environment, as this primitive tadpole-like larva swims through the water. Upon finding a suitable substrate, the larva proceeds to implant its head end into the selected location and becomes sessile. In doing so, it absorbs much of its brain and returns to the rather primitive condition of the adult form of the species (a process paralleled by some human academics upon obtaining university tenure). In some circumstances, probably related to the ability that the larva has to utilize its primitive digestive system, it may proceed to reproduce prior to becoming sessile. This step is believed to have generated a class of brainy organisms (our distant ancestors) known as the chordate filter feeders (figure 23.4). The lesson of this evolutionary stage is, of course, very clear. It is that brains are needed only in those multicellular beings that

Evolution of Nervous Systems

An interneuron, in the strict sense, is any nerve cell which does not communicate directly with the outside world either as a sensing device (a sensory neuron) or by means of a motor terminal on a

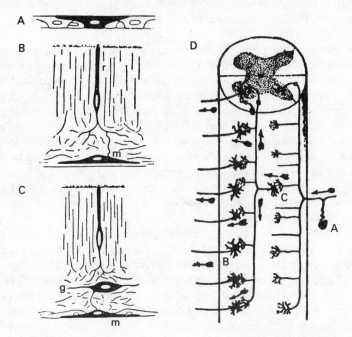

muscle (a motor neuron). Interneurons, therefore, receive and send information to other nerve cells exclusively. Their evolution and development represents the basis for the elaboration of the central nervous system. The diagrams that follow represent stages of development present in early invertebrates.[4] In A, a motile cell (in black) from a primitive organism (a sponge), responds to direct stimulation with a wave of contraction. In B, in more evolved primitive organisms (e.g. the sea anemone), the sensory and contractile functions of the cell in A have been segregated into two elements; 'r' is the receptor or sensory cell and 'm' is the muscle or contractile element. The sensory cell responds to stimuli and serves as a motor neuron in the sense that it triggers muscle-cell contraction. However, this sensory cell has become specialized such that it is incapable of generating movement (contraction) on its own. Its function at this stage is the reception and transmission of information. In C, a second neuron has been interposed between the sensory element and the muscle (also from a sea anemone). This cell, a motor neuron, serves to activate muscle fibres (m) but responds only to the activation of the sensory cell (r). In D, as the evolution of the central nervous system progresses (this example is the vertebrate spinal cord), cells become interposed between the sensory neurons (A) and motor neurons (B). These are the interneurons, which serve to distribute the sensory information (arrow in A) by their many branches (arrows in C) to the motor neurons or to other neurons in the central nervous system (from Ramon y Cajal).[5]

move actively. Indeed, it is only then that such forms must interact with the environment at speeds that are sufficiently fast to require a rapidly acting organ specialized for the forecasting of external changes with sufficient anticipation (prediction) to afford corrective behaviour.

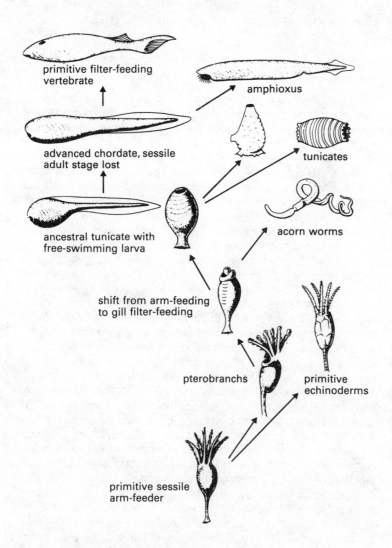

Figure 23.4 A simplified diagram of chordate evolution. In its early phases this process led to an end point in the production of efficient filter feeders, such as the tunicates. The development of a motile larva, presumably in a pre-tunicate stage, began a new evolutionary series leading toward true vertebrates (from Romer[6]).

The Embedding of Coordinate Systems in the Brain

How can a system such as the developing brain, initially devoid of any knowledge of the properties of the external world, acquire such information by evolutionary means so that it may, in turn, predict? The answer here seems to be straightforward. Natural selection has favoured those living organisms having cell-biological rules by which neurons (through their connectivity) may incorporate sensory referred properties of the external world *into the internal functional states*. This internal embedding of external properties allows actively moving forms to deal with the vicissitudes of existing in an ever changing environment. This internalization is attainable by cellular specializations which specify neuronal connectivity. These include most importantly cell adhesion, cell differentiation and the intrinsic electrical properties of the neurons. The internalization of the properties of the external world into an internal functional space is at this stage the central problem regarding brain function. Addressing this problem, one may ask two principal questions:

Internalization

By internalization is meant the ability that the nervous system has to fracture external reality into sets of sensory messages (carried to the brain by millions of sensory nerve fibres) and to simulate such reality in brain reference frames. Andras Pellionisz and I consider that this internalization process can be formally treated using mathematical concepts. Thus a sensory input can be represented as a dynamic point vector in a system of sensory coordinates (the peripheral sensory systems) where the electrical activity in each fibre represents a component of such a vector. These sensory vectors represent, then, external objects (invariances) whose existence is independent of the system of sensory coordinates that encode them. In order to represent any such invariant in our brain, the sensory vector (in a multidimensional frequency space, since it is generated by impulses in many fibres) must be transformed into an internally meaningful vector. A truly fundamental problem becomes apparent here, since the reference frames intrinsic to the brain are different, of necessity, from the reference frames of the external sensory systems. Indeed, sensory responses arise from a direct interaction between the external world and a set of receptors which may respond to stimuli such as light, or sound or angular movement. Their messages in the form of nerve impulses (see box on pp. 346–7) must, therefore, be decoded by a set of internal neurons that do not share the external physical arrangement or the functional properties that receptor systems have in the periphery. This difference between the external and the internal reference frames relates to both the direction and the number of coordinate axes. The issue of direction relates to the fact that the axes of the sensory coordinate system, being the 'natural' coordinates of the body, are oblique (non-orthogonal). The same property exists for the internal reference frames. A similar problem arises with respect to the number of coordinate axes (represented by the number of nerve fibres). The number of fibres arriving at a given site in the brain may be larger or smaller than the numbers of fibres that leave such a brain site. What is needed then is a type of vector transformation that does not depend on the properties of the coordinate systems that encode or decode them. These types of coordinate system-independent vector transformations are known in mathematics as tensorial transformations. Thus, Pellionisz and I introduced the concept of tensor network theory in an effort to develop a formal approach to the study of the nervous system. Our approach in fact suggests that neuronal networks actually implement tensorial transformations by means of their electrical activity and connectivity.

(1) If nerve nets represent a functional embodiment of the properties of universals, how is this embodiment implemented?

(2) Even if a mechanism is found to internalize external properties in a functional geometry, how may this functional geometry make sense of 'universals' beyond the blind transformation of sensory inputs into motor outputs? Indeed, how can such a network understand (in the sense that we, as brain networks, understand) or, stated differently, how can a neuronal network develop semantics?

Development of Connectivity

At this point I should like to review possible mechanisms by which intrinsic properties of neurons may specify the details of connectivity. While this may appear to be far more detailed than necessary in a general account, I feel that describing the possible relation between the cellular and the global levels must be done as strictly as possible, as it is in this realm that we need to define and understand the problem.

Amongst the more recondite aspects of brain development is the mechanism by which neuronal nets are organized, in a dynamic sense, during development. The prevailing view considers that such organization is basically a product (a) of genetic information unfolded in time; and (b) of epigenetic (or non-genetic) variables relating to the position of nerve cells, growth of nerve fibres in the embryo, position of the targets of growing fibres,[8] and chemotaxis (growth following a chemical substance).[9] Recently several deeply clarifying concepts have been added to the mechanisms above – the specific regulation of cellular movement through gated adhesiveness[10] as described in the 'regular hypothesis' of Gerald Edelman,[11] and the 'selective stabilization' of synaptic connectivity as proposed by Jean Pierre Changeux.[12] This connectivity is assumed to proceed, via 'natural selection' (only those connections that are effective become stabilized) to determine the specificity of neuronal contacts that characterize the adult central nervous system. Another basic concept which may be considered as an organizing principle in the generation of such networks relates to the intrinsic electrical responsiveness of nerve cells (see box) and their ability to entrain electrical events in other cellular elements. This hypothesis I would like to refer to as 'dynamic linkage'.

Dynamic Linkage (Coordinate Embedding Residing in Oscillation and Resonance)

Electrical kinship as determined by the membrane potential oscillation of given nerve cells, and by the electrical resonance generated by such oscillator neurons in related nerve cells, seems to be an important key in the organization of networks (see box on pp. 346–7). Historically, one of the basic tenets in theories about development of the nervous system has been that it is initially organized from a perspective of muscular movement, as suggested on morphological grounds by the anatomist Santiago

How Neurons Work

Nerve cells have a variety of shapes and sizes but share certain important characteristics, especially those involved in their key function – the transmission of signals from one neuron to another, and ultimately to muscles or glands.

Like the other cells of the body, neurons are enveloped by a membrane which is of central importance in its function. This phospholipid membrane has embedded in it a diverse population of specialized structures such as structural proteins, enzymes, channels, pumps and receptors. The last three give the nerve cell its remarkable electrical properties and its sensitivity to external chemical substances. Among the anatomical features that set neurons apart from other cells (see figures 15.2 and 15.3) is the presence on the cell body of two types of filamentous processes: the *dendrites*, which are relatively short, and an *axon* or nerve fibre, which can be long (up to about one metre in the human adult). Generally speaking, the dendrites are mainly responsible for receiving signals from the axons of other neurons through junctions called *synapses*. Synaptic transmission serves to activate the axon of the next cell in line and thus electrical signals can move from one cell to the next.

The composition of cytoplasm of a neuron is different from that of the surrounding medium. From an ionic point of view the interior of a cell has a concentration of potassium that is about thirty times higher than the extracellular fluid. Sodium has a concentration inside that is about one-tenth that of the surrounding fluid. These facts, combined with the *selective permeability* of the membrane (which allows potassium to leak out more easily than sodium to leak in), create a small voltage difference of about 0.07 volts (70 mV) between the inside and the outside, the inside being negative. This potential difference is called the *resting membrane potential*. During active transmission of nerve impulses, sodium ions can gradually leak into the cell and eventually change the intracellular ionic concentration for this ion. This increment in sodium concentration is opposed by an active mechanism known as a pump which can extrude sodium ions, even against a concentration gradient.

Most neurons have the capacity to generate and transmit *impulses* or *action potentials* – very fast pulses of voltage change across the cell membrane which sweep over the cell body and along the axon at speeds from a few centimetres to 100 metres or more per second. The basic events underlying the action potential were worked out by Alan Hodgkin and Andrew Huxley in Cambridge in the 1950s.[13] It turns out that specialized molecular structures in the nerve membrane, called channels, are sensitive to changes in the membrane potential. In particular, if the difference in voltage between inside and outside decreases (that is, *depolarization*, the inside becoming less negative), *sodium channels* tend to open, altering the *sodium conductance* and allowing positively charged sodium ions to rush into the cell. This entry of sodium exaggerates the local depolarization of the cell: the membrane potential very rapidly changes and actually overshoots zero, the inside becoming positive compared with the outside. The situation is restored by a selective but delayed increase in potassium conductance, due to the opening of potassium channels, which are themselves activated by the depolarization. The resulting outflow of positive potassium ions *repolarizes* the membrane and the resting potential is restored. This whole remarkable 'all-or-nothing' sequence lasts only a thousandth of a second or so.

The propagation of the impulse along the axons results from local electric currents flowing between the depolarized region of the membrane and neighbouring resting areas. This local current flow causes a gradual depolarization of the nearby membrane, which in turn triggers the impulse mechanism.

Of course, something has to cause an initial depolarization to start off the whole process and this usually happens in the cell body or its dendrites. If the neuron happens to be a sensory receptor, its membrane is especially sensitive to physical stimulation from the environment (for example, pressure on the nerve membrane in the case of touch fibres innervating the skin), which sets off the initial change in membrane potential. For neurons inside the nervous system it is a *chemical* change in the fluid bathing the cell that starts the process. The *terminals* of each nerve axon secrete minute quantities of a *transmitter substance* (of which there are many different sorts) whenever the terminal itself is depolarized by the arrival of an impulse. This transmitter substance diffuses rapidly (in about 0.5 milliseconds) across the gap and acts on special *receptors* in the membrane of the dendrites or cell body of the next neuron, which in turn change the local ionic conductance; the resulting movements of ions across the membrane cause a local change in membrane potential (a synaptic potential). Synaptic transmitter substances can be *excitatory* (causing a depolarization of the next cell and hence an increase in the probability of an impulse starting) or can be *inhibitory*, causing changes in membrane properties that tend to counteract local depolarization. The receptors in nerve membrane are not only sensitive to transmitter substances produced at synapses by other nerve cells; some of them can be activated by hormones and by drugs in the fluid around the cell.

It must be said that not all transmission between nerve cells is chemical, that is, depending on transmitter substances. There are in the central nervous system also *electrical synapses* where the membranes of the two cells are tightly fused together, forming a low resistance junction across which the nerve impulse can sweep directly. This direct electrical transmission, known as electrotonic coupling, is especially common early in the development of the brain.

Since Hodgkin's and Huxley's original experiments there has been an enormous amount of research on the properties of nerve cells, which turn out to be considerably more complicated than originally thought. For instance, there are not just two sorts of channels in the membrane (one for sodium, the other for potassium), but many different kinds. There are channels for the positively charged ion, calcium, which plays a very important part in triggering the impulse and in causing the release of transmitter substance at the nerve terminal. The interplay between all these channels, some activated by local potential change, others by ions or other molecules inside the cell, can lead to *oscillation of the membrane potential* and hence *spontaneous* patterns of impulses (as in the heart beat, which depends on similar mechanisms).

This kind of inherent rhythmicity (called *intrinsic autorhythmicity*) is especially pronounced in immature neurons during development of the nervous system. Since embryonic nerve cells are also often electrically coupled, impulses set up by autorhythmicity tend to spread repetitively through networks of neurons. Spontaneous rhythmic firing in nerve nets is now being studied *in vitro* in isolated slices of brain tissue which can be kept alive in a dish and which allow the electrical properties of cells to be determined by direct electrical recording using fine glass micropipettes, which can penetrate cells without injuring them (*intracellular recording*). Inherent rhythmicity can also be seen in tiny transplanted fragments of embryonic nerve tissue (see Szentágothai's chapter in this book).

Ramón y Cajal, in his model of the spinal cord,[5] and in functional studies by Preyer[14] and Tracy.[15] This motor primacy, generated by nerve cells and imposed on muscle (or sometimes generated by muscle cells themselves)[16] is followed by the organization of the sensory systems to include, in order of appearance, propioceptive (sense of position) and cutaneous, followed by vestibular, auditory and visual, inputs.[17] The issue that has remained open relates to what aspects of cell function serve as the linkage between single cell properties and the development of neuronal nets, with respect to interaction with the external world.

During development, neurons are known to have electrical autorhythmicity.[18,19] This intrinsic autorhythmicity, which is beginning to be defined in mammalian CNS *in vitro*,[20,21] I consider to be one of the central mechanisms in the early organization of nerve nets (see box on pp. 346–7). Autorhythmicity and cell-to-cell communication through direct electrical contact (electrotonic coupling), which characterizes embryonic tissue,[22,23] can generate synchronous firing by entrainment of co-existing intrinsic oscillatory properties (for example, coupled oscillators). One example of such coupled oscillation is the early bursts of action potentials in motor nerve cells recorded in chick embryo ventral spinal cord after administration of the drug curare, which blocks chemical transmission from the nerves to muscle.[18] These properties, together with chemical synaptic transmission (see box on pp. 346–7) also present in early embryos, are thus the essential electrical substrates of the organization of brain circuits. The point here, then, is that once a primitive network is assembled by adhesion and chemotaxis, *a further selection must occur on the basis of intrinsic electroresponsiveness* allowing the electrical recognition of dynamic kinship (electrical resonance) in the form of coupled oscillation. However, such electrical resonance *may be different from those ultimately present in the adult brain*. Indeed, neural connections are initially made and broken and intrinsic electrical properties do change. An example of the latter is the neurons of the dorsal root ganglion (the sensory cells innervating the periphery and sending signals into the spinal cord). In early developmental stages, these neurons demonstrate rebound calcium conductances[24,25] which are lost in the adult stage.

An example of such transient connectivity is seen in the development of the cerebellum where, in the embryo, mossy fibres (see figure 23.5) may contact Purkinje cells directly.[26,27] These transient connections most probably serve to organize certain components of the circuit: for example, setting in anatomical register the mossy fibre and Purkinje cell connectivity on to cerebellar nuclear cells. The mossy fibre/Purkinje cell synapse is known to disappear later in development and to be replaced by an indirect connection via the granule cells. However, in early development undifferentiated inputs reach the Purkinje cells directly and can generate synaptic potentials (see box on pp. 346–7) which have been recorded intracellularly *in vitro*.[27] Moreover, this direct connectivity between mossy fibres and Purkinje cells may remain if the granule cell system is lost.[28] A similar process may also take place in the Purkinje cell/climbing fibre system where multiple innervation is replaced by one-to-one junctions.[29] These intermediate nerve nets, which exist transiently during development of the central nervous system, I would like to refer to as 'proto-networks'.

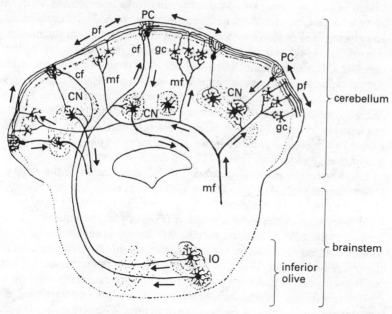

Figure 23.5   *Ramón y Cajal's illustration of connections and neurons of the cerebellum and the inferior olive – important parts of the motor system. IO, inferior olive (a nucleus in the brainstem); PC, Purkinje cell – the main cell type in the cerebellum; CN, deep cerebellar nuclei, to which the Purkinje cells send inhibitory signals; cf, climbing fibres – the axons of neurons in the inferior olive, which excite Purkinje cells directly; mf, mossy fibres, carrying other information (mainly sensory) into the cerebellum; they excite granule cells (gc), whose axons are parallel fibres (pf), which contact the dendrites of Purkinje cells.*

The Concept of 'Proto-networks'

The basic hypothesis here is that the final organization of the circuits of the brain does not occur as a simple continuous selection of connectivity but rather in a piecemeal fashion. Indeed, the thesis presented here is that nerve nets, which are momentarily assembled during development, will interact to generate 'internal functional states' during a critical but limited time period. These internal states are truly intrinsic to the central nervous system and do not relate at this point to any aspect of the external world. Following this proto-network state, neurons will give way to new, more complete, circuits by the incorporation of, or amalgamation with, other proto-networks developed in parallel. The organization of these proto-networks must be ruled, at least in part, by electrophysiological means, in particular by the ability of individual neurons to resonate to specific inputs at given moments in development, in accordance with their intrinsic electroresponsiveness. The actual ionic mechanisms capable of generating intrinsic oscillations (see box on pp. 346–7) are quite varied. In mammals several specific ionic conductances have been described which are capable of inducing intrinsic oscillations in neuronal ensembles[30] and endowing neurons with the ability to resonate at given stimulus frequencies.[21]

It must be emphasized then that proto-networks represent an amalgam of several factors, including neuronal location, period of development, and electrophysiological character, the last being governed by the maturation of individual cell types. The existence of proto-networks further suggests that the ultimate functional states that characterize the adult nervous system are produced through a set of evolving interactive stages. These initial organizational stages are ephemeral and serve only as a set of discrete steps towards a more general order. A clear example of these steps can be observed even in infants, where maturation of the nervous system can be well established by the appearance and obliteration of given sets of muscle sequences.[31]

The advantages of proto-networks in the organization of the nervous system are threefold. First, they afford the nervous system a simple method for selection based on direct cell-to-cell interactions (see box on pp. 346–7) such as electrotonic coupling and synaptic transmission.[32] This permits many cells to oscillate together, as has been demonstrated, even in the adult nervous system, for a group of cells in the brainstem, called the inferior olivary nucleus,[30] which send their axons to the cerebellum. Such oscillatory behaviour serves to organize, by resonance leading to reverberation and by the reinforcement of synaptic interactions, the structure of the circuit at a given moment in time. The actual detail of the biophysical–biochemical mechanisms by which cyclic electrical activity reinforces synaptic interactions in order to generate network order is currently at a stage of active investigation at both invertebrate and vertebrate levels.

Secondly, because the organization of these proto-networks occurs at different times during development, it is possible for such networks to coalesce into functional units that may have formed part of another primitive network at a previous stage, but which slightly later in development may no longer be interconnected. As an example, Bekoff and colleagues demonstrated that the motor nerve cells controlling flexor and extensor muscles in chick embryos begin to discharge in a reciprocal manner very early in development.[33] However, at an even earlier stage most motor neurons were shown to fire synchronously.[34] In some cases protoconnectivity may remain, to be modified dynamically by either inhibition or by the embellishment of the circuit by other inputs, as in the case of the inferior olive.[35]

Thirdly, there is the possibility that the next level of organization is modulated by electrophysiological mechanisms similar to those generating the primitive proto-networks, but acting on a grander scale, again via common oscillatory and resonant properties amongst cell ensembles, that is, by means of 'dynamic linkage'. An example of such oscillatory behaviour, even in the adult brain, is the presence of regular oscillations in the electroencephalogram including the alpha rhythm and the so-called thalamocortical spindling. This resonance may occur with reference to intrinsic electrical properties or due to the sharing of sensory input, which would then conjoin proto-networks through co-variant messages from the periphery.[36] This co-variant sensory input may refer either to oscillatory sensory activity generated by muscular tremor (and its readmission by so-called corollary discharge, that is, impulses re-entering the central nervous system via branches of the axons of motor neurons)[35] or by the presence of co-variant sensory messages arising from external stimuli.

In short, then, it is proposed that networks evolve during embryogenesis by 'natural selection' based, among other variables, on a commonality of intrinsic electrophysiological frames of reference. These electrical properties are basically single cell oscillation and ensemble resonance via coupled oscillation and reverberation. This commonality of electrical behaviour is proposed as serving to reinforce synaptic interactions and growth.[37] In conjunction with this hypothesis, the formal treatment elaborated by Pellionisz and myself[36,38] as the tensor network theory of nervous system function (see box on p. 344), is based partially on mathematical deductions[39,40] and partly on deductions from the electrophysiology of neuronal systems.[30,35,37]

Given the above, then, one may say that mind is a computational state of the brain generated by the interaction between the external world and an internal set of reference frames. These latter frames are being generated, initially, as an internal embedding of the body's natural coordinate systems.

The Development of Semantics

An essential point of debate in this book has been raised by John Searle on the question of semantics. I agree that the question of semantics is pivotal in the understanding of 'mindness'. However, I consider that the issue of semantics goes beyond language to include the action of placing sensory inputs 'into internal context' so that those inputs may be *understood* by the nervous system. The concept of semantics, even in a purely linguistic sense, seems then to be ultimately related to the problem of sensorimotor transformations. This term is used here to address far more than a simple set of reflexes. Indeed, these transformations are viewed as utilizing sensory input to modify ongoing internal functional states. These internal functional states are then homomorphic with external reality. The sensory input feeds and modulates an internal state of intrinsic origin, that is, perception is a dream modulated by sensory input.

In order to put this issue into context, we may ask, for instance, 'How do we see?' Indeed, among the many upsetting experiences encountered as a professor of physiology at a medical school, one in particular is relevant here. It relates to a student who, having been particularly interested in our teaching of the nervous system, said, 'But, now that I have learned neuroscience, I find that I still do not understand, for instance, how I see'. The student may be able to recite the functional and anatomical properties of the visual system from retina to motor neurons and yet may say to me in all candour, 'I can follow the whole system and its properties but I still have no conception at all of what it is to see.' This problem arises because we forget to tell our students that seeing is reconstructing the external world, based not on the reflecting properties of light on external objects but, rather, on the transformation of such visual sensory input (a vector) into perception vectors in *other sets of coordinate systems.* Indeed, we should have reminded our students that in order to see one requires first to have moved within the world and to have established, via the use of natural coordinates, the properties of objects with respect to our own physical attributes (the weight of each object, its size with respect to that of our body, etc.). It would be clear then that it is only through the ability that our brain has to transform measurements in one set of coordinates (the visual system) into comparable sets of measurements (visually guided motor execution) provided by other sensory inputs (for example, touch from fingertips) that one can truly develop the necessary semantics to be able to understand what one sees. The point is that understanding the functional connectivity of the visual system is not sufficient to understand vision. Rather, putting vision into the context of coordinates that are intrinsic to the body is the essential step needed to 'make sense' of the visual information. It is easy to demonstrate that in order to see we must interact with the external world by means of movement. In adult man, visual reversal following the wearing of inverting prism goggles can occur only if the subject is allowed to move about while wearing the goggles.[41] *In short, then, we are able to measure and recreate universals on the basis of our own physical properties because, through interactions between our brain and the rest of our body, a set of natural coordinates has been embedded in our central nervous system.* The next question then may be, 'But what about thinking? How is that related to movement?'

Thinking as Internalized Movement

Let us consider the possibility of thinking as internalized movement. What sort of brain events have to occur in order to generate the necessary movement to reproduce an internal image of the external world (for example, using brushes and paints)? It seems most likely that the methodology by which the brain develops the coordinate systems required to deal with the external environment in a predictive manner can be further elaborated to generate thinking. This process reaches a maximum level of sophistication in man where the ability to predict and the desire to do so represents a very important component of our intellectual life. This becomes quite clear when we consider how we generate a given 'voluntary' movement.

Given a particular set of sensory stimuli or a particular motor goal, a number of pre-motor vectors control strategies must be evaluated in order to choose the right solution, especially given that the motor system is over-complete.[42] The point here, however, is that as the number of possible motor strategies increases, their evaluation given a motor task becomes more involved. Indeed, a reconstruction of possible movements and their possible consequences becomes, in fact, the substrate of 'thinking'. The more complete the evaluation of the strategies of movement, the more complex and perfect the motor execution. Finally, spoken language and its special semantics also fall into the same general category. Meaning (general semantics) must be transformed into pre-motor speech (or pre-motor writing) and then executed as a motor act.

How Can Sensory Messages be Transformed into Pre-motor Patterns?

The particular way in which the computational properties of nerve networks can be transformed into the ability to generate thoughts will then be related in a non-trivial manner to the properties of single cells and the functional states that such connectivities may generate. A possible way to look upon these functional states (following work done by Andras Pellionisz and myself) is to consider the nervous system as operating in organized patterns of electrical activity in neurons, which may be described and formally treated as implementing a functional space.[36,40,42] The advantage of this general approach is that *any* sensory input coming through *any* set of nerves can be transformed by sets of internal coordinate systems and so can relate different sensory stimuli to each other to form an image. Thus all inputs produced by sensory messages relating to an external object send messages that, having a common origin, are co-variant vector components of such stimuli (I see, feel, smell and 'measure' the orange with my surrounding fingers as I bring it close to my mouth). Following this view, the firing in each nerve fibre in a nerve bundle represents a vector component of the sensory vector (the message), each component being totally independent of the presence of other vector components (firing in other nerve fibres), despite the fact that the different vector components are co-variant components of the same sensory stimulus.

This method of introducing information into the nervous system allows the acquisition of information in a piecemeal and parallel fashion where each nerve responds to a particular aspect of the sensory stimulus depending upon the properties of its peripheral receptor or the particular distribution of the receptors over the body (that is, their receptive fields). From the superposition of the activity in each fibre, an internal image of the stimulus may be constructed, but only after the central system knows what the firing of each fibre represents in the outside world (that is, only after semantic development). Thus, transforming a set of such sensory vectorial components into a functional state that represents the outside world requires the summation of these vector components into a vector image. This image resides in a functional space having a large number of coordinate axes (as many as the number of nerve fibres in the sensory nerve in question). From an experimental point of view the actual number of vector components (action potentials in single fibres) that must be considered in studying sensorimotor transformation is many orders of magnitude smaller than the total number of nerve fibres involved in any one vector-to-vector transformation. The ultimate transformation of sensory functional space into motor functional space requires that the sensory message be 'put into context' as a pre-motor vector in order to generate goal-directed movements. The particular set of ideas developed from this point may be read in detail in other publications.[36]

The point of interest here is that the tensorial approach is at least one possible description of nervous system function capable of formally describing aspects of mindness arising by evolutionary steps through the development of nerve networks. These nerve networks, by embedding the natural coordinates of the animal and then of the external world in relation to these natural coordinate systems, can develop an image of universals, particularly when helped by such tools as language and mathematics. A significant aspect of this account is that, in principle, such a type of solution may be utilized in constructing brain-like machines. Indeed, the properties of mindness are probably implementable by means other than biological order. In this account, while the brain is at this time the only system capable of embodying this particular set of transformations, in principle other non-biological implementations of the same type of vector–vector transformation are possible. In saying this, I also want to convey the type of unity that I see between the object capable of generating the functional state and the functional state itself. I choose to ignore as trivial the dualistic distinction that is sometimes made between hardware and software as relates to brain function, as I seriously believe that these concepts are not applicable to the body–mind issue. Whether or not one can make a virtual machine (supported by a very large computer) capable of mimicking the complex activity of the brain, I cannot say. However, given that the complexity of a computer cannot increase beyond a certain level without being seriously compromised by its own complexity, it is my feeling that only special-purpose computers would be ultimately capable of functional states in any way similar to our own.

Of Consciousness and Invariance

Given the parallel and distributed nature of brain function, our ability to focus on any particular aspect of the external world requires the 'extraction' of the object or invariant from the perceptual background. This object–background separation, similar in every way to attention,[43] developed rather early in evolution and is present in invertebrates as well as in all vertebrate forms. In man, and probably in other higher mammalian forms, it encompasses the perception of one's own body and, thus, it underlies the development of the concept of 'self'. There appears to be an important pragmatic reason for the development of self-awareness, having to do with 'global' integration. Specifically, the concept of self serves to fuse the total conglomerate of sensorimotor transformation (to include higher nervous functions) into a singular computational space. A good argument for the existence of this singular computational space is provided by the perceptual deficits of neurological patients with damage to the cortex of the parietal lobe, especially of the non-dominant hemisphere. Following such a lesion, the perception (and the actual existence) of one side of external reality is denied by the patient (for example, right parietal lobe lesion produces the disappearance of the left half of external reality to vision, hearing, touch, etc.). More importantly, this condition, known as the parietal lobe neglect syndrome, is accompanied by the inability to recognize the existence of the corresponding side of one's own body. This damage of the image of 'self' is acute to the point that one may shave only one side of one's face, not recognize one's left hand as belonging to one, omit to draw a leg into one's trousers and an arm into the corresponding sleeve, and actually deny the existence of any problem when asked if anything is wrong or odd. Furthermore, during alcoholic hallucinations one may argue with internal images that exist only in one side of one's 'hallucination space' (cf. Mesulam[44]). In this context, 'self' is clearly a neuronal computational construct in every way similar to all other perceptual states fed by our sensory inputs, and has no independent existence from other perceptual realms. A point of interest here is that while invariances exist in the external world (corners and carrots exist independently from the coordinate systems with which they are measured), invariances are also computational constructs of the brain, and so is self-awareness.

Finally, that the nervous system constructs invariances from the external world ('exteroception') or the inside of our body ('interoception'), and operates with them, is agreed by all. It is less well known, however, that the nervous system can perform motor tasks that demonstrate, directly, that motor execution is coordinate-system-independent. In fact, in attempting to obtain a graphic demonstration of internal pre-motor invariance, I asked an artist friend in Budapest (Arnold Gross) to make a *large* drawing of the face of a young woman, utilizing mainly his elbow and shoulder joints and using an appropriately large drawing pencil (see A in figure 23.6). Then I asked him to draw another face, similar to the first, with his drawing hand against the table so that the drawing would be executed by finger movements alone (that is, by a completely different set of muscles and joints) and on a different size scale (small). On returning to New York I photographically enlarged the small face (figure 23.6B) and superimposed the two faces (figure 23.6C). Note the similarities between the two drawings. The issue here, then, is that the internal functional representation of the face of a young woman can be externalized (drawn) with little distortion using totally different sets of motor and sensory coordinate systems. This example demonstrates that the internal vector which represents such a face may be transformed into motor space in a coordinate-system-independent manner; or, to put it in other terms, that tensorial properties are operant in our sensorimotor transformations.

Indeed, we may find that, as in the case of powered flight (once believed the exclusive realm of living organisms), machines may in principle do as well as brains. Ultimately, understanding the mind may not be as intricate as our vanity hoped or our intellect feared.

Figure 23.6 Externalization using different sets of motor and sensory co-ordinates. A: Composite showing a large drawing made by the artist Arnold Gross of Budapest when allowing movement of his elbow and shoulder, and a small version of the same drawing made when restricting movement to the hand alone. B: Enlargement of the small drawing in A. C: Superimposition of A and B showing the great similarity between the two drawings.

Notes and References

1 By 'mindness' I mean high-level awareness, including self-awareness.

2 A functional state is defined in terms of 'functional geometry' in the sense that brain networks, formed by the connections between nerve cells, can implement coordinate-system-independent transformations of inputs to outputs by means of the computational properties of the network. These computational properties are envisaged as different from those of present-day computers in that they are 'non-von Neuman', i.e. not simple yes/no statements but rather an explicit transformation of, for instance, external physical geometry into an internal functional geometry in a 'multidimensional space' (i.e. comprising many coordinate axes).

3 This general scheme of sensorimotor transformation has not changed much during evolution to include *Homo sapiens*. Even our advanced brain can receive information only through sensory cells in our body and can only externalize its internal functional states by muscle activity or by secretion (i.e. we either move or drool!).

4 Grundfest, H. (1959) Evolution of conduction in the nervous system. In A. D. Bass (ed.), *Evolution of Nervous Control from Primitive Organisms to Man.* Washington, D. C.: Amer. Assoc. Adv. Science.

5 Ramón y Cajal, S. (1911) *Histologie du système nerveux de l'homme et des vertébrés.* Paris: Maloine.

6 Romer, A. S. (1969) Vertebrate history with special reference to factors related to cerebellar evolution. In R. Llinás (ed.), *Neurobiology of Cerebellar Evolution and Development*, pp. 1–18. Chicago: Amer. Med. Assn.

7 The statocyst is an organ that senses the direction of gravitational pull and serves as a sensory apparatus for equilibrium and upright posture.

8 Cowan, W. M. (1979) Selection and control in neurogenesis. In F. O. Schmitt and F. G. Worden (eds), *The Neurosciences: Fourth Study Program*, pp. 59–79. Cambridge, Mass.: MIT Press.

9 Gottlieb, D. I. and Glaser, L. (1980) Cellular recognition during neural development. *Ann. Rev. Neurosci.* 3: 303–18.

10 By gated adhesiveness is meant adhesiveness between cells that can appear and disappear at different times during development depending on chemical clues.

11 Edelman, G. M. (1984) Cell adhesion and morphogenesis: the regulator hypothesis. *Proc. Natl. Acad. Sci., USA*, 81: 1460–4.

12 Changeux, J. P. and Danchin, A. (1976). Selective stabilization of developing synapses as a mechanism for the specification of neuronal networks. *Nature* (London), 264: 705–12.

13 For a fuller account of the biophysics of nerve cells, see Kuffler, S. W., Nicholls, J. G. and Martin, A. R. (1984) *From Neuron to Brain.* Sunderland, Mass.: Sinauer Associates.

14 Preyer, W. (1885) *Specielle Physiologie des Embryo.* Leipzig: Grieben.

15 Tracy, H. C. (1926) The development of motility and behavior reactions in the toadfish (*Opsanus tau*). *J. Comp. Neurol.* 40: 253–369.

16 Harris, J. E. and Whiting, H. P. W. (1954) Structure and function in the locomotory system of the dogfish embryo. The myogenic stage of movement. *J. exp. Biol.* 31: 501–24.

17 Gottlieb, G. (1976) Conceptions of prenatal development: behavioural embryology. *Psychol. Rev.* 83: 215–34.

18 Provine, R. R. and Rogers, L. (1977) Development of spinal cord bioelectrical activity in spinal chick embryos and its behavioral implications. *J. Neurobiol.* 8: 217–28.

19 Woodward, D. J., Hoffer, B. J. and Lapham, L. W. (1969) Correlative survey of electrophysiological, neuropharmacological and histochemical aspects of cerebellar maturation in rats. In R. Llinás (ed.), *Neurobiology of Cerebellar Evolution and Development*, pp. 725–41. Chicago: Amer. Med. Assn.

20 Llinás, R. and Yarom, Y. (1981) Electrophysiology of mammalian inferior olivary neurones in vitro. Different types of voltage-dependent ionic conductances. *J. Physiol.* (London), 315: 549–67.

21 Jahnsen, H. and Llinás, R. (1984) Ionic basis for the electroresponsiveness and oscillatory properties of guinea pig thalamic neurones *in vitro*. *J. Physiol.* (London), 349: 227–47.

22 Furshpan, E. J. and Potter, D. D. (1968) Low-resistance junctions between cells in embryos and tissue culture. In A. A. A. Moscona and A. Monroy (eds), *Current Topics in Developmental Biology*, vol. 3, pp. 95–127. New York: Academic Press.

23 Spitzer, N. C. (1979) Ion channels in development. *Ann. Rev. Neurosci.* 2: 363–97.

24 Carbone, E. and Lux, H. D. (1984) A low voltage-activated calcium conductance in embryonic chick sensory neurons. *Biophys. J.* 46: 413–18.

25 Nowycky, M. C., Fox, A. P. and Tsien, R. W. (1984) Two components of calcium channel current in chick dorsal root ganglion cells. *Biophys. J.* 45: 36a.

26 Rakic, P. and Sidman, R. L. (1970) Histogenesis of cortical layers in human cerebellum, particularly the lamina dissecans. *J. Comp. Neurol.* 139: 473–500.

27 Llinás, R. and Sugimori, M. (1979) Calcium conductances in Purkinje cell dendrites: their role in development and integration. *Progr. Brain Res.* 51: 323–34.

28 Llinás, R., Hillman, D. E. and Precht, W. (1973) Neuronal circuit reorganization in mammalian agranular cerebellar cortex. *J. Neurobiol.* 4: 69–97.

29 Crepel, F., Mariani, J. and Delhaye-Bouchaud, N. (1976) Evidence for a multiple innervation of Purkinje cells by climbing fibers in the immature rat cerebellum. *J. Neurobiol.* 7: 567–78.

30 Llinás, R. (1984) Rebound excitation as the phsyiological basis for tremor: a biophysical study of the oscillatory properties of mammalian central neurons *in vitro*. In L. J. Findley and R. Capildeo (eds), *Movement Disorders: Tremor*, p. 165–82. London: Macmillan.

31 McGraw, M. B. (1946) Maturation of behavior. In L. Carmichael (ed.), *Manual of Child Psychology*. New York: Wiley.

32 Bennett, M. V. L. (1966) Physiology of electrotonic junctions. *Ann. N.Y. Acad. Sci.* 137, 2: 509–39.

33 Bekoff, A., Stein, P. S. G. and Hamburger, V. (1975) Coordinated motor output in the hindlimb of the 7-day chick embryo. *Proc. Natl. Acad. Sci., USA*, 72: 1245–8.

34 Hamburger, V. (1977) The developmental history of the motor neuron. *Neurosci. Res. Progr. Bull. 15*, suppl. 1–37.

35 Llinás, R. (1984) Possible role of tremor in the organization of the nervous system In L. J. Findley and R. Capildeo (eds), *Movement Disorders: Tremor*, pp. 473–78. London: Macmillan.

36 Pellionisz, A. and Llinás, R. (1985) Tensor network theory of the metaorganization of functional geometries in the CNS. *Neuroscience*, 16: 245–73.

37 Llinás, R. (1979) Calcium regulation of neuronal function. In F. O. Schmitt and F. G. Worden (eds), *The Neurosciences: Fourth Study Program*, pp. 555–71. Cambridge, Mass.: MIT Press.

38 Pellionisz, A. (1983) Brain theory: connecting neurobiology to robotics; tensor analysis: utilizing intrinsic coordinates to describe, understand and engineer functional geometries of intelligent organisms. *J. Theoret. Neurobiol.* 2: 3.

39 Pellionisz, A. (1984) Tensorial brain theory in cerebellar modelling. In J. R. Bloedel, J. Dichgans and W. Precht (eds), *Cerebellar Functions*. Heidelberg: Springer.

40 Pellionisz, A. and Llinás, R. (1979) Brain modelling by tensor network theory and computer simulation. The cerebellum: distributed processor for predictive coordination. *Neuroscience*, 4: 323–48.

41 Dolezal, H. (1982) *Living in a World Transformed.* New York, London: Academic Press.

42 Pellionisz, A. and Llinás, R. (1980) Tensorial approach to the geometry of brain function: cerebellar coordination via metric tensor. *Neuroscience*, 5: 1125–36.

43 Crick, F. (1984) Function of the thalamic reticular complex: the search light hypothesis. *Proc. Natl. Acad. Sci.* 81: 4586–90.

44 Mesulam, M.- M. (1981) A cortical network for directed attention and unilateral neglect. *Ann. Neurol.* 10: 309–25.

24

The Biological Role of Consciousness

Horace Barlow

Horace Barlow has been actively involved with the physiology and psychology of perception for forty years. He was guided on this path by E. D. Adrian, who showed where neurophysiological research was leading, and William Rushton, who showed that research might be enjoyable as well as informative. He has worked on the frog's retina (discovering lateral inhibition and 'fly-detectors'), the rabbit retina (directional selectivity), cat retina (responses to single photons) and cat cortex (disparity selectivity). He has also been interested in the physical and biological factors that limit sensation and perception, such as photon fluctuations, the dynamic range of nerve fibres as signal channels, and their large though limited ability to interconnect with each other.

Horace Barlow is now a Royal Society Research Professor at the Physiological Laboratory in the University of Cambridge.

What is the selective advantage conferred on the human race, or any other species, by consciousness? Is it just an epiphenomenon of our brain mechanisms – the whine of the neural gears, the clicking of the neural circuitry? Or can one identify a more important role for it in the survival and future of our species? Like many others, I feel untuitively certain that consciousness is of paramount importance, and it therefore becomes an intriguing task to search for and try to define this role.

The answer I shall put forward is that consciousness links the individual to the community within which he lives, a link that is crucial to all that is human. Normal perception, learning and memory are thought to be involved – nothing paranormal – but the individual's need for consciousness and its impossibility without social experience means that consciousness itself is what forces an individual to interact with the community. This interaction occurs in both directions, for one's consciousness is much concerned with other individuals, while past experience with other individuals has much influence on the content of each individual's consciousness.

This idea places consciousness in the border regions between the individual and the community; this is quite different from the border between dualism and identity theories that Jeffrey Gray has been concerned with,[1,2] but the two ideas are complementary, not conflicting, and if it is correct that consciousness haunts the intersection of these two boundaries we shall have made good progress in delimiting the types of

William Shakespeare (1564–1616). His acute perception of the human condition reveals a superlative consciousness.

nervous activity with which it is concerned. But let me start by explaining the converging paths which have brought me to this viewpoint; in a sense these are digressions, but I hope they will move you gradually towards my way of looking at the problem.

Consciousness and Single Units

I started thinking about consciousness because of my interest in the role of single nerve cells in sensation and perception.[3,4] Briefly, one can find neurons in sensory centres and pathways that show discriminative powers not unlike those of an intact human being. You find cells in the rabbit retina that respond when things move up but not down, and we can tell if things are moving up or down (see figure 24.1). Likewise you find cells that discriminate between different velocities of movement, and between stereoscopic disparities, and colours, and the various categories of cutaneous sensation. More recently cells have been found in the monkey cortex that respond to human faces,[6] and appear to be able to discriminate between the faces of particular individuals.[7] Such cells have much of the discriminative capacity of our own sensations, and when you come across these facts you are bound to say to yourself, 'Well, I know that when I discriminate between red and green this is accompanied by a conscious sensation. When this single nerve cell shows the same sort of

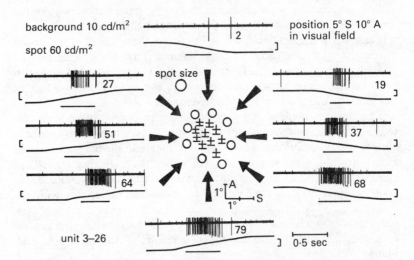

Figure 24.1   Example of pattern discrimination at the cellular level. This ganglion cell in the rabbit's retina gave a vigorous burst of impulses (lowest record) when a spot of light moved upwards through the appropriate part of the visual field, very few when it moved downwards (highest record). Other directions gave intermediate responses (records at the side). The receptive field was first mapped with a stationary spot turned on and off, and this region is represented in the centre of the figure by the ± symbols, indicating that a brief response occurs at on (+) and off (−); no responses occurred outside the ring of O's. Then a spot was moved through the receptive field in the direction of the arrows, and the records at the bases of the arrows obtained. Here the vertical lines are action potentials or impulses, which are the messages signalled to the brain, with the numbers of impulses (from 2 to 79) imdicated. The lower trace in each record shows the movement of the spot of light (from Barlow, Hill and Levick, 1964).[5]

discriminative capacity, am I to suppose that it is actually having some kind of rudimentary sensory experience?' Although there may be some people who think that a primitive form of sensation occurs in a single cell, that doesn't make sense to me, and I cannot accept it.

I think this is a problem of levels of analysis: if one cannot find the explanation for consciousness at the level of single cells one has the choice of looking at a lower level or at a higher level. The lower, more analytic, level does not seem promising to me, for transmitter substances and receptor molecules are surely even further from consciousness than single neurons. Going one step in the other direction, to nerve nets and groups of neurons, does not seem to introduce any very interesting new possibilities, but the picture changes dramatically if you consider whole brains, for then types of behaviour occur that result from one brain interacting with another. This seems to me the level at which one must look for a better understanding of consciousness, and especially of its biological role.

Conscious Thought and Social Understanding

The second digression is to compare my position with that of Nick Humphrey. Even though we had never previously talked to each other on the subject, we found that we had rather similar views when we gave talks at a conference in Cambridge about seven years ago,[8,9] for we agreed that consciousness is closely connected with the social behaviour of animals; however, I think I have carried this initial insight to its logical conclusion and shall try to clarify my viewpoint by comparing it with Nick's better-known position.[10]

He points out that knowledge of the working of one's own mind can be very important in social behaviour; one understands the motivation and causes of the behaviour of others by analogy with one's introspective knowledge of the motivation and causes of one's own behaviour. While fully agreeing that the survival value of consciousness derives from its influence on social problems and their solutions, I think he has much too much confidence in the validity of the knowledge gained by introspection about the working of one's own mind. I do not think it gives accurate knowledge of the causes and motivation even of one's own behaviour, let alone that of others. Introspection only leads one to *think* one understands the reasons for one's actions, and the limitations of this partial knowledge are crucial. Furthermore, his view does not emphasize the influence of social experience, particularly early experience, on the nature of an individual's consciousness. This experience may control the quality, depth and validity of an individual's introspection, thus making consciousness a joint product of the individual and his social environment.

Of course this is to some extent simply an echo of Freud, but once it is admitted that introspection is fallible, one must look at the errors it leads to, as well as the advantages if confers, when considering its survival value. Some may find this cynical, but there are other sources of knowledge than introspection, and in this post-Freudian, post-Marxist age it seems to me a much sounder viewpoint. My mistrust of introspection is also the basis of my last digression.

Biological Roles are not Introspectively Obvious

The third and most important pathway to my viewpoint arises from a difficulty in the direct introspective attack on the question. A few analogies will show how deceptive such an approach can be.

First consider pain: introspection tells us that pain is unpleasant and that pain-producing objects and situations are to be avoided, but it does not tell us that pain preserves our lives and limbs. The fact that this is indeed the case becomes abundantly clear when one encounters unfortunate individuals who lack a sense of pain, for they suffer repeated and potentially dangerous minor injuries from burns or abrasions that others reflexly avoid. Furthermore when they have received a minor injury, they lack the automatic reactions that rest and protect the injured part, allowing it to recover.

The important point to realize is that direct introspection about pain does not lead one to appreciate its value and it is instructive to see how to circumvent this difficulty. Instead of contemplating pain directly, ask the question 'What is the principal action associated with the sensation of pain?' I think one would answer, either by introspection or by observing others, that it leads to withdrawal from painful objects or situations, and avoidance of these in the future. From there it is of course a small step to understand the survival value of a system of nerve fibres that can only cause unpleasantness, and to see the benefits derived from them.

Now take another example – falling in love. Poetry books are full of introspections on this subject, and as before they somehow miss the point we are interested in. On the other hand, asking what principal action is associated with falling in love makes it obvious that the propagation of the species and future survival of the human race are at stake. The poets are unintentionally instructive on the devious fallibility of introspection, for they avoid emphasizing the fertility and motherliness of the person concerned and dwell on very different qualities.

EXPERIENCE	INTROSPECTIVE MESSAGE	SURVIVAL VALUE
Pain	Unpleasant and to be avoided	Minimizes injuries
Love	Desire for lifelong attachment, feelings of unbounded admiration, etc.	Propagation of the human species
Redness	Attribute of a physical object	Ability to communicate about this attribute

Introspection on our experiences does not directly tell us their survival value (more on redness at pp. 369–72)

I think this brief consideration of pain and love has shown how hopelessly misleading it can be to try and draw conclusions about the biological survival value of a subjective experience by direct introspection. That doesn't mean to say that one should ignore one's introspections altogether, for when the misleading aspects are pointed out we may be able to say, 'Well yes, perhaps this does make sense.' But the survival value of a subjective experience is certainly not the first thing revealed to introspection, and it helps to look at the principal associated actions which it brings about in yourself and other people.

This could be pursued further by talking about hunger or thirst, and I shall return to the sensation of redness later, but it is time to leave these digressions and attack consciousness itself, applying the lessons learnt in these preliminary skirmishes with pain and love.

> No longer mourn for me when I am dead
> Than you shall hear the surly sullen bell
> Give warning to the world that I am fled
> From this vile world, with vilest worms to dwell:
> Nay, if you read this line, remember not
> The hand that writ it; for I love you so,
> That I in your sweet thoughts would be forgot,
> If thinking on me then should make you woe.
> O, if, I say, you look upon this verse
> When I perhaps compounded am with clay,
> Do not so much as my poor name rehearse;
> But let your love even with my life decay;
>   Lest the wise world should look into your moan,
>   And mock you with me after I am gone.

Figure 24.2   Sonnet no. 71 by Shakespeare.

Conscious and Unconscious Neural Activities

If our consciousness is limited, what is it limited to? Upon what types or classes of neural activity can we obtain an introspective viewpoint? At first one is inclined to think that, without consciousness, all mental life would cease, but it is certainly not true that all neurally mediated behaviour would cease. Consciousness is therefore associated with the working of only part of the brain, and we want to find what part this is.

We have seen that one path to the answer may be to look at the principal actions that are associated with it, and also of course at those that can occur without it. It would also be illuminating if one could find pathologies of consciousness analogous to the absence of the sense of pain, or colour blindness, for then one might be able to point to the direct consequences of its absence or faulty functioning. Let us start by trying to decide what parts of the working of the brain are accessible to consciousness and what parts are not.

I think everybody will accept that there are many things one's brain does for one that are not associated with consciousness. For instance, I walk towards my front door or my car, and I find my hand in my pocket getting out the key. That part of my brain is actually rather stupid because it usually gets out the wrong key, but one must give it credit for doing a quite complicated action without any conscious thought passing through one's mind. I am sure everyone can think of many equivalent neural computations that their brain performs without their awareness: picking footfalls on a mountain path, many aspects of driving a car or returning a shot at tennis, brushing one's teeth or putting on one's clothes, for example. Maybe these are consciously initiated, and maybe when first performed one has to pay conscious attention, but in normal life one's brain does many complex operations for one without the breath of consciousness. What then is the general characteristic of those brain operations that *do* accompany consciousness?

The answer I would give is that they are concerned with social interactions, and especially with the preparation and execution of communications with other individuals. Of course this mainly means communication with other humans, though I wouldn't want to deny consciousness to the person who is talking to his dog. Somebody might object that all forms of neural activity must be brought about in the same way, by nerve impulses, synaptic potentials and so on, so that it is inadmissible to suppose that some forms of activity are accompanied by consciousness, others not. An analogy may make clear why this objection is invalid. Consider speech and sound: again it might be said that both are transmitted by the vibration of air molecules, hence one cannot attribute an important property to the one and not the other. But speech is not *just* the vibration of air molecules; speech sounds form only a very small subset of all vibrations of air molecules, and when talking about speech it is that sub-set we are interested in, not the general question of how sound is transmitted to the listener. In the same way, it is quite reasonable to say that the nervous activity associated with consciousness is only a small part of all the activity of the brain, namely the part which is concerned with communications with other individuals; that is the important aspect of conscious activity, not the fact that it is mediated in the same way as most other operations of the brain.

Now, of course it is true that you can have mutual communication between two individuals without consciousness. If we recognize that unconscious communication is possible, we are not forced to say that bees, for example, are conscious even though they certainly communicate with one another very freely and effectively. But one can also have consciousness without concurrent communication with another individual, and this needs more careful consideration.

If I'm shut in a room by myself I don't become unconscious, so that the relationship between consciousness and communication isn't simple and immediate; consciousness continues when communication is cut off. But I would claim that whenever one is conscious, even in one's deepest introspections, one is in a sense addressing some other individual. Are others aware of an audience when they are thinking to themselves? I could often name the individual or individuals to whom my thoughts are addressed, but I don't know how universal this is. Even when the audience cannot be specified, I believe it is reasonable to insist on the importance, for all conscious thought, of some internal model of one or more other human minds.

As Kenneth Craik argued, our brains are adept at modelling the environment,[11] and the characteristics of other individuals must be among the most important candidates for such modelling. If you have doubts about the importance of human models in introspection, ask yourself what language your thoughts are couched in, and from whom you learnt that language. For me at least it makes sense to suppose that the dawn of an infant's consciousness comes with its early communication with its parents, and that ever afterwards the image or model of the communicatee is a partner in conscious experience.

The importance of interaction and communication for one's consciousness will probably be challenged, so my first task is to make the idea acceptable to common sense. I shall try to do this in two ways: first, see whether these ideas fit in with common usage; and second, find whether they are plausible when we introspect about them.

Common Usage of 'Conscious'

I have chosen three rather different examples to show that communication is an important part of consciousness, as this term is commonly applied. If someone says 'he's unconscious', to test this you would immediately try to establish reciprocal communication with the individual concerned, and if you failed you would be likely to agree that he was unconscious. This would be so even if, for example, the person was sleep-walking and showed many indications of being in a normal state. In such a case you might go up and tap him on the shoulder, and if you didn't get sensible responses you might say, 'Well, he appeared at first to be conscious, but he is not responding to me and his consciousness must at least be impaired.'

Another example indicates what seems to be a very different usage of the word 'conscious'. In a train coming back from London once, I heard two football fans talking about a third person whom they both knew; they were saying, 'he's not even conscious.' It turned out that what they meant was that this third party didn't support the same team; so it seems that they were imputing unconsciousness simply because they couldn't communicate on this one issue.

Conscious (kɒnʃəs), *a.* [f. L. *consci-us* knowing something with others, knowing in oneself, privy to, conscious + -OUS. L. *consci-us* f. *con-* together + *sci-* knowing, as in *scīre* to know: cf. *nescius* unknowing, *præscius* foreknowing. There is no such word in F., which uses *conscient* in some of the senses (as did also Bacon); but It. has *conscio* privy, accessary, guilty, from 16th c.]

†1. Knowing, or sharing the knowledge of anything, together with another; privy to anything with another. *Obs.* [With quot. 1651, cf. L. *alicui alicujus rei conscius.*]

1651 HOBBES *Leviath.* 1. vii. 31 Where two, or more men, know of one and the same fact, they are said to be Conscious of it one to another. 1664 SOUTH *Serm.* (1823) I. 394 Nothing is to be concealed from the other self. To be a friend and to be conscious are terms equivalent.

2. *fig.* Attributed to inanimate things as privy to, sharing in, or witnesses of human actions or secrets. Chiefly *poet.*

(The earliest recorded use–the word being one of those ridiculed by Ben Johnson. Frequent in the Latin poets: with 1667, cf. Ovid 'quorum non conscia sola est'.)

Figure 24.3   The Oxford English Dictionary's definition of conscious agrees that shared knowledge, implying communication, is an important aspect of consciousness (reproduced courtesy of Oxford English Dictionary, Oxford University Press).

Now let's just take a third example. I made a conscious decision this morning to miss my dentist appointment. And what I mean by that is that I didn't accidentally miss it; I went through a stage when I could have told you, or the dentist, that I was going to miss it. So what the word 'conscious' adds to the meaning of the above sentence is the fact that I was in a position to communicate my decision to another person.

In all these three examples, which are really quite diverse, it is the ability to communicate that is the crucial test of consciousness, so I wonder if anyone can think of a good example of the proper use of 'conscious' which would disprove this statement: the person who is said to be conscious is in a position to communicate, and the person who is said to be unconscious is not. In common usage, communication or the ability to communicate appears to be a crucially important aspect of consciousness.

Introspective Acceptability

Does this attempt to delimit the types of neural activity that are involved in consciousness seem plausible introspectively? As I've mentioned, there are pitfalls here, but no idea about consciousness is likely to survive unless it can at least be reconciled with our introspections on the subject.

Many people will point out that although one's conscious thoughts are largely composed of words and language, they are not exclusively composed of them. I'm sure musicians can consciously think in terms of musical phrases and harmonies, but music is after all a form of communication, so that objection is answered. I'm also told that if a champion skier is to have any chance of winning he must, just before he starts a race, rehearse in his mind exactly how he will take every gate. Well, at first those don't seem to be communications that pass through his mind, but I wonder if the skier is not actually rehearsing messages from (or to) his trainer, rather than rehearsing the motor actions he will perform. In any case these two examples are unusual, and the prevalence of language in consciousness will probably be conceded.

Even with my more elaborate conscious thoughts I can often make myself aware of an audience whom I am addressing; this is important because I would have different thoughts if the audience were different. Perhaps many of you would agree that, when you are thinking in a particular mode, this is sometimes because you have in your mind a particular person or audience. If you accept this, then you have admitted that consciousness is not a property of a single brain, but also involves the representations in that brain of others. This is particularly important for those introspections about one's beliefs and actions that, as Nicholas Humphrey points out,[10] help one to understand other people, for it means these others are having a reciprocal action on one's own thoughts. Thus conscious introspection is not just a simple aid to social behaviour, but is itself moulded and formed by social experience.

I find that this comparatively small change in how I think of consciousness makes an important difference, and now that it has been incorporated in my thoughts, it is not only acceptable but also attractive to realize that consciousness is not all my own brain's work, but is partly caused by those with whom I communicate.

Autism – Life Without Consciousness?

Can one point to pathological conditions of consciousness, analogous to the lack of a sensory system subserving pain, or to congenital colour blindness? It was suggested before that childhood autism, whose pathognomic symptom is the failure to develop normal social relationships, might represent such a condition,[9] and recent experimental[12] and theoretical[13] studies add some plausibility to this. Baron-Cohen, Leslie and Frith found that 16 out of 20 autistic children failed a test that required them to understand that another being could hold a false belief because it had incomplete information;[12] a group of normal children of mental ages matched to the autistic group passed the test without difficulty, as did a group with Down's syndrome similarly matched. Thus the autistic children were unable to do a simple version of precisely the task that Humphrey said consciousness facilitated – understanding the causes of another individual's actions and beliefs. As I have emphasized, our own introspective knowledge is incomplete, but autistic children appear to lack even our limited conceptualization of mental states and their origins.

One wonders if some impairment of the mechanism and range of consciousness might not be the cause of ill-defined 'psychopathic personalities', habitual criminals, and others whose principal problem lies in their relationship with other individuals and society. This may amount to no more than saying 'they do not think like us', but it may also draw attention to the aspect that is different, namely the capacity to introspect on one's own mental state and recognize the existence of similar mental states in others.

It is also interesting to speculate about an individual whose introspection could extend far beyond the limits restricting those of the majority. Such an individual would have access to superior understanding of the causes of his own and also of his friends' beliefs and actions: he or she would make a good playwright or novelist, but would we regard such an individual as unusually understanding and sympathetic, or as cold, calculating and unsocial? Greater introspective power, like any other improved mental faculty, could clearly be advantageous to the individual, but it might be disruptive to the group and species. How much then does social morality depend, not on the validity of our introspections, but on each individual's introspection having limitations and errors similar to those of others in the community?

Raw Consciousness

Consciousness of course means many things. So far I have talked mainly about the aspect that decides one's future actions in the light of introspection on one's own mental state and that of others. Because so little is known of the underlying physiology and psychology of these processes, there is little temptation to think about them in over-simple, over-mechanistic terms; but this is not true of supposedly more elementary forms of consciousness such as 'raw' redness, which some would

Figure 24.4   Jane Austen (1775–1817), another super-conscious person. Did she have introspective powers that exceeded normal bounds and limits, thus giving her superior knowledge of the causes of people's beliefs and actions (Mary Evans Picture Library).

hold to be just our brains' direct response to a stimulus in the external world. The rather complete physiological and psychological knowledge we possess of such peripheral sensory processes seems at first to support this notion, for it might be thought to imply that there is no room for communication and interaction in generating the experience. I do not think this view is correct because current knowledge does not explain how sensory experiences acquire their labels, and for a number of other reasons.

First, we often *do* want to communicate about sensations like redness, and I claim this is why they form part of the content of our consciousness. We want to be able to say, 'That strawberry is red enough to pick and eat', or 'The red sunset forecasts good weather'; no one can deny this need to communicate about our immediate sensations. Furthermore the influence of language, and hence necessarily of social experience, upon the raw sensations themselves is greater than one normally admits. Consider a colour-blind individual who completely lacks one of the three types of cone photoreceptor possessed by those with normal colour vision (that is, a 'dichromat', instead of a 'trichromat' like most of us). There are irrefutable reasons for believing that such an individual's experience of colour must be very different from that of the rest of us, yet most of them would understand what I have said about colour in this essay, and could carry on a normal conversation about colours without a slip. Quite a number of them are actually unaware of their abnormality until it is revealed to them by testing: surely such a person's knowledge of colour must have been derived from sources that are certainly not accessible to us when we introspect on our sensations.

It is interesting to speculate about a colour-blind individual who, as is the case with many of them, has a normal mother and a colour-blind father: on my views he might have a thoroughly schizophrenic consciousness of colour, since his early verbal knowledge of it would come from a mother who might seem to him 'funny about reds and greens' and a father whose experiences matched his own much better, but who would have suffered the same problem as the son in matching these experiences to the spoken words of the majority.

The Recipe for Redness

1 Form an optical image.
2 Measure the light in long, medium and short wavebands in each part of it.
3 Compare amounts locally in each waveband.
4 Make comparisons over larger regions of the image.
5 Classify the results and make an array of possible results. These are the possible *unlabelled* colour sensations, and the current perceptual computations allot each part of the image to a position in this array.
6 Form an array of colour words by listening to adjectives for surfaces of objects, etc.
7 Observe how they are used and attempt to match them to positions in array no. 5.
8 As you succeed, attach labels of array no. 6 to the appropriate positions in array no. 5.
9 Forget you ever did nos. 6, 7 and 8 but retain labels in no. 5.
10 Use these labels to describe your sensations, e.g. 'that apple is red'.

Redness is never raw: it is the result of a complicated sequence of operations. (NB: the physiological mechanisms of steps 1–3 are understood quantitatively; steps 4 and 5 are beginning to be known; steps 6–10 are almost guesswork, but something of this sort must happen.)

These facts are less surprising when one realizes that the sensation of redness is the end result of an elaborate sequence of neural operations (see box The 'Recipe for Redness'). This is what Edwin Land has been

telling us recently,[14] and a long time ago Hermann von Helmholtz was saying that perceptions were the products of unconscious induction.[15] It makes a lot of difference where you think the sensation of redness occurs in the sequence of events from physical stimulus to the final consequence of that stimulus, namely the utterance 'it's red', or the ability to communicate or make use of that fact in some other way. If you think only a few easy steps intervene between the physical stimulus and the sensation, whereas many steps intervene between the sensation and the communication, then you may have a problem with my view of consciousness. But if you think (like Helmholtz and Land) that many logic-like processes go on before even the simplest sensations occur, then there is plenty of room for social experience to interject its effects, and the point of view that I am presenting becomes much more acceptable. If the sensation is much nearer the utterance than the physical stimulus, it becomes reasonable to say that the sensation of redness is merely preparing you to communicate the fact that something is red; this is another case where introspection is misleading, for redness is a carefully cooked product and is never as raw as it seems.

Figure 24.5   Hermann von Helmholtz (1821–94) who is as famous for his contributions to sensory physiology and neurophysiology as for his achievements in physics.

Having defended the view that consciousness involves communication, even in the case of raw sensations, I want to make it clear that I do not think this communicative role *explains* it. There would probably be something mysterious about the subjective sensation of redness that would remain after one had a complete account of the underlying mechanisms, even if this account included a description of the mechanisms relating it to social interaction and communication. This 'something' seems likely to lie beyond the range of current scientific approaches, but linking it to the extraordinary complexities of social interaction at least relieves one of the urge to attempt explanations in over-simple physiological terms.

Implications

What are the implications of the view that consciousness is an aspect of communicating, interacting, brains? Well, the first idea one must discard is that consciousness is simply a property of a brain by itself. This is where I started, for it was because I had accepted the usual view that consciousness is just an attribute of the brain, like mass or colour, that I was puzzled when I realized that there was probably no remnant of this attribute in the single cells I was recording from. Consciousness becomes a bit less bizarre and paradoxical if you accept that it has to do with communication and interaction between brains, and not with a single brain by itself or any part of it by itself.

To illustrate the benefit of this change, take the problem of giving the reason why brains can be conscious but stones cannot. If consciousness was a simple attribute of either by itself, you would have to say the difference was the result of some physical difference between the two, and this would start you on a lengthy, but ultimately false, trail. Once you accept that consciousness is a matter of communication and interaction, the problem vanishes, for these interactions have a quite different degree of complexity in stones and brains. We may have landed ourselves with a little problem about bees, because they obviously communicate freely and effectively, but I think there is still a sufficient gulf between the complexity of their interaction and that of humans for one to be justified in making a qualitative distinction between them.

The Biological Role of Consciousness

If what I have been saying is correct, one can begin to see that the biological consequences of consciousness are immense, for it must determine the whole form and quality of human social behaviour. Let us see how this happens.

Let us suppose that consciousness in the infant is awakened by the first mutual communication with another person – perhaps the first smile that is returned – and that the trace or memory of this interaction is an essential part of subsequent conscious experience. To enlarge this experience and bring it partly under his control the infant brain must build a model of what it is interacting with, that is a model of the mother and her brain which will tell the infant when smiles will be returned, and when other responses and interactions will occur. Just as in a conversation two people can explore a subject in greater depth than either of them alone, so remembered partners in introspective 'conversations' can allow deeper insight than would be possible for a mind that did not possess good models of others. Thus the content and validity of introspection can be enlarged, but only by social experience leading to the incorporation of models of other people's minds. On this view the crucial feature of consciousness is that it *requires* a remembered partner for its introspections: consciousness is taught, awakened and maintained by interactions with other modelled minds, and its characteristics in any individual depend to some extent upon these other minds. Thus consciousness becomes the forum, not of a single mind, but of the social group with whom the individual interacts.

A mind without an inner life is not a human mind, but the same postulate that explains the biological importance of this inner life also goes some way towards explaining another crucial human characteristic, namely the production of an objective, permanently recorded, culture. This could be the expression of the mind's desire to communicate and interact, not just with the remembered minds of others, but also with the minds of future generations. If consciousness depends on interaction, it is not surprising that people seek to leave traces for later minds to interact with.

I have proposed that the survival value of consciousness results from the particular patterns of social behaviour it causes us to follow. The important part that this has played in our evolution justifies our intuitive sense that consciousness is not an epiphenomenon of neural machinery but is of paramount importance to our species. Thus it can be claimed that some progress has been made towards the goal of finding its biological role. Two cautions are, however, needed. First, consciousness is unlikely to be the only mechanism that promotes and makes possible our social behaviour; hence the most that can be realistically claimed is that the powers and limitations of consciousness are important in this respect. Second, this insight certainly does not *explain* the aspect of consciousness that is mysterious and apparently beyond the range of the reductionist scientific approach; by relating it to the enormously complex area of our social interactions it may, however, point us in the direction that will enable us to understand it better.

References

1 Gray, Jeffrey A. (1971) The mind–brain identity theory as a scientific hypothesis. *Philosophical Quarterly*, 21: 247–54.

2 Gray, Jeffrey A. (1986) The mind–brain identity theory as a scientific hypothesis: a second look (this volume).

3 Barlow, H. B. (1972) Single units and sensation: a neuron doctrine for perceptual psychology? *Perception*, 1: 371–94.

4 Barlow, H. B. (1985) The role of single neurons in the psychology of perception. (The Bartlett Lecture of the Experimental Psychology Society) *Quart. J. exp. Psychol.* 37: 121–45.

5 Barlow, H. B., Hill, R. M. and Levick, W. R. (1964) Retinal ganglion cells responding selectively to direction and speed of image motion in the rabbit. *J. Physiol.* (London), 173: 377–407.

6 Perrett, D. I., Rolls, E. T. and Caan, W. (1982) Visual neurons responsive to faces in the monkey temporal cortex. *Exp. Brain Res.* 47: 329–42.

7 Perrett, D. I., Smith, P. A. J., Potter, D. D., Mistlin, A. J., Head, A. S., Milner, A. D. and Jeeves, M. A. (1985) Neurons responsive to faces in the temporal cortex: studies of functional organisation, sensitivity to identity and relation to perception. *Human Neurobiology*, 3:197–208.

8 Humphrey, N. K. (1980) Nature's psychologists. In B. D. Josephson and V. S. Ramachandran (eds), *Consciousness and the Physical World*, ch. 4, pp 57–80. Oxford: Pergamon.

9 Barlow, H. B. (1980) Nature's joke. In ibid., ch. 5, pp. 81–94.

10 Humphrey, N. K. (1984) *Consciousness Regained*. Oxford: Oxford Univ. Press.

11 Craik, K. J. W. (1943) *The Nature of Explanation*. Cambridge: Cambridge Univ. Press.

12 Baron-Cohen, S., Leslie, A. M. and Frith, Uta (1985) Does the autistic child have a 'theory of mind'? *Cognition*, 21: 37–46.

13 Leslie, A. M. (1987) Pretense and representation: the origins of 'theory of mind'. *Psychological Review* (in press).

14 Land, E. H and McCann, J. J. (1971) Lightness and Retinex theory. *Journal of the Optical Society of America*, 61: 1–11.

15 Helmholtz, H. von (1896) *Handbuch der Physiologischen Opik*, Zweite Auflag. Hamburg und Leipzig: Voss.

25

The Inner Eye of Consciousness

Nicholas Humphrey

Nicholas Humphrey was until recently Assistant Director of Research at the Sub-Department of Animal Behaviour in Cambridge. He has combined academic research in neuropsychology and experimental psychology with speculation on a larger scale about man's place in nature. His writings include Consciousness Regained *(Oxford Univ. Press, 1983), and* In a Dark Time *(Faber & Faber, 1984), for which he won the Martin Luther King Memorial Prize in 1985.*

A note tucked away in Denis Diderot's *Elements of Physiology* (1774) reads: 'If the union of a soul to a machine is impossible, let someone prove it to me . . . If it is possible, let someone tell me what difference it would make.' Replace the term 'soul' with the term 'consciousness', and we have what are still the two central questions in the science of mind. Could a *machine* be conscious? What *difference* would it make to it?

Although Diderot must have meant his question to be a direct challenge to Descartes – who considered that men alone had souls – the form of the question suggests he still went along with the view that bodies and minds are made of different kinds of stuff. The question was whether a machine could be *united* to a soul – as, say, England might be united to Scotland, or a man united to his shoes. Yet elsewhere Diderot explicity opposed this kind of dualism. 'Oh! ridiculous writer,' he said of a Cartesian dualist, 'if I once admit these two distinct substances [body and soul], you have nothing more to teach me. For you do not know what it is that you call soul, less still how they are united, nor how they act reciprocally on one another.

This is one issue that the philosophy of mind has done something to resolve. First has come the realization that there is no reason to believe that mind – soul, consciousness, etc. – is something distinct from the activity of the physical brain; rather (in John Searle's terms) it should be regarded as a 'surface feature' of it. Second – and in some ways equally important – has come the realization that the human brain itself is a machine. So the question now is not *could* a machine be conscious, but what *kind* of machine could be conscious. How much more and how much less would a conscious machine have to resemble the human brain – nerve cells, chemicals and all? The dispute has become one between those who argue on the one hand that it's simply a matter of having the

Charles Darwin (1809–82) photographed towards the end of his life. It did not occur to him that if souls exist at all, they exist as properties rather than as adjuncts to the mechanism (Mary Evans Picture Library).

appropriate programs, and those who say it's a matter of the hardware too.

With Diderot's second question, 'What difference would it make?', we are however not much further forward. When Diderot asked it – again as a challenge to Descartes – my guess is he was asking rhetorically for the answer 'None'. A machine, he imagined, might have a soul – and yet, for all practical purposes, be identical to an unconscious machine. 'If a soul were joined to a watch, what would it produce therein?' As a time-keeper, it would be just the same watch as it was before. But if consciousness is no *use* to a watch, the same could well be true for human beings.

The realization that consciousness might be useless was, I suspect, something of a breakthrough. I remember my own surprise and pleasure with this 'naughty' idea when I first read Wittgenstein and J. B. Watson – something to tease one's schoolfriends with. But it is a naughty idea which has, I think, had a good run, and now should be dismissed.

When Diderot wrote he knew nothing about evolution by natural selection. He had his own ideas about evolutionary progress occurring through struggle between competing forms to produce increasing 'harmony'. But even if it had occurred to him that consciousness was part of this harmonious scheme, the condition for its survival would have been simply that it did not get in the way: there was no reason why it should be in any way adaptive.

The theory of natural selection, however, makes the condition for something's evolving and surviving much stricter. Apart from the very simplest structures, almost nothing exists that does not contribute to an organism's biological success. 'What difference does it make?' The answer must be that it helps in some way to keep the animal alive.

Then either we throw away the idea that consciousness evolved by natural selection, or else we have to find a function for it. We can of course throw it away (Darwin himself seems to have done); but let us not – at least not until we've tried. 'Surface features' of organisms are in fact the very features on which natural selection is most likely to act. The fur on an animal's body is, if you like, a surface feature: no one doubts that fur evolved.

The problem is first to escape from a definition of consciousness that renders it self-evidently useless and irrelevant, for example, private states of mind of which the subject alone is aware, which can neither be confirmed nor contradicted, whereof no one can speak and we must all remain silent, etc.

Neither biologically nor psychologically does that feel right. Such definitions, at their limit (and they are meant, of course, to impose limits), suggest that statements about consciousness can have no *information value* – technically that they can do nothing to reduce anyone's uncertainty about what is actually going on. I find that counter-intuitive and wholly unconvincing. When a man describes his states of mind, either to us or to himself, common sense tells us that he is in fact communicating something, namely information about certain inner processes – feelings, sensations, memories, etc. If he says, for example, 'I'm in pain', or 'I'm in love', we reckon we actually know more about him, and for that matter that *through being conscious* he knows more about himself.

But what kind of information is this? What is it about? For a materialist

Figure 25.1   Denis Diderot (1713–84). He challenged Descartes' opinion that men alone have souls, but still went along with the view that bodies and minds are made of different kinds of stuff (Mary Evans Picture Library).

there can be only one answer. It is about something that is going on inside his *brain*. True, that's not how most ordinary people see it. The gulf between brain states, as described by physiologists, and mind states, as described by conscious human beings, is practically – and some would argue, logically – unbridgeable. Yet who doubts that a mapping between the two descriptions does in fact exist: that consciousness is in fact a picture of the workings of the brain?

Let's take the metaphor of conscious 'insight' seriously. Imagine the situation of an animal that does not possess this faculty of insight (figure 25.2). It has a brain which receives inputs from conventional sense organs and sends outputs to motor systems, and in between runs a highly sophisticated information-processor and decision-maker. But it has no picture of what this information-processor is doing or how it works. The animal is unconscious.

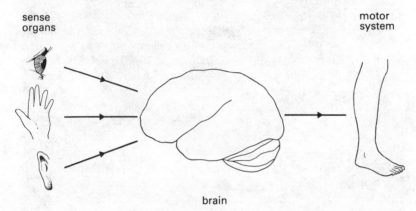

Figure 25.2 The workings of an animal without insight.

Now imagine that a new form of sense organ evolves, an 'inner eye', whose field of view is not the outside world *but the brain itself* (figure 25.3).

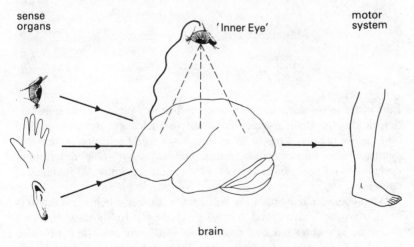

Figure 25.3 The added role of an 'inner eye'.

Figure 25.4   Thomas Hobbes (1588–1679), philosopher and contemporary of Descartes. He described how consciousness provides us with an extraordinary effective tool for understanding – by anaology – the minds of others like ourselves (Mary Evans Picture Library).

Like other sense organs, the inner eye provides a picture of its information field – the brain – which is partial and selective. But equally, like other sense organs, it has been designed by natural selection so that this picture is a useful one – in current jargon, a 'user-friendly' description, designed to tell the subject as much as he requires to know. This animal is conscious.

What could such an inner eye be for? The answer, I believe, is that it is for doing what I have called 'natural psychology'.[1] By showing each and every one of us how our own mind/brain works, consciousness provides us with an extraordinarily effective tool for understanding – by analogy –

the minds of others like ourselves. Thomas Hobbes, Descartes' contemporary, said it clearly: 'Whosoever looketh into himself and considereth what he doth when he does think, opine, reason, hope, fear &c. and upon what grounds, he shall thereby read and know what are the thoughts and passions of all other men upon the like occasions.'[2]

What difference does that make? It makes the difference, I suspect, between being a man and a monkey. Human beings have evolved to be the most highly *social* creatures the world has ever seen. Their social relationships have a depth, a complexity, and a biological importance to them which no other animals' relationships come near. No accident, I think, that human beings are so far as we know unique in their ability to use *self-knowledge* to interpret others.

If that ability could exist without consciousness, let someone prove it to me. If any other animal possesses it, let someone tell me what evidence he has.

References

1 Humphrey,N. K. (1983) *Consciousness Regained*. Oxford: Oxford Univ. Press.
2 Hobbes, Thomas (1648; 1946) *Leviathan*, ed. M. Oakeshott. Oxford: Oxford Univ. Press.

26

The Nature of Conscious Awareness

John Crook

John Crook began his research career in ethology at Cambridge with a detailed field study of the social organization of weaver birds in Africa and India. His monography on this topic stimulated similar studies on the evolution of animal societies, including those of primates. He initiated research on the Gelada baboon in Ethiopia in 1966, and in 1968–9 spent a year as Fellow at the Center for Advanced Study in the Behavioral Sciences at Stanford and became interested in the early development of humanistic psychology and psychotherapy in experimental groups. He is currently engaged in field studies of Himalayan Buddhist villages where he is involved both in socio-ecological studies and in work on the meditational practices of monks in the local monasteries. He also runs retreats for Zen practitioners at a college in Mid-Wales several times each year.

Introduction

I am going to discuss the nature of conscious awareness and its origins and need to begin by stating my basic position on the subject. In explaining performances of people or animals, some may think that there is no call to discuss awareness if, as with Cruise missiles or computers, one can see how the job is done. All that seems necessary is an analysis in terms of information-processing, for this may give an adequate and predictive account of what happens. With some such account of a mechanism or system the investigation of its function may then proceed through the analysis of the contexts of its use and its likely effects on the fitness of individuals. In this way an analysis of the evolution of cognitive systems can proceed and indeed this is one main thrust of contemporary cognitive ethology. Consciousness or awareness is then perceived as an epiphenomenon, a secondary effect, without great significance in theory.

I am going to argue, none the less, that since you and I can almost certainly agree that both of us are conscious there is therefore a phenomenon to be discussed. We may also agree that consciousness is often particularly vivid as an aspect of problem solving, whereas many of our bodily functions and apparent motivations are rarely experienced as such. Furthermore, the term consciousness, as used conventionally and

An old villager rests during circumambulation of the monastery of Sani in Zangskar, Ladakh. His visualizations and mantra repetitions constitute an elementary meditation bringing a peace of mind which is also quantified as gaining merit by the spinning prayer wheel and the counted beads (photograph by John Crook).

described in the *Oxford English Dictionary*, refers clearly to personal or mutual knowledge of the fact of experiencing (see figure 24.1). It is tempting therefore to treat consciousness as a property of a person or of certain classes of organism. It would be more precise to argue that consciousness is a property attributable to certain cognitive activities, in particular those concerned with the representations of the world used in relating the organism or person to the world. Susan Blackmore argues that consciousness is a property of models that perform this function; and is inclined to think that all forms of representation are conscious.[1] My view is less embracing; mirrors or cameras or Cruise missiles are not, in my view, conscious but I agree that it is in a comprehension of the organismic modelling process that an understanding of consciousness must lie. And, since such processes are inherent in the cognition of higher organisms, consciousness may often be attributed to such an organism also.[2]

We may therefore reasonably pose a series of questions. What are the constraints on consciousness? Why is only certain information accessible? What are the functions of consciousness and the rules of access to it? What is the evolutionary origin of consciousness?

Recent hypotheses regarding the evolution of conscious cognition have drawn attention to its especial significance for sociable animals. In this view consciousness is a result of social evolution calling for a mechanism for the representation and inspection of multilateral processes inherent in social interaction.[3,4,5] Consciousness is viewed as an aspect of intentionality with respect to the goals of social strategies of an evolutionary, flexible kind. My argument in this chapter accepts this basic viewpoint but adds an emphasis on the awareness of bodily sensing or proprioception, which seems an equally essential aspect of the phenomenon. This emphasis reintroduces the topic of feeling and emotion to an area that is too easily treated only within its purely cognitive dimension (see box below).

Knowing What the Body is Doing

Action depends not only on knowing what is happening in the immediate environment but also on knowing what one's own body is doing in it. Body awareness involves feedback from body organs and limbs. There are three sources of such knowing:

(1) *Proprioceptive feedback*: Information from specialized receptors in muscles, tendons, joints and skin that record movement and report back to the brain (figure 26.1).

(2) *Reafferent feedback*: When an action is ordered the nervous system copies the order as a neural trace. Comparison between these command copies and actual performance is important, for example, in vision where compensation for eye movements is taken into account when evaluating the perception of moving objects (figure 26.2).

(3) *Exteroceptive feedback*: Direct observation of the movements of limbs, etc.

It is postulated that exteroceptive feedback is a higher nervous function and 'conscious' while proprioceptive and reafference are lower brain functions (medullary and cerebellar) and 'unconscious'.

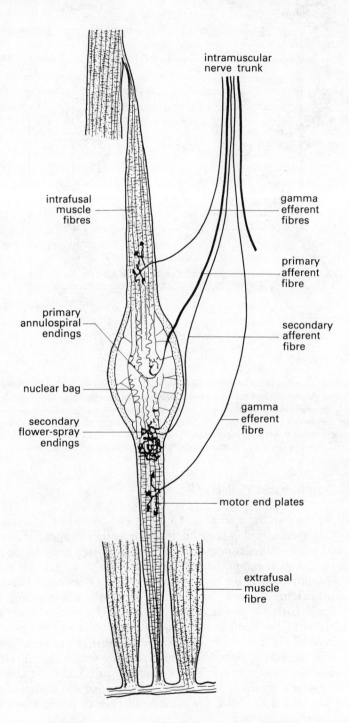

Figure 26.1   The intricate structure of a muscle spindle, a sense organ found in between the normal fibres (extrafusal fibres) of skeletal muscles. These spindles provide proprioceptive sensory feedback to the nervous system, indicating the degree of stretching or shortening of the muscle (redrawn from Strong and Elwyn's Human Neuroanatomy 5th edn, 1964, Williams and Wilkins).

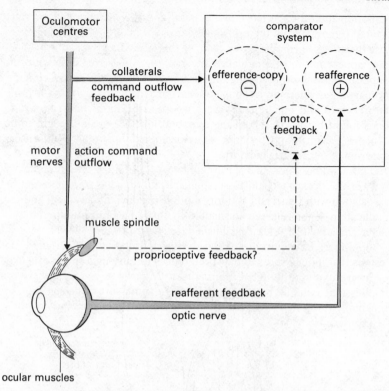

Figure 26.2   A hypothetical flow diagram to show the relationship between outflow of movment signals from the oculomotor centres in the brain to the eye muscles, the visual information coming in along the optic nerve and the possibility of proprioceptive feedback from muscle spindles in the eye muscles. Comparison of all the signals in the 'comparator system' would allow the brain to distinguish between movements of the retinal image caused by movements of the eye and movements of the visual world (redrawn from von Holst and Mittelstaedt, 1950, Naturwissenschaften, *37, 464–76).*

Proprioception and Models of Reality

Accepting our own consciousness as a simple fact allows us to examine, at least in our species, and in some inferences from the behaviour of others, how and when consciousness appears. The approach must be one in which physiological and phenomenological knowledge are related. In his valuable contribution to the book *Self-Awareness in Domesticated Animals*,[6] the neuroanatomist David Bowsher surveys evidence concerning the neurological basis for proprioceptive awareness. He distinguishes between tracts to the brain bearing inputs that produce experiences of generalized bodily sensations, which the neurologist Henry Head called protopathic sensory experiences, and tracts responsible for precisely point-located sensations (epicritic) of specific pain. Acute and chronic pain systems are separable and there is evidence that stimulation of the former can inhibit the latter – a mechanism perhaps important in the application of acupuncture.

There is also a possible separation between the occurrence of pain sensation and the experience of it as painful. Bowsher reports that certain limited removals from the prefrontal cortex of the brain cause patients to lose the affective component of pain, so that while they are reporting pain they appear not to be troubled by it. The prefrontal area is thus deeply implicated in the experiencing of sensation. The cerebral cortex contains primary areas where direct somatic sensations including sight and hearing are received and non-primary areas where associations between sensations might be processed. In the temporal lobe are areas thought to be concerned with the 'association of associations', including multisensory experiences recalled as memories.

These studies show that we are already on the track, in a preliminary way, of the brain mechanisms responsible for somatic sensation and its association with visual and auditory input. Prefrontal involvement and the implication of the reticular formation, the hypothalamus and the intralaminar thalamus are at least established (see figure 26.3).

On a more ethological level David Vowles proposes that certain brain lesions that induce shifts in paw preferences in rats suggest that rats may be aware of the differential efficacy of their paws in certain tasks.[7] He implies that rats like humans may possess 'some sort of body image or schema', which they use to predict and control the outcomes of their behaviour.

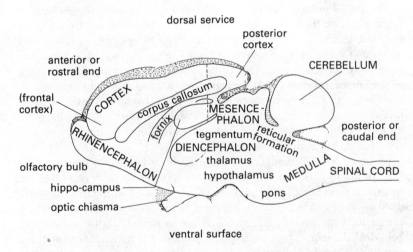

Figure 26.3 A schematic view of the brain of a primitive mammal, the rat, cut down the middle from front to back (redrawn from Altman, 1966, Organic Foundations of Animal Behavior, Holt, Rinehart and Winston, 207, reprinted by permission of CBS College Publishing).

The existence of such a schema as a resource governing intentional behaviour has been postulated by neurologists and psychologists such as Henry Head[8] and Kenneth Craik[9] and is implicit also in Freud's neurophysiological model of the human mind,[10] and again in Piaget's idea of the sensorimotor schema,[11] the logic of which underlies the basis of language. The wider psychological implications of the body schema are discussed by Fisher and Cleveland,[12] who point out that ideas about the body acquired during socialization play major roles in the way the body is experienced.

The idea that the brain generates a *model* of the sensory inputs from the body has considerable power for psychological theory. Indeed without such a model effective action in the environment, including the social environment, would be impossible, since the integration of bodily movement and situational adaptation could not then be achieved. O'Keefe and Nadel review neuroethological evidence on the brain areas involved.[13] MacKay and Inglis have both argued that such a model is not merely the direct presence of the sensory input data but is rather a *re-presentation* of that data in a form designed to preserve stability, perhaps by emphasizing and focusing on key features in a pattern and discounting slight fluctuations in experience.[14,15] The inputs are thus used to create a 'portrait' of the inner and outer sensorium. This amounts to an organizing system that is being constantly updated by fresh information and which maintains a 'conditional readiness' of the organism in relation to strategically related environmental demands. In my view it is this conditional readiness that constitutes a prime aspect of consciousness.

We can see that we have here a model based on the detection of 'dissonance' in which the matching or mismatching of novelty against an established image is a continuing process. The temporal stability of the model in time is a vital property, for it is this that allows the updating process to occur. I am going to argue, in common with others, that consciousness is one aspect of this cognitive system and that the continuity of awareness arises from the temporal properties of the model.

Yet not everything that may be modelled is necessarily represented in consciousness. Indeed we know awareness to be *serial*: we are aware of only one theme at a time. We therefore need to describe a process that accounts for the decision-making implied in the explicit presentation of material in consciousness. This is the function of attention. Clearly some allocation of priority based probably on a comparison of degrees of dissonance at differing levels or stages of representation is involved. The orderliness of awareness – its apparent stability within time – is what gives us the feeling that we live in a world rather than within experiences conjured up by capricious senses.

Some ethological models of the occurrence of activities under conditions of motivational thwarting or conflict may give us clues regarding the control process here. David McFarland has argued that when an animal is drinking (say) and its activity is thwarted, then the output copy of its motor command (that is, its 'intention') is not matched by the subsequent behavioural event.[16] In a comparison process that matches the intended output with *feedback* describing the consequences, a mismatch between the feedforward information and the behavioural outcome produces an inhibition on the ongoing activity such that some other system of inputs can gain momentary control of the brain and a 'displacement' activity arises (see box below). Similarly, when feedforward expectancies of familiarity are mismatched with novel occurrences, orienting or alarm reactions may often occur.[17] John Archer has produced a model for the occurrence of aggression based on similar principles.[18]

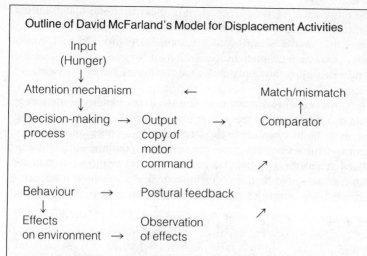

Outline of David McFarland's Model for Displacement Activities

Input
(Hunger)
↓
Attention mechanism   ←   Match/mismatch
↓   ↑
Decision-making →   Output   →   Comparator
process   copy of
                              motor
                              command   ↗

Behaviour   →   Postural feedback
↓   ↗
Effects   Observation
on environment →   of effects

Activities that are quite out of context often happen in the behaviour sequences of animals. A brooding gull may suddenly make nest-building movements or a mobbing finch start frantically preening. Human beings scratch heads or bite nails. In this model attention to an ongoing activity (feeding, say) flips when the effects of action do not match the output copy of the animal's motor command. An alternative activity takes over for a short time before the system flips back under the prevailing input control.

It seems likely that mismatches between expectations originally fed forward intentionally for confirmation and the form of the actual event may provoke marked shifts in the focus of attention and hence in the contents of the stream of consciousness. Several ongoing models of an organism's existence may be running concurrently but only one will be most applicable or relevant to its situation at any one time. This one is likely to be selected for attention and hence experienced, whereas others will not then gain access to awareness.

The orderliness of the consciousness process is emphasized by recent studies where degrees of disorder intrude upon normal consciousness. Susan Blackmore in her study of out-of-body experiences suggests that explanations of these unusual states may be couched more usefully at present in terms of models of the experiential processes involved rather than by attempts at a physiological theory.[19,20] Such 'top–down' psychological explanations may be more stimulating to thought than 'bottom–up' biological ones at the present time.

Susan Blackmore argues that:

(1) The brain maintains *models of reality* based upon the input of sensory information and on information drawn from memory to control for stability.

(2) The most stable model is consistent in that match–mismatch testing confirms its value as a basis for action.

(3) The stable model is attributed the status of reality and this 'reality status' is then attributed by projection on to the assumed outside world. 'Reality' is thus a psychological attribution rather than a matter of external fact.

(4) When this model is disturbed by illness, drugs, emotional imbalance or stress, an attempt is made to restore it. The best way to restore it may be to build a replica model from memory. This may restore the input control – essential if an organism is to continue with survival-related behaviour. Only when a model based on memory becomes for a time more stable than the defective or degraded input model is it attributed the status of reality. Examples are out-of-body states.

Similar arguments can perhaps be applied to dreams, although here memory itself is remodelled under the influence of 'repressions' retained in the 'unconscious'; and to certain other altered states of consciousness.

I would like to distinguish here between the *somatic model*, the partly conscious model, we have of the integrated body we appear to inhabit, the *soma-situational model*, whereby we appear placed in certain topographic relationships with what we call this 'room', 'hillside' or 'town', and the *socio-focal model*, which, in addition to subsuming the other two, places us within the appearance of our social relationships. All three are seen as closely integrated and overlapping in a single functional system.

Where we experience ourselves to be within this tripartite schema of 'reality' is a function of the current focus of attention. This focus is itself a function of the current state of intention, which will be concerned normally with the resolution of some current biological need, situational challenge or ideational problem. This intentionality will in turn be subject to some set of rules as to the importance of currently present *issues*.

In this viewpoint, then, conscious experience is a concomitant of an intentional direction of attention upon some *issue* selected within some hierarchy of criteria, perhaps ultimately based in *evolutionary stable strategies* of the species. Awareness arises in the targeting process of attention as directed within such an intentional hierarchy. This means that awareness will move between the somatic, the soma-situational and the socio-focal areas of consciousness in a more or less orderly fashion structured by the strategic concerns and contemporary inputs of an individual.

The stability of our experience of reality is, however, not always derived from our perception of the environment so much as its re-creation, making use of memories to fill in the picture; reality is essentially an attribution of the mind, which can become illusory. It seems likely that the representational material of the three areas constitutes a modelling hierarchy and that access to consciousness is normally given to higher levels, low levels being processed without awareness, even though access to these levels is possible if sufficient dissonance draws attention to them. We all know that in normal conscious states our awareness of bodily sensation is limited – pushed aside by the fact that our attention is locked upon some social or situational issue. It is almost as if (as in the learning of a task) the functions of the body are on automatic pilot and do not usually have to be attended to consciously.

What happens if the somatic model is made the object of deliberate attention? The most interesting literature here is not within the Western tradition but found within the technical writings of phenomenological Buddhism – specifically the Tibetan tantra, in which attention is often deliberately directed to the bodily condition – especially upon the somatic consequences of especial patterns of breathing. A recent yogic commentary by Geshe Kelsang Gyatso illustrates the complexity of the awareness that may then arise.[21] In brief synopsis the following points may be made.

Figure 26.4   The monastery of Karsha in Zangshar, Ladakh where experienced monks still practise and study Tantric meditation (photograph by John Crook).

(1) By directing attention to the inner feel of the trunk, limbs, face, genitals or other specific locations, conscious access to bodily sensation is obtained. Meditation involving a tour of the inner feel of the body is invigorating and may be termed meditational massage.

(2) Observation of breathing, particularly during holding the breath, shows that certain foci of awareness have a natural prominence: these are near the navel, in the chest, throat and head. It seems this is likely to be so because sensation from the functions of particular organs arises in these areas; the abdominal and diaphragmatic muscles in opposition, the lungs and heart, the vocal apparatus and visual/auditory perception. We may suppose that access to these sensations is acquired by a top–down process whereby incoming signals are released from an inhibition by other mental activities which otherwise prevent them from becoming experienced.

(3) Deliberate placing of awareness in these foci, referred to as the *cakras* in the original Indian accounts written in Sanskrit, produces sensations as if a form of energy or local tension were being generated. If the *cakras* are meditated upon for long periods they appear to 'open'

so that upward and downward energy streamings of sensation occur. Thinking may then be inhibited and a condition of equanimity and a perception clear of the interpretative interpolation of thought arises, a condition called the 'clear light' of the mind.

(4) Practice allows the meditator with closed eyes to experience himself totally in terms of the inner energy field, free from situational contact. This is termed the subtle energy body or the illusory body. In the practices of mind transformation, this energy body, plus the 'clear light' of the mental state, may be evoked as a directly experienced meditational 'being' which then replaces the usual hassling mind.

Such practices, which can be dangerous without careful tuition from an expert, open the meditator to a holographic-like experience of inner space constituted by the apperception of proprioceptive and reafferent body information usually withheld from conscious access due to the priority of social or situational issues. The facts show that such awareness is normally implicit – that is, accessible to awareness – but only occasionally made explicitly so. Other features of the yogic system discussed by Geshe Kelsang Gyatso implicate dream and apparent out-of-body experiences and these become open to analysis in terms of the account of consciousness we are considering here.[22]

The Emergence of Self-consciousness

I am arguing that conscious awareness is a conditional property of the reality model in its tripartite form. It may be said to be the subjective aspect of the continuing re-presentation of a temporally stabilized informational display within which multilateral processing of an issue can occur. Issues are chosen according to a hierarchy of criteria and become intentionally the focus of attention. Issue resolution removes the intention, whereupon attention is focused upon a further issue. Since most issues can be presented only one at a time, conscious awareness has a serial form. However, within the processing of an issue arising at the social level, say, the information at the somatic level is still potentially accessible – and a shift of attention will move it from implicit to explicit awareness.

What exactly is meant by 'subjective' aspect as applied to cognition? Why should this particular process give rise to phenomenal experiencing. If attribution of reality is accorded only to the most stable model irrespective of the momentary balance between input and recall from memory, what sort of relationship with the 'external' environment is desirable or achieved? These are difficult questions.

Firstly 'subjective' refers to ontology, 'being' itself, rather than the phenomenology of experience. It may be more correct to say that you and I *are* the process of re-presentation of cognitive materials rather than that we *have* such a property as consciousness or that consciousness is a property of cognition. When certain forms of cognitive processing arise the modelling itself is consciousness. What, then, is the key element in making a representational process a conscious one? I suggest the essential ingredient is the temporal continuum of the detection of dissonance, which maintains and updates the integrity of the model and its coherence as a meaningful set of relations between intentionality and the 'reality' frame within which it is set. The model of reality is stabilized by a feedforward process that predicts the relations between its features in immediately future time. This prediction is then confirmed or denied by a form of match–mismatch comparison. The continuity of this processing is a figure–ground relationship, the appearance of patterning against a background within which issues receive attention and which constitutes in itself a psychological 'time', the awareness of process itself. This awareness constitutes the subjective basis (ontology) of the experiencing of phenomena. There are indeed certain states of awareness in which input processing and imaginative thought are both drastically reduced: here the sense of time alters; temporal change may become imperceptible; time stops. Consciousness then virtually disappears in a condition called *samadhi* in the Indian literature.

If a focus on the role of the processing subject is included in the calculus governing behaviour, then a degree of self-awareness in the continuum of the organism's present moment exists. Sentient self-awareness, as we normally use the term, requires, however, a secondary metacognition whereby the temporal stability of the self-process is realized; and this can probably arise only when symbolic reference to past, present and future is possible. In other words it requires language or at least conceptuality. This distinction between a primary and a secondary metacognitive process of self is similar to that made by Duval and Wicklund between subjective and objective self-consciousness.[23]

The experiencing of self doubtless varies in many ways but in this presentation I want to emphasize two key dimensions. One concerns the extent to which the subject looks inward at his own mental 'world' or outward at the phenomena he experiences. The other concerns the degree to which awareness is characterized by a forward-looking, anticipatory intentionality or a present-centred attentionality – a there/then versus a here/now polarity. The crossing of these two dimensions produces a mandala-like representation of the experiential world with four quadrants (figure 26.5). Intentionality with Extension characterizes the analytical thought processes of socio-situational referencing. Intentio-

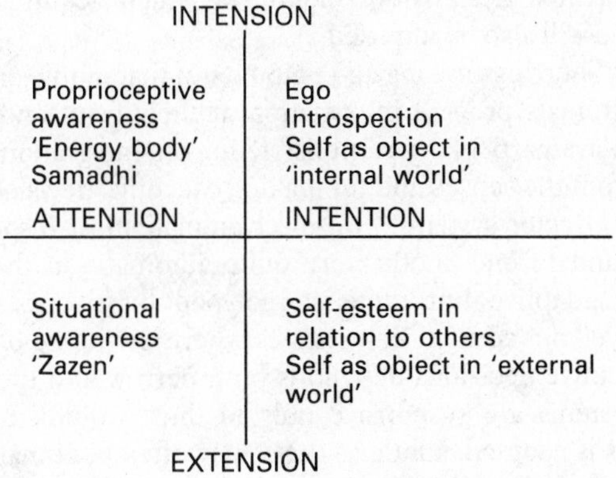

INTENSION

Proprioceptive awareness 'Energy body' Samadhi	Ego Introspection Self as object in 'internal world'
ATTENTION	INTENTION
Situational awareness 'Zazen'	Self-esteem in relation to others Self as object in 'external world'

EXTENSION

Figure 26.5   Two dimensions of experience defining the locus of personal awareness.

nality with Intension is introspection. High levels of Attention with Intension produce states of inward observation or meditative trance (*samadhi*); the same levels of Attention with Extension give rise to clear states of environmental awareness – as in the Zen-based martial arts.[24,25]

Eastern meditation manuals are largely concerned with developing the ability of the subject in moving the locus of attention at will between these four broad types of experiencing. Success gives the yogi a high degree of control over his own mental life.

The Comparative Psychology of Consciousness

To what extent may we attribute consciousness to non-human animals?[26] We may suppose that conscious awareness, in that it involves the maintenance of a continuum of re-presentational display, requires more neural apparatus than basic decision-making based on the simple record-ing and processing of sense data.[2] This implies that any such apparatus will be developed only if there is natural selection favouring its evolution. It follows that only those species that need conscious processes will have them. Nicholas Humphrey is probably right that animals with complex social lives evolve not only the intellect for the analysis of social relations within the socio-focal model, but also, necessarily, the capacity to feel somatic changes associated with social hopes and fears and which involve the basic somatic model.[27,4] Such ideas are supported by findings that the form of the body image in people is influenced by socialization and introjection of motivations from parental figures.[12]

Species may thus vary in the extent to which:

(1) inputs are accessible by representational awareness;
(2) inputs are stored as information accessible by focused attention under certain conditions;
(3) the quality of the representational continuum of day-to-day con-sciousness; and
(4) the specific criteria providing a hierarchy whereby decisions to attend to an issue intentionally are made and categorized.

In general, of the information available to an animal, that part of it which is accessible to consciousness will be determined by filtering processes of a biological nature on top of which acquired social and cultural criteria will also be imposed.

Sir Charles Sherrington long ago pointed out that motile and bilaterally symmetrical animals process information at their front ends where the neural ganglia are particularly responsible for the integration of informa-tion coming from the senses and for making executive decisions which are passed to the effector system.[28] In lower animals most responses to the environment and to one another are quite automatic in that presented stimuli evoke adaptive but quite stereotyped behaviours. These be-haviours are well suited to circumstances where the range of stimulation on which executive decisions depend is both narrow and highly predict-able. Such systems are responsive only to those stimuli to which the responsiveness is adapted, subtle as these may often be. Innate or 'wired-in' reflexive behaviour of this sort is clearly not suited to circumstances in which stimulation is highly variable, with much fluctuation in environ-mental conditions requiring many short-term adjustments in behavioural orientation.

Among lower organisms a capacity to adjust to frequent change involves the provision of mechanisms that allow associative rather than automatic behaviour to develop. At the most elementary level there are two adaptive processes here – conditioning and habituation, which in more advanced learning are paralleled respectively by the acquisition and the extinction of operant behaviour. Associative behaviour is vital to all advanced animals, as it is this that allows the differential reinforcement of responses that optimize the use of time and energy in complex and variable environments. The old principles of reinforcement and extinc-tion simply point to the fact that an animal, within the context of its evolved and stabilized strategies, monitors its behaviour in relation to its, ultimately physiological, well-being. A stable state of the organism is maintained while growth and reproduction occur.

We are beginning to know something now about the awareness of the environment by animals, against which associative choices are made. Since the 1950s a prime idea in cognitive study has been the notion, originally from Tolman and his latent learning rats,[29] that, to use his metaphor, animals 'map their environments' in their heads not only with respect to space, but also with respect to time. They do this through perceptual exploration.

Early behaviourists believed animals learnt through the reward or punishment of actions. Tolman and his colleagues ran two groups of rats for food in mazes. One group had had prior experience of the maze without food in it. When they found the food more quickly and efficiently than rats without such prior experience Tolman was able to argue that learning could come about through observation and the building up of a 'map in the head'. This also drew attention to the importance of exploration in animal behaviour.

The 'map' depends upon the acquisition of perceptual norms, which represent the animal's experience of its environment and which depend upon the storage of experience in memory. It then becomes possible for the animal to compare novel with familiar experience. Commonly animals seek out the novel until its investigation is so complete that interest wanes with the object's increasing familiarity. Animals service their maps with recurrent exploration, seeking out and making familiar stimulation which is novel to them, yet always within limits set by the animal's tolerance of intensity and type of stimulation.

Work in Holland by Rudi Drent and his colleagues shows clearly how important these internalized spatio-temporal maps must be.[30] For exam-ple, a hunting kestrel times its forays to hours when mice have been previously located and chooses routes with high probabilities of success based on past experience. Similarly, a wagtail having a territory alongside a stream spends sufficient time there to deplete the bank of renewable food items deposited there by the brook. It then goes away for a time, not so long, however, as to allow a competitor to become established, and, having foraged for a while in a flock, returns when a valuable amount of new food has been deposited.[31] Clearly in such examples the availability of food items, their frequency in certain locations and their temporal

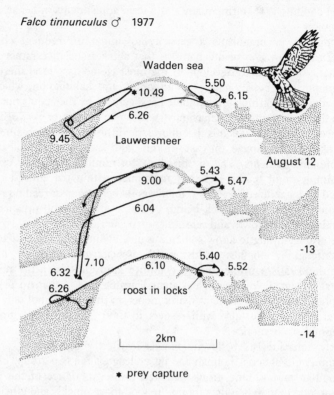

Figure 26.6   Daily routines of hunting as observed in a male kestrel followed with the aid of radio telemetry on five successive dates. Note the correspondence in time and site of capture of voles on three successive days (redrawn from Drent, 1986. 'Risk/benefit assessment in animals', Animal Mind – Human Mind, Springer Verlag).

variation are all well 'mapped' and the information is used in calculating behavioural tactics that are highly predictive of success.

Predictive monitoring of the environment by using a cognitive map leads us to suppose that two processes at least are in operation. Firstly, differential attention to objects of contrasting significance to a strategically performing individual; secondly, cognitive representation of objects and their availability in space and time for use in comparisons between situations then, now and future. Richard Andrew,[32] for example, has made effective use of the attention theory of Donald Broadbent[33] and other psychologists to explain the performances of chicks in selecting food items from contrasting backgrounds, some demanding the use of simple categorizations and some of quite complex ones.

Models of performance involving complex cognitive discriminations are now beginning to appear. Thus pigeons in a Skinner box exposed to a range of pictures can learn to respond for food only when a 'tree', which may come in several forms, appears in the picture. Clearly a concept of 'tree' has been formed and used in decision-making. The hungry pigeon can scan a picture and discriminate between categories that appear in it.[34] An African grey parrot has been trained to vocalize real words so as to identify, refuse or request objects by using verbal labels.[35]

Norton-Griffiths has studied the behaviour of parent oyster-catchers

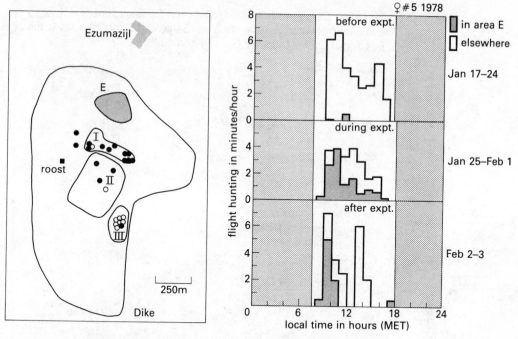

Figure 26.7   Manipulating the allocation of hunting time by a female kestrel. The map on the left shows the home range and prey captures in January 1978 before the experiment (solid dots – prey taken in flight, open dots – from perches), and the experimental area (E) where prey were deliberately provided in the 8–day period 25 January–1 February (the great majority between 09.00 and 10.00 hours). Shown on the right is the dramatic effect of this supplementary feeding on allocation of hunting time, including a pronounced peak in visitation corresponding to the main feeding time after the supplementary feeding ceased (bottom panel) (redrawn from Drent, 1986, 'Risk/benefit assessment in animals', Animal Mind – Human Mind, Springer Verlag).

feeding their young on mud flats.[36] His analysis enabled him to propose a computer flow diagram as a model for the decision processes involved. He assumed that as parents and chicks arrive on the flats hungry from the high tide roost, the brain of the parent is producing an output that creates a sensation of hunger. This causes the parent first to feed itself but, as the output signal drops to a threshold, it turns to feeding its chicks. The position of this threshold against the output signal scale depends upon (i) the residual hunger of the parent; (ii) the behaviour of the chicks, which changes with age (K); and (iii) the time elapsing after a chick is fed before is responds again, and yet other factors. The parent has to carry through a number of computations involving Yes or No answers at decision points. The resulting performance allows the adult both to feed itself and to care effectively for its young. In cognitive terms the parent seems to be able to integrate physiological indicators of its own degree of satiation with several sorts of input from the behaviour of its young. Information is thus processed and tactics performed which ensure the strategic goal of rearing chicks without self-sacrifice.

The information-getting function of flocking[40] has received much

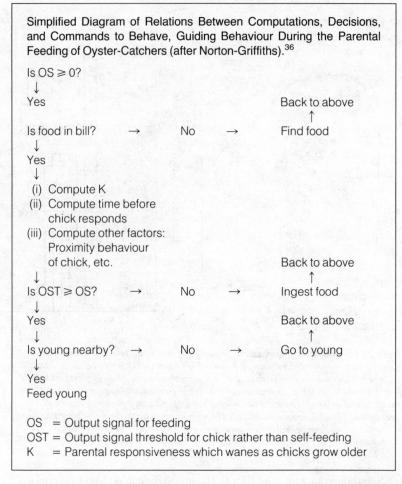

Simplified Diagram of Relations Between Computations, Decisions, and Commands to Behave, Guiding Behaviour During the Parental Feeding of Oyster-Catchers (after Norton-Griffiths).[36]

Is OS $\geq$ 0?
↓
Yes   Back to above
                                                                         ↑
Is food in bill?   →   No   →   Find food
↓
Yes
↓
 (i) Compute K
(ii) Compute time before
      chick responds
(iii) Compute other factors:
      Proximity behaviour
      of chick, etc.   Back to above
↓   ↑
Is OST $\geq$ OS?   →   No   →   Ingest food
↓
Yes   Back to above
↓   ↑
Is young nearby?   →   No   →   Go to young
↓
Yes
Feed young

OS = Output signal for feeding
OST = Output signal threshold for chick rather than self-feeding
K   = Parental responsiveness which wanes as chicks grow older

attention recently,[37] and my research student Peter de Groot has provided the first laboratory demonstration of its occurrence.[38] Using small flocks of hungry weaver birds (*Quelea quelea*), he showed that where only 6 of 12 birds in an aviary knew which of 4 exits to take to find food, the ignorant 6 rapidly oriented their behaviour to the knowledgeable birds and followed them to the goal. He found that birds fed on poor-quality food (seed and sand) would also discover good-quality food (seed only) in the same way. In addition, hungry birds given the choice of fed or unfed birds as companions chose the former. It seems clear that hungry birds pay very close attention to the demeanour of their companions and are able to infer which ones have fed well and are confident about the direction to take to find food or which have already fed well. De Groot's work emphasizes the importance of paying close attention to social companions as a means of gaining information about the environment. Chimpanzees also show attention to food-knowledgeable animals and thereby reach good food sources quickly.[39] Michael Chance and his colleagues have also emphasized the importance of social attention in primate groups.[40]

Although relatively simple, these cognitive activities in animals seem to imply the presence of an updating process in the maintenance of cognitive models, which I suggest to be the prime requirement for the temporal continuity that constitutes conscious awareness. Yet the quality of such experiencing must be relatively simple, lack metacognition and be confined to the continuous present. The ability to *reflect* on experiences of the past, or to *imagine* plausible scenarios of the future may be absent. The movements of sleeping dogs or cats do suggest dreaming, however, so that free-running information-processing from memory alone (that is, past experience) may occur in these and other higher animals; and the use of implicit knowledge of past experiences is probably an important component of plans underlying the action of cooperative hunters such as wolves.

The complexity of decision-making in the societies of baboons and apes may mark a step nearer the human condition.[41] Decisions regarding choice in the formation of alliances (which have considerable effects on invidivuals' fitness in reproduction) depend on assessments of relations between two other animals (say) and each of these with self. Such a calculus must involve some conceptualization, at least implicit, of self's involvement in the process.[42,43] I have argued that activities involving reciprocal altruism in which cheating is a possibility require an empathic insight into the motivations of another to detect a risk of allying with one who cheats. Such empathic sensitivity to another must, however, be distinguishable from experiences of self,[4,44] so that categorizations of self-experiences are likely to be enhanced and categorized as such. Nick Humphrey stresses the idea that reciprocal communication in such organisms involves the capacity to have feelings (of self, about self, of another, as of another, etc.) and to express them.[5] Conscious awareness

Figure 26.8 Complex interactions develop between individuals when three 'harem' groups of Gelada baboons rest together showing much mutual attention. Semyen Mountains, Ethiopia (photograph by John Crook).

Figure 26.9 What consciousness would you attribute to this male Gelada collectedly gazing back at the observer only a few feet away? (photograph by John Crook).

of feelings is seen to be an essential component in relating to others in sociable groups – and in the assessment of such relations according to criteria that ultimately involve indices representing personal reproductive fitness. The objectification of such inner events in language (that is, secondary metacognition, see above) opens the way to the sharing of the rehearsal of past scenarios (for better comprehension) with others and to creating together potential scenarios (for better outcomes) in imagination. Actual behaviour is then guided by a complexity of understanding and illusion which we humans refer to by such words as consciousness, conscience, intentionality and so forth. At this point the mental worlds of a complexity discoverable in the analysis of the 'object-relations' of individuals participating in psychotherapy come into being.[45,46]

Marian Dawkins has done much to show how animal preferences can indicate to us how they may feel about things and settings to which we expose them in domestication and economic exploitation.[47] The level and quality of the conscious awareness involved in, say, chickens as opposed to cows, pigs, horses, dogs or caged cougars has, however, been little explored. Conscious awareness must be conditional on the evolution of a species' cognitive skills related to the maintenance of fitness in its environment of origin. These adaptations constrain the elaboration of cognitive apparatus and the capacity for experience in both input comprehension and imaginative reflection from memorized sources. The consciousness or *Innenwelt*[48] of animals will vary specifically and their appropriate care and treatment by humans necessarily requires an analysis of their cognitive capacities and adaptations.

I submit that we now have ways of conceptualizing consciousness in humans and animals that will allow us to conduct more subtle and effective research, and also that the origin and nature of our own modes of awareness and understanding are now open to psychobiological investigation in ways that may at last break the mould of long-standing paradigms of the past. An integrative perspective of the type proposed above seems essential if we are to advance beyond the naive reductionism of information science on the one hand or the tendency to treat ideas about consciousness solely in terms of cultural projections on the other.

Figure 26.10 An Ethiopian village musician in the Semyen Mountains relaxes after performing. What consciousness do you attribute here? (photograph by John Crook).

References

1 Blackmore, S. J. (1987) Who am I? Changing models of reality in meditation. In G. Claxton (ed.), *Beyond Therapy: The Impact of Eastern Religions on Psychological Therapy and Practice*. London: Wisdom.

2 Crook, J. H. (1983) On attributing consciousness to animals. *Nature*, (London), 303, 11–14.

3 Hallowell, A. I. (1956) The structural and functional dimensions of a human existence. *Quart Rev. Biol.* 31: 88–101.

4 Crook, J. H. (1980) *The Evolution of Human Consciousness*. Oxford: Oxford Univ. Press.

5 Humphrey, N. (1983) *Consciousness Regained*. Oxford: Oxford Univ. Press.

6 Wood-Gush, D., Dawkins, M. and Ewbank, R. (1981) *Self-Awareness in Domesticated Animals*. Potters Bar: U.F.A.W.

7 Vowles, D. (1981) Neuropharmacology and awareness of the body in rats. In ibid.

8 Head, H. (1920) *Studies in Neurology*. Oxford: Oxford Univ. Press.

9 Craik, K. J. W. (1952) *The Nature of Explanation*. Cambridge: Cambridge Univ. Press.

10 Pribram, K. H. (1968) The foundation of psychoanalytic theory: Freud's neuro-psychological model. In Pribram, K. H. (ed.), *Brain and Behaviour, 4. Adaptation*. Harmondsworth: Penguin.

11 Piaget, J. (1971) *Biology and Knowledge*. Edinburgh: Edinburgh Univ. Press.

12. Fisher, S. and Cleveland, S. E. (1958) *Body Image and Personality*. New York: Van Nostrand.

13 O'Keefe, J. and Nadel, L. (1978) *The Hippocampus as a Cognitive Map*. Oxford: Oxford Univ. Press.

14 MacKay, D. (1965) A mind's eye view of the brain. In N. Wiener and J. P. Shade (eds), *Progress in Brain Research, 17*, Cybernetics of the Nervous System, pp. 321–32. Amsterdam: Elsevier.

15 Inglis, I. (1980) Towards a cognitive theory of exploratory behaviour. In J. Archer and L. Birke (eds), *Exploration in Animals and Humans*. New York: Van Nostrand.

16 McFarland, D. (1966) On the causal and functional significance of displacement activities. *Z. für Tierpsychol.* 23: 217–35.

17 Sokolov, E. N. (1960) Neuronal models and the orienting reflex. In M. A. B. Brazier (ed.), *The Central Nervous System and Behavior*. New York: Macy.

18. Archer, J. (1976) The organisation of aggression and fear in vertebrates. In P. Bateson and P. Klopfer (eds), *Perspectives in Ethology*. New York: Plenum.

19 Blackmore, S. J. (1982) *Beyond the Body*. London: Heinemann.

20 Blackmore, S. J. (1984) A psychological theory of the out-of-body experience. *J. Parapsychology*, 48: 201–18.

21 Gyatso, Geshe Kelsang (1982) *Clear Light of Bliss*. London: Wisdom.

22 Crook, J. H. Cognitive psychology and the Six Yogas of Naropa (in preparation).

23 Duval, S. and Wicklund, R. A. (1972) *A Theory of Objective Self-Awareness*. New York: Holt, Rinehart & Winston.

24 Herrigel, E. (1950) *Zen in the Art of Archery*. London: Routledge & Kegan Paul.

25 Leggett, T. (1978) *Zen and the Ways*. London: Routledge & Kegan Paul.

26 Griffin, D. (1976) *The Question of Animal Awareness*. New York: Rockefeller Univ. Press.

27 Humphrey, N. (1976) The social function of intellect. In P. Bateson and R. Hinde (eds), *Growing Points in Ethology*. Cambridge: Cambridge Univ. Press.

28 Sherrington, C. (1906) *The Integrative Action of the Nervous System*. New York: Scribner.

29 Tolman, E. C. (1948) Cognitive maps in rats and men. *Psy. Rev.* 55, 4: 189–208.

30 Drent, R. H. (1982) Risk–benefit assessment in animals. In D. Griffin (ed.), *Animal Mind – Human Mind*. Dahlem Life Sciences Report 21. Berlin: Springer.

31 Davies, N. and Houston, A. I. (1981) Owners and satellites: the economics of territory defence in the pied wagtail. *J. Anim. Ecol.* 50: 157–80.

32 Andrew, R. A. (1976) Attentional processes and animal behaviour. In Bateson and Hinde, *Growing Points in Ethology*.

33 Broadbent, D. E. (1958) *Perception and Communication*. London: Pergamon.

34 Herrnstein, R. J., Loveland, D. H. and Cable, C. (1976) Natural concepts in pigeons. *J. exp. Psychol: Animal Behavior Processes*, 2: 285–302.

35 Pepperberg, I. (1981) Functional vocalisations by an African Grey Parrot. *Z. für Tierpsychol.* 55: 139–60.

36 Norton-Griffiths, M. (1969) The organisation, control and development of parental feeding in the oyster catcher. *Behaviour*, 34: 55–114.

37 Ward, P. and Zahavi, A. (1973) The importance of certain assemblages of birds as 'information centres' for food finding. *Ibis*, 115: 517–34.

38 Groot, P. de (1980) Information transfer in a socially roosting weaver bird (*Quelea quelea*): an experimental study. *Animal Behaviour*, 28: 1249–54.

39 Menzel, E. W. (1974) A group of young chimpanzees in a one-acre field. In A. M. Schrier and F. Stollnitz (eds), *Behavior of Non-Human Primates*. New York: Academic Press.

40 Chance, M. and Larsen, R. R. (1976) *The Social Structure of Attention*. New York: Wiley.

41 Dunbar, R. (1984) *Reproductive Decisions. An Economic Analysis of Gelada Baboon Social Strategies*. Princeton: Princeton Univ. Press.

42 Colvin, J. (1982) Ph. D. Thesis. Cambridge University Library.

43 Premack, D. and Woodruff, G. (1978) Does the chimpanzee have a theory of mind? *Behav. Brain Sci.* 4: 515–26.

44 Gallup, G. G. (1975) Towards an operational definition of self-awareness. In R. H. Tuttle (ed.), *Socio-ecology and Psychology of Primates*. The Hague: Mouton.

45 Altman, I. (1979) Privacy as an interpersonal boundary process. In M. von Cranach, K. Foppa, W. Lepenies and D. Ploog (eds), *Human Ethology, Claims and Limits of a New Discipline*. Cambridge: Cambridge Univ. Press.

46 Guntrip, H. (1983) *Schizoid Phenomena, Object Relations and the Self*. London: Hogarth.

47 Dawkins, M. (1980) *Animal Suffering: The Science of Animal Welfare*. London: Chapman & Hall.

48 Uexküll, J. von (1909) *Umwelt und Innenwelt der Tiere*. Berlin: Springer-Verlag.

Part 5

Problems:
What is Mind?

Despite our forays into psychiatry and anthropology, into the inner workings of nerve cells and the bizarre notions of quantum physics, into computers, cognition and animal communication, the question remains, what is mind? *We have been told how it might benefit animals and man, how it might have emerged during evolution and how it could develop in social groups and individuals. But what is it?*

The stimulus for this book was the hope that modern brain research, hugely productive as it has been, might now be in a position to explain mind, intention and consciousness in functional terms, or at least to offer hope of an experimental attack on this subject. We thought that it would be timely to bring together philosophers and scientists to compare notes and see how closely their ideas have converged.

In this final section of the book we look at the gap between the two worlds of test tubes and tautologies, of syllogisms and scintillation counters. Is the gulf between them too wide to be bridged; do the two worlds lie at such different levels that bridge-building is impossible; or might it even be the case that, like alcohol to the Redskins, or the common cold to the Eskimos, contact with strangers and new ideas isn't always a good thing?

Ed Hundert, a neurologist, starts on a positive note by asking how advances in the scientific study of the brain can contribute to philosophy's attempt to understand the mind. He points out the similarity between Immanuel Kant's ideas about the nature of human experience and present knowledge of the structure and organization of sensory pathways in the brain. Nevertheless he warns that the distinct vocabularies and technologies of philosophy and neuroscience often prevent the insights of one field from contributing to the other. This problem is likely to become more urgent as advances in brain research begin to define the neural basis of cognitive processes.

Paul Seabright, economist and philosopher, looks at the relationship the other way round and wonders how philosophy can help scientists to understand the mind. In the disparate approaches of philosophy and science he analyses the fundamental tension between the concept of the mind as we experience it and the nature of mind as viewed through the eyes of an inquisitive scientist. He attempts to relax the tension of conflicting concepts by analogies with the relationship between levels of description in many other fields. Just as the style or school of a painting belongs to all of its physical parts yet is not a property of any single dab of pigment, so conscience or memory could be a property of widely distributed activity in the brain without there being any such thing as a 'neuron of guilt' or a 'remembering cell'. This approach still leaves unexplained the phenomenon of conscious awareness. A painting doesn't need to know *that it is an impressionist work in order for this higher-order property to emerge. Why then are the emergent functions of the human brain – perception, emotion, intention and so on – embraced by awareness?*

Philosopher Ted Honderich looks critically at the gamut of approaches to the philosophy of mind. Some axioms, he argues, are secure: mentality, described in terms of subject and object, does indeed exist; the concept of the mental and of persons he finds indispensable. These axioms, combined with the functional perspective of brain research that he calls 'psychophysical intimacy', limit us to certain pictures of the mind. He raises doubts in turn about identity theories and the dualism of the self-conscious mind. Even a more acceptable determinist theory, of psychophysical nomic connection faces a damaging if not fatal objection from quantum theory.

Jeffrey Gray, psychologist, also casts doubts on mind–brain identity theory. Even in the sophisticated form advanced by John Searle it tends to prevent the asking of scientifically relevant and important questions about the necessary features of the processes to which consciousness is linked and about its survival value in Darwinian terms. The common view that identity theory (mind states are identical to brain states) is preferable to dualism on scientific grounds may not be valid.

Finally, neuroscience and psychology are castigated for their misleading use of language by philosopher Peter Hacker and scholar of comparative linguistics Roy Harris. Hacker finds a deep conceptual confusion in talk of the brain 'receiving information from the senses, decoding and interpreting it', of the brain 'containing maps, representations and models of the world that are expressed in a neural language or code'. Such terminology may be a fruitful metaphor, but if it is taken literally it is, he argues, a misdescription of important empirical discoveries, based on unclarity about the concepts of a language and a code of convention, information and communication, of maps and representations. He sees such misuse of concepts as an example of the widespread homunculus fallacy, criticized by Ludwig Wittgenstein, namely the attribution to parts of a creature (in particular to its brain), of predicates that only make sense in application to the whole creature. Such confusions, Hacker says, lead scientists to misrepresent their results, to ask questions that make no sense, and to the mystification of nature.

Roy Harris takes not only brain researchers but also many philosophers and linguists to task for the fashionable view that the grammatical structure of human language must be matched by a 'grammar-in-the-head'. Harris rejects this hypothesis: far from having any explanatory value, it is born of both terminological and conceptual confusion.

If anything constructive emerges from these two final chapters and from the doubts, caveats and contradictions in this book, it is the recognition that neuroscience cannot crack the nut of the mind by sheer weight of scientific effort. What must come first is the establishment of predicates and axioms, the definition of where the nut is, what kind of nut it is and how the cracking should be planned. What we can surely all agree on is that discovering the nature of mind, the kernel of the nut, is the richest prize for brain research, psychology and philosophy.

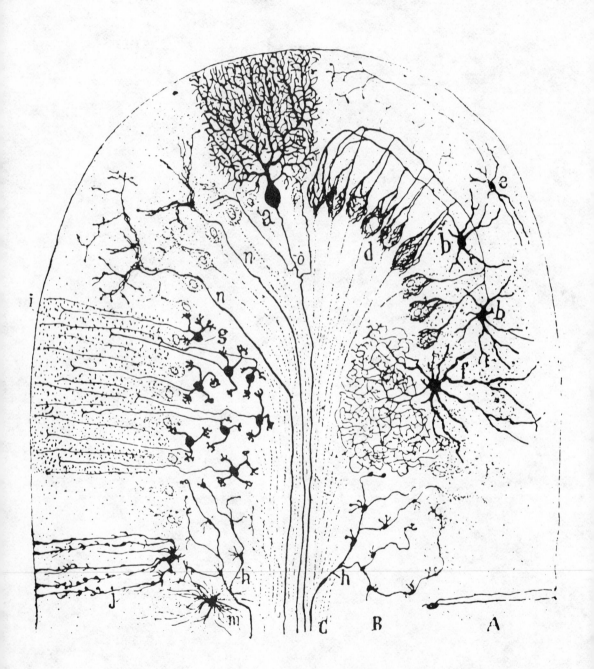

27

Can Neuroscience Contribute
to Philosophy?

Edward Hundert

Edward M. Hundert holds degrees in mathematics and the history of science from Yale University, in philosophy, politics and economics from Oxford University, and in medicine from Harvard Medical School. He has been the recipient of numerous academic honours and prizes, including Yale's R. H. Chittenden Prize for highest standing in mathematics and the natural sciences, the G. Batterby Prize for highest First Class Honours while at Hertford College, Oxford (which he attended on a G. C. Marshall Scholarship), Harvard's S. Sanger Prize for research in psychiatry, and the R. Sleyster Scholarship of the American Medical Association for outstanding scholarship in psychiatry. He is a psychiatrist at McLean Hospital in Belmont, Massachusetts, a lecturer on medical ethics at Harvard Medical School, and is currently working on a major book entitled Philosophy, Psychiatry, and Neuroscience – Three Approaches to the Mind. *Dr Hundert's contribution is based on chapter 7 of that book, soon to be published by Oxford University Press, whose kind permission to reprint it in this volume is gratefully acknowledged.*

In addressing the interdisciplinary task of exploring common ground between neuroscience, cognitive and behavioural science, and philosophy, the essays in this collection seem to be more concerned with how philosophy might contribute to the sciences than vice versa. This is understandable. Philosophy, concerned as it is with such amorphous questions as 'What constitutes a good argument', sounds at least initially like the sort of discipline that *might* contribute to any other field at all. (Some philosophers would say 'to any other field worth studying'.) The reverse question which interests me, however, sounds at least initially like a *non sequitur*, even in its most general form: 'Can neuroscience contribute to philosophy?' This problem is only made worse when we get more specific and ask, for example, 'Can all the years neurophysiologists like Colin Blakemore have spent putting microelectrodes into cats and monkeys to record impulses from nerve cells possibly shed some fresh light on the sort of research Immanuel Kant was up to when he wrote *The*

The tangle of cells and fibres that makes up the brain. This drawing, published in 1911 by the great Spanish neuroanatomist, Santiago Ramón y Cajal, shows a section through the cerebellum, a region of the brain involved in the control of movement. The tissue has been stained by the Golgi method, which causes intense staining of a tiny fraction of all the nerve cells and fibres. What can the knowledge of the structure and function of the brain contribute to the philosophy of mind?

Critique of Pure Reason?' In spite of such initial reservations, I think it is only fair to begin a discussion whose title is a question by providing the answer up front. My goal in this case is to demonstrate that the answer to the question is: 'Yes – under one condition.'

This 'one condition' sounds much easier to fulfil than it actually is. The condition is that we agree to remain open-minded enough to view neuroscience and philosophy as two *perspectives*, so that when the two tell us different things about how the mind works, we can view them not as two competing points of fact, but as two differing points of view. You would like to think (or at least I would like to think) that the human mind is complex enough that *any* given description or explanation of it would *always* be taken as a perspective – as a point of view rather than as a point of fact. Yet, philosophers and neuroscientists (and psychologists who have yet a third perspective) all treat one another as if the others were *wrong* about something! And by insisting that they are all perspectives, I am not saying that any given description or explanation cannot be wrong, only that none is truly complete, however accurate it might be.

The best way (or perhaps the only way) to demonstrate how these diverse disciplines can be viewed as two 'perspectives' – and how a synthesis of the two can enable one to contribute to the other – is by providing an example, and I shall therefore provide one as follows. First, I shall introduce one of the most basic problems of philosophy. Then I shall introduce (what for philosophers will be a grossly oversimplified account of) one of this problem's most famous solutions: namely, Kant's solution in *The Critique of Pure Reason* (1781). Then, using the field of artificial intelligence as a bridge over to neuroscience, I shall introduce (what for neuroscientists will be a grossly oversimplified account of) some basic neuroanatomy and neurophysiology that just might shed some fresh light on Kant's solution to the original problem – if we are willing to let it.

The philosophical problem I have chosen is the very basic question of where all of the various properties come from which we attribute to the objects of our experience. We all think of objects in the world as having many properties. We think of objects as having shapes and colours, odours and temperatures, motion or rest, etc. We think of objects as substances which persist through time, which obey various laws of nature, and which can influence one another through various causal mechanisms. We think of objects as existing in the dimensions of space and time. We also think of some objects as especially beautiful or valuable and others as hideous or unpleasant. And so forth.

Particularly since Descartes, philosophers have always been quick to point out the fairly obvious distinction that must be made between physical objects (or 'things') and our experiences of those objects (or 'thoughts'). Even a moment's reflection informs us about this distinction between 'things' and 'thoughts', 'things' being physical objects which are meant to exist somehow 'out there' in the world, while 'thoughts' (which is to say our experiences of those objects) happen in our own minds and result from an *interaction between the physical objects and ourselves*. This is especially easy to see in the case of optical illusions. A consideration of the Müller–Lyer arrows (figure 27.2) reminds us of the difference between the properties we assign the two lines as they are 'out there on the page' (by hypothesis, equal length) and our experience of them (one appearing longer) which arises from an interaction between the physical objects 'out there on the page' and ourselves.

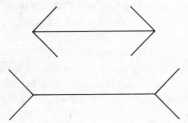

Figure 27.2   The Müller-Lyer illusion.

Since *all* of our experiences of objects arise from such an interaction between ourselves and external objects, a basic question immediately arises: of the many properties we attribute to the objects of our experience (that is, shape, colour, motion, substance, causation, space, time, beauty, etc.), which are really properties of those external objects, and which really arise from properties of ourselves?

Many answers have been given to this basic philosophical question. Bishop Berkeley suggested that *all* of the properties come from us. John Locke suggested that we should use the science of physics to distinguish 'primary' qualities such as shape (which objects would be assigned in and of themselves) from 'secondary' qualities such as colour (which arise from our interaction with the objects). Locke's suggestion is especially interesting here since he first suggested the contribution that science (in his case, physics) might make to this philosophical problem.[1]

Kant's Model of the Mind

As mentioned above, I would like to discuss yet a third answer: that of Immanuel Kant.[2] Kant's 'apportionment' of properties between physical objects and ourselves was so incredibly ingenious that to this day a lot of philosophers spend a lot of their time trying to figure out exactly what it was he actually meant! Kant's answer (on at least one interpretation of what he meant) was that what there is 'out there' supplies only the crudest sense-data, such as shapes, colours, texture, etc., while *we* supply the properties of substance, causation, time, space, and so on. Furthermore, Kant emphasized, as no one before him had, that *nothing* can ever enter our experience without acquiring these characteristics which *we* bring to our experience. Thus, says Kant, it is *meaningless* to speak about knowledge of objects existing outside of space or time because our mind constructs all of our experience spatially and temporally.

In keeping with this creative 'apportionment' of properties, Kant's model of the mind is divided into two departments, or Faculties: Sensibility and Understanding. The Faculty of Sensibility is the relatively passive faculty whose job it is to collect the raw sense-data from the world. It then becomes the job of the more active Faculty of Understanding to organize those data into our experience of the world. One conception of this model is shown in figure 27.3 where Sensibility is drawn in circles receiving the raw sense-data (shapes, sounds, etc.) from the world; and Understanding is drawn in crosses as a grid which is thrown over those data, organizing it according to the properties (substance, causation, etc.) which we bring to our experience. (I have intentionally left out the dimensions of space and time for now, but will return to them below.)

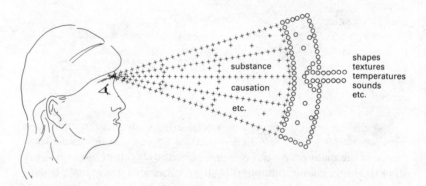

Figure 27.3   Kant's model of the mind.

It is important to see this model against the background of Kant's larger project. Kant takes as his starting-point experience as we all know we have it. He says, in effect, 'We all know what experience is like', and asks: 'What must be true about the workings of these faculties, grids, and so forth in order for experience to end up that way?'

In answering this question, Kant was actually a bit vague about the detailed workings of Sensibility (for example, he never attempts to generate a minimally sufficient list of raw inputs needed to produce the sort of experience we all have). But he saw as one of his greatest contributions to philosophy the generation of a minimally sufficient list of concepts which must be used by Understanding to produce the sort of experience we all have. As drawn in figure 27.3, Kant's 'grid' was composed of twelve of these concepts (the so-called Categories of Understanding), which he naturally saw as an important step toward specifying the 'necessary conditions' of human experience. Unfortunately for Kant, philosophers have long since discarded his particular list of twelve, and in fact the whole 'faculty approach' to the mind has been out of philosophical favour for many years.

Fodor's Model of the Mind

Recently, however, the 'faculty approach' has been making a come-back. As Jerry Fodor explains in his recent book, *The Modularity of Mind*,[3] this revival is partly due to developments in the field known as artificial intelligence, which approaches questions about the mind by analysing actual or conceptual computer models of the brain. Fodor's thesis is especially interesting in light of the above discussion, since his 'project' is really very similar to Kant's. That is, Fodor says, in effect, 'We all know what experience is like', and asks: 'What sort of functional architecture would a computer need if it were to be a good model for a brain capable of having that sort of experience?'

Some of the features such a computer would need are obvious. If, like us, the computer is to be aware of what is going on around it, it would obviously need a set of transducers capable of converting external stimuli into a form of information the computer could handle. (These transducers would do the job done for our brains by our retinas *vis-à-vis* visual stimuli, our inner ears *vis-à-vis* auditory stimuli, etc.) Equally obviously, if the computer is going to model our mind, it will need some very fancy central processing systems which can manipulate the information it gets in all sorts of interesting ways, remembering information, believing it, expecting it, ignoring it, etc.

But (and this is not so obvious) Fodor argues that in order to be a really good model of our mind, our computer would need – in addition to transducers and central processing systems – a functionally distinct set of *input analysers* which take the information coming from the transducers and process that information into a different form: the form which is then used by the central processors. Since each of these input systems analyses only one type of input (for example, visual information, auditory information, etc.), we might draw Fodor's model of the mind as indicated in figure 27.4.

In this figure Fodor's 'central systems' are drawn in crosses, 'input systems' are drawn in circles, with the star at the bottom of each representing its transducer. I shall not review here all of the evidence Fodor offers to support this model, except to comment on a few features which I have built into my diagram. (The ideas I am presenting here come

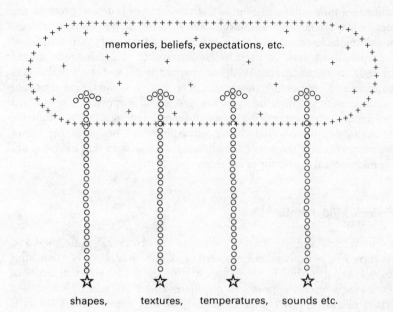

Figure 27.4   Fodor's model of the mind.

from Fodor's book, but figure 27.4 does not: it is merely my vision of Fodor's model.) In addition to being 'domain-specific' (that is, processing only one type of information), input systems are 'informationally encapsulated'. Informational encapsulation means that each input system analyses its input in ignorance of what is going on in all of the other input systems and, more importantly, in ignorance of what is going on in the central systems. (This is why most of each 'circular' input arrow is drawn outside the 'crossed' central systems in figure 27.4.) There is a lot of evidence that the 'upward' processing of information in input systems takes place in ignorance of the information available to central systems, but perhaps the most straightforward is the persistence of optical illusions. One of the most striking things about figure 27.2 is that the Müller–Lyer arrows continue to look unequal in length even when we have measured them – indeed, even when we know that the whole point is that the percept is an illusion. Being an ignorant input system, our visual input system analyses the lines as unequal and presents them to us that way even when *we* know they are not.

The other side of the fact that input systems analyse their input in isolation of central systems is that central systems have access only to 'higher' levels of already-processed input. Central system access to input representations diminishes as we move downward in figure 27.4, with virtually no direct access to the representations being processed nearest the transducers. (If all of the representations emanating from our retinas 'took' higher up, we would all know a lot more trivia than we do!)

Central systems, in contrast to input systems, obviously cannot be informationally encapsulated if they are going to do their job. Indeed, for central systems, the more crossing of informational domains, the better. This is why central systems are represented as a horizontal faculty, whereas input systems are represented as vertical. As Fodor explains, this model can be translated into psychological terms as endorsing a functional distinction between 'perception' (input analysis) and 'cognition' (central processing). That is, although we often use these terms ambiguously, 'perception' considered as input analysis should not properly be considered a species of 'thought'.

It is easy to see the evolutionary advantage of this whole scheme, with its 'upward' input analysis: if our transducers were hooked directly to our central systems, we would spend most of our time seeing (hearing, etc.) the world the way we remember, believe, or expect the world to be. The recognition of novelty – of *unexpected* stimuli – has extremely obvious evolutionary advantage, and is made possible only by the separation of transducers and central systems by 'dumb' input analysers.

A Synthesis of Perspectives

Thus far I have been discussing some of Kant's ideas and some of Fodor's ideas. I would now like to discuss a few of my own. My suggestion is that we view Kant's model and Fodor's model as two *perspectives* in the way I have tried to make obvious by my 'circles and crosses' scheme. That is, I suggest we explore what might be gained by thinking of Kant's Faculty of Sensibility in terms of Fodor's input systems and Kant's Faculty of Understanding in terms of Fodor's central systems. What makes these two so complementary as perspectives is that Kant seems to have been a bit vague about how his input systems work, but went into great detail about the functional architecture of his central systems; while Fodor does the opposite, providing much more detail on the input system side. (In fact, Fodor offers an explanation for why he provides more detail on the input system side, which I shall return to shortly.)

Two structural modifications of Kant's model are suggested by this synthesis. First, the amorphous 'input arrow' of figure 27.3 should be broken into a number of distinct arrows better to reflect the domain-specificity and informational encapsulation of input systems. Second, and more important, although Fodor's model endorses and emphasizes the functional distinction between input systems and central systems, his model also demonstrates the overlap of the two: a 'grey zone' (or in this case, a zone of circled crosses) blurring the boundary of Sensibility and Understanding (figure 27.5). This zone of overlap reminds us that central systems *do* have some access to higher-level input representations, so that presumably input systems are no longer informationally encapsulated at these higher levels. Fodor's 'modularity' is, as Fodor himself stresses, a matter of degree.

This blurred boundary between input systems and central systems is crucial inasmuch as it accounts for a certain degree of feedback in the system. Such feedback is well illustrated by the example of 'blind spots'. Patients with tumours on their optic nerves can lose surprisingly large fractions of their visual fields without becoming aware of a 'hole' in their world. Presumably, their central systems correctly assume that the world

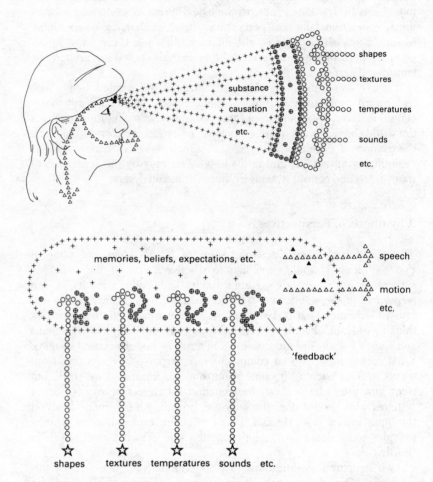

Figure 27.5   Synthesis of models.

does not have such holes and fill in the visual input at higher levels of processing by assuming (usually correctly) that the world is fairly redundant (see box 'Blind Spots in a Redundant World'). Such a feedback mechanism would also account for the lack of subjective awareness we all have of our own physiological blind spots. (This sort of feedback has led some people to suggest that 'downward' rather than 'upward' input analysis is the rule, but the weight of current evidence is in favour of Fodor's model.)

It is tempting to think that Kant was sensitive to this blurred boundary between Sensibility and Understanding. Many a commentator has discussed what Kant may or may not have meant by always emphasizing that Understanding can only do its synthetic work with the inspiration and assistance of its 'first lieutenant', The Faculty of Imagination. Kant made it clear that he did not mean imagination in the usual creative sense, and it is tempting to take him to be referring to just this sort of 'filling in of blind spots' left by Sensibility. But let me set aside such matters of historical speculation and turn to yet a third model of the mind – the neuroscientist's model.

Figure 27.6

Blind Spots in a Redundant World

There are no receptor cells (Fodorian 'transducers') on the retina at the spot where all the nerve fibres come together and leave the eyeball as the 'optic nerve', and so we all have a blind spot on each eye where no sensory input is collected. Using figure 27.6 you can locate your own blind spot, and also demonstrate how a pattern is 'filled in' or 'completed' across the blind spot. Close your left eye and look at the dot-circle, holding the book about ten inches in front of your eyes. Adjust the distance until the x-circle disappears. Does this blind spot leave a 'hole' in the chequered background or does it appear continuous? The fact that the pattern appears continuous when the x-circle disappears is a demonstration of the idea that central systems use an assumption that the world is fairly redundant (and free of 'holes') as they fill in such holes at higher levels of processing. Now repeat the procedure, closing your right eye and looking at the x-circle. The figure demonstrates the relatively small physiological blind spots we all have. A similar demonstration could be done, however, by a patient with a relatively large blind spot, say because of an optic nerve tumour. Although half the actual input may be lost, the pattern would still appear continuous and the individual would still have no subjective awareness of a 'hole' in his world. (adapted from Mussen, Rosenzweig *et al.*)[4]

A Neuroscientist's Model of the Mind

One of the more interesting things about Kant's and Fodor's models of the mind as I have interpreted them is that the brain works more or less in the way they describe. Although I am not interested in a complete and exhaustive account of the brain according to this scheme, I offer in figure 27.7 a crude conception of the brain in terms of the models discussed above. In this 'neuroscientist's model of the mind', each of the primary sensory areas is drawn in circles as an 'input system'. The areas drawn in crosses again represent 'central systems', here covering the regions of the brain susggestively known as the 'association cortex'. Just how many circled crosses should be put between the two is a bit arbitrary, but since each sensory region is divided, loosely speaking, into 'primary', 'second-ary' and 'tertiary' areas, I have chosen to label the secondary areas as zones of 'overlap', so that the tertiary areas are to be considered already part of 'Understanding'. (I have labelled these regions for the visual sensory area: a similar scheme could be shown for each of the others.)

In moving on to the brain, we are also forced to remember that we humans have, in addition to input systems and central systems, a set of what might be called 'output systems'. These output systems are often lumped together as 'motor systems', but might usefully be divided into a few discrete systems for movement, speech, and a few others. These were shown in figure 27.5 in triangles (along with overlapping areas of crosses in triangles where their boundary with central systems is blurred in analogous fashion to input systems). They complete figure 27.7's account of (the left side of) the human brain.

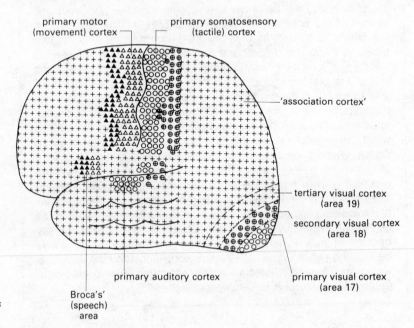

Figure 27.7 A neuroscientist's model of the mind.

Microscopic Anatomy of the Human Cortex

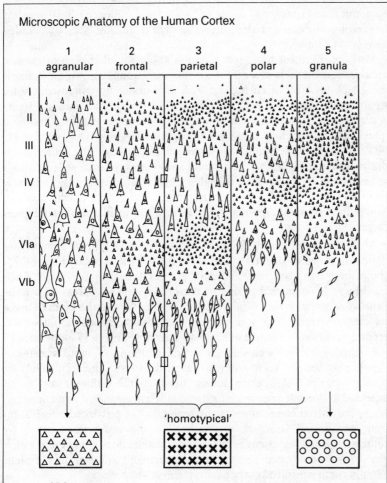

Figure 27.8

Over most of its surface, the human cortex can be divided into six layers according to the distribution of cells and fibres. Based on the varying pattern of smaller and larger cells found in each layer in different parts of the brain, Economo[5] identified five fundamental types of cortex: 1. agranular, 2. frontal, 3. parietal, 4. polar, and 5. granular (figure 27.8). Granular cortex, containing only smaller ('granular') cells, is characteristic of primary sensory areas of the brain, just as agranular cortex, containing only larger cells, is characteristic of motor output areas. Frontal, parietal and polar types all contain varying layers of smaller and larger cells and are sometimes called collectively 'homotypical' cortex. This representation of photomicrographs of each type of cortex is adopted from Carpenter and Sutin.[6] It demonstrates the allocation of cortical regions in figures 27.7 and 27.9.

This conception of the brain is supported by two sorts of evidence: anatomical and functional. Since the anatomical evidence is relatively less interesting to discuss, I shall dispense with it quickly (see box, 'Added Levels of Complexity').

Perhaps the most basic way to think about the allocation of cortical areas in figure 27.7 is in terms of the microscopic anatomy of the brain. If you pluck off a bit of cortex and look at it under the microscope after treatment to stain the cells, the cortex can be divided into six layers according to the distribution of cells and fibres no matter where you 'pluck' from. Which of these layers contains large cells vs. small cells, however, depends very much on where you pluck. Basically, figure 27.7 is drawn in circles wherever you would see relatively small cells in all six layers ('granular cortex'), in triangles wherever you would see relatively large cells in all six layers ('agranular cortex'), and in crosses wherever you would find various alternating layers of large and small cells ('homotypical cortex').

Much more intuitive anatomical evidence for this scheme comes from the connections of our 'transducers' to these various areas. Figure 27.9 shows how our eyes, ears and skin are connected to the brain. Each transducer is connected to one of the primary sensory areas by a well-defined neural pathway. (I have drawn the eyes behind the brain to make the diagram neater. The optic nerves, tracts and radiations run under and around the brain to connect our retinas in front with area 17 at the back.)

Having noted the well-defined neural pathways of input systems, I should note too the sharp contrast this provides with the architecture of central systems. In Fodor's terms, fixed neural pathways are to be expected in domain-specific, informationally-encapsulated input systems, where hardwired connections facilitate the flow of privileged information from one neural structure to another. In the association cortex, by contrast, the neuroanatomy is diffuse, with connections going every which way – as we would again expect from a department where any sub-system might want to consult any other sub-system at any time.

(I should digress here to note that it is this anatomical point which Fodor uses to explain why his scheme gives us more detail about the workings of input systems than central systems. A correspondence between form and function is to some extent a prerequisite for successful neuropsychological research. The presence of this form–function correspondence in input systems explains why neuroscientists have made most of their advances in the 'circled' regions of the brain. The apparent absence of such a form–function correspondence in the association cortex gives rise to Fodor's pessimism about how much we will *ever* know about the detailed workings of the 'crossed' regions of the brain. I am actually a bit less pessimistic than Fodor on this point. This is probably because the division of the brain into parts with known anatomy and parts with unknown anatomy also divides it into the areas cared for by neurologists and the areas cared for by psychiatrists when things start to go wrong! Viewed in this way, research on the crossed regions can take many forms Fodor might not have considered. But now I digress too far.)

My final anatomical point is that the microscopic anatomy of the cortex provides evidence not only for the identification of systems according to

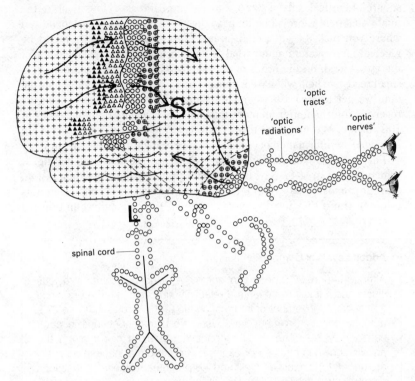

Figure 27.9 The neuroscientist's model with transducers and hierarchy of information flow added.

our previous models, but also for the hierarchy of information flow built into those models. That is, although almost all areas that are connected together have *reciprocal* connections (that is, in both directions), there is an asymmetry between 'feedforward' and 'feedback' directions as to which cortical layers these connections are sent to and from. As we would expect, the 'feedforward' direction (shown by heavy arrows in figure 27.9) moves from primary to secondary to tertiary areas in the sensory regions, but from tertiary to secondary to primary areas in the motor region.[7] But enough of the anatomy lesson.

The more interesting evidence for this scheme comes from functional considerations. The most obvious of these functional considerations is what happens if you stimulate these different areas of someone's brain with an electrode and ask them what they are experiencing. What you find is that stimulation of 'circular', primary sensory areas (for example, area 17 in the case of vision) produces the experience of very simple hallucinations (points or lines of flickering light, whorls of colour, etc.); whereas stimulation of 'crossed', tertiary areas (for example, area 19) produces the experience of complex hallucinations (formed, complex visual images). (It almost goes without saying that flashes of light send people to neurologists, while formed, complex hallucinations send them to psychiatrists!)

Some of the most convincing evidence for our 'hierarchical scheme' comes from the notion of 'receptive fields', which increase in size as we move along the heavy arrows in figure 27.9. That is, if we randomly pick a square of cortical cells of size 1 mm × 1 mm and ask 'How much of the total visual field is providing input to these cells?', the answer depends on where you pick the square. In area 17, that square of cells would be receiving information about what is happening in a very small sector of the visual field: on the order of one degree (1°) of arc in diameter. This small receptive field will have increased by two orders of magnitude by the time we get to area 19, where the same size square of cells would be receiving information from more than half the visual field: on the order of 100° of arc. We may take this as strong evidence that more and more *integration* of information occurs as we move along these heavy arrows.

The effects of various lesions on experience are also illuminating. If someone loses area 17 (say, because of a tumour), they lose their vision; they go almost totally blind (see Larry Weiskrantz's chapter in this volume). But if they just lose areas 18 and 19, they manifest an unusual

---

Added Levels of Complexity

Although figure 27.9 begins to look more complicated than previous illustrations, it still represents a relatively simplistic picture of mental functioning. Movement of information along the arrows in figure 27.9 actually occurs via many interposed cellular connections in each sensory system. The cellular connections which occur along the arrows shown in circles (for example, from the eye back to area 17) are understood relatively well, and it is presumably these connections along the way which help account for the *analysis* in input analysis. (Inputs are modified via these cellular connections into a form which can be used in 'central processing'.) The detailed anatomy of the heavy arrows shown over the cortex in figure 27.9 is understood relatively less well, but is currently an exciting field of discovery. Van Essen and Maunsell discuss twelve separate visual areas in the macaque monkey, for example, with some 33 pathways interlinking them.[8] This added complexity has thus far supported the model discussed here, since the hierarchy of visual areas begins at 'VI' (area 17) and proceeds forward toward the temporal, parietal and frontal lobes, with receptive fields increasing at each of the 6 hierarchical levels into which Van Essen and Maunsell divide their 12 visual areas. Van Essen and Maunsell also note the existence of 'projections from areas 18 and 19 back to 17',[9] helping to explain the presumed mechanism by which blind spots are filled in, as demonstrated above and as represented by 'feedback' arrows in figure 27.5. (They also discuss in some detail the distinct functional anatomy of motion analysis and form and colour analysis in the visual input system, supporting the concept of Modules as anatomically defined inputs which are used by the brain to synthesize a complete experience of the world – see below.) For even further levels of complexity, see also the review of object vision and spatial vision by Mishkin, Ungerleider and Macko,[10] who also report the discovery of multiple distinct 'multisynaptic corticocortical pathways' in the monkey's visual system, but again using a language which supports Fodor's functional distinction between input systems and central systems.[11]

condition called visual agnosia. In this condition, visual acuity is normal (the person could correctly identify the orientation of the 'E's' on an eye chart). But they lose the ability to identify, name or match even simple objects in any part of their visual field. In Fodor's terms we might think of this disconnection of input and central systems as a separation of 'cognition' from 'perception' – which is why 'perception' thought of in this way cannot properly be considered a species of 'thinking'.

Having divided the brain into input, central and output systems according to anatomical and functional evidence, the last point I would like to make in this regard has to do with how much of the brain has been allocated to each. If we divided up the brains of various animals according to the scheme of figure 27.9, we would find that man has the largest area of crosses as compared to circles plus triangles. And in fact this fraction would get smaller as we went down the evolutionary scale in sequence (figure 27.10). I am not sure that I would put much faith in this whole project if this were not true, and I get great relief knowing that it is.

Building Bridges Between Models

Now that the neuroscientist's model of the mind has been described in the same terms as our previous models, we are in a position to see what this model might contribute to the others. To begin with, since 'input systems' are anatomically defined, we can now tell how many input systems there are. Our naive answer might have been that there are five input systems corresponding to the 'five senses', but this would be a very low estimate. We know, for example, that 'taste' is really the product of four taste inputs, detecting sweet, bitter, salt and acid, plus further important input from olfaction. In figures 27.3, 27.4 and 27.5 I listed separate inputs for temperature and texture (rather than 'touch') for similar anatomical reasons: each has a separate pathway to the brain. (In fact, temperature runs up the front of our spinal cord while texture runs up the back. Thus, a lesion (say, a tumour) at location 'L' on figure 27.9 would cause a person to lose temperature sensation below the level of the lesion. That person would, however, still be able to tell that he was being touched with a piece of cotton wool, for example.)

Some of the most exciting neuroscience research of the past 20 years has centred on the uncovering of the basic input systems which make up vision. Thus far, neuroscientists have identified anatomically distinct systems of neurons in area 17 selectively sensitive to the properties of shape (that is, orientation), size, direction of movement, colour and depth (that is, binocular disparity). Although scientists have not yet identified all of our basic 'building-blocks of perception', I shall refer to these anatomically defined properties as Modules (to follow the idea of Fodor's 'modularity thesis'). Modules, then, would include such properties as 'sweet' rather than 'taste', 'temperature' rather than 'touch', and 'colour' (or 'motion', or . . .) rather than 'vision'. As Fodor suggests,[3] 50 might be a better guess than five for the total, but only time will tell.

This neuroscience perspective on Fodor's model complicates his input systems a bit. We no longer have one transducer per input system, but a

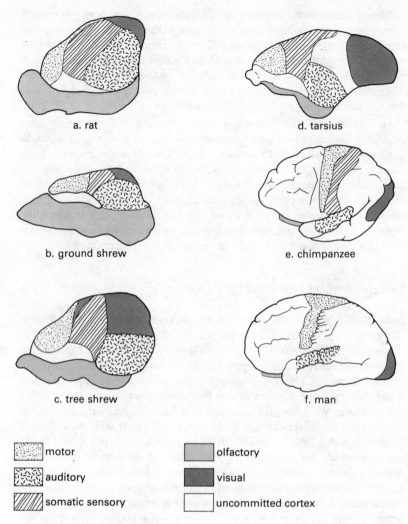

Figure 27.10   *The traditional view of the progressive increase, during mammalian evolution, in the amount of the cerebral cortex 'uncommitted' to a specific sensory or motor function (shown white in these diagrams). In fact, recent research suggests that much of the 'uncommitted' cortex is occupied by additional sensory and motor regions, which increase in number up the evolutionary scale. For instance, in monkeys about half or more of the cerebral cortex consists of an array of visual areas, each of which may be concerned with analysis of a particular aspect of the visual stimulus, such as colour, movement, distance, etc. (redrawn from original illustrations by Stanley Cobb in* The Purposive Brain *by Ragnar Granit, 1977, MIT Press.*

set of parallel inputs which all arise from the same transducer. Thus figure 27.11 shows that visual input is not broken into the Modules found in area 17 until long after that input has left the retina. One interesting thing about this new twist is that, from a 'naive realist's' perspective (and a scientist's perspective), the visual information as represented in area 17 'looks' even less like the world than does the representation of that information on the retina (which at least preserves the two-dimensional configuration of the pattern of shapes it analyses – even if upside-down and mirror-reversed!). But presumably this dissection of the information by the input systems pays off by enabling our central systems to use this abstracted information in constructing a representation of the world which is very accurate indeed. (As noted above, the accuracy of this ultimate construction presumably provided these systems with their evolutionary edge.)

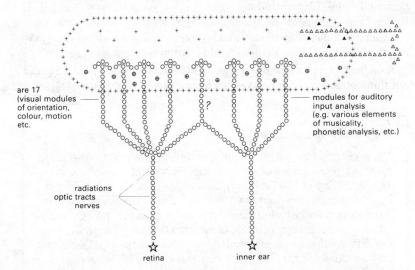

are 17
(visual modules
of orientation,
colour, motion
etc.

modules for auditory
input analysis
(e.g. various elements
of musicality,
phonetic analysis, etc.)

radiations
optic tracts
nerves

retina   inner ear

Figure 27.11   Fodor's model reconstruction in the light of the neuroscientist's model.

Input systems, then, hardly constitute a 'passive' faculty. In fact, input systems are continually organizing and analysing their inputs to ever greater degrees as they approach our central systems. Thus, even if we had no evidence for 'feedback' at high levels of input analysis, we could have deduced the fact that there is no sharp boundary between input systems and central systems: at their highest levels, input systems are doing so much work to get information into the form central systems, 'then' organize, that it becomes arbitrary whether or not we decide to designate that work as the central system organizing itself.

A Contribution to Philosophy

Having dealt briefly with the above contributions which the neuroscientist's model can make to Fodor's model, I shall now turn at last to the point of all of this: the contribution of neuroscience to philosophy. We saw above the contributions Fodor's model could make to Kant's model by thinking about Sensibility in terms of input systems and Understanding in terms of central systems. The question of how many Modules there are in total also carries over to Kant's model. We must leave to the neuroscientists the task of determining the complete list of Modules: a very different task from Kant's attempt to determine the complete list of Categories! Thus, although these scientists' work will affect our ultimate 'apportionment' of properties between Sensibility and Understanding, there is little more that can be said about that side of the problem right now (except, perhaps, *support research*!).

Although I think that the above synthesis of perspectives can contribute to any number of problems in philosophy (see box 'The Problem of Language'), I should like to stick with the 'apportionment of properties' problem here and discuss the question of dimensionality. I noted originally that I left out space and time when I drew Kant's model and I can now explain why. The reason is that, within Kant's own framework of Sensibility and Understanding, this analysis suggests a rethinking of Kant's 'apportionment' of space and time. I shall therefore focus my remaining comments on dimensionality to exemplify the sort of contribution to philosophy I have in mind for this 'synthesis of perspectives'.

Kant 'apportioned' space and time to the Faculty of Sensibility. He did not think of space and time as items of raw sense-data, however. Rather

---

The Problem of Language

The problem of language is another problem to which the proposed synthesis might contribute. Fodor spends a good deal of energy in *The Modularity of Mind* showing why language ought to be (counterintuitively) considered an input system.[3] I shall not review here his arguments demonstrating how language shares each of the properties which characterize all input systems (domain-specificity, informational encapsulation, hardwiring, etc.). But one reason this claim is counterintuitive is that language can 'get in' through more than one sensory modality (we can hear it or read it). I do not think that this is a problem, so long as we remember that 'domain-specificity' refers to Modules, not sensory modalities. If Fodor is right, language is an input system which crosses sensory modalities. This possibility is shown as a '?' in figure 27.11.

I actually find Fodor's arguments convincing, but will complicate matters by pointing out that language is also an output system (we also speak and write it). And furthermore, in the abstract sense in which philosophers discuss language, any symbolic representational system which transfers information is a 'language'. We must therefore also confront the 'language' of central systems in the sense in which artificial intelligence theorists refer to 'machine language'. My point here is that language is unique in having input, central, and output system roles; but these are three *different* roles. I think that much of the confusion in contemporary analytical philosophy results from a failure to recognize this tripartite function of language *in its three different guises*. (An example of this confusion is seen when philosophers dismiss Fodor's claim about the input system role of language by saying that language cannot be informationally encapsulated: after all, we can talk about other input systems and about central systems. These philosophers confuse the issue even as they make their point since they take evidence from language in its central and output system roles to rebut a claim made about its separate input system role!) Recognition of the tripartite nature of language, suggested by the above considerations, can clarify a great deal in the philosophy of language. It constitutes an important example of how our synthesis of perspectives can 'contribute to philosophy'.

than being 'sensible intuitions' like shapes, colours, etc., space and time are called the 'forms of sensible intuitions' by Kant. Kant's Sensibility is thus not entirely passive: whatever data are received by Sensibility are received by it in the 'form' of spatial and temporal arrays *of* shapes, textures, sounds, etc. (From the neuroscientist's perspective, we might think of this claim as reminding us that the patterns of shape and colour represented on the retina already have spatial and temporal relationships.) Our experience of the world as spatial and temporal thereby comes to us, according to Kant, via the good offices of Sensibility.

If we are willing to see our three models as three perspectives of a single subject (rather than three models of three unrelated subjects), we have reason to rethink Kant's claim about dimensionality and Sensibility. While it is true that the data come to us in a certain order in space and time, we have seen that Sensibility's job is in fact to abstract the data from that form and reorganize it into a form better suited to the synthetic work of Understanding. In fact there is good evidence that our experience of the world as spatial and temporal is a product of the labours of Understanding: the central processing systems of our association cortex.

Although we know very little about the functional anatomy of the association cortex (for reasons discussed by Fodor and mentioned above), we do know that the spatiality of our experience happens somewhere in the inferior parietal lobe, which I have marked with an 'S' in figure 27.9. (This is actually the ideal spot, situated between inputs about how the world feels and how the world looks, as the heavy arrows indicate.) Thus, if patients develop a tumour at spot 'S', their visual acuity is fine (from area 17) and they can identify, match, and name objects (connections through areas 18 and 19), but they cannot locate objects in space. The most dramatic examples of this are patients with the syndrome known as 'hemispatial neglect' (figure 27.12). These people have lost their right inferior parietal lobe and are completely unaware of the left side of their world – including their own left arm! (As I mentioned above, now that we know a little bit about the anatomy, people who begin ignoring half of their spatial world – say, only retaining interest in the right half and ignoring the left half – are no longer considered 'crazy': they are sent to a neurologist, not a psychiatrist. Unfortunately, we have had less success in identifying the functional anatomy of time, so if people begin ignoring half of their temporal world – say, only retaining interest in the past and ignoring the future – they are called 'psychotically depressed' and sent to a sympathetic psychiatrist!)

The important point is that when we use the neuroscience model to rethink the Kantian model, we have reason to remove the properties of space and time from Sensibility and give them over to Understanding. That is, staying with Kant's own project of starting with experience as we know we have it and asking what the workings of the mind must be like for experience to end up that way, neuroscience can inform us about the workings of Sensibility and Understanding in helping us sort out 'where the various properties of our experience come from'.

Of course, Kant would not be very happy with all of this. He conceived of his project as a purely conceptual one (which is why he derived his Categories from a logic table) and his 'apportionment' had many huge

*Figure 27.12   An example of
'hemispatial neglect'. The
drawing on the right was
performed by a patient who was
asked to copy the examiner's
drawing shown on the left (from
Heilman, Watson and
Valenstein[13] reproduced by
permission of Oxford University
Press, Inc.).*

burdens to bear: Kant's entire theory of mathematics and much of his
moral theory rested upon the assignment of space and time to Sensibility.
What I am suggesting, in contrast, is the synthesis of a bit of factual
analysis and a bit of conceptual analysis. (In fact, I would suggest another
important contribution from the field of psychology and epistemological
analysis, but have confined myself here to 'neuroscience and philosophy'.)
This is not to say that a purely conceptual philosophical approach is
invalid; it is only to suggest that a synthesis of approaches has something
to offer as well.

Kant himself would feel no need to respond to claims made by
neuroscientists or psychologists about how our brains or minds actually
work. Kant was much more interested than I am with the question 'What
exactly is philosophy?', and this concern led him severely to limit his field
to the 'demonstration of a priori truths'. It was this bias that enabled Kant
to say that it is a philosophical matter that beings need Sensibility to have
experience, but that it is not a philosophical matter which precise sense-
data they need (the latter being a contingent matter and hence a subject
for psychologists and other scientists – not philosophers).

Kant would, however, feel the need to respond to a request for a
justification of his distinction between 'forms of sensible intuitions' and
'Categories of Understanding'. In fact, his justifications would be based
on just those parts of his philosophy (his theory of geometry and its
associated doctrine of the transcendental subjectivity of space, his
'deduction' of the Categories from basic elements of logic, certain aspects
of his moral theory, etc.) that have been the most heavily criticized by
philosophers over the past hundred years. There are, that is, independent
philosophical reasons to consider reapportioning space and time to the
Faculty of Understanding (not to mention additional support from
psychology), but, again, I shall limit myself here to the 'contributions of
neuroscience'.

Perhaps the contribution from neuroscience to philosophy I am
suggesting would become clearer by comparison with John Locke's
proposal that we look to the science of physics to contribute to the same
problem.[1] The most important difference is that the present scheme is

concerned with apportioning only properties *of our experience*. Locke's scheme is often read as a proposal for dividing all of the properties which we deem objects to have. The question thus arises: 'Is *mass* a primary or secondary quality?' Since mass is a property physicists attribute to matter but one which we do not *experience* when we experience objects, the question does not arise as to whether mass is a Module of Sensibility or a Category of Understanding. (At the risk of upsetting philosophical purists, I shall continue to use Kant's term for the properties Understanding brings to experience. Context will always tell whose sort of Category is being discussed.)

Neuroscientists must concern themselves with physics, of course, in considering how photons interact with the retina to produce colours, etc. But physics is only secondary in this scheme. Thus, when it is determined that temperature is nothing but motion (the motion of small particles), Locke must decide whether to eliminate a property from his list of primary qualities. The neuroscientist, however, does not change his list of Modules; temperature may *be* motion on a different scale, but our input systems treat motion and temperature as totally different kinds of input.

The biggest advantage our synthesis offers over Locke's suggestion is that, in the present scheme, appearance at least sometimes (in fact most times) actually does reflect reality! Locke's is certainly a coherent way of dividing up properties, but at the expense of appearance *never* reflecting reality (which makes the whole project slightly uninteresting). Objects, for example, never 'have' colour in reality in Locke's scheme, but always appear coloured. Perhaps I am just optimistic, but if there is one feature I would like an 'apportionment' to have it is that appearance and reality at least have a chance of coinciding!

A Few Words of Caution

I have tried to make a case for the contribution neuroscience can make to philosophy by taking one example in which neuroscience might contribute to what one philosopher said about one philosophical problem. It would not be honest to conclude without asking whether there is anything special about Kant that enabled us to achieve such a synthesis. Indeed there are some special features of Kant's philosophy which made this synthesis possible, and so I would like to identify a few of these as a way of limiting my optimism for the contribution of neuroscience to 'philosophy' in general.

First, although Kant saw his philosophy as a reaction against empiricism, he began his story by considering things like 'sense-data' – an interest shared by scientists and psychologists alike. If, in contrast, his starting-point was a concern for radical subjective freedom, there would be less common ground upon which to build a synthesis of perspectives. I am less optimistic about the contribution neuroscience might make to Kierkegaard or Nietzsche than about its contribution to Kant.

Second, Kantian philosophy is Western philosophy, which shares with science some very basic logical constraints. Like scientists, Kant takes for granted, for example, that opposites contradict one another and cannot both be true. Such a common logical framework is a prerequisite to a synthesis of perspectives. I am therefore less optimistic about the contribution neuroscience might make to certain Eastern philosophies, which take for granted the existence in this world of the continuing contradictions of Yin and Yang, etc.

Finally, I should note that in developing a synthesis of the 'neuroscientist's model of the mind' and Kant's 'model of the mind', I have separated Kant's 'model' from the rest of his metaphysical theory. I do not intend to argue here for the coherence and integrity of this separation. I would like to note, however, an interesting difference between my approach and P. F. Strawson's in his essay on Kant, *The Bounds of Sense*.[14] Strawson also separates Kant's model from Kant's metaphysical theory. But Strawson's project is precisely to reconstruct the metaphysical theory in isolation from the model; whereas I have been doing the opposite – working to reconstruct the model in isolation from the theory.

At some points, Strawson suggests that a reconstruction of the model might be 'an interesting project in the philosophy of mind'. But elsewhere he accuses the model of being no more than a bit of 'speculative psychology'. In this mode, Strawson seems to be claiming to be addressing himself to Kant's 'philosophy', leaving the 'model' to the field of psychology. (And hardly anyone denies the contribution neuroscience can make to psychology in this day and age.)

This is perhaps a final cause for pessimism – the claim of the philosophical purist who blindly accepts Kant's definition of philosophy (above) and, though he might find a synthesis of perspectives interesting, would also say that it is not philosophy at all. I think this is a coherent and consistent position, but a rather sterile one. I cannot see a justification for denying potential contributions of psychology and neuroscience to our understanding of the mechanisms which make human experience possible as we explore the philosophical questions concerning the necessary conditions of that experience. My example of space and time as aspects of Kant's 'model' which would be 'reconstructed' in the light of neuroscience was chosen precisely because so many metaphysical issues depend upon them. The burden of proof surely rests with those who would claim that this has nothing to do with philosophy.

Notes and References

1 Locke himself did not really think in terms of science 'contributing' to philosophy. He simply took for granted that physicists are the ones who describe the world as it 'really' is, leaving philosophy in the very subordinate position of making what it could out of the world science offers it. Although I am limiting myself here to the contributions of a science to philosophy, I see the two existing in much more of a reciprocal relationship than did Locke. See John Locke (1690) *An Essay Concerning Human Understanding*. Reprinted with introduction and glossary by Peter H. Nidditch (1975) Oxford: Clarendon Press.

2 Kant, Immanuel (1781) *Critique of Pure Reason*. Reprinted in English translation by J. M. Mieklejohn (1934) London: Dent.

3 Fodor, Jerry A. (1983) *The Modularity of Mind*. Cambridge, Mass.: MIT Press.

4 Mussen, P., Rosenzweig, M. R. *et al.* (1977) *Psychology*, colour figure 8. Lexington, Mass.: D. C. Heath.

5 Economo, C. F. V. (1929) *The Cytoarchitectonics of the Human Cerebral Cortex.* London: Oxford Medical Publications.

6 Carpenter, M. and Sutin, J. (1983) *Human Neuroanatomy*, 8th edn., p. 654. Baltimore: Williams & Wilkins.

7 In the forward direction, most (at least 85–90 per cent) of the projections arise from superficial layers of the cortex and terminate in layer IV. (This is called 'forward' by similarity with the pathways coming *from* the retinas *to* area 17, where the pathways terminate preferentially in layer IV.) In the 'feedback' direction, projections arise from both superficial and deep layers and terminate preferentially outside layer IV, mostly in layers I and/or VI. See Van Essen and Maunsell,[8] especially pp. 371–2, for more detail.

8 Van Essen, D. C. and Maunsell, J. H. R. (1983) Hierarchical organization and function streams in the visual cortex. *Trends Neurosci.* 63: 370–5.

9 Ibid., p. 371.

10 Mishkin, M., Ungerleider, L. G. and Macko, K. A. (1983) Object vision and spatial vision: two cortical pathways. *Trends Neurosci.* 64: 414–17.

11 Mishkin, Ungerleider and Macko (ibid., pp. 416–17) summarize, 'A major question posed by the present analysis is how object information and spatial information, initially carried together in [the pathway which projects to area 17] but then analysed separately in . . . two [distinct] cortical visual pathways, are eventually reintegrated.' They suggest that such reintegration may well occur in the 'limbic system and frontal lobe', where memories and emotions are thought to reside. This language can be understood as a neuroanatomical tour of figure 27.11, where information ascends the vertical input systems which separate it into Modules to be reintegrated in the horizontal central systems where memories and expectations are found.

12 Granit, Ragnar (1977) *The Purposive Brain*, p. 57. Cambridge Mass.: MIT Press.

13 Heilman, K. M., Watson, R. T. and Valenstein, E. (1985) Neglect and related disorders. Chapter 10 of Heilman and Valenstein (eds), *Clinical Neuropsychology*, p. 246. Oxford: Oxford Univ. Press.

14 Strawson, P. F. (1966) *The Bounds of Sense.* London: Methuen.

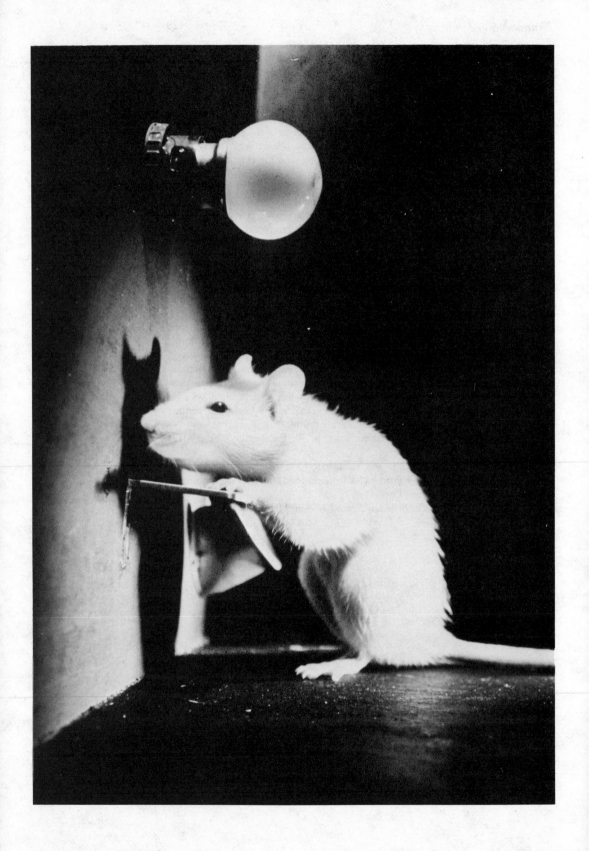

28

The Order of the Mind

Paul Seabright

Paul Seabright graduated from New College, Oxford in Philosophy, Politics and Economics in 1980, since when he has been a Fellow of All Souls College, Oxford. After considering a career as a philosopher, he decided instead to concentrate on economics. He has retained a strong interest in current developments in philosophy, and has written on these and other themes in a variety of publications.

Shortly after delivering the lecture on which this chapter is based, he began a stay of fifteen months in South India, investigating attitudes towards risk among rural communities.

How can we reconcile the understanding that scientists have in their capacity as investigators of the world with the subjective, colourful and insistent reality we continue to experience as human beings? The sense that there is a tension between these two perspectives is one of the most ancient sources of anxiety in the whole history of man's attempts to think, and the problem it poses is one that may never be solved. But philosophy in its consoling role works less by solving problems than by inducing us to stop worrying about them (just as in its irritant role it rarely poses new questions, preferring to panic us into reconsidering old and dormant ones). The compulsion to loiter around impenetrable intellectual thickets has a long history, which is the only excuse I can offer for retreading this much-explored ground.[1]

This essay is intended as a companion to Edward Hundert's, which shows how scientific advances in psychology and neuroscience can contribute to the understanding of the mind attempted by philosophy. My brief is the reverse: how can philosophy contribute to the scientist's understanding of the mind? The answer I shall develop is of philosophy as a discipline that soothes rather than solves, but is no less important and constructive for that. Specifically, I want to consider three forms commonly taken by the general tension just referred to: the tension, that is, between the human mind we explore with the tools of science and that which we experience as a part of living. It is a tension that often leads us to question the reality of one or other of these two perspectives, giving an odd sense of dislocation, as though we were reading a pedestrian biography of a very dear friend. These three forms of tension are particularly real to scientists, but many laymen have been troubled by them at some time. They can be described as the problem of conflicting

A rat in a Skinner box, taught to press the lever when the light turns on (photograph by Mike Salisbury).

laws, the problem of conflicting descriptions, and the problem of conflicting claims about what exists (or ontologies, as these are sometimes called). I shall discuss a way of viewing mental phenomena that helps to relax these tensions, not solving them so much as relocating the fundamental tension elsewhere, at a point where it more properly belongs and where we can more easily come to terms with it.

The Three Tensions

The first tension is caused by the problem of conflicting laws. Psychology, both as an academic discipline and as an art of everyday living, involves our appealing to certain (often crude) generalizations about the way people and animals behave. 'He cancelled the appointment because he was afraid that we were angry with him.' 'The rat pressed the lever because it had been given food for doing so in the past.' In each case such explanations appeal to an assumed background of reliable generalizations, such as that both people and rats tend to seek out rewards and avoid unpleasant experiences. (The controversial question of whether these must be viewed as strict laws need not trouble us here.) The progress of psychology depends on our being able to refine and improve such generalizations. But the problem is that we and our brains are also subject to the laws of physics, laws that do not admit of arbitrary exceptions and whose scientific investigation has yielded spectacular predictive results. If physical laws ultimately determine our movements as physical bodies in space, it seems to follow that any psychological generalizations we make either contradict physical law and so have to be discarded, or predict the same as physical law and are therefore redundant. If physical law determines whether your body will come to my office at 11 o'clock tomorrow, there seems to be no scope left for your psychology in determining whether or not you keep the appointment. Progress in psychology has been slow and messy; has it all been a waste of effort?

It is worth remarking as an aside that there is no comfort to be derived here from the fact that quantum physics is not strictly deterministic (see Roger Penrose's chapter in this volume). Apart from the fact that subatomic indeterminism is compatible with a fairly rigid near-determinism on a slightly larger scale, quantum indeterminacy is governed by statistical laws. These require every undetermined event to be strictly random (given certain parameters determined by physical law). Strict randomness is no more compatible with psychological law (or intentional choice, for that matter) than with physical law. So whether the foundations of physics are ultimately deterministic or not makes no difference to the problem of conflicting laws.

The second tension is due to the problem of conflicting descriptions. When we describe what is going on at a certain moment in the life of an individual, say a poet at work, we can talk in terms of the thoughts or feelings which pass through his mind, or we can talk of the patterns of electrical and chemical activity taking place in the neurons in his brain. Many of us are inclined to believe two, apparently contradictory, things about the relation between these two kinds of description of the event.

Figure 28.1 A poet at work on a sonnet. Percy Bysshe Shelley (1797–1877). Are his writings more correctly described as the result of thoughts and feelings or of patterns of electrical and chemical activity in the neurons in his brain? (Mary Evans Picture Library).

On one hand, we feel that thoughts and feelings cannot be free-floating, as it were: if he were thinking different thoughts at that moment this would be reflected in a different pattern of activity in his brain. Likewise, if the activity in his brain at some moment of intense pain took a particular form, we believe it could not have taken exactly the same form but have represented a strong feeling of pleasure. This is sometimes expressed by saying that mental descriptions are 'supervenient' upon physical descriptions; for our purposes we can remember it with the help of the slogan:

No mental difference without a physical difference.

On the other hand, most of us also remain convinced that mental descriptions cannot be just reduced to, or translated into, physical descriptions. Take a particular mental activity such as 'thinking of England'. What might this involve? A host of different possibilities springs to mind: a mental picture of Big Ben, the memory of a snatch of Elgar, the murmuring of a line of Blake, an involuntary stiffening of the upper lip. When we think of the multitude of different kinds of brain activity that might accompany these, it seems almost inconceivable that we could ever come up with a set of rules for translating mental descriptions into physical descriptions. In part, of course, this is because a mental activity such as 'thinking of England' is only vaguely specified, and might include a great variety of activities even characterized in purely mental terms. But in part it is due to the very nature of the difference between mental and physical description. Consider a highly specific mental event, such as the thought that the square on the hypotenuse is equal to the sum of the squares on the other two sides. This thought might occur in the process of writing it out as a sentence. It might occur in the process of writing down a proof. It might occur in the process of speaking, or in reply to a question to which we formulate the answer 'yes'. There is no reason why the patterns of neural events that accompany these physical actions should have a common physical description. They don't need one: what unites them is the common role they play in the structure of our mathematical discourse. In the same way, what unites the various mental activities describable as 'thinking of England' is the role they play in our language. They might play a common role even without having a common pattern of the sort we could discern on an oscilloscope connected to microelectrodes in the brain (just as a bank manager and the front half of a pantomime horse may have a common role in a production of Cinderella without a more than passing physical resemblance). So in general it appears that any one kind of mental activity might be embodied in an infinite number of possible physical ways. Yet how can we reconcile this intuition with the apparently much closer view of the mental–physical relationship implied by the slogan above?

The third form of tension is caused by conflicting claims to existence. Many people, particularly practising scientists, believe everything that exists is a physical object. We might express this more graphically by saying that the physical world is everywhere; it has no pockets into which non-physical objects could fit. There is nowhere in the brain where the scientist's scalpel and electrodes cannot in principle reach. But most of us also think many things that exist are not *just* physical objects. A neuroscientist once put it to me this way: 'I can dissect and analyse any part of the brain I want to, and I can do so in an ever more detailed and sophisticated way. Yet it is frustrating to think that however hard I probe I cannot find where someone's conscience is, or their sense of humour.' Is this sense that a physical inventory of the universe will not tell us the whereabouts of everything we want to find just nostalgic obscurantism? Or does it mean that we are wrong to think that only physical objects exist?

It is worth remarking how closely these three tensions are related, despite the differences in the way they are expressed. After all, the reason we think the laws of physics govern everything in the world is that we think everything is a physical object. Conversely, our primary reason for thinking everything to be a physical object is precisely our discovery that the laws of physics seem to apply to everything in a regular way, without suspension. Likewise the close relationship between mental and physical descriptions is made plausible by the clear evidence that physical events cause mental events and can be caused by them; that is why we take aspirin for headaches. In fact, we can state the connection between the second and the third tension more precisely. The claim that there can be no difference in non-physical properties without a difference in physical properties has among its implications that there exists at most one non-physical object, because all objects with no physical properties are identical to each other. (This argument is said to have been used to demonstrate the superiority of monotheism over polytheism.) So the claim that everything is a physical object can be seen as slightly stronger than but very similar to that embodied in the slogan that preceded it.

A Way Out

What are we to make of these problems? There is a way of viewing mental phenomena that can certainly help to make the tensions I have discussed seem less acute. This will be a beneficial effect of any theory that takes mental properties to be higher-level, organizational or (as the jargon has it) 'functional' properties of physical objects called brains. Now I don't propose to defend any such theory as a comprehensive solution to all aspects of the so-called mind–body problem: I wouldn't know how to do that. I want only to discuss this one specific benefit that such theories can bring. The benefit arises in part because there are a number of other fields of understanding where we are familiar with the relationship between higher- and lower-level properties, and do not see it as posing any problem. The analogy with these fields may make the problem of the mind–brain relationship seem less acute in those areas where the analogy is apt. Where the analogy breaks down (as it certainly will somewhere) the problem will remain, but it may show a less alarming face.

What does it mean, then, to talk of some properties as being higher-level, organizational or functional properties? Two familiar examples are the way we talk about paintings, and about the activities of groups or

Figure 28.2 Chadlington Football Club, 1950. The men have a certain relationship to one another that would not be captured by simply listing their names (photograph courtesy Philip Pratley).

teams. Suppose I describe a painting as 'impressionist'; what I mean by the term is that the bits of paint on the canvas are arranged in a certain kind of way relative to one another, that its shapes and colours bear a certain relationship to each other, a relationship that would not be captured by my simply listing the different pigments, brushes and canvas the painter had used. Similarly, if I describe a group of men as making up some football team, I imply that their actions are related in certain ways, that these men have a certain relationship to one another that would not be captured by simply listing their names. The point of these analogies is to suggest that we may find it helpful to see certain mental properties – anxiety, optimism, anger, thoughts of all kinds – as corresponding not to properties of individual nerve cells, but rather to patterns and relationships among the events in the cells in the whole brain. Such a situation is familiar within science itself: chemical properties, for example, are properties not just of individual atoms but also of how they are arranged.[2]

Reconciling Laws

How does this help to resolve the three tensions? Take first the conflict of laws. At first sight this might look like the old problem of free will and determinism, but in fact it is really one of a clash between two kinds of law. Except in rare moods, I don't believe I understand what the free-will problem even is – but fortunately, whatever deep foundations our sceptical worries may shake, the practical threat that physical law poses to our habit of using psychological language (or the language of free choice) about the mind is negligible. The reason for this confidence has to do with the fact that even systems rigidly governed by physical law may prove forever impossible for physics to predict satisfactorily. At the turn of this century the French mathematician Hadamard proved a remarkable theorem. He distinguished two kinds of path along which a particle could travel: closed trajectories, in which particles remained always within a finite distance of their starting-points, and open trajectories, in which they travelled further and further away without limit. Think of a circle and a straight line in Euclidean space. What Hadamard showed was that in some systems, if a particle was set in motion along an open trajectory characterized by a certain velocity and a certain direction, it was always possible to find a closed trajectory which differed from the direction of the open one by as small an angle as one cared to specify. In other words, two particles setting out upon trajectories that differed to the tiniest imaginable degree could eventually end up indefinitely far apart. And however accurately one measured the initial trajectory of a particle, one

Figure 28.3 Open and closed trajectories. Hadamard's theorem considers whether the two paths could be distinguished at the start point, where the angle of divergence between open and closed trajectories becomes vanishingly small.

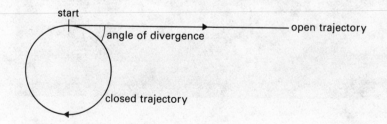

*Figure 28.4   Cartoon of a painting by Seurat. Studio cast-off or prize for a rich collector?
(reproduced courtesy of the National Gallery of Scotland).*

*Figure 28.5   Les Baigneurs by Seurat. Definitely not a studio cast-off. Flecks of paint in exactly
the right place are critical (reproduced courtesy of the Trustees of the National Gallery, London).*

would eventually make indefinitely large errors in predicting its movement.

Now it so happens that it is frequently the physical systems that are hardest to predict for these reasons, which can be most readily understood by means of higher-level or organizational principles. Take the example of a computer controlling a sophisticated piece of machinery like an aeroplane. An electric charge passing down one part of the circuit may make the aeroplane turn right. One passing down another part a tiny distance away may make the aeroplane turn left. If we tried to predict the movement of the aeroplane using physical laws alone, given the position and velocity of all its constituent subatomic particles, a tiny error in predicting the position of a few electrons could, by confusing a left with a right turn, lead to our mistaking the aeroplane's position by thousands of miles. So instead we use our understanding of the computer's functional or organizational structure – its software – to help us understand and predict the movement of the plane.

This is not to say that human brains just are computers, a claim that tends to be overdone nowadays. It merely explains how brains can share with computers the feature of being impossible to predict satisfactorily using merely physical law, so long as our measurements remain liable to error, as they forever will. The example of paintings may reinforce the point. Suppose an impressionist portrait is admired and bought by an American collector: if we tried to predict *that* by physical law we should have difficulty. For if a few flecks of paint in the eyes and nose had been a fraction of an inch to the left the effect of the painting might have been spoiled, and the painting have ended up among the studio cast-offs instead of in America: Thus initial conditions that are very hard to discriminate in physical terms may be much more distinct according to the categories of art appreciation – so predictions may always be more accurate when the laws on which they rely are cast in these higher-level terms (see box below). No one need worry that physics will ever make psychology obsolete.

Higher-level Conditions

It is often true that the vagueness of many high-level terms limits their usefulness in the formulation of predictive laws. Take a statement like 'When he is angry he bangs his fist on the table'. This is likely to be much more useful as a retrospective explanation of someone's behaviour than as a means of predicting it in advance. For when, exactly, is someone angry? When is he merely a little irritated? Terms like 'angry' usually cover a number of clear central cases, and an often larger number of uncertain or doubtful ones. (Our statement is best interpreted to mean something like: 'When he is angry he tends to bang his fist on the table, and the more unambiguously angry he is the more likely he is to do it.') So even if there were exact psychological laws, the vagueness of the vocabulary of psychology would limit our ability to know when they applied. Explaining the mind would be like trying to paint a landscape using only primary colours.

Reconciling Descriptions

What of the second tension – the conflict of descriptions? It was generated, remember, by two claims; first, that differences in mental states must be reflected in physical differences; and second, that mental descriptions are not just translatable into physical descriptions. The examples of paintings and teams can explain the point and compatibility of these two claims. Differences in style have to be reflected in physical differences: two physically identical paintings cannot be different in style. However, an impressionist painting is not composed of impressionist atoms and molecules; and it is virtually inconceivable that anyone could (even in principle) draw up rules stipulating when a painting was or was not impressionist purely in terms of the properties of its individual particles.

A different view from the functional one about mental states (namely Descartes's view that they are in some sense free-floating, only contingently related to states of the brain) has been claimed by Sir Karl Popper to be an inextricable part of common sense. Now it is always dangerous for philosophers to argue about what is and what isn't common sense (they often end up claiming a popular mandate for the most bizarre views). But I think I can claim the support of a great many television viewers for the approach advanced above. The programme *Star Trek*, like many science fiction fantasies, plays with the idea of a teletransporter that disintegrates people and transmits information about all the constituent particles to a receiver station, which reassembles them. Now when Mr Spock is beamed down to Mars, of the many accidents that might happen *en route*, the ones that worry us all consist in the failure of his body and brain to arrive. As far as I know, no one ever worries that Mr Spock's body and brain might arrive exactly as they left, but that his mind might somehow have got lost on the way. Yet if the audience were all neo-Cartesians, this thought should be keeping them on the edge of their seats. For there is no reason to think that an invention that could teletransport brains could also teletransport minds, unless minds were in some sense constituted by the higher-level properties of brains.

The Cartesian View

If we took the Cartesian view seriously, all kinds of activity that are quite harmless or even beneficial for our brains might be feared for their effect on our minds. Any new drug might snuff out mental activity altogether while leaving the brain unaffected, a thought that is all the more disturbing when we reflect that we should never know whether it did or not – because the behaviour of others who had already tried the drug might be quite unaffected and we might not know that they had lost their minds.

The thinking behind this is not at all mysterious. If a painting were being teletransported for an exhibition of impressionists on Mars, someone who told us that it had arrived physically exactly as it set out, but had become a cubist painting *en route*, would be met with justified scepticism. The same reaction would greet a football manager who claimed that though all his players had turned up for the final of the Milky Way Cup, his team had unaccountably failed to arrive. Yet none of this makes talk of teams reducible to talk of individuals. For a team to score a goal is not the same as for any one of eleven individuals to score a goal. A goal scored by a particular individual counts as a goal scored by the team only when the right conditions hold, such as that the individual concerned has been selected to play for the team, that he has not been fielded as a substitute for another team, and so on. Reference to the team may be an essential part of these conditions.

In the same way, talk of artistic styles or subjects is not reducible to talk of individual dabs of paint. A certain pigment may be characteristic of a particular style, but only when observed in conjunction with other stylistic traits. A dab of black paint may represent the pupil of one of the sitter's eyes, but only because of its relation to the rest of the paint on the canvas. The functional relations that determine the style or subject of a painting can in fact be very complex ones, referring even to things outside the painting itself. We may identify a Monet as a painting of the Japanese-style garden at Giverny; this is to identify a property of the painting, along with its physical properties. But suppose we discovered that the garden at Giverny contained no such view, which was rather to be found in a park in a neighbouring town? The painting would now have a different property, namely that of being a painting of the park. What would be different would be nothing about the physical qualities of the painting, but rather of the physical qualities of something else to which it was related. Philosophers have generated a surprising amount of heat arguing about how a thought can be dependent for its content on something outside the mind, while at the same time being embodied in a state of the brain. The problem becomes gratifyingly unmysterious when we use the analogy of painting – for the higher-level properties of brains which determine thoughts can be properties not simply of the brains considered in isolation from all other objects, but may include their relation with other objects in the world.

Reconciling Mental and Physical Objects

By now the solution to our third tension should have made itself clear. A team is not something that exists independently of its members. Although any one member may be unnecessary to the existence of the team, when someone asks us to point out the team, what we do is to point to its members. Likewise, a painting is a physical object. Its style is not something else, a non-physical object, that is mysteriously attached; it is a property of the object itself. Now some stylistic features of a painting may be very localized, as when we say that a portrait shows a sense of humour in its treatment of the sitter's eyes. So it may be that some mental phenomena (pain, for instance) are traceable to activity in highly localized areas of the brain. There *may* be a seat of the sense of humour. But for many phenomena that we are interested in (like conscience or memory) the trend of current neurophysiological research strongly suggests otherwise. This doesn't matter in the least: a conscience or a memory is no less real for being diffused over the brain rather than dug into a single corner. It would be an absurd prejudice to think that the only real properties of objects were physical properties – if we believed that, we should think molecules no less fictitious than memories. Whereas in fact – on the best of current evidence, I should say – memories no less than molecules are physical objects, part of the physical universe, but objects we are capable of recognizing under names other than physics gives them.

Remaining Puzzles

The briskness with which this conclusion has been reached should not mislead us. These analogies for the brain do break down. For instance, an important philosophical tradition emphasizes a privacy in mental experience: there are some features of mental life that only the subject itself can know. This is uncertain ground, but if such a claim is true there is no analogy for it in the case of paintings or teams. We cannot claim that seeing mental properties as functional properties of brains will solve the mind–body problem. What we can claim is that any solution is likely to involve seeing mental properties in such a way – and this is not a negligible advance, for it helps to dispose of the unnecessary tensions I have already discussed. What it leaves is the problem of consciousness: functional properties of brains ought to be specifiable objectively, so there seems no reason why the brain itself should have better access to them than an outside observer. How should we react to the possibility that a brain will always be able to perceive high-level functional patterns in its own activity that an outside observer cannot see? Would this be indicative of some deep non-empirical fact about 'what it is like' to be a certain individual? Or would it be merely a puzzling contingent fact that no amount of hand-waving, no appeals to the irreducibility of consciousness or the difference between syntax and semantics can explain? To date the two views are ranged against each other as opposing dogmas, for no one has given a justification (as opposed to a rousing affirmation) of either. The way the argument develops may well depend on our reaction to certain discoveries in artificial intelligence (what do we think of a computer that beats its programmer at chess, not because of a superior memory but because it has adopted rules of thumb for winning that are superior to any the programmer had devised? Does this indicate a perception of high-level patterns and relationships beyond the capacity of an outsider to see?)

I should not like to guess whether it will eventually seem reasonable to view the ability to perceive complex, unprogrammed similarities between patterns of organization as the effect of some underlying phenomenon called consciousness, or as the very stuff of consciousness itself. But as I have tried to show, philosophy can contribute to the science of the brain by pointing to abstract and complex analogies with other areas of discourse. There is no doubt that the activity of perceiving and developing complex similarities amid diversity, one which it shares with art and with imaginative science, is one of the very highest engagements of the human mind.

Notes

1 None of the important arguments, and not all of the examples in this essay, are original to me. To refer to all sources would be too intrusive in a general introductory article such as this one, but particular mention should be made of Jaegwon Kim's article 'Supervenience and nomological incommensurables'. *Am. Ph. Qu.* (1978).

2 Throughout this essay I write of physical properties as though they were clearly distinct from functional ones. But the more physics discovers about the divisibility of matter, the more physical properties turn out to be functional ones after all. There is no necessary reason why this process should halt: *all* properties may turn out to be functional ones relative to properties at some lower level.

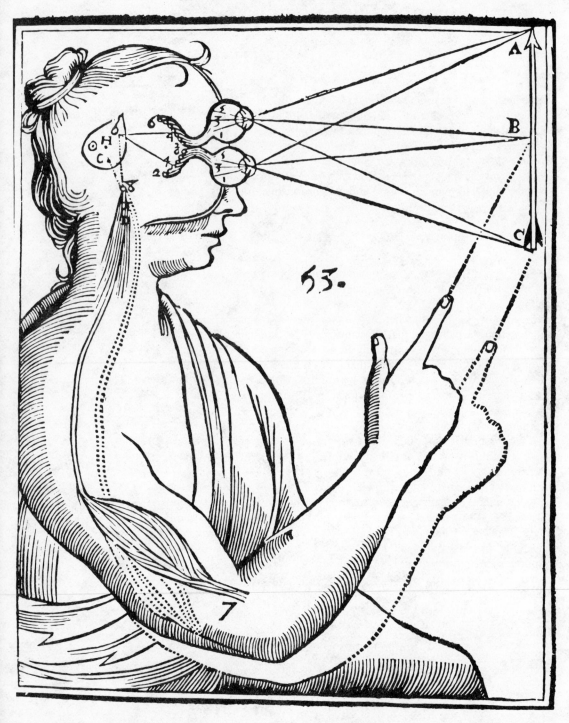

29

Mind, Brain and Self-conscious Mind

Ted Honderich

Ted Honderich is Professor of Philosophy at University College London. He is the author of Punishment: The Supposed Justifications *and* Violence for Equality: Inquiries in Political Philosophy, *and of philosophical articles on various subjects. He is also the editor of a number of books and the general editor of several series. His main interest, however, has changed from moral and political philosophy to the philosophy of mind. His forthcoming* A Theory of Determinism: The Minds, Neuroscience and Life-Hopes *defends three hypotheses about neural and mental events and their relations to other things, and contains a new and different resolution of the traditional problem of free will.*

Consciousness is elusive, and trying to think about it can make you unhappy. It is possible to feel *some* sympathy with Colin Blakemore, who with just a touch of querulousness asks a certain question. What, he asks, is the poor scientist to do when he is confronted with 'the rumour of a phenomenon – which is all that consciousness is'?[1] Still, consciousness *is* more than a rumour. We can readily agree, although we will worry later about the terms of the agreement, that there is a certain amount of it in me or anyway with respect to me as I write this, and so with you as you read it. There are, that is, two individual sequences of mental episodes – states, events, acts, and so on.

What is fundamental to consciousness, in so far as we can discern it, is what can be briskly described as *the interdependent existence of subject and object*. To think back on any mental state, event or act is to get into uncertain view two things which can be so named, and which seem to be such that neither could exist without the other. In many cases of mental episodes, such as beliefs and desires, the objects within them represent third things. In other cases, such as aches and some moods, they do not. I freely admit that these uses of the terms 'subject' and 'object' are something like metaphorical, and that they are not specific. I have recourse to them for want of better, and because they are needed. They convey the entirely ordinary ideas or perceptions of our consciousness which have issued in, among others, the speculative and disputable

The influence of the soul on the machinery of the brain, according to René Descartes, from the 1664 French edition of the Treatise of Man. *Descartes thought of the pineal gland (the pear shaped object in the middle of the head) as the interface between the soul and the brain. He suggested that it receives messages from the senses, for instance from the eyes in this diagram, by means of waves of vibration through the fluid in the chambers of the brain. In turn, by subtle movements and deflections, conveying the will of the mind, it influences the transmission of signals from the brain to the muscles.*

conception of consciousness of Franz Brentano, as activity which has reference to a content, or activity which is directed upon an object.[2]

Many contemporary philosophers, alarmed at the idea of metaphor and the like, hope to define consciousness in a related but wholly formal way – following Roderick Chisolm[3] – as that which is the subject-matter of a class of statements with certain logico-linguistic features. One such logico-linguistic feature is that the statement concerned is not made false by containing a description which applies to nothing. The logico-linguistic enterprise runs into the trouble of counter-examples, but, to my view, it was always hopeless. More precisely, there is no hope of characterizing the episodes of consciousness, of getting hold of their nature, by way of *only* the given logico-linguistic features of statements. Take the statement 'He wants a perfect wife'. There is no hope of characterizing consciousness by not worrying about what 'wants' means, and so on, and simply fastening on to only such facts as this, that the statement may remain true despite the non-existence of the object. The failure has many analogies. Suppose it were true, miraculously, that all and only the statements in English about that splendid species of tree, Turner's Oak, had certain grammatical properties, perhaps some unique structure in deep grammar. We would then in a sense have a definition of Turner's Oak: that alone which, when it is talked of in English, is talked of by way of sentences of a certain grammar. In virtue of having this knowledge we would have no characterization of Turner's Oak. It is proper to say that we would have no knowledge of the tree. So with consciousness, and the like enterprise.

There is not much more hope in following John Searle and attempting to characterize the nature of consciousness by way of the idea of an ordinary symbol, say a piece of English, and of what is symbolized.[4] The relation of symbolization, certainly, is like the relation between an object within consciousness – one of the two bits – and a represented third thing. But this is not a relation involved in all of consciousness, and certainly does not tell us *at all* about the fundamental subject–object relation. The *subject* is certainly not anything of the character of a *symbol*, let alone a symbol of the object.

This is not the time to see what better can be done with what we can all discern of consciousness, its fundamental subject–object nature. Rather, it is the time to assume, in my case to take as an axiom, that there *is* what has this fundamental character, whatever else may be true of it. *Consciousness, truly described by the metaphor of interdependent subject and object, does exist.*

To assume this is to part company from a number of schools and traditions. It is to abandon the view that consciousness is only behaviour: bodily movements. It is, however, a bit hard to abandon behaviourists, since those who can be abandoned need first to be found, and behaviourists appear to have gone to ground.[5] There may be one in Harvard, that other home of lost causes.

We do part company from more vigorous schools – Turing machine functionalism[6] and artificial intelligence,[7] or rather that part of artificial intelligence which offers a philosophy of mind. There is an argument from the premise that consciousness at bottom is subject and object, somehow conceived, to the conclusion that it cannot adequately be captured by what it is proper to call *merely abstract states* – Turing machine states or computer programs, as distinct from any instantiations of them. The argument, in part, is that the episodes of consciousness *do* have spatio-temporal location, and are thus distinct from abstract states. It may or may not be that programs, sets of rules which connect a propositional input with a propositional output, are a necessary condition of our ordinary intelligent carry-on. What *cannot* be true, given the perceivable character of consciousness, is that it is no more than a program, no matter the complexity or the external causal relations of whatever physical system instantiates it. With respect to Artificial Intelligence, there is also Searle's 'Chinese room' argument, repeated in his contribution to this book, which rests on a plain fact and is to my mind conclusive.[8]

We can be confident of the existence of consciousness characterized in the given way, and we can be as confident of a second thing. That each of us is where we are and doing what we are – on the assumption that we are more or less willing, and have been for a little while – is something whose explanation requires the mentioning of his or her prior conscious or mental episodes – states, events, acts, and so on. This is an instance of the efficacy or indispensability of the mental, the fact that mental episodes make a difference to certain physical facts about us: our actions and activities. Mental episodes also make a difference to many other later mental episodes. This is not only a view that there is *an* explanation of my action, or my desire, that includes a reference to an earlier mental episode. It is the view that *any* full explanation of an action, and of each of many mental episodes, has an essential part. The explanation has as an essential part an earlier mental episode, something with the subject–object character.

This is the axiom of *the indispensability of the mental*. Its recommendation, one can say, is the futility of contemplating its denial. It is futile to contemplate that even if we had quite different beliefs and desires than we had, or none at all, we would still be in the places where we now are. It is futile to suppose that there is a full explanation of action, or of such mental events as desires and intentions, which leaves out the earlier mental. It is fair to say that the denial in question, true epiphenomenalism, has been wandered into unawares by occasional philosophers and a few more neuroscientists. It has hardly ever been reflectively chosen as an account of the mind. Perhaps T. H. Huxley was the last to do so.[9] Off the page, no one believes it.

A third proposition about the mind has no less claim to the name of axiom. It is that in addition to a mental event, a *person* is an indispensable part of any full explanation of a human action, and of each of many human mental episodes. This is no soulful, spiritual or Wittgensteinian proposition. It derives from what is easy enough to say vaguely, that the explanation of your doing what you do necessarily includes a reference to the person you are. It is persuasive to say, certainly, that the occurrence of an identical desire in another person might well not be followed by the same things. An action is in part owed to standing dispositions, physical in character – which standing dispositions are fundamental to the identity of the person. There is then the axiom of *the indispensability of persons*: they too are needed to explain human actions and mental episodes.

It would be wonderfully impertinent of me to try to sum up neuroscience to those who are engaged in it, or to try to sum up that part of it which is relevant to our present concern, and which yields a fourth axiom. That is the part of neuroscience which has to do with what is sometimes called the interface between mind and brain. To speak differently, consider the sequence of facts beginning with a drop of rain on one's hand and ending with a conscious sensation. This part of neuroscience has to do with the relation between the last physical fact, whenever it is in relation to the conscious sensation, and the conscious sensation. Or, consider the sequence of facts beginning with an intention, and ending with the muscle movements which get the umbrella up. The presently relevant part of neuroscience has to do with the relation between the intention and the first physical fact, whenever it is.

Any adequate summary of this part of neuroscience, I am sure, must yield a certain conclusion. There is what can be called the intimacy of mind and brain, of mental and physical episodes – what we can call, a bit racily, *psycho-physical intimacy*. More precisely, there are three things in question: localization, co-occurrence, and the internal explanation of co-occurrence:

(1) Types of conscious or mental episodes stand in a certain relation to larger or smaller locales in the brain.
(2) Individual or token mental episodes occur simultaneously with individual neural events and processes in these locales. That is, there is co-occurrence.
(3) The explanation of co-occurrence is – so to speak – within itself.

Figure 29.1   The scientist Thomas Henry Huxley (1825–59), who chose epiphenomenalism as an account of the mind (Mary Evans Picture Library).

As may not need saying, the proposition about localization is not to the effect that every type of mental event stands in relation to a numbered bit of the brain, a single or simple area of tissue, or a single or simple neural structure. Further, the brain involves redundancy – what was associated with one part may come to be associated with another. For all of that, some recent work in neuroscience seems to have more in common than was expected with what is sometimes called the 'narrow localization' of the nineteenth century.[10] As may not need saying either, the second proposition does not assume the individual neural events and processes are in any way simple.

Neuroscience, as it seems to me, must change the philosophy of mind, and to a great extent it has already done so. It must do so, mainly because it establishes the axiom or proposition of psycho-physical intimacy. What is most important is the third element of that intimacy, having to do with the explanation of co-occurrence. It is of course unthinkable that this has no explanation. It is unthinkable that what we have is a mere parallelism, or a parallelism of which the only explanation is a divine one, a remarkably diligent God. What is different, and fundamental, is that neuroscience establishes that *there is a certain sort of explanation* of the co-occurrence of a mental and a neural event. That is, there is some explanation *in terms of the related events themselves*. Some substantial relation holding between a mental event and a certain simultaneous neural event is the explanation of their co-occurrence. There is no third thing needed.

The way in which neuroscience must change the philosophy of mind is therefore by limiting a range of options. It limits us to a choice between certain philosophical theories as to mind and brain, mental and physical events. We can only have theories in accord with psycho-physical intimacy. There are, I think, three of these theories, or three worth thinking about. Each, to speak metaphorically, is somehow to the effect that mental events are bound up with neural events – that it is no accident that a part or structure of my brain is exactly as it is when I think or feel exactly as I do. I shall look at these three possible theories, the first one very quickly, and then, to show generosity of spirit, give some time to what I take to be an impossible one.

One of the three possible theories, or rather families of theories, allows that some neural events *cause* simultaneous mental events, and some neural events are *caused by* simultaneous mental events. This messy proposal, if it is not unthinkable, is to be put aside for several reasons. One is that the second idea, that some brain events are caused by simultaneous mental events, involves us in the very unwinning idea of overdetermination. That is, we may be involved in trying to believe in the existence of *two* sufficient causes for each of myriad numbers of neural events. Each of these events surely has a sufficient wholly physical cause – this too is confirmed by neuroscience – and we are now to suppose that it has a second sufficient cause as well, a mental one. That is unpersuasive. So are variants of the view, which make mental episodes causally necessary rather than causally sufficient.

If we put aside this first family of pictures of the mind, we are left with this choice: either the mind *is* the brain, which is to say mental events *are* neural events, or the mind and the brain are *in a certain nomic connection*, which is to say that mental events are in this nomic connection with neural events.

The idea of nomic connection, sometimes called necessary or lawlike connection, although its analysis is a matter of philosophical dispute, is one of our two or three really fundamental ideas about reality. It is expressed in ordinary language in many ways – for example, by saying that since one particular thing happened, another *had* to happen, or if one thing happened, only one thing *could* happen after that. It is also expressed in the various mathematical formulations of scientific law. Nomic connections, at bottom, are of a number of kinds, one of them being causal connection, others not involving a causal side and an effect side – both sides, so to speak, are on a level. Two examples of the latter kind of nomic connection are provided by the interdependent variation of the pressure of a gas and its volume and temperature, according to the Boyle–Charles law for ideal gases, and the orbits of the two stars which make up a double star, which are held close together by mutual gravitational attraction. (I here pass by what cannot be discussed, the current idea that causal connection and presumably all nomic connection is itself probabilistic in nature. It is an idea dear to some of those whose first interest is probability theory, but to my mind is not well defended. For example, it does not follow from the fact that a cause, my striking the match, made probable its lighting, as we can all agree, that the striking plus other conditions did not make necessary the lighting.)[11]

The first thing to be said of the family of Identity Theories, which of course do need careful consideration, is that we need to be told what is meant by talk of identity. What is meant by saying that a certain *mental* event, say your wanting to scratch your ear a moment ago, which we can label ME_1 *was identical with* a certain complex *neural* event NE_1 in you, constituted by the firings of neurons of some system, the traffic of transmitter-substances and so on? We are told ME_1 was or was the same as NE_1, but what does that mean? Most Identity Theorists have not stopped to ask, and others have not stopped to think of the implications of their answer.

For various reasons, one of them having to do with the axiom of the indispensability of the mental, there seems to me only one usable answer, essentially the traditional one owed to Leibniz. It was his general view that to say one thing *is* another is to say that the first has *all and only the properties, parts, features, characters or whatever* of the second. We can speak a bit more carefully, and thus avoid that sentence's irritating suggestion that two things are one thing. To say that a thing named or described in one way *is* the thing named or described in another way – that is to say that what is named or described in the first way has all and only the properties and the like of what is named or described in the other way.

What we have, then, is that your wanting to scratch, mental event ME_1, had all and only the properties, parts, features, characters or whatever of a certain complex neural event, NE_1. As I have said elsewhere before now, a crucial question arises. *What* properties and the like were had by the mental event? There are two possible sorts of answer, very different.

One very natural one, to which we shall attend for a few moments, is that ME_1 had only the fundamental property of interdependent subject and object, together with related mental properties which are distinctive of wants, notably an attitude to a possibility. If the answer is natural, it nevertheless produces a disaster. Taken together with the proposition that in the given sense ME_1 *was* NE_1, the answer entails that NE_1, which we described as a neural event, had only *mental* properties and the like. Some perfectly respectable bits of the physical world located in your head are, one might say, *mentalized.* They are deprived of their physical properties. The philosophical doctrine of idealism, in part that *all* of what appears physical is mental or spiritual, here has a most curious descendant, what might be called *Local Idealism.* There is a related disaster if we start on the other side of the equation of the mental and the physical. What properties and the like did neural event NE_1 have? Suppose we say, naturally enough, that it had only physical properties. It follows that ME_1, which we described as a mental event, becomes wholly physical. What seemed a perfectly respectable bit of your conscious life, a want, comes to have had only the properties of action potentials, transmitter substances and the like. This, unlike Local Idealism, is perhaps a view that has found a philosopher or two to defend it, although that is uncertain. This materialism of the *Eliminative* or *Radical* or, as some might say, *Australian* sort, cannot detain us. It offends against the first axiom of the philosophy of mind: that there does exist the mental conceived in a certain way.

Certainly it is possible to give a very different answer to the questions about the properties and the like of ME_1 and NE_1. It is possible to give the *same* answer to each. What properties and the like did ME_1 have? *Both* mental and physical properties and the like. What of NE_1? *Both* mental and physical properties and the like. It is important to see what we now get. The fundamental proposition of the resulting Identity Theories is to the effect that mental event ME_1 was neural event NE_1 in the sense that there was one entity that had both physical and mental properties. This is certainly not the most natural understanding of the claim that one event *was* another, or *was identical with another*. But it is what we get if we avoid Local Idealism and Eliminative Materialism.

It seems to me that virtually all contemporary Identity Theories are of this form. They assert, somehow, that the mental and the neural are one thing in the sense that there is but one thing which has two fundamentally different sorts of properties. It is typically said, as by Donald Davidson about his Identity Theory, that there is a thing which *as physical* stands in some relation to something else, or which *under a physical description* stands in that relation.[12] However, the thing *as mental* or *under a mental description* does not stand in the given relation.

Searle's recent book (cf. his chapter in this book) is partly a defence of his somewhat different Identity Theory.[13] We have it that a thing at one level or at one level of description, the physical, stands in a certain relation to something else. But *at another level* or *another level of description*, it does not. Searle asserts, with respect to his one thing, that there can be causal relations holding between levels of it. That entails, of course, no matter how often it is said that there is but one *entity* in question, or that this is not a Dualism, or not a Bad Old Dualism, that there are *two of something*. I have spoken of properties, parts, features, characters or whatever, and I shall not try to be more precise. Hereafter, by the way, I shall simply speak of properties.

The conclusion that virtually all contemporary Identity Theories entail the existence of *two* of something is as true of those theories – such as Davidson's – which do not assert causal relations between levels of an entity. What *can* be meant by saying that some entity, *as* such-and-such, or *under one description*, is in some relation, while *as* such-and-such, or *under another description*, is not in that relation? All that can be meant, very evidently, is that the entity has two properties. The philosophical usages are in fact not far from certain ordinary usages which are to precisely the same effect. It is as something to keep out the draught that he wants the thing as the door, not as an object of beauty.

My present aim, however, is not to point out that virtually all contemporary Identity Theories misname themselves, as they do, despite the small fact that there is some reason for their name: that they do assert that what has two properties is one thing. My aim, rather, is to show that nothing whatever is gained by saying that it is one thing that has certain mental and physical properties, and that any account of the mind which comes to no more than this must fail. It must give way, in my view, to the account of the mind in terms of psycho-physical nomic connection. Davidson's Identity Theory, although I shall not discuss it here, provides an engrossing but salutary example.[14]

What we have, on these views, is that your wanting to scratch your ear, ME_1, was or was identical with the neural event NE_1. That means there was one thing which had both a mental and a physical property. Do we, in saying just that, allow for what we have taken as established by neuroscience, that the explanation of their co-occurrence is in themselves? It may well seem we do not. By way of distant analogy, that it is one thing, *a pear*, which is both yellow and hard, does not explain the co-occurrence of yellowness and hardness in the pear in terms of those properties. But leave that. There is something that can be settled more quickly.

Does saying, with respect to ME_1 and NE_1, that there was one thing which had both a mental and a physical property allow for the axiom of the indispensability of the mental? Suppose you didn't only want to but *did* scratch your ear. The axiom is to the effect that your want to do so is an essential part of any full explanation of your action. Is your want made into this by saying that *it was a property of a thing which also had a physical property*? Identity Theorists suppose so. Indeed, their desire to be true to the axiom is one root of their theories. They typically suppose, rightly, that an action is a sequence of physical events, say the moving of an arm – an *intended* physical sequence, of course, but still a physical sequence. They suppose too, partly as a result of neuroscience, that the physical sequence is in part caused by a neural event and in part by other physical events. They attempt to get the mental into the story in an essential way by *identifying* the neural event with, say, a want. Thus the want, they suppose, becomes an essential part of the explanation of the action.

They suppose wrongly. Your want does not become part of the explanation of your scratching in virtue of its being true that it is a property of what also has a neural property, which latter property is a cause of the scratching. By easy analogy, suppose a pear is yellow, and a half-pound in weight. When it is put on the scales, the pointer goes to the half-pound mark. Does the explanation of that latter event necessarily include the colour of the pear? It does not. Its yellowness does not become part of the explanation of the pointer-event in virtue of being a property of a thing which also has the property of being a half-pound in weight.

With the failure of these Identity Theories we come to the other alternative, the hypothesis that mental and physical events are in nomic connection or correlation. That, in my opinion, is the basic truth about the interface between the mental and the physical. To that hypothesis can be added two others. One, which I have made a mistake or two about in the past, has to do with the causation of the psycho-physical pairs.[15] The bare bones of the other is that each of our actions is the effect of a certain causal sequence involving such a psycho-physical pair. The latter two hypotheses, although I shall not look into the matter, seem to me strongly confirmed by neuroscience. The relevant parts of neuroscience, of course, are those having to do with neural traffic to the psycho-physical interface in the brain and away from it.

The three hypotheses seem to me very arguable, and indeed the best available philosophical theory of the mind. The theory is a *kind* of dualism and satisfies, I think, all the four axioms that have been mentioned, having to do with the existence of the mental properly conceived, mental indispensability, personal indispensability and psycho-physical intimacy. Having had a good deal to say of the theory elsewhere, I shall in this philosophical and scientific book only make some remarks, no doubt inflammatory ones, pertaining to the fact that it is indeed a *determinist* theory of the mind. The remarks, or reminders, will also introduce my last subject, which is the very, very different dualism – it *does* deserve the name – of Sir John Eccles and Sir Karl Popper.

Any determinist must be shaken by what is a popular interpretation of Quantum Theory, that there occur physical events such that it is physically possible that they might not have happened even though the world was just exactly as it was before their occurrence. In a fundamental sense, then, not having to do with probability, they have no explanation whatever. A determinist must be shaken, but it is possible for him not to be overwhelmed, for a number of reasons. If he is not too much a victim of consensus, which he need not be if he remembers the fate of scientific and like consensus in the past, he can think that the future may well go his way.

One reason for not being overwhelmed by Quantum Theory, in a relevant way, is that there is indeed a distinction between the theory, taken as several bodies of mathematics, and its interpretation or semantics, which is to say the nature of its application to reality. It is possible to have no competence with respect to the mathematics, but a view of interpretations. The latter have for good reason been a matter of controversy, including great controversy among physicists. How, exactly, are the referents of certain mathematical expressions to be conceived? Obviously the question is crucial to anyone concerned with more than the mathematics.

A second and related point has to do with a standard interpretation by physicists of Quantum Theory, indeed what is labelled the orthodox interpretation. It is not the plainer idea that there are undetermined and inexplicable events, in an ordinary sense of 'events'. It is, if a sentence can come near to catching it, that the theory is concerned with what can be called *observer-dependent* entities and properties. These include what are *called* particles, positions, momentums, and so on. Evidently, as has often been remarked by physicists, such terms as 'particle' are not used in any classical or ordinary sense. *How akin* are these items to – say – numbers and propositions? The latter, certainly, are not of the right logical category to be causes or effects, or to be the terms of any nomic connections. That one of the positive integers, in itself, causes nothing is not an effect, and is no nomic correlate, is no worry to any determinism – no more than a view of the positive integers is weakened by not applying to things that for logical reasons cannot be positive integers.

Thirdly, and disgracefully quickly, it is common to read that when the momentum, in a sense, of a particle, in a sense, is ascertained, the 'particle' lacks a 'position'. Not that it *has* a 'position' that cannot be ascertained, which incidentally would be no threat to determinism, but that it does not have a 'position'. It is unclear to me how *that* central conclusion can be taken to threaten determinism, as certainly it has been. Determinism does not include the proposition that what does not exist (a 'position') is caused to exist.

Fourthly, on the popular supposition that there are undetermined *events* at the level with which Quantum Theory is concerned, the microcosmic level, there is the matter of whether they give rise to indeterminism at the macrocosmic level, the level of things as we ordinarily know them, including neurons and their discriminable parts. There are different views on this. One is that there is no macrocosmic indeterminism – in which case the relevance of Quantum Theory to our concerns is at least obscure. Another view, my own, is that if Quantum Theory is as some take it to be, such as to establish the existence of undetermined events, there *should* be macrocosmic evidence. It is in very short supply. In fact, despite what is said of randomness and radioactive decay, it can be argued that none exists.

Fifthly, and above all, I find myself wholly on the side of a cast-iron proposition. From the fact that no causal circumstance or nomic correlate for an event has been discovered, it does not follow that there exists no such causal circumstance or nomic correlate. Most relevantly, from the fact that a theory admits of no such thing, it does not follow that there is no such thing. It is accepted, I note, even by physicists unsympathetic to determinism, that von Neumann's supposed proof to the contrary depends on Quantum Theory, and hence can be said to beg the question. Other such physicists are unpersuaded for other reasons.[16] John Bell is taken by some to have improved upon von Neumann.[17] I cannot believe that he has done much damage to the cast-iron proposition.

Finally, merely to mention the *bête noire* of some physicists, there do exist the rudiments of a deterministic physical theory – owed to de Broglie and Bohm.[18] It is of course to the effect that there are 'hidden variables', hidden causes and the like, which do explain supposedly undetermined events. It is not popular. But that, given the history of science, might unkindly be taken as not fatal.

To come round to doctrines of classical free will, and to speak very informally indeed, their proponents have very rightly ceased to suppose that events of *pure chance* could conceivably give us a desired freedom, responsibility, and so on. If determinism is the frying pan, pure chance is the fire. Something else needs to be conceded. Such doctrines, as in the case of Eccles and Popper, typically include a proposition of quantum indeterminacy in the brain as a premise. That, to speak again very informally, must be that there are neural events which in the most fundamental sense have *no* explanation, whatever is said about their probability. The proposition of physics is *not* that they have no such explanation of one kind, but may perfectly well have an explanation of another kind. To the proposition of quantum indeterminacy, however, proponents of free will *add* the proposition that the given neural events *do* have such an explanation. They are the work of such a thing as the Faculty of the Will, or a Creative Self, or the Self-conscious Mind. This is self-contradiction. Determinist pictures of the mind, by contrast, have the charm of self-consistency.

To turn now to the Self-conscious Mind, as conceived by Eccles and Popper, it is said to do three things.[19] It surveys the brain in its workings, it crucially influences those workings and, in the course of these activities, it gives rise to the unity of our experience. The Self-conscious Mind is certainly quite other than the mere totality of an individual's mental events. As certainly, it is not to be conceived as in nomic connection with the brain. It is in some sense *above* the brain. For what the descriptions are worth it is *an independent entity*, it is *active*, it has *primacy* with respect to the brain, it has *the master role*. I should like now to look quickly – there are more details elsewhere[20] – at what can be taken as the main neuroscientific argument advanced for this view. There is an additional reason for looking at the argument. It is presented not only as confirmation of the Self-conscious Mind, but also as falsification of the theories we have had under consideration, those of psycho-physical identity and psycho-physical nomic correlation. The argument is based on experimental findings of Benjamin Libet, who is perhaps a bit sympathetic himself to the Self-conscious Mind.[21]

Such a peripheral stimulus as a touch or a pulse of electricity to the skin of one's hand issues very quickly indeed in a train of action potentials – nerve impulses – to the brain. But, according to Libet, it takes a relatively long time, about half a second, before there then occurs in the brain what is called *'neuronal adequacy'* – physical sufficiency – for the conscious experience. To repeat, it takes a half-second before there is neuronal adequacy for the conscious experience. However, Libet has devised experiments of which the upshot is that subjects in effect report their conscious sensation as occurring much *earlier* than about a half-second after the stimulus, perhaps only a tenth of a second after. These seemingly conflicting propositions – that it takes a half-second for neuronal adequacy, and that subjects in effect report experiences coming earlier – are said to issue in a certain crucial and defensible hypothesis. That single hypothesis in turn, in Eccles's words, calls for something that can 'play tricks with time'. It calls for the supposition of the Self-conscious Mind. We are also told that the crucial hypothesis falsifies ideas of psycho-physical identity and psycho-physical nomic correlation between simultaneous events.

What is the crucial hypothesis? Well, Libet and his colleagues write: 'The subjective experience of the skin stimulus occurs relatively quickly after the delivery of . . . [the skin stimulus], rather than after the expected delay of up to about 500 ms for development of neuronal adequacy . . .'[22] They give the same hypothesis on other pages – in effect that the conscious experience itself is *not* delayed in the expected way, until the time of neuronal adequacy. Eccles says effectively the same thing on several of his pages: 'There can be a temporal discrepancy between neural events [neuronal adequacy] and the experience of the self-conscious mind.'[23]

That is not the end of the story. Libet and his colleagues also write: 'There is an automatic *subjective referral of the conscious experience backwards in time* . . . after the delayed neuronal adequacy at cerebral levels has been achieved . . .'[24] That is, the conscious experience *is* delayed the statutory half-second, but in having it the subject somehow 'refers it back in time' or 'antedates' it. They say this elsewhere as well. Eccles, on others of his pages, says the same thing, for example: '. . . although there is this delay in experiencing the peripheral stimulus, it is actually judged to be much earlier, at about the time of cortical arrival of the afferent input . . .'[25]

It is pretty clear, and still clearer in diagrams and other more technical passages, that Libet and his colleagues, and Eccles and Popper, have *two* hypotheses on their hands, not one, and that they have not distinguished them. It is fair to say that what they seem most often to have in mind is the second one. It is what we can call the *delay-and-antedating* hypothesis – that the experience *is* delayed and does actually happen only about a half-second after the stimulus, but the subject somehow 'antedates' it.

Why do they suppose this hypothesis is evidence for the Self-conscious Mind? The main reason, I suspect, is that they have confused it with the other one, which can be called the *no-delay* hypothesis. That is that the experience is not delayed but actually happens a lot earlier. Certainly *that* hypothesis, if it were true, would call out for something pretty miraculous, a real trick, to explain its truth. *That is so because it is a self-contradiction.* Neuronal adequacy for an experience evidently must be understood, as remarked earlier, as neural events which are sufficient for the experience. They are said to come into existence only about a half-second after the stimulus. It is then self-contradictory to hypothesize that the experience was earlier than that time. *If* the no-delay hypothesis were true, there *would* of course be trouble for Identity Theories and the theory of simultaneous nomic connection of neural and mental events. A self-contradictory objection is no reason to stay awake at night.

What of the other hypothesis, the one our authors most often have in mind? Does the delay-and-antedating hypothesis, if it is true, give us reason to favour the idea of the Self-conscious Mind? None whatever. *This* hypothesis does not put a conscious experience at a different time from a neural event, and so call out for an extraordinary intervention, and make an Identity Theory of a theory of simultaneous nomic connection impossible. That a conscious experience has an odd or indeed a bizarre character, involving what is called antedating, is no barrier to either theory, although that too is supposed. It is no more a barrier than a kind of hallucination involving a mistaken belief or impression as to time.

Is the delay-and-antedating hypothesis true? It does not much matter for our present concern, but I doubt it. So far as one can understand it, it is the claim that a subject has an experience at a certain time, which experience is at that time accompanied by the false belief or impression that it really happened earlier. But just having the experience, as in the case of any experience whatever, surely includes or is accompanied by the true belief or impression that it is happening then. The delay-and-antedating hypothesis, therefore, seems to require that subjects are *at one time aware of, and nevertheless hold,* self-contradictory beliefs. Do they? I wonder.

The last thing to be said here is that the doctrine of the Self-conscious Mind also offends against the axiom of psycho-physical intimacy. One's Self-conscious Mind is not in lawlike connection with one's brain, or identical with it, but only in what is called 'liaison' with it, or rather with parts of it. Given its rather impressive nature, incidentally, akin to what needs to be called the Soul, it is no surprise that it is in liaison only with one's dominant cerebral hemisphere, likely to be the left but possibly the right. This leads Popper to the speculation, admittedly a light-hearted speculation, that the Self-conscious Mind, in childhood, may *choose* the side of the brain, right or left, on which it will concentrate.[26] I guess it chooses the side it likes best. It is an engaging idea, but I don't think it will catch on.[27]

Notes and References

1 Blakemore, Colin (1977) *Mechanics of the Mind*, p. 32. Cambridge: Cambridge Univ. Press.

2 Brentano, Franz (1973) The distinction between mental and physical phenomena. In Oskar Kraus and Linda McAlister (eds) *Psychology from an Empirical Standpoint*, London: Routledge & Kegan Paul.

3 Chisolm, R. M. (1957) *Perceiving*. Ithaca, NY: Cornell Univ. Press; cf. Davidson, Donald (1980) Mental events. *Essays on Actions and Events*. Oxford: Clarendon Press; Lycan, W. G. (1969) On intentionality and the psychological. *American Philosophical Quarterly*.

4 Searle, J. R. (1983) *Intentionality: An Essay in the Philosophy of Mind*. Cambridge: Cambridge Univ. Press.

5 Mackenzie, Brian D. (1977) *Behaviourism and the Limits of Scientific Method* London: Routledge & Kegan Paul.

6 Putnam, Hilary (1975) *Mind, Language and Reality. Collected Papers*, vol. 2. Cambridge: Cambridge Univ. Press.

7 Newell, Allen and Simon, Herbert (1963) GPS: a program that simulates human thought. In E. Feigenbaum and J. Feldman (eds), *Computers and Thought* New York: McGraw-Hill; Hofstadter, Douglas R. and Dennett, Daniel C. (eds), (1981) *The Mind's I*. New York: Basic Books, cf. Boden Margaret (1981) *Minds and Mechanisms*. Brighton: Harvester Press.

8 Searle, J. R. (1980) Minds, brains, and programs. *Behav. Brain Sci.* 3:. Reprinted in Hofstadter and Dennett, *The Mind's I*.

9 Huxley, T. H. (1896) Animal automatism. *Collected Essays*, vol. 1. London.

10 E.g. Perrett, D. I., Smith, P. A. J., Potter, D. D., Mistlen, A. J., Head, A. S., Milner, A. D. and Jeeves, M. A. (1985) Visual cells in the temporal cortex sensitive to face view and gaze direction. *Proc. R. Soc. Lond.* B223.

11 Suppes, Patrick (1970) *A Probabilistic Theory of Causality*. Amsterdam: North-Holland; (1984) *Probabilistic Metaphysics*. Oxford: Blackwell.

12 Davidson, Mental events.

13 Searle, *Intentionality*, ch. 10.

14 Honderich, Ted (1984) Smith and the champion of mauve. *Analysis*.

15 Honderich, Ted (1981) Psychophysical lawlike connections and their problem. *Inquiry* (1981) Nomological dualism: reply to four critics. *Inquiry*.

16 Pagels, Heinz R. (1983) *The Cosmic Code: Quantum Physics as the Language of Nature*, pp. 165–6. London: Michael Joseph.

17 Bell, J. S. (1964) On the Einstein Podolsky Rosen paradox. *Physics*. (1966) On the problem of hidden variables in quantum mechanics. *Review of Modern Physics*.

18 Bohm, D. (1957) *Causality and Chance*. London: Routledge & Kegan Paul; (1962) A proposed explanation of Quantum Theory in terms of hidden variables at sub-quantum-mechanical level. In S. Korner (ed.), *Observation and Interpretation in the Philosophy of Physics*. New York: Dover; Broglie, L. de (1953) *The Revolution in Physics, tr.* R. W. Neimeyer. New York: Noonday.

19 Eccles, J. C. and Popper, K. R. (1977) *The Self and Its Brain*, Berlin, Heidelberg, London. New York: Springer Internat.

20 Honderich, Ted (1984) The time of a conscious sensory experience and mind–brain theories. *J. Theor. Biol.* 110; Libet, B. (1985) Subjective antedating of a sensory experience and mind–brain theories: reply to Honderich. *J. Theor. Biol.* 114; Honderich, T. (1986) Mind and brain and time: rejoinder to Libet. *J. Theor. Biol* 118.

21 Libet, B. Wright, E. W. Jr., Feinstein, B. and Pearl, D. K. (1979) Subjective referral of the timing for a conscious sensory experience. *Brain*, 102:1.

22 Ibid., p. 200.

23 Eccles and Popper, *The Self and Its Brain*, p. 362.

24 Libet *et al.*, Subjective referral, pp. 201–2.

25 Eccles and Popper, *The Self and Its Brain*, p. 364.

26 Ibid., pp. 495, 507–8.

27 All of the contentions of this chapter are more fully stated and defended, and
    sometimes given different definitions, in my forthcoming *A Theory of Deter-
    minism: The Mind, Neuroscience and Life-Hopes*. Oxford: Oxford University
    Press.

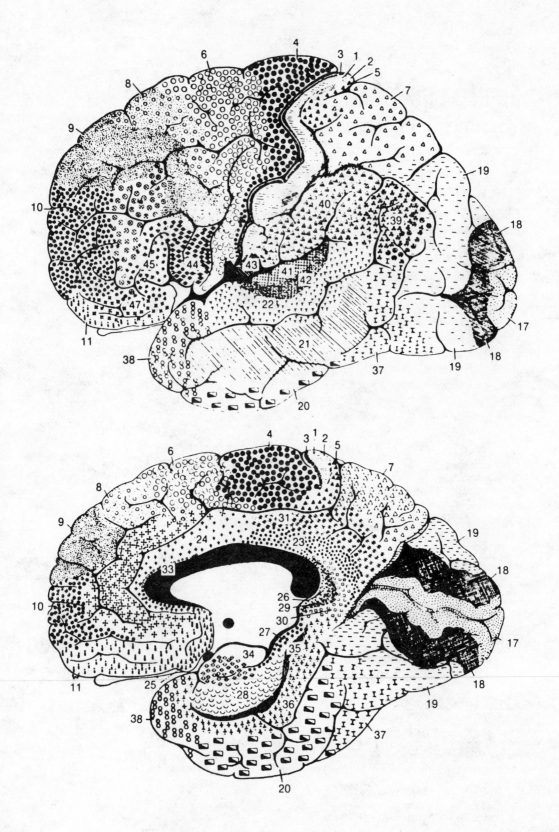

30

The Mind–Brain Identity Theory as a Scientific Hypothesis: A Second Look

Jeffrey Gray

Jeffrey Gray is an experimental psychologist with an interest in the way in which the brain controls behaviour. He has mainly worked with rats, concentrating on the role played by particular brain systems in emotion and learning. His most important contribution to this field is a general theory of the psychology and neurology of anxiety (see The Neuropsychology of Anxiety, *Oxford University Press, 1982). He has also contributed to the development of biologically based theories of human personality, in part by acting as a conduit for Soviet research findings in this field (see* Pavlov's Typology, *Pergamon, 1964). After 19 years as a Lecturer in the Department of Experimental Psychology and a Fellow of University College, Oxford, he moved to London in 1983 to succeed Hans Eysenck as Professor of Psychology at the Institute of Psychiatry (Maudsley Hospital), where he is supplementing his work in the field of brain and behaviour with clinical research into the problems of the mentally ill.*

In 1970 a volume of papers appeared, devoted to the mind–brain identity theory,[1] that is, to the view that mental states are identical to brain states and that a given mental state will be fully accounted for if and when one has accounted for the corresponding brain state. Until I read them I had supposed that, as a scientist working in the field of brain and behaviour, I was myself a mind–brain identity theorist. However, as I read through the volume I experienced an increasing sense of unease and felt impelled to write a critique of the theory from the standpoint of a working scientist (published in the *Philosophical Quarterly* in 1971). The year 1984 saw a major reawakening of interest in these issues in the United Kingdom (although, in this as in so many other things, the Americans have been several years ahead of us). Two particular events have given rise to the present writing. First was the series of seminars on 'Minds and Matters' organized in Oxford by Susan Greenfield and Colin Blakemore, which this book records. Second, the distinguished American philosopher John Searle delivered the 1984 Reith Lectures on BBC Radio, on the subject

Imagine the cerebral hemispheres of the human brain split down the middle. Here we see the left hemisphere, viewed from the outside (top) and the inside (bottom), divided into regions by the anatomist, Brodmann (1909). He classified these cortical regions according to subtle differences in the layering, and in the types and densities of nerve cells visible in microscopic sections. Many of Brodmann's anatomical regions do indeed correspond to areas with distinct functions. But do those functions include the mind?

of 'Minds Brains and Science'.[2] These events have caused me to reconsider the arguments I put forward in 1971. Arrogantly, no doubt, I have concluded that nothing much has happened in the intervening years to lessen their force. Section I of this chapter, accordingly, reprints my 1971 article (slightly modified) in its entirety. In the second section I go on to consider Searle's position (which may be regarded as a contemporary and highly sophisticated version of the mind–brain identity theory) in the light of the arguments deployed in section I.

I   The Mind–Brain Identity Theory, 1971

In recent years a number of philosophers have advanced views about the relationship between mind and body which have come to be known as the 'mind–brain identity theory'. I wish, in this chapter, to consider the possible fruitfulness, from a scientific point of view, of adopting one particular version of this theory. According to this version,[3] (a) there are no philosophical objections to the hypothesis that mental states are identical with brain states; (b) there is, or will be, available scientific evidence which is compatible with a range of hypotheses, including dualism, epiphenomenalism, psycho-physiological parallelism, mind–

Some Definitions

Dualism: the view that there are separate physical and mental realms that causally interact. **Epiphenomenalism**: the view that mental events are caused by physical events but have no causal effects themselves. **Psychophysiological parallelism**: the view that physical events are caused by physical events and mental events by mental events, that the two different kinds of event do not causally interact, but that the two different kinds of event do not causally interact, but that there is a regular temporal coincidence between a given type of physical event and a corresponding type of mental event.

---

brain identity, etc. (see box); and (c) philosophico-scientific criteria, such as parsimony, simplicity, concordance with the rest of the corpus of scientific knowledge, etc., make the mind–brain identity theory the most reasonable hypothesis to choose from this range. We shall take it for granted that (a) and (b) are correct, and consider only what kind of a hypothesis the mind–brain identity thesis is, and whether or not it is likely to be of value to scientists concerned with the nature of consciousness.

From a scientific point of view there are two main ways of approaching the problem of consciousness. (I sometimes talk of 'conscious experiences' or 'conscious events' and sometimes of 'consciousness'. No stand is implied on the issue of whether there is a unitary property of consciousness or many kinds of qualitatively different conscious events. If the latter is the case, the problem indicated in this paper would arise for each class of conscious events. For simplicity's sake, therefore, the argument is pursued here as though there is but once class of conscious events.) One way of approaching the problem of consciousness is to consider it within an evolutionary framework, so that one is impelled to ask: 'How did it evolve?' and 'What survival value does it confer on organisms which possess it?' The other is to consider the problem mechanistically, so that one is impelled to ask: 'How is consciousness linked to the physiology of the brain?' and 'How does consciousness affect the control of behaviour?' (The answers to the two sets of questions would, of course, need to be linked together in any adequate account of consciousness.)

The Privacy of Conscious Experience

In the approach to either set of questions we are faced with the problem which philosophers have considered as the distinction between the public nature of the world about us and the private nature of conscious experience. From the scientist's point of view this problem may be put as follows. For any individual scientist concerned with psychology or physiology, his own conscious experience is a *datum* and therefore stands *in need of explanation*; as far as the behaviour of others is concerned, however, consciousness can only function as a *hypothesis* by which to *explain* this behaviour. The reason why the problem posed by consciousness for the behavioural scientist is at present so acute is the following. Nothing that we know about behaviour, physiology, the evolution of either behaviour or physiology, or the possibilities of constructing automata to carry out complex forms of behaviour, is such that the hypothesis of consciousness (which, in any case, would not be suggested by these kinds of data if we did not find it already present in our own experience, where it is itself a datum) provides a good explanation for them. Conversely, nothing that we know about the evolution of behaviour or about its physiological control gives us any clue as to how to explain the occurrence of conscious events as data in our own experience.

It may be thought that it is the *privacy* of conscious experience which poses the problem. I do not think that this is so. Scientists need have no more difficulty in principle in agreeing about observations of their private conscious experiences than they do about meter readings, although it is usually more difficult for them to agree on the former in practice. On occasion, however, even the practical difficulties may be overcome in a suitable experimental situation. Consider, for example, this quotation from a paper in *Nature* by O. Lippold:

Anyone who has prominent alpha rhythm [a regular electrical rhythm, with a frequency of about 10 cycles per second, recorded from the region of the human scalp, at the back of the head, that overlies the visual cortex] can make a simple observation to show that eye tremor can occur. A bright point-source of light is viewed against a completely dark field. If the gaze is now swept at a suitable speed (from top to bottom of the field of view in one second), vertically past the source, the resulting after-image can be examined. It will be found to be an approximately sinusoidal trace.[4]

It is clear that, in the experiment described, the characteristics of the after-image are being used to test a physiological hypothesis in a manner which does not differ in principle from, say, the way one might use an electromyogram to record from the muscles of the eye.

Lippold's experiment shows how the scientist's *own* conscious experiences may be used as *data* to test hypotheses about physiological events. It is also possible, using other experimental designs, to test the *hypothesis* that certain kinds of conscious experience exist in *others*. Roger Shepard and his colleagues, for example, have tested the hypothesis that people have mental images of a quasi-visual kind.[5] Suppose you have to judge whether two line drawings are of the same or different shape; and that, in fact, they are the same but one is presented as a rigid planar rotation of the other. If you solve this problem (as subjects report) by forming an image of the shape and mentally rotating it, then one might expect that the time you will take to detect that the two shapes are the same will increase with the degree of angular disparity between them. This is exactly what Shepard has reported. Such experiments should serve to quell any residual philosophical doubts as to the existence and accessibility of conscious events in general and mental images in particular.

The Gulf Between Consciousness and Behaviour-plus-Physiology

It seems, then, that if the problem of consciousness were due essentially to the privacy of conscious experience, we would just need to wait until the scientists developed sufficiently ingenious tricks to get around their practical difficulties. But the problem goes much deeper than that.

I have claimed that nothing we know about behaviour or physiology would prompt us to develop the hypothesis that there are conscious experiences; that this hypothesis has no explanatory force in accounting for the form our observations of behaviour and physiology actually take; and that nothing we know about physiology or behaviour offers us a clue as to how either of these could take part in any causal relationship with the conscious experiences we actually have as data. Although I doubt that these propositions will meet with much opposition, it might be worth while giving an example of our state of ignorance.

In the last two decades or so our knowledge of the physiology of sleep has vastly expanded as a result of research on animals. In the course of this research it has been discovered that there are, in fact (at least) two kinds of sleep which alternate with each other during the time an animal is curled up 'behaviourally' asleep.[6] These two kinds of sleep differ from each other on a variety of physiological indices: the electroencephalogram recorded from the surface of the intact brain, the electrical activity of a large number of different structures deep in the brain, the tension of the muscles in the limbs and the neck, the activity of the respiratory and cardiac systems, and movements of the eyes. Furthermore, the same two kinds of sleep appear in essentially the same ways in (at least) all mammalian species. There is nothing in these observations which could possibly prompt the hypothesis that one kind of sleep is to do with consciousness and the other not; such a hypothesis, if proposed, would in any case fail to explain the particular differences between the two states of sleep which are observed; and, finally, there is nothing in these observations which can help explain the fact – which we discover *only* by asking the members of our own mammalian species what is going on when we wake them up from the two kinds of sleep – that the one kind is accompanied by dreams and the other is not.

Lest it be objected that research on this problem has only just begun, and that further observations may reveal *why* the one kind of sleep is accompanied by dreams and the other not, I shall make my point stronger and say that, at present, we know of no conceivable observations which could provide the answer to that question. The fact that we cannot (at present) conceive of such observations might perhaps be taken by some philosophers as an indication that there is a logical confusion somewhere in our even asking about the link between physiology and consciousness. I would suggest, rather, that it stems from the fact that no one has yet proposed a scientific theory with the power to guide us towards the right kind of observations. And I take it that the proponents of the mind–brain identity theory are either putting forward such a theory, or, alternatively, proposing a model to which any such theory offered in the future ought to conform. I hope to show that they are certainly not doing the former; and that, if they are attempting to do the latter, then there is a better model which can be put forward.

Let us first be clear about where the problem of consciousness arises. It is sometimes mistakenly believed that this is at the point in a chain of behaviour (or in the evolution of behaviour) at which the most natural language to use employs the vocabulary of goals, intentions, etc.[7] But there is no reason to suppose that a language in terms of goals and intentions implies the existence of conscious experiences in the behaving system. There are many ways in which one can design machines or program computers so that they display goal-directed behaviour (that is, so that they have 'intentions'). But we have no reason to suppose (given the absence at present of a suitable theory to guide us) that in so doing we are in some way 'wiring in' consciousness.

The problem of consciousness arises at a simpler stage in the business of machine construction than the stage at which it is necessary to build in goal-directed behaviour: it arises at the point of sensation. If we design a machine to react to certain kinds of physical energy and to display certain kinds of goal-directed behaviour in response to it, we need not suppose that the occurrence of the goal-directed behaviour implies that sensations occurred upon reaction to the appropriate kind of physical energy. Yet this is what occurs (as a datum) in the case of human beings. The problem which concerns us then is, roughly, the problem posed by pain or after-images rather than the problem posed by intentions (which is not a problem at all).

Statement of the Problem

We are now in a position to state our problem more clearly. This problem consists in the way in which the hypothesis of conscious events in others is to be linked to observations about behaviour and about physiology. The usual case, when a scientist proposes a hypothesis to account for some body of data, is that the hypothetical constructs he uses possess features from which the relevant properties of the observed data may be deduced. If the hypothesis is testable by further observations and is in fact upheld by them, the question of how it accounts for the data (if it is a well-constructed hypothesis) cannot arise. The hypothesis of consciousness (for others) is peculiar in that it is *not* equipped with features from which the behaviour and physiology of others may be deduced. This is because, rather than being constructed as a hypothesis able to generate such deductions, it has itself arisen as a datum (in our own experience) and has then been extended to others by inductive generalization only. This has the consequence that, even when (as in the experiments on the rotation of mental images described earlier) we are able to test a particular hypothesis that there are particular conscious events, the successful outcome of such a test may add to our belief in the reality of, for example, mental images in others without contributing to our understanding of the way in which either these particular conscious events or conscious events in general are related to either behaviour or physiology. Furthermore, since our hypothesis of consciousness for others does not contain any description of the properties of consciousness (other than the description, 'like the sort of thing that goes on in one's own experience'), there are no observations by which we could test whether systems (either biological or artefactual) rather different from ourselves do or do not have conscious experiences, whether of a particular kind or in general.

Thus we stand in need of a scientific account of how conscious experiences (in the sense which is best illustrated by the experience of primitive sensations) (a) evolved and (b) confer survival value on organisms possessing them (the evolutionary questions); and of how they (c) arise out of brain events and (d) alter behaviour (the mechanistic questions). Let us consider whether the mind–brain identity theory can itself either be such an account or provide a model for the construction of such an account. (We shall consider below what is meant by 'providing a model for the construction of an account'.)

The Mechanistic Questions

Let us approach the problem first from the mechanistic standpoint. Consciousness occurs in (i) a system which (ii) displays behaviour in (iii) an environment and which (iv) is composed of biological tissue. We do not know a priori which of these conditions, alone, in combination, or in interaction, are necessary for the occurrence of conscious experience.

If we consider the question 'What are the distinguishing features of those processes which are accompanied by consciousness and those which are not?' in the light of this analysis, at least the following answers are possible:

(1) All the conditions (i)–(iv) are involved: that is, consciousness occurs in a certain kind of system displaying certain kinds of behaviour in certain kinds of environments, provided the system is composed of certain kinds of biological tissues (to wit, neurons).

(2) Only conditions (i)–(iii) are involved: consciousness occurs in a certain kind of system displaying certain kinds of behaviour in

certain kinds of environment. This implies that, if we put together the right kind of artefactual system and placed it in the right kind of environment with which it could interact in the right kind of way, it would have conscious experiences.

(3) Only the nature of the system (i) matters. This implies that, if we mimicked the system correctly on a computer, conscious experiences would occur in the computer.

(4) Only condition (iv) matters. This implies that conscious experience is somehow a property of biological cells, or perhaps of nerve cells only. We might then have access only to certain 'macroscopic' aspects of conscious experience which arise when a lot of neurons come together, each neuron having its own 'microscopic' consciousness. (If this sounds absurd, consider whether the half of the brain that can't talk after a 'split-brain' operation in man[8] does or does not have conscious experiences alongside the conscious experiences of the half of the brain which can talk to you – see Donald MacKay's chapter in this volume.) If it does, what happens if you halve each half of the brain, and halve again, and so on? Can we be sure – without the kind of theoretical understanding which, it is claimed in this chapter, we lack – that consciousness drops out at some minimal quantity of brain tissue greater than one neuron?)

It appears that the proponents of the mind–brain identity theory usually entertain only possibility (1), that is to say, that the critical features which allow the occurrence of consciousness are only possible in brains. Indeed, it is not clear that one would wish to speak of a mind–brain *identity* theory if the properties of brain which gave rise to conscious experience could be instantiated in robots, computers or isolated neurons. Yet none of these possibilities can be ruled out a priori and none of them is in any obvious way less plausible than possibility (1) as a scientific hypothesis about the nature of consciousness.

The Evolutionary Questions

Let us now approach our problem from an evolutionary point of view. Although certain minor characteristics of organisms might arise by association with other characteristics themselves possessing survival value, that is, as epiphenomena, it seems implausible that such a major characteristic as the possession of consciousness could do so. The existence of consciousness as a datum in one species, our own, implies therefore, that since it has evolved it must have survival value, which in turn implies that it must alter the behaviour of the organisms which possess it. Now suppose that there are in the brain two classes of physiological process, those which are accompanied by conscious experiences and those which are not. The evolutionary point of view compels us to believe that, if we were able to allow the former class of physiological processes to occur as usual except that we somehow prevented the occurrence of the conscious experiences by which only they are accompanied, the resulting behaviour would in some way be different and, indeed, in some way less advantageous to the animal's survival.

It is not at all clear that the mind–brain identity theory would even allow us to talk in the way I have just done. For, if the physiological processes are identical with the conscious events, it would not be possible for the one to occur without the other. Yet, since the mind–brain identity theory is in part advocated on the grounds that it is good science,[9] it would seem reasonable to say that, if it does not allow us to talk in a way which the most widely accepted theory in biology makes natural, then it falls short of its self-appointed standards. It is true that a proponent of the mind–brain identity theory is able to consider the Darwinian survival value of the brain states which are identical with conscious events. But it seems undesirable that the question, 'What would happen if we suppressed the conscious events without altering the neuronal events normally accompanying these?' should be ruled out a priori by our philosophical biases (even though it may well turn out to be an empirically impossible question to put).

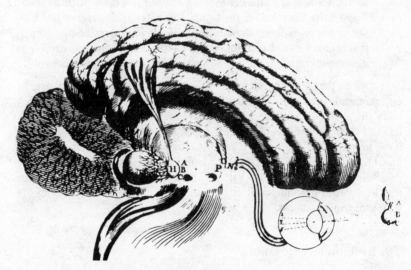

Figure 30.1 Descartes' dualist view of visual perception, from the Latin edition (1661) of the Treatise of Man. *The optics of the eye form an inverted image (5,3,1) of the apple (A,B,C) which sets up a matching pattern of activity (6,4,2) in the walls of the fluid-filled ventricles of the brain. Waves of vibration spread across to the site of communication with the soul, the pineal gland (H), to form a re-inverted image of the apple (A,B,C), which gives the soul perception of the world.*

Which Model for a Theory of Consciousness?

It seems, then, that viewed from the standpoint of mechanism and from that of the theory of evolution, the mind–brain identity theory leaves something to be desired. Yet some of the arguments I have used against this theory may seem to be tainted with dualism; and dualism, of the Cartesian kind, is rightly under great suspicion. But the point of view which I am advocating – which can best be termed a kind of 'double-aspect' theory – can be distinguished from Cartesian dualism and, when it is so distinguished, it can, I believe, offer a better model for what a scientific theory of consciousness should eventually look like than the mind–brain identity theory.

In Cartesian dualism, the properties of consciousness are due to the nature of the psyche itself; the properties of the organismic machine are equally their own; and the two different kinds of stuff merely interact in the pineal gland. The difference between this and the view proposed here are that: first, on the present view, the properties of conscious experience will need to be derived (when we have an adequate theory with which to perform the derivation) from the properties of the processes which give rise to conscious experience (and we have seen above what different kinds of possibility there are as to the kinds of properties which could prove to be necessary); and second, the nature of the behaviour changes to which consciousness gives rise will need to be such that we can see how they confer Darwinian survival value on creatures possessing consciousness. Thus the properties of consciousness would be entirely explicable within the framework of the unified science which is equally the goal of the proponents of the mind–brain identity theory; but to achieve this goal it is not necessary to regard conscious experiences as identical to the brain processes with which they are linked. On the contrary, to regard conscious experiences as identical to brain processes in this way makes it very difficult to ask certain sorts of question – about the necessary features of the processes to which consciousness is linked, and about the Darwinian survival value of consciousness – which may precisely be the critical ones to ask.

It can now be seen what it means to talk of a 'model' for a scientific theory, as I have done earlier in this chapter. It is clear that neither the mind–brain identity theory, nor the double-aspect theory advanced here is itself a scientific theory. For neither makes any proposal about the nature of the critical features of brain processes which could give rise to conscious experiences and by reference to which one could explain the properties of conscious experiences; nor does either make any explicit proposals about the way in which consciousness could control behaviour and so confer Darwinian survival value on a species possessing it. However, to adopt the mind–brain identity theory – or the Cartesian theory, the epiphenomenalist theory, or the double-aspect theory advanced here – alters the nature of the scientific questions one subsequently asks and the nature of the kinds of answers one looks for. A Cartesian would not think of asking 'What properties of brain processes determine the properties of consciousness?' since he believes the properties of consciousness are *sui generis*. A mind–brain identity theorist might ask this question, but still be precluded from asking about the survival value of consciousness (as distinct from the survival value of the brain processes with which consciousness is considered to be identical). Yet these, from a scientific point of view, are the vital questions to ask.

II   The Mind–Brain Identity Theory, 1987

The position expressed by John Searle (see chapter 15) appears to be a version of the mind–brain identity theory. But it is scientifically more sophisticated than most earlier versions. These have generally supposed that the identity between brain processes and mental processes posited by the identity theory will gradually come to be established by ever more detailed observations of spatio-temporal correlation between the two apparently different kinds of event, of the kind 'whenever mental process X occurs brain process Y can be observed, therefore $X = Y$', and so on for all X and Y. This is the kind of reductionism that occurs when one repeatedly enters clouds (flying through them, say, in an aeroplane), observes that all clouds consist of water droplets, and concludes therefore that clouds just *are* collections of water droplets. Reductionism of this kind is theoretically weak, and plays a greater part in ordinary, everyday reasoning than in the developed sciences. In its place Searle has proposed a reductionist model that is much more typical of scientific reasoning and which (usually) possesses great theoretical power.

Micro- and Macro-features of Systems

This model turns on the distinction made in the physical sciences between 'the micro- and macro-properties of systems'. Searle explains this distinction as follows:

Consider the desk at which I am now sitting, or the glass of water in front of me. Each object is composed of micro-particles. The micro-particles have features at the level of molecules and atoms as well as at the deeper level of subatomic particles. But each object also has certain properties such as the solidity of the table, the liquidity of the water, and the transparency of the glass, which are surface or global properties of the physical systems. Many such surface or global properties can be causally explained by the behaviour of elements at the micro-level. For example, the solidity of the table in front of me is explained by the lattice structure occupied by the molecules of which the table is composed. Similarly, the liquidity of the water is explained by the nature of the interactions between H_2O molecules.

It seems to me that these rather banal examples provide a perfectly ordinary model for explaining the puzzling relationships between the mind and the brain. In the case of liquidity, solidity, and transparency, we have no difficulty at all in saying that the surface features are caused by the behaviour of elements at the micro-level. At the same time we accept that the surface phenomena just are features of the systems in question. The clearest way I know of stating this point is to say that the surface feature is caused by the behaviour of micro-elements, and at the same time is realised in the system that is made up of the micro-elements. There is, indeed, a cause and effect relationship, but at the same time the surface features are just higher-level features of the very system whose behaviour at the micro-level causes them . . .

If we apply these lessons to the study of the mind, it seems to me there is no difficulty in accounting for the relations of the mind to the brain in terms of the brain's functioning to cause mental states. Just as the liquidity of the water is caused by the behaviour of elements at the micro-level, and yet at the same time is a feature realised in the system of micro-elements, so, in exactly that sense of 'caused by' and 'realised in', mental phenomena are caused by processes going on in the brain at the neuronal or modular level, and they are realised in the very system that consists of neurons.[10]

Searle's model for the cause-and-effect relationship between brain and mind has many attractive features. It has impressive scientific antecedents, and these demonstrate exactly how the model can work. Furthermore, it allows one *both* to see how the brain and the mind can be aspects of the same physical system (thus satisfying the identity theorists' major demand), *and* to talk in a natural manner of the brain's 'causing' mental processes, so permitting the working scientist to ask such questions as 'How does the brain cause mental processes?', 'What evolutionary function is served by the brain's causing mental processes?', etc. (questions whose importance I have stressed in the first section of this chapter). A final advantage of Searle's model is that it focuses attention on the need for a theoretical linkage between the micro- and macro-levels of the brain–mind system. Indeed, this is its chief advantage over the earlier, essentially correlational approaches to the mind–brain problem that I have alluded to above. Discovering that wherever there is a cloud there are water droplets tells us nothing about *how* water droplets take on the macro-features of clouds. But the relationship between particles and solidity or water molecules and liquidity (as in Searle's examples) is of a kind that allows one to show in detail how the properties of particles give rise to solidity or those of water molecules to liquidity.

The Flaw in Searle's Model

Alas, however, it is at just this, its apparently strongest, point that Searle's model is most seriously flawed. The reason why the properties of the micro-elements of systems are usually able to explain their macro-features is to be found in the process by which scientists construct and test theories. Typically, the macro-features (for example, the liquidity of water) are observed first; the scientist then constructs a hypothesis about micro-elements (for example, water molecules) which, if correct, can account for the macro-features; he then derives predictions from his hypothesis and tests them by further observations; these observations are usually carried out first at the macro-level and then, as techniques and knowledge improve, more directly at the micro-level. Now, given this process of theory–construction, the question of *how* the micro-level explains the macro-level (assuming that hypotheses are well constructed, predictions appropriately derived and successfully tested, and so on) can scarcely arise: the validity of the explanation is guaranteed by the fact that the hypothesis was explicitly constructed so that it *would* explain the macro-features of the system.

But this is by no means the case in the linkage that Searle proposes between neuronal events (his micro-elements) and mental phenomena (his macro-features). The properties of neurons have been postulated in the light of observations that concern either behaviour (from which psychologists infer various high-level features of brain activity, for example, that the brain must contain mechanisms by which rewards increase the probability of emission of behaviour that is followed by rewards) or the physiology of largish chunks of nervous tissue (for example, that there exist sensorimotor reflex arcs interrupted by synapses). More recently, with the great advances in neurophysiological knowledge and techniques, the properties of neurons have been largely inferred from observations made on neurons themselves. At no point in the development of neuronal physiology have the properties of neurons been postulated so that they might account for the features of conscious mental events. Thus there is no way to establish for brain and mind the kind of theoretical linkage between micro- and macro-level which makes the examples given by Searle (solidity, liquidity, etc.) work. In short, he has offered us a blank cheque that no one can (at present) guarantee.

This is not to say that Searle's arguments are valueless. On the contrary, it seems likely (but, in the absence of an explicit hypothesis about the linkage between micro- and macro-levels, that is the best one can say) that he has correctly anticipated the shape that a theory of the relationship between brain and mind will eventually take. However, by treating the problem as though it was largely resolved by the (philosophical) demonstration that mind and brain *could* relate to one another as macro- and micro-features of a single system, Searle runs the risk of deflecting attention from the much more important (scientific) issue of how they *in fact* relate to one another.

The Conditions for Consciousness

Let us turn to a second issue that was raised by section I of this chapter and which is raised again by Searle:[2] namely, the necessary and sufficient conditions that must hold for conscious experience to occur.

We know, as a matter of fact, that consciousness is related to the activity of the human brain. We may paraphrase this fact by the statement (recapitulated from section I) that conscious events occur in (i) a system which (ii) displays behaviour in (iii) an environment and which (iv) is composed of biological tissue, namely neurons. Like other mind–brain identity theorists, Searle appears to believe that all four of these conditions must be met for consciousness *ever* to occur. But, in the absence of a tried and tested theory of the linkage between neuronal and mental events, this position is one of mere assertion. I suggested above that there are (among others) the two following alternative possibilities:

(1) Only conditions (i)–(iii) are necessary, implying that, if we put together the right kind of artefact and allowed it to interact in the right kind of way with the right kind of environment, it would have conscious experiences; let us call this the 'conscious robot' possibility.

(2) Only the nature of the system (i) matters, implying that, if we mimicked the system correctly on a computer, conscious experiences would occur in the computer; let us call this the 'conscious computer' possibility.

Searle argues strenuously against these two possibilities, especially the latter. Let us examine his arguments and see if they succeed in restricting the range of possibilities left open in the earlier part of this paper.

Searle attacks in particular what he calls the 'strong artificial intelligence' or 'strong AI' position,[2] namely, the view that 'any physical system whatever that had the right program with the right inputs and outputs would have a mind in exactly the same sense that you and I have minds'. As phrased, this view lies ambiguously between the conscious robot and conscious computer possibilities distinguished above; but for the most part Searle's attack is aimed at the conscious computer. A further ambiguity lies in the interpretation of the word 'mind'. This term is normally used to cover both conscious and unconscious mental events, and the 'sense in which you and I have minds' undoubtedly includes both. It is not clear, however, whether the view that Searle calls 'strong AI' is intended to claim merely (1) that a run of the right kind of computer program would process information in the manner that mental events (conscious or unconscious) process information, or (2) that the computer in which the program is run would house conscious events while it is running. (One reason, I believe, why Searle is able to disregard this second ambiguity is that his micro/macro-feature argument has first been used, in the manner outlined above, to finesse the whole issue of consciousness.) A final ambiguity is that Searle's attack on the strong AI position can be read in two ways. The less extreme version would merely refute the claim, attributed to proponents of strong AI, that the running of a computer program of sufficient information-processing complexity *must* automatically involve or generate 'mind'. The more extreme version holds that the running of a computer program, no matter of what kind, *could not* of itself involve or generate 'mind'. Among these ambiguities I shall choose that set of alternatives which is most relevant to the concerns of this essay: the *more* extreme attack, reading 'mind' as *including* conscious experiences, and applied successively to the conscious computer and then to the conscious robot.

The Conscious Computer

What Searle claims, therefore, is that no digital computer (we come to the robot possibility later), no matter what program it runs, could ever generate conscious experiences. This claim, if true, would eliminate one of the sets of conditions for consciousness (namely, those of the conscious computer) which my earlier discussion left open as one among several empirical possibilities. In making this claim Searle relies on the following central argument:

(1) Computer programs have syntax (rules for transforming symbols into other symbols) but no semantics (the symbols that are transformed do not represent anything outside the program).
(2) Minds have 'semantic contents', that is, mental events refer to or represent things other than themselves – things, moreover, that are usually located in the world outside the person experiencing the mental events.
(3) Therefore 'no computer program by itself is sufficient to give a system a mind'.

The argument is persuasive. The first premise, that computer programs possess syntax but not semantics, is not in dispute. The second premise is almost equally beyond reproach. It is typical of conscious experiences that they represent something or other outside the experiencing subject (for example, one might see a house, recognize a face, smell a rose or hear a bird sing). Indeed, it is difficult to think of conscious events that do not, in at least some degree, possess this characteristic. There are, none the less, some. Pains, for example (which have an unrivalled claim to *being* conscious events), refer to nothing beyond themselves; they are sometimes so far from referring to the organ in which one experiences them that it is often difficult to localize them as occurring in any precise spot. Stars before the eyes (after a blow), ringing in the ears, and itches are other, similar examples. But these are probably the last kinds of conscious events that anyone is likely to wish to attribute to a computer or computer program, so that they do not offer any serious impediment to Searle's argument. Thus, while the conclusion (3) is not absolutely watertight, it is certainly compelling. At the very least, we must accept that Searle has greatly weakened the plausibility of the view that a computer might house conscious events just because it runs a certain kind of program. And, since this view is currently very popular, this is an important step forward: it will free energies to concentrate on other, more likely possibilities.

The Conscious Robot

So much for the conscious computer. What of the conscious robot? Here Searle is on much weaker ground. He extends his argument to a robot that picks up a hamburger and causes the digital computer that consti- tutes its central processor to receive the symbol for 'hamburger'.[2] This system too, he says, will lack mental life. The argument on which this assertion is based appears to be the following. First, we have already proved (as above) that a digital computer cannot itself have a mental life, because it has no knowledge of the meanings of the symbols it manipu- lates. Second, 'the causal interactions between the robot and the rest of the world are irrelevant unless those causal interactions are represented in some mind or other. But there's no way they can be if all that the so- called mind consists of is a set of purely formal, syntactical operations'.[2]

I find it difficult to attribute any precise meaning to the second part of this argument. Searle has previously committed himself to the (plausible) view that the key feature that minds have, and computers lack, is the capacity to form representations of, and attach meanings to, events external to themselves. How do those creatures that possess minds (human beings, say, as the only case we are sure of, but certainly not the only case) come to have this capacity and to exercise it? They must surely achieve this feat by virtue of their 'causal interactions with the world'. And, if they can form representation in this way, how does Searle know that a robot (of sufficient, though undetermined, powers) cannot? If we designed a robot with complex sensory devices and taught it that it must activate the symbol for 'hamburger' only upon receipt of complex conjunctions of visual, chemical, thermal, textural, etc., inputs, plus perhaps certain movements of its own made in relation to the source of these inputs, do we know whether or not the robot's representation of the object that it labels with the 'hamburger' symbol would count as a 'mental event' or give rise to a 'conscious experience'? I do not know; and, if Searle knows, he does not disclose the source of his knowledge. If it is just that the robot (by definition) is not made of biological tissue (neurons, etc.), then he is asserting the identity theory, not justifying it.

On this last point (the requirement that mind be generated by biological tissue) Searle (uncharacteristically) wavers. At one point he remarks: 'brains are biological engines; biology matters; it's not just an irrelevant fact about the mind that it happens to be realised in human brains.' But in the very next paragraph he supposes that Martians have arrived on earth, that we have concluded that they have mental states, but that when we open up their heads all we discover inside is green slime. 'Well, still,' he says, 'that green slime, if it functioned to produce consciousness and all the rest of their mental life, would have to have causal powers equal to those of the human brain.' The argument is in principle unexceptionable (though there may be much lower levels of consciousness, and perhaps therefore of the relevant 'causal powers', than those possessed by the human brain). But why is it not equally applicable to an artefact, if we could construct it, made of non-biological tissue but displaying the full range of complexity of behaviour and the full range of interaction with the environment that is displayed by *Homo sapiens* (or even a rat or a cat)? Searle gives no reason to distinguish between the two cases, biological non-terrestrial tissue and non-biological terrestrial tissue, and it is hard to see how he could. But note that, in rejecting Searle's assertion, I am not asserting the contrary. We do not know whether non-biological tissue can generate conscious events: it is an open question to be decided by empirical observations guided by an appropriate scientific theory (if and when we have one), not by a priori philosophical debate. (In his chapter in this volume Searle himself adopts this position.)

Searle's Attack on Cognitive Science

Searle next attacks the claims of cognitive science (or, indeed, to judge from the tenor of his argument, any branch of theoretical psychology) to 'fill in the gap' between brain and mind (taking the latter to mean the conscious events, beliefs, desires, etc., that we all know from our everyday experience).[2] Cognitive science, Searle says, cannot fill this gap because there is no gap to fill: there is just neurophysiology (at differing levels, ranging from, for example, the single neuron to an area of neocortex) which gives rise to everyday mental events in the micro/macro-feature way outlined above. It is a mistake to try to insert into this non-existent gap any set of additional cognitive, computational or psychological concepts (of which those derived from AI simply happen to be the ones that are currently most fashionable). Such concepts only obfuscate what would otherwise be a transparent relationship between brain micro-events and mental macro-features.

It is presumably Searle's espousal of a version of the mind–brain identity theory that motivates this attack on cognitive science, since, if we admit a level of theoretical concepts between the brain and mental phenomena, we open the way to claims that consciousness is linked to these concepts (which might, say, be instantiated in a computer or a robot) rather than directly to the brain. So let us follow the argument through and see how good it is.

The particular gap-filling exercise which Searle chooses as the target of his attack is the one that seeks to characterize the brain as processing information, following rules, making computations, etc. The heart of his attack is a distinction between, on the one hand, *true*, or *'psychological'*, rule-following or information-processing (which is what people do when they consciously follow rules or think about things they know and understand) and, on the other, *as-if* rule-following or information-processing (which is what computer programs do). Searle argues that as-if rule-following and information-processing lack key features that define true rule-following and information-processing. He describes these key features as follows. *Rule-following*: 'In order that the rule be followed, the meaning of the rule has to play some causal role in the behaviour.' *Information-processing*: 'The sense in which I do information-processing when I think is the sense in which I am consciously or unconsciously engaged in certain mental processes.'

It will be clear that, if we take these key features of true rule-following and true information-processing together with Searle's view, discussed above, that computers have no semantic contents and thus no mental processes, we must conclude (as he does) that computers cannot truly follow rules or truly process information. However, since we have already conceded most of what Searle has to say about the possibility of there being a conscious computer, this conclusion need not detain us further here. But Searle then goes on to claim that application of the concepts of rule-following or information-processing to the brain (other than to those features of brain activity that are themselves experienced as psychological rule-following and information-processing in the fullest sense) is no less of the as-if variety than when these concepts are applied to computers. It is *this* claim that poses the threat to cognitive science, and which we must examine more closely here.

I shall frame the argument around an example used by Searle, that of Chomsky's proposal that all human languages share a universal grammar. Searle writes about this in the following terms.

Chomsky's search for a universal grammar is based on the assumption that if there are certain features common to all languages, and if these features are constrained by common features of the human brain, then there must be an entire complex set of rules of universal grammar in the brain. But a much simpler hypothesis would be that the physiological structure of the brain constrains possible grammars without the intervention of an intermediate level of rules or theories. Not only is this hypothesis simpler, but also the very existence of universal features of language constrained by innate features of the brain suggests that the neurophysiological level of description is enough to do the job. You don't need to suppose that there are any rules on top of the neurophysiological structures.[11]

Searle's treatment of universal grammar is attractive in its simplicity and parsimony. But it misses out something important. It will be easier to show what this something is, if we consider the ordinary production and comprehension of language, rather than the so-called universal rules of grammar (whose very existence is still in doubt).

Language Rules

There can be little doubt that all human languages are stuffed full of rules. The discipline of linguistics is entirely concerned with establishing the nature and content of these rules. Major departure from the rules in the production or interpretation of a given language has the serious consequence that the intended communication is misunderstood. Where are these rules contained? Not in the language itself, since this is a mere abstraction from the utterance of particular speakers and their comprehension by particular hearers. The rules, then, must be contained in the heads of these speakers and hearers. But are they, in Searle's sense, true, psychological rules? That is to say, does the meaning of the rules of language play a causal role in the production and comprehension of language? Surprisingly, it turns out that Searle's answer to this question has to be 'no', with the consequence that the rules of language production and comprehension are only 'as-if' rules.

In case the reader should doubt that I am correctly interpreting Searle's distinction between true and as-if rule-following, let us take a more careful look at the way in which he draws it.

I want to make this point completely clear, so let me give you another example. When my children went to the Oakland Driving School, they were taught a rule for parking cars. The rule was: manoeuvre your car towards the curb with the steering-wheel in the extreme right position until your front wheels are even with the rear wheels of the car in front of you. Then turn the steering-wheel all the way to the extreme left position. Now notice that if they're following this rule, then its meaning must play a causal role in the production of their behaviour. I was interested to learn this rule because it's not a rule that I follow. In fact, I don't follow a rule at all when I park a car. I just look at the curb and try to get as close to the curb as I can without bashing into the cars in front of and behind me. But, notice, it might turn out that my behaviour viewed from outside, viewed externally, is identical with the behaviour of the person who is following the rule. The formal properties of the behaviour are not sufficient to show that a rule is being followed. In order that the rule be followed, the meaning of the rule has to play some causal role in the behaviour.[12]

With this passage in mind, let us look again at the case of the rules of language. It would appear that, according to Searle, one would be following a true, psychological rule in the production or comprehension of language only if one had actually learnt the rule and were capable of describing it and applying it to one's own behaviour. One would need, for example, to be able to say of oneself something like, 'I added the sound "s" to the word "cat" just now because I wanted to refer to more than one cat and that's the way you make plurals in English'. Well, one might be able to talk honestly in this way about the manner in which one uses a foreign language, learned painfully through grammar books. But is this the way a native speaker of English does the trick? And, just in case you are in any doubt about the answer to that question, how about a four-year-old native speaker? Surely not. When we learn our native tongue at mother's knee we do so without understanding any rules at all in the sense that we could express the meaning of the rule or that this meaning could 'play a causal role' in our use of language. So the rules of language that are contained in our heads (except perhaps for those parts of our heads that deal with foreign languages) are, in Searle's terms, only 'as-if' rules.

In that case, according to Searle's argument, cited above, we 'don't need to suppose that there are any rules on top of the neurophysiological structures' that mediate language. So we must ask again, where *are* the rules of language, if they are neither in the language nor in the heads of language-users? Faced with this Searle would say, I think, that it is a non-question, that I am inventing a gap where there isn't one so that I may engage in another one of those spurious gap-filling exercises that he abhors. As for his own position, this is stated thus: 'We are neurophysiologically so constructed that the stimulation of hearing other people talk and interacting with them will enable us to learn a language.'

But, for a full understanding of what is going on in language learning (and the many other cases like language learning), we have to ask one further question: *why* are we neurophysiologically constructed in just this way? The answer to this question is, in principle, both clear and uncontroversial: we are neurophysiologically constructed in this way because the behaviour that neurophysiology of this kind produced among our ancestors was conducive to their survival and reproduction. This, of course, is the standard Darwinian answer to any such question; but in the present context it contains some interesting implications.

Top–Down Determinism

Above all, it illustrates an important feature – one that Searle himself ignores – of the causal relationships that may hold between micro-elements and macro-features in the explanatory model which, on the analogies of solidity, liquidity, etc. (see above), Searle wishes to apply to the mind–brain problem: namely, not only do micro-elements give rise to the macro-features of the system that they compose, but also macro-features can determine the characteristics of micro-elements. In short, there is top–down as well as bottom–up determinism. To illustrate this point with regard to the examples from which Searle starts, consider the molecules that make up a stream of water. It is the properties of the molecules that determine the liquidity of the water; but it is the liquidity that determines the location of the water molecules (by causing them to run downhill). Similarly, the solidity of a table (determined by the properties of its atomic constituents) will help determine the location of those constituents (by, say, withstanding collapse when the roof falls in). These are relatively trivial examples of top–down determinism, and largely a matter of definition. But there are much more interesting cases. Before we return to the topic of language, it will be worth spending time on a particularly important case, pointed out by the late Michael Polanyi.[10]

Polanyi's example concerns the sequence of bases (adenine, A, guanine, G, thymine, T, or cytosine, C) that make up a single-stranded length of DNA (for example, a chromosome fragment) that codes for one or more genes (figure 30.2). Any one of these bases may follow any other in the sequence (including itself), and the laws of chemistry (for example, with respect to energy minima) will be equally well satisfied. So something other than the laws of chemistry must determine *which* base is found at a particular point in the sequence. What is this something else? An initial answer to this question would be: the ancestor from which *this* length of DNA has most recently replicated, and so on from ancestor to ancestor (we leave aside questions of mutation, faulty replication, etc.). But then a further question will arise: how did the ancestors of our length of DNA acquire and keep their particular sequence of bases? The answer to *this* question takes us beyond chemistry and into biology: namely, our length of DNA has its particular sequence of bases because organisms

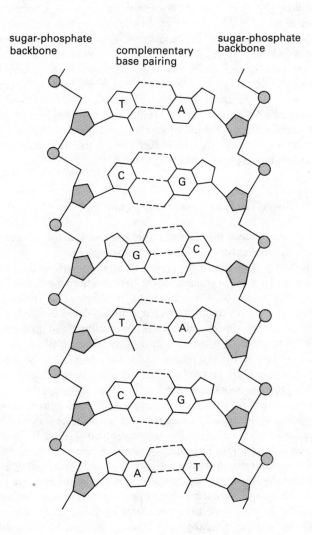

Figure 30.2 The base pairing of two DNA chains. According to the laws of chemistry, any one of these bases (labelled T, A, C or G) may follow any other in the sequence (including itself). Something else must determine which base is found at a particular point in the sequence (redrawn from Watson, Tooze and Kutz, 1983, Recombinant DNA, *Scientific American Books, fig. 2.6).*

carrying *this* sequence were genetically endowed with mechanisms that enabled them to survive and reproduce more efficiently. Thus the lower-level (micro-element) laws of chemistry leave open four options at each point in the sequence of bases; and selection among these options is accomplished by the (equally deterministic) higher-level (macro-feature) laws of biology. Determinism is *both* bottom–up *and* top–down, and in neither case is it trivial.

With this lesson in mind, let us return to our question concerning the rules of language: why are we 'neurophysiologically so constructed that the stimulation of hearing other people talk and interacting with them will enable us to learn a language?' Answer: because people (or their simian forebears) who could produce and understand language were better able to survive and reproduce. But, in order to produce and understand language, the brains of these people had to contain mechanisms that could follow the rules that are essential for linguistic communication. Thus, far from its being the case (as Searle argues) that neurophysiological properties determined the capacity of language users to behave *as if* they were following rules, it was the necessity genuinely to follow such rules that constrained (in a manner analogous to that described in Polanyi's DNA example) the brains of language-users to contain mechanisms capable of doing so. It follows that the level of psychological description (the following of rules, etc.) that Searle wishes to proscribe as an unnecessary fiction forms an essential component in any complete explanation of the way in which the unitary mind–brain system that produces language operates and has evolved.

The Conditions for Consciousness – Again

A further consequence flows from this argument, one that brings us back to our central theme: the conditions for consciousness.

If it is correct to suppose that particular neurophysiological mechanisms have evolved in the human brain because they mediated the rule-following that is essential for language, it follows that quite different neurophysiological mechanisms might similarly have evolved, provided only that they were able to subserve the same functions (in the way that quite different kinds of wing have evolved in different phyla, all permitting their owners to fly; see figure 30.3). This possibility (of convergent evolution) is unlikely in fact to have been realized in the case of language, since this appears to have evolved only once. But suppose we take a cognitive skill that is much more widespread in phylogenetic terms, that of responding to the regular sequence of two stimuli, A followed by B, in such a manner as to prepare for B when given A (that is, classical or Pavlovian conditioning). This skill is found in the sea-slug (*Aplysia*) in much the same form as in the rat, cat, dog and Man; but it is highly unlikely that the sea-slug uses the same neural machinery as we do when forming and using Pavlovian associations. When we form such associations, we are at least sometimes conscious of doing so. So the equation arises: is the sea-slug similarly sometimes conscious? Searle would have us (I think) answer this question by looking at the neurons with which we

BEE, HUMBLE.

BRITISH GLOW WORM,
Male—Flying.

DRAGON FLYING.

CROSSBILL.

EAGLE, GOLDEN.

J. W. Wood.

FLYING SQUIRREL.

Figure 30.3 Convergent evolution exemplified by the variety of wings found in nature. Insects, birds, flying mammals and gliding reptiles all evolved wing-shaped appendages completely independently as separate but similar solutions to the problem of how to fly through the air (illustrations from Beeton's Dictionary of Natural History*).*

and the sea-slug do this particular trick: if they are the same, then the sea-slug is also likely to be aware of the associations it forms. But there is an equally plausible alternative: namely, that the particular neural machinery with which a cognitive skill is performed is unimportant; rather, it is the nature of the skill itself that matters (in which case we perhaps already know that the sea-slug has some rudimentary form of consciousness). As between these two alternatives I see no way at present of choosing (see section I of this chapter).

Conclusion

So how does the mind–brain identity theory stand today? Searle has put forward a persuasive case for his new version of this theory. But, in spite of his forceful advocacy, I fear that the theory is in barely better shape than in 1971.

Searle's basic explanatory model for the relation of mind (as a macro-feature of the mind–brain system) to the functioning of neurons (as micro-elements of this system) is much more satisfactory than the correlational approaches that have largely preoccupied earlier identity theorists; it has impressive scientific antecedents; and it allows one to pose the scientifically interesting questions in a way that previous identity theories have often prevented. And the model would be even stronger if full use were made of top–down (from macro-feature to micro-element) determinism, as well as the bottom–up determinism with which Searle is exclusively concerned.[2] (Among other things, I believe, top–down determinism, along the lines of Polanyi's DNA example, would eliminate the paradox of free will with which Searle grapples unsuccessfully. But, since this problem is rather separate from that of consciousness, I have not considered it here.)

None the less, in spite of these assets, Searle's model suffers from a fundamental weakness: it suggests no theoretical linkage between the neuronal micro-elements and the macro-feature of consciousness. Nor could it, since (unlike the scientific precedents upon which Searle draws) the properties of the micro-elements have not been constructed with the object of explaining the macro-features. Thus, as outlined in section I of this chapter, the link between consciousness and neurons remains at the level of brute fact – consciousness being a datum from my own experience (and, of course, yours); neurons being concepts drawn from the quite separate universe of discourse that encompasses physiology and behaviour; and the two meeting only because they both occur in the same heads. And this must perforce continue to be the case until someone proposes a principled theory to account for the detailed manner in which the properties of neurons and/or neuronal systems give rise to conscious events. Neither Searle nor (so far as I am aware) anyone else has yet been able to propose such a theory.

I said above that one advantage that Searle has over previous identity theorists is that his position allows one to ask the interesting scientific questions about consciousness (which I considered in section I of this chapter). But further scrutiny shows that this feature of Searle's position derives from the fact that his micro/macro-feature model does not necessarily lead to the mind–brain identity theory that Searle himself seems to hold. This point will have become clear, I think, from my discussion of the rules of language. From that discussion I concluded that, to the question 'What properties of neuronal micro-elements might give rise to the macro-feature of consciousness?', it would be as legitimate to answer 'Such-and-such an aspect of the following of rules' as 'Such-and-such an aspect of neuronal functioning'. Indeed, it is probable that Searle's explanatory model can be a useful framework within which to pose the scientifically interesting questions (of evolution, mechanisms, etc.) *only* to the extent that it allows such alternative answers.

We come again, therefore, to the conclusion reached in section I of this chapter: to espouse the philosophical theory of mind–brain identity in the absence of a specific scientific model as to how the properties of brain actually give rise to mind (and, most importantly, to the conscious aspects of mind) is prematurely to close off potential avenues of scientific exploration. We should instead continue to keep all our options open.

References

I am indebted to my former philosophical colleagues at University College, Oxford, J. L. Mackie, M. G. J. Evans and J. H. McDowell, for their comments on an earlier version of the first part of this chapter and for many valuable discussions.

1 Borst, C. V. (ed.) (1970) *The Mind–Brain Identity Theory*. London: St Martin.
2 Searle, J. R. (1985) *Minds, Brains and Science*. London: BBC Publications. See also Searle's chapter, this volume.
3 E. g., Smart, J. J. C. Sensations and brain processes. In C. V. Borst, op. cit., pp. 52–66.
4 Lippold, O. (1970) The origin of the alpha rhythm. *Nature* 226: 616–18.
5 Cooper, L. A. and Shepard, R. N. (1973) Chronometric studies of the rotation of mental images. In W. G. Chase (ed.), *Visual Information Processing*, pp. 75–176. London: Academic Press.
6 Dement, W. C. (1965) An essay on dreams: the role of physiology in understanding their nature. In F. Barron *et al.*, *New Directions in Psychology*, vol. 2. New York.
7 See, e.g., Taylor, C. Mind–brain identity, a side issue? In C. V. Borst, *The Mind–Brain Identity Theory*, pp. 231–41.
8 Sperry, R. W. (1968) Hemisphere deconnection and unity in conscious awareness. *American Psychologist*, 23: 723–33.
9 See, e.g., Armstrong, D. M. The nature of the mind. In C. V. Borst, *The Mind–Brain Identity Theory*, pp. 67–79.
10 *The Listener*, 8 November 1984, pp. 14–16.
11 *The Listener*, 22 November 1984, pp. 17–18.
12 *The Listener*, 22 November 1984, p. 17.

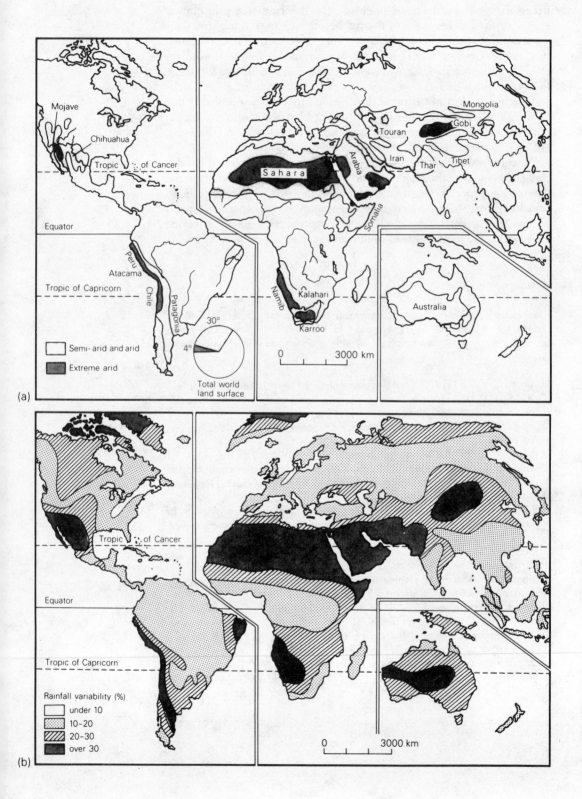

(a)

Mojave
Chihuahua
Tropic of Cancer
Equator
Peru
Atacama
Chile
Patagonia
Tropic of Capricorn

Mongolia
Touran
Gobi
Iran
Thar
Tibet
Arabia
Sahara
Somalia
Namib
Kalahari
Karroo
Australia

Semi-arid and arid
Extreme arid

30°
4°
Total world
land surface

0   3000 km

(b)

Tropic of Cancer
Equator
Tropic of Capricorn

Rainfall variability (%)
under 10
10–20
20–30
over 30

0   3000 km

31

Languages, Minds and Brains

Peter Hacker

Peter Hacker has been Fellow and Tutor in Philosophy at St John's College, Oxford since 1966. He has recently been elected to a British Academy Research Readership. He read PPE at The Queen's College, Oxford, wrote his doctorate under the supervision of Professor H. L. A. Hart while at St Antony's College, Oxford, subsequently enjoying a Junior Research Fellowship at Balliol before going to his present college. He has held various Visiting Chairs in North America. He has written extensively on the philosophy of Wittgenstein, on philosophy of logic and of language, and on philosophy of mind. He is author of Insight and Illusion *(Oxford University Press, 1972), co-editor (with J. Raz) of* Law, Morality and Society *(Oxford University Press, 1977), co-author (with G. P. Baker) of* Wittgenstein: Understanding and Meaning *(Blackwell, 1980), and author of* Frege: Logical Excavations *(Blackwell, 1984),* Language, Sense and Nonsense *(Blackwell, 1984),* Scepticism, Rules and Language *(Blackwell, 1984),* Wittgenstein: Rules, Grammar and Necessity *(Blackwell, 1985). He is currently writing a book entitled* Appearance and Reality, *concerned with perception and perceptual qualities.*

Analogies

Fruitful analogies are the go-cart of creativity. The hydrodynamic analogy proved immensely fruitful in the development of the theory of electricity, even though electrical current does not flow in the same sense as water flows and an electrical wire is not a kind of pipe. Voltage is indeed analogous to pressure; it is fruitful to consider amperage as akin to current and to view electrical resistance as being similar to hydrodynamical resistance. But if a schoolchild – after having his first lesson about electricity – proceeded to cut electrical wires, turn them up vertically and shake them in order to get some of the electricity to pour out, we would, with justice, think that he had not understood the lesson, not grasped the character of the 'model' of electrical current, and wholly misconstrued the concepts of flow of electricity, electrical potential, and so forth.

Analogies can be equally fruitful and illuminating in non-theoretical intellectual disciplines. The art historian who describes works of art is not

*What may rightly be called a 'map'? Major world zones showing (a) the distribution of world deserts; (b) rainfall variability. A map is a 'symbolic description' using an array of symbols to yield a true (or false) characterization of a certain aspect of the world. To be a map, the conventions of representation used by the map-maker must be known to the map-reader (*The Nature of the Environment, Blackwell, 1985).

constructing theories in the sense in which the physicist is. Although, like the physicist, he pursues understanding and insight, the nature of the understanding is categorially distinct. But here too analogies may often be immensely fruitful. When Sir John Summerson, in *The Classical Language of Architecture*,[1] talks about the architectural vocabulary of classical architecture, of the grammar of Renaissance building, he is employing a most illuminating analogy. It is enlightening to view classical architecture under the aspect of a grammatical structure. A column is 'meaningless' unless it supports something. The orders are 'as categorical in the grammar of architecture as, say, the four conjugations of verbs in the grammar of the Latin language'. They are not ready-mades to be slotted together, rather 'it is much better to think of them as grammatical expressions imposing a formidable discipline, but a discipline within which personal sensibility always has a certain play'. The elements of classical architecture, the orders, arches, vaults, pediments, etc. are, in architectural practice, governed by a multitude of (once) well-known rules as to what is possible, what makes sense, what is proper (and respectable), what is slightly improper, and what is downright nonsense. The analogy is important and can be used to further our understanding.

Nevertheless it should be noted how profoundly different the role of such an analogy is in the aesthetics of architecture from the role of analogies in empirical science. It does not generate hypotheses that can be tested in experiments, nor does it produce a theory that can be used to predict events. The understanding that is the product of such an analogy is not the result of new information, nor does it lead to new empirical discoveries. It does not lead to the asking of fresh factual questions which can then be answered by further empirical research. It is a new form of description which involves a rearrangement of familiar facts. It makes formal connections between descriptions of architectural features and characterizations of linguistic ones. Thenceforth we can significantly say of architectural features: 'That makes sense (or, is nonsensical)', 'This is rhetorical (or, is bombastic)', 'That is witty (or, ambiguous)', 'This is a solecism', and so on. The analogy yields new forms of comparison, changing our understanding of buildings and affecting the way we look at things. We see them under the aspect of the analogical concept. This is a salient feature of aesthetic criticism and description.

Classical architecture, then, can illuminatingly be said to be analogous to a language. But if Summerson started to tell us that on a dark night on the Acropolis he can hear the Parthenon speaking to the Erectheum, if he insisted that we must decode what the Colosseum has to say to the Arch of Severus, then we would think that either his prose was getting excessively purple and his metaphors running out of control, or that he was suffering from a fit of madness.

There is a widespread view among neurophysiologists and psychologists, particularly those who study the mechanism of perception, that the brain receives information from the senses, that this information is duly encoded in the brain and interpreted by the brain. By interpreting this information, the brain builds up a representation of the 'external world' and then issues instructions which will ensure the survival of the organism. Of course, if information is received, encoded, decoded, interpreted and provides grounds for making plans, then there must be a language or system of representation in which this is all done. It will, therefore, come as no surprise at this point that scientists who discuss the functioning of the brain in this manner are perfectly happy to talk about the brain's having a language. Is this just a picturesque metaphor or helpful analogy? Or is it a symptom of widespread confusion in the presentation, description and explanation of experimental data painstakingly and ingeniously achieved, which are then mangled by misdescription? This is the subject I shall address.

J. Z. Young, one of the most influential living British biologists, announces in the opening pages of *Programs of the Brain* that what he hopes to show is 'how the organization of the brain can be considered as the written script of the program of our lives'.[2] What neuroscience can do, he explains, 'is to translate the language in which the brain programs are written into ordinary language . . . we are using the analogies of language and of writing to understand the entities [brains] that produce them'. One might presume that analogies employed in a biological science would be akin to the model-generating analogies of physics rather than the aspect-seeing analogies of art history. For neurophysiology aims, I take it, to construct verifiable theories, testable hypotheses, and prediction-yielding explanations. This appears to be Young's view:

The proposal is to use the analogy of the encoding of information by writing to speak about the way in which the brain contains the scripts of the programs that issue in human action. This is not merely to use a picturesque metaphor. Discoveries made by physiologists in recent years show the detailed characteristics of the cells in the brain that provide the code signs for features of the world, such as a particular line or sound, or the colour red. (p. 11)

I shall suggest that Young is at best employing an analogy of the aspect-seeing variety in the belief that it is of the model-generating and hence essentially explanatory kind. (I am not suggesting a sharp dichotomy of types of analogy here, but of *uses* of analogy.) More importantly, it leads Young himself, and those of his colleagues who are similarly deceived, into conceptual confusions on a par with the supposition that electrical current is a kind of liquid or that one building can and does talk, in the language of classical architecture, to another. To show this I must first sketch out the beguiling picture that is, as we shall see, widespread among neurophysiologists and psychologists.

The Language of the Brain

Why should anyone think that the brain has or uses a language in the first place? One pattern of reasoning runs as follows: when we perceive an object by means of our perceptual organs, electrical impulses are transmitted along nerve fibres to highly specific parts of the brain. For example, when we see something, light from the object is reflected into our eyes, falling upon the light-sensitive retina. The cells of the retina, duly stimulated, respond by transmitting impulses along the optic nerve. The pattern of impulses must, it seems, in some sense contain all the information for the brain to go on about what is seen. But, of course, there is no *picture* in the visual cortex representing what we see. Yet surely, there *must* be some kind of representation in our heads of what we see, otherwise we would not *be* seeing: So a distinguished psychologist of perception, J. P. Frisby, argues: 'it is an inescapable conclusion that there must be a symbolic description in the brain of the outside world, a description cast in symbols which stand for the various aspects of the world of which sight makes us aware.'[3] A parallel pattern of reasoning is applied to other senses to yield similar conclusions.

A 'symbolic description' is presumably an array of symbols which are so combined as to yield a true (or false) characterization of a certain aspect of the world. It must be cast in a certain language which has a vocabulary and grammar. If one knows the language, then one will understand such a 'symbolic description'. Since, on Frisby's view, for a person to see something just is (*inter alia*) for his brain to construct a symbolic description, the brain must have, use and understand a language, the language of the brain. 'The problem of seeing is the problem of building up a symbolic description of a scene using information contained in the input visual image', and it is evident, Frisby argues, that this must be done by 'encoding symbolically all the useful information contained in the input image in terms of a vocabulary of feature symbols' (p. 26), that is, symbols which stand for such features of what is seen as edges, corners, lines, etc. In fact, nerve cells in the visual cortex (the striate cortex) are sensitive to, that is, respond electrically to, just such features as lines or edges in the visual field.[4] However, in order to produce a feature description, the activity of these cells must be interpreted. *The* great question, Frisby contends, is:

what is the code in which the outcomes of the interpretative process are written? What is the feature description lodged in the brain which is the neural correlate of our conscious awareness of features? If we see a 'sharp edge oriented at 23° clockwise from the vertical and of medium contrast', what is the neural representation of this feature description, this percept? (p. 53)

Of course, he concedes, we do not know the answer to this question. In fact, we have 'almost no idea' of what the feature code might be. 'A Nobel prize surely awaits the discoverer of this elusive language' (loc. cit.).

Much is unclear in this sketch, but the following points are evident. The general conception at work involves the supposition that the brain has a *language* of its own, which consists of *symbols* that *represent* things. It uses the *vocabulary* of this language to *encode information* and it produces *descriptions* of what is seen (or, more generally, perceived). Precisely the same general conception informs J. Z. Young's speculations about the 'programs of the brain'. He goes to some length to clarify these important ideas.

The brain, Young contends, 'is an agent issuing instructions, after it has decoded (understood) the signals it receives about what is going on around it' (p. 43).[5] The task of the neurophysiologist is to study the language of the brain so that we may 'learn to recognize and interpret the elements of the script and the meanings of the signs in which it is written' (p. 2). A language, we are told, is a *code*. Indeed these expressions are used more or less interchangeably: a code is 'a set of visible signs, sounds or other physical events adopted to form a system of communication of messages' (p. 290) and a language is a 'system of signs used for intentional communication by one or more codes' (p. 294). 'The concepts of signs and information, and of coding and language', Young argues, 'are closely related to the nature of life itself' (p. 2). Far from being essentially, conceptually, tied to the notions of convention and normativity, they lie much deeper in the very roots of the biological.

A sign is *symbolic* when it 'somehow corresponds to features of the surroundings in such a manner that it communicates a lot of information that is used by the organism in its business of keeping alive . . . a symbol is a special sort of signal because it represents features of the surroundings in such a way that the organism immediately recognizes its significance and acts accordingly' (p. 60). The lives of all organisms are, Young suggests, governed by programs, that is, plans of procedures, schedules or systems under which action may be taken towards a desired goal (p. 8). Each individual creature follows programs written in two main languages embodied in different media: (a) the fundamental inherited program written in the DNA code; (b) programs written in the language of the brain. 'Its units are the groups of nerve cells so organized as to produce the various actions at the right times' (p. 10). Men, Young adds interestingly, follow programs written in two further languages, namely 'the organized sounds of spoken language' and 'writing and other forms of speech'[6] (p. 10).

What does the brain do with its language? Among other things, it makes *maps* on the basis of the information communicated to it by the senses. This startling, indeed amazing idea, is widespread among scientists who study the brain:

The nerve cells that analyse the information of the senses are laid out on the brain to make actual physical maps of the surface of the body or retina. What goes on in the brain must provide a faithful representation of events outside, and the arrangement of the cells in it provides a detailed model of the world. (Young, p. 11)

Note that Young, like Frisby, is moved to use necessitarian language: there *must* be a representation of what we see in the brain, otherwise we would not see; this conclusion is 'inescapable'. The startling idea that the brain contains maps arose out of the experimental work of many neurologists and neurophysiologists including D. H. Hubel and T. N. Wiesel who successfully mapped out systematic correlations between the electrical responses of groups of cells in the visual cortex and differently oriented lines, etc. in corresponding parts of the visual field.[4] On the assumption that arrays of brain cells *represent* states of affairs in the world, it evidently seems plausible to many theorists to conceive of nerve cells as words of a code. One can then 'compare the problem of how they represent the world to understanding how a grammar allows the combination of words to make meaningful statements' (p. 51), and the primary clue to the character of this brain language or code is, Young argues, the fact

that the information from the sensory surfaces of the retina, or skin, or from the ear is laid out in a topographically precise way on the surface of the brain. Moreover for each such sense there is a series of such maps, each recombining in a new way the words of information provided by the cells. So the grammar of this language has something to do with spatial relations. It communicates meanings by topological analogies. (p. 52)

Figure 31.1   David Hubel (left) and Torsten Wiesel at a conference in the mid-seventies. Their work on the visual systems of cats and monkeys has greatly advanced our understanding of the mechanisms of vision. But is it right to say that they have discovered visual maps in the brain or that they have deciphered the language of vision? (photograph by Colin Blakemore).

On the basis of such 'maps' or 'representations' the brain 'constructs hypotheses and programs' (pp. 11, 57). The task of the theorist is 'to show how the brain cells provide the code in which these hypotheses and programs are written' (p. 11).

The picture that I have outlined is a mythology of neural processes, in the sense in which Platonism in mathematics might be said to be a mythology of a symbolism. It is not a theory, for if it were a theory it would at least make *sense* for it to be true and one might try to devise experiments to confirm it. Equally, it would make sense for it to be false, and one might endeavour to confute it. But this picture does not make sense *as such a theory*, any more than does the personification of forces of nature in Greek mythology. For one can devise no *experiment* to confute the idea that the passage of the sun through the sky is Apollo upon his fiery chariot. There is, of course, nothing *wrong* with the myths, unless one treats them as theories. Then, however, they are deeply misleading, neither fulfilling the expressive function of mythology nor the explanatory function of empirical theories. As far as I can see, speculative neurophysiology, through misconstruing a range of analogies, has generated a kind of mythology which it treats as incipient empirical theory if not established empirical fact.

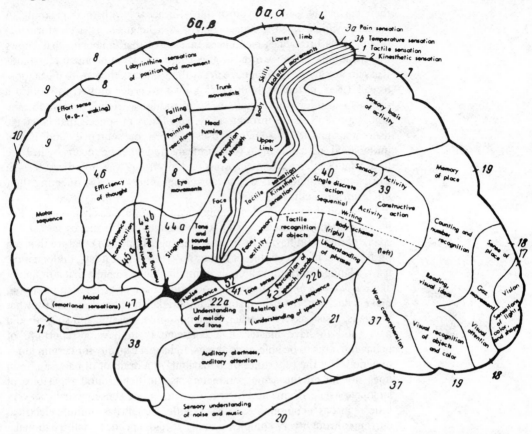

Figure 31.2 Modern phrenology. A diagram based on the work of K. Kleist showing the presumed locations of functions in the left hemisphere of the human brain. Each function is ascribed on the basis of the effects of damage to that part of the brain in humans. This may be a useful summary of the results of a great deal of research, but is it correct to call it a map?

In the rest of this chapter I shall try, rather schematically, to sustain the verdict that this account makes no sense (it is not empirically false but conceptually awry), that it is born of the inadvertent misuse of language, misunderstandings of crucial concepts such as *language, code, representation, understanding* and equivocation over, for example, *information, sign, map*, as well as confusing a rather unhelpful analogy with a genuine empirical hypothesis.

Disentangling the Knots

I shall not try to formulate a definition of 'a language'. What I mean by this expression is just what other English speakers typically mean by it. English, German, French, Chinese, Japanese, etc. are languages. The only speakers of any language that we are acquainted with are human beings, though there is a lively debate going on about a select few chimpanzees. Someone who *has* a language has mastered a technique, acquired or possesses a skill of using symbols in accord with rules for their correct use, or – if you prefer – in accord with their meaning. A creature which *has* a language or *knows* a language is a creature that understands utterances (sentences in use) of that language, that knows the meanings of the words of the language. If someone understands Russian he can *use* the language to say things, to ask the way to the station, to call a taxi, to tell a tale or crack a joke, to order dinner, to request a drink, to wonder what time it is, to introduce a friend, to describe the landscape, and so on through a myriad of acts of speech that language users engage in. If someone uses a word or sentence, and is not understood, he can explain what it means and what he means by it. If he understands a language he can respond in various ways to others' uses of words and sentences, as well as correcting others' errors, querying their unclarities and equivocations.

I mention these platitudes simply because they are easily forgotten. For if one remembers them, it should be obvious that it makes *no sense* to speak of the brain having or using a language. Only of a creature that can perform acts of speech does it make sense to say that it has, understands, uses, a language. But it is literally unintelligible to suggest that a brain, let alone *a part of a brain*, might ask a question, have or express an intention, make a decision, describe a sunset, undertake an obligation, explain what it means, insist, assert, instruct, demand, opine, classify, and so forth. To have, and to have mastered, a language is to have a repertoire of behaviour. It is to be able to do things, to have a capacity for certain kinds of action. But the repertoire of 'behaviour' of a brain or of part of a brain does not lie on the same parameters as the behavioural repertoire of language users. Brains and their parts can, in one sense, actually *do* very little[7] – just as a computer can do very little, namely pass minute electrical currents through very complex circuits at high speed. I shall try to make this clear in the following pages; the point is not a trivial linguistic one but an important observation concerning the bounds of sense – hence about our concepts of language and language users.

It makes no sense to talk of the brain containing knowledge or information written in its own language. It is worth reminding oneself how these phrases are used. We may say of a book that it contains the knowledge of a lifetime, or of a filing cabinet that it contains all the available knowledge (duly card-indexed) about Julius Caesar. This means that the pages of the book or the cards in the filing cabinet have written on them *expressions* of a large number of known truths. In this sense, to be sure, the brain *contains* no knowledge at all. There are no symbols in the brain that by their array express a single proposition, let alone a proposition that is known to be true. Of course, in this sense too a human being *contains* no knowledge either. To possess knowledge is not to contain knowledge; I have a smattering of knowledge about sixteenth-century woodcuts, but I contain none, and Hind's history of early woodcuts contains a great deal of knowledge but has none. To possess knowledge is to know that such and such is the case, and that in turn is an ability (or is at least ability-like), not a matter of containment.

Likewise with information. A great deal of information is amassed in the *Encyclopedia Britannica*. In that sense, there is none at all in the brain. Much information can be *derived* from a slice through a tree trunk, or from a geological specimen. And no doubt too from the dissection of a brain. But that is *not* information which the brain *has*. Nor is it *written* in the brain, let alone in 'the language of the brain', any more than the information 'in' the tree trunk about the severity of winters in the 1930s is written in arboreal patois.

Do not computers contain knowledge, and does not the brain contain knowledge and information in just the same way? One may certainly store information on computer discs. Of course, the computer no more knows the information which is stored in it or the knowledge it contains than does a book, filing cabinet or bookcase. Unlike the book or file, the storage of information in a computer does not take the form of written symbols that express propositions. Rather we, having several millenia ago developed one method of recording and storing what we know, namely writing and storing documents, have recently evolved a means of recording and storing what we know in a way which, for certain purposes, is more economical and efficient, namely on computer discs. But to say that the information we have about a certain subject is contained or stored in the computer is not to attribute any cognitive capacities to the computer. It is rather to say something about what we *use* the machine for. In the wholly unmysterious sense in which a computer can be said to contain knowledge or information, *brains do not*. For we do not *use* brains as we use computers. Indeed it makes no more sense to talk of storing information in the brain than it does to talk of having dictionaries or filing cards in the brain as opposed to having them in a bookcase or filing cabinet.

This may seem a dogmatic piece of 'ordinary language philosophy'. For it must surely be *obvious* that the brain contains information: Phillips, Zeki and Barlow, in their survey paper 'Localization of Function in the Cerebral Cortex, Past, Present and Future', contend that neurophysiologists at the 1981 meeting at Hertford College, Oxford 'were ... searching for more sophisticated ideas about representation. They were not asking how the retina is projected on to the visual cortex, but how motion, form or colour information may be organized there; not how the sensory surface may be mapped in the somatosensory cortex, but how different modalities of sensation are organised'.[8] I shall briefly examine the concept of representation below, but I confess that I find incoherent the idea that *information* about motion, form or colour might be 'organized' in the visual cortex, in the requisite sense of information.

The neurophysiologist may patiently explain that of course by 'information' he does not mean an array of known propositions expressed in a symbolism. Rather, he employs the expression as engineers, 'communication theorists', or 'information theorists' do. '"*Information*"', Warren Weaver writes, 'in this theory is used in a special sense that must not be confused with its ordinary usage. In particular, *information* must not be confused with meaning. In fact, two messages, one of which is heavily loaded with meaning, and the other of which is pure nonsense, can be exactly equivalent from the present viewpoint as regards information.'[9] And Claude E. Shannon, who invented the mathemathical theory of information, wrote, 'the semantic aspects of communication are irrelevant to the engineering aspects'.[10] What then is *information* in this sense? It is a measure of one's freedom of choice in transmission of a signal. So it applies not to individual 'messages' and their content, but to the choices between possible 'messages' or signals. The amount of information is measured by the logarithm to the base 2 (the binary system) of the number of available choices. The unit of information (a choice between two options) is commonly called a 'bit' (binary digit). And the communication theorists have developed elaborate mathematical theories to measure the amount of information carried by an 'information' source that produces a sequence of 'signals' according to certain probabilities which themselves depend on the previous distribution of 'signals' in the sequence.

Is this actually what neurophysiologists mean? I think not, or at any rate, not unequivocally. Young introduces the information–theoretic notion (on p. 42 of his book) and immediately stumbles into the natural ('semantic') concept of information:

So far we have not spoken about the nature of the changes that convey information along a communication channel. Some physical events in the nerve must provide the units of a code, which together stand for or represent the events in the outside world to which the organism must react. Evidently this correspondence must be a *pre-established* property of the communication system ... the correspondence of the words of a human language with what they are to signify, however it becomes established, is mostly arbitrary. But somehow in the process of production of effective communication channels there must be correspondence with what is to be communicated. We have therefore to enquire what are the units of the neural code and how did they come to represent events in the world. (p. 43)[11]

Dr Pangloss would have been delighted at such pre-established harmony. It is, however, evident that two quite different senses of 'information' are here conflated, the information–theoretic one which has nothing to do with 'representing' and the 'semantic' one, which has nothing to do with 'bits'. Young is not unique here. Phillips, Zeki and Barlow similarly wander unawares from the information–theoretic sense to the common-or-garden one:

Zeki proposed that the so-called 'colour-coded' cells of V1 do not respond to specific colours at all, but only to the presence of sufficient amounts of their preferred wavelength in the light reaching the eye. The information is then *used* by the cells of V4 *to assign colours to surfaces*, and the pattern of activity in these cells corresponds simply with the subjectively seen colour.[12]

As far as I understand the phrase 'using information to assign colours to surfaces', it is not something a *cell* can intelligibly be said to do in *either* sense of 'information'. My qualms are magnified by subsequent remarks:

We think that nerve cells use the same inductive logic as the detective [the statistical operation, not the high-level conscious process that goes on in the detective's mind], and that statistically significant coincidences are the informational fodder that they grab hold of and devour to build higher perceptual concepts and more complex forms of organized behaviour.[13]

I flounder in the mixed metaphors; but to one thing I hold firm: cells are not in the business of building perceptual concepts – or any other kinds of concept – on the basis of statistically significant coincidences – or any other kind of information in either sense of the term.[14] This should be evident if one reflects upon what it means to say that a creature has or 'builds' (constructs) a concept. Of what creatures does it *make sense* to say that they have concepts, and in what circumstances do we attribute conceptual abilities to a creature? A creature that has concepts is one that makes true or false judgements, that believes certain things to be the case, disbelieves others, doubts or is certain. It is (with marginal qualifications, perhaps, for the recognitional capacities and associated behavioural repertoire of the higher mammals) a symbol-employing creature. It makes sense to say of a human being that it has perceptual concepts such as the concepts of seeing, hearing, or tasting, or concepts of perceptual qualities, such as the concepts of magenta, B-flat, or acrid. For of a human being it makes sense to say (and is often true) that it has mastered the use of expressions such as 'to see (hear, taste)' or 'magenta (B-flat, acrid)'. But it is literally senseless to attribute conceptual abilities *to cells*. Cells no more construct or possess concepts, let alone use inductive logic, than they write sonnets to their mistresses' eyebrows, philosophize or undertake obligations.

It is here, in such remarks of biologists and physiologists, in the questions which they pose and present as the frontiers of knowledge that they hope to assail, that one can see vividly the effects of their muddled and misunderstood analogies. For an analogy which leads to the wrong side of the frontier between sense and nonsense *and misleads its users* into thinking that they are on the brink of astonishing and extraordinary discoveries is pernicious. It is noteworthy that Young gives divergent explanations of what a language is. On the one hand it is 'a system of signs used for intentional communication by one or more codes' (p. 294), on the other it is 'a system of relations of parts constituting the signs that organize the actions necessary for the self-maintenance of the living system' (p. 10). On the first specification brains cannot be said to have a language, since they cannot be said to have any communicational intentions. I may intend to communicate my ideas about philosophy to my undergraduates. I may intend to convey my wishes and desires, I may aim to let my wife know when I'll be home. But a brain can no more be said to intend to do something than it can be said to fall in love, make a promise, or get married. On the second specification, assuming that 'sign' is taken not symbolically, but causally, then any homeostatic system within an organism that is requisite for preservation of the organism has a language. But, in this bogus sense of 'language', a language has nothing whatever to do with such familiar phenomena as English, French and German, that is, what we use, speak, hear and understand.

It is important to notice that the acts and activities of using a language are typically intentional. (Of course, words may be involuntarily forced from me, expletives and exclamations spring involuntarily from my lips. But what may happen some of the time may be, and in this case is, inconceivable as happening all of the time.) The words of a language have a conventionally assigned use, and one who has mastered a language must know the use, the correct employment, of an expression and be able to distinguish a correct from an incorrect use. For a sound or mark on paper to have a use, to be used in accord with a standard of correctness, there must be a practice of so using it, typically a social practice. For only where there is a practice of employing a sign can there also be an activity of matching the application of the sign against a standard of correctness. Since signs have a meaning, a use, only in so far as there is a convention, a standard of correctness for their application, there must be a *possibility* of correcting misuses by reference to the standard of correctness for the use of the expression which is embodied in an explanation of meaning. The use of language is essentially a normative activity.

It follows that neither brains nor cells, let alone DNA molecules, can intelligibly be said to have a language. (Nor indeed *not* to have a language, any more than it makes sense to say that my pen does not speak English or that my fingernail does not have a bank account). Nor can they be said to follow conventions. It does not make sense to suggest, as Phillips, Zeki and Barlow do, that 'it would be very hard to believe that a functionally sensible outcome could arise from these connections [of cells in the cortex] unless the communications transmitted down them followed a set of conventions, and these conventions might be termed the cortical language'.[15] For to follow conventions, there must be conventions to follow, standards of correctness for certain kinds of behaviour. For there to be conventions there must be practices of using the conventions in teaching and learning, in correcting mistakes, in explaining and justifying action. Only of a creature who has the *ability* to make a mistake, who can *recognize* his mistake by reference to a standard, who can *correct* his action for the *reason* that it was erroneous, only of such a creature can one say that it follows and uses conventions.

Perhaps one source of error here lies in misunderstandings and misuses of the term 'code'. A code is *not* a language, it presupposes a language. When we wish to transmit a message that expresses an array of propositions to a person and also ensure that others should not understand it, we encrypt, encipher or encode it into a cryptogram. To do this we may employ a cipher system, which treats of letters or groups of letters (usually only up to three) by transposition or substitution, or a code system, which is a substitution system that treats words, phrases or sentences. Be it code or cipher, a cryptogram *is* a cryptogram only if the array of signs is being used in accord with rules to encrypt information that is *expressed* in sentences of a language. It is true, and possibly a source of confusion, that with the invention of telephone, telegraph and television there developed methods of concealment *analogous* to cryptography, namely ciphony (speech), cifax (facsimile) and civision (television). It is important to note that these are only analogous to literal cryptograms (the 'unit' is not a simple character, letter or word, but a timed portion of the continuously varying audio or image-scanning signal). A language, such as English, is not a code. Understanding utterances of a language involves no decoding or deciphering, for there is nothing encoded which needs decoding. *Sometimes* a remark may need *interpreting*, but not very often. And interpreting, unlike decoding, is a form of *explanation*.

It follows also that when biologists talk of the 'genetic code' they are not using the word 'code' in the sense in which a code is essentially related to a language, that is, in the sense that what one encodes is a sentence or set of sentences in a language. It may be harmless (or rather, it should have been harmless) to refer to adenine (A) guanine (G) thymine (T) and cytosine (C) as 'letters', although they are no more letters than numbers are objects. It should have been at worst picturesque to say that DNA contains the genetic code of 1.5–3.5 million letters which incorporates the genetic *information* that builds and controls the cell, all encoded in nucleotide sequences. But, as far as I can see, it has been profoundly misleading! The sense in which there is a 'program' embodied (not written) in the genetic material has no significant relation to the sense in which human beings make a program, namely (as Young says), 'a plan of procedure, a schedule or system under which action may be taken towards a desired goal . . . a plan of action that is chosen from a set of possible plans and with specific objectives'. DNA molecules, cells, unicellular organisms have neither plans nor goals, they do not *choose* courses of action from among alternatives, nor do they have objectives.

Similar considerations apply to cerebral events. Nothing in the cortex constitutes a 'symbolic representation' of the creature's environment. Confusion is doubtless caused by misuse and misunderstanding of the much overworked expression 'representation'. Much can and should be said about signs 'representing' or constituting 'representations', but I must confine myself to three observations. First, if one insists that linguistic expressions *represent* features of the world, one had better first decide which linguistic expressions – words or sentences? Do all words represent, or only some? And what is it for a word to represent? If one wishes one can indeed say that virtually all words represent; thus 'horse' represents a horse (which horse, one wonders), 'heat' represents heat, 'if' represents conditionality, 'not' represents negation. But, of course, this is to say virtually *nothing*. Secondly, what does it mean to say that a word or sentence represents something? A painting can be said to represent X if it is a painting *of* X. What is it for a word to represent X? (Don't reply: it is the name of X! For that simply replaces one vacuity and obscurity by another.) Similar difficulties attend the claim that sentences represent. Do all sentences represent (declaratives, imperatives, interrogatives, optatives), or only some? What is it that they represent? Facts or states of affairs? – that is a path which has suffered such heavy traffic that nothing but mud remains of it. One might bypass this ruined track: one can say of a significant sentence that it means the same as another, one can explain what it means; one may use a sentence and, in certain contexts, explain what one meant by what one said. Does one either want or need more? Thirdly, it is indeed common to talk of systems of representation. Cartography can be said to be a system of representing the lie of the land, topographical features or demographical ones, rainfall or geological features. There is, however, no such thing as representing a territory on a map without employing a particular set of conventions of representation involving a specific method of projection, for example, cylindrical (Mercator), conic or azimuthal. So there are no representing maps without conventions of representation. There are no conventions of representation without a *use*, by intelligent, symbol-employing creatures, of the representation. And to *use* a representation correctly one must *know* the conventions of representation, understand them, be able to explain them, recognize mistakes and correct or acknowledge them when they are pointed out. Whether a certain array of lines is or is not a map is not an *intrinsic* feature of the lines, nor even a *relational* feature (that is, the *possibility* of a 1:1 mapping), but a *conventional* one (that is, the *actual* employment, by a person, of a convention of mapping).

What is meant by the claim that neural events represent features of the surroundings of the organism? Young explains as follows:

We say that a sign is symbolic when it somehow corresponds to features of the surroundings in such a manner that it communicates a lot of information that is used by an organism in its business of keeping alive . . . a symbol is a special sort of signal because it represents the features of the surroundings in such a way that the organism immediately recognizes its significance and acts accordingly. (p. 60)

This is ill conceived. That a given cell on the retina reacts to a pattern of quanta that hit it and accordingly transmits an electrical impulse does not make that nerve impulse into a symbol. It is not even a signal, save perhaps in the sense in which a flash of lightning is a signal of thunder, that is, a causal concomitant (so *not* in the sense in which railway signals signal the train drivers when to stop or go). The electrical impulse does not *represent* anything at all, it does not *stand for* or *signify* or *mean* anything (save perhaps in the sense that clouds mean, that is, are causally related to and provide inductive grounds for predicting, rain). The response of a cell in a given column in the visual cortex to the activity of a group of light receptors of the retina signifies to the *neurophysiologist* that certain cells of the retina have been stimulated in a certain way (for example, by an orientation slit moving across it), for, with the help of Hubel and Wiesel, the neurophysiologist has discovered a causal correlation. But if we call the electrical impulse 'a sign' it is obvious that the *organism* does not 'recognize its significance', since the 'organism' (cat or monkey) has not read Hubel and Wiesel. (I take it as given that Hubel and Wiesel have demonstrated that the visual cortex is arranged in columns of orientation-sensitive cells. What they have *not* shown and, I noticed with relief, do not claim to have shown (in the papers I have read) is that 'nerve impulses are signals that act as symbols'.)[16]

The fact that very specific arrays of cells respond electrochemically to electrical impulses transmitted from a group of cells in a given part of the retina neither shows nor suggests that the impulse or the neurons *represents* that part of the retina, let alone an object in the visual field. Consequently there is great danger of conceptual confusion if physiologists insist upon talking, as many do, of cerebral *maps*. If a topographic map is, as Zeki says it is, a 'means of representing [a] body surface',[17] then the visual cortex does not have a map of the visual field either *on* or *in* it. Zeki, as far as I understand him, thinks that there are literal maps in (on) the cortex,[18] for in the same article he notes that the 'cortical maps are not at all precise, geographic representations of the retinal surface, but are distorted in accordance with the functions of the area in question'. One might complain thus of 'distortions' on a genuine map, for example, distortions involved in the representation of Canada on a cylindrical

Mercator projection. But, of course, there is only a distortion if there is a *scale* which does not adjust to the particular method of projection, a scale which is *used* in measuring distance. (One does not complain that a picture is *distorted* if the figures are not life size, or if certain parts are foreshortened, on the contrary.) Even more obviously there is only room to talk of map distortion if there *is* a method of projection. And for there to be a method of projection there must be map-makers employing *conventions* of representation.

The only sense in which there could be maps on the brain is the sense in which I might draw a map on my hand. What seems to be true is that the *physiologist can map* the retina on to the visual cortex or part of it. But that does not make it a map of the retina, let alone of the visual field. If, *per impossible*, there were a map on the cortex, that would no more solve the neurophysiologists's problems than a picture on the pineal gland solved Descartes's. For like Descartes the modern neurophysiologist is trying to explain the processes involved in seeing an object. And he comes perilously close to saying that when a person sees an object there is a map, a representation of the object, not on the pineal gland, but on the visual cortex. But now he must explain who or what sees or reads the map. If it is neither the mind nor a gnostic cell, what can it be? Will future science tell us? I quote Young once more:

We have now given some meaning to the statement that the signals from the retina 'represent' visual events and are 'decoded' in the brain. But we have not explained in what sense these activities of the cortical cells can be said to 'interpret' or 'understand' the messages from the retina. Somehow the actions of all these cortical nerve cells must cooperate to receive and 'interpret' the signals. Often they are answers to the questions that the cortex itself has asked, and it goes on to ask others . . . At present we do now know either how the brain asks its questions or how it uses the answers. The knowledge we have of the principles of coding has been acquired only in the last few years. We may expect that physiologists will pursue the problem further. (pp. 126ff)

I do not think that physiologists are likely to fare any better with the question of how the brain asks and answers questions than with the question of how the mind sees pictures on the pineal gland. These are not deep and challenging questions to be answered, but conceptual confusions masquerading as empirical problems.

I shall round off these critical remarks with two methodological observations that may help to avert misunderstanding. First, the arguments I have mustered are not reliant upon any particular prejudice in favour of ordinary language. I have not argued that the man on the Clapham omnibus would not say that neurons communicate information to each other or that the brain receives message in code from the senses, or that a cell recognizes a configuration. It is probably true that he would not and he would be right not to. Nor would he say that the amount of information carried by a sequence of signals is measured in bits, or that two messages, one heavily loaded with meaning and the other pure nonsense, may carry the same amount of information. For he would not understand such a proposition in the sense in which it is perfectly true. My argument does not turn on ordinary usage as opposed to technical usage, but only on *what makes sense* and what does not. The bounds of sense can be violated by the misuse of technical, non-ordinary expressions no less than by the misuse of ordinary ones. And, in particular, they can and – in the cases I have examined – are violated by unconsciously crossing ordinary uses of expressions with half-understood technical ones. Secondly, it is not open to the neurophysiologist or psychologist to shrug off these criticisms on the grounds that he *is* using 'language', 'represent', 'communicate', 'recognize', etc. in a special technical sense, and that it is not *he* but his gullible reader (such as myself) who is guilty of crossing the ordinary use with his special technical one. For were he so to argue, the initial analogy with which his story began, and which so impresses us all, is no analogy whatever, and the various exciting questions which he raised *en passant* are either unexciting or absurd.

Concluding Remarks

If my argument is on the right track, what is the source of the conceptual confusions with which neurophysiologists and biological scientists surround their empirical investigations? There are manifold conceptual confusions about certain key terms such as 'language', 'symbol', 'sign', 'representation' or 'map'. There are disastrous equivocations over crucial expressions such as 'code', 'information', 'transmission of information' in which information–theoretic uses of expressions are unconsciously or wilfully allowed to merge with quite different uses of these expressions. I have touched on these. But there is also a further conceptual muddle running through the writings of these scientists. It has been felicitously dubbed 'the homunculus fallacy' by Anthony Kenny,[19] and his account of it rests on an observation made by Wittgenstein: 'Only of a living human being and what resembles (behaves like) a living human being can one say: it has sensations; it sees; is blind; hears; is deaf; is conscious or unconscious'.[20] The homunculus fallacy is *not* merely the supposition that one might, for example, explain our perceiving objects by reference to a homunculus (such as the mind or brain) perceiving pictures on the pineal gland or interpreting maps on the visual cortex, but also the more important incoherence of attributing predicates, such as 'sees', 'understands' or 'knows', which can only sensibly be predicated of what is human or akin to human, to *parts* of a human being. To attempt to explain perception or the understanding of an utterance by reference to the transmission of information to the brain which then decodes, interprets and understands what was encoded in a neural signal is to fall victim to precisely this incoherence. Not only is it incoherent, but also, far from being a step to the resolution of the questions addressed, it merely reduplicates the question. For we replace the question 'How does a person see, understand, interpret?' with the question 'How does the brain (or visual cortex or gnostic neuron) see, understand, interpret?' And while some sense can be made of the former questions, the latter merely enshroud in a veil of mystery a conceptual incoherence. The homunculus fallacy is rife in neurophysiological *speculation*.

I conclude with a final question: does it matter? Neurophysiology has made great progress in the last decades. If the arguments I have adumbrated are correct, or even half-correct, then there are widespread confusions in much speculative neurophysiology. Nevertheless it does not seem to have impeded work. Perhaps these linguistic analogies are readily misinterpreted, but how does that affect the serious scientific research programmes? After all, it might be said, neurophysiologists must use *some* language to describe their subject-matter and results, and would it not be self-mutilation rather than self-restraint to renounce all use of analogies? To these questions I have three answers.

First, if scientific misconceptions that are rooted in conceptual muddles rather than empirical ignorance lead scientists to construct misconceived research programmes and hypotheses that are not true or false, but rather lack sense, then these confusions *are* important. Whether this happens in neurophysiology I am not competent to judge (it certainly happens in empirical psychology). If it leads them, as it quite evidently does, to ask questions that make no sense, then the misleading analogies and metaphors they employ are not a harmless *façon de parler*.

Secondly, if the scientist's quest is *understanding*, then the conceptual confusions that inform his reports on his discoveries are disastrous. For they mask the truths he has discovered and their significance from his own eyes. This, to be sure, is not a new phenomenon. Newton's work on optics was great science; but he ended up arguing that colours are sensations in the sensorium. However, it makes no more sense to say that green is a sensation than to say that a number is an idea and an imaginary number an imaginary idea.[21] Hence it is evident that Newton did not achieve his goal, namely an understanding of the phenomena he was investigating. His famous qualms about action at a distance signify a similar failure of understanding in respect of his great work in mechanics. In both cases the flaw is not remediable by more experimental research, but only by conceptual clarification.[22]

What is, to my mind, much more important is the fact that these conceptual muddles mask the nature of scientists' discoveries from the eyes of their audience. This contributes greatly to the transformation of science into popular witch-doctory, a transformation that is enthusiastically encouraged by many scientists themselves. To be told that the brain has a language of its own, that its language has a grammar, consists of symbols that have meanings, that it represents the extra-cranial world to itself, and that it makes and interprets maps or representations is, after all, *sensational*. It is immensely exciting: it sounds like a discovery on a par with discovering that whales or chimpanzees have languages, only even more extraordinary and astonishing. But it is not at all like that. And it is not, in this sense, in the slightest exciting. For so to describe what neurophysiologists have discovered is like describing the discovery of infra-red photography as discovering how to see what people look like in the dark. The astonishment is akin to the schoolchild's astonishment at being told that mathematicians have discovered that a line which does not cut a circle at any point really does intersect it – at imaginary points.[23] The correct response to the neurophysiological misdescriptions is not amazement at the ubiquity of semiotics in nature, as Young suggests (p. 9), but 'The way you have described what you have done makes no sense; so please tell me precisely what happened.' When these discoveries have been properly described, they are not particularly surprising – or not surprising in anything like the same sense, but only in the sense in which it was surprising to find black swans in Australia.

Finally, I do not suggest for a moment that scientists should abjure analogies or metaphors. On the contrary, I started this chapter by pointing out how fruitful analogical reasoning is in science. What is worrying about some aspects of speculative neurophysiology, exemplified beautifully in Young's book, but also evident in the work of the professionals working at the coal face, is that a large part of their motivation seems to rest on a misleading analogy. Not only do they seem motivated by pseudo-mysteries, but a striking range of their 'most exciting' questions rest on a metaphor. Analogies and metaphors, I said at the beginning, are the go-cart of creativity. But it should be very worrying if one cannot give *sense* to one's problems without them. Neurology should not provide an excuse for neural mythology.

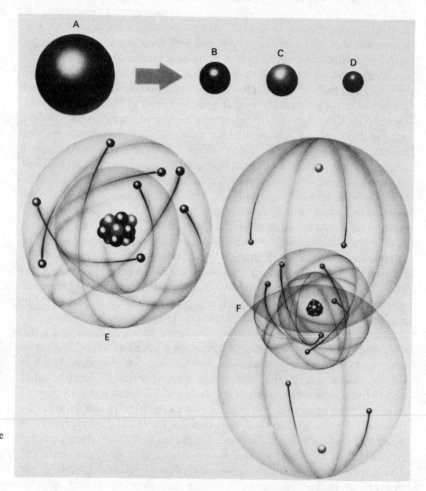

Figure 31.3 A pictorial metaphor for the structure of atoms, from a children's encyclopaedia. The nucleus (A), neutrons (B), protons (C) and electrons (D) are shown as little balls. E is an atom of oxygen and F a molecule of water. All very well, as long as it is intended only as an analogy (based on an illustration in The Hamlyn Younger Children's Encyclopaedia, Hamlyn, *1972).*

Notes

I am indebted to Dr T. P. S. Powell for guiding me through some of the outlying thickets of neurophysiology and for his advice and encouragement, and to Dr O. Jacobs for clarification of elementary points about information theory. I am grateful to Dr G. P. Baker, Dr R. Frey, J. Hyman, Dr J. Raz and Dr S. Shanker, all of whom read and commented upon an early draft of this paper. My greatest debt is to Professor Roy Harris, who both suggested the topic and identified the target. He read, and suggested improvements to, successive drafts, and at the actual meeting where I presented a shorter version of this paper he acted in that rarest of academic roles, a supportive co-symposiast. The final draft of the paper was delivered as one of the Milton C. Scott Lectures at Queen's University, Kingston, Ontario.

1 Summerson, J. (1980) *The Classical Language of Architecture,* revised edn. London: Thames & Hudson.

2 Young, J. Z. (1978) *Programs of the Brain.* Oxford: Oxford Univ. Press. This volume is based on Young's Gifford Lectures at the University of Aberdeen, given in 1975. Young's work as an experimental scientist is indisputably very distinguished. If a scientist of such eminence attempts to articulate the achievements and problems of contemporary neurophysiological understanding of the brain, the picture he paints is likely to represent a style of thought widespread among his colleagues working upon these topics.

3 Frisby, J. P. (1980) *Seeing: Illusion, Brain and Mind,* p. 8. Oxford: Oxford Univ. Press.

4 Hubel, T. H. and Wiesel, T. N. (1979) Brain mechanisms of vision. *Scientific American* (September), 241.

5 In parallel manner Colin Blakemore writes: 'Somehow the brain knows about the properties of the retina and fills in the missing information . . . why does the brain not also know about the physiological processes in the visual cortex, which lead to changes in signals about orientation when more than one line is present? Surely it should be possible for the brain to re-interpret information from the cortex and compensate for illusory distortion.' – The baffled brain (1973). In R. L. Gregory and E. H. Gombrich (eds), *Illusion in Nature and Art,* p. 33. London: Duckworth.

6 Neither 'human language' nor 'writing and other forms of recording speech' are language*s* on a level with the putative DNA language and the alleged 'neural language'. 'Human language' is, if anything, the multitudinous language*s* of mankind, not one language in contrast with Neuralese. *A fortiori, writing* is not a language.

7 Not of course because they are so incompetent, but because it is senseless to attribute such capacities to objects like a brain. Confusion on this matter is strikingly evident in the following passage by the psychologist R. L. Gregory: 'Eye and brain combine to give detailed knowledge of objects . . . we know now that specific features of objects are selected and combined to give an internal account of the object world . . . The ease with which we see, apparently by merely opening our eyes, hides the fact that this is probably the most sophisticated of all the brain's activities: calling upon its stores of memory data; requiring subtle classifications, comparisons and logical decisions for sensory data to become perception.' – The confounded eye (1973) in Gregory and Gombrich (eds), *Illusion in Nature and Art,* p. 50. For, of

course, it is not the brain that sees, but the human being; the brain has no 'stores of memory data', and can no more classify, compare and make logical decisions than you or I can transmit information by neural pathways (rather than by telephone).

8 Phillips, C. G., Zeki, S. and Barlow, H. B. (1984) Localization of function in the cerebral cortex, past, present and future. *Brain*, 107: 338.

9 Weaver, W. (1949) Recent contributions to the mathematical theory of communication. In C. E. Shannon and W. Weaver, *The Mathematical Theory of Communication*, p. 8. Urbana: Univ. Illinois Press.

10 Shannon, C. E. in ibid., p. 31.

11 The disastrous effect of such a conception is again vividly displayed in Gregory, e.g.: 'The major lesson from physiology is that a limited number of features of objects are available to the brain, at any one time ... Current physiological knowledge ... is providing evidence of what features are accepted by the brain from the sense organs; especially what features of retinal images are accepted for vision ... Briefly, the orientation of lines, movement and certain shapes, such as corners or angles, are represented by the firing of single cells in the "visual" striate cortex ... This ... leaves the question: how are these selected features, as neurally represented, combined to give perception of objects? ... If perceptions are inferences, based on signalled data from the senses and stored in memory, then we should ask: what are these inferences like? Are they like other kinds' of inferences? ... We may not as yet know the physiology behind all this; but at least we can ask and hope to answer, this kind of question.' – In Gregory and Gombrich, *Illusion in Nature and Art*, pp. 54f. But, of course, we can only ask the question if it *makes sense*; and it makes *no* sense to conceive of seeing or hearing as an inference, let alone an inference made by the brain, based on signalled data (electrical impulses) from the sensory organs. To be sure, to repudiate these absurdities in *no way* affects the discoveries of Hubel and Wiesel correlating retinal stimulation with reactions of columns of cells in the visual cortex.

12 Phillips, Zeki and Barlow, Localization of function in the cerebral cortex, p. 339.

13 Ibid., p. 345.

14 Having castigated neurophysiologists for uncomprehendingly adopting the unfortunate technical terminology of information theorists, I must confess that the information theorists are just as bad. Weaver explains that a 'communication system' consists of an *information source* that selects a *message* out of a set of possible ones, the *transmitter* changes the message into the *signal* which is sent over the *communication channel* to the *receiver* which changes the signal back into a message for the *destination*. So far so good – for telephone engineers. But then Weaver explains: '... in oral speech, the information source is the brain, the transmitter is the voice mechanism producing the varying sound pressure (the signal) which is transmitted through the air (the channel). When I talk to you, my brain is the information source, yours the destination; my vocal system is the transmitter, and your ear and the associated eighth nerve is the receiver.' Saussure, I fancy, would have been delighted.

15 They suggest two conventions, on analogy with conversational conventions around a conference table: first, for everyone to keep generally silent (otherwise no message will be heard); second, when silence is broken, the duration and strength of an utterance should be proportional to its importance. (Are important items of information at physiology conferences always prolix and delivered at the top of one's voice?) As a *metaphor* this is tolerable. Do they take it to be any more than a metaphor?

16 Young, *Programs of the Brain*, p. 117.

17 Zeki, S. M. (1978) Functional specialization in the visual cortex of the rhesus monkey. *Nature*, 274: 425.

18 Young indisputably does. A similar confusion is evident in Blakemore: '. . . the harder the map is studied the less accurate it is seen to be. For one thing the scale of the map is peculary stretched with a disproportionate area devoted to the fovea, particularly in the cortex. For another thing the map is only a two-dimensional one, spread across the surface of the brain, whereas perceptual space is not only three-dimensional, in spatial terms, but has such extra dimensions as the colour of objects, that have no simple place in the brain's maps.' (*op.cit..* p. 15).

19 Kenny, A. J. P. The homunculus fallacy; repr, in his (1984) *The Legacy of Wittgenstein*. Oxford: Blackwell.

20 Wittgenstein, L. (1953) *Philosophical Investigations*, §281. Oxford: Blackwell.

21 It is, unfortunately, nonsense which philosophers have, both then and now, eagerly embraced. Very briefly, sensations are not in the sensorium or mind. In the only sense in which it does make sense to attribute location to sensations, then, they are in the body (toothache is no more located in the mind than in the toe). Furthermore, colours are not sensations, since coloured objects such as chairs, flowers, pictures do not have sensations but do have colours, and while colours are visible, sensations are not. Finally in the only sense in which the sensorium has contents they are not coloured. For elaboration of these contentious points, see my *Appearance and Reality* Blackwell, 1987.

22 To be sure, some scientists have, in the past, grasped this point. In a justly famous passage Hertz wrote: 'We have accumulated around the terms "force" and "electricity" more relations than can be completely reconciled amongst themselves. We have an obscure feeling of this and want to have things cleared up. Our confused wish finds expression in the confused question as to the nature of force and electricity. But the answer which we want is not really an answer to this question. It is not by finding out more and fresh relations and connections that it can be answered; but by removing the contradictions existing between those already known, and thus perhaps by reducing their number. When these painful contradictions are removed, the question as to the nature of force will not have been answered; but our minds, no longer vexed, will cease to ask illegitimate questions.' Hertz, H. (1899) *Principles of Mechanics*, tr. D. E. Jones and J. T. Walley. Introduction, pp. 7ff. London: Macmillan.

23 Cf. *Wittgenstein's Lectures on the Foundations of Mathematics, Cambridge, 1939* ed. C. Diamond (1976) pp. 16ff. Brighton: Harvester Press.

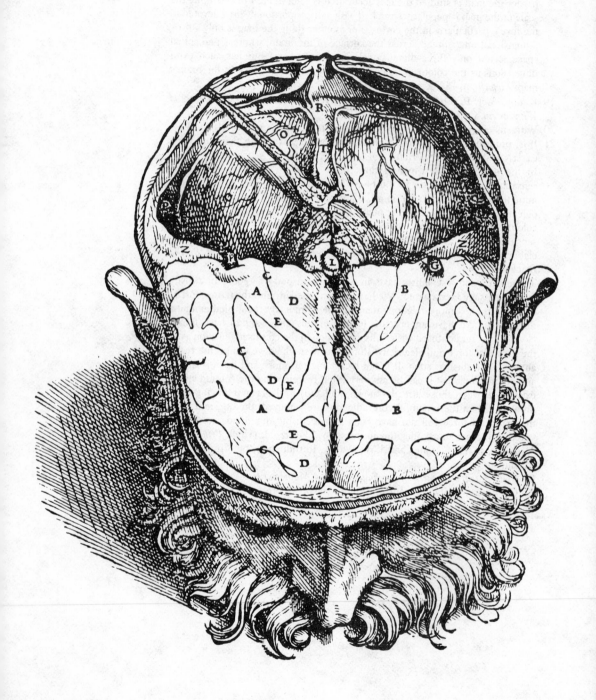

32

The Grammar in Your Head

Roy Harris

Roy Harris is Oxford's first holder of the University's Chair of General Linguistics, established in 1978. He read Modern Languages at St Edmund Hall, Oxford, and later studied at the School of Oriental and African Languages in London, under the late C. E. Bazell, from whom he inherited a healthy scepticism about the pretensions of modern linguistics. He thinks the subject has suffered in recent years from preoccupation with abstruse formalisms, and from anxiety to be recognized as a 'science'.

Introduction

In much currently fashionable talk about the brain, language enters the discussion in two ways. On the one hand, what goes on in the brain is explained in terms of language. On the other hand, language itself is explained in terms of what goes on in the brain. It is not without significance that scientists who use linguistic metaphors when describing what goes on in the brain are often those who apparently find no difficulty in accepting that human linguistic abilities are explicable in terms of brain activities. There seems to be some connection between the two; at least enough of a connection to take it as an initial question for investigation.

A case in point is J. Z. Young, described a few years ago as 'arguably the most influential living British biologist'. The first chapter of his book *Programs of the Brain* has the title 'What's in a brain?'.[1] Among the very many things in the normal brain, according to Young, is a grammar of one's native language. He goes so far as to define *grammar* as: 'the set of brain programs by which sentences are generated'. What the evidence is for postulating this as-yet unidentified set of programs is never explained. One might infer from this that the matter is too obvious to need explaining. But is it?

The first question one might ask about this grammar is: 'What language is it formulated in?' For many neuroscientists this would be a quite reasonable question, because they evidently hold that the brain has a language of its own, or perhaps several languages, in which its programs are written. Assumptions of this kind may in turn raise problems; but it is worth noting how they connect with the thesis under discussion. Postulat-

A non-metaphorical analysis of the human brain, from Vesalius' De Fabrica (1543). He found no grammar inside the head.

ing the existence of neural languages allows the theoretical possibility that one of the things such languages might be used for in the brain is recording a grammar. Without that, the grammar-in-the-head hypothesis would not even be a candidate for consideration.

Languages and Codes

A second question might be this. Since there are an infinite number of possible grammars of English, all defining exactly the same set of sentences, which is the one in my brain? Or are there an infinite number of them? Or just a restricted sub-set? The question is not a frivolous one if the grammar-in-the-head hypothesis is to be taken seriously. It would doubtless be unfair to ask neuroscience to specify exactly what form the brain's grammatical rules take, because neuroscience, on its own admission, has not yet 'cracked the neural code' in which they are formulated. It is fair, however, to observe that neuroscience is never likely to make much progress in code-cracking if in fact there is no code to crack.

It is relevant to note *en passant* that one of the characteristics of the

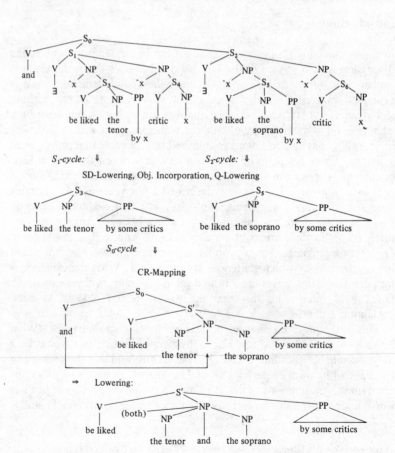

Figure 32.1   One academic version of the grammatical structure presumed to underlie the sentence, 'Some critics liked (both) the tenor and the soprano.' Does this structure exist somewhere in the head of the speaker of the sentence? (from Seuren Discourse Semantics, *Blackwell, 1985).*

current communications jargon about what goes on in the brain is a constant muddling of the terms *code* and *language*, as if they were interchangeable. But a language is not a code; and a code is not a language, either. Only languages in the ordinary sense – languages such as English, French and Latin – have grammars. A code does not have a grammar; nor could a code somehow 'generate' a grammar. Codes do not need grammars. A code does not even need words. A code is simply a cipher. A code is devised in such a way that any desired type of text can be encoded, and the result decoded by anyone who has the key to the cipher. Decoding is a process of recovering the original text. If I know the Morse code, I can put any Latin text into Morse; and I can also reverse that operation and recover the original Latin text. But I can do all this without knowing a word of Latin. That is the crucial difference between a language and a code.

Even those who see the importance of distinguishing between languages and codes nevertheless sometimes fall into the trap of supposing that because using a code does not involve knowing a language, it follows that encoding and decoding are purely mechanical processes; processes of the kind that, say, a telephone system performs. Nothing could be more grossly misconceived. When I pick up the telephone and talk to someone on the other end of the line, the telephone does not encode my English and then transmit it along the wire for decoding by the instrument on the desk of the person I am speaking to. If it could do that, the telephone would have been a far cleverer invention than it was; and it was certainly a very clever invention in any case. But encoding and decoding English was never something it could do. It did not need to. It operates in a far simpler way by a direct process of energy conversion. If telephones could handle languages (as distinct from mere sound waves), and if neural processes were in that respect telephonic, then there might be some sense in saying that a grammar was a certain set of brain programs. But if ifs and ans were pots and pans, there'd be no need of tinkers.

Once languages are confused with codes, and coded messages in turn confused with transmissions, it is almost inevitable to make the consequential mistake of assuming that if scientists concentrate hard enough on analysis of the transmissions and the transmission mechanism, that in the end is bound to yield the key to a hitherto undeciphered code. That is just like supposing that by studying the electrical impulses in telephone wires one might eventually learn English (or whatever language the telephone users happened to speak). One would not learn anything of the kind; for the simple reason that there is no English passing along the telephone wires.

Perhaps another term needs to be mentioned here: *translation*. Translation is an operation which involves linguistic knowledge; and in particular knowledge of at least two languages. The record-holder to date is the legendary Cardinal Mezzofanti, who is said to have been able to translate 114 languages. But not even Cardinal Mezzofanti could have translated a Latin text into Morse code; for the Morse code is not a language. Nor does a telephone translate English into electrical impulses; because electricity is not a language either. If a telephone could do translation, then it would be the most astonishing translation machine ever invented.[2]

Sentences and Utterances

Returning to the brain-program definition of grammar, so far only the problems clustering about the term *grammar* itself have been mentioned. There is a no less awkward set of muddles clustering about the notion of what the grammar (that is, set of brain programs) is alleged to do; which, according to Young's definition, was 'generate sentences'. What this claim fails to make clear is whether what the brain programs generate are speech-events in the real world 'outside', or items somehow stored in one's head, or merely potential items or events of some kind. This makes a significant difference to the substance of the claim in question. If the claim is that brain programs generate speech-events in the real world 'outside' (that is, audible utterances) then the term *grammar* is evidently being misused: for grammars do not produce utterances. Only human beings do that. If the claim is that what is generated are just pre-speech items recorded in one's head, but ready for use in actual speech whenever needed, then presumably such items have to be recorded in some kind of linguistic notation, or otherwise they would hardly count as 'sentences'; and here we are back again with those enigmatic neural codes. Thirdly, if the claim is that the sentences are envisaged merely as potential verbal output items from a generative system, that really explains nothing at all. We are left with the unsolved problem of how these potential items are actualized and utilized in the processes of speech. The difficulty here is that a program is presumably just a set of instructions. But instructions, like grammatical rules, do not of their own accord generate anything. It is only their implementation which results in an end-product. But about their implementation the account so far given is silent. Until that lacuna is filled, language remains a mystery. For it is the decision to utter particular words at a particular time in a particular context and to do so appropriately which is the hallmark of human linguistic ability. And this requires situational judgements, communicative intentions, and self-awareness – all of which are properties of the human being, not of the human brain.

There is no great mystery as to where this gobbledegook about grammar in your head comes from. It has two main sources. One source is the writings of those linguistic theorists who speak of people having 'internalized grammars'. These internalized grammars correspond alleg- edly to the sets of generative rules devised externally by the theorists themselves as a means of specifying the set of well-formed sentences of a language. Biologists and others may perhaps be forgiven for taking this linguists' talk of internalized grammars quite literally, as implying that speakers have somehow picked up or learnt off and committed to memory a set of recursive rewrite formulae specifying the sentences of English. But it would take a grammarian of the extreme lunatic fringe to claim that. There is a less bizarre way of justifying talk of internalized grammars, simply as a shorthand for generalizing about an individual's linguistic practice. If that linguistic practice consistently exemplifies certain pat- terns and avoids others, we can say, for example, that the speaker speaks 'as if' knowing such a rule as 'adjectives agree with the noun in gender and case', or 'rewrite S as NP + VP', etc. It does not follow that the speaker actually has 'internalized' anything at all corresponding to the rule as the grammarian formulates it. To put the point another way, one must not construe the term *generate* as used by linguists as implying anything about real-time production of potential or actual utterances. Yet that is precisely, one presumes, what a real live brain program would be concerned with.

The other source of this gobbledegook is the terminology employed by the computer scientists. Computer science, as the darling of modern technology, has simply assumed the right to baptize any old system it uses and call it a 'language'. But that baptism does not guarantee that the system in question has any linguistic status at all. No intelligent person believes that because a certain state officially calls itself a 'democracy', it follows that the state in question must actually be a democracy, or that the procedures of government it has institutionalized must therefore be democratic procedures. For exactly the same kind of reason, no one should take it on trust that what computer science calls 'languages' must be languages. They are, in fact, not even codes, as is clear enough even from the entry *languages* in the current *Penguin Dictionary of Computers*. Computer scientists do indeed talk of programs 'communicating' with the computer, giving it instructions, etc. But this is on a par with saying that I communicate with a light bulb by switching it on, or that the movement of the switch 'tells the bulb to light itself up'. Because computer scientists say programs are 'communicating' with the computer, they call FORTRAN, BASIC, etc. 'languages'. But such 'languages' are in the final analysis sets of symbols corresponding to operations in the machine (corresponding because the machine has been designed that way – it cannot fail to 'understand'). The objective of the programmer's 'communication' is to reorganize the state of the machine so that the machine will carry out certain tasks. The 'language-like' character of FORTRAN, BASIC, etc. is due to the fact that it makes the programmer's task simpler if the symbols corresponding eventually to the operations in the machine are organized so as to be handled via a typewriter keyboard. But if a typewriter were wired up to an electric circuit in such a way that when the typist types the letters ON in that order a light goes on, and when the letters OFF are typed in that order the light goes off, we should not take very seriously the idea that the typist was sending written messages to the bulb, or that the bulb could understand English. Likewise, if the letters A, B, C, D, E, F, and G are painted on the appropriate keys of a piano keyboard, a learner can pick out certain tunes by following certain alphabetic sequences. But it would be absurd to call that a 'piano language', and even more absurd to suppose that the learner was using it to 'communicate' with the wires in the body of the instrument.

Metaphors and Experiments

The question could nevertheless be raised whether in some sense or other talking about a grammar in the brain might not be 'right' after all. There seems to be only one way in which scientists might be justified in

*Figure 32.3   The opening
sentences of the entry on
'Languages' in* A Dictionary
of Computers, *by A.
Chandler, J. Graham and R.
Williamson (Penguin, 1977).*

languages   In order to communicate with each other, men use language: in the same way, 'languages' of one sort or another are used in order to communicate instructions and commands to a computer. The unique feature which distinguishes a computer from other man-made tools and devices is its versatility in dealing with vastly different problems. This means that some very versatile method of communicating these enormously varied problems has to be devised.

that hope. While recognizing the current metaphorical status of this terminology, they might believe that in the fullness of time the metaphor would turn out to be a plausible description of reality. After all, the history of science provides us with well-documented examples of this kind. For instance, to quote a case cited by Rom Harré, the resistance to corrosion of aluminium was at one time explained by talking about a protective 'skin' allegedly formed at the beginning of acid or alkali attack.[4] Originally, this term 'skin' was just a metaphor. But subsequently it proved possible, by advances in experimental technology, to show that there was a layer of substance which could be separated from the underlying metal, and produced as the barrier accounting for corrosion resistance. Thus, as Harré puts it, 'the "skin" of the model became the skin of fact'. In one sense, we are still left in the realm of metaphor, but what has happened is that terms intuitively used to talk about the phenomenon turned out to have 'real-world' counterparts. We pass from analogy to description.

Now it does not matter for present purposes what exactly the facts of the case were about this particular episode in the history of science. All that matters is that we see that there could be such a type of case. The example is not automatically confined to the natural sciences. Suppose certain politicians feel that whenever British workmen go on strike it is 'as if' Moscow had succeeded in damaging the British economy: so they are led to talking about strikes as Russian plots. Then, as in the case of aluminium and corrosion, the 'Russian plot' hypothesis is a candidate for a certain explanatory role in the story; and it may – or may not – prove possible to demonstrate the existence of actual Russian plots in a convincing range of test cases. Again, there is the possibility of passing from analogy to description.

The important point is that if this is the kind of justification offered for the talk about grammar in the brain, it just will not do. For in order to upgrade the status of any tentative hypothesis or scientific metaphor, what is needed is what Harré calls an 'ontological experiment'; and a decisive one. In the case of aluminium and corrosion, scientists produced just such an experiment. They succeeded in detaching the alleged 'skin' from the metal it protected. But in the case of the brain as a communications system, there is no ontological experiment which would validate the metaphor.

It is worth spelling out the reason why. A grammar of a language is not just any relevant set of rules or procedures. In order to qualify as a grammar, it must be formulated in a language or in a notation which contains symbols designating or standing for classes of grammatical elements and grammatical relations. It would be perfectly possible to list all the sentences of the King James version of the Bible in alphabetical order and to store them in a computer for retrieval as required. But that would not constitute writing a grammar of Biblical English. There would be nothing to say what the grammatical relations between the sentences were.

So what kinds of ontological experiment are conceivable which would settle the question of whether we have grammars of our native language in our heads? Perhaps it would be useful here to distinguish two versions of what needs to be proved. Those who take the position associated with what is sometimes called 'strong AI' (Artificial Intelligence) might urge that the grammatical rules in our heads will turn out to be components of programs in a rather high-level language which organize and coordinate what goes on in particular instances when speech is called for. For 'strong AI' makes the claim that there is a level of mental operations which can be defined over formal units and relations, irrespective of how that is concretely instantiated in neurophysiological terms. So here we must be looking for structural analogues, rather than for specific, individual processes or pieces of mechanism. The trouble with this is that candidates for structural analogues will doubtless turn out to be embarrassingly numerous, because the simplest form of a grammar is exceedingly simple. It is no more, in effect, than a multiple-branching tree-structure with occasional loops. But such structures, obviously, can be used for myriad purposes apart from grammar. The problem would be to devise a test which distinguished a neural grammar-program from any other program: and since we do not know at all what form the alleged grammar-program takes, we cannot even begin to tackle the problem. So let us turn to a less abstract version of the grammar-in-the-head thesis and suppose that there will turn out to be direct clues to specific grammatical rules in the immediate patterns of brain activity accompanying speech.

Now consider the question: how could we ever prove by ontological experiment that one of my sets of brain programs did actually employ symbols for classes of English grammatical elements or relations? Suppose we had available extremely powerful techniques for showing exactly what goes on in the brain when we talk. And imagine it could be shown, for instance, that the regular neural concomitant of turning an affirmation into a corresponding negation (as, for example, *John hit Bill* into *John didn't hit Bill*) was that a certain firing-pattern of neurons in the affirmative case was fired exactly in reverse order in the negative case. That would be extremely interesting. But would it show that we have discovered a grammar employing the concept of 'Negation'? Clearly not. Anyone who supposed that merely establishing the correlation between the firing-patterns and the negative transformation proved that the brain program has a 'Rule of Negation' would be making the same logical error as someone who thought that the regular correlation between the states of the electrical device which ensures that the red, amber and green lights of a traffic signal come on in the right order and the observable behaviour of the traffic when they do so proved that the traffic signal must have internalized rules of the Highway Code.

This argument against the 'strong AI' position, it should be noted, is entirely different from the objection to 'strong AI' advanced by John Searle in his Reith Lectures, *Minds, Brains and Science*.[5] To argue, as Searle does, that brain programs are inadequate to explain mental events because the programs themselves are definable in purely syntactic terms is question-begging. It would make no difference at all if the programs were defined in semantic terms too. Consider the following analogy. It is possible to define a program for a grandfather clock purely in terms of internal wheels, weights and levers, without making any reference to the time shown by the hands on the dial. It is equally possible, on the other hand, to specify exactly the same set of operations, but making quite explicit reference to the time shown by the hands on the dial. Whichever specification is chosen will not prove that a clock which carries out the program can tell the time. Only human beings can tell the time. All a clock (even a chiming clock) can do, if appropriately programmed, is keep time.

It does not follow from the fact that the words of the National Anthem can be specified in terms of a formal sequence of letters of the alphabet, in themselves meaningless, that the National Anthem is meaningless. What follows is merely that that particular mode of formal specification does not say anything about what the words mean. So what would be a mistake here is identifying the formal specification as an account of the meaning; or, alternatively, taking the mere fact that the formal specification can be given to be a guarantee that the object thus specified is meaningful. But that leaves untouched the apparently more interesting claim of 'strong AI' that the implementation of a brain program is itself constitutive of a mental event (which includes our awareness of the semantic value). The crucial question is: 'Can we make sense of such a claim?'

In trying to evaluate the claim, it is important to note that it does not equate the meaning of the program with its processes of physiological implementation in a brain. That is to say, to revert to the example of the National Anthem, the claim is not that the meaning of the words consists simply in uttering or writing them on a particular occasion, or indeed of rehearsing them silently to oneself, going through them 'in one's head'. The claim is, rather, that the mental event which we call thinking or remembering or conjuring up the words of the National Anthem (including not merely their sounds and shapes but also what they mean) is – and is nothing other than – the implementation of some brain program or programs which could in principle be specified in purely formal terms. Now the trouble with this claim is not so much that it is obviously false or meaningless, as that even if both meaningful and true it is so very weak as to be trivial and quite unenlightening. Far from being an exciting claim, it turns out to be almost totally devoid of interest; for semantics is no less amenable to formalization than syntax. One of the (few) lessons that may have been learnt from the great debates which have racked linguistic theory during the past quarter of a century was just that: almost anything linguistic under the sun can be formalized if need be, and in any number of ways. So to oppose syntax to semantics on those grounds is naive. Even more naive is to suppose that where language is concerned the formalization of syntax is trouble-free, whereas the formalization of semantics bristles with problems. If anything, it is the other way round. Thus Searle's attack on 'strong AI' is a non-contest, because not only is it utterly misdirected, but 'strong AI' was never strong enough for a fight in the first place. (Its proponents may have said it was: but shouts of encouragement from the corner of the ring are no substitute for punches.)

At the end of the day we have still not managed to prise the 'skin' off the aluminium, because there is no 'skin' to prise off. Our conclusion must be that one thing advances in neuroscience will never be able to tell us anything about is why the words *the cat is asleep* form an English sentence whereas *cat asleep is the* do not. Furthermore, it would be fatuous to believe that the explanation is that I have brain programs which produce one of those sequences but not the other. For clearly I can say either if I want to.

Language and Thought

Why, then, would anyone wish to insist that there is a grammar of English somewhere inside my head? The answer is that taking it for granted that there must be works to the advantage of those who do not wish to be restricted by accepting the traditional distinction between 'mind' and 'brain'. Many quotations could be cited in support of this; but here one will have to do duty for many. It does not come from a neuroscientist or a biologist, but from one of our present-day cultural gauleiters: the television journalists. This particular journalist supports 'defiance of the old convention that mind is what the psychologists deal with, in contrast with the material brain that the surgeons and physiologists handle. To a reporter taking some trouble to be objective there is plainly a movement under way, in the laboratories of several countries, which makes this distinction thoroughly out of date.'[6]

The reporter is not wrong. J. Z. Young on the same subject writes: 'At present the word "brain" means only a little more than a reference to a convoluted whitish mass of stuff. Is it possible to change all that and to give so full a meaning to the word "brain" that it will no longer be a semantic mistake to say that brains think?'[7] The question is one which verges on what old-fashioned linguists used to call 'rhetorical'. But the motivation is clear. The biologist wants to be in on the act when it comes to solving those ultimate scientific mysteries: 'how do human beings think?' and 'What is thought?'

Thinking, or an important part of thinking, is usually taken to involve language. So a languageless brain would not be a very plausible candidate as the human organ of thought. What better way round the problem than simply to postulate that the brain has a grammar, of which eventually neuroscience will be able to reveal the detailed rules? In the meantime, the clearest indication of the presence of such a grammar seems to be merely the fact that one of the things human beings can do is talk. But now we have come full circle: for that indeed was the starting-point of our inquiry. We knew long ago that human beings talk, and that grammarians identify certain linguistic units as 'sentences'. But have we explained how the two things match up, or what that has to do with thinking?

It would be wrong to suggest that only neuroscientists rely on grammar-in-the-head jargon in order to fudge the answers to awkward questions about minds and brains. In recent years linguistic theorists have increasingly come to rely on it too, and for much the same reason. They do not want to miss out when it comes to sharing the academic honours for solving the mysteries of human thought. But they are more reluctant than the neuroscientists to get their hands experimentally dirty. So they profit from letting the assumption go unchallenged that what grammarians do by their armchair methods complements what the scientists do in the laboratory. Both teams of investigators are investigating what goes on in your head, but at 'different levels of description' (as the current cop-out phrase puts it).

The common factor in all this is the assumption that the explanatory task will be easier if we can somehow dispose or take care of the brain–mind distinction, and just concentrate on configurations of internal rules or processes. But that is to fall victim to much the same kind of fallacy as Descartes, only with certain differences of emphasis and with the problems dressed up in modern scientific terminology. To be a creature that thinks is to be a creature with certain kinds of capacities; and these capacities are studied by studying how the creature makes use of them in the business of living; not by trying to see what internal mechanisms distinguish the class of thinking creatures from the class of creatures who are thoughtless.

In short, the objection to talking about grammar as a set of brain programs is not that this way of talking is stylistically novel or outlandish; nor that it is logically impossible for a brain to operate with procedures structurally analogous to the formulation of grammatical rules. The objection is to its reliance on a linguistic dud cheque that no scientific bank in the world will ever cash. If we are to understand language as a human experience, we certainly need to understand what grammar is. But that understanding can only be hindered, not advanced, by falling for neuro-nonsense about grammatical programs in the brain.

References

1 Young, J. Z. (1978) *Programs of the Brain.* Oxford: Oxford Univ. Press.

2 The invention of a 'telephone that talks in several tongues' was announced in *The Times*, 19 March 1985. This machine, on display at a science exhibition in Tsukuba, is a telephone linked to a computer system. It can translate phone calls from English into Japanese and vice versa, but is not speaker-independent and can 'recognize' only a limited number of messages.

3 Chandor, A. (ed.) (1977) *The Penguin Dictionary of Computers*, 2nd edn., p. 236, Harmondsworth: Penguin.

4 Harré, R. (1961) *Theories and Things*, p. 26. London: Sheed & Ward.

5 Searle, J. R. (1984) Beer cans and meat machines. *The Listener*, 112, no. 2884: 14–16.

6 Calder, N. (1970) *The Mind of Man*, p. 10. London: BBC Publications.

7 Young, *Programs of the Brain*, p. 3.

Index

Index by Fiona Barr